FOURTH EDITION

HEALTH, ILLNESS, AND THE SOCIAL BODY

A CRITICAL SOCIOLOGY

Peter E. S. Freund
Montclair State University

Meredith B. McGuire
Trinity University

Linda S. Podhurst
University of Medicine and Dentistry of New Jersey

Prentice
Hall

Upper Saddle River, New Jersey 07458

Library of Congress Cataloging-in-Publication Data

Freund, Peter E. S.
  Health, illness, and the social body : a critical sociology /
Peter E. S. Freund, Meredith B. McGuire. Linda S. Podhurst.—4th ed.
    p. cm.
    Includes bibliographical references and index.
    ISBN 0-13-098230-X (pbk.)
    1. Social medicine. 2. Medical care–Social aspects. 3. Sick–Psychology. 4 Body, Human–Social aspects.
  I. McGuire, Meredith B. II. Podhurst, Linda S. III. Title.
  RA418.F753 2002
  306.4'61–dc21   2002027070

Publisher: Nancy Roberts
Senior acquisitions editor: Chris De John
Managing editor: Sharon Chambliss
Editorial/production supervision and
   interior design: Interactive Composition Corporation
Copyeditor: Melissa Messina
Prepress and manufacturing buyer: Mary Ann Gloriande
Senior marketing manager: Amy Speckman
Marketing assistant: Anne Marie Fritzky
Cover art director: Jayne Conte
Cover design: Bruce Kenselaar

This book was set in 10/12 Baskerville Book by Interactive Composition Corporation
and was printed and bound by Maple Vail.
The cover was printed by Phoenix Color Corp.

 © 2003, 1999, 1995, 1991 by Pearson Education, Inc.
Upper Saddle River, New Jersey 07458

Printed in the United States of America
10 9 8 7 6 5 4 3 2 1

ISBN   0-13-098230-X

Pearson Education LTD., *London*
Pearson Education Australia PTY, Limited, *Sydney*
Pearson Education Singapore, Pte. Ltd
Pearson Education North Asia Ltd, *Hong Kong*
Pearson Education Canada, Ltd., *Toronto*
Pearson Educación de Mexico, S.A. de C.V.
Pearson Education–Japan, *Tokyo*
Pearson Education Malaysia, Pte. Ltd
Pearson Education, Upper Saddle River, *New Jersey*

CONTENTS

PREFACE

The world is, increasingly, a single place. The crisis events, epidemics, and environmental pollution in seemingly remote countries can and do affect our own health and well-being. In 2001, as we began writing this text, events surrounding attacks on the World Trade Center and the Pentagon, American troops in battle in Afghanistan, fear of an epidemic of anthrax, and a serious economic recession, reminded Americans that our health and our lives cannot be taken for granted. Yet, as we seek greater security for our people, we must remember that real security requires much more than military security. It requires *social* security—the assurance that the society will support its members, mutually protecting each other through our institutions and social policies. Enduring security, thus, involves society-wide health security.

This volume addresses that larger image of the kind of health security we need. Sickness and death are not random but occur in discernible patterns. Carefully using societal resources to address the sources of those patterns of sickness and death can promote real health security. For example, rather than focusing narrowly on trying to prevent bioterrorist contamination of city water supplies, we could address *all* sources of water contamination, such as industrial pollution and inadequate sewage treatment. Instead of wondering merely how to protect government office and postal workers from anthrax spores, we could ask how to make work in the whole society safer and less stressful. Rather than pay profiteering pharmaceutical corporations for a stockpile of treatments for bioterrorism, we could address the problems of drug pricing and the failure of the system to make needed pharmaceutical available to all citizens. Instead of worrying about preventing terrorists from aerial spraying of toxic substances, we could create adequate environmental controls to prevent agribusinesses from aerial spraying of toxic pesticides and manufacturers from releasing sickening air pollution. Rather than focusing on providing temporary relief for those unemployed in the aftermath of terrorist attacks, we could assure *all* citizens that they could earn an adequate living-wage to support themselves and their families.

Despite the fact that the United States spends far more (per capita and as a percentage of the Gross National Product) on health care than any other country in the world, our citizens do *not* enjoy better health or longer lives. In fact, as Chapter 11 shows, on most measures of health, Americans fare worse than nearly all other economically advanced countries. National security of health, in this wider sense, would address the causes of so many Americans' premature deaths. The sociology of health and illness identifies many of these causes.

This is not a standard medical sociology text; instead, it presents a critical, holistic interpretation of health, illness, and human bodies that emphasizes power as a key social-structural factor in health and in societal responses to illness. Some of the most interesting recent health-related research explores precisely those areas of social life where power differences are evident: gender, race and ethnicity, poverty and wealth, work and professions, abuse and violence, the physical and social environment, and health care financing and delivery, among others. The politics of the debate over U.S. health care "reform" also illustrates the importance of power and wealth—especially of corporate actors—in setting the very terms of discourse, not merely affecting the policy outcomes.

This text does not attempt to cover every relevant topic, but is organized as a set of core essays around which to build a course. Thus, for example, the topics of women's health issues, race and ethnic factors in health and illness, and HIV/AIDS are discussed in several different sections, rather than all under one heading. Students using the Index will find a wealth of information and references for further research on these and other important issues. Using this text as a core reading, instructors can assign related articles, monographs, or readings to complement their own emphases.

Chapter 1 outlines relevant problems and key concepts in the field, and especially shows how this text links materialist and social-constructionist theories of health and illness through the unifying theme of power. Chapter 2 introduces students to social epidemiology, and outlines broad patterns of morbidity and mortality. This fourth edition emphasizes international health and illness comparisons and issues, especially in Chapters 2, 3, and 11. Chapters 3 through 5 describe the social production of unhealthy bodies and develop interpretations of the nature of connections among mind, body, and society. Chapters 6 through 9 discuss the social context of ideas and experiences of health and illness. Chapters 10 through 12 examine social and cultural factors in the medical system's treatment of sick persons and the political economy of health care in the United States.

Appendix A outlines major resources for a search of the literature in the field. Students preparing term papers or theses will find these resources essential. The book's extensive bibliography should also be invaluable for researchers. Appendix B is an annotated list of new video resources. We have found good visual presentations to be excellent aids for concretizing and illustrating points that are often far from students' personal experiences, as well as for stimulating discussion. These Appendices (including the full annotated list of recommended films), together with a chapter-by-chapter list of Recommended Readings and other pedagogical aids, will be available with links at http://www.trinity.edu/mmcguire.

Previous users of this text will recognize that we now have the assistance of a third author, Dr. Linda Podhurst, a medical sociologist at the University of Medicine and Dentistry of New Jersey. Even as this book was being written,

Dr. Podhurst began work on an important new international public health initiative in pediatric AIDS treatment and prevention. Her work in Newark, New Jersey, sub-Saharan Africa, and other places hard hit by the global epidemic of HIV/AIDS is highly relevant for our emphasis on seeing U.S. health and illness in a global context.

In writing this fourth edition, we have received additional help from several persons, whose assistance we gratefully acknowledge: Miriam Fisher, Lauren Johnson, Debra Kantor, Liana Knudsen, George Martin, Bob Podhurst, Jim Spickard, Sheryl Tynes, and Freda Zackin. Special thanks to Jim Spickard for constructing our charts and graphs and for giving much IT support. We appreciate the advice and encouragement of our editors, Nancy Roberts and Sharon Chambliss. Also, we very much appreciate Kieran McGuire's graphic design tailored to this text. We thank Kristen Carney, Irma DeLeon, Ashley Fry, Kathryn Hammond and Franke Johnson for assistance in manuscript preparation. Finally, we want to thank our partners and families for putting up with us during the writing of this book and for illustrating by their very lives why sociologists should care about health.

Chapter 1

A SOCIOLOGICAL PERSPECTIVE ON HEALTH, ILLNESS, AND THE BODY

❀ ❀

"Individuals who enjoy good health rightly think of themselves as fortunate: But luck has little to do with the broad patterns of disease and mortality that prevail in each society. The striking variations in health conditions among countries and cultural groups reflect differences in social and physical environments. And increasingly, the forces that shape health patterns are set in motion by human activities and decisions. Indeed, *in creating its way of life, each society creates its way of death.*" [emphasis added]

> *Source:* Erik Eckholm, *The Picture of Health: Environmental Sources of Disease.*
> New York: W. W. Norton, 1977, pp. 18–19.

- **The Social Construction of the Body**
- **The Social Construction of Ideas about the Body**
  Health Beliefs and Practices
  The Medical Model
- **The Centrality of Power in the Sociology of Health and Illness**
- **The Perspective of This Text**

When we think of health and illness, we usually think of eating properly and other healthy habits, of institutions such as hospitals, and of health professionals such as doctors and nurses. Although we may be dimly aware that health has its social dimensions, we may not think of health as a topic for social scientists.

Sociological analysis emphasizes that the occurrence of illness is not random. Different kinds of societies produce different patterns of illness and death. As Eckholm's statement on the preceding page shows, our material social and cultural way of life is linked with our way of death. The sociology of health and illness studies such issues as how social and cultural factors influence health and people's perceptions of health and healing, and how healing is done in different societies. Social structures and cultural practices have concrete consequences for people's lives.

We like to think that a newborn infant is as yet untouched by these abstract forces and has possibilities for health limited only by the child's genetic makeup. Even at birth, however, these abstract forces have begun to inscribe themselves on the baby's body. The very life chances of this infant, including the probabilities that she will live, be well, acquire the skills for success in her culture, and achieve and maintain that success, are powerfully influenced by all of the social circumstances and forces she will encounter throughout her life. In short, the baby's life chances, including possibilities for health and long life or sickness and death, are shaped or constructed by society itself.

The baby's birth weight, for example, is influenced by her mother's diet, which in turn is partly a product of her society, her culture, and her social class. Other features of the mother's social context have direct consequences for the newborn's health, including the mother's smoking or drug habits, the housing and sanitary conditions in which the infant is born, and the like. Later, whether the baby is a victim of cholera, bubonic plague, schistosomiasis, or lead poisoning depends on public health measures taken in her environment. What other factors in the baby's home life and environment will shape her sense of self and self-esteem, and her ability to cope with stress and manage her environment? As she matures, how will her gender, race, ethnicity, and social class influence her life chances?

Later in life, her experiences as a worker will place her in various physical environments and social relationships that will affect her health. Her culture will shape what she likes to eat, how she experiences stress, whether she drinks alcohol, and how she feels about her body. How she experiences the process of giving birth will be shaped by her culture's meanings of childbirth as well as by the social context of birth, such as whether it takes place in a hospital under the supervision of an obstetrician trained in Western notions of pregnancy as a medical problem.

The infant is born into a social structure and culture that also powerfully influence what will be considered illness and how that illness will be treated. When this person gets sick, social forces play an important role in determining her chances of becoming well. How does she decide when she is sick and needs help? If she is sick, for example with a bad cold, how will others respond? If she develops multiple sclerosis, how will the attitudes and responses of others, and the quality of her social and physical environment affect her very life chances? What will happen if she develops a stigmatizing illness, such as leprosy or AIDS?

What resources are available to her in dealing with her needs when ill? If she approaches the medical system for help, how does she pay for it? How do her social class, age, race, and ability to pay influence the quality of her medical care? How does the institutional context of her medical care (for example, a public versus a for-profit private hospital, or a nursing home compared to a hospice or home care) help determine its quality? In addition to the quality of life, even the quality of death is linked with such social contexts.

Medical systems involve concrete organizations that reflect the economic interests of such groups as doctors and other professionals, insurance companies, pharmaceutical industries, manufacturers of medical equipment, hospitals, research organizations, government agencies, and medical schools. They all compete for resources, influence policy, and try to set health care and research agendas. Health care systems differ greatly from society to society in how they define and meet the needs of individual citizens. The baby's life chances are intimately intertwined, therefore, with these seemingly remote social organizations.

The fates of individual bodies are thus linked to the workings of the social body. A person's life chances are neither some deterministic fate nor a purely accidental, random result. Rather, a person's chances for illness and successful recovery are very much the result of specifiable social arrangements, which are in turn products of human volition and indeed deliberate policy choices made by identifiable groups and individuals. In large part, illness, death, health, and well-being are socially produced.

THE SOCIAL CONSTRUCTION OF THE BODY

To construct is to make or build something. Clearly, societies do not literally make or produce bodies, but they can influence, shape, and misshape them. Just as an artist can mold clay to construct an object (which is constrained by the physical properties of the clay), social groups and the cultures they share can shape members' bodies. Obvious examples of cultural shaping of the human body include the foot binding practiced in traditional Chinese society, the cradle boards used to shape infants' heads among the Kwakiutl Indians, the stays and corsets worn by nineteenth-century middle-class European and American women, and the high heels and pierced earrings favored today. Similarly, having to live in a polluted environment or to sit at a desk, to work on an assembly line, or to bend over all day in a mine shaft are examples of social conditions that can indirectly shape the body and in turn the body's health.

A biologist illustrates the physical consequences of social practices:

> If a society puts half its children in dresses and skirts but warns them not to move in ways that reveal their underpants, while putting the other half in jeans and overalls and encouraging them to climb trees and play ball and other active outdoor games; if

later, during adolescence, the half that has worn trousers is exhorted to "eat like a growing boy" while the half in skirts is warned to watch its weight and not get fat; if the half in jeans trots around in sneakers or boots, while the half in skirts totters about on spike heels, then these two groups of people will be biologically as well as socially different. Their muscles will be different, as will their reflexes, posture, arms, legs and feet, hand-eye coordination, spatial perception, and so on. They will also be biologically different if, as adults, they spend eight hours a day sitting in front of a visual display terminal or work on a construction job or in a mine. (Hubbard, cited in Vines, 1993: 93–94).

Those things that happen to human bodies are closely related to the working and anatomy of the social body. Illness is not merely a physical experience but also a social experience. The sick body is not simply a closed container, encased in skin, that has been invaded by germs or traumatic blows; rather, it is open and connected to the world that surrounds it. Thus, the human body is open to the social body. Similarly, our material (or physical) environment, such as the urban landscape, the workplace, or our foods, are influenced by our culture, social structure, and relationships. And these, in turn, influence our bodies.

THE SOCIAL CONSTRUCTION OF IDEAS ABOUT THE BODY

Ideas, too, are constructions. Every society has many levels of shared ideas and practices regarding bodies: What is defined as healthy and beautiful in one society might be considered unhealthily fat and ugly in another; what is seen as thin and lean in one group might be defined as sickly in another. Aging may also be defined as a process to be either conquered, feared, accepted, or revered. Likewise, some societies picture the body as working like a machine, whereas others see it as a spiritual vessel.

Health Beliefs and Practices

Because they are social constructions, our ideas of the body and its health and illness are influenced by both our culture and our social position, such as class or gender. Both cultural and social structural factors are important in understanding people's behavior and health. People act as they do not only because of their beliefs about health (the cultural aspects) but also because of structural aspects, such as how power is distributed and relationships are organized. Thus, although we conceptually distinguish cultural and social structural aspects, in actuality they overlap.

Culture is the beliefs, values, practices, and material objects shared by a people. Culture includes such elements as language, beliefs about the universe and the nature of good and evil, ideals such as justice or freedom, and more mundane considerations such as what constitutes appropriate food, dress, and manners. It also encompasses objects that a people produce and share. Cooking utensils, automobiles, plays, cemeteries, blueprints, crucifixes, tools, musical scores, and flags are among the items that represent cultural values and notions.

How do our cultural conceptions of a person's physical abilities affect those abilities? In our society, we used to believe that women were unable to carry heavy objects. Although biology contributes somewhat to women's physical abilities, so do cultural ideas. In a patriarchal society, women's expectations that they will be weak, together with the experience of being treated as weak because of their social status, have a self-fulfilling result: Women do not become strong. Culture can affect health by shaping behaviors, such as diet, or by influencing how people change their environments, which in turn affects their health (Brown and Inhorn, 1990).

Social structure (or social organization) is the relatively stable, ongoing pattern of social interaction. In a particular society, recognizable patterns of interaction are appropriate to different social positions and relationships, such as parent-child, supervisor-employee, teacher-student, and friend-friend. Behavior in these relationships is regulated through a number of mechanisms, including social control and shared cultural values. Various persons in social relationships occupy different social statuses. These relationships are often part of larger social organizational contexts; for example, the supervisor and employee positions may be part of a business corporation.

One feature of social structure is how it is stratified. People can be stratified or ranked according to such dimensions as class, ethnicity, age, and gender. Socioeconomic status (SES), or **social class,** is often measured by income, occupation, or wealth. A person's social location in socioeconomic stratification influences how much power the individual has to manage his or her body and external environment. Socioeconomic position can be used analytically to understand the social location and power of neighborhoods and communities, as well as individuals (Lynch and Kaplan, 2000).

Other determinants of power affect health. The particular position of power we occupy in our family (for example, child or parent) and our gender, race, and ethnicity are also all important factors. Even health status (being chronically ill, for instance) determines the stressors to which we are exposed and the coping resources available to us.

In understanding health and illness, cultural aspects to consider might include people's eating and hygienic practices and their ideas about health, illness, and healing. By contrast, structural elements might include a person's position and relationships in the workplace, family, and medical settings, as well as such social status indicators as gender, race, age, and class.

Both scientific and nonscientific ideas about health, illness, and the body are the result of social construction, as are the facts we assemble as evidence for our ideas about the world. All descriptions, including medical descriptions, are constructions in that they include some information and exclude other information. Similarly, definitions of health are social constructions. For example, the *International Dictionary of Medicine and Biology* defines health as "a state of well-being of an organism or part of one, characterized by normal function and unattended by disease" (Becker, 1986: v. 2, 1276). This definition delineates well-being only in terms of bodily functioning and the absence of disease. But are we necessarily healthy if we simply lack disease? And are all diseases necessarily unhealthy? Is it healthy to function under all (however miserable) conditions? Why should functioning be such an important criterion? Is it because our society places so much cultural emphasis on certain forms of functioning?

The Medical Model

Our culture derives many of its ideas about the body from the Western biomedical model. A sociological perspective on health and illness, however, does not take this model as truth. Rather, medical ideas of the body and its diseases are also seen as socially constructed realities that are subject to social biases and limitations. Biomedical ideas are based on a number of historical assumptions about the body and ways of knowing about the body; the following are some of these historically created assumptions that have become embedded in the Western medical model. Chapter 9 develops these concepts in more detail.

One biomedical assumption is *mind-body dualism*. The medical model assumes a clear dichotomy between the mind and the body; physical diseases are presumed to be located solely within the body. As a result, biomedicine tries to understand and treat the body in isolation from other aspects of the person inhabiting it. The history of Western medical science suggests several of the sources of this image of the body as separate from mind or spirit.

Not only does the medical model dichotomize body and mind, but it also assumes that illness can be reduced to disordered bodily (biochemical or neurophysiological) functions. This *physical reductionism* excludes social, psychological, and behavioral dimensions of illness. One result is that medicine sees disease as localized in the individual body. Such conceptions prevent the medical model from conceiving of the social body or how aspects of the individual's social or emotional life might affect physical health. Thus, medicine generally ignores social conditions contributing to illness or promoting healing.

A related assumption of the biomedical model is what Dubos (1959) called the *doctrine of specific etiology*. This belief holds that each disease is caused by a specific, potentially identifiable agent. The history of Western medicine shows both the fruitfulness and the limitations of this assumption. Dubos noted that although the doctrine of specific etiology has led to important theoretical and practical achievements, it has rarely provided a complete account of the causation of disease. An adequate understanding of illness etiology must include broader factors, such as nutrition, stress, and metabolic states, which affect the individual's susceptibility to infection. As noted in Chapter 2, the search for specific illness-producing agents works relatively well in dealing with infectious diseases but is too simplistic to explain the causes of complex chronic illnesses. Also, as Dubos observed, this approach often results in a quest for the "magic bullet" to "shoot and kill" the disease, producing an overreliance on pharmaceuticals in the "armamentarium" (stock of "weapons") of the modern physician.

The *machine metaphor* is another implicit assumption in the medical model. Accordingly, the body is a complex biochemical machine, and disease is the malfunctioning of some constituent mechanism (such as a "breakdown" of the heart). Other cultures use other metaphors; for example, ancient Egyptian societies used the image of a river, and Chinese tradition refers to the balance of elemental forces (yin and yang) of the earth (Osherson and AmaraSingham, 1981). In combination with the assumption of mind-body dualism, the machine metaphor further encouraged the notion that the physician could "repair" one part in isolation from the rest (Berliner, 1975).

Partly as a product of the machine metaphor and the quest for mastery, the Western medical model also conceptualizes the body as the proper *object of regimen and control* (Foucault, 1979), again emphasizing the responsibility of the individual to exercise this control in order to maintain or restore health. This assumption meshes with other values, resulting in the medical and social emphases on such standardized body disciplines as diets, exercise programs, routines of hygiene, and even sexual activity (Turner, 1984: 157–203).

THE CENTRALITY OF POWER IN THE SOCIOLOGY OF HEALTH AND ILLNESS

One of the unifying themes of this text is the social construction of both ideas about the body and the body itself. In this process, power and control play an important role. In the most general sense, **power** is the ability to get what we want and to get things done.

Power is a ubiquitous factor in our daily lives. It both enables us to accomplish tasks (such as to get enough food) and constrains the number and types of possibilities open to us. This text emphasizes the relationship between health and power, such as the power of workers over their work pace; the power of people to control the quality of their physical environments; the power of various groups or societies to shape health policy or to deliver what they consider healing; the power of people of different statuses to control, receive, and understand information vital to their well-being; and the power of the mass media to shape ideas about food and fitness. In addition to these objective manifestations of power, we also subjectively experience power. Our sense of personal empowerment–a feeling that we can handle stressful situations, for instance–is important to health and well-being and strongly related to our ability to manage our environment and feel safe and secure in it. The power of individuals is not simply personal but also usually has a social basis.

The concept of social power in particular implies that the will of one individual or group can prevail over that of others. Our statuses (such as age and social class) in society determine the resources available for the exercise of power. For example, if I own a business and control its resources, I can decide how they will be used; generally, I have power in my workplace and have more resources to enforce my will than do the workers in my business.

Often our experiences deal not with overt power or control but relative, implicit power. For example, if I feel in control of my family life, I thus feel able to resist others' attempts to wrest control, whether by direct confrontation or by subtle manipulation. For this reason, power is typically enhanced when its exercise is accepted as legitimate. Likewise, when people do not recognize that power is being exercised, they may submit to control unwillingly and unknowingly. Concepts like "social status" and "social control" thus are significant in understanding the relationship between power and the body. Control refers to the exercise of power in a particular situation. Like a sense of empowerment, control is related to our ability to manage our environment and to feel safe and secure in it.

Social control may be defined as those ways in which a society assures itself of its members' proper and respectable behavior, appearances, productivity, and contributions. Social control assures the relatively smooth functioning of the social order and the maintenance of hierarchical relationships such as class.

This control may rely on violence, force, persuasion, and/or manipulation. Internalized forms of control, such as individual conscience, are far more subtle and effective means of assuring uniformity. The standards by which people learn to measure themselves are another way in which society uses the social self as a means of control. Social organizations also use their control of information to maintain power. For example, the regulation that workers have to punch a time clock is a device for assuring work attendance. Social control measures also affect those who are in power, as when they become their own slave drivers.

THE PERSPECTIVE OF THIS TEXT

Although our focus is sociological, we have drawn from many other disciplines and subdisciplines, such as medical sociology, medical anthropology and economics, socio- and psychophysiology, sociology and anthropology of the body, sociology of health and illness, social psychology, history, philosophy of the body, and ethics. Each has its separate focus, and persons contributing to one discipline are often unaware of related work in other fields. We emphasize synthesizing work from several disciplines to achieve a more holistic appreciation of health and illness that views healing and prevention in the broadest sense: The body is not treated as a self-enclosed machine, and health and illness are understood in their social, cultural, and historical contexts.

A holistic perspective is necessary, but difficult because it requires us to go beyond the rigid separations of concepts about the body, mind, and society. As Scheper-Hughes and Lock (1986: 137) wrote:

> We are without a language with which to address mind-body-society interactions, and so are left hanging in mid-air, suspended in hyphens that testify to the radical disconnectedness of our thoughts. We resort to such fragmented concepts as the biosocial, the psychosomatic, the psychosocial, the somatosocial, as feeble ways of expressing the complex and myriad ways that our minds speak to us through our bodies, and the ways in which society is inscribed on the expectant canvas of our flesh and bones, blood and guts.

We stress the interactions of mind, body, and society, and the importance of symbols and subjective experience in understanding health and illness. The narrow focus and unifactorial models of disease characterizing much of modern medicine and some of the sociology of health and illness deflect attention from the social issues implied by persisting inequalities in health status within most modern societies (Comaroff, 1982: 61), as well as the yet greater gaps of inequality between so-called developed and less developed nations. A critical sociology, thus, emphasizes the interconnected factors of social inequality, power, and social control in producing both illness and health.

SUMMARY

This text on the sociology of health and illness deals with the social construction of bodies, with an emphasis on how power shapes this construction. How cultural and social-structural factors and central power relationships influence us physically and how we perceive, care for, maintain, and "repair" our bodies constitute the major questions to be addressed. Our perspective is holistic, emphasizing the interpenetration of mind, body, and society.

The first part, Chapters 2 through 5, deals primarily with the ways in which society and culture affect physical functioning, and the material environments in which people exist. The second part, Chapters 6 through 9, emphasizes people's experience of their own and others' bodies, especially social aspects of the illness experience. The last part, Chapters 10 through 12, examines social and cultural factors in the medical systems' treatment of sick persons, and the political economy of health care in the United States.

WHO BECOMES SICK, INJURED, OR DIES?

❈ ❈

" 'You know,' [*a physician describing the dilemmas of practicing medicine*] said, 'sometimes it feels like this. There I am standing by the shore of a swiftly flowing river and I hear the cry of a drowning man. So I jump into the river, put my arms around him, pull him to shore and apply artificial respiration. Just when he begins to breathe, there is another cry for help. So I jump into the river, reach him, pull him to shore, apply artificial respiration, and then just as he begins to breathe, another cry for help. So back in the river again, reaching, pulling, applying, breathing and then another yell. Again and again, without end, goes the sequence. You know, I am so busy jumping in, pulling them to shore, applying artificial respiration, that I have *no* time to see who the hell is upstream pushing them all in.' "

Source: attributed to Irving Zola, cited in John B. McKinlay, "A Case for Refocusing Upstream: The Political Economy of Illness," pp. 516–529 in P. Conrad, ed., *The Sociology of Health and Illness.* New York: Worth, 2001.

Sickness does not just happen. Rather, discernible patterns are evident in the distribution and frequency of sickness, injury, and death in human populations. **Social epidemiology** is the study of the distribution of patterns of health and illness in human populations and of the social factors that shape them (Berkman and Kawachi, 2000).

REFOCUSING UPSTREAM: WHY *SOCIAL* EPIDEMIOLOGY

The wry anecdote on the preceding page reminds us that we, as a society—indeed, as a whole world—spend enormous energy and expense trying to save lives and rescue the sick *after* they have already fallen ill and suffered physical damage due to **preventable causes.** In order to "refocus upstream" and address those causes pushing people into the stream of sickness and death, we need to understand how *social* factors promote sickness and death. All humans die eventually, but many premature deaths are preventable. Some sickness is inevitable, but "refocusing upstream" could greatly reduce the amount and severity of sickness, allowing people to function better and live fuller—not just longer—lives. When people are being pushed into the stream of sickness and death by human social arrangements or identifiable human actions (and inaction), then social epidemiology can identify which social arrangements need to be changed for the well-being of all.

Noticing relationships between specific illnesses and people's social situation is hardly a new phenomenon: Early Greek and Egyptian writers made such connections (Sigerist, 1960). Popular lore also includes awareness of the linkage between, for example, an occupation and a sickness. *Alice in Wonderland*'s Mad Hatter was a plausible madman because people had recognized a connection between the occupation of hatmaking and bizarre behavior long before the relationship was traced to the effects of the mercury with which hatmakers regularly worked (Stellman and Daum, 1971: 255). Similarly, long before medicine identified the problem, villagers living by the Niger River in Africa recognized that their proximity to the river was related to the prevalence of a horrible sickness characterized by intense itching and eventual blindness. Often they would move away, abandoning valuable farmlands, when the sickness had affected too large a proportion of the community (Eckholm, 1989).

Before there was a formal discipline to study the social distribution of sickness or death, astute observers noticed the significance of social class and occupational variables. For example, more than 150 years ago, one chronicler noted:

> "In Bethnal Green in the year 1839 the average age of deaths in the several classes was as follows: Gentlemen and persons engaged in professions, and their families . . . 45 years; Tradesmen and their families . . . 26 years; Mechanics, servants and labourers, and their families . . . 16 years. . . . Although the average age of deaths in the different classes varied somewhat from area to area, the differences between the classes existed in all areas of the country" (cited in Blane, 1986: 113).

During the late eighteenth and early nineteenth centuries, industrialization set the stage for the development of the disciplines of both sociology and epidemiology (Spruit and Kromhout, 1987). The changes that accompanied industrial capitalism created radically different conditions for health and illness:

> The rates of smallpox, typhus, typhoid fever, diphtheria and scarlet fever all increased: two cholera epidemics had swept through the warrens of the Great Towns, a third was on its way. . . . The reordering of the circumstances of everyday life . . . ensued. Industrial capitalism gave rise to novel physical arrangements for work and dwelling (the factory, the company town), created new patterns of economic exploitation (mass displacements from land, urban migration in unprecedented numbers, wage labor). . . . Hazardous and fatiguing work, damp cold and stifling living quarters, cheap gin and adulterated foods, demoralization–the legacy of disease bequeathed by early capitalism stems from such an environment. (Susser et al., 1985: 4)

Epidemiology, as a discipline, evolved from early studies of epidemics among people living in such environments. Like sleuths tracing the path of a suspected criminal, epidemiologists examined clues to the path of a suspected source of infection. For example, in 1854 a cholera epidemic broke out in London. Sir John Snow pinpointed known cases of the disease on city maps, thus narrowing the search to certain neighborhoods. He then interviewed survivors and neighbors of cholera victims about everyday behavior, such as what the victims had eaten, where they had played, and so on. Snow discovered that all of the victims had obtained their water from the same pump. He concluded that there was a relationship between this source of water and cholera infection, and he had the pump shut down, thereby ending the epidemic (Snow, 1855).

Although modern epidemiologists have far more sophisticated tools such as computers and complex bacteriology laboratories, their underlying method remains much the same as Snow's. They search for patterns linking the types and incidence of sickness of a people with their way of life. Thus, epidemiological studies often highlight the political and social contexts of health and illness (see Box 2.1). The famous nineteenth-century epidemiologist Rudolf Virchow declared, "Medicine is a social science, and politics is nothing but medicine on a grand scale" (quoted in Susser et al., 1985: 6). Political and social factors are readily evident in studies showing certain diseases to be characteristic mainly of the rich; others occur almost exclusively among the poor. Political implications also follow, for instance, from epidemiological studies demonstrating certain occupations to be the causes or major contributing factors in certain illnesses and death. Epidemiology is only one of many approaches to understanding the connections between social arrangements and sickness or death, but epidemiological data receive special attention from policymakers because they describe large-scale differences applicable to entire industries, communities, or nations.

Complex Webs of Causal Factors

Epidemiology examines the interaction of complex disease-producing factors: a "web of causation" (MacMahon and Pugh, 1970). This web is composed of

Box 2.1

Fur Fashions and Plague

"The outbreak of Manchurian plague at the turn of this century constitutes a well-documented example of the role of living patterns in disease causation. The plague bacillus is widely distributed among the wild rodents of Asia. Manchurian marmots normally harbor this microbe, but they do not suffer from the infection under usual circumstances. Around 1910, a change in women's fashions in Europe suddenly created a large demand for the fur of the Manchurian marmot, and a number of inexperienced Chinese hunters began to hunt this wild rodent. Until then it had been hunted only by Manchurians who had a taboo forbidding them to hunt sick animals. In contrast, the inexperienced Chinese trapped every animal within reach, especially the sickest who were slower and easier to catch. As it turned out, the sick marmots were suffering from plague, and many Chinese hunters contracted the infection from them. When the hunters met in the crowded and ill-ventilated Manchurian inns, those who had caught the microbe spread it to their neighbors, thereby initiating a widespread epidemic of pneumonic plague. A change in women's fashions in Europe thus indirectly caused an epidemic of pneumonic plague in Manchuria."

Source: René Dubos, *Man, Medicine and Environment.* Baltimore: Penguin, 1968: 113.

three main, intertwining aspects: agent, host, and environment. The agent is the source of a disease, such as a virus in an infection or asbestos fibers in asbestosis. The agent is a necessary but not sufficient cause of disease; disease does not occur without an agent, but the agent alone is not sufficient to produce the disease.

The site within which an agent creates a disease is called the host. The host and agent interact within a biosocial environment, which includes the external conditions linking the agent to the host (such as unsanitary living conditions); the vector, or the means through which the agent is carried (such as diseased marmots or contaminated drinking water); and the condition of the internal environment of the host (such as relative immunity). To cause disease effectively, an agent must be able to survive in the environment and find a susceptible, fertile host (Johnson and Sargent, 1990). For example, a human body (host) may harbor tubercular bacilli (agent), but if the body's resistance is high, this disease agent cannot produce infection. Thus, disease is not the outcome of just one factor; rather, many factors contribute to the complex web of causation.

As the name implies, epidemiology arose from the study of widespread infectious diseases, or epidemics. The maturing field now includes study of the distribution, spread, and causes of noninfectious diseases (for example, heart disease, cancer), as well as of other conditions of ill health or death (for example, violence and abuses) which are not diseases of individual bodies. The epidemiology of these noninfectious sicknesses is more difficult than infectious diseases, however, because they develop more slowly, often over decades. The causal factors are thus obscured by time. A 60-year-old victim of a heart attack is not likely to be able to recall accurately relevant information about his life as much as 40 or 50 years earlier.

Noninfectious diseases also often involve multiple contributing factors rather than a single infectious agent. It is difficult to identify all possible factors and determine their relative weight. For example, the hormones in birth control pills have been implicated in the development, many years after their use, of breast cancer. But determining just how significant a factor they may be is complicated for several reasons. The disease does not develop in clinically observable forms immediately upon use of the pill. Other factors (such as the age of the onset of menstruation) are also involved and, in combination, greatly increase probability of developing the disease. Evaluating the relative importance of these various other factors (such as the woman's leanness, her age at the birth of her first baby, and whether she breastfed her babies) or even whether some possible factors are not being considered is difficult. It is hard to determine, many years after the fact, exactly how much or which type of hormones women received; formulations for early contraceptive pills contained much higher dosages of hormones and in different combinations than more recent formulations. If a woman is now 48, she may have taken several different formulations for many periods of varying length since the age of 18.

Although web of causation stresses *multiple* causes, this approach has a number of limitations. First, it still assumes disease to be a feature solely of *individual* bodies, divorced from their sociocultural contexts (Link and Phelan, 1995). Few epidemiological studies consider the "spiders" that "spin the web" (Krieger, 1994), that is, the fundamental social, cultural, and biological factors that interweave agent, host, and environment. Epidemiology needs an ecosocial approach incorporating historical, evolutionary, and sociopolitical determinants of health (Susser and Susser, 1996a, 1996b; see also MacIntyre and Ellaway, 2000).

Epidemiology's quantitative focus on separate, discrete variables is a different approach and level of analysis than those of qualitative studies of health and illness. Epidemiological approaches, alone, tend to treat data out of their social and historical contexts, thus reducing their complexity. Epidemiology should be combined with qualitative approaches (such as ethnography) to refine categories (for example, "race," "ethnicity") and to provide a richer, more textured picture of illness and health (Fenton and Charsley, 2000). In the chapters that follow, we suggest some of the spiders that weave the web of illness causation, for which we must look beyond epidemiological studies. Epidemiological studies, however, are a good starting place to describe *general* demographic factors linked to patterns of disease and death.

Methodological Issues

Epidemiology proceeds by observing statistical correlations between two or more variables pertaining to health, sickness (that is, morbidity) or death (that is, mortality). The data for these statistical procedures are often drawn from records kept for other institutional purposes; researchers must therefore contend with discrepancies or errors created by the original records.

Statistical Associations The existence of a statistical correlation between two variables is not sufficient evidence of a causal link between them. Many statistical relationships are spurious. For example, a nineteenth-century observer noted that the incidence of cholera was inversely correlated with the altitude of a community; low-lying places had higher rates of the disease than did those at higher altitudes. This correlation seemed to confirm a prevalent notion that stagnant air (miasma) caused cholera; accordingly, because their air was supposedly fresher, communities at higher altitudes had less miasma and thus less cholera. Later epidemiological discoveries showed that impure water was actually the vector (means of spreading the agent) for cholera. Because low-lying places were more likely to have both stagnant air and impure water, investigators had been led to a spurious correlation between the disease and miasma (Mausner and Bahn, 1985).

Historically, many epidemiological uses of statistical correlations have been seriously biased by racial or ethnic prejudice. Many late nineteenth- and early twentieth-century U.S. public health measures were justified by reference to epidemics allegedly caused by immigrants. An epidemic of smallpox in San Francisco between 1876 and 1877 was attributed to the immigrant Chinese, although deaths among Chinese San Franciscans accounted for only 77 of the 482 smallpox deaths in that epidemic. The city's public health officer attributed the epidemic to "unscrupulous, lying, and treacherous Chinamen who have disregarded our sanitary laws," merely on the basis of the statistical correlation between the influx of Chinese immigrants in the years prior to the outbreak and the increased morbidity compared to the previous epidemic (Kraut, 1994: 82).

Although epidemiology as a science has become more careful methodologically, similar misuse of epidemiological evidence arose in the early years of the AIDS epidemic, when oversimplified statistical correlations made AIDS appear to be linked to Haitian immigrants. In the early 1980s, the U.S. Centers for Disease Control announced that Haitian immigrants had been classified as a high-risk category for AIDS. A few years later, when it dropped this classification, the director of the Center for Infectious Disease acknowledged the spurious relationship, stating, "The Haitians were the only risk group that were identified because of who they were rather than what they did" (cited in Kraut, 1994: 261).

It is often difficult to determine whether a statistical correlation is the product of an indirect relationship actually explained by intervening variables. For example, epidemiological data from the rural southern regions of the United States may show a statistical correlation between low birth weight and childhood deaths from diarrhea. Does that mean that low birth weight causes subsequent death from diarrheal dehydration? This is a plausible interpretation because birth weight may affect the child's susceptibility to illness, but birth weight may be only a by-product of some other causal factors. One clue is to ask a somewhat oversimplified question: What kind of children are likely to experience both low birth weight and diarrhea? The profile of children with these conditions suggests several related features: They are likely to be from poor families in which the mother was young and received little or no prenatal care (Stevens, 1988). To establish a direct causal link between low birth weight and death due to diarrhea, it would be necessary to identify and hold constant all other factors. Any causal analysis must take into account multiple factors that may operate at several levels in the web of causality.

Bases of Data   Epidemiological studies may be based on seriously flawed records. Some statistics come from the records of schools, industries, insurance companies, hospitals, and public health departments. Because these data are kept for various other institutional reasons, they are often of limited accuracy for epidemiological purposes. For example, industrial accident statistics can be distorted by an industry's attempt to give the impression of a low accident rate.

Likewise, death certificates are very inaccurate and unreliable sources of information about the causes of death (Hill and Anderson, 1988, 1991). A Connecticut study found that 29 percent of death certificates inaccurately stated the cause of death, based on autopsy reports and patients' medical records (Kircher et al., 1985). In a further 26 percent of the cases, the autopsy and death certificate gave the same general disease category but attributed death to different specific diseases. More than half of the certificates thus provided seriously flawed data about the cause of death. Similarly, interviewing doctors in a Scottish city, Bloor (1991) found wide variations in how deaths were certified.

The usefulness of data from both medical records and death certificates may also be diminished by judgments made by the medical personnel who keep the records. Deliberate misrepresentations often occur when the cause of death is a stigmatizing sickness, such as alcoholism or AIDS. Such reporting problems make it difficult to assess the scope and actual impact of these important health problems. Political, economic, and ideological considerations also figure into the deliberate underreporting of the incidence of stigmatized diseases.

Death certificates also often state only a final cause of death, rather than the initial or contributing causes. For example, a person who dies of a gunshot wound may be listed as having died of internal bleeding. Although the bleeding is a fact in the case, the gunshot wound does not appear in the mortality statistics. Certain causes of death, such as adverse reactions to prescribed medications, are also systematically underreported (Altman, 1988).

The *International Statistical Classification of Diseases, Injuries and Causes of Death,* revised about every ten years by the National Center for Health Statistics of the United States, specifies standards to be used by attending doctors, coroners, and others in an attempt to produce internationally comparable data. Changes in these guidelines for classification, however, yield different rates of morbidity and mortality. One revision of the manual required coders to disregard medically induced (iatrogenic) causes of death, such as postsurgical bleeding or drug reaction, and instead to record the medical condition that first necessitated the treatment (Bloor et al., 1987). The most recent classification guidelines code asks for the immediate cause of death and a sequential listing of *all* underlying causes. These new data will likely result in the discovery of comparatively high rates of medically induced conditions leading to death.

Despite recent efforts to change the format of U.S. death certificates to allow for more complex and thorough reporting, the data entered on them remain problematic. Most death certificates are based on doctors' clinical judgments about the cause or causes of death; autopsies are expensive and performed for a decreasing proportion of cases. Whereas in the 1950s, autopsies were performed on about half of all patients who died in a hospital, current rates are only about 5–10 percent, performed disproportionately for forensic (that is, legal) evidence and, thus, hardly a representative sample. Even when an autopsy subsequently contradicts the certificate or adds significant new information (which is the case for 20–40 percent of autopsies), physicians often do not amend it (Brody, 2001).

Even if autopsy findings are included on death certificates, these data may be slanted by the criteria used to select cases for autopsy. Women are less likely to be autopsied than men. In some states, nonwhite deaths are less likely to be investigated than those of whites (Bloor et al., 1987). Social status and/or the perceived social worth of the victim may also influence the thoroughness with which a death is investigated (see, for example, Sudnow, 1967). The cases autopsied are not a representative sample of all deaths.

So-called errors or variations in diagnosis are not random; they are often socially produced. For example, medical personnel's judgments may vary according to the perceived social class of the dead person. In earlier medical reporting, the cause of a professional person's death from heart disease was likely to be labeled "angina," whereas the cause of death of a working-class person with the same condition was usually classified as something else (Marmot et al., 1987). Similarly, diagnoses (and thus morbidity statistics) are influenced by doctors' attitudes toward patients' social characteristics, such as gender, social class, or occupation, as discussed further in Chapters 9 and 10. For example, earlier data indicated that the rate of deaths due to alcoholism in Scotland was about twice those in England and Wales; these data are now in question, because studies show that doctors in England and Wales are much less likely than those in Scotland to attribute death to alcohol-related diseases such as cirrhosis (see Altman, 1988).

Cultural differences in medical practice, even among Western industrial nations and among doctors trained in modern biomedicine, account for some variations in diagnoses. For example, blood pressure readings considered hypertensive in the United States would be considered normal in England (Payer, 1988). Doctor characteristics may also affect the diagnosis or reported cause of death. Because of differences in their training, younger British doctors were less likely than older ones to report stomach cancer as a diagnosis (Bloor et al., 1987). Thus, a falling rate of mortality due to stomach cancer may be at least in part an artifact of differences in doctors' education.

These examples show that many health statistics may be *artifactual,* or produced by the social arrangements by which the statistics themselves are gathered and processed. Such artifactual evidence is misleading and often altogether incorrect. With these limitations in mind, let us examine some results of epidemiological investigation. The cautious use of epidemiological information can give us a broad picture of health.

CHANGES IN LIFE EXPECTANCY AND OTHER HEALTH INDICATORS

The twentieth century saw dramatic increases in life span, worldwide—particularly in the richer countries that became economically "developed."[1] Most of this gain was achieved by reducing "premature" mortality; that is, the average life expectancy rose particularly due to the reduction of deaths among infants, children, and young adults. It is worthwhile to examine and compare such health indicators as infant and child mortality rates, both between countries and over time. These comparative data suggest clues about where to invest efforts and money in order to improve people's health and to prevent illness and untimely death. The last part of this chapter examines some variables in the United States for such clues.

American males born in 1900 could expect to live 46.3 years, and females, 48.3 years. By 1999, the life expectancy for both sexes had increased, but so had the gap between male and female rates. Males born in 1999 can expect to live 73.9 years; females born that same year could live on the average to the age of 79.4 years (USDHHS, 2001a). Figure 2.1 shows the dramatic increase in life span in the United States by decades from 1900 to 1999.

A general decline of infant mortality and increasing difference in life expectancy between men and women began to emerge around 1920. In 1999, the infant mortality rate[2] for the United States was 7.1 deaths per 1,000 (USDHHS, 2001a). Figure 2.2 shows U.S. patterns of infant mortality between 1920 and 1999. There are also dramatic differences between blacks and whites in both general life expectancy and infant mortality. Infant mortality rates are a crude indicator of a nation's health status. Relative to other economically developed nations, the United States has a very high infant mortality rate, ranking twenty-sixth among the world's "developed" nations (USDHHS, 2000: 157). Similarly, the United States has a high under-five child mortality rate, ranking behind all other developed countries in a worldwide comparison, and tying for thirtieth place with Cuba, which has a "developing" economy (UNICEF, 2000).

---

[1]The terms "developed" and "underdeveloped" are unfortunately laden with connotations of superiority and inferiority and fail to indicate the extent to which wealthier and more powerful nations have historically prevented other countries from becoming "developed." Because these are the terms used by the United Nations and other data-gathering agencies, however, we have continued to use them.

[2]The infant mortality rate is the number of children who die within the first year, calculated per 1,000 live births.

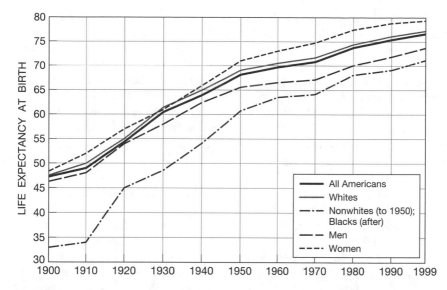

FIG 2.1   **Changes in U.S. Life Expectancy, 1900–1999.** *(Sources:* USDHHS, *Health United States, 2001; U.S. Bureau of the Census,* Historical Statistics of the United States, Colonial Times to 1970. *Bicentennial edition, part 2. Washington, DC, 1975.)*

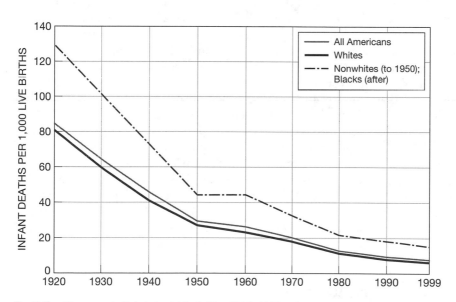

FIG 2.2   **Changes in U.S. Infant Mortality, 1920–1999.** *(Sources:* USDHHS, *Health United States, 2001; U.S. Bureau of the Census,* Historical Statistics of the United States, Colonial Times to 1970. *Bicentennial edition, part 2. Washington, DC, 1975.)*

Along with life expectancy changes have also come changes in the causes of death in Western industrial societies. Despite the recent development of some infectious diseases such as AIDS, there has been a long-term decline in death rates due to infectious diseases and an increase in death rates due to chronic degenerative diseases (McKinlay et al., 1989). In 1900, acute infectious diseases (pneumonia, influenza, and tuberculosis) were the foremost causes of death in the United States. Chronic diseases (heart disease, cancer, cerebrovascular disease, and chronic lower respiratory disease) were the major killers in 1999. In the last two decades of the twentieth century, the death rate from coronary heart disease decreased, but rates of death from cancer and diabetes increased (USDHHS, 2001a).

This shift from infectious to chronic degenerative diseases is part of **epidemiological transition,** characterizing changes in societies as they become more developed. Nevertheless, infectious disease can also be chronic (as is the case with AIDS) and infectious diseases are still a source of morbidity and mortality in developed societies (Radley, 1994). Some evidence indicates that since 1980, mortality from infectious diseases in the United States has been increasing, after years of steady decline. In 1980, infectious diseases ranked fifth as cause of death; by 1992, they ranked third (Pinner et al., 1996). Possible reasons for these increased rates include the spread of AIDS and diseases such as tuberculosis (of which some strains are resistant to antibiotics), especially in contexts of increased poverty (Pinner et al., 1996; Radley, 1994). Nonetheless, chronic degenerative diseases (including heart disease and cancer) still predominate as causes of death.

The increased incidence of chronic degenerative diseases cannot be attributed simply to the fact that people are living longer. It is true that the longer people live, the more likely they are to develop a chronic disease; however, increased longevity does not account for the fact that, beginning in the 1950s, even *younger* age groups have shown an increased incidence of these afflictions (Eyer and Sterling, 1977; McMurray and Smith, 2001). This premature development of degenerative sickness may be the result of contemporary dietary, environmental, and social factors. Evidence that the social, biochemical, and physical environment of industrialized societies create new health problems, such as increased rates of cancer, comes from a comparison with preindustrial societies, which have lower incidence of these problems (McMurray and Smith, 2001). Aspects of the way of life in industrialized societies are implicated because the rates of chronic degenerative diseases increase among groups that migrate from agricultural to industrial communities (Janes, 1986).

THE MYTH OF MEDICAL PROGRESS

Many people believe miracles of medical progress have been responsible for the improved health and longevity in Western industrial countries since the turn of the century. Media imagery often contributes to this notion, but much evidence suggests the contribution of medical intervention to increased life expectancy has been rather limited. McKeown (1979) argues that improved nutrition and population control, the control of predators, and improvements in urban dwelling conditions and hygiene have played a much greater role in extending life expectancy than has medical technology. The impact of these various factors on health can be documented through epidemiological studies.

A study of mortality rates in the United States shows that medical intervention (such as inoculations) accounts for only a small percentage of the decline in mortality from infectious diseases during the early part of the twentieth century (Kates, 1996: 57; Wilkinson, 1996: 66–67). Another study (Bunker et al., 1994) calculated that only about five to seven years of the 30 years by which U.S. life expectancy increased in the twentieth century have been due to any form of preventive or therapeutic *medical* care.

Figure 2.3 shows that, of nine common infectious diseases, only poliomyelitis began to decline significantly *after* the introduction of the vaccine. All the other major infectious diseases had declined dramatically prior to the introduction of a vaccine or antibiotic (McKinlay and McKinlay, 1977). The near-eradication of smallpox was *not* due mainly to new technologies (for example, vaccines), but to international surveillance and communities' rapid and concerted response to outbreaks (Baxby, 1995). The decline of tuberculosis likewise preceded the introduction of chemical therapies (Friedman, 1987). Nonmedical factors, such as improved nutrition, clean water, garbage and sewage disposal, and other public health measures, may account for the primary decline in mortality due to many infectious diseases.

The precise contribution of medicine to increased life expectancy, to the reduction of morbidity, and to the quality of life is difficult–if not impossible–to assess. Some have argued that the iatrogenic (that is, medically induced) health risks of modern medicine and its institutions outweigh its benefits (Illich, 1975). This position probably overstates the harmful effects of modern medicine. Nevertheless, any evaluation of the contribution of medical intervention must take into account its iatrogenic consequences, such as unneeded surgery, over- and misprescription of drugs, the negative side effects of medication, and infections transmitted in medical settings.

Without a doubt medicine has made significant contributions to human health. It is effective in treating many acute diseases. Emergency medicine has saved many lives, and technological innovations in medicine since World War I have made it possible for many to survive previously mortal health crises. Medicine has also played a major role in the virtual eradication of some infectious diseases, such as smallpox and polio. The ability of medicine to treat or prevent chronic, degenerative diseases is more limited, however. Furthermore, the benefits from medical progress must be distinguished from social-environmental changes and public health measures that have played a major part in improving people's health. The contributions of public health measures are often devalued by modern medicine, resulting in social policies that allocate the vast majority of health care expenditures

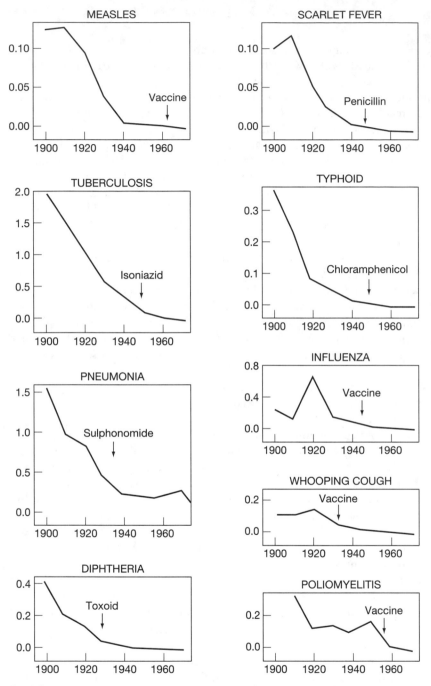

FIG 2.3 **The Fall in the Standardized Death Rate (per 1,000 Population) for Nine Common Infectious Diseases in Relation to Specific Medical Measures in the United States, 1900–1973.** *(Sources: John B. McKinlay and Sonja M. McKinlay, "The questionable effect of medical measures on the decline of mortality in the United States in the twentieth century," Milbank Memorial Fund Quarterly 55, 1977: 422–423.)*

to medical research and treatments rather than to preventive programs such as maternal nutrition or workplace safety.

MORBIDITY AND MORTALITY IN A GLOBAL PERSPECTIVE

The pattern of high rates of mortality due to infectious diseases that was evident in industrialized societies at the beginning of the twentieth century still characterizes the health situation of many parts of the world. International comparisons corroborate the historical comparisons: Life and health are largely the product of healthy living conditions. When people's living conditions—nutrition, sanitation, clean water, adequate shelter, safe workplaces—improve, then sickness and "premature" death are greatly reduced. Life expectancies in economically advantaged countries are substantially higher than in the rest of the world.

On average, compared to people in poorer countries, those in economically advantaged countries live more of their life span in relative good health. In 2000, the World Health Organization (WHO) changed its method of calculating longevity, taking the expected overall life longevity and subtracting years "lost" to disability and debilitating diseases (weighted for severity). Thus, for example, Uganda—a desperately poor country, struggling with epidemic AIDS, malaria, and tuberculosis—has the low overall life expectancy at birth of about 42 (World Bank, 2001b), but many people are living with diseases so debilitating that the average "healthy life expectancy" at birth is closer to 32.7 years. In the WHO rankings, all of the countries in the lowest ten were in Sub-Saharan Africa, where overall life expectancy has been dropping dramatically since about 1990, as discussed further in this chapter (WHO, 2000).

By contrast, the top countries for healthy life expectancy were all relatively economically advantaged: Japan (74.5 years), Australia (73.2), France (73.1), Sweden (73.0), Spain (72.8). Not only was their overall average life expectancy greater than lower-ranked countries, but also the years "lost" to debilitating disease or injury were fewer. In this rating system, the United States ranked twenty-fourth (70.0 years)—lower than most other economically advantaged countries (WHO, 2000). Some of the reasons for this low ranking, as compared with many countries with far less per capita income, are discussed further in this chapter and in Chapter 11.

Average life expectancies and mortality rates are somewhat misleading statistics, however, because they do not reflect the variations between subgroups (such as class, gender, and rural-urban differences) within each society. For example, the "healthy life expectancy" rate for Brazil is relatively low (59.1 years), but the southern half (where wealthier citizens are concentrated) has a relatively high rate (WHO, 2000). Extreme disparities between the living conditions of the wealthy and the poor explain most of this difference. The average infant mortality rate for Brazil is 43.2 and the average under-five mortality rate is 116.7. The richest quintile (20 percent) of Brazil's population, however, experiences only a 15.3 infant mortality rate, while the poorest quintile has a rate of 72.7 (nearly five times as great). The richest quintile has an under-five mortality rate of 18.7, compared to

113.3 for the poorest quintile—more than six times as great (World Bank, 2001b). Thus, in countries with great disparities between the richest and poorest citizens, the average rates may lead us to underestimate the amount of suffering and death of a large proportion of the populace.

In developing countries, as in nineteenth-century Europe and America, such factors as inadequate diet and unsanitary conditions contribute greatly to the high mortality rate and prevalence of infectious diseases. (Chapter 3 discusses further the problem of world hunger.) As of the beginning of the twenty-first century, nearly one-quarter of people in developing countries lacked access to safe drinking water, and approximately half lacked adequate sanitation (World Bank, 2001a). Childhood diseases such as measles are much more likely to result in death where nutrition and sanitation are poor. Indeed, communicable diseases account for 59 percent of all deaths among the poorest quintile of the world population, compared to only 8 percent among the richest quintile (World Bank, 2001b).

Many Westerners consider Third World countries to be inherently disease ridden, eagerly awaiting the benefits of modern civilization. In reality, the intrusion of so-called civilization from the West has introduced devastating infectious diseases to Third World peoples. Native peoples of the Americas and Polynesia were decimated by diseases introduced by European explorers, sailors, merchants, and colonists (Kraut, 1994). Since Captain Cook's voyage there in 1778, more native Hawaiians have died of infectious diseases introduced by foreigners than of all other causes combined (Bushnell, 1993).

In the nineteenth century, Africa was viewed as a "white man's grave," a disease-filled "dark continent." Many diseases, however, such as smallpox, syphilis, measles, influenza, cholera, and tuberculosis, were introduced to Africa from Europe and Asia, devastating native populations, which had no immunity to diseases to which they had never been exposed. The colonization of Africa and the slave trade created massive sociocultural dislocations and altered patterns of land use. Migration to the cities and the attendant overcrowding, as well as the ecological disruption of the land, generated conditions that bred and spread certain infectious diseases. In epidemiological terms, alterations in the environment made for a changed relationship among host, agent, and environment. For instance, in western Africa the development of logging, commercial agriculture, roads, railways, and other changes in the landscape created sites (infection reservoirs) for breeding mosquitoes and thus for spreading malaria (Epstein and Packard, 1987).

In countries such as South Africa, radically different pictures of health exist side by side in the same society. As a whole, South Africa has a highly developed economy. Nevertheless, the policy of apartheid (1950–1993) produced the social and economic domination of a white minority over a nonwhite majority by radical segregation of housing, education, occupations, and legal status. This social arrangement resulted in very different living conditions for whites and nonwhites, and hence in different patterns of morbidity and mortality. The infant mortality for blacks in South Africa is approximately six times higher than that of whites.

One-quarter of black children under 14 years of age are chronically malnourished or undernourished. By contrast, hardly any malnutrition or undernutrition exists among whites, and whites generally die of "diseases of affluence," which are linked with lifestyles characterized by high-calorie diets and sedentary occupations. Blacks are more likely to die of infectious diseases, such as cholera, tuberculosis, and measles (a disease that is rarely fatal in affluent societies). Thus, in one nation, two very different ways of life produce different health profiles. These differences are a dramatic illustration of how social-structural arrangements (that is, apartheid) can produce different patterns of health, illness, and death (Frankel, 1986).

Another socially produced cause of illness, disability, and death is human violence toward other humans. Assault, homicide, and domestic violence take an enormous toll on the health and well-being of people worldwide. When the person who is killed or maimed by such violence is also economically and/or emotionally the support of a family, the long-term health of many people can be harmed. War and other organized violence harm people indirectly, by destroying or siphoning off valuable resources that people need for their subsistence. Many countries spend a large portion of their gross domestic product (GDP) on military expenditures, rather than social needs. For example, Pakistan bought 40 fighter jets from a French transnational corporation for an amount that could have supplied safe drinking water for two years for the 55 million Pakistanis who lack it, plus essential medicine for the 13 million Pakistanis who lack it, and basic education for 12 million Pakistani children who lack it (cited in Millen and Holtz, 2000).

War and war-related injury and death are particularly devastating to the health and well-being of an entire country. For example, Afghanistan (a desperately poor country that came to most Westerners' attention only when the United States and its allies pursued their "war on terrorism" on Afghan territory) had experienced more than two decades of warfare, in which U.S.-backed Afghani tribes fought Soviet-supported tribes. Warfare and drought had created conditions of extreme deprivation, causing Afghanistan to suffer the fourth highest rate of under-five mortality in the world (more than 25 percent of all Afghani children die before the age of five) (UNICEF, 2000). Many of those who survived had serious injuries and disabilities, indirectly due to the years of war. An estimated 5–7 million undetonated land mines (many supplied by the United States[3]) had been left buried in the fields and byways, and many civilians—especially farmers and children—were killed or maimed by them (Bearak, 2001). Long after such active violence ends, the people must struggle with deprivation, injury, and illness brought on by warfare (see Taipale et al., 2001).

Not only are diseases themselves spatially and socially segregated, but various forms of segregation also reduce people's ability to know and understand

---

[3]The United States has been the world's foremost arms supplier. Between 1993 and 1994, U.S.-supplied weapons were used on one or both sides in 45 of the 50 largest conflicts; between 1993 and 1997, the U.S. government sold, gave away, or let industry sell $190 billion in weapons to almost every country in the world (cited in Millen and Holtz, 2000: 212).

others' way of life. Probably most members of the white minority in South Africa did not fully perceive the physical consequences of apartheid. The ability of the affluent to see the world of the hungry and poor is blocked by their spatial and social segregation from each other. Similarly, a reporter in Ethiopia noted that many members of the urban middle and upper classes did not have any knowledge of the famine in their own country until foreign correspondents wrote about it (May, 1985). A censored press can thus mute social conscience. In many cities in the United States, economically comfortable middle-class persons may likewise live only blocks from squalor and never be truly aware of it.

INFECTIOUS DISEASES: THE EPIDEMIOLOGY OF HIV/AIDS IN THE GLOBAL PICTURE

The myth of medical progress, together with belief that the world was engaging in economic development and "progress," led many people in the 1960s and 1970s to believe that infectious diseases were being eradicated. Many proponents of spreading technological development throughout the world argued that, partially in response to improvements in pharmaceutical and agricultural technologies, developing societies would, likewise, pass from conditions of high mortality due to infectious diseases to concern about chronic diseases of aging (see Garrett, 1994: 32).

The same political and economic forces that spurred such globalized "development," however, have also brought new (and the return of old), **globalized** sources of infection, disease, and death. By the end of the twentieth century, it was clear that economic globalization had dramatically increased the worldwide epidemiological "web of interconnectedness" (Zielinski Gutiérrez and Kendall, 2000). The global picture of HIV/AIDS infection illustrates this interconnectedness.

In the early 1980s, Americans and Europeans began to become aware of a new epidemic (eventually attributed to the Human Immunodeficiency Virus, HIV) in their midst. The HIV/AIDS epidemic has shaken that faith in "progress" and, in many places, completely reversed previous trends toward improvements in life expectancy and health. In the 20 years since what had been an animal virus apparently mutated and began infecting humans, it has killed an estimated 28 million people and has spread rapidly worldwide (WHO, 2001). Other infectious diseases have reached epidemic proportions in recent years, as well. Tuberculosis and acute febrile diseases (like malaria and dengue fever) have reappeared and spread—often in drug-resistant mutant forms—even in developed countries. Threats of biological warfare and bioterrorism have also heightened our awareness of the threat of epidemics of dangerous infectious diseases, such as smallpox.[4]

---

[4]This heightened awareness of our vulnerability to outside sources of infection simultaneously reveals how relaxed *internal* regulation in recent decades has made us vulnerable, as well. In the United States, water, air, and food are far more likely to be dangerously contaminated by internal agents (such as improperly handled meats, factory emissions of radiation or air pollutants, and chemical contamination of wells and reservoirs) than by foreign terrorists.

Epidemiology—especially social epidemiology—has grown more sophisticated as it tries to understand and respond to these urgent health issues worldwide. The epidemiology of HIV/AIDS is a good illustration of how a disease spreads and affects populations differently in different cultural and socioeconomic situations. The history of our understanding of the AIDS epidemic also illustrates many of the blind spots that often prevent effective and rapid response to epidemics and their victims, both in the United States and throughout the world.

In 2000, there were an estimated 3 million deaths worldwide due to AIDS—the highest total since the beginning of the epidemic more than two decades ago. The United Nations estimates that, by the end of 2001, 40 million people worldwide were infected with HIV. Of those infected, more than 96 percent live in developing countries. About 940,000 people in North America (mainly the United States) were living with HIV/AIDS. The infected proportion of the U.S. population is much higher than in other developed countries (about three times the rate in Europe and six times the rate in Australia and New Zealand). It is, nevertheless, much lower a proportion than in severely affected regions, such as the Caribbean (where HIV/AIDS is about four times as prevalent as in North America) and Sub-Saharan Africa (where it is about 15 times as prevalent) (UNAIDS, 2001a).

Table 2.1 shows the distribution of HIV/AIDS as of December 2001. This epidemic is rapidly changing. For example, in 2001, the epidemic was spreading most rapidly in Eastern Europe and Central Asia, where the economies and public health systems collapsed after the Soviet Union dissolved. East Asia and the Pacific also showed dramatic increases in new HIV/AIDS cases, as parts of China and other countries that had been politically and culturally isolated began to experience economic conditions promoting spread of the disease (UNAIDS, 2001a).

The transmission of HIV depends on the geosocial and cultural context in which it is spread. In the early years of the epidemic, in North and South America, Western Europe, Australia and New Zealand, HIV/AIDS affected mainly males. The mode of transmission often involved men having sex with men (MSM), whereas the rate from heterosexual intercourse was relatively low. In these countries, AIDS was concentrated primarily among MSM, who may or may not self-identify as homosexual, contributing to the myth that it is essentially a "gay plague." This misperception, however, may have initially blinded researchers and the public alike to the breadth of HIV infection. We now know that HIV transmission is the result of sexual (heterosexual as well as homosexual) contact with an infected person, sharing needles and/or syringes with someone who is infected, and blood transfusions with infected blood supplies. Babies born to women with HIV infection may become infected before or during birth or through breastfeeding after birth.

This early misinterpretation illustrates how researchers' categories for classifying groups can misguide the interpretation of data. These categories are far from neutral. In this case, in the early years of the epidemic, the notion that AIDS was a "gay plague" classified homosexual males as the prime risk group. Thus, some American physicians could not believe intravenous drug users who developed

TABLE 2.1   **Global Distribution of HIV/AIDS, 2001**

Regions (Listed in Order of Proportion* of Population Infected)	Adults & Children Living with HIV/AIDS	2001 Deaths Due to HIV/AIDS	Adults & Children Newly Infected in 2001
Australia & New Zealand	15,000	120	500
East Asia & Pacific	1,000,000	35,000	270,000
North Africa & Middle East	440,000	30,000	80,000
Western Europe	560,000	6,800	30,000
Eastern Europe, Central Asia	1,000,000	23,000	250,000
Latin America	1,400,000	80,000	130,000
South Asia, South East Asia	6,100,000	400,000	800,000
North America	940,000	20,000	45,000
Caribbean	420,000	30,000	60,000
Sub-Saharan Africa	28,100,000	2,300,000	3,400,000
TOTALS	40,000,000	3,000,000	5,000,000
Children under 15	2,700,000	580,000	800,000
Women	17,600,000	1,100,000	1,800,000

*Note: These ratios underrepresent the effects of AIDS in countries where a high proportion of those infected have died rapidly after infection. Thus, countries like Brazil, where death rates among HIV/AIDS-infected persons are much higher than in the United States, may appear to have comparable proportions of the population infected; in reality, though, their devastation may be much greater than these ratios suggest.

Source: UNAIDS, "AIDS epidemic update, December, 2001" retrieved from the World Wide Web at www.unaids.org/worldaidsday/2001.

AIDS but denied any homosexual contact (Bloor, 1995: 56). Rather than oversimplifying data into "risk groups," it makes sense to focus on the variable sociocultural, political, and economic contexts in which HIV transmission occurs.

This focus better enables us to understand changing patterns (such as the increasing proportion of women and children) in HIV/AIDS infection in developed countries. The rates of new infection in the gay community had leveled off until the mid- to late-1990s because of dramatic changes in sexual practices. Such changes preceded large-scale government health education campaigns and were due, in part, to social organizing, education, and condom distribution by the gay community (Bloor, 1995). More recently, however, rates of new infection among MSM have increased again, especially among young men. In 2000, 59 percent of reported HIV infections among adolescent males aged 13–19, and 53 percent of cases among men aged 20–24, were transmitted by MSM contact (USCDC, 2002a). At the same time, however, rates of HIV infection among men of color—especially gay men of color—are increasing. The stigma attached to homosexuality in the communities of color may prevent men from being tested and from identifying themselves as gay or bisexual (Altman, 2001). Research among gay and bisexual men indicates that some are now less concerned about risk of infection than in the 1980s, perhaps assuming (incorrectly) that AIDS is no longer difficult to treat and fatal (USCDC, 2002a).

When the AIDS epidemic was first recognized, some epidemiologists referred to groups (such as homosexuals and Haitian Americans) with disproportionately high rates of HIV infection as "risk groups." The designation of groups as "high risk" is itself problematic. First, no one is at risk of HIV infection because of their membership in a group but because they engage in certain risky practices. Intravenous drug users are at risk, not because they inject drugs, but because they share needles (Bloor, 1995: 29). Second, researchers' use of broad categories (such as "Hispanic") to label so-called "high-risk" groups obscures the wide variation *within* groups. Higher rates of poverty and substance abuse increase the risk of infection in some Hispanic American communities. For example, among Puerto Rican-born Hispanics, high-risk behaviors associated with drug abuse are far more common than MSM as a mode of transmission. By contrast, for those born in Mexico, Cuba, and Central and South America, MSM is the primary mode of transmission (USCDC, 2000). Thus, clearly, an individual's risk for HIV infection is *not* a product of being Hispanic. Even "risk groups" identified on the basis of risky behavior (such as prostitution) show considerable variability in HIV incidence. For example, prostitutes in Las Vegas, Nevada (where prostitution is legal and regulated) had none, while prostitutes in Newark, New Jersey had a 55 percent rate of HIV infection (Bloor, 1995). Third, to single out certain groups as "high risk" may contribute to stigmatizing them, leading to discrimination and further poverty, as happened to many Haitian Americans earlier in the epidemic.

Although HIV/AIDS strikes rich and poor alike, *new* AIDS cases in *developed* countries are disproportionately among poor people (World Bank, 2001). Thus, it would be a mistake to conclude that the growing rates of infection among certain minority groups are mainly about race or ethnicity, per se. One grassroots organization of AIDS activists, ACT UP (AIDS Coalition to Unleash Power), has shifted the focus of its protests accordingly. First formed in the late 1980s as a coalition of white, middle-class gay and lesbian activists, the organization now emphasizes racism and poverty (both in local and global contexts) as its main AIDS-related targets (Kim, 2001). The growing differential between the situation of the poor and peoples of color, on the one hand, and the rich, generally white, developed world, on the other hand, leads some critics to suggest that the HIV/AIDS epidemic is but one product of a "global apartheid"—an international system of minority rule (comparable to that of whites under the South African policy of apartheid) based on differential access to basic human rights (Booker and Minter, 2001).

The global pattern of HIV/AIDS infection has been a disproportionate burden for the poor—of sickness, death, orphaned children, increased poverty, and the loss of entire generations of prime-age adults. Worldwide, an estimated 96 percent of those infected are in the developing countries (World Bank, 2001). The greatest devastation of HIV infection has been in Sub-Saharan Africa (as Table 2.1 shows). There, the patterns of transmission and of the course of infection are very different from those in Europe and the Americas. In Sub-Saharan Africa, one-third to one-half of all persons infected with HIV/AIDS are women, with a particularly high concentration of cases among prostitutes. This prevalence suggests that, in that region, heterosexual intercourse is a more common means of transmitting AIDS than other means, such as homosexual contact and intravenous drug use (Ateka, 2001). In Sub-Saharan Africa alone, an estimated 2.2 million children are at risk of HIV infection through mother-to-child transmission (UNAIDS, 2001b).

What cultural and socioeconomic factors account for these differences? Diseases are spread when populations are forced to move, due to violence (such as the 1994 exodus of millions from Rwanda), or natural disasters (such as drought, urbanization, and displacement). Such displacement often separates young men from their families and breaks cultural patterns that previously constrained sexual behaviors. The United Nations (1998) reports that, worldwide, the number of refugees, returnees, and internally displaced persons has increased more than fourfold in less than two decades. Africa accounts for a vastly disproportionate number of those displaced persons (in 1997, 4.3 million refugees, 1.7 million "returnees," and 16 million internally displaced persons).

In parts of Africa, the practice of migratory labor (residual from the colonial past), together with dire poverty, make prostitution a common practice. Millions of couples are separated for months at a time, while men leave their families to work in the cities or on plantations (Lear, 1996). Men who resist the use of condoms yet have multiple sex partners, transmit the virus from place to place during their travels for work. And when they return to their families, even if they are obviously sick, their wives are not free to refuse to engage in sex (see du Guerny and Sjoberg, 1999; Zielinski Gutierrez, and Kendall, 2000). Women cannot insist their husbands use condoms. One South African schoolteacher explained that, in their culture, "the woman has no power with the man," because having paid the bride price, he believes "she is supposed to do everything I say" (quoted in McNeil, 2001a).

At the same time, African women who become infected and transmit HIV infection may have few or no alternatives for their subsistence and survival. An estimated 65 percent of AIDS infection in females occurs by age 20, due in part to older infected males taking very young women as partners, to increasingly very young women resorting to prostitution for survival, and to widespread and growing rates of rape in many African cities (Zielinkski Gutierrez, and Kendall, 2000). Cultural myths that sex with a virgin will cure AIDS have resulted in dramatic increases in the number of child rapes by HIV-infected men (Swarns, 2002). Rape itself is epidemic in many parts of Africa. One doctor in a rural South African province where there is about a 40 percent chance that a young male rapist is HIV positive explained that it was nearly impossible to obtain anti-AIDS drugs for rape victims, in part because "forced intercourse is not regarded as a hell of a crime by the average rural Zulu; it's very accepted" (quoted in McNeil, 2001b). Thus, women's already low status and lack of power renders them more vulnerable to HIV infection (see Crossette, 2001; Schoofs, 1999). Cultural pressures on women define their status as child bearers and mothers (Bassett and Mhloyi, 2001); hence, they are expected to bear children, even when there is a likelihood of transmitting HIV to them. Furthermore, the burden of home care for people with AIDS falls mostly on women, thus increasing their burden of poverty (du Guerny and Sjoberg, 1999).

Poverty is a significant factor in the pervasiveness and intensity of the HIV/AIDS epidemic in Sub-Saharan Africa, as well as in other developing countries. People who are already malnourished, have parasitic and other infections, and lack access to health care, succumb more readily to HIV infection (Stillwagon, 2001). Women are particularly affected in this respect, too, because they constitute 70 percent of those living in extreme poverty in the world (Schoofs, 1999). A combination of domestic, socioeconomic, and cultural factors shape the epidemiology of AIDS in Sub-Saharan Africa differently from the patterns of other countries, especially economically developed countries. Particularly important factors in Sub-Saharan Africa include rapid urbanization, the migrant labor system (a legacy of colonialism), extreme gender inequality, and abject poverty.

Dire poverty is not only a causal factor but also a growing *result* of the HIV/AIDS epidemic in Sub-Saharan Africa. Victims' families and the entire economy lose the productivity of younger, skilled workers who die of AIDS. The epidemic is creating a generation of orphans—12.1 million in Sub-Saharan Africa as of 2001 (UNAIDS, 2001b). HIV/AIDS is putting a strain on already limited health care resources (Danzinger, 2000). Lacking money to provide infected patients with expensive antiretroviral drug therapies, hospital staffs are often overwhelmed with the emotional, as well as financial, drain of tending large numbers of inexorably dying patients (Swarns, 2001).

The epidemiology of HIV/AIDS (and many other diseases) in Africa and other developing countries is, thus, linked with economic globalization—especially the policies of the World Bank, the International Monetary Fund (IMF), the World Trade Organization (WTO), and transnational pharmaceutical corporations. In developed countries like the United States, many HIV-infected persons can obtain the costly treatments that may enable them to live and continue to work, sometimes turning HIV infection into a chronic disease. Transnational pharmaceutical companies control the patents on these drugs and want to protect their worldwide profits.

In 2001, U.N. Secretary General Kofi Annan called on rich countries to allocate $7–10 billion annually to a global fund to address infectious diseases (particularly HIV/AIDS, malaria, and tuberculosis) in developing countries.[5] At the same time, Doctors Without Borders, the Nobel Prize-winning NGO (nongovernmental organization), and other international health activists tried to arrange for large-scale purchase of antiretroviral drug treatments from generic producers, like the Indian manufacturer CIPLA. At meetings of the World Trade Organization, the United States sided with the patent-owning transnational pharmaceutical corporations, which vehemently argued that sales of the generic drugs violated their "intellectual property rights." If the U.N. AIDS Fund and developing countries' health agencies are forced to pay the "market" prices of patented drugs, they will be able to help

---

[5]The United States was quick to shirk its fair share of contribution, offering only $200 million for the fund—less than two-tenths of 1 percent of a tax cut given earlier that year to the upper quintiles of American taxpayers (Weissman, 2001). Nine months after the call, donations and pledges had fallen far short of the goal, and the U.S. pledge was particularly low proportionate to its national wealth (Stolberg, 2002).

only a small portion of the infected population (Rosenberg, 2001; Weissman, 2001). Now that epidemiologists understand how HIV/AIDS is spreading and other researchers have developed treatments that, while not curing, prevent AIDS from killing and debilitating its victims, the world needs the political will to address the causes and effects of this global epidemic. Meanwhile, millions of preventable cases of new infection are developing; millions of needless deaths are occurring.

VARIATIONS IN MORTALITY AND MORBIDITY: THE CASE OF THE UNITED STATES

The wide range of mortality (that is, death) and morbidity (injury and disease) *within* societies is distributed along basic sociological variables such as region, age, gender, ethnicity, and class. Variations in health and death are linked to people's different locations in social space and structure. The following discussion examines major variables in mortality and morbidity for the United States.

Age

As expected in a developed country, U.S. death rates increase with age. Figure 2.4 shows population pyramids for the United States, which indicate, for a given year, the relative numbers of males and females in each age bracket. The data for 1910 take a conventional "pyramid" shape, because the birth rates are balanced by death rates for both sexes, in a somewhat even pattern. The U.S. pattern for 1910 resembles that of many moderately well-off developing countries today. The U.S. pattern for 2000, however, is less conventionally shaped because of decreased (but varying) birth rates and lower death rates, a pattern that characterizes economically developed countries.

This trend, in which fewer people are born and more live past the age of 50, has been called the **graying of society** because larger proportions of the population survive into old age. Between the Census 1990 and Census 2000, the proportion of people aged 85-years-and-over grew dramatically; however, the growth rate of the proportion of 65-and-over decreased, due to low birth rates in the 1920s and 1930s (U.S. Census Bureau, 2001b). By Census 2020, the older members of the "baby boom" generation will have swelled the ranks of the 65-and-over population. There are socioeconomic consequences to a changing age structure of a society. For instance, in a "graying" society, one can anticipate increased health costs and a greater demand for care (McMurray and Smith, 2001).

Although chronic degenerative diseases have been increasing in all age groups, their rates increase most dramatically for older people (Radley, 1994). Only rates for death due to homicide, accidents, and suicide decline with age; rates of death due to chronic illnesses and disabling conditions increase. Many chronic conditions are not a natural result of aging. For example, the rate of hypertension (high blood pressure) increases with age in U.S. society but not in hunting and gathering societies, such as the nomadic !Kung bushmen of the Kalahari

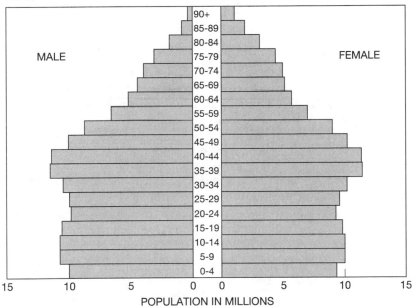

FIG 2.4 **Age Composition of the U.S. Population, 1910 and 2000.** *(Sources: Population Reference Bureau,* Population Bulletin *37 (2), 1982; U.S. Bureau of the Census,* Census 2000).

Desert in Africa (Schnall and Kern, 1981). Similarly, the U.S. rate of death and chronic illnesses, such as chronic lung disease and cancer, associated with tobacco use is higher than in most other countries; aging Japanese, by contrast, are far less likely than their American counterparts to experience these health problems (WHO, 2000).

Although aging seems inevitably to involve increased morbidity, some researchers suggest the possibility of "compressing" morbidity. They argue that although the life span is biologically limited, it may become possible to limit the period when an aging person is infirm (Fries, 1990). The "compression of morbidity" thesis helps to challenge stereotypes about aging (such as the inevitability of deterioration), but it may be overly optimistic about health problems associated with aging.

Although compression of morbidity may be occurring, it pertains mostly to higher socioeconomic groups. Widespread compressed morbidity would require greatly increased social equality (Bury, 2000). One study examined healthy life expectancy by gender and education for U.S. whites and African Americans in 1970, 1980, and 1990. The study found evidence of the compression of morbidity in the last decade among those of higher educational status. Lower-status persons, however, are still experiencing an expansion of morbidity (Crimmins and Saito, 2001). Clearly, in order to achieve widespread compression of morbidity or a significant societal increase in healthy life expectancy, the United States needs a much higher level of social equality.

Gender/Sex

Before the twentieth century, women typically died younger than men. One explanation of the difference is that frequent pregnancies and childbirth involved considerable health risks. Also, under conditions of general material scarcity, women often got what food was left after men and children ate their share. Poor nutrition then compounded women's health difficulties (Shorter, 1982). Today, in some developing countries, male life expectancy is greater than, or the same as that of women (Doyal, 1995). In several countries of North Africa and the Middle East, where the male-female ratio of healthy life expectancy is even or reversed, female mortality rates may be adversely affected by the disadvantaged position of women in these societies (WHO, 2000).

The female advantage in life expectancy became apparent in the United States and Europe by the late nineteenth century (Doyal, 1995). In the early 1900s, women's life expectancy was about two to three years longer, on average, than men's in the richer countries around the world. By 1999, women were living seven to eight years, on average, longer than men in those countries (WHO, 2000). As Figure 2.1 shows, the United States exemplifies this pattern, with the female "advantage" of 2.0 years in 1900 growing to 5.5 years in 1999 (USDHHS, 2001a).

Biological factors may partially account for the higher mortality rates of males, especially early in life (Carpenter, 2000). Higher fetal mortality rates have been reported for males (Harrison et al., 1992). Because the male-female mortality rate difference occurs cross-culturally, it cannot be explained fully by social or cultural factors. Female life expectancy is also higher among many other animal species (Sagan, 1987). This biological advantage for women may come from hormonal differences, although such differences may also produce higher rates of some sicknesses in women (Friedman, 1987). Although biological factors may contribute to differences in men's and women's health and longevity, social factors linked to *gender*—rather than *sex*—differences often create, maintain, or exacerbate biological health differences (Bird and Rieker, 1999).

In the United States, men die earlier and have more life-threatening illnesses, but in general women become ill more frequently (Carpenter, 2000). Chronic illnesses are more prevalent among women than men, but they are less life-threatening than those of men (Marks, 1996). Some researchers argue, however, that rates of debilitating chronic degenerative diseases are rising among older women, such that their *healthy* life expectancy is much lower than their overall life expectancy. Women may live longer, on average, than men, but are likely to spend most of those extra years in conditions of disability and dependency (Litt, 1997).

Women also report more episodes of illness and more contact with physicians (Susser et al., 1985: 71). Women's higher rates of sickness and doctor visits can be partly explained by gynecological or reproductive problems, which men do not have, but the incidence of these problems is not great enough to account for the difference in morbidity rates between men and women. Perhaps women are more willing than men to admit they are sick and/or to visit physicians. If this is true, then lower morbidity rates for men are deceptive, because they are a function of the underreporting of sickness rather than differences in rates of actual disease (see Waldron, 1994). Perhaps women learn more effective coping skills and ways of caring for themselves, but no firm evidence exists for this hypothesis. Gender differences in morbidity may be underestimated, however (Carpenter, 2000). For such conditions as flu and the common cold, men are more likely than women to overstate the severity of their symptoms. Thus rather than being stereotypical "chronic complainers," women may be underreporting their sickness.

Men are more likely than women to engage in high-risk behavior, such as smoking, violence, or unsafe driving (Stillion, 1995). Likewise, risks associated with work roles may be higher for men (Krieger and Fee, 1994; Woods, 1995). The health effects of women's employment outside the home are mixed. There is evidence that women's health benefits from employment, but such work may also force women to carry the stressful "double burden" of paid employment and work at home (Bellaby, 1999). Many women's income is essential for their subsistence and that of their children; paid employment may give them not only greater resources for health and well-being, but also greater control over household resources. Gender-specific barriers to women's good health may be, at root, caused by inequality and relative lack of power. Those women who experience ill effects from paid employment are most likely to be those who are underpaid and overworked, who bear unequal burdens of work in the home, and who experience discrimination in the allocation of household resources (see Doyal, 1995). This inequality thesis is corroborated by a comparative analysis of men's and women's health in the 50 states, which found that women experience higher mortality and morbidity in states where they have lower levels of political participation and economic autonomy (Kawachi et al., 1999b).

The mortality gap between men and women may be narrowing in recent years. The gap may narrow further as women adopt such high-risk behaviors as smoking and enter workplaces with job stressors and other risks, while men, by contrast, improve their health behaviors (Woods, 1995). Death rates due to lung cancer (a disease caused primarily by cigarette smoking) rose among U.S. women by 600 percent between 1950 and 2000, making lung cancer the leading cause of preventable deaths among women (USCDC, 2001b). Although such biological factors as hormonal differences play some role, sociocultural factors linked with differences between men's and women's roles probably account for much sex-linked variation in mortality and morbidity rates (see Bird and Rieker, 1999).

Race and Ethnicity

Patterns of morbidity and mortality also vary among ethnic and racial groups[6] in a society. Some differences may be explained by hereditary factors that are disproportionately characteristic of certain groups. Genetically transmitted sicknesses include sickle-cell anemia (among blacks and some other groups) and Tay-Sachs syndrome (among persons of Eastern European Jewish descent).

Hereditary factors may also combine with sociocultural factors to produce ethnic differences in morbidity and mortality. For example, Mexican Americans are more likely to have inherent lactose intolerance than Anglo Americans; lactose intolerance combined with social factors (such as higher rates of poverty) produces serious nutritional deficiencies (Schreiber and Homiak, 1981: 283). Similarly, genetic tendencies may be a component factor that, together with environmental factors and changed diet, leads to disproportionately high and increasing rates of obesity and diabetes among Mexican Americans (Guendelman, 1998).

Patterns of variation are linked indirectly to ethnicity through other factors: nutrition, housing and sanitary living conditions, employment and types of occupation, family patterns, and lifestyle. For example, inner-city black preschoolers have a higher incidence of childhood lead poisoning than their suburban black counterparts, suggesting that the causal factors are not race but living conditions— in this case, substandard, older housing where the crumbling lead paint may be

---

[6]We must remember that both race and ethnicity are socially constructed categories, rather than innate biological characteristics of an individual. The identification of individuals as "members" of racial or ethnic groups is clearly a social process, which varies widely in different societies and eras (Smith, 1999). Although people of a common ethnic background may have a high probability of sharing certain genetic traits (discernible, for example, by DNA testing), there is so much genetic variation within ethnic and racial groups that very few physical conditions can be biomedically explained by race or ethnicity alone. Nevertheless, because racial and ethnic minority groups often suffer socioeconomic disadvantage, discrimination, residential segregation, stress produced by racism, and other social factors connected with morbidity and mortality, it is useful to study their epidemiological patterns (Krieger, 2000).

ingested by young children (Melnick and Rouse, 2001). The following discussion gives some of the highlights of U.S. data about racial and ethnic variation in morbidity and mortality.

African Americans constitute by far the largest racial/ethnic minority in the United States. Epidemiological data referring to "nonwhites" are thus mainly describing blacks. The pattern of health of black Americans is very different from that of white Americans. In 1999, black life expectancy was 71.4 years compared to 77.3 years for whites (USDHHS, 2001a). These rates represent a dramatic improvement since 1920, when life expectancy was 45.3 years for blacks and 54.9 years for whites. Nevertheless, African Americans are at higher risk for almost every health problem compared to other racial or ethnic groups (Dressler and Bindon, 2000).

One major factor in the lower life expectancy for blacks is their high rate of infant mortality. Figure 2.2 shows differences in infant mortality between white and nonwhite Americans between 1920 and 1999. Even though infant mortality has been steadily declining for both groups, the rate for blacks is more than twice that of whites (USCDC, 2002b). Infant mortality is especially high among newborns with low birth weight or very young mothers or both. The rate of live births of babies with low birth weight (less than 2,500 grams) was 12 percent for blacks compared with 6 percent for whites; 38 percent of black mothers did not receive prenatal care until after the first trimester of pregnancy, compared to 20 percent of white mothers (Anderson et al., 1987). These factors are clearly linked with socioeconomic factors. Low birth weight is often the direct result of poor maternal nutrition and inadequate prenatal care. Maternal tobacco and other drug use also contribute to poor infant health among African Americans. Fetal alcohol syndrome is also disproportionately higher among African Americans and Native Americans compared to other ethnic groups (Collins, 1996). Compared to other industrialized countries, the U.S. infant mortality rate is appallingly high, largely due to this country's failure to address the problems of poverty, especially nutrition and health care.

The proportionately higher rates of hypertension and hypertensive heart disease among blacks compared with whites illustrate the complexities of causal factors with which epidemiological studies must contend. Factors accounting for these differences include genetic factors in susceptibility, greater stress due to racism, lower socioeconomic status, less access to good medical care, and a higher rate of obesity among blacks (Krieger, 2000). The genetic susceptibility explanation seems doubtful, because cross-cultural studies found no such patterns among genetically comparable peoples of Africa (Dressler and Bindon, 2000). Whereas American blacks show a rapid increase in blood pressure after about the age of 24, African blacks living in tribal communities do not have increased blood pressure as they age. Their migration to industrialized, urban settings, however, does promote increased blood pressure (Janes, 1986). The lower socioeconomic status of many blacks and other racialized ethnic groups accounts for much of the health inequality (Howard et al., 2000; Smith et al., 2000). Even after taking social class into consideration, however, some significant differences remain (Crimmins and Saito, 2001; Smaje, 2000). Such factors as stress produced by racism, residential segregation,[7] and inferior quality of these residential spaces, which influence even the more affluent blacks, may explain some of these remaining "racial" differences (Adler et al., 1999; Krieger, 1990, 2000; Schulz et al., 2000; Smaje, 2000; Smith et al., 2000; Williams, 2000).[8]

Hispanics[9] (among them, Mexican Americans, Puerto Ricans, and Cuban Americans) are the fastest growing sector of the U.S. population. Some "Hispanic" groups are at increased risk for diabetes, hypertension, tuberculosis, AIDS, alcoholism, cirrhosis, specific cancers, obesity, and violent deaths. Among subgroups of Hispanics, Puerto Ricans have the poorest health, due mainly to lower socioeconomic status, lower education levels, and an extremely high (60 percent) rate of female-headed households. An epidemiological paradox, however, is that Hispanic women have favorable birth outcomes (that is, rates of low-birthweight babies and of infant mortality that are more similar to Anglo women's than to blacks'), despite the fact that they are impoverished, poorly educated, and medically underserved (Guendelman, 1998).

Some American ethnic groups comprise individuals whose families came to the United States in different waves of immigration. Comparative studies thus have the potential of identifying which factors in sickness and death are due to the particular living situation and lifestyle of a group in the United States compared with the country of origin. For example, although the rate of tuberculosis among Chinese Americans is higher than among the general population, it is nevertheless lower than in the old country. Similarly, both first- and second-generation Chinese Americans have more coronary heart disease than Asian Chinese; diet and stress are both implicated (Gould-Martin and Ngin, 1981). The experience of migration itself may contribute to poor health (Sundquist, 1995).

In the last three decades of the twentieth century, both the volume and sources of new immigrants to the United States changed dramatically. By the year 2000, only 15 percent of the foreign-born population of the United States had come from Europe; far more, at least one-fourth, had come from Asia (U.S. Census

---

[7]Residential segregation may also mean less access to decent education, health services, housing, and recreational facilities. Toxic waste dumps, waste incinerators, and air pollution from traffic appear to be disproportionately found in black neighborhoods (Brown, 1995b).

[8]Race and ethnicity can confound standard measures of class. Thus, while a middle-class white woman and a middle-class African American woman may be in the same occupational and socioeconomic categories, the white woman may still have higher pay and better working conditions (Smith et al., 2000).

[9]The term *Hispanic* is a contested term for nonblack persons of Latin American descent. Because it arbitrarily lumps together, for national census categories and other record keeping, persons of highly diverse and often mixed ethnic backgrounds, it results in confusing generalizations. For instance, for hypertension, Mexican women are at lowest risk, Central American women at higher risk, and Cuban and Puerto Rican women are at highest risk (Krieger and Fee, 1994). We need to question such categories, recognizing that they are not "natural" divisions of populations but socially constructed categories that are much more complex and heterogeneous than they appear to be (Fenton and Charlsley, 2000).

Bureau, 2000a). Thus, the diversity of racial and ethnic minority groups complicates interpreting epidemiological data. For example, in order to understand health-related data for blacks and Asian Americans in Minnesota, we would need to realize that many of them are Somali and Hmong refugees, whose ways of life and illnesses reflect both their native cultures and the traumas of the refugee experience (see Faust et al., 1998).

Demographic transition refers to the changes populations undergo (usually in the course of so-called modernization) as they move from a situation of high mortality and fertility to a stage in which mortality has declined but fertility is still high. The third phase is characterized by low fertility and mortality (Omran, 1971). Native American groups have experienced more decline in mortality than in fertility, and the decline in mortality is largely due to the reduction of epidemic infectious diseases. The resulting rates of morbidity and mortality, at this stage of transition, reflect a shift in causes of death. Between 1950 and 1999, overall mortality rates for Native Americans declined dramatically, especially mortality due to influenza, pneumonia, and certain diseases of early infancy. At the same time, mortality due to accidents, violence, and alcohol-related diseases remained relatively high, and deaths due to diabetes, lung cancer, and chronic respiratory disease have increased (USDHHS, 2001a).

There thus appears to be considerable racial and ethnic diversity in the United States in rates of mortality and morbidity, but precise figures are not available because national epidemiological data do not differentiate among white ethnic groups or nonwhite ethnic groups (for studies on minority groups' health and immigrant groups' health issues, see Hogue et al., 2000; Loue, 1998; Polednak, 1989). Most differences, however, appear to be largely due to social-structural factors, especially class. Nonetheless, purely materialist explanations (that is, those that focus on the impact of different material conditions on health differences) may not always completely explain ethnic differences in such health indicators as infant mortality (Andrews and Jewson, 1993). Cultural factors also influence diet, reproduction, and such health-related behavior as smoking and drinking. Yet cultural explanations of health inequalities should not become deterministic ones that emphasize differences between cultural groups and obscure what humans have in common, while neglecting within-group cultural diversity (Karlsen and Nazroo, 2000).

Social Class

Social class is probably one of the most useful shorthand indicators of a person's power. Class is usually measured by income, education, or occupation; wealth (or durable income) is more difficult to measure but also very useful (on issues of measurement and indicators, see Lynch and Kaplan, 2000; Robert and House, 2000). Generally, a consistently significant relationship exists between socioeconomic position and health (Link and Phelan, 1995). The lower the social class, the higher the rates of morbidity and mortality. This relationship is not surprising, considering the important part that our socioeconomic situation plays in the quality of our everyday lives.

Numerous social epidemiological studies have documented, for many countries—both developing and economically well off—that socioeconomic disparities are correlated with differentials in death from a wide range of causes, longevity, and morbidity rates for a wide range of illnesses (Lynch and Kaplan, 2000; Marmot, 2002; Wilkinson, 2000). Inequality affects people's health even before they are born, as reflected in rates of low-birthweight babies, infant mortality, and under-five mortality. These disparities in childhood may continue to affect people's health in adulthood, even if they change socioeconomic position (for an overview of key studies, see Kawachi and Berkman, 2000; Kawachi et al., 1999a; Link and Phelan, 2000; Lynch and Kaplan, 2000; Marmot, 2000; Robert and House, 2000). Increasingly, researchers are finding that these within-society differences in mortality rates and other health indicators are *not* attributable mainly to absolute material standards or absolute poverty. Conditions of poverty obviously have a direct relationship with causing disease and death; absolute poverty results in malnutrition, high rates of infection, unsanitary living conditions, and so on. However, the degree of social inequality within the society appears to be a more powerful explanatory factor than the degree of absolute poverty (Wilkinson, 2000).

A major study in England (the Whitehall Study) found pervasive differences by social class (defined by occupation) in morbidity rates for a wide range of diseases (Marmot et al., 1987). A follow-up study 25 years later was able to identify the actual ages at death and cause of mortality for the same subjects. It found the same gradient by social status for most causes of death: Nearly regardless of cause of death, persons in the lowest "class" occupations died younger than persons in the middle classes, and those in the middle classes died younger than persons in the top class (Marmot, 2000).

The specific features of social inequality that might account for this strong correlation with morbidity and mortality are hotly debated. Is it due to the "hidden injuries of class," such as humiliation and disrespect? Is, perhaps, race and ethnic inequality an intervening variable that explains most of income inequality? Is the correlation with morbidity and mortality due to psychosocial factors, such as insecurity, stress, or sense of hopelessness or lack of control? How are class-linked health behaviors involved? Is any of the differential due to variations in access to the health care system? Several chapters of this book address these questions further.

How serious is socioeconomic inequality? In the United States and the United Kingdom, socioeconomic disparities have increased (Graham, 2000; Navarro, 2002a). Despite its national rhetoric of equality in the "land of opportunity," since 1980, the United States has seen growing inequality in wealth, income, consumption, and proportional share of tax burden. Of all "wealthy" countries, the United States now has the *greatest inequality* between its upper and lower classes. In 1973, mean income of the highest income quintile (fifth) of all American households was 10.3 times that of the lowest income fifth, and 2.5 times that of the middle-income quintile. By 1997, the disparity had grown to 13.9 times the income of the lowest income fifth, and 3.3 times that of the middle-income quintile. The incomes of the very wealthy (top 5 percent) American households grew even more dramatically, relative to all others' (U.S. Census Bureau, 2000b). The Congressional Budget Office (CBO) found even more marked increases in inequality of after-tax income, due largely to tax reductions that favored the rich (and this was before the further tax cuts of 2001). The CBO data showed that, as of 1997, the highest income 20 percent of the population, in aggregate, received as much after-tax income as the entire other 80 percent (CBO, 2001).

Social class stratification shows up more dramatically in measures of household wealth (that is, net worth), and wealth is more likely than income alone to be linked with access to power and privilege. In the last two decades, the United States has experienced considerable consolidation of wealth in the hands of its richest citizens. By 1998, the wealthiest 1 percent of all households owned 42.1 percent of all wealth—the greatest concentration of wealth at the top since 1929 when the Great Depression began (Wolff, 2000).

Other economically developed (OECD) countries had much greater equality: Sweden, Finland, Belgium, Norway, Denmark, and Luxembourg all had miniscule levels of inequality, compared to the United States. Other European countries were somewhat more unequal but still considerably less so than the United States. Of OECD countries, only the United Kingdom approached the high level of inequality characterizing the United States, and disparities between high- and low-income groups have continued to grow, although not so fast as in the United States (cited in Navarro, 2002a: 70).

Differences in mortality between socioeconomic groups have generally increased in the United States since the 1960s (Kennedy et al., 1996). In recent decades, similar increases in mortality-rate disparity have been noted between socioeconomic groups in other countries (for reviews of this literature, see Deaton, 2002; Robert and House, 2000). In Scandinavia, long-standing illness is reported more frequently among blue-collar than white-collar groups (Rahkonen et al., 1993). There is a relationship between people's self-assessment of health and their income levels. The higher the income level, the more likely self-assessed health is excellent; the lower a person's income, the more likely health will be self-rated as poor (Blaxter, 1990; Graham, 2000).

These data illustrate that differences that at first appear to be individual are often actually social variations. Although smoking is an individual behavior, for example, those in the lowest socioeconomic positions are almost three times as likely to smoke as those in the highest positions (Marmot et al., 1987), which may partially explain the higher rates of respiratory diseases among the lower classes. Similarly, alcohol consumption is highest among the lower classes, as is the incidence of obesity (Dutton, 1986). Deaths due to accidents also increase as socioeconomic status decreases (Quick, 1991).

The Black report, a famous British study on the relationship between class and health, concluded that lack of personal control over one's life was an important factor linking low social status with poor health (Black, 1980; see also Gray, 1982). A 1987 update of the Black report not only documented persisting class differences in morbidity and mortality, but also showed a widening gap in health between the upper and lowest classes (Townsend, 1990). Similar conclusions can be found in the Acheson Report (Independent Inquiry into Inequalities in Health, 1998).

Syme and Berkman (1976) have argued that this lack of control and other adverse features of lower-class life create a "generalized susceptibility" to disease (see also Blaxter, 1990). The conditions of lower-class life include living and working in more polluted and crowded environments, exposure to higher noise levels and risks of accidents, and inadequate housing and transportation. Medical care for the poor is less accessible and of lower quality than that for higher social classes. Furthermore, health problems of the poor are typically more serious, complex, and difficult to treat (Dutton, 1986).

As the Black report shows, for England, improved access to medical care does not by itself significantly reduce social class differences in health. Scandinavian countries, which provide citizens with excellent access to high-quality health care, nonetheless exhibit some class differences in health. A study of the Scandinavian situation concluded that "health care without social welfare and economic policy will be ineffective in reducing social inequalities in health" (Rahkonon et al., 1993: 77). To seriously reduce the effects of social class on health requires far more basic economic and social reforms (Hurowitz, 1993).

Measuring social class variables is difficult. Occupation is one indicator of social class, but occupational categories are often broad and not neatly tied with a single social stratum. For example, how would the classification scheme distinguish between a farmer who owns 50 acres and cultivates them for family subsistence, and a "farmer" who owns 4,000 acres and hires numerous workers to cultivate them (Susser et al., 1985)? Measures of class using occupation may use the husband's occupation as a measure of the wife's socioeconomic status, but such measures do not indicate whether a husband is, indeed, sharing his socioeconomic advantage with his wife and children. As the occupational structure of society changes, older occupational categories may no longer be useful, and many persons may be excluded or mismeasured (Blaxter, 2000). Most researchers currently use some measure of income, education, and/or wealth to identify degrees of socioeconomic inequality.

Despite such definitional problems, studies of many societies document a consistent relationship between social class and health. Rates of mortality and social class are clearly linked, but the relationship between class and specific causes of death is not so consistent, and may change over time. The epidemiology of poliomyelitis also illustrates how the relationship between class and mortality from specific diseases may change over time. In lower-class areas, characterized by overcrowding and poor sanitation, children often developed antibodies and hence immunity to polio after being exposed to the virus early in life. Thus, the poor had lower risk of paralysis and death than the more "sheltered" middle and upper classes. When the polio vaccine was introduced in the mid-1950s, however, this relationship between class and vulnerability to the disease changed. Those upper- and middle-class children who were first vaccinated were the first to benefit. An education campaign eventually resulted in the widespread acceptance of immunization, but pockets of underimmunized persons still exist in the United States, particularly among lower-class minority groups (Susser et al., 1985: 229–231).

Thus, the relationship between specific kinds of morbidity or causes of mortality may not follow the usual relationship with social class and may shift over time. At present, however, there are no major causes of mortality for which death rates are not higher among lower-class than upper-class persons. On the whole, the lower classes bear higher burdens of mortality and morbidity (Blaxter, 1990).

Even when data show a strong correlation between two variables, such as social class and health status, the direction of causality is sometimes difficult to determine. Does variable A produce variable B; does variable B produce A; or are they related in even more complex ways, mutually influencing each other or indirectly influencing each other through some third (intervening) variable? For example, do lower social status and the poor living conditions that accompany it produce poor health, or does poor health lead to downward mobility and lower income, or do both situations interact (Dutton, 1986)? The explanation that poor health results in downward mobility has been called the *drift hypothesis,* which suggests that those who acquire disabling diseases "drift" down the social ladder in the course of their lives (Lawrence, 1958).

Some evidence hints that serious illness in childhood is related to downward mobility in later life. Boys who were seriously ill are more likely than those who were healthy to gravitate to a social position below that of their fathers (Wilkinson, 1986b). Downward drift may be linked only to specific "diseases" such as schizophrenia (Adler et al., 1999), so the drift hypothesis does not explain satisfactorily most of the relationship between class morbidity and mortality (Graham, 2000; Marmot, 1996; Wilkinson, 1996). While the drift hypothesis may not sufficiently account for the relationship between class and health, it does remind us that health inequalities between individuals are the outcome of "cumulative differential response to adverse material conditions and to behavioral and psychological risks" (Graham, 2000: 15). Young bodies influenced by such adverse conditions may have health problems later in life.

Some of the relationship between social inequality and specific kinds of morbidity and mortality may be more artifactual—a product of the way the variables are measured—than real. An extensive critique of the Black report argues that the correlation between social class and mortality due to chronic degenerative diseases is essentially artifactual (Bloor et al., 1987). For example, the perceived social class of the deceased person influences whether the cause of death was classified as heart disease. The significance of such artifacts in the correlations between social class and health is not clear. Other reviews (compare Graham, 2000; Marmot et al., 1987) consider artifacts to be relatively unimportant in explaining the social class differences in health. They observe that a large number and variety of studies, done in several societies, indicate a strong relationship among class, health, and death.

SUMMARY

There are observable patterns to the frequency and incidence of mortality and morbidity. As opposed to the clinical-medical model, which focuses on individual bodies and a limited number of causal factors in disease, the epidemiological approach looks at social patterns of morbidity and mortality and the complex "web of causation." Epidemiological studies show that many patterns of morbidity and mortality are connected with social variables, such as the kind of society, race, ethnicity, age, social class, and gender. These epidemiological variables are also rough indicators of the social distribution of power and of the different power relationships people experience. However, epidemiological studies are limited because of their tendency to decontextualize health and illness, and their purely quantitative orientation. Yet with its broad generalizations, social epidemiology sets the stage for a more refined analysis of the ways a society produces, defines, experiences, and treats sickness and death.

Chapter 3

THE MATERIAL FOUNDATIONS OF HEALTH AND ILLNESS

� ✿ ❀ ✿ ❀ ✿ ❀ ✿ ❀ ✿ ❀ ✿ ❀ ✿ ❀ ✿ ❀ ✿ ❀ ✿ ❀ ✿ ❀ ✿ ❀ ✿ ❀ ✿ ❀ ✿

"In his *Discourse on the Diseases of Occupations* (1713), Ramazinni claims to identify the mark left by each occupation. For example, a middle aged taylor [tailor] is known by his bent back, crooked legs, and short sightedness, produced by sitting cross-legged over his sewing in dim light. So exact is the correspondence between impairment and occupation that a physician might shortcut a diagnosis if he first finds out what a man's occupation has been."

Source: Paul Bellaby, *Sick from Work: The Body in Employment,* 1999, p. 2.

- **Food**
  Hunger
  Sociocultural Dimensions of Eating Habits

- **The Social Organization of Space and Practices**
  Space, Practices, and Occupational Health
  Space, Practices, and Transportation
  Accidents

- **Environmental Pollution**
  The Individual as Polluter
  Pollution in the Workplace

Certain social practices contribute to the production of a healthy body; others lead to its destruction. The very condition of our bodies—whether we are healthy or sick, whether we live or die—depends not on luck but on social circumstances.

In Chapter 2 we discussed some of the patterns of distribution of sickness and death according to social variables like socioeconomic status, ethnicity, race, and gender. In this chapter we examine certain social environments and practices that produce physical conditions contributing to these differences in health and illness. Basic health requirements—a satisfactory diet and a safe, clean physical environment—are very much influenced by many cultural and social-structural arrangements.

Both nationally and globally, many social and economic structures and practices seriously endanger people's health. Increasingly, the health threats to impoverished Americans are different from—yet ironically linked with—the health threats to the affluent. Similarly, disease and death in places remote from affluent nations are increasingly linked with social and economic problems in those nations. The societal and global arrangements for production and consumption are central to people's health or sickness, life or death.

One aspect of the social production of health and illness, as Chapter 2 demonstrates, is that basic social-structural inequalities lead to disproportionate rates of sickness and death among, for example, poor women and children, persons of color, and people in developing countries.[1] Social structure also shapes the amount of power different groups have to control physical resources (such as food and shelter) and the quality of their physical environment (such as workplace safety or a neighborhood's safe air and water).

Another aspect of the social production of health and illness is the influence of culture (such as people's beliefs and values, ethnic and religious practices). Globalization does not mean "Americanization," although many corporate commercial practices imply that the entire world should consume American culture—films and music, jeans and sneakers, tobacco and fast food. Rather, in the contemporary period, communications media, immigration and travel, and globalized marketing as well as production, have multiplied the daily contacts of diverse cultures. The world is increasingly a "single place" (Robertson, 2001), with cultures in contact, mingling or conflicting, in new and unforeseen ways. Cultures can affect the material well-being of people directly. For example, when a culture puts greater value on males' lives than on females', a family with little food may give

---

[1]We use the term "developing countries" here, because it is the term adopted by the United Nations for its reports on world health and poverty issues; however, the term has ideological connotations with which we do not agree. For example, calling their work "aid" to developing countries, the World Bank makes large development loans to poor countries whose poor people subsequently suffer misery and hunger to pay the interest on such huge external debt. The Report of the Commission on Macroeconomics and Health of the World Health Organization (December 2001) called on the World Bank and other global finance operations to relieve dramatically or forgive altogether the staggering debt burden of the poorest countries. (see also, Gershman and Irwin, 2000; Kim et al., 2000; Stillwagon, 1998)

less nourishment to girl children. If a culture values certain body shapes that require restrictive clothing (such as corsets or tight shoes), then the physical malformations of the bodies that have been thus shaped are cultural products (McMurray and Smith, 2001: 36).

Why do so many people, in this nation and in this world, lack the basic material requirements for health and life? Why are environmental degradation and sickening pollution distributed unequally around the nation and world? What are the *social* sources of preventable death and disease at the beginning of the twenty-first century?

FOOD

By examining the social-structural and cultural factors shaping people's food and eating, we can better understand how both health and illness are socially produced. Because of our global interconnectedness, we first view the problem of hunger in the context of world hunger.

Hunger

Sufficient nourishment is so basic to human life and well-being that the United Nations recognizes it as a fundamental human right (see United Nations, HCHR, 2000). Every few years the news media alert the public in economically developed nations to widespread starvation in parts of the world such as Somalia or Bangladesh. The public conscience is mobilized, and money and food are collected. The furor then dies down, and for a while the public forgets the routine starvation that plagues much of the world. During 1996–1998, an estimated 825 million people were undernourished; the vast majority of these (792 million) were in developing countries. Significant numbers in developed countries (34 million people) also lacked food security; a large proportion (28 million) of these were in places like the former U.S.S.R., where formerly "developed" economies were being drastically restructured[2] (United Nations Food and Agriculture Organization, 2000). Table 3.1 illustrates the correlation between food insufficiency and other indicators of well-being. Although the level of poverty of a country is a predictor of hunger and undernutrition, Table 3.1 shows that *inequitable distribution of resources* causes extreme hardship and death for the poorest citizens of developing (and developed) countries. For example, India had a much higher poverty rate than Bolivia, but the differences in health and nutrition indicators between the richest 20 percent of its people and the poorest 20 percent were far less extreme than in Bolivia (World Bank, 2001).

More common than outright malnutrition is undernutrition, or a diet that lacks enough basic nutrients such as protein or vitamins. Iron deficiency anemia is

---

[2]The proportion of persons living in dire poverty (that is, less than the equivalent of US$2.00 per day) has risen dramatically in Eastern Europe and Central Asia, from 3.6 percent in 1987, to 20.7 percent in 1998 (World Bank, 2001). (on the health crisis in the former U.S.S.R., see Field et al., 2000)

TABLE 3.1   **Health, Nutrition, Poverty, and Mortality: International Comparisons**

Rates of Infant Mortality, Child (Under five) Mortality, and Nutrition Problems by Poverty Status (Poorest and Richest Quintiles, Compared to Population Mean) for Three Developing Countries

	Kenya (1998)			Bolivia (1998)			India (1992/93)		
	Poorest	Richest	Population	Poorest	Richest	Population	Poorest	Richest	Population
% in poverty*			62.3			51.4			86.2
IMR*	95.8	40.2	70.7	106.5	25.5	73.5	109.2	44.0	86.3
U5MR*	136.2	60.7	105.2	146.5	32.0	99.1	154.7	54.3	118.8
% Children Stunted	44.1	17.1	33.0	39.2	6.0	24.2	55.6	30.9	47.1
% Children Underweight	38.7	12.4	26.9	20.1	4.2	10.6	88.8	45.2	73.1

*Definitions used in World Development Indicators:

Population in Poverty = % of total population living on less than US$2.00 per day

IMR = Deaths under age 12 months per thousand births

U5MR = Deaths under five years per thousand births

(For comparison: The IMR and U5MR are under eight per thousand for the United States and under six for nearly all other developed countries.)

Source: The World Bank, "World Development Indicators, 2001," "Income Poverty," "Social Indicators," and "Poverty and Health," data retrieved from the World Wide Web at www.worldbank.com/poverty/data/ on 22 December, 2001.

common, affecting 43 percent of people in developing countries, compared to one out of three worldwide (United Nations Food and Agricultural Organization, 2000: 232). Anemia, which results in symptoms of fatigue, persists in an estimated 51 percent of children under the age of five and in 60 percent of pregnant women. An estimated 40 million preschool children in 37 countries have vitamin A deficiency (McIntosh, 1995). Iodine deficiency affects approximately 200 million people and about another 1 billion are at risk (McIntosh, 1995). Mortality rates from measles are much higher in developing countries. One-third of all children under the age of five in developing countries are undernourished to the point of permanent developmental impairment (Cohen and Hoehn, 1991). Although not starving, many people in the world suffer from stunted physical development, a greater vulnerability to disease, and a lowered quality of life brought on by undernutrition.

An adequate diet is characterized partly by the quality of food consumed and by a certain amount of various vitamins, protein, fiber, and other components. An adequate diet also requires the consumption of a sufficient number of calories to support the body's activity. (A calorie is a measure of how much energy is generated by food eaten.) In the last two decades of the twentieth century, developed countries increased their per capita calorie consumption from 3,220 to 3,240 (some of which is due to *over*eating). In contrast, in developing countries, per capita calorie consumption went from 2,300 to 2,650; this means that many people in developing countries do not get enough calories to sustain their work and other activities of daily living. All regions experienced some increase, except "transition economies" (for example, countries of the former U.S.S.R.), which decreased caloric intake from 3,390 to 2,890 kcals per day.

There are currently 33 developing countries with per capita food consumption levels so low that they experience chronic food insecurity, with large numbers of the populace at risk of malnutrition or outright starvation (United Nations, FAO, 2001). Per capita figures, however, do not show how these calories are distributed within the population. As Table 3.1 shows, per capita indicators obscure age, sex, and social class differences within countries or regions, understating the existence of malnutrition (McIntosh, 1995: 42–43).

Although undernutrition and malnutrition are more prevalent in developing countries, many people in rich countries also suffer hunger and undernutrition. This is an ironic problem in the United States, where an entire industry is devoted to producing foods that taste like the real thing but lack caloric substance, and where many overeat to the point of obesity. The U.S. Department of Agriculture's analysis of the 1999 annual survey of food security in American households revealed that—despite unprecedented national prosperity and productivity—more than 31 million Americans (a third of them children) were hungry or "food insecure" (that is, having to rely on emergency help from a food bank, or parents skipping meals in order to feed their children). While the proportion of "food insecure" households was one in ten nationwide, households with children experienced food insecurity at a rate of nearly one in five, and the proportion of "food insecure" households headed by single women was nearly one in three. Households categorized as

"Hispanic" had the highest rate of total food insecurity (more than one in five), but "Black, non-Hispanic" households had the highest rate of regular hunger (more than 8 percent of all households, more than double the national average). Although food insecurity was more prevalent in the southern and western regions of the United States, it was disturbingly widespread in all regions (Tufts University, Center on Hunger, Poverty and Nutrition Policy, 2001).

In response to the problem of hunger, the 1960s "War on Poverty" and other federal initiatives included the introduction of food stamps, increased health care and welfare benefits, expanded school lunch (and later, school breakfast and summer meal) programs, and WIC (a food program for infants and expectant mothers). Despite their effectiveness, these programs have been cut back several times since the 1980s, leading to continual problems of hunger in America (see Cohen and Hoehn, 1991). In the 1980s, increased unemployment and underemployment created a "new poor" (former members of the middle and working class) and contributed to increased hunger. Neither wages nor public assistance benefits grew to keep pace with greatly increased costs of shelter, forcing many families to choose between hunger and homelessness (Poppendieck, 1995). By 2000, the United States had become one of the most extremely stratified of all developed countries, with the richest 1 percent of Americans receiving more after-tax income than the entire poorest 38 percent (Center on Budget and Policy Priorities, 2001).

Many states with the greatest inequality are those with the highest proportion of hungry families. For example, considering its average per capita income, Texas has very high rates of child poverty and of food-insecure households, because a small proportion of the state's population receives incomes extremely higher than that average. The state also has enrolled an abysmally small proportion (47–54 percent) of eligible participants in the federal Food Stamp program—one of the three worst states in the nation. Table 3.2 compares Food Insecurity Rates, as well as related social indicators, for three states: Kentucky (with less than the national average incidence of hunger), Kansas (with average proportions), and Texas (with greater than average proportions of hungry households). Note, for example, that

TABLE 3.2   **Food Insecurity, Hunger, and Poverty in Three States, 1999**

	Texas	Kansas	Kentucky
Per capita average income	26,858	26,824	23,237
Percent of all households that are food insecure	12.9%	9.9%	8.4%
Child poverty rate (national average = 16.9%)	22.1%	18.5%	16.7%
Percentage of eligible people who participate in Food Stamp program	47–54%	46–60%	62–77%

Source: Food Research and Action Center, "State of the States," (December, 2000) retrieved from the World Wide Web at www.frac.org, 22 December, 2001.

Kentucky (despite a lower average per capita income than Texas) has a significantly lower rate of child poverty and of food insecurity.

At the turn of the century, so-called "welfare reform" forced many single mothers off welfare and into low-paying jobs. At the same time, many eligible families ceased receiving Food Stamp assistance, resulting in an increase in "food insecure" households. Without federal food assistance, people increasingly turned to private charitable food banks, but the food banks did not have enough to meet the increased need. The subsequent recession that began early in 2001 affected all workers, but disproportionately hurt the working poor (U.S. Conference of Mayors, 2001).

Overpopulation and Scarcity   One common theory explains world hunger as a matter of overpopulation combined with lack of natural resources, such as arable land and favorable climate. Accordingly, poor people exceed their ability to feed themselves by reproducing too fast. This is often called a Malthusian explanation, after Thomas Malthus, a nineteenth-century British economist whose theories of population growth still have influence (Hess, 1987). Malthus ([1798] 1965) argued that the growth of the world's food supply would not be able to keep pace with the growing population unless it were reduced by "natural" forces such as war or famine, or by poor people's abstinence from sex. Innovations in agricultural productivity, which were already apparent in Malthus's time, cast doubt on his theory. His interpretations nonetheless influenced many social scientists and policymakers, particularly the nineteenth-century social Darwinists, who argued that social life and survival could be explained using the principles of evolution and that evolution favored the "survival of the fittest." Malthus's predictions were "dismal" and led some (including the social Darwinists) to believe that although food aid might help the poor in the short run, it would simply encourage them to breed more, thus creating more long-term suffering (Hess, 1987).

The Malthusian notion of an absolute scarcity of food and thus the need for poorer nations to control population growth still prevails (McIntosh, 1995). Although there is some truth to this position, advocates often refuse to consider policy measures, such as land reform, that would more equitably redistribute the resources needed to grow food. Malthus, of course, could not fully grasp the potential of modern technology to stimulate the food supply. With existing levels of technology, some estimate that it is possible to feed a much greater number of people than the world's current population. However, in many countries hunger seems to have increased just as the world food surplus has grown. In fact, many poor countries in which undernutrition and malnutrition prevail are *exporting* large quantities of food. While Brazil dramatically increased its soybean exports (to feed livestock in Japan and Europe), hunger spread from one-third to two-thirds of its own people (Moore-Lappé et al., 1998).

Emphasis on population control as the primary solution to hunger problems often places the burden of solutions on poor people whose attitudes toward birth control appear irrational to outsiders. High birth rates in developing countries may, however, be very rational to the people themselves, who believe they need more babies (in the face of high infant mortality) to care for them in old age and to provide a family labor force. Population growth is thus not simply the *cause* of poverty. Large families are a way of coping with impoverished conditions, and hence a *result* of poverty (George, 1982). Developing peoples with successful rapid reductions in population growth rates, such as China and the Kerala region of India, show that the lives of the poor (particularly poor women) must improve before they can choose to have fewer children (Moore-Lappé et al., 1998).

The scarcity argument also holds that many countries lack sufficient natural resources such as arable land. Less than half of the world's cultivable land is being used to grow food. Moore-Lappé and others (1998) have argued that every country has enough land to feed itself, and that hunger is often the result of patterns of land use and ownership due to the social distribution of power in these societies (see also Buttel, 2000; McMurray and Smith, 2001). Although overpopulation and geography contribute to world hunger, more important reasons involve sociopolitical and economic factors, as well as technology and knowledge.

Technology and Knowledge   Modern technologies, such as farm machinery, allow people to work the land more effectively and often to increase food production. Indeed, some improvements in health in the Western world were the consequence of advances in agricultural production. Yet these technologies must be viewed in their sociopolitical and economic contexts.

Toxic substances are often a part of modern agricultural technologies, but developing countries do not have effective regulatory controls (Millen and Holtz, 2000). Many pesticides such as DDT and DBCP, which have been banned in the United States, continue to be sold and used in developing countries. Pesticides have widespread and deadly effects on farmers who often do not know of their risks (Hunt et al., 1999), and they pollute water supplies. These toxic chemicals often come back to our dining room as residues on vegetables and fruits, thus completing a "circle of poison" (Weir and Shapiro, 1981).

The high yield these agricultural technologies produce has other negative consequences. They are typically energy intensive, requiring considerable quantities of oil to build and fuel machinery, and to make pesticides and fertilizers. Thus, a great deal of nonrenewable resources, like oil, is required to produce relatively little food energy. The need to import such resources for energy and for agricultural technology increases the foreign debts of many Third World countries, which means that more land must be devoted to producing export crops to pay those debts.[3] Energy-intensive technology is a mixed blessing for many people. Small farmers cannot afford it, and its uncontrolled use may deplete the land and

---

[3]A new biotechnology that may prove to be a disadvantage for the world's poor is genetically modified crops. These new seeds have the potential to expand harvests and improve the nutrient content of staple crops, like rice and wheat. At the same time, they are very expensive and produce sterile progeny (that is, subsequent years' seeds cannot be locally produced but must be purchased annually at great expense). Thus, the ones who will benefit from the new agricultural technologies are the corporations selling them and the agribusinesses that can afford to buy them (Millen and Holtz, 2000).

cause extensive pollution (McMurray and Smith, 2001). Many farmers would benefit from less energy-intensive ways of growing food, but such possible options are not likely to be developed by the companies that profit from existing technologies. In short, technologies do not develop in sociopolitical and economic vacuums.

Land as a Resource: Use and Distribution In the last decades of the twentieth century, massive disruptions occurred to the way of life of farmers and farmworkers worldwide. Their very means of providing subsistence for themselves and their families were taken away "in the name of development, modernization, industrialization, growth, globalization, progress, and profit" (Araghi, 2000). In Brazil, for example, the top 1 percent of landowners controls 45 percent of the arable land, while the bottom 80 percent owns 13 percent of the land and there are five million landless families. In all of Central America, 94 percent of all farms utilize only 9 percent of agricultural land. Richer land-owners typically control better farmland, and can afford to let it lie idle (for example, when cash crop prices are too low to pay for the labor of cultivation). An estimated 1 billion rural people in the world are landless or near-landless, and the rate of their displacement has increased in the last two decades of the twentieth century (Araghi, 2000).

The global commercialization of agriculture, as promoted by the World Bank and the International Monetary Fund (IMF), has pressured developing countries to shift from producing food crops for local consumption to planting crops for export. For example, in order to get some relief from its external debt, Zimbabwe was pressured to reduce corn cultivation from 895,000 acres to 245,000 acres in order to grow tobacco for export. Similarly, Lesotho exports large quantities of asparagus, while its people suffer high rates of malnutrition. Kenya, which has serious problems of malnutrition and stunting due to food insufficiency (see Table 3.1), is a major beef exporter to Europe (Araghi, 2000; see also Gebremedhin, 1997). Rural people have also been displaced from arable land in order to make way for building dams, industrial parks, and resorts. In short, farmers' access to land and their ability to grow what their family needs are prerequisites to subsistence (Buttel, 2000). Land reform or other equitable distribution of resources that would make this subsistence possible is very difficult to institute. Wealthy landowners and new business elites control the political systems and have a vested interest in the so-called development projects that displace poor farmers (see Araghi, 2000; Gershman and Irwin, 2000).

In southwestern India, the state of Kerala managed to improve its life expectancy and infant mortality rates, despite the fact that it has one of India's lowest per capita income rates. (In 1993, life expectancy in Kerala was 71 years, compared with the national rate of 61 years; its infant mortality rate was 13 per 1,000 live births, compared to 80 per 1,000 for India as a whole.) The lower infant mortality rate and increased life expectancy were due to improved food intake. In 1969, a new state government instituted land reform, government control of food prices, large-scale public health actions, accessible medical care, and literacy training. Kerala was able to improve its health and nutritional status through political and social change rather than increased economic development and production (Franke and Chasin, 1994).

Hungry Bodies Are Socially Produced A basic requirement for health is a good diet. Most countries have the resources to feed even very large populations, but the key factors in determining whether they do so appear to be political considerations as well as corporate control of technologies and, often, of large amounts of land used to grow export crops. The basic requirement of health, a good diet, is linked therefore to the distribution of power. It is easier to blame nature, scarcity, a lack of technology, or individual reproductive practices than it is to indict social systems. Yet it is the social systems and the way power is distributed within them that create world hunger.

The Sociocultural Dimensions of Eating Habits: "You Are What You Eat"

A society's practices of food consumption also play a role in nutritional problems. These eating habits are in turn influenced by sociocultural factors and issues of power. So-called affluent societies, with their diets high in animal fat, salt, and sugar, are often characterized by poor eating habits. At the end of the eighteenth century, sugar consumption in Europe (13 pounds per person per year) was already relatively high compared to previous times. With time, sugar found even more and more uses as a flavor enhancer and preservative. By the middle of the twentieth century, sugar consumption in the United States was over 120 pounds per person per year (Mintz, 1979). In some respects our diets have become healthier (increased consumption of protein, for instance); however, in other ways (significantly increased consumption of food additives, sugar, animal fat, and salt), they have become unhealthier. We tend to view eating habits as a matter of individual free choice. Although this is partly true, they also reflect sociocultural preferences, and the way we eat is shaped by sociopolitical and economic factors (see McMurray and Smith, 2001). In this section, we examine the interrelationships among society, power, and food from that perspective.

We do not eat merely to survive or because food provides us with sensuous pleasure. For humans, food takes on symbolic meanings, and activities related to the consumption of food have social functions and dimensions. Sharing food reflects social bonds. A family dinner is an occasion to communicate, affirm social ties, and remind members of their respective social statuses. Tastes in food are used by people to distinguish themselves socially. Middle-class people pride themselves in "good" taste in food choices, preparation, and consumption, as opposed to the "unhealthy," "unrefined" eating practices of the lower class. There are some gendered food preferences in our society: Men may prefer red meat and "man-sized" portions; women, salad and vegetables (Lupton, 1996).

Food taboos exist in virtually every society. For instance, Muslims and Jews prohibit the consumption of pork. A breach of a food taboo can affect one physiologically. A person who knowingly eats a proscribed food may get sick or even die. For example, when the Ponape, a people of the South Pacific, ate a forbidden fish, they would break out in hives (Farb and Armelagos, 1980). Cultures define what is edible or not, what is "good" food and "bad" food. For example, rural North American folk beliefs hold that eating too much pork, red meat, or salt is "bad," causing high blood pressure (Lupton, 1996: 28).

Culturally rooted aversions to particular foods are not restricted to religious groups or preliterate societies. A priest in San Francisco once suggested that because Asian refugees in the area liked to eat dogs and cats, the humane society could supply them with stray animals (which unless adopted, would be killed anyway) to use as food; his proposal was met with a great deal of opposition. Many Americans would get physically ill if they discovered they had just eaten "puppy parmigiana," yet in some parts of the world dogs are a normal source of meat protein and even considered a delicacy. Americans enjoy cheese, but most Chinese people find it disgusting (Lupton, 1996). Cultural factors thus shape our food preferences, our reactions to food, and our very appetites.

The diets of specific cultures are often well suited to the physical environments and biological constitution of the people who inhabit them. A genetic intolerance of lactose, a prime component of milk, is not uncommon among *most* peoples of the world (Overfield, 1985). Such physical intolerance, common among the Chinese, may partially explain their aversion to cheese, for example. Cultures also adopt certain food habits for practical benefits. Some foods may be too costly in their demand on land, human, and fuel resources. The Chinese custom, for example, of rapidly cooking food in a wok over a high flame developed because of fuel scarcity (Farb and Armelagos, 1980).

Sociocultural Change, Eating Habits, and Transnational Corporations

When external forces alter the eating habits or way of life of a culture, new nutritional problems can ensue. In many societies, dental cavities were rare until Western influences introduced large amounts of refined sugar into the diet (McElroy and Townsend, 1985). Several decades ago the Zuni Indians of the American Southwest had a very low incidence of diabetes. As farmers and hunters, their bodies had developed a capacity to store fat efficiently to survive periods of food shortage. Their cultural values defined being fat as healthy. As they "modernized," their lifestyle became more sedentary, and they replaced their traditional diet with the low-income food culture of fast food that was high in salt and sugar. Their biological capacity to store fat then became a liability, as they burned less energy and consumed more food. The incidence of diabetes subsequently increased (Peterson, 1986).

In recent years, transnational corporations (TNCs) have found new markets for their food products in developing countries. Often these products are promoted in sociocultural environments in which their widespread use may be inappropriate and unhealthy, producing a pattern of poor health (dubbed "the new world syndrome" [Shell, 2001]) in many consumers. Soft drinks and white bread, for example, have been aggressively promoted in countries like Malaysia and Mexico (Kaur, 1990). Advertising campaigns and the fact that these products are seen as coming from a "high-status" culture make them prestigious, and they may come to symbolize modernity and social status. Given the people's limited cash income however, such products consume disproportionate amounts of the family budget and provide little nutritional return. In a marginally nourished population, this exchange is a poor trade.

In the 1960s and 1970s, several TNCs such as Nestlé promoted commercial baby formula in developing countries. Their advertising presented bottle feeding as modern and healthy for babies. Bottle feeding, however, required much of the family cash income (from 15 to 85 percent, depending on the country), and many mothers diluted the milk to stretch supplies, thus unintentionally starving their babies. The lack of the clean water, fuel, and sanitary conditions needed for formula preparation and storage also prevented the product's safe use (Kaur, 1990). Even a marginally nourished mother can usually produce breast milk, which also transmits to the infant her natural antibodies that fight infection. As bottle-feeding practices were adopted in much of Africa, infant malnutrition increased. Doctors gave this form of commercially encouraged malnutrition a medical label: "bottle-baby syndrome." In 1981, in order to prevent such abuses, the World Health Organization adopted an international marketing code for infant formula, and eventually (after an effective international boycott of the TNCs) the infant formula manufacturers agreed to abide by the code. A 1997 study, however, found that several major TNCs were still routinely violating the code (Meier, 1997).

The world's eating habits are increasingly influenced by global corporate interests, which not only control much food production but also influence the information disseminated through advertising. One author concluded, "Backed by such powerful advertising, the standardization of food values at a global level at the expense of the local specificities has divorced people's eating habits from their history and culture" (Mansour, 1987: 16). Large corporations have more and more control not only over the growing and processing of food, but also over advertising and information about their products. These factors increasingly shape the food habits of the world.

Nutritional and Commercial Practices in Industrialized Countries

Commercial messages that promote foods are often directed at such vulnerable targets as children. A considerable portion of Saturday morning commercials on U.S. television, for example, promotes sugar-laden cereals and snack food. Most commercials imply that such food is consumed by the viewer's heroes, and that eating it will result in personal pleasure and status among one's peers. One study indicated that children influenced by these commercials may exert significant control over their mothers' shopping habits (Barnouw, 1978: 91–93).

Not only do individual advertising messages affect eating habits, but their cumulative tone also suggests a cultural attitude toward food. The more implicit messages often have a greater effect. Bottled drinks, such as beer and soft drinks, are heavily advertised. The implicit message is less a matter of which product one drinks, but rather that one should want a commercial drink instead of water or a home-produced beverage to satisfy thirst. Advertising has thus sold a behavior, not just a product (Gussow, 1978: 222). Some ads suggest that when people are hungry and do not have time to eat, they should deaden hunger pangs by consuming a candy bar, which produces a sugar "high." Other ads urge the audience to eat or drink more, even after the hunger or thirst is satisfied; expanded appetites are thus created. To sell products, commercials often urge people to override their bodies' signals by either deadening them or overconsuming. Their messages are often contradictory: "Be thin," "control your eating," "eat, drink, and be merry," and "gorge, gorge, gorge."

Affluent societies often consume overly rich diets with too much sugar, fat, and salt, and too little fiber. The U.S. Department of Agriculture's studies found that, although other aspects of U.S. diets improved, Americans' excessive consumption of fat and sugar has increased in recent decades. The recommended level of fats is 38 grams, while Americans consumed, on average, 49 grams during the study's baseline years (1970–1975) and 60 grams in 1996. For sugar, the recommended level is 12 teaspoons, but Americans consumed 27 a day in 1970–1975 and 32 in 1996! (Melnick and Rouse, 2001: 20). A related problem is increased use of highly processed foods. Food processing enables producers to preserve, store, and transport a wide variety of foods, and it increases the convenience of preparing many foods. By its very nature, however, processing causes the loss of many nutrients (Farb and Armelagos, 1980: 211). It also frequently takes away some of the natural flavors; to compensate for lost flavor, manufacturers then add sugar, salt, or artificial flavoring (Silverstein, 1984).

The diet of our modern society is more varied, interesting, and in many ways more nutritious than that of our medieval ancestors, who, prior to the fifteenth or sixteenth centuries, subsisted on a plain fare mainly consisting of grains and vegetables with few spices (Braudel, 1973). Increased trade, the availability of new foods and seasonings, and advances in agricultural technology and food processing have made an improved diet possible. The growth of capitalism helped stimulate trade and technology to the benefit of many. Food processing, however, is also used to increase profit. Technologies have been developed to store foods longer, to increase yield of products (for instance, hormones make chickens grow faster and fatter), to enhance flavor in place of using expensive ingredients, and to disguise products with artificial colors, scents, and shapes (Center for Study of Responsive Law, 1982). Yet rather than reducing food prices, processing often increases costs (Silverstein, 1984). Corporate control over food production and distribution also affects the choices available. Relatively few people have access to and can afford to buy unprocessed foods, which are now sold as part of a growing health food industry. In many places, supermarket fare is the only option. The diet of affluent societies, with its high-fat, high-salt, low-fiber, and processed nature, is being globalized, spreading to the rest of the world, often displacing more appropriate, healthier local diets (McMurray and Smith, 2001).

Dieting and Fitness   An estimated 61 percent of U.S. adults are overweight, as are 13 percent of U.S. adolescents and children. Among adults, obesity has doubled since 1980, and it has tripled among adolescents. The problem has been increasing so dramatically that the U.S. Surgeon General named overweight as one of the most pressing public health challenges; he noted that obesity now contributes to nearly as much preventable disease and death as does cigarette smoking (USDHHS, 2001b). Socioeconomic and cultural factors contribute to this nationwide health problem.

The motivation and opportunity to consume a healthy diet and to exercise are socially distributed (Goldstein, 1992). Several studies show a relationship between social class and obesity (Chrisler, 1994). One study indicated that women from lower-class backgrounds are six times more likely to be obese than upper-class women. Eating disorders, such as anorexia, are more common in upper-class women (Yates, 1991). Some of this variation is explained by differences in availability of adequate nutrition (that is, starchy food satisfies hunger and is cheaper). The increasing access to high-fat, high-salt, low-fiber food has fueled the growth of obesity among the poor (Critser, 2000).

Another factor is that people overeat to manage stress; also, different classes assign different social meanings to obesity. Obesity is not as heavily stigmatized in the lower class. Dieting and fitness rituals are primarily a middle- and upper-class phenomenon (Goldstein, 1992), not motivated simply by a concern for better health. In some cultures fat is a sign of prosperity (McMurray and Smith, 2001). In middle-class American culture, however, fat symbolizes loss of self-control. In addition to socioeconomic factors, cultural-ethnic factors may also contribute to attitudes about fat (Critser, 2000) and the tendency to be overweight.

What constitutes being overweight, and how much excess weight is unhealthy? Questions of overweight and overnutrition are difficult to calculate with precision. Although supposedly objective scientific facts bear on what is defined as normal weight, the standards change, and various groups challenge particular standards of evaluation (Sobal, 1995). In short, no tidy, universal standard exists for how much we should weigh (Chrisler, 1994; Sobal, 1995).

Our cultural obsession with dieting and fitness reflects a concern not merely with health but also with self-control and physical appearances. In our society, looking good and feeling well tend to be confused (Lupton, 1996). In all societies, health is judged to some degree on the basis of appearances, but in our society, a person's image is especially important, due to the influence of mass media and other political-economic factors.

Concern about weight and fat is one expression of a generalized societal anxiety about physical appearances. Since the 1880s, societal criteria for acceptable weight have become more demanding (Schwartz, 1986). Eating disorders are on the increase, and cultural standards for women's bodies have shifted from fat to thin. Women's and increasingly men's anxiety about weight and fat constitutes a major source of profit. A 1985 survey found that in comparison to 1972 data, respondents (both male and female) showed more dissatisfaction with their body image. Although the proportion of women expressing such dissatisfaction was still higher than in 1985, the differences in the level of dissatisfaction between the sexes had narrowed. Weight was the one physical feature that evoked the most anxiety among these males (Cash et al., 1986). One study found that 63 percent of high school girls were dieting the day they were surveyed (compared to 16.2 percent of boys). Children become concerned about weight as early as seven or eight years old (Way, 1995).

Such fears are not totally without foundation. Obesity is strongly stigmatized in our culture, particularly among the middle and upper classes (Lupton, 1996; Sobal, 1995). Negative attitudes toward obese people are learned at an early age (Yates, 1991). One study showed ten- and 11-year-olds pictures of a "normal" child, one with an amputated limb, one with facial disfigurement, one in a wheelchair, one with crutches and a wheelchair, and an obese child. Asked to rank the pictures in terms of their preference for a friend, most children made the obese child their *last* choice (Richardson et al., 1963). Discrimination against people who are obese has been found in education, rental housing, employment, and other areas of life. A number of groups have emerged to combat the stigma of overweight and to advocate "fat power" and "fat pride" (Sobal, 1995).

Obesity does contribute to physical problems such as high blood pressure. Although obesity functions to raise blood pressure because of the physical strain it puts on the body, other factors may also be involved. Because obesity is perceived as a negative attribute, it may affect an individual's self-esteem. Anxieties about one's body may also contribute to increased blood pressure (Lynch, 1985).

Although obesity may result from inherited traits and metabolic disorders, social factors are important too. To regulate our appetites, we need to know whether we are hungry. It is possible that obese people are more vulnerable to social forces that short-circuit hunger signals from their bodies. One study found that "normals" were more oriented to internal cues as signals when to eat, whereas obese people relied on external cues such as the appearance, taste, and smell of food and the time of day. In one variation of the experiment, a wall clock had been moved forward a few hours, displaying the wrong time. Subjects of normal weight did not eat the available food, even though the clock falsely signaled meal time, whereas the obese subjects ate (Schachter, 1968).

Some have observed that our culture encourages people to rely on external signals for eating. Snack ads urge us to deaden hunger signals; meal schedules encourage us to look to the clock for signs of hunger. If there are natural limits to human appetites (and this is debatable), advertising messages try to overcome them. This factor does not explain individual differences in responding to social pressures, but it does suggest that cultural pressures may affect the way people perceive their bodies, and hence how they control their eating.

All societies value some degree of self-control, but in modern societies such a concern is pervasive. Turner (1984: 112) observes:

> We jog, slim and sleep not for their intrinsic enjoyment, but to improve our chances at sex, work and longevity. The new asceticism of competitive social relations exists to create desire—desire which is subordinated to the rationalization of the body as the final triumph of capitalist development. Obesity has become irrational.

The contemporary emphasis on fitness, especially among the middle class, is not simply a matter of health but of conformity to the norms of an eternally youthful, lean body. Moreover, fitness activities may be a way of displaying control over one's body and hence over one's self in a culture in which control is valued and yet powerlessness seems to be a pervasive experience (Glassner, 1989). The "ideal" body is not only slender, but also firm—tightly self-managed, self-constrained; this changed ideal may reflect society's increased emphasis on self-control and management, rather than externally imposed control and coercion (Bordo, 1990).

A study of workers in California's Silicon Valley suggests that their almost compulsive tendency to exercise and diet (along with compulsive shopping and extensive drug abuse) represents a way of coping with the powerlessness, alienation, stress, and loneliness of much of their lives (Hayes, 1989). As with dieting, a vast industry has arisen to meet fitness needs, producing endless streams of commodities and specialized technologies, from electronic rowing machines to digital pulse meters. Commercialized diet and fitness thus transform simple needs into marketable commodities (Glassner, 1989).

In modern society, appearances are very important in achieving success in work, play, and sexual relationships. A competitive society makes such successes important to the individual's sense of self. To achieve them, a rational mastery over the body and appearances becomes a central concern in life. By these norms, then, obesity reflects an irrational inability to control oneself, whereas dieting and fitness activities promote a sense of self-mastery (Lupton, 1996).

Gender, Power, and Eating Disorders Much concern about weight is a concern about appearances. The standards for physical appearances or somatic (body) norms vary from time to time and place to place. The importance of conforming to such standards also varies. Our society tends to evaluate women by their appearances and men by their performance (such as occupational, athletic, and sexual). Despite some shift in attitudes, men are generally more anxious about functioning and women about appearances (Lakoff and Scherr, 1984). Furthermore, the responsibility for whether one is successful in one's area of competence rests with the individual:

> Ours is a culture of personal responsibility; we are told to captain our own souls and "take responsibility" for our successes and failures. Traditionally, men have been able to demonstrate success through their achievements in work, but it has mainly been through what a woman does with her appearance that she has been able to exhibit her mastery and achievement to others and to herself. (Millman, 1980: 155)

Although this double standard is changing somewhat, it still prevails (Way, 1995).

Women are more likely than men to believe they are overweight when in fact they are not, if judged by so-called objective standards (which themselves are not so objective). A 1980 survey of college women found that 70 percent believed they were overweight, although only 30 percent actually fit the insurance chart definitions. Women's anxieties about weight are thus out of proportion to the facts. Fears about one's body and appearances are fueled by the mass media, which reminds audiences how inadequate their bodies are. One woman observes:

> The mass media tells us all day and all evening that we are inadequate, mindless, ugly, disgusting in ourselves. We must try to resemble perfect plastic objects, so that no one will notice what we really are. In ourselves we smell bad, shed dandruff, our breath has an odor, our hair stands up or falls out, we sag or stick out where we shouldn't. We can only rook people into liking us by using magic products that make us products too. (quoted in Hatfield and Sprecher, 1986: 291)

Concerns about weight are a source of chronic stress for many women (Attie and Brooks-Gunn, 1987). Pressures on women to look thin may contribute to eating disorders like anorexia and bulimia, which are much more common among women than men. Anorexics lose the desire to eat and starve themselves. Bulimics binge, consuming vast amounts of food, and then purge themselves by vomiting or using laxatives. Although the initial motivation for disordered eating practices is cultural or social (Way, 1995), these practices over time may modify the body physiologically to make the person "addicted" to such practices (Brumberg, 1988). Self-starvation may become pleasurable and satisfying (Lupton, 1996).

Our culture gives members seriously conflicting messages about eating. On the one hand, people are urged to control their appetites and to diet in order to be sexy and desirable. At the same time, there is a conflicting message to enjoy life, to consume, to indulge ourselves and our appetites. The cultural contradiction of our times lies in the conflict between one set of messages, which emphasizes the importance of discipline as producers (that is, the work ethic), and another, which stresses our role as pleasure-seeking consumers (Brumberg, 1988). Turner (1992: 224) argues that anorexia may, to some extent, be regarded "as an ascetic and moral response to contemporary consumerism." We are thus asked to be both ascetic (disciplined and in control of our flesh) *and* hedonistic (pleasure seeking and indulgent) at the same time. This dual expectation compounds problems for women, whose traditional role as nurturers and food providers places them in frequent contact with food (Charles and Kerr, 1987). Anorexia can be interpreted as a woman's body discipline carried to an extreme. Families of anorexic adolescents often stress perfection and success (Yates, 1991). Eating disorders are extreme, self-destructive ways of responding to cultural conflicts that affect most women to some degree.

Eating disorders are not really problems of appetite for food but rather self-destructive responses to cultural constraints and contradictions. Somatic norms of femininity limit female appetites (not only for food but also for public power, independence, and sexual gratification). Gender-role norms expect women to feed and nurture others, and not the self.

Similarly, overeating is sometimes a means of asserting control. Millman (1980) found that some of the obese women she interviewed experienced eating as the one area of a controlled life where they felt able to "let go," and others used eating as a way of protecting themselves against parental domination. One respondent reported that she ate and gorged herself as a defiant response to her mother, who was always harassing her about her appearance. Millman (1980: 73) observed:

> This woman (like several others I interviewed) has throughout her life used food and weight to assert and feel control in her relationships and her place in the world. And when these assertions run against the wishes of parents or husbands, eating and weight become associated with a refusal to bow to social control.

Others have argued that fat may represent a form of "armor" by which some women can protect themselves from unwanted sexual advances. Eating may also help alleviate the anxieties about identity and devalued sense of self that our society engenders in women (Chernin, 1981). The double standards of physical appearances, together with the strong link that our culture encourages between women's looks and their sense of self, have led some writers to declare that "fat is a feminist issue" (Ohrbach, 1981). This approach suggests that eating disorders are not simply a loss of control but may reflect an attempt to assert control (albeit in ultimately self-destructive ways). It is simplistic to view eating disorders as a sign of personal weakness or as a purely individual matter, independent of social factors (Lupton, 1996).

THE SOCIAL ORGANIZATION OF SPACE AND PRACTICES

Our fitness, health, and physical comfort depend in part on the quality of the physical space we inhabit and our options for activity within it. Those options depend greatly on the social organization of space, as well as the opportunities or constraints that social forces place on our movement. The social organization of space and activities (that is, practices) is affected by the distribution of power in any given society. Some people have more influence in shaping their physical surroundings than others; some have more freedom of movement.

Space, Practices, and Occupational Health

The design of physical environments reflects social status. One indicator of social status is the amount and quality of an individual's space. Large private offices with windows, for example, are reserved for executives (Lindheim, 1985). The vast majority of jobs in the expanding information service sector are low-level positions in which workers have little control over their environment, which is designed to maximize cost effectiveness and worker control. The following arrangement is characteristic of white-collar offices:

> Of the people surveyed in one large modern office building by our Columbia University research team, 34 percent could not decorate or personalize their work areas in any way. They couldn't even hang a picture or keep a plant. Ninety percent could

not control the number of people passing by their desk area, and 69 percent had no say over whether others could come directly up to their desk at any time without permission. Eighty-four percent of the office workers reported that they were always in the view of someone else and had no way to avoid this contact; 80 percent also reported that they had no control over whether their work or conversations were overheard. The overwhelming majority of office workers could not alter the ventilation (88 percent), open the windows (96 percent), adjust the lighting (83 percent), rearrange the furniture or equipment (75 percent), or change the temperature (75 percent). (Stellman and Henifin, 1983: 112)

How the workplace regulates our movements may literally shape or misshape our bodies. Friedrich Engels ([1845] 1973: 282–283), writing over 145 years ago, describes the crippling effects of their work on the bodies of women and children coal carriers:

> The first result of such over-exertion is the diversion of vitality to the one-sided development of the muscles, so that those especially of the arms, legs, and the back, of the shoulders and chest, which are commonly called into activity in pushing and pulling, attain an uncommonly vigorous development, while all the rest of the body suffers and is atrophied from want of nourishment. More than all else the stature suffers, being stunted and retarded.

These damaging effects result from how environments are organized, the design of tools and equipment, the pace of work, and the fact that certain repetitive work practices can cause disproportionate wear and tear on the body. Although musculoskeletal problems are more likely to be associated with certain work practices, the injurious impact of such practices can be significantly reduced by frequent breaks, job rotation, and the proper ergonomic design of work spaces and equipment. Musculoskeletal problems are often the result of a poor fit between the social organization of space, time, and practices, and the person's body.

The occupational link with musculoskeletal injuries, such as "washerwoman's sprain," "bricklayer's shoulder," and "telegraphist's cramp" has long been recognized by medical science (Goldoftas, 1991). In the early twentieth century, certain musculoskeletal injuries were attributed, not to workplace conditions, but to the special "sensitivity" of certain groups, especially women and Jews. This gender and ethnic bias among physicians was related to societal fears about the movement of women and immigrants into the U.S. labor force (Dembe, 1996).

In the last quarter of the twentieth century, most economically developed countries experienced significant reductions in the proportion of the workforce employed in manufacturing and corresponding increases in the proportion employed in the service sector of the economy. In the United States, nearly 70 percent of jobs were in the service/information sector. While many (though by no means all) types of service jobs are physically less hazardous, this does not mean that service jobs are free from health hazards (Bellaby, 1999: 164–165). For instance, not only assembly line workers, but also data entry clerks, can sustain repetitive strain injuries.

People whose occupations require the use of their arms, wrists, or fingers in quick repetitive motions (such as cashiers, meat packers, computer operators), may suffer from inflammation of their tendons (tendonitis) or from compression of their nerves (carpal tunnel syndrome) (Dembe, 1996). As the use of computers in universities becomes more common, cumulative trauma disorders are becoming more prevalent among students (Rimer, 1997). Among meat packers, carpal tunnel syndrome is estimated to be as high as 15 percent of the work force (compared to a prevalence of 5 to 10 percent in the industrial work force). The rise of carpal tunnel syndrome in the United States has been attributed to the intensification of work pace and the alteration of work practices so that the range of motion is decreased (Goldoftas, 1991).

Ergonomics is the study of the relationship among the workers, their movements, and the physical features of their work environment. For example, is the chair designed to minimize backaches after long hours of sitting? Is the control panel easily readable and within comfortable reach? Ergonomic studies have tended to emphasize designing machines and workplaces to enhance productivity; however, less attention has been given to worker health or comfort (Goldsmith and Kerr, 1982). Furthermore, ergonomists design workplaces based on the average person with little provision for those whose bodies are not average.

In many workplaces, even basic ergonomic considerations are often ignored to enhance productivity and profits. Workers may be forced to work in cramped, uncomfortable positions. For instance, one welder comments:

> I got moved to a new job spot-welding where I had to stand on my toes with my head all the way against my back and my arms stretched out all day long. I told my boss that we had to disassemble the piece in order for me to do the job without injuring myself, and he insisted that I could do it the way it was. Well, I did it until finally I hurt my back so bad that I was out for 5 months. (quoted in Back, 1981: 24–25)

Until a few decades ago, farm laborers were forced to use short-handled hoes, which raised productivity by increasing traction but also caused serious back pains. It was only after pressure from unions and workers that the farm owners finally allowed workers to use long-handled hoes. Healthy movements are thus related not just to the nature of the activity, but also to the design of the tools and environment.

Varying the position of the body frequently during the workday is important for orthopedic health and psychological well-being. Some workers come to experience themselves and their bodies as "split" when their work involves uncomfortable, uninterrupted, repetitive motions:

> I sit in one place all day facing a wall. My fingers are moving all the time, my eyes are staring into a machine that is placed so I have to hold my neck stiff to see the words clearly. Everyone is typing or using machines so there is a lot of noise. It's impossible to talk or even to turn around and look at someone else. My job is basically to copy numbers and letters all day, but most of the time I'm not even aware of them. *It's like*

my hands and my eyes are alive and my mind and my body are dead. (quoted in Back, 1981: 41–42 [emphasis added])

People can adapt to unhealthy environments, but often at a cost. A significant portion of time in our everyday lives is spent on such unnoticed forms of body activities as walking up and down, pacing, stretching our limbs, tapping our feet, drumming our fingers, smoothing our hair, and hugging our body. These kinds of activities are integral to our self-image and contribute to stress reduction and to fitness (Csikszentmihalyi, 1990). They may also foster a sense of self-control and physical-emotional satisfaction. The social arrangements of many workplaces affect workers' ability to engage in these natural activities.

The workplace illustrates the relationship between the organization of space and the regulation of motion, and workers' psychophysical well-being. Disempowering spaces force people's bodies into standard forms or the motions of a machine. Workers need to vary their movements and to distribute more evenly the stressors that cause bodily wear and tear. The ability to control movements and to adapt work spaces to one's own well-being in turn depends on various political and economic factors.

Space, Practices, and Transportation

Transportation is another arena in which the organization of space and practices affects health. In many parts of the United States, someone with no automobile transportation has severely curtailed access to medical care, shopping, leisure activities, friends, and work. It has been estimated that more than 38 percent of U.S. households with incomes under the poverty level do not possess a car. About 24 percent of households of elderly persons lack a car (Freund and Martin, 1993). Similarly, most youths and many persons with disabilities are unable to transport themselves (M. Hillman et al., 1990). In American society access to transportation is thus unequally distributed, based on race, income, age, and class (Holtz Kay, 1997). The system of transportation dominated by the individual passenger car was created not merely by individual consumer choices but also by political and corporate interests. The major portion of public funds spent on transportation in the United States goes for highways as opposed to mass transit (Freund and Martin, 1993).

Reliance on automobile transportation is related to various problems of physical fitness. Difficulties in commuting can increase stress; for example, the heart rate of a train passenger is lower than that of a passenger in a private car (Lundberg, 1976). Driving causes increased levels of stress hormones, blood sugar, and cholesterol (Robinson, 1988), and can create problems like "motorist's spine" and "driver's thigh" (Homola, 1968). Persons who drive a car for 20 miles or more a day are at special risk for lumbar disk herniation (lower back injury). Truck drivers suffer a high rate of back injuries (National Institute on Disability, 1987).

The shape of modern transportation networks is the result not merely of society's love affair with the automobile but also of concrete economic and political decisions that affect the location of offices, shopping malls, industrial parks, and restaurants. These decisions thrust individuals into relying on private automobiles, whether they love or hate them. Advertising campaigns of automobile companies, furthermore, have imbued the car with symbolic meanings of masculinity, freedom, and social status; reliance on cars is thus not simply a matter of preference. Through their various interventions in the marketplace, manufacturers have shaped social space to the needs of automobile transportation. According to Snell (1982), from the 1930s to the 1950s the automobile industry (specifically General Motors) promoted the homogenization of the urban landscape by dismantling alternate transportation networks (such as trains and trolleys) and replacing them with inefficient, polluting trucks, buses, and automobiles. Once other modes of transportation had declined, the automobile became a virtual necessity rather than a luxury (Freund and Martin, 1993).

Accidents: An Individual or Social Problem?

Accidents are the fifth most common cause of death in American society. Automobile accidents constitute a large percentage of total accidents; work-related injuries are another important component (USDHHS, 2001a). Accidents result from the interplay among an unsafe environment, unsafe equipment and tools, and the behavior of the individuals involved. Accidents are usually treated as the results of individual fault, but often social and environmental problems also play a significant causal role. Accidents are not random, unpredictable events but follow patterns (Smothers, 1991). The very definition of events as "accidents"—as opposed to socially produced, preventable incidents—has political and social policy implications (Freund and Martin, 1993).

Auto Accidents   Despite long-term declines in the rates of fatalities and injuries from automobile accidents in the developed world, absolute levels of death and injury remain high and stubbornly resist reduction. In 1999, there were 42,401 U.S. deaths by motor vehicle (USDHHS, 2001a) compared to 34,763 in 1950 (Freund and Martin, 2002). Improvements in safety (both in vehicle-roadway technology and in driver behavior) have been offset by increases in auto use fostered by the expansion of auto-centered transport. In both the United States and the United Kingdom, reduction in the rate of traffic accidents has lagged behind declines in the rates of home and workplace accidents (Leichter, 1991: 181–182). Driving an auto remains a far riskier activity than other means of travel: Risk of death from an auto accident over a 50-year period is estimated to be one in 100, whereas risk of death from an airplane crash is one in 20,000 (*New York Times,* 1991; see also Royal Commission on Environmental Pollution, 1994). Auto accidents are a leading cause of death for males 15 to 44 (Freund and Martin, 2001). Just as auto accident fatalities are socially distributed along lines of gender and age, they also vary by social class. In Britain, lower-class persons have the greatest risk of auto accident fatality; because fewer lower-class persons drive, not surprisingly, their pedestrian death rate is also high (Quick, 1991).

Each year in the United States, approximately 4 to 5 million motor-vehicle related injuries occur. Of these, 500,000 people require hospitalization (averaging a stay of nine days). More deaths occur from automobile accidents than from any other injury-producing event. Motor vehicle accidents are the largest single trauma-induced cause of paraplegia and quadriplegia, and a major cause of epilepsy and head injuries in the United States (Holtz Kay, 1997).

Although traffic deaths and injuries remain an intractable problem—and an underappreciated public health issue—in the developed world, the worldwide picture is also not promising. About 1 million traffic deaths and about 40 million traffic injuries occurred in 1990 worldwide. Traffic accidents were the ninth leading cause of death, and the World Health Organization projects that deaths from traffic accidents will rise by 2020 to about 2.3 million, more than doubling the toll for 1990. Deaths will increase as developing nations adopt auto-centered transport systems, at the same time the proportion of young adults in their populations (those at most risk) grows (Murray and Lopez, 1996).

Why the automobile exacts such a high health risk is a complex question. Much public attention focuses on drunk driving. In 1990, 39.7 percent of U.S. road fatalities involved drivers with blood alcohol levels of 0.1 percent or more (a level defining intoxication). This figure represents a decline from 1982 when it was 46.3 percent (Smothers, 1991). These figures are somewhat misleading, however, because they include all traffic deaths in which any of the parties involved consumed alcohol, even if the person who was drinking was not at fault. Other estimates place the figure of alcohol-related deaths at 25 percent (Ross and Hughes, 1986). Many alcohol-related traffic fatalities, furthermore, involve cofactors such as fatigue, inexperience, poorly designed or inadequately lit roads, and unsafe cars (Gusfield, 1981).

Although individual drivers have a responsibility to drive safely, focusing merely on individual behavior neglects the social, cultural, and environmental dimensions of auto accidents. In many parts of the United States, the automobile is the only available means of transportation, pressuring drunken drivers and other impaired persons (for example, those with vision problems) into driving. Such factors in traffic fatalities are the result of social policies and an automobile-dominated social organization of space (Freund and Martin, 2002).

Policy responses to traffic accidents emphasize raising the *drinking* age, but few legislators would consider raising the *driving* age because in many parts of the country to be without a car is to be helpless, especially given an atrophied public transportation system. Social factors also explain why males are at particularly high risk. Many young males are socialized into taking lots of risks and into feeling or appearing invulnerable; media messages glorify speed and risk taking; many car-chase scenes convey a relatively carnage-free image of fast or reckless driving; advertisements glamorize cars as images of masculinity, speed, power, and excitement; and young men often view the use of seat belts as not "macho" (Horton, 1985b; Quick, 1991).

Economic pressures may also contribute to vehicular accidents by promoting reckless behavior on the road. Truck drivers have a high rate of drug consumption (especially stimulants). Economic considerations lead them to drive longer hours with unsafe equipment and larger payloads. Thus, social-structural forces contribute to trucking accidents (Freund and Martin, 2001).

Public policy has not given much attention to the health costs of a transportation system centered on the auto (Freund and Martin, 1997). Accidents are only one of the costs, which also include health consequences from auto emissions, noise pollution, and so on. Diet, smoking, exercise, and alcohol are in the limelight as health-lifestyle issues, but because we take cars for granted as the primary means of transport and because of the political power of auto interests, there has been inadequate analysis of the health implications of pervasive auto use (Freund and Martin, 2001).

In addressing the problem of automobile accidents, most policy focuses on changing individual behavior through education or various sanctions (Gusfield, 1981). However, individuals are hard to reach, influence, and control; traffic penalties are not consistently and rapidly imposed on violators; and to monitor and educate all drivers is difficult and not very cost effective. By contrast, an ecological approach to the problem emphasizes changing the social and physical environment (for example, building safer highways), producing safer cars, and making many alternative ways of traveling available to drivers (Syme and Guralnik, 1987). These kinds of preventive measures have been consistently constrained by the marketplace, however. The political and economic power of the automobile industry, in consideration of the cost of designing safer vehicles and highways, seriously limits the government's power or willingness to choose and implement solutions to prevent auto accidents (MacLennan, 1988).

Workplace Accidents: Unsafe Behavior, Unsafe Conditions?   Workplace accidents (some prefer the term *injury* because an accident implies a random occurrence) differ from occupational diseases: In the former, the exposure to the source is sudden, and the damage as well as its cause is readily apparent (Baker et al., 1987: 177). By contrast, the cause of work-related diseases is not always apparent, and the effect may be gradual. Accidents are thus discrete, clearly identifiable events that happen suddenly but involve a multitude of causal factors (Dembe, 1996).

Between 1992 and 1995, occupational injury claimed the lives of more than 6,000 U.S. workers each year (USDHHS, 2000). Workplace accidents caused 5.7 million injuries in 1997 (USNIOSH, 1999). Like other health problems, their incidence and severity tend to be socially distributed. Lower-status jobs generally involve more accidents (Dutton, 1986). Because black males tend to work in high-risk occupations with little control over their work environment, they have a 37 percent greater likelihood than whites of suffering occupational injuries or illnesses (Goldsmith and Kerr, 1982). The rate of injuries, particularly fatal ones, has generally declined somewhat in the past 50 years (Baker et al., 1987). The legislation of safety regulations, such as the 1969 Federal Mine Safety and Health Act, seems to have helped reduce injuries. Since 1994, however, the Occupational Safety and Health Administration's (OSHA) safety inspections have dropped by 43 percent (Cooper, 1997).

Data on workplace safety are highly problematic. Job injury rates are sometimes calculated in terms of the number of workdays lost per week, month, or year due to injury. However, employers often keep injured workers on the job or move them temporarily to easier jobs to keep injury rates down (Goldsmith and Kerr, 1982). Some companies simply do not report all injuries. In 1986, the Chrysler Corporation was fined a substantial sum for failing to report 182 injuries at one work site alone (Noble, 1986). Because official government data are based on company self-reports, these figures also tend to underestimate injuries. In 1985, the U.S. Bureau of Statistics reported that 3,750 workers died on the job, whereas the National Safety Council (an independent agency) reported 11,600 worker deaths (Noble, 1986). Part of this discrepancy is due to the fact that the government does not count injuries in private businesses employing fewer than 11 people.

The concept of accident proneness, first coined in 1926, became the focus for whole generations of industrial psychologists who searched for specifiable characteristics causing some individuals to be especially likely to have accidents. In a chapter on industrial and occupational psychiatry, the 1966 *American Handbook of Psychiatry* described the "accident syndrome" as involving an "impulsive character" and "reaction of anxiety." The handbook does not suggest, however, that the psychiatrist should take into account the characteristics of the workplace in which the "accident-prone" behavior occurs (Berman, 1978: 23–24). Empirical research has been unable to isolate any personality traits, independent of specific situations, that could be categorized as "accident proneness" (Members of the Working Party, 1975).

Environmental factors also contribute to accidents. Workplace accidents involve "accident-prone" tools and environments, as well as social pressures that encourage risky behavior. The ecological model appears more useful than the individual behavior model for understanding workplace accidents. As the meat-packing industry came under increased competitive pressure, wages decreased, but productivity pressures grew, simultaneously increasing the rate of on-the-job injuries (Dembe, 1996; Novek et al., 1990). Especially when linked with job alienation, situational pressures enhance the likelihood of accidents (Back, 1981).

Design of equipment itself is sometimes the source of accidents. Although machines can be built in an ergonomically sound fashion to reduce accidents, more often they are designed mainly to enhance productivity (Goldsmith and Kerr, 1982). The burden of accident prevention in these environments is thus on the individual worker. An assembly-line worker commented:

> When there are accidents they always blamed us for not using safety equipment. Six of us had to work with an acid solution and we were all given plastic goggles. But no

one could wear them because they didn't fit and you couldn't see very well with them on. This was a piece work job and there was no way we were going to make our bonus if we wore our glasses. I always felt caught between being worried about my health and being worried about not making production. You know it could've been fairly easy to put a shield over the whole operation so we wouldn't have to worry about it. (quoted in Back, 1981: 15)

Engineering controls that alter the environment, such as putting a protective "shield over the whole operation," are typically more expensive than giving workers individual safety equipment, such as respirators to prevent breathing dust. So-called passive safety approaches, which rely on safe equipment and environment more than on behavior, are more effective but also more expensive (Baker et al., 1987). Although respirators are cheaper for corporations, they create problems for workers. Respirators are physically uncomfortable, especially if worn the whole day under conditions of high temperature and noise. They may also be ineffective or create such side effects as breathing difficulty or heart strain. Workplace physical stressors, such as high noise levels and toxins, may also affect workers' perception, alertness, and reflexes, thereby producing "accident proneness."

Some social scientists consider accidents to be related to the social structure of the workplace. In many work situations, there is a split between those who plan and organize work and those who execute it. This division may influence the perception and treatment of occupational health problems (Dembe, 1996). Experts who study accidents and occupational health problems are often far removed from the day-to-day routine of the workplaces they analyze. Furthermore, management concerns with productivity and cost effectiveness are not often compatible with workers' needs for safe workplaces. Human error (for example, due to drug use) and carelessness *are* significant factors in workplace injuries. It is also important, however, to focus on how such variables as style of managerial control also contribute to workplace health problems (Members of the Working Party, 1975: 74–75). One basic issue in occupational injuries is the conflict between, on the one hand, managerial pressures to enhance productivity and profit margins, and, on the other hand, the needs of workers to work in the safest technologically feasible working environment. Box 3.1 illustrates some structural ways of reducing workplace injuries.

"Safety" experts tend to focus on the individual and to minimize the importance of *social* organization of space and practices (Williams et al., 1995). For example, one study concluded that safety experts overemphasized individualistic and psychological factors, such as "safety values," and needed to pay more attention to participants' local knowledge about the safety of environments (for example, poor housing, unsafe play spaces, transport and traffic conditions). Although having the right attitude about safety *is* important, to prevent accidents, it is also very important to consider such environmental arrangements as the organization of space, time, and practices (Roberts et al., 1995).

Box 3.1

Swedish Road to Better Conditions

"The Swedish approach to health and safety has four main features.

First, Swedish workers have won real power at the local level to prevent hazards. Sweden's OSHA–the National Board of Occupational Safety and Health–sets standards and inspects workplaces, but unions view its role as secondary to their own efforts.

Second, Swedish workers have the information and training to enable them to use that power.

Third, unions have a major voice in safety and health research and research is often geared to finding practical solutions to hazards.

Fourth, Swedish unions are concerned about the total work environment, not just safety and health as narrowly defined in the U.S. They consider physical safety hazards, chemical and noise exposures, heat and cold, speed-up, boredom, and stress as related problems. The Swedish unions are concerned not only about injuries and illnesses but also discomfort, an unpleasant work place, and lack of job satisfaction.

They believe that workers are entitled to a humane work environment and control over their jobs."

Source: *In These Times,* January 18–21, 1986: 17. Reprinted by permission.

ENVIRONMENTAL POLLUTION

The concept of pollution usually carries the connotation of the fouling of the environment by humans, but volcanoes pollute the air and various nonhuman species pollute the environment with their excreta. In fact, most atmospheric pollution is not of human origin. About 9 percent of the carbon monoxide in the air comes from human sources, such as automobile use. Various industrial processes account for 16 percent of the hydrocarbons in the atmosphere. About 45 percent of the sulfur dioxide in the atmosphere comes from human activity (Botkin and Keller, 1982: 172–173).

Approximately 130 million Americans are exposed daily to harmful levels of air pollution. An estimated 60,000 Americans die prematurely each year of heart attacks and respiratory illnesses linked to air pollution, and 250,000 children a year suffer from asthma attacks and respiratory disorders triggered by air pollution (St. Clair, 1997). Clean air is not equally available in the United States. Table 3.3 shows the number of people residing in areas that met U.S. air quality standards.

A significant decrease of lead emissions between 1976 and 1980 coincided with an approximately 50 percent decline in the use of leaded gasoline. Between 1974 and 1991, the lead levels in the blood of Americans, aged 1–74, declined by 78 percent (Kitman, 2000: 38). Nevertheless, one-third of poor black American

TABLE 3.3 **The Number of People by Race/Ethnicity in the United States Residing in Areas that Meet Air Quality Standards for Pollution (for CO, Ozone, SO_2, NO_2, Lead, and Particulates)**

	Percentage of Population						
All Pollutants	1990	1991	1992	1993	1994	1995	1996
All Persons	71.0	65.2	78.4	76.5	75.1	67.9	81.3
White	71.8	66.0	79.1	76.9	76.4	69.7	81.9
Black	71.5	63.4	76.5	75.2	70.4	59.4	80.8
American Indian or Alaskan Native	76.8	75.2	83.0	82.4	80.0	77.9	83.2
Asian or Pacific Islander	49.6	46.7	64.4	62.8	55.6	48.2	64.4
Hispanic	49.3	45.2	56.8	57.7	54.8	44.5	56.3

Source: U.S. Department of Health and Human Services, *Health United States 2000,* Hyattsville, MD: National Center for Health Statistics, 2000: 249.

children between the ages of one to five, who live in large cities, have hazardous levels of lead in their blood. Seventeen percent of Hispanic American children and only 6 percent of white children living under similar conditions have such high lead levels in their blood (Brody, 1995). Lead poisoning stunts the development of children's brains, and nearly a million U.S. children under five are believed to suffer from it (Pear, 1999). Leaded gasoline continues to be sold in most developing countries. Indeed, 93 percent of all gasoline sold in Africa is leaded, as is 94 percent in the Middle East, and 35 percent in Latin America. This means that 1.7 billion urbanites in developing nations are at risk for lead poisoning (Kitman, 2000: 39).

Motor vehicles are a major source of carbon monoxide, a gas that interferes with the blood's ability to carry oxygen. Sulfur dioxides and nitrous oxides come from fuel combustion used to heat dwellings, generate electricity, and power motor vehicles (Renner, 1988). These emissions are important components of acid rain, which has a destructive impact on forests and the life in lakes and rivers, contributes to the erosion of building surfaces, and may contribute to human respiratory problems. Because acid rain often falls in regions distant from where the pollution originates, the economic activity in one region damages the environment in another, causing political strains between regions and nations, such as the United States and Canada.

Although humans are not the only sources of global pollution, their activities have increasingly produced ecological changes in climate, atmosphere, and the very shape of the earth's surface. Our social institutions may not be able to regulate the impact effectively (Shabecoff, 1987: A6). This impact of humans on the spaceship earth is not merely the result of technology or so-called progress but is also linked to the failure of political, economic, and social policy to regulate the use of technology or to create healthier technologies.

Poorer communities are more likely to be victims of corporate pollution. Several studies document the fact that toxic waste dumps are disproportionately likely to be located in poor neighborhoods, especially poor African American neighborhoods (Krieger and Fee, 1994). Roughly three out of five African Americans and Hispanic Americans live in communities with one or more hazardous waste sites. Childhood cancer rates are several times the national average in Latino farm communities where pesticides are used. Primarily because of poor air quality in inner cities, young black men die of asthma at three times the rate of young white men (Muwakkil, 1996a).

Along the U.S.-Mexico border, the waterways are becoming chemically and bacterially polluted. Unscrupulous U.S. developers have not provided safe water or sewage disposal in many new housing developments for poor workers, and many *maquiladora* workers on the Mexico side live in unregulated shantytowns (Brenner et al., 2000). The border region has become an attractive area for legal and illegal dumpers of toxic chemicals and radioactive waste (Skolnick, 1995).

Sometimes it is community-based groups that call attention to the health consequences of polluting activities of corporations in their communities. In one Massachusetts community, ordinary citizens collected information to understand the sources and effects of pollution in their area. Their efforts led to lawsuits against two corporations that had been dumping toxic wastes (Brown and Mikkelsen, 1990). Increasingly, local lay activists fight against placing toxic waste dumps in their communities. These struggles for environmental justice have led to the emergence of what has been called "popular epidemiology" (Brown, 1995b), which involves the participation of community members who collect data and collaborate with experts using epidemiological methods. Popular epidemiology grows out of the concern of people living in communities that are polluted or in other ways perceived to be unhealthy (Brown, 2000a, 2000b; Couch and Kroll-Smith, 2000).

Discussions of pollution often pronounce that "we" (referring to humans in general) pollute. This expression, however, masks the sociopolitical dimension of environmental health by equating the individual litterbug with the corporate polluter whose impact on the environment is more far reaching and potentially dangerous than that of the individual (Bookchin, 1962). Not all of us citizens pollute equally, nor are we all equally affected by pollution. Not unlike passive smoking, polluted air affects even those who do not themselves pollute.

"Don't Let the Smoke Get in Your Lungs": The Individual as Polluter

Although tobacco smokers do not contribute significantly to atmospheric pollution, their habits do have a significant impact on health. Cigarette smoking is the leading cause of preventable disease and premature death in the United States and other developed countries. One of every five U.S. deaths is smoking related (USCDC, 2001a). Cigarette consumption has been rising in developing countries as the tobacco industry has increasingly pursued new markets outside the United

States and Western Europe. According to the World Health Organization, in 1997, about one-third of the world's population over the age of 15 were smokers; this proportion is a significant increase over just two decades ago. If current smoking patterns continue, more than 500 million people alive today will eventually be killed by tobacco use (cited in Stebbins, 2001).

Experts argue that smoking is as serious an addiction as heroin and, in the long run, perhaps even more damaging to the body (Weil and Rosen, 1993). In addition to nicotine, a highly addictive substance, cigarette smoke contains some 40 cancer- and other disease-causing chemicals. Because nearly 60 percent of all smokers became addicted to tobacco as adolescents, much tobacco advertising continues to target young consumers. In 1999, 23 percent of American twelfth-graders reported smoking cigarettes daily in the previous 30 days (U.S., Forum on Child and Family Statistics, 2000). The number of teenagers who began smoking each day grew steadily in the 1980s and 1990s, reaching a peak in 1997 (when there were more than 3,000 new smokers daily), and declining somewhat since 1998 (2000 National Household Survey on Drug Abuse, USDHHS, cited in American Cancer Society, 2001). In the United States, an antismoking campaign began in the late 1960s and gained considerable momentum in the 1980s and 1990s, aided significantly by several successful lawsuits that held tobacco companies responsible for failure to disclose their knowledge about the damaging effects of tobacco. Smoking among U.S. adults has declined steadily since 1974 (Feder, 1996). Many workplaces, universities, restaurants, and other indoor public spaces have adopted bans on smoking. Rates of smoking vary inversely by socioeconomic status (Adler et al., 1999). Increases in the rates of smoking by African American and Hispanic males are particularly high. Cigarette industry advertising has increasingly targeted these vulnerable groups (Baer et al., 1997).

Individuals who smoke also affect the quality of air shared by others in the enclosed spaces of offices, homes, and restaurants. Passive smoking (the inhaling of someone else's cigarette smoke) causes lung cancer and promotes heart disease. Among American adults, exposure to secondhand tobacco smoke causes an estimated 3,000 deaths annually from lung cancer (USCDC, 2001a). Parents' smoking affects their children's respiratory health, contributing to diseases such as asthma. The effect of the smokers' habit on nonsmokers raises fundamental issues regarding individual rights as opposed to collective rights:

> Air pollution makes us take seriously the fact that we exist, not as isolated entities secure behind our fences, but as fellow creatures in a shared and threatened environment. While in some settings—when looking at second-hand smoke or workplace hazards—we can insist that individual consent remains fundamental, in others we may have to look beyond consent to autonomy and beyond the individual to a deeper sense of community. If anything is our birthright, it is the air that we breathe. (Center for Philosophy and Public Policy, 1985: 5)

The passive smoking issue has helped to define "personal" habits as a social problem (Chapman et al., 1990). Might other "habits" such as the "excessive" use of automobiles also be viewed as social problems because of their pollution of "community" air (Freund and Martin, 1993)?

Tobacco-producing corporations form a major industry in the United States, using extensive lobbying and political muscle to try to prevent further regulation of tobacco sales in this country. The tobacco industry has compensated for its loss of revenues in the United States by increasing its exports, particularly to the developing countries in Asia, Latin America, and Eastern Europe (Stebbins, 2001; see also Baer et al., 1997; Millen and Holtz, 2000). In the 1980s, at the same time that the U.S. Surgeon General was calling for a complete ban on tobacco advertising and sales, the Reagan and Bush administrations exerted pressure on several Asian countries to allow American cigarette sales and advertising or to face trade sanctions (Stebbins, 2001). In his final speech as Surgeon General, C. Everett Koop said:

> It is the height of hypocrisy for the United States, in our war against drugs, to demand that foreign nations take steps to stop the export of cocaine to our country while at the same time we export nicotine, a drug just as addictive as cocaine, to the rest of the world (cited in Millen and Holtz, 2000: 210).

Rather than deal with such massive economic and political issues, however, policymakers find it easier to focus on changing individuals' habits (Milio, 1985). Although smoking is an individual behavior and only the individual can decide to stop, the practice of smoking is firmly rooted in a sociocultural context (Bellaby, 1999). Advertising has glamorized smoking, associating it with vigor, sexiness, and sophistication. Other social factors supporting the habit include peer pressure among teenagers and the use of smoking for sociability and for stress reduction (Lupton, 1994: 155). Smoke cessation programs, some argue, have little impact, because their focus is on changing individual behavior rather than addressing the habit's sociocultural sources (Syme and Guralnik, 1987). As with accidents, we need an ecological approach that considers individuals and their relationships to their social and cultural environments to address supposedly personal addictions like smoking.

Pollution in the Workplace

Between 70,000 and 100,000 Americans die each year from occupational diseases—*not* including occupational injuries (Elling, 1986; National Safe Workplace Institute, 1990). About 390,000 new cases of disabling occupational diseases are diagnosed annually (Moeller, 1992). These estimates vary according to criteria for the category of "occupational diseases." Many respiratory problems experienced by coal miners, for example, were not immediately classified as black lung. They were so designated only after years of political conflict between mine owners, workers, unions, and various health professionals (Smith, 1981). The same symptoms were previously diagnosed as bronchitis, emphysema, or health problems resulting from workers' personal habits. In fact, occupational diseases are often hard to distinguish from "ordinary," nonwork-related problems (Elling, 1986: 18). To a physician untrained in diagnosing occupational diseases, lung cancer caused by asbestos looks like cancer due to smoking. Many cases of brown lung (a disease caused by inhaling cotton fibers) among textile workers go unrecorded because the symptoms may be misinterpreted as emphysema (Guarasci, 1987). Stress-related diseases (discussed in Chapter 4) are also not included in occupational disease statistics.

Obtaining sound statistics on occupational disease is a complicated process because they vary depending on who decides which health problems are job related. Company doctors, for example, are less likely to view symptoms as work related than union-affiliated doctors. One doctor working for the textile industry claimed that brown lung is "best described as a 'symptom complex' rather than a disease in the usual sense":

> We feel that this term may be preferable, first in order not to unduly alarm workers, as we attempt to protect their health and secondly, to help avoid unfair designations of cotton as an unduly hazardous material for use in the textile industry, raising the fear that the engineering control of it may be costly, and that it may be better, therefore, to switch to some less costly material. (quoted in Berman, 1978: 93)

Industry has focused on individuals, their lifestyle, and their "susceptibility" to occupational diseases (Epstein, 1990a). For years, instead of cleaning the air of cotton dust, the textile industry tried to identify hypersusceptible workers or "reactors" (Green, 1983). Employers' concern with workers' health is often inextricably tied to economic interests that influence what is or is not perceived and treated as occupational disease. As with accident prevention, management favors individual devices rather than passive engineering controls for the prevention of occupational disease. The issue of having the worker adapt to the workplace rather than adapting the workplace to the worker is thus not merely an economic one. Nelkin and Brown (1984: 70) observe the following:

> [T]he dispute over precautions extends beyond the question of immediate cost. Personal protective equipment places responsibility for protecting health on the workers themselves. Ill health can then be blamed on their failure to comply. Conversely, engineering controls place responsibility on management, shifting both the burden and the blame. To insist on personal precautions is to reinforce the belief that individuals are responsible for their own health and safety. To accept engineering controls is to accept the notion of corporate responsibility.

Because the people who study or make policy decisions about occupational health are often remote from the workplace (Dembe, 1996), workers' reports of symptoms are often ignored or invalidated, despite the fact that workers are often the first to recognize occupational health hazards. A Labor Department study found workers' self-reporting of health hazards to be highly reliable, except that workers tended to underestimate the effects of chronic diseases caused by occupational exposure (Nelkin and Brown, 1984: 31). Coal miners have known of "miner's asthma" for generations; their awareness is documented in song and popular writings. Such knowledge was dismissed as unscientific or as excuses for malingering, however. Although workers' reports are not based on scientific observation, ignoring their observations delays effective responses to occupational health hazards.

Workers do not always report work-related health problems, however; some may not complain out of fear of repercussions. Many others do not make the connection between low-level, long-term exposure to hazards and diseases that developed slowly or gradually. For example, the symptoms of asbestosis appear 20 to 40 years after asbestos exposure. Most private physicians have little training in environmental or occupational medicine and may not recognize patients' symptoms (Brown and Kelley, 2000; Dembe, 1996). One study of worker deaths from asbestos exposure showed that only 48 percent were correctly diagnosed on the death certificates. Only about half of U.S. medical school programs require course work in occupational health; among those that require the topic, the median time spent on occupational health topics is four hours (National Safe Workplace Institute, 1990: 18). Physicians are not oriented to public health, and only 1.4 percent of all U.S. medical students study environmental medicine (Brown and Kelley, 2000: 52). Many doctors do not record a patient's occupational and work history, and often they fail to connect symptoms to work conditions.

Tens of thousands of different chemicals are used in commercial production processes, and the list grows at the rate of about a thousand a year. Of the 2 million known chemicals, only a few thousand have been tested for their dangerous properties, and only a few hundred of these have been thoroughly tested. Production processes often use several chemicals in conjunction with each other, but very little is known about health hazards created when these chemicals (which individually may be harmless) interact with each other (Nelkin and Brown, 1984). Regulatory standards are typically set only after a problem has been identified among workers. In this sense, workers often function as human guinea pigs.

As Epstein (1990b: 455) notes:

> The regulatory system is potentially only as valid as the information generated is reliable. When the ingredients are not identified, when the proper studies are not conducted, when the results of studies are not published for review, and when the results of studies state conclusions contrary to the actual data, effective regulation becomes virtually impossible. . . . An overwhelming record confirms the premise that scientific information generated and interpreted by institutions and individuals with direct or indirect economic interests in its outcome must be regarded as suspect until proven otherwise by independent validation.

Institutional interests do not necessarily intentionally alter data. Sometimes, however, industries such as asbestos mining and manufacturing have collected occupational health data and then systematically suppressed it (Lilienfeld, 1991).

Regulatory agencies such as the Environmental Protection Agency (EPA) or OSHA must rely on company data about various chemicals. However, the very companies with an economic interest in producing the chemicals are often the ones that test them. Cutbacks in funding to regulatory agencies further limit effective research to determine regulatory standards. In many cases, OSHA has not set standards even for those chemicals known to cause cancer.

Many dusts and particles inhaled by workers produce serious health problems. Workers who inhale such common particles as cotton fibers, coal dust, sand, fiberglass, or asbestos can suffer debilitating and often fatal lung diseases. Exposure to chemicals used in many manufacturing processes has also been linked to cancer and various other serious diseases.

Pollution in the workplace is not confined to blue-collar or industrial jobs. For example, the computer industry, which seems high-tech and clean, exposes workers to solvents, chemicals, and gases that may be toxic (Hayes, 1989). Supposedly clean office work sometimes involves inhaling ozone, a gas that can aggravate respiratory problems, from photocopiers or chemical copier fluids (Stellman and Henifin, 1983). Several studies document "office sickness" due to the high pollutant content of modern office buildings that are often airtight and rely on centralized air sources (Sterling et al., 1983).

The World Health Organization estimates that 30 percent of new and remodeled buildings, with efficient but "closed" ventilation systems, have indoor air quality problems (cited in National Safe Workplace Institute, 1990). Closed systems can spread infections such as the flu (Gilbert, 1997). Ironically, some workers in the EPA building itself wore respirators shortly after it was built because of indoor air pollution.

Workplace pollution spreads beyond the confines of the workplace, affecting workers' families. Factory pollution also tends to spread into the immediate vicinity. A high percentage of urban dwellers have some asbestos fibers in their lungs, even though they have not worked with asbestos. Atmospheric pollution from asbestos plants, construction sites, and even from auto brake linings spreads asbestos fibers into public spaces.

Just as the fruits of production are not equally distributed, so too are the costs of production, such as pollution, unequally shared. The average age at death of blue-collar workers is many years less than that of white-collar workers (National Safe Workplace Institute, 1990: 11). People living in urban poverty areas are exposed to larger quantities of chemical and air pollution than their middle-class suburban counterparts (Dutton, 1986). Likewise, developing countries experience increasing pollution and industrial hazards, even while already industrialized countries are achieving greater environmental and workplace health and safety regulations (McMurray and Smith, 2001). Many developing countries want to attract industry, but they lack technical information to evaluate processes, resources for testing products, effective power to set and enforce standards, and worker organizations to voice concerns (Millen and Holtz, 2000).

In the United States, the Occupational Safety and Health Act of 1970 was passed to "assure as far as possible every working man and woman in the United States, safe and healthy working conditions." This assurance has not been realized, however, in large part due to political abuses and to underfunding of the vast task of researching and enforcing standards (see Howard, 1985). The United States spent $0.63 per worker on job health in 1986, whereas Finland spent $12.29 in 1986 and Sweden $12.33 in 1988 (National Safe Workplace Institute, 1990). Compared to Sweden, Finland, Germany, and the United Kingdom, the United States ranked last, or tied for last place, on five out of six criteria for effective occupational safety and health: a strong national policy mandate for occupational health and safety; the provision and organization of services related to occupational health; workers' ability to control their work environment; the level of financing for occupational health activities; worker education; and the information about the workplace available to workers and experts (Elling, 1986).

Comparative data on actual levels of occupational health and safety in each of these countries are scant and difficult to evaluate because countries use different methods of collecting and categorizing information. Elling (1986) argues that those countries with the most protection have the lowest rates of occupational disease and injury. Calculating admittedly crude work-related death rates, he found that the United States had the highest rate, with 50 such deaths per 100,000 workers; the United Kingdom had 2.5 per 100,000, and Sweden had 3.6 per 100,000 (Elling, 1986: 22). The other developed countries appear to have stronger regulations and generally safer working conditions than the United States (Goldsmith and Kerr, 1982). For instance, Swedish workers have the right to veto plans for new machines, work processes, or construction on health and safety grounds. They are also trained in health and safety (including ergonomics) at the employers' expense. In one Saab automobile plant, the accident rate decreased 33 to 50 percent after some of these policies were implemented (Engler, 1986). Because a significant proportion of disease and disability in the United States is work related, issues of regulation and the politics of regulation have become important health considerations (National Safe Workplace Institute, 1990).

SUMMARY

Sociopolitical factors and culture construct our physical environments, our access to such resources as food, and hence our bodies. Cultural meanings, shaped by social status as well as corporate and other political interests, influence physical activities: working, eating, and fitness. Social, political, and cultural factors shape people's opportunities for a safe and healthy material environment and lifestyle.

MIND, BODY, AND SOCIETY

�֎ �֎ ✖

"Industrial and, no less so, post-industrial forms of work require a rhythm which over-rides the seasons and even the difference between day and night. Global commerce and financial dealings are even more demanding in this respect than local shift working. These work patterns are as much at odds with the agricultural cycle that preceded them as that, in its turn, was with the hunting and gathering economy of the stone age."

Source: Paul Bellaby, *Sick from Work: The Body in Employment,* 1999, p. 59.

We have briefly reviewed some of the ways in which social and political factors affect the quality and our use of our material environment. In previous chapters, we looked at physical determinants of health and at their social contexts. Here we examine other ways our bodies are affected less visibly, but perhaps more directly, by social relationships and structures. In this chapter and the next, we focus on the issue of sociopsychological stress and health. Stress and related concepts provide the basis for a holistic perspective in which individual minds and bodies are integrally interrelated with social environments.

"STICKS AND STONES MAY BREAK MY BONES, AND NAMES CAN ALSO HURT ME"

In everyday life, we are sometimes aware that sociopsychological factors affect our health. We might say, "I always get a cold after a tough exam."[1] Conversations contain various psychosomatic references such as, "You're a pain in the neck!" "She'll be the death of me yet!" "Grandma died of a broken heart!" These references show a commonsense awareness of the connections among the mind, body, and society. Particularly among middle-class persons, there appears to be a recent increase in self-consciousness about bodies and stress.

Despite this recent interest in mind-body relationships, psychological and social factors are not perceived to be truly important in determining health because they are not "real," that is, countable and tangible. Viruses, radiation, chemicals, and smoking are physical factors whose effects on the body can be measured and observed. Because medical science has viewed mind and body as separate entities to be studied and treated separately, doctors often do not assign these factors much reality or tangibility. Thus, although we may intuit the reality of psychosomatic connections, we also believe that "sticks and stones may break my bones, but words will never hurt me" (at least not physically!). Yet is this adage really true?

Some evidence suggests that a conversation with another person (even a nonthreatening one) will automatically raise our blood pressure; a conversation with our boss, even more so (Lynch, 1985; Lynch and Rosch, 1990). What are we to make of accounts of "voodoo death," when a chieftain utters a death curse at a woman who violates a tribal taboo, and the woman, who believes her death to be inevitable, soon dies of no clear physical causes (Cannon, 1942)?[2] Modern

---

[1]In fact, studies show that immunity to disease among medical students is lower than usual during finals (Kiecolt-Glaser and Glaser, 1991).

[2]Other mechanisms may be involved in voodoo death besides being scared to death. For example, other people, such as relatives, friends, and neighbors, withdraw their emotional support from the victim. Funeral rites may be carried out while the person is still alive, thus symbolically defining the individual as dead. (This has been called social death.) However, there may also be a withdrawal of material support. The literature on voodoo death differs on how the process works. Some argue that dehydration (loss of body fluids) is a vital factor. Relatives may withhold water, and the victim, believing he is doomed, loses the desire to drink or obtain water (Eastwell, 1982). Thus, according to some, voodoo death has mainly physical causes, with psychological causes being secondary. Others argue that although physical causes are important, psychologically giving up on life produces lethal physical consequences (such as cardiac arrhythmia). Some laboratory evidence indicates that animals who give up die because their physiological systems have been depressed to a point of death (McElroy and Townsend, 1985).

equivalents of voodoo death occur in such cases as sudden death after retirement or widowhood. Engel (1971) argued that such phenomena are due to intense emotional arousal, which interrupts the regular rhythm of the heart; in other words, it causes a cardiac arrhythmia that can be deadly. We do not wish to overstate the case that words can kill, but we do want to make the point, developed further later, that human physiology is responsive to its social environment and symbolic meanings can physically affect us.

Placebos: A Case of Mind or Body?

Research on placebos provides some suggestive linkages between mind and body. A placebo is a chemically inert or inactive substance (for example, a sugar pill) that looks like real medication. It is a sham treatment that is supposed to have no actual physical effects. The Latin word *placebo* means "I will please." Doctors sometimes give placebos to patients who want and expect treatment yet seem to have no physical, organic basis to their complaints. Placebos are also used in tests of drugs and treatments to determine how much of a drug's effectiveness is due to its specific physical properties and how much is due to subjective or psychological factors. The placebo is used as a standard (or a control) against which a drug being tested can be compared.

Although chemically inert, placebo "pain medication" can actually reduce pain in as many as 35 percent of patients (Beecher, 1959). In the late 1950s, there was even a controversial experiment with placebo surgery. (Recent tighter rules for experiments with human subjects prohibit such experiments.) It was found that an early version of coronary bypass surgery (called mammary artery ligating surgery) was no more effective than sham surgery, in which patients were put to sleep and had an incision made, although no actual surgery was performed on the heart arteries (Cobb et al., 1959). Some observers have suggested that current coronary bypass surgery may likewise derive part of its success from a placebo effect. Many bypass patients experience considerable relief, even though their surgery produced *no* working grafts (that is, surgery did not improve ventricular function). The operation's symbolic and metaphorical effects may thus account for much of the patients' relief from angina pain (Moerman, 1997). Because patients usually hope that treatment will work, almost all treatments involve an element of the placebo effect. Medical settings—with their impressive equipment, diplomas and certificates on doctors' office walls, white uniforms, clipboards, and stethoscopes—contribute to this faith or expectancy. Even the color of placebo "medication" can increase its effectiveness. Placebo effectiveness varies, depending on the condition being treated. Cultural factors (such as the meaning of a condition or symbolism of a treatment) often influence how well a placebo works (Moerman, 2000).

Some researchers view the placebo effect as being all in the mind, with no physical basis. Others suggest that placebos actually induce internal physical changes in the body (Bakal, 1979; Cousins, 1989; Eisenberg et al., 1993a; Horwitz et al., 1990; Weil, 1988). For instance, placebos may stimulate the body's production of natural opiates, called endorphins (Davis, 1984; Levine et al., 1978). If this is true, it may be an oversimplification to consider the pain-relieving properties of a placebo merely psychological. Doctors' bedside manner, or communication, may likewise have concrete physical effects, such as reducing pain or speeding recovery (see Moerman, 2000). As one physician notes,

> But what if it is demonstrated in the future that reassurance provided by a health professional is capable of releasing endogenous morphine-like substances within a patient's brain? Without doubt, the phrase "laying on of hands" will acquire a new meaning. (Bakal, 1979: 251)

The Western assumption of a division between mind and body is not shared by all cultures. In many cultures being sick or being healed is neither all biological nor all psychological, but a psychophysiological process (Grossinger, 1990; Kleinman, 1978). We examine this issue in later chapters. For our present purpose, research on placebos illustrates that they have a psychophysiological effect and that biomedicine's assumption of a mind-body split is not supportable. Indeed, the assumption of such a mind-body dualism limits medicine's ability to understand health and illness.[3] Furthermore, mind and body exist in a social environment with which they also interact. Thus, social meanings, pressures, and relationships have at least *some* impact on us. The following sections sketch some of the possible pathways through which social pressures (or stressors) can become the source of psychophysical troubles.

The value of placebos is sometimes misconstrued as a simplistic mind-over-matter argument, which leads to the trap of another form of mind-body dualism: the mind ruling the body. Mind and body must be seen as interacting and not as separate elements. Diseases clearly have biological components, but they also have a psychosocial dimension. Psychosocial factors, however, do not magically transform bodies. Psychosocial pressures generally take years to exact their toll; for instance, social stress does not generate coronary heart disease or hypertension overnight. Some health problems experienced in adulthood may have begun much earlier in the person's life, even early childhood, when the organism is not yet fixed in its patterns of physical responses. Physical damages brought on by long-term stress, for example, may not be easily reversible. The fact that a health problem is affected by social factors, however, does not make it any less real.

The Open Quality of Human Bodies: Dogs Don't Brood

All creatures interact intimately with their environments; they have an impact on their environmental conditions and in turn are affected by them. When studying organisms and their surroundings, we have a tendency to make a sharp

---

[3]Evidence comes from a host of disciplines with a bewildering array of names, including psychological medicine, psychosomatic medicine, psychophysiology, health psychology, sociophysiology, and psychoneuroimmunology. A central theory underlying much research in this area is that the immune system may be the connecting point between psychosocial experiences and diseases (Solomon, 1985). Such factors as social stress may have an impact on immunity, which in turn lowers a person's resistance to disease.

distinction between the environment and the creatures inhabiting it (Levins and Lewontin, 1985), but this distinction is misleading. Animals adapt to their environments, but they also transform the world they live in, often modifying it to their needs and in turn being shaped by the world they have shaped. Humans, more than other creatures, can transform their social and physical environments, but they are also more affected physically and mentally by the world they create.

Creatures are shaped not only by physical surroundings but also by their social relationships and expectations. Social relationships affect physical responses. The social position of animals, for instance, affects their behavioral responses to amphetamines. Given amphetamines, both dominant and submissive monkeys increased dominant and submissive behaviors "appropriate" to their status. When a monkey changed its social position, so did its response to the drug. Thus, under amphetamines, a monkey with increased status changed its behavior from being submissive to being more threatening and making more dominant displays (Haber and Barchas, 1984).

In a similar experiment with humans, four subjects were told they would be given a sleeping pill, but one of the four was actually given a stimulant. All four subjects became drowsy and quiet (including the one who had unknowingly been given the stimulant). This study shows the importance of social expectations, the influence of the experimenter, and the behavior of one's peers (in this case the other three subjects) for one's physical response. Psychosocial factors were thus as important as the drug's biochemical properties in influencing people's behavior (Bakal, 1979: 180). Culture and social learning affect how the individual experiences the effects of drugs (Becker, 1967). The ability of the hallucinogen LSD, for example, to produce a psychotic episode does not depend merely on the chemistry of the drug but also on the sociocultural setting in which it is experienced.

Human physical functioning is more responsive than that of other animals to its environment (Berger and Luckmann, 1967: 47–50). This is true for a number of reasons:

1. Human beings leave the womb more unfinished than other creatures and exist in an extrauterine social womb of dependence on others. Social learning begins before we are biologically complete (for instance, our central nervous system is not fully developed) for an extended period after birth. Because human young are more open and malleable, early social learning has a deeper impact on them both physically and mentally. Although rats are far more "closed" than humans, studies show that activity and social stimulation can modify the brain of infant (and even adult) rats (Diamond, 1988). The role of early stimulation in constructing human physiology is much greater. Indeed, there may be critical periods in which the body is particularly "open" to social-environmental influences. Experiences early in life may influence how we respond physically to stressors later in life because they "become built into our nervous, immune and endocrine systems—our selves" (Evans, Hodge, and Pless, 1994: 184). Because human interdependence is partly a result of biology, human physiological functioning is more deeply affected by social surroundings (Birke, 1986: 85).

2. Humans communicate through the use of symbols, which allows them—unlike other creatures—to reflect on themselves and their bodies, and to attach meanings to events (Berger and Luckmann, 1967). Symbols allow humans to remember experiences in a way that other creatures cannot. Humans reflect on their past and anticipate their future, but dogs cannot brood about old grudges. This is not to say dogs do not remember past pain or wait in anticipation, but relative to humans, they tend to be more grounded in the here and now. Such a capacity to reflect on the meaning of events may generate a chronic, low level of stress because our brooding can contribute to a constant degree of psychophysical arousal. The capacity to symbolize widens the range of events to which humans respond as psychologically and physically stressful. A human can respond to the fear of being humiliated in the same way that an animal responds to physical threat. Unlike animals, however, humans do not generally respond to threats motorially (that is, by running or fighting) but by mulling them over in their minds. This response has an impact on our health, because the wider range of anxiety and guilt about our past, present, and future that may result can affect us physically.

3. Research shows ways in which seemingly involuntary physical processes, such as blood pressure, digestion, and the functioning of the immune system, can be changed in "lower" animals by conditioning (namely, reward and punishment) and in humans by learning (such as learning through biofeedback). People are capable of a great deal of voluntary self-regulation and, as yogic practitioners demonstrate, can initiate the regulation of even "involuntary" aspects of physical functioning (Pelletier, 1992). Whereas one can *condition* an animal to lower its blood pressure, humans can *place themselves* into states of mind that will alter their blood pressure. This means the regulation of blood pressure and other supposedly involuntary physical functions are not closed systems that simply operate automatically, but rather they are responsive to the psychosocial environments of which the person is a part. Human sexual responses are modulated by "higher" cognitive functions. Fantasies may amplify or diminish excitement (Cohen and Taylor, 1976). All organisms are capable of *self*-organizing their physical functioning; in humans this capacity seems greater. This capacity may be affected by moods, emotions, and feelings about ourselves that are in turn connected to our social existence (Buytendijk, 1974).

In sum, one might loosely characterize human physiology, relative to that of other creatures, as more responsive to its environment and more capable of self-regulation. Humans have more open and more controllable bodies; hence, we are more "makeable." Our bodies have greater access to the outer physical and social world because humans are free from fixed instinctual patterns and have greater capacity for self-regulation. One human aspect of our bodily nature is this particular openness to the world. "Our body in its relative independence has an opening to a formed outer world" (Buytendijk, 1974: 19).

Through these mind-body thoroughfares, our movements are shaped by the physical constraints of our world, and our internal environment fluctuates to some extent with our experiences in the social and physical world. The way in which conversation can raise blood pressure serves as an example. Our way of life in a society and how we experience this way of life are linked to the functioning of our bodies through muscular, neurohormonal, cardiovascular, respiratory, and other systems. Due to our developed self-consciousness and capacity to reflect, the self can dampen or incite the physical systems and in turn be affected by them.

The ability to communicate symbolically (which is intrinsically tied with this open quality) makes us susceptible to a wider range of stressors than other forms of life experience. Humans respond physically to both physical and socially symbolic threats. Most psychosomatic illnesses are therefore peculiarly human. Humans also possess a greater ability to modify stressors' impact by the way we interpret them.

Body and society can intersect in many ways. We have reviewed some obvious connections, such as the impact of cultural and social factors on our diet and hence on our physical condition. Other interrelationships between body and society are more subtle, such as ways our biochemistry may be influenced by the temporal rhythms of social environments or relationships. Some body-society influences involve surface modifications of our muscular-skeletal structure, including our posture, movements, and the shape of our bodies. Others may penetrate our body by changing blood pressure or the responsiveness of our nervous system. Although showing relative internal stability, our bodily systems are "never completely withdrawn from a relationship to a way of existence" that is constantly changing and affecting these bodily systems (Buytendijk, 1974: 29).

Respiratory functioning, which is both voluntary and involuntary, exemplifies such body-society connections. We breathe automatically, yet can hold our breath. How we breathe may be affected by our mood. Anxious people breathe more shallowly. Anxiety in turn may be produced by social settings. What we have here is a kind of society-mind-body bridge (Lupton, 1994). Similarly, blood pressure, blood sugar, and immunity are affected by patterns of neuroendocrinological arousal (Gruchow, 1979), which are themselves linked to the way we live and respond to our life experiences. The early empirical and theoretical foundations for such linkages can be found in the pioneering works of W. B. Cannon (1929) and his student who became the father of contemporary stress research, Hans Selye (1956).

The Neurohormonal Connection: Stressor and Stress Response

The body's response to stressors appears to involve the immune, hormonal, and nervous systems. Previously considered self contained, these systems are now increasingly seen as interconnected (Evans, Hodge, and Pless, 1994).

A stressor, or a stress situation (Suter, 1986), refers to stimuli, or environmental conditions or events, that elicit stress. We include here those stimuli that come from our minds, such as recalling a frightening event. The threat of a dog's bite is a stressor, and our body's response to that stressor is called the stress response or fight-or-flight response. The stress response is the body's way of getting ready to deal with the stressor by mobilizing itself to either fight or to flee. This "fight-or-flight reflex," as Cannon (1929) called it, involves neurohormonal changes in the body (Suter, 1986: 73), which elicit a particular pattern of arousal or excitation in the nervous system and the release of certain hormones. One function of these hormones is to "stimulate and coordinate distant organs" (Selye, 1975: 148).

Hormones are released by the endocrine glands directly into the body, and they stimulate or depress various physical functions. These hormones act as the body's chemical messengers, telling it to step up or to slow down its activities. Adrenaline (also known as epinephrine) and noradrenaline (norepinephrine) are examples of a class of stress hormones known as catecholamines. The stress response involves changes in the central nervous system (CNS; the brain and nerves in the spinal cord) and the release of some of these hormonal substances.

Other examples of stress hormones are the corticosteroids. Research since Selye, however, has suggested that many other hormonal substances, including peptide hormones (for example, endorphins) play a role in the stress response. Thus, to speak of specific stress hormones may be misleading (Pelletier and Herzing, 1988; Weiner, 1992). We could think of hormones as "information substances" (Hill, 1989). One function of hormones is to stimulate and coordinate distant organs (Selye, 1975). Another may be to provide communication links between different physiological systems. Thus, peptide hormones, for example, influence communication between the brain and immune system (Pelletier and Herzing, 1988). Both the organism and its relationship with its environment can be conceptualized in informational terms, with neuroendocrinological functions acting as information networks within the organism (Weiner, 1992).

The fight-or-flight response, according to Selye, is a general physiological response that involves a number of systems throughout the body and can be evoked by any number of nonspecific stimuli (stressors) in the environment. Selye noted that his medical training encouraged a blind spot for the idea of nonspecific factors. In the course of his medical education, specific diseases and their causes "assumed an ever increasing importance and pushed the syndrome of just being sick, the question 'what is disease in general?' out of my consciousness into that hazy category of the purely abstract arguments that are not worth bothering about" (Selye, 1956: 17). In contrast to Selye, other researchers (Weiner, 1992) argue that stressors evoke physiological responses specifically attuned to those specific stressors. Furthermore, prior rhythms of the organism, genetic predispositions, social contexts, and other factors influence physiological responses to stressors. We examine some sources of variability in physiological responses to stressors later in this chapter.

The stress response, in the form of this neurohormonal activity, creates a number of nonspecific changes in the body[4] that adapt the organism for fight or

---

[4]The stress response can never be measured directly. In a sense, a stress researcher is like an investigator who tries to deduce what is happening inside a factory on the basis of noises he or she hears while standing on the outside (Suter, 1986). Some measures of stress include the calculation of the amount of electrical activity in the nervous system and the biochemical analysis of blood and urine, but all of these methods have problems. For instance, although the quantity of catecholamines in a person's urine reflects different levels of stress, it may also be a function of that person's unique way of metabolizing (processing) such substances because some people will excrete such hormones more rapidly than others.

flight (Sapolsky, 1990):

1. Blood pressure is increased. Blood flows to the muscles and heart, and much is diverted from the peripheral (outer) parts of the body; this is why cold feet and hands are often a symptom of stress. Blood is also diverted away from functions, like digestion, not needed for fleeing or fighting.
2. Sugars and fats (including cholesterol) are released to give the body energy.
3. Immunity is temporarily depressed to allow the body to tolerate possible invasions, such as wounds.

These changes suggest how prolonged, uninterrupted stress might create physical problems. For example, does the continued release of fats and sugars into the blood help explain the connection between stress and coronary heart disease? Can prolonged stress affect the mechanisms that regulate blood pressure? These are some of the issues investigated by stress research.

Weiner (1992) suggests that research should focus on disturbances—what he calls "perturbations" of neuroendocrinological rhythms and ways in which stressful experiences relate to those disturbances. He advocates looking at both organic (disease) and functional (ill health) problems from this holistic model. Some researchers believe that stress-induced neuroendocrinological changes generally only contribute to causing disease (as a cofactor along with others, such as prior structural damage and genetic factors). Furthermore, they argue stress-induced changes contribute more to ill health than to the onset of disease. *Disease* (such as coronary heart disease) has a relatively clear biological basis. Bodies also manifest *ill health* in a wide range of symptoms such as sleeplessness, fatigue, hyperventilation, chronic pain, and so on. These symptoms, on the other hand, do not have a clear-cut organic basis (Weiner, 1992). Even though such forms of distress are common medical complaints, medicine has neglected them because they lack clear organic sources. Given the tendency for medicine to see mind and body as separate, often doctors do not take such problems seriously.

The events in modern life that elicit the stress response in humans are not usually physical but more typically social and symbolic in nature (for example, the threat of being humiliated). Furthermore, modern conditions do not always make the adaptive response of fleeing or fighting a practical one. We may be provoked by a boss to fight or run, but we have learned that neither response would be appropriate. Thus, the body may be continuously geared up for action but not allowed by the rules of civilized behavior to act.

Any demanding situation, such as climbing a dangerous trail for enjoyment or mining coal in a dangerous mine shaft for a living, can be stressful. Not all stressors are negative, however; some can energize and challenge. Stress itself is not inherently unhealthy. It is a part of life, and a totally stressless environment would be both impossible and boring.

Negative and positive stressors are not necessarily equal in their impact on us. Are there qualitative differences in how people respond to negative or positive stressors? Research (Dohrenwend and Pearlin, 1982) suggests that it is not just change or environmental demands that are stressful. The uncontrollability of the stressor event seems to increase its destructive consequences for the body. Stressors are likely to have a negative effect when the individual feels helpless in the face of them.

The Relationship Between Physical and Sociopsychological Stressors

Just as physical factors affecting health (such as diet) cannot be separated from sociocultural ones (such as eating patterns), so too sociopsychological stressors may be difficult to separate from physical stressors. A physical stressor may have an impact on psychological states like mood (Bullinger, 1990). For example, noise levels may not only have physical consequences, such as damage to hearing, but may also influence mood and act as a psychological stressor. Furthermore, evidence indicates that physical and sociopsychological stressors interact with each other. By lowering immunity, stress can aggravate an individual's vulnerability to infectious microorganisms. Being physically rundown may also make it harder to cope with social stresses. Often different kinds of stressors interact with each other and may in fact increase one another's impact on the body. Such a mutually enhancing interaction is called a synergistic relationship. Each factor may "feed" into the other, amplifying effects that either one alone might have had.

The relationship between diet and stress exemplifies synergism. In our fragmented ways of looking at health and illness, we often focus on one factor (such as diet) as *the* determinant of health. Some think that eating properly will save them from heart disease and other woes, yet diet cannot be considered in isolation from other factors. A high cholesterol diet *combined* with high levels of social stress can increase the likelihood of atherosclerosis (hardening of the arteries), over and above the effect of diet by itself (Eyer, 1984; Kaplan et al., 1983). Smoking and stress combined may interact synergistically to raise blood pressure and heart rate (Karasek and Theorell, 1990; Ratliff-Crain and Baum, 1990).

Not only physical stressors (for example, workplace ergonomic conditions) but also mental ones can influence levels of muscular tension leading to musculoskeletal disorders (Lundberg et al., 1994). Mental stress can produce muscular tension in the absence of a physical workload; it can be aggravated by the fact that muscles are being "readied for use" but *not* being used. Mental and physical stressors can get together synergistically to increase muscular tension. For example, the combination of the inability to relax at home because of a "second shift" of household labor and physical work conditions (at a computer terminal, for instance) may lead to the high incidence of neck and shoulder problems among women (Lundberg et al., 1994).

A QUESTION OF SUSCEPTIBILITY

Why do two people react very differently to the same stressors? Some of us face stress with confidence; others with fear, despair, and a sense of hopelessness. Some people seem to weather life's crises without much damage; others break easily. Clearly, it is not only the stressor itself that determines the reaction, but also how the individual experiences and deals with the stressor. Furthermore, research suggests that even physiological reactions to stress vary from person to person. Some people's bodies react very strongly to a stressor; others' less so. What factors account for such variations in individual susceptibility?

Although there are important individual variations in reactions to stress, we should avoid individualistic interpretations that ignore the social circumstances contributing to these variations. Such approaches tend to blame the victim of stress rather than to examine the social situations that might account for variations in individual susceptibility. Three interrelated kinds of individual variations in stressor reaction exemplify this problem; the mere presence of a stressor does not account for a person's physical reaction to it. First, there are differences in the way people's bodies respond to stressors (**physiological reactivity**). Second, there are variations in how people perceive stressors and assess what is happening to them (**cognitive-emotional appraisal**). Third, there are differences in the way people manage stressors (**coping**).

Physiological Reactivity

Although the basic pattern of the stress response remains essentially the same from person to person, researchers have found recurring *individual* patterns in the way people's bodies respond to stress. Some individualized physical responses are more fixed or rigid than others. Two people faced with the same stressor will show differences in the level to which their blood pressure rises. The pressure of persons who have hypertension tends to fluctuate more dramatically than that of those whose blood pressure at rest is "normal" (Buytendijk, 1974; Suter, 1986).

Individuals also differ in their patterns of neurological excitation. In some people the ergotrophic response, in which sympathetic arousal is high, is more easily elicited. Other people respond more quickly with a tropotrophic response, in which parasympathetic excitation predominates (Suter, 1986). Individuals may also differ in how readily their bodies shift between these two responses, physically changing from being in a state of fight or flight to being in a state of relaxation (Gellhorn, 1969).

Individuals have varying hormonal reactions (Bieliauskas, 1982: 5). In some laboratory studies, men produced more epinephrine in response to stressors than women did. A study of women in nontraditional "male" occupational roles, however, showed that women meet demands with almost no sharp increase in epinephrine like the men's (Frankenhaeuser, 1991). It is nonetheless possible that this difference has genetic and natural bases. Perhaps men overreact to stress, thus producing an inefficient excess of stress hormones (Frankenhaeuser, 1991; Overfield, 1985; Polefrone and Manuck, 1987). Some physiological variations may reflect differences in biological makeup. Perhaps men and women *do* differ biologically to some extent in hormonal reactions. Perhaps some individuals are genetically predisposed to hypertension or coronary heart disease. Such issues are by no means resolved, and the research results are mixed.

Variations in physiological reactivity, such as differences in catecholamine reactivity, may also be the result of social factors, at least to some extent. Men and women are socialized to deal with stress in different ways. It may well be that these learned patterns also affect their way of responding physically (Birke, 1986). The fight-or-flight response tends to elevate blood pressure. A long-term exposure to stressors and a learned typical way of responding to them might eventually lead to a regular pattern of reacting physically, as some animal studies suggest (McCarty et al., 1988). One study suggests that chronic occupational stress in blue-collar workers may, over an extended period, modify the way the heart and blood pressure respond to stressors (Siegrist and Klein, 1990).

Moss (1973) has argued that given a certain cognitive-emotional orientation to stressors, over time the nervous system might become "tuned" into a particular pattern of arousal. Thus, the sympathetic nervous system's reaction to situations might become amplified and fixed in that amplified pattern. This idea of "tuning" raises interesting possibilities. Our bodies are "open" to our environments to greater or lesser degrees at different phases of our lives. Exposure to an extremely stressful situation (for example, child abuse) at one point in one's biography may alter one's pattern of responding physiologically to a stressor at later times in one's life. Some research suggests that physically and sexually abusive childhood experiences can disrupt cardiovascular and neurohormonal activity in adulthood (Taylor et al., 1999; Heim et al., 2000) and even brain development (Ito et al., 1998; Mustard, 2000).

Primate studies show that early social experiences may have impact on not only subsequent *behavior,* but also physiological *reactivity* throughout life (Suomi, 2000). Emotional and social insecurities in early childhood may, for instance, lead to higher basal levels of stress hormones, like cortisol. In this way, insecurities and intensely stressful experiences may cast a long shadow over health in later life (Wilkinson, 1996: 494). Individual physiological patterns in responding to stress might be partly the result of learning and other social experiences (Suter, 1986: 84). The distinction between physiological factors and social factors in health is thus not always clear cut.

Cognitive-Emotional Appraisal

Cognitive-emotional appraisal is the physiological impact of a person's interpretation and emotional reaction to a stressful event. In one study of this phenomenon, Lazarus (1966) and his associates showed male students different versions of a film that depicted ritual operations on the genitals: circumcision (cutting around the penis to remove the foreskin) and subincision (cutting the penis lengthwise). One version of the film had no sound and showed only the operations. Another version had a soundtrack that emphasized the harmlessness of the procedures and the fact that the participants in the rites saw them as an honor. A third version contained the narration of an anthropologist who, in an intellectual tone, constantly commented on events as the interesting and "exotic" customs of other societies.

The researchers measured the level of physiological stress response of each member of the audiences. Those exposed to the second or the third version of this film showed lower physiological levels of stress. Lazarus concluded that one's physical reaction to a stressor is affected by how one interprets it. In this case, the soundtracks helped the audiences interpret the stressor as less threatening. Although watching a stressful event on a film is not the same as seeing it in person or having it done to oneself, such experiments illustrate that our interpretations of events have a significant effect on how we react to them.

Several theories emphasize the importance of an individual's cognitive-emotional appraisal of situations in linking stress to illness. Antonovsky (1987: 13) proposes that people with a high "sense of coherence" are healthier:

> [They have] a global orientation that expresses the extent to which one has a pervasive, enduring though dynamic feeling that (1) the stimuli deriving from one's internal and external environments in the course of living are structured, predictable and explicable; (2) the resources are available to one to meet the demands posed by these stimuli; and (3) these demands are challenges worthy of investment and employment.

Antonovsky (1990) conceptualizes this sense of coherence as "dispositional orientation" (rather than personal "trait") toward experiencing stressors as comprehensible, manageable, and meaningful.

Cultural factors and an individual's position in a social structure can affect this sense of coherence. Antonovsky does not, however, thoroughly examine the ways environments disempower people, nor does he systematically consider how conditions that attack a person's sense of coherence are built into the social organization of institutions such as the workplace and the family. He also does not explore in sufficient depth the impact of social and economic systems such as capitalism on individuals' sense of coherence.

These theories emphasize the importance to health of feeling a sense of empowerment or control.[5] What they clearly do not distinguish is how a person feels or perceives the world, as opposed to conditions that lead a person to emotionally and mentally appraise the world a certain way. The emphasis on cognitive appraisal

---

[5]Antonovsky (1979: 127–128) claimed that it is important to differentiate a sense of control from one of coherence, because a sense of control implies that "I am in control," which reflects a cultural bias equating sense of control with self-control. However, people do not have to be in control to have a sense of coherence. Rather, they need simply to be participants in shaping their fate, believing that who- or whatever is in control (their god or leader, for instance) is controlling events in the people's interest and is a legitimate authority. One can feel that the world is relatively safe and in control and yet not be in control.

But two issues must be raised: First, self-control is important in Western industrialized societies. Second, however much events can be "in the hands of the Lord," so to speak, individuals still must feel the world is manageable and not working against them. It is inconceivable that persons could tolerate feeling they were puppets or that their actions were not their own. To be unable to connect one's actions with more or less predictable outcomes would be most disturbing. Antonovsky admitted that, although control need not be totally in individuals' hands, they must feel themselves to be participants in their actions.

in the stress literature often implies that how one perceives an event is the result of a psychological attribute or quality inherent in the person, independent of the event itself (Evans, Hodge, and Pless, 1994). This approach treats *how* we perceive things as almost unrelated to what we are perceiving. Such a focus may downplay common, objective environmental stressors such as poverty (Moos and Swindle, 1990). Furthermore, people may react physiologically to a stressor but not be consciously aware of it (Krohne, 1990).

Although individuals do vary in the way they appraise stressors at any given time, these differences are often the result of former social experiences with past stressors. Feeling helpless may come from some set of previous objective experiences. If, for instance, people were once overwhelmed and made to feel powerless by social class, economic, or familial events, later in life they may find it harder to believe that a stressor now confronting them is a manageable one (even if it is!) (Evans, Hodge, and Pless, 1994).

Seligman (1992) observed that animals placed in laboratory conditions of helplessness for a long enough period were unable to cope with subsequent stress or possible activity. He has linked such "learned helplessness" to depression, poor health, and a generally heightened susceptibility to stressors. Female monkeys in subordinate statuses are at greater risk for depression (Shively, 2000; Shively et al., 1999). Being a lower-status monkey means less control, being more isolated and a more likely target of oppression.

The experience of powerlessness in everyday situations at work or home may produce a similar learned helplessness in humans (Lennerlof, 1988). Other authors have introduced similar concepts, for example, the "giving-up complex" (Schmale, 1972) and the "paralysis of will" (Bakal, 1979). Likewise, the notion of "surplus powerlessness" (Lerner, 1992) suggests that if individuals were once made to feel powerless, the expectation that they will again be powerless builds up and keeps them from acting when confronted with stressors (even when they are able). People's present reactions to stressors are thus linked to their past experiences with empowering or disempowering situations. A lifetime of social exploitation or domination will certainly have an impact on whether a person feels empowered.

Coping

Coping refers to all of the ways of managing the tension a stressor produces (Mechanic, 1978: 51). As Syme and Berkman (1976: 6) observed:

> Generalized susceptibility to disease may be influenced not only by the impact of various forms of life change and life stress, but also by differences in the way people cope with such stress. Coping, in this sense, refers not to specific types of psychological responses but to the more generalized ways in which people deal with problems in their everyday life. It is evident that such coping styles are likely to be products of environmental situations and not independent of such factors.

One's cognitive-emotional appraisal of a situation is in itself a way of coping or managing stress. Some people overact emotionally; seeing the glass as half empty, they give up. Others see a glass that is half full and keep striving. Coping is not merely a matter of attitude, perception, or emotional response, however; it also involves action—that is, doing something about the stressor.

The focus of much stress literature on individual coping leads to two blind spots. First, these studies fail to consider how power affects people's ability to do something about stress. How does social class, ethnicity, gender, or work situation influence resources for effective coping? Second, much research tends to separate coping and stressor, thereby missing the fact that the conditions creating stress often also limit both the possibility of and options for coping. One's social position (such as one's status as a woman) often limits options for coping. In some areas of life, such as in friendships, certain personal styles of coping strategies are possible, but in much of everyday life people's options for managing stress are very limited. The world of work, for example, allows most people only limited coping strategies (Pearlin and Schooler, 1978). Coping ability tends to be viewed as primarily an individual phenomenon. This misconception comes from separating individuals from the social and cultural *contexts* in which they cope (Peterson, 1994; Valach, 1995).

The early literature on stress gives the impression that stress is a problem primarily for high-powered, white-collar workers. Yet research indicates that although these groups do face a great deal of stress, they also have access to resources that allow them to cope with it more effectively than those who lack resources. Even among animals the "top dog" generally has more resources to handle stressors than the "bottom dog." One study of baboons found that, in response to stress, high-ranking males showed faster increases in cortisol, a stress hormone, than subordinate baboons; however, their basal level (that is, the ordinary amount when not exposed to stress) of the hormone was lower than that of the subordinates. Furthermore, when the stressful event ended, the amounts of cortisol in high-ranking baboons returned more rapidly to the basal levels than did those of their subordinates. The more effective coping of these "top bananas" was attributed to such advantages as better choice of food, mates, and living conditions (Sapolsky, 1982, 1989, 1990; Wilkinson, 1996). Another researcher found that rats that can control the source of stress or predict when stress will occur also cope more effectively and show fewer pathological effects of stress than do rats that cannot control or predict stressors (Pelletier and Herzing, 1988: 32). The blood pressure and cardiovascular reactivity of rats in response to stressors have been shown to be linked to their position in the social hierarchy (Bohus et al., 1991). Lower-status female monkeys had higher levels of coronary artery blockage than higher-status ones (Shively, 2000; Shively and Clarkson, 1999).

A wide range of physiological patterns is associated with subordinate rank in animals; these patterns vary as the social status of the animal changes. They are thus a function of the animal's social status (Weiner, 1992: 176). Although animal studies cannot be used uncritically to generalize about human situations and behavior, executives and other "top bananas," whose job conditions allow for control and provide resources for coping (such as more control over the use of one's time), can probably cope with stress more effectively than those who do not experience such advantages.

One might argue that nonexecutive stress is a more serious health hazard than executive stress. A study of 5,100 Swedish and American men found the highest risk of coronary heart disease among workers with both heavy job demands and a "low ability to influence how their tasks are done" (Karasek and Theorell, 1990; Peterson, 1994). Thus, one's social position (such as on the job) may influence both the amount of stress one faces and the resources one has for coping. The most stressful occupations are those that combine high levels of stress with little control over those stressful conditions. Being a telephone operator or a waitress may therefore be more stressful than being a bank officer, sales manager, or physician. For example, a National Institute of Occupational Safety and Health study found that clerical women who had low control over their work with VDTs (video display terminals) showed higher levels of job stress than the highly pressured air traffic controllers, who also work with such terminals (Howard, 1985: 73). Similarly, a survey of U.S. Post Office mail handlers find them to be largely in the "high strain" job category—high job demands and low decision latitude (Cahill and Landsbergis, 1996). Thus, the social circumstances in which people find themselves influence not only the demands to which they are exposed but also their ability to handle those demands.

Corporate health programs have proliferated in the United States. Sponsored mainly by larger corporations, they emphasize exercise, meditation, diet control, and smoking cessation (Conrad, 1988; Pelletier, 1985). Although programs for blue-collar and lower-echelon white-collar workers exist, many are directed toward executives, who present potentially more expensive health-related losses for the corporation. These programs seem to have developed in an economic environment of escalating medical costs to corporations and governments (Alexander, 1988). However, there is no definitive evidence yet that, in the long run, they do prevent illness (Conrad, 1988). Indeed, they may be attempts to impose new forms of social control on the workers through a new corporate health ethic, by shaping values and attitudes of workers toward their lifestyles and also toward work. Such an ethic stresses the *individual* worker's fitness, strength, diet, and health habits while avoiding scrutiny of social contexts that affect health (Conrad and Walsh, 1992).

Although their overt function is to use prevention to reduce health care costs and loss of workdays, corporate health programs may also direct attention away from political and environmental issues in the workplace. They do not generally encourage workers to examine critically the social conditions under which they work, such as work pace, vacations, breaks, or participation in decisions affecting their work. The implicit message to employees is that their health (and the costs they incur by being sick) are their individual responsibility (Glassner, 1989). Such programs may even be used to justify cutting back on medical benefits. The corporate image also benefits by such programs, and other parts of the business sector profit by selling the equipment and services for these programs (Alexander, 1988).

Stress and Power

Young (1980: 133) observes that both scientific and lay discussions of stress tend to "subvert sociological reasoning" by removing people from their social contexts and from class and group conflicts. They tend to emphasize subjective factors and the way individuals *perceive* events, or in other words, psychological as opposed to sociological factors.[6] The way people see things gets confused with the way things are (Young, 1980: 145). Instead of beginning analyses of stress and health by looking at coping responses, cognitive-emotional appraisal, or individual forms of coping, why not begin by examining social conditions of inequality or structural arrangements, such as those that force a person to work under pressure or do not allow time to relax?

The incidence of diabetes among Mexican American migrant farm workers illustrates the relationship among psychosocial stress, limited options for managing stress, and social inequality. Much research on diabetes has focused on genetic factors, together with nutrition, obesity, and health behavior. Although these variables are important influences, exclusive emphasis on them obscures the role of such factors as social inequality. Diabetes is more common among low-status and low-income people. The exact role that psychosocial stress plays in the disease is not clear; however, some evidence suggests stress may influence its onset and course (Jacobson and Leibovich, 1984; Scheder, 1988).

Stress can also affect health behavior, such as excessive eating and drinking. The neuroendocrinological arousal generated by high levels of chronic stress may also affect blood sugar metabolism (Jacobson and Leibovich, 1984). One study found that rates of adult-onset diabetes (Type II diabetes mellitus) were much higher among those who had spent a long time as migrant farm workers and had frequent experiences of stressful life events. Obesity did not distinguish those who got diabetes from those who did not. Rather, the high levels of stress experienced by these migrant workers as a result of their low social position, disrupted social networks, social marginality (that is, being outsiders in American culture), discrimination, heavy workloads, job insecurity, poverty, and feelings of hopelessness and helplessness contributed to catecholamine-produced impairments in glucose levels (Scheder, 1988).

Folk diseases such as "nerves" (*nervios* or *nervos*) also reflect the links among stress, power, and sickness. "Nerves" are a form of ill health characterized by physical symptoms that appear to have no clear organic source, such as fatigue, trembling, headaches, fainting, and feeling of imbalance. "Nerves" are physical responses to situations of extreme powerlessness that characterize the lives of many poor people, especially women. That similar illness is widely experienced cross-culturally suggests the importance of issues of power, personal sense of

---

[6]We therefore do not agree with Mechanic (1978: 71), who after reviewing literature on helplessness and health, concluded that whether we in fact control our external environment is a "philosophical issue." What is significant, he said, is our subjective response to conditions, or our sense of helplessness.

control, and psychosocial stress for people's health and well-being (Duffie, 1996; Low, 1994; Scheper-Hughes, 1992).

The social organization of time provides an excellent example of the complex interrelationship of physical, sociopsychological, and political (that is, relationships of power) sources of stress and illness. Our social material environments (such as the design of our work spaces and the pace of work demanded of us) are important influences on our bodies. Our everyday lives take place in social contexts in which time is organized in specified ways. These contexts constrain or empower us and can have an impact on our health.

SICKENING SCHEDULES

Control over time—our own or other people's—is a form of power. Powerful persons have the ability to regulate other people's time and labor. The ability to manage our own schedules is limited by our position in society. Wealthy persons have more resources for managing the stress of demanding schedules. A teacher can keep a student waiting, but students should not be late for their appointments with a teacher because a teacher's time is assumed to be more valuable. *Time is socially organized, and the ability to schedule time and to manage it is socially distributed.* Those with more power have more control over time (see Bellaby, 1999).

From the moment we enter the world as babies, we are subject to a social calendar that is not of our own making, and we are taught to respect the constraints of time. The fragmentation and structuring of time and space in adult terms begins early. In some societies, however, adults and children do not experience such sharp time distinctions between work and play (Cherfas and Lewin, 1980).

In our society, the emphasis is on productivity. The social organization of our economic life is the basis of much of our social scheduling of time. This organization demands intense productivity. How members of a society collectively use time and the different degrees of control over their own or other people's time are central sociopsychological factors in health. They determine the frequency and intensity of stressors as well as the effectiveness of means of dealing with those stressors. For example, work time can be stressful for many people; factors such as social or occupational status influence how well they can cope with work time.

Time and Work

In general, employment is a power relationship. The employer, using rewards and sanctions and controlling workers' time, pursues the goal of maximizing the labor productivity of employees. Employees, by contrast, have an interest in conserving their energies and ability to function and in controlling their own time, as much as possible. These divergent interests mean that workplaces are often the sites of struggles over temporal control (Bellaby, 1999: 114).

In the first half of the twentieth century, employers extended their intense control over workers' time. The rhythms of the machine increasingly paced workers themselves. With the emergence of the assembly line, new systematic and rational-ized forms of control (subsequently called "Fordism"—named for Henry Ford) pre-dominated in the workplace, encompassing not only manufacturing but also office work. For instance, standards for workers were increasingly set by time-and-motion studies.

The work of Frederick Taylor epitomizes the attempt to impose rationalized, scientific controls over time and motion. In *The Principles of Scientific Management* ([1911] 1947), Taylor argued for a sharp division between those who plan work and those who do it. The planning was to be carried out exclusively by managers trained in scientific management. Jobs were to be divided and subdivided into the smallest, easiest-to-learn unit of activity. Time-and-motion studies would deter-mine the most efficient way to move and the optimum unit of time each sub-divided task should take. These studies would then set standards for precisely how and how fast all the workers would move. Taylor argued that such a system of management should take precedence over the idiosyncratic rhythms and needs of individual workers (Karasek and Theorell, 1990). Although his system is no longer widely applied in most workplaces, the attitudes and assumptions of Taylorism still prevail among many managers.

Work in industrial manufacturing in particular was highly regulated by machines and specific, limiting instructions. Tasks were broken down into short, simple, repetitive units of activity (Braverman, 1974). The result of this form of control, used in the pursuit of productivity, was to place workers increasingly into environments that moved too fast, were deadeningly boring, and controlled the motions of the body in an unnatural and uncomfortable way.

The pace and motion of factory work has been extended to white-collar office work. The movements of some keyboard operators and other office machine operators have taken on "automaton-like characteristics" (Stellman, 1977: 55). Computer technologies opened up new work possibilities, but have also led to more highly repetitive, boring, machine-paced work in the office. Computer tech-nology provides for increased control over individual workers. A terminal on a supervisor's desk can monitor the number of strokes made by each individual keyboard operator (National Safe Workplace Institute, 1990).

Bell Telephone computers print 15-minute summaries of how many opera-tors were on duty, how many calls each operator handled, the average speed of an operator's answer, and how long they spent talking to each customer (Howard, 1985: 63). Citicorp Bank uses a computer information system that provides man-agement with data about workplaces hundreds of miles away. Each clerk's printout shows the amount of time spent processing records, talking on the phone, and the like. The records are then evaluated according to standards set by Citicorp's time-and-motion specialist (Howard, 1985: 30–31). A National Association of Working Women's survey found that 35 percent of its members, in jobs as diverse as bank teller, data entry clerk, waitress, and truck driver, were monitored by computer (Howard, 1985: 62). Even middle-level managers and executives are subject to closely monitored time controls; some must submit accounts of work done every half hour (Garson, 1988). Thus, in bureaucratically controlled workplaces (including office and professional work) one trend, exacerbated by computerization, is toward greater standardization of work and control over time (Burris, 1993; Garson, 1988).

Load Balance   Some environments demand too much, too fast; others demand some degree of involvement but make too few demands and are boring. The different rhythms of working (and of living in general) may be conceived of in terms of load balance: Do they demand too much or too little? How much of a load is imposed on a person? Load imbalance may involve overload or underload (or both) as temporal rhythms. A chronic load imbalance may adversely affect one's health. Although our examples of time rhythms are drawn from the workplace, the problem of load balancing may apply equally to the lives of the unemployed, the elderly, and persons with disabilities (Frankenhaeuser, 1981).

Underload and overload are products of the degree of control one has over the rhythm of one's work. Temporal demands are not as stressful when self-generated. However, they are stressful when they are imposed and combined with little control over how one's work is done (Karasek and Theorell, 1990). Such jobs are likely to be held by low-status workers. Overload may involve piecework, such as being paid by the number of letters typed each hour. Overload usually results from a work environment that moves too fast for comfort. Underload often involves machine-paced work, such as an assembly line. Workers' movements are standardized but also demand their attention. Underload tends to be boring and tiring work. Clearly some boring work need not be stressful. A night watchman can read, walk, and chat; this work may thus not be as stressful as boring work that requires sustained alertness and attention, such as watching a machine.

Work often involves both underload and overload (Frankenhaeuser and Gardell, 1976). A dramatic example is the labor process at a meat packing plant:

> Two lines run during the day, one on the night shift. The pace is maintained by the skinning machine operators who place the hams with skins removed on the conveyer. . . . Workers holding razor sharp knives are forced to match the pace of machine operators. If a worker cannot keep up, the others down the line must work faster just to maintain the pace. Arguments occur among workers, accusations of going too fast or too slow. Stress on the job is high due to the surrender of control to the machine-paced line combined with the need to maintain a constantly high level of attention. A momentary loss of attention can lead to error or injury. Indeed, the sense of stress is heightened by congestion as workers are sandwiched between the moving table and large vats for waste and trim located two feet away. From management's perspective, however, the changes are viewed positively, because workers put pressure on each other to keep up production speeds. (Novek et al., 1990: 49, 292–293)

One can imagine the multiplicity of health risks that characterize this job, such as the danger of injury from knives and sharp machines, as well as repetitive strain injury. There is also the psychosocial stress produced by the pressure of time and the boredom coupled with the demand for constant alertness. Many jobs involve such a combination of extremes of hectic and boring work, together with strict control over time and movements that is physically and psychologically uncomfortable. Postal and delivery service workers, particularly those like mail handlers whose work is machine paced, are under considerable stress aggravated by recent industry moves to increase productivity often at the expense of safety (Cahill and Landsbergis, 1996; Drew, 1995). The "tyranny of the schedule" is a risk factor in occupational health (Syme, 1996: 29).

Overload and underload have been linked to increased excretions of stress hormones (Frankenhaeuser, 1981). A study of sawmill workers found that those whose jobs were characterized by a lack of control over their situation (as a consequence of overload and underload) were most likely to have increased stress hormones in their urine. These workers also reported feeling tired, tense, anxious, and ill more frequently than other workers (Frankenhaeuser and Gardell, 1976). Low control coupled with fast pace increases cortisol and adrenaline excretions (Karasek and Theorell, 1990). Some research has linked chronic work overload among blue-collar workers to heart disease (Weiner, 1992: 88). Higher hospitalization rates for heart attacks were related in another study to hectic monotonous work, lengthy and irregular work hours, and low degree of influence over timing holidays (Haynes, 1991: 159).

Such research shows that the social organization of time can be both *physically* stressful (that is, contribute to bodily wear and tear) and *psychologically* stressful. It can contribute to ergonomic stress, affecting the body "directly" by forcing workers to a pace that puts an excessive strain on the musculoskeletal system and makes work unsafe (see Bellaby, 1999). It can also be psychologically stressful, creating unhealthy neurohormonal changes in the body.

The machine-paced nature of much work means that, in a sense, the human body must function like a machine. Because machines can tolerate what humans cannot, the gearing of the body to the rhythm and movements of a machine may have destructive physical effects. A sociologist who worked in a Hungarian tractor factory described how the time pressure of machine-paced work affected the way workers paid attention to physical signs that they are tired or uncomfortable:

> The best way I can put it is like this: I cease to exist. When the huge side doors of the workshop are opened and the transporters rattle in loaded with material, I know—without having a thought as such, I simply know—that I am in a freezing draught, but I do not feel that I am cold. My back aches, there is a cramp in my fingers, the piece rate is ridiculous: I don't feel or think any of this. (Haraszti, 1978: 112)

Time pressures can thus put one out of touch with one's own body.

To argue that our contemporary work hours are long may seem absurd in comparison to the nineteenth-century workweek of around 70 hours (Friedmann, 1961: 105). That period, however, was not typical. Industrial capitalism was then becoming a dominant force in Western society, and productivity was being enhanced mainly by lengthening the workday. By contrast, in agricultural societies the workweek was shorter (around 30 hours a week) and more in gear with sea-sonal rhythms, and workers frequently labored only about 15 weeks a year (Eyer and Sterling, 1977; Johnson, 1978).

In the United States, the number of hours per year that people work has in-creased since the late 1960s. From 1969 to 1987, the increase for men was nearly 100 work hours per year and for women, about 300 more hours a year. Currently, approximately 25 million U.S. workers are laboring more than 49 hours a week. Most of them are white-collar workers (Fraser, 2001). In the economic boom of the late 1990s, the U.S. economy increased productivity primarily in the service sector (for example, transportation, banking, business services, and professional services—including health care), which collectively employs 77 percent of the workforce (not counting government employees and farm workers).

Government productivity figures fail to take into account the extra (unpaid) work done by many (especially salaried) white-collar workers. One economist commented: "To the extent that work time is being understated, productivity is being overstated. . . . Acceleration of productivity growth through hard work alone isn't sustainable: people simply can't work harder and harder indefinitely" (Roach, 2000). Salaried "managers" are not covered by the Fair Labor Standards Act (FLSA), so employers evaded overtime and minimum wage laws by labeling service jobs "assistant manager." Other employers changed professional jobs (for example, computer software development and stock broking) from salaried work to the status of "independent contractors." This arrangement saves the employer from having to pay for the worker's pensions, health care benefits, social security taxes, and wages for the full time the job takes. Productivity is overstated also when wage workers are not paid their full due. For instance, restaurant workers are expected to clean up after closing time—often, "off the clock." Although the 1938 FLSA made this practice illegal, the federal agency which enforces the law has had its budget cut repeatedly in the last 20 years, so employers flaunt the law regularly with impunity (Geoghegan, 1999).

In Europe in recent decades, work hours have generally decreased, perhaps because of stronger unions than in the United States, but globalization of labor markets has created increased pressures on workers in Europe, as well as the United States, to work harder and longer. Paid vacation time required by law in Europe ranges from four to five weeks a year (Schor, 1992). The United States has no requirements for paid vacations, and the standard paid vacation (when em-ployers offer one at all) in the United States is less than half as long as in Europe.

Shift Work   Working on shifts is another kind of temporal rhythm that is utterly unknown in many societies. As capitalism became the predominant form of economic and social organization in Western society, shift work became more com-mon. By 1980, 11 percent of full-time U.S. workers were on late shifts (U.S. Depart-ment of Labor, 1981). Roughly 20 percent of U.S. workers are on some form of shift work (Klinkenborg, 1997). In Europe the proportion of workers on shifts has increased overall since World War II, with the greatest increases among women and nonmanual (white-collar) workers (Blyton, 1985). Shift work became more common as the investment in machinery became greater and as it became profitable to sustain production around the clock. Some shift work is needed for technical reasons, such as a specific manufacturing process that cannot be interrupted. Certain service jobs (like those in hospitals) also require round-the-clock coverage. Most shift work, however, is instituted because it increases profits by maximizing the use of the equipment and space in which capital has been invested.

There are many different systems for arranging shifts. The most common is to have an early morning, late afternoon, and night shift (for example, 5 a.m. to 1 p.m., 1 p.m. to 9 p.m., and 9 p.m. to 5 a.m.). The number of days worked on the same shift is called the rotation period. The most common rotation period is one week (Baker, 1981: 109).

Shift work often goes against the rhythms governing many bodily functions. Heart rate, body temperature, the production of various hormones, and metabolic rates all vary with the time of day, and seem to follow a 25-hour cycle called a circadian rhythm (Åkerstedt, 1990). One researcher suggests that shift work often violates workers' physiological rhythms by not giving them enough time to adjust from one cycle to another (Levi, 1981, 1978). One study exposed 100 volunteers to rotation periods that shifted between three days and three nights of continuous work. It was found that the circadian rhythms, geared to being awake during the day, persisted. The author concluded that although the endocrine system will eventually adapt to the shift, long rotation periods are necessary to adapt (Levi, 1978). However, most shift arrangements do not allow for this.[7] Studies show higher rates of sleep and digestive disorders among shift workers (Åkerstedt, 1990). Although some argue that shift work has not demonstrated long-term serious effects on health (Poole et al., 1992), one study found a connection between cardiovascular disease and the amount of shift work done. Higher levels of serum cholesterol also were found among shift workers (Knutsson et al., 1986).

The time of the day a person must work affects sensory-motor performance (for example, quickness of reflexes). It also has an impact on the metabolism (the body processing) of various chemicals and toxins to which individuals are exposed in the course of their work. How quickly the body absorbs a medication depends on what time of day it is taken. Similarly, how chemicals and other physical stressors affect the body may depend on the time of day of exposure, an issue that has not received much attention in research on time, work, and health (Baker, 1981: 117). Social factors often interact with psychophysical stressors in complex ways.

Shift work, like overtime, may be formally voluntary in the terms of a union contract, but often financial pressures or fear of denying a superior's request may

---

[7]Some individuals adjust better than others; some prefer certain time cycles, and there are sometimes ways of arranging shifts so that workers have an opportunity to adjust. However, most workers do not have sufficient control over their work time to effect schedules compatible with their individual needs.

make what is formally voluntary in practice almost compulsory (Pfeffer, 1979: 87–88). Working overtime or on different shifts, furthermore, has social consequences for workers and their families. Shift work often intrudes into the worker's personal life, affecting leisure and social networks such as family and friendships. These changes in turn influence eating habits and sleep patterns, and may produce such adverse health consequences as digestive disorders (Klinkenborg, 1997). For these reasons, some countries, such as Sweden and Belgium, have laws that strongly limit the prevalence of shift work.

Some experiments allowing employees to have some control over their own time, by choosing to work longer days and shorter weeks or other alternatives to nine-to-five daytime hours, have been tried in the United States and Europe. In West Germany and Switzerland about 40 to 45 percent of the work force is on flextime; it is mainly a white-collar prerogative, but more blue-collar workers are on flextime in those countries than in the United States. About 8 percent of the U.S. work force has flextime, and those workers are concentrated in the service sector and among nonmanual workers in large-scale business enterprises (Blyton, 1985). Unfortunately, flextime experiments are often limited by overriding fears of declining productivity and managerial control. Unlike flextime, U.S. industrial use of "compressed" work weeks (more hours per day over fewer days per week) and mandatory overtime to achieve "just-in-time" production, is often not a matter of choice for employees. A 1996 survey found that 34 percent of large companies used compressed work weeks for some of their employees (Kilborn, 1996). Although this compression may be preferable for some workers, for others it is highly stressful.

Work Time, "Free" Time

The increasing use of cell phones, pagers, and computer technologies makes it possible for work time to seep into "free" time. Such "job spill" (Fraser, 2001), when work tasks invade free time, is a new and growing source of work stress. White-collar and professional workers are increasingly pressured to check and respond to voice and e-mail messages during their free moments (such as while commuting) and even on vacation.

A time urgency characterizes behavior not only in work time but also in free time. In fact, the character of leisure time is affected by work time. The two-week vacations common in the United States (compared to the average of four to six weeks in many other industrial countries) are directly affected by the other 50 weeks of work. Temporal rhythms of underload and overload affect life experiences other than work (Antonovsky, 1979: 187). A college professor who worked in a factory on his year of academic leave observed:

> Except for shopping at supermarkets that are open all kinds of hours, I could hardly run errands, go see a doctor, or do anything in the community. . . . I found myself torn between spending those few precious hours of waking leisure with my son, with my wife or by myself. I found myself, in short and with some important

differences no doubt, trying to live with drastically curtailed and compressed free time as millions of American workers have learned to live, snatching moments of personal satisfaction largely from time not sold to others. (Pfeffer, 1979: 41)

People who work in dull and restricting jobs tend to be less likely than those with interesting jobs to engage in "leisure activities requiring planning, participation and effort" (Frankenhaeuser, 1981: 492). Workers do not typically compensate for dull jobs with exciting, challenging leisure-time activities.

Not only may the rhythms of work time seep into the lunch hour, weekends, and holidays, but the physiological responses to work stress may also continue long after the workday is done. The physiological effects of work overload may spread to leisure hours, thus delaying their full impact (Frankenhaeuser, 1991). Many of us have experienced a form of work time carrying over into our free time when we are unable to adjust our sleep patterns during vacations and continue to wake up to an inner alarm clock geared to the memories of work time. The inability to unwind is accompanied by the hormonal system's inability to slow down, even in the absence of environmental demands. Thus, workers who have been working overtime show elevations of catecholamines not only at work but through the next evening as well. The process of unwinding may be accompanied by an increase in psychosomatic problems (Levi, 1981: 53).

The inability to relax during free time is also the consequence of media and peer pressures to consume frenetically. Although some people may shop for enjoyment, often free time ends up as rigidly scheduled as work time. The activity of consuming requires that commodities be bought, kept, and maintained. More time must be spent shopping, getting to sales on time, and having goods repaired, waxed, shampooed, trimmed, and polished. Because time spent consuming must to some extent be scheduled, leisure time is therefore regimented. Sports and amusements may also mirror the rhythm and movement of the work world. One observer commented:

> Even days ostensibly outside daily routine, holidays, are occupied with "organized" sports and amusements which, far from being liberating forms of leisure facilitating participation in subjective atemporality, are ritualistic reaffirmations of the daily grind, veritable sermons or morality plays on the value of efficient use of "on" time and the rewards of synchronized cooperation. Indeed, unprogrammed, "idle," or "non-productive," time, eagerly sought and jealously safeguarded in more subjective cultures, is experienced as malaise in machine culture. (Dye, 1981: 58–59)

A disciplined worker and a disciplined consumer go together hand in hand in our society.

So-called leisure time is often consumed by unpaid labor in the form of housework and the care of dependent children and elderly. In our society, this burden falls disproportionately on women. Parenting and housework are work, even though they are not socially recognized as paid, "productive" labor. These forms of work are characterized by recurring, boring, repetitious tasks; long hours; social isolation in the home; and many features, such as underload and overload, that characterize factory work (Doyal, 1995; Popay and Bartley, 1989). Working mothers thus carry a double burden from both paid work and housework (Hochschild, 1989; Schor, 1992).[8] Furthermore, those household tasks for which women are responsible tend to be those that must be done daily at a fixed time, whereas men's household tasks (such as fixing the car) allow for more flexibility in scheduling (Frankenhaeuser, 1991).

In one study, male managers "wound down" physiologically more rapidly after leaving work than did female managers, indicating the continued work pressures of a "second shift" that women face. Similar results have been found for women physicians (Theorell, 1991). Another study concluded that if men's and women's roles were more equal and they spent their time in the same way, "women would experience better health than men, more consistent with their greater longevity" (Bird and Fremont, 1991: 126).

The standardization of work time (such as the practice of working for eight hours from nine to five) also means that many people are excluded from paid work, including mothers who cannot afford child care, elderly people who must rest more often, and disabled people who may not function as effectively on a nine-to-five schedule. Since the industrial revolution, there has been a trend to separate spheres of activity. Paid work is increasingly done outside the home; in earlier days it was often done at home. This segregation of activities of work and home, together with the standardized workday, makes it difficult or impossible for mothers and others who cannot function on "normal" time to participate in the paid labor force.

It would be simplistic to assume that the unemployed poor merely have time on their hands, without examining the quality of this time. The poor, both unemployed and employed, are unable to enjoy the privileges of time use that go with higher social class levels. For example, they spend a great deal of time waiting for various services in places such as emergency rooms, clinics, welfare offices, and courts. Such waiting can cost precious wages, especially because many services are not available after working hours. Middle-class people can take time off, and upper-status people can have the service brought to them (Henley, 1977). One's social position also influences the degree of access to other people's time and control over one's own use of time (Henley, 1977).

Elderly persons or people with disabilities sometimes find themselves in surroundings that overwhelm them because they are unable to function at the speed demanded. In the right context, however, they might still be able to function well. Older people's disorientation and inability to function are sometimes interpreted as signs of senility; others' inability to function at "full speed" may be seen as a sign of mental or social disturbance. Thus, instead of seeing these problems as responses

---

[8]Despite the stress of this double burden, many women employed outside the home experience *positive* effects on health compared to women working only at home; the net health effects of the "second shift" thus are mixed (Hibbard and Pope, 1993; Lennon, 1994).

to environments that move uncomfortably fast or slow, we tend to treat them as personal, internal states of mind. When the environment of college students was experimentally sped up so that they could not maintain the pace, they also began to show irritability and the inability to function (Kastenbaum, 1971). Retirement and institutionalization lead people to experience "standard" time as irrelevant, thus atrophying time-related coping skills and contributing to behavior that may be incorrectly interpreted as evidence of senility.

An important relationship exists between time and health. The standard ways of socially scheduling activity often conflict with one's personal pace or bio-rhythms. A sharp discrepancy between the two will have an impact on one's health. Scientists studying sleep and sleep disorders note the tension between the sociocultural organization of time and the rhythms of our bodies (Klinkenborg, 1997). Such a split between social time and our ability to keep up is prevalent in time-pressured, production-oriented societies. In a society as productive as ours, a shorter workweek with longer breaks, more flexible hours, and less time-pressured work should not be impossible. Despite two-day weekends and labor-saving devices, we seem to live in a world that is more time pressured than past societies and many present ones.

SUMMARY

Material environments and our interactions with them affect our bodies. Symbolic and social factors, however, may also influence bodies through neurohormonal and other physical changes, which in turn may even mediate the interaction between our bodies and the physical environments they inhabit.

Stress is not merely in the eyes of the beholder, nor are the ways in which people handle stressors merely a matter of our individual resourcefulness. The economic organization of a society, the various social pressures—such as time pressures—to which its members are subjected, and their membership in sociological categories such as class, race, ethnicity, gender, and age are very important considerations. In the next chapter, we continue to explore these ideas by looking at the emotional aspects of social relationships, power, and health.

SOCIAL ORGANIZATION, HEALTH, AND ILLNESS

✤ ✤

Researchers placed blood pressure and pulse monitors on participants in one study and corre-lated the changes in these stress indicators with activities and social pressures throughout the day. The case of one hospital administrative aide exemplifies workplace stress.

"Her peak reading at the office—a diastolic pressure of 77—came in the morning when she was mediating a dispute between two secretaries. She hit this level again just before lunch when she was in that perennial secretarial bind: politely taking orders from someone who annoys you.

In this case, it was a patient, a tense, well-dressed suburban matron convinced that something was wrong with her despite repeated tests showing she was healthy. At that moment, there were two real emergencies going on—doctors were rushing in and out of the office to consult about a woman near death on an operating table, and a cardiac patient from another hospital needed to be transferred by helicopter to the medical center. In the midst of all this, Collins spent 15 minutes negotiating appointments for the matron; her voice remaining pleasant, but her diastolic pressure peaking and her pulse hitting 90."

Source: John Tierney, "Wired for Stress," *New York Times Magazine,* May 15, 1988, p. 81.

As indicated in Chapter 4, social encounters—particularly those characterized by a great deal of social inequality—can be stressful. Because of powerful and complex links between our emotions and our physical responses, some social relationships can promote sickness and inhibit healing. At the same time, social relationships and a sense of being connected to others can positively influence our health. Social networks can protect us from stressors; they can influence our appraisal of, and our ability to cope with, stressors. Our daily social relationships are not random, however; they are organized in institutional contexts, such as the workplace, religious group, and family. Thus, society influences our health through its institutional arrangements and our social positions in those arrangements. This chapter examines some social-emotional aspects of interaction, their institutional contexts (especially work and family), and their link to social inequality in everyday life.

"I GET BY WITH A LITTLE HELP FROM MY FRIENDS": SOCIAL SUPPORT AND HEALTH

Humans' biological makeup, as Chapter 4 shows, makes them open to influences from the social environment, including relationships with other people. The importance of social relationships for health is demonstrated by studies that find loss of a spouse or intimate friend leads to risk of coronary problems (Pilisuk and Parks, 1986: 33), lowered immunity (Bartrop et al., 1977), or death (Engel, 1971). Mourning and separation from loved ones can affect levels cof stress hormones (Pilisuk and Parks, 1986: 45). The absence of social support can affect immune competence. Strong relationships with others can increase resilience against illness (Fonagy, 1996: 128). Although the withdrawal of social support or a diminished quality of social relationships can have a sickening impact on us, social bonds also have the potential to heal us.

Social support is one source of the individual's sense of empowerment. It may seem strange and perhaps a bit clinical to think of our relationships with lovers, family, friends, and fellow workers or students in terms of *power,* yet social ties can serve as nets that hold us up or keep us from falling when we are threatened. They function as sources of information and financial or other kinds of aid and as mirrors that help reflect messages of self-affirmation back to us. Just as a fetus needs a womb to receive nourishment, shelter, warmth, and life support, human beings do not function effectively as isolated individuals.

Social support is a general term for the many different resources that aid persons in times of crisis and help them cope with life. Social relationships empower individuals by making them feel they are part of a larger social order. They are also a source of self-validation and a sense of personal security (Pilisuk and Parks, 1986). As symbols of those relationships, physical contact and intimacy can be empowering. Other people can remind us that we are alive and have someone to lean on and depend on when necessary. They can enhance our sense of security and self-confidence. Emotional support is one of the most important ways that social support empowers individuals (House, 1981).

This support may involve touch. Because many measures of social support use paper-and-pencil methods such as questionnaires, human touch has not been adequately investigated as a medium of emotional support. Giving social support may involve subtle cues like body language and tone of voice, which often go unnoticed by the researcher-observer (Pilisuk and Parks, 1986: 39). Although the effects of social contact may not be mentally perceived, nonetheless they may have an impact on our bodies. For example, a nurse's touch can affect the blood pressure of even a comatose patient (Lynch, 1979). Under the stress of electric shocks, dogs who were petted responded to these stressors with fewer pathological consequences than animals who were not touched. Similarly, rabbits on a high-fat diet that were not touched were more likely to develop heart disease than those that were cuddled and petted (Marmot and Mustard, 1994). Rats handled during infancy recovered from stress neurohormonally, more rapidly than non-touched rats; indeed, non-handled rats may age more rapidly (Berkman et al., 2000). Social support also reduced the stress of lower status in monkeys (Shively et al., 1999). Animal experiments should be used cautiously when generalizing to humans, but these studies do suggest that nonverbal aspects of social relationships may have health consequences.

Social support may have physical benefits by preventing the loss of self-esteem and aiding a sense of mastery (Pearlin, 1983). Social support empowers by giving individuals a sense that they are valued, esteemed, cared for, and belong to a network of mutual obligation. These are primarily *emotional* functions, but social support also serves *instrumental* purpose. A person's support networks often provide useful information and material resources (such as financial aid) as well as other help (Levin and Idler, 1981). Support can also encourage recovery from an illness, for example, by encouraging a family member to do therapeutic exercises. Other social networks also promote such health habits as regular exercise, good eating habits, and adequate sleep.

In the classic study *Suicide,* Durkheim ([1897]1951) found a relationship between rates of suicide and the degree to which individuals were integrated into their group, which he measured with indicators such as divorce rates. Thus, a group with high rates of divorce should show a high rate of suicide. Conversely, a more integrated group should have a lower rate.[1] Durkheim was the first social scientist to demonstrate that suicide was not simply an individual psychological issue but also to some extent a social and cultural phenomenon influenced by such factors as the strength of social bonds (see Berkman et al., 2000). Much of the literature on social support and health follows in this tradition by making similar associations between social isolation and poor health. We must also consider

---

[1]Durkheim also recognized that groups fostering *too much* integration could encourage what he called "altruistic suicide," such as the deaths of Japanese kamikaze pilots who crashed their planes into Allied warships during World War II.

the possibility of a reverse causal relationship; that is, poor health may lead to social isolation (House et al., 1988).

Social isolation itself can be stressful. Some research indicates that low integration into social networks (or low social cohesion) contributes to poor health, even when significant stressors are absent (Gore, 1978: 158). In a comprehensive study of a large population in Alameda County, California, Berkman and Syme (1979) measured four types of social contact: (1) marriage partners, (2) close friends and relatives, (3) members of a church, and (4) informal or formal associations. Persons who had contacts with any of these groups evidenced lower mortality rates than those who did not. The authors of this study recognized the problem of causal direction: Does illness cause a person to withdraw and others to withdraw from that person, or does social isolation generate sickness? Therefore, they analyzed groups with every kind of health status and found that, even among those who were sick, persons with higher levels of social contact had lower mortality rates. Persons with extensive social connections were likely to smoke and drink less, and to eat and sleep more regularly than those with few social connections. This finding suggests that social relationships also protect health by encouraging good health habits (Wallston et al., 1983).

Another study found that neither high stress nor lack of support, in and of themselves, increased pregnancy complications. When major stressors were combined with a low degree of social support, however, there were significantly higher numbers of complications. Women who had high stress and high levels of social support experienced fewer difficulties than those who had a lot of stressful events but not much support. When the levels of stress were low, the absence of social support did not have a notable impact on complications (Nuckolls et al., 1972). Most research finds social support to be either a primary *causal* factor in determining health or a *mediating* factor, which may protect the person from the full impact of the stressor. Over the last two decades of the twentieth century, 13 large prospective cohort studies in the United States and several other developed countries demonstrated that people who are isolated and disconnected from others are disproportionately likely to die earlier (see Berkman and Glass, 2000, for a review of this literature).

The Quality of Social Support

Lynch (1979) argues that social isolation can both contribute to coronary heart disease and adversely affect a person's recovery from a heart attack. Lynch emphasized that social contact (or what he calls "dialogue") is of chief importance for health. Corroboration of his thesis comes from studies that find mortality rates are considerably lower among married persons than among those who are single or formerly married. Between 1970 and 1988 in Poland, changes in death rates among married men and women were low, but they were substantially higher among divorced men and women. A similar pattern was found in Hungary, where the highest increases in death rates were among widows (Wilkinson, 1996: 123–124). Likewise, death rates from such diseases as cirrhosis of the liver, tuberculosis, and pneumonia are higher for those who are not married (Levin and Idler, 1981; Lynch, 1979). Although such evidence is in line with our cultural assumptions about the importance of family life, it must be interpreted cautiously. Marital status tells us nothing about the *quality* of social contact. Many people are formally married but psychologically live alone and feel isolated from each other, whereas divorced and other single people may participate in rich social lives. Unhappy marital relationships can cause greater health risk than can the absence of a partner (Kiecolt-Glaser and Glaser, 1991: 860–861).

Social support is also important in the workplace, where it buffers work-related stress (Hibbard and Pope, 1993; House, 1981; Waxler-Morrison et al., 1991). A study of NASA workers found that good work relationships protected them from the effects of such stress (Caplan, 1972). Unemployment can have negative health effects, but social support may buffer them by offering a sense of empowerment. A longitudinal study of men who were laid off from work found that those with higher degrees of social support reported fewer symptoms of illness and showed lower levels of cholesterol (Gore, 1978).

Further investigation is needed on how particular organizational forms encourage or discourage social support. For example, how do cultural factors, such as an emphasis on competitiveness and individualism, affect the possibility for supportive relationships in the workplace? Pilisuk and Parks (1986: 59) observed "social currents of careerism, autonomy, mobility, privacy and achievement that disrupt our traditional roots and ties also make difficult the continuity of new bonds." Not only do we need further research on how social support may be health promoting, but also we need to examine how control over work conditions (and other institutional settings) makes social support possible.

A Critical Appraisal of Social Support

Much of the social support literature makes several assumptions that are problematic. First, social support should not be treated as a stable, constant factor; levels of social support do not necessarily remain the same over time. Second, stressful events (stressors) and social support are not independent factors, but rather interact with each other (Atkinson et al., 1986). Just as social support may protect a person against a stressor (such as unemployment), so too may a stressor (such as unemployment) affect levels of social support. For example, a spouse's unemployment may put a strain on the entire family relationship and thereby reduce the support given by family members. High levels of kin involvement and family leadership have been associated with high blood pressure among low-income people. For those with more economic resources, such family involvement and status have been linked with low blood pressure (Corin, 1994: 107–108).

The main failing of social support research is its blindness to the larger contexts of power relationships in which social support takes place (see Berkman et al., 2000). For example, people in economic need may have difficulties with their social networks. Their social and economic powerlessness may strain their social networks, and may also limit their access to supportive social relationships.

Working-class people on the whole have less developed social networks and group affiliations than middle-class people (Fischer, 1983). One study showed how poverty limits social involvement because of a lack of funds for transportation, recreation, or association dues (Pilisuk and Parks, 1986: 60). Income and education seem to affect how much social support can reduce stress (Ratliff-Crain and Baum, 1990).

Existing research tends to focus only on the *beneficial* aspects of social support. Although it is popularly believed that it is always good to have family and friends around in times of trouble, social support is not necessarily helpful and at times can be counterproductive. For example, persons experiencing a health crisis can be overprotected, which slows recovery. Family members may also try to communicate supportive messages ("You can do it!") that may be interpreted by the ill person as a form of pressure to get well (Horton, 1985a). Social support may undermine sick people's sense of personal competence by making them feel that they cannot do anything on their own or they cannot possibly reciprocate the help they have been given (Pilisuk and Parks, 1986: 39; Taylor et al., 1999). Indeed social contact (including intimate relationships) can be stressful and affect our ability to cope with and appraise stress. One study indicates that perceived support may be more important than received support in coping with stressful events.[2] It concluded that it is possible that "the perception of one's network being ready to act can be as important—if not more important—than actual supportive behavior" (Wethington and Kessler, 1986: 84).

Western researchers typically assume that social support essentially means support from close family or friends. Yet people from various cultural backgrounds differ in what they perceive as social support and where they turn for support. In some cases, it is one's spouse or one's children; in other cases, friends and neighbors. The feeling of "belonging" to a neighborhood may be more important than any specific source of interpersonal support (Corin, 1994: 124–125). Lack of social support, as well as lack of (socially affirmed) self-esteem and sense of mastery, may account for "differential vulnerability" in the face of illness and other life struggles (Thoits, 1983: 90). Thus, an important factor in determining individuals' ability to cope with stress is how *empowered* they feel themselves to be.

Nevertheless, there are problematic *ideological* biases implicit in emphasizing social support and deemphasizing other factors that produce illness. The social support approach puts the responsibility on the individual and private sphere institutions such as the family. One consequence of overemphasizing social support may be to force people to fall back on their own *private* resources (Fischer, 1983), for it is in the private sphere of family life and friendship in which people have some control (Pearlin, 1983). In such public settings as the workplace or school, social support may not be available—indeed, may be organizationally discouraged—and individual coping mechanisms may not be effective. Research and health policies

---

[2]A problem in this study is that measures of both perceived and received support were based on the recall of subjects; they are therefore highly subjective and may have been perceptually modified by the respondents.

need to address the health problems exacerbated by coping difficulties and limits to social support created by societal structures *outside* the private sphere (Wadsworth, 1996: 165).

Studies of social support make little mention of class and power. For example, how do controls in the workplace affect social support as well as self-esteem and self-mastery? How does the distribution of power in existing social networks such as families affect social support? How do institutional structures under capitalism generate competitiveness, individualism, and social mobility that make social support difficult? Social support can be a means of empowering the individual, but it exists in social and cultural environments that often reduce its quality and availability. The research emphasis on social support should not blind us to the many other ways these social environments can disempower individuals, making it more difficult for them to control their own bodies and well-being (see Carpenter, 2000).

Social Inequality, Support, and Health

Evidence from animal studies indicates that physiological changes, some of which contribute to illness, are associated with subordinate status. When the social status of an animal is altered, these physiological patterns change (Weiner, 1992: 176). Obviously, relationships between top-ranking baboons and bottom bananas (as studied, for instance, by Sapolsky, 1982, 1989, 1990) are in many ways unlike those between office worker and boss. The "underlying threat among humans is not of being bitten so much as that of economic sanctions like losing your job or missing promotion" (Wilkinson, 1996: 196).

Human relationships are more complex and involve symbolic aspects. We are creatures capable of reflecting on our situation. Thus, unlike other creatures, we can dramatize insults and injustices in our minds—either playing them down or dramatically enhancing them. The very process of talking to ourselves and others about events can function to minimize or dramatize their significance. Animal studies can suggest some ways by which social status affects human bodies (Evans, Hodge, and Pless, 1994). A number of similarities exist in the way risk factors for coronary heart disease are affected by social status both among baboons and humans (Brunner, 1996; Wilkinson, 1996: 195). The activities involved in establishing and maintaining hierarchies—such as activities of social control—may have physical consequences for humans and other animals (Weiner, 1992: 195).

It has been argued that there is a relationship between the distribution of power in a society (such as levels of economic equality or inequality), levels and quality of social support, and health (see Berkman et al., 2000). Once societies have gone through an epidemiological transition (see Chapter 2) and most of their members have an adequate minimum material standard of living, then psychosocial factors (such as lack of social support and stress) become more important as determinants in disease (Wilkinson, 1999a; Williams, 2000, 2001). Some evidence links U.S. income distribution, social cohesion, and mortality (Kennedy et al., 1996). Both economic stressors and social support tend to be socially distributed by class: "It's as simple as that. If you are poor, you have more stress and less supportive resources" (Pilisuk and Parks, 1986: 58). Indeed, some observers argue that the more egalitarian a society is, the more socially integrated, and thus healthier, it is (Wilkinson, 1996).

Social inequality thus not only affects the distribution of material resources available to individuals, but one's position in a social structure also influences the psychosocial resources available (Brooker and Eakin, 2001; Evans, Hodge, and Pless, 1994). Inequality damages the social fabric of a society, affecting the quality of social relationships not only in the family but the public sphere as well. In societies characterized by relatively equal income, one finds that "Instead of a moral and social vacuum mediated only by market relationships, life beyond the family has a well developed social structure. . . . [P]ublic life is explicitly part of social life" (Wilkinson, 1996: 133–134).

LIFE AS THEATER: SOCIAL INTERACTION IN DRAMATURGICAL PERSPECTIVE

Social interactions are often not only not beneficial, but downright harmful. What makes everyday social encounters, such as talking to one's boss, particularly stressful? Viewing social interaction from a *dramaturgical perspective* can help us understand some of the sources of stress in social relationships. In his early work, *The Presentation of Self in Everyday Life* (1959), Goffman views social life as theater, describing dramaturgical strategies as means of information control through which individual actors, small groups, institutions, and even whole societies manage how information is presented and expressed, in order to accomplish a desired impression. Using such resources as costumes, props, and settings, actors seek to control their *presentation of self* (that is, how they show themselves) and to monitor information presented to them by other actors. If everyday life is to some extent theater, then being a competent actor requires correctly interpreting "cues" provided by others and managing the information one presents to them. Actors seek to maximize the visibility of some information, to minimize the visibility of other information, and to gain access to information about others. How we feel about ourselves (our self-image) is related to how effectively we present ourselves and whether various encounters validate or invalidate our self-conception. Because much social life involves performing, it is easy to identify with the "stage fright" of an actor about to go on stage or that of a social actor about to present herself as a competent candidate at a job interview. Performances in everyday life can be stressful—indeed, under some circumstances, very stressful.

Emotion Work as Stressful

The stress connected with one's presentation of self and with dramaturgical strategies for monitoring other people's displays, we call *dramaturgical stress* (Freund, 1982, 1990, 1998). Dramaturgical stress is generated by role playing, the effort of managing the impressions one makes on others, and particularly by struggling to keep up social appearances that are inconsistent with deeply held feelings and conceptions about oneself.

A significant part of performing in social life involves managing our own and other people's emotions. Everyday situations call for appropriate emotions and feelings as well as appropriate displays of emotions. Many skills of self-presentation thus require what Hochschild (1983) calls **emotion work**—the activities through which we manage our own and other people's emotions. Emotion work involves repressing displays of undesirable or inappropriate emotions and evoking appropriate ones. For example, it is considered improper to laugh during a funeral. What does one do to keep from displaying such inappropriate emotions? One might try to think of something sad, engaging in emotion work to both appear to have the proper demeanor and to "feel" the appropriate emotions.

Performing is part of all social life, so some dramaturgical stress is inevitable. Societies such as ours, however, exacerbate dramaturgical stress because the manipulation of appearances and emotions is an important skill and a highly complex and self-conscious act. Not only are emotions and bodily expressions highly controlled, but also the activity of manipulating appearances is itself stressful (Elias, [1978] 1994). It takes energy to constrain feelings and actions and to manage emotional communication while monitoring that of others. Self-presentation and role playing, together with the emotion work required by these roles, can be dramaturgically stressful (Williams and Bendelow, 1996: 41). Under certain social conditions stress becomes particularly intense and chronic, promoting illness.

Dramaturgical Stress and Social Inequality

Dramaturgical stress is heightened when a person's performance in a given situation is inconsistent with his or her concept of self (Cockerham, 1978: 49). Stress may be generated by "the task of managing an estrangement between self and feeling and between self and display" (Hochschild, 1983: 13). Considerable pressure may come from the effort to protect and to control emotional information. Actors in subordinate social statuses (that is, those with less power) may be more likely to encounter such stressful situations and lack the dramaturgical resources to cope with them.

As noted in Chapter 4, some actors are in social positions that make them particularly vulnerable to stress: those who occupy subordinate positions in various institutional contexts (such as school, family, or work), members of minority groups, and those whose identities are potentially stigmatized (disabled or gay people, for instance). Actors in subordinate positions may lack *status shields* (Hochschild, 1983) to protect their sense of self (Freund, 1998). Lower-status individuals often lack such dramaturgical resources, leaving their very selves vulnerable to attacks by those in power (Williams and Bendelow, 1996). For example, institutional rules protect teachers from having their authority, character, or competence challenged in class, whereas students lack such status shields.[3]

Inability to protect the boundaries of self and to counter the intrusion of others may lead to depression and anxiety. Individuals' social positions determine their resources for protecting their self-concepts and for controlling how they experience themselves. Subordinate status, combined with social controls that prevail in a situation (such as a service job that demands emotion work), require intense feelings to be suppressed, denied, or relegated to another sphere (such as family). Persons in subordinate status are thus especially vulnerable to dramaturgical stress, and the stress is intensified by their powerlessness in the face of controls and demands of others (Williams, 2001). Box 5.1 illustrates how degrading work and demands to be cheerfully deferential compound the physical distress of "menial" laborers.

The social organization of time and social/physical space influences our emotion work and dramaturgical competence, the availability of "backstage"[4] respites, and our levels of security about our psychological space, and hence levels of dramaturgical stress. Having to interact in the same physical space with coworkers, bosses, or family members, we are less likely to express disruptive emotions there. "Physical containment may support emotional containment" (Newton, 1995: 84).

Social status is a key factor determining how much each individual can control this organization. For example, higher-status persons enjoy more private space and means of segregating audiences (such as a secretary who controls who is allowed into one's private office). Their dramaturgical stress is likely to be reduced because these spatial arrangements enable them to sustain a consistent presentation of self and effective performance. The organization of space and time also influences the degree of surveillance to which an actor's performance is subject and hence levels of stress.[5] Actors in subordinate statuses are more likely to find themselves subject to greater surveillance than persons in dominant statuses. For example, a reservations clerk is more likely to have her phone conversations electronically monitored by her supervisor than is the hotel sales manager. Subordinate status also reduces power over one's body and personal space. For instance, a boss can touch employees, but the employees cannot freely reciprocate.

Humans in subordinate social positions are particularly vulnerable to dramaturgical stress, not only because they often face heightened and conflicting emotional demands, but also they lack resources and options for coping or resisting. Williams and Bendelow (1996: 41) observe, "Less powerful people, therefore,

---

[3]A poignant example of how such vulnerability translates into ill health is the response of a woman living in an extremely poor community in Brazil to a question about "anger nerves," a culturally recognized illness. She replied, "That's like when your 'patron' says something that really ticks you off but because she's your boss you can't say anything but inside you are so angry that you could kill her. The next day you are likely to wake up trembling with anger nerves" (Scheper-Hughes, 1992: 175).

[4]Backstages are "places" (for example, a restaurant kitchen), where a waiter, for instance, can relax in his role, share talk about troublesome customers, and rehearse his role.

[5]Goffman (1961) argued that the social and physical arrangements in "total institutions" (such as monasteries, prisons, mental hospitals, and nursing homes) may work to short-circuit inmates' abilities to *control* their self-presentation.

Box 5.1

Social Inequality and Dramaturgical Stress:
Not-so-"Merry-Maids"

Author Barbara Ehrenreich spent several months doing low-wage service work, try-ing to learn how it was possible for women driven off welfare to live and support their families on wages barely above the federally mandated minimum. One of the jobs she took was with a housecleaning service:

> "Maddy assigns me to do the kitchen floor. OK, except that Mrs. W. is *in* the kitchen, so I have to go down on my hands and knees practically at her feet. No, we don't have sponge mops like the one I use in my own house; the hands-and-knees approach is a definite selling point for corporate cleaning services like The Maids. 'We clean floors the old-fashioned way—*on our hands and knees*' (author's emphasis), the brochure for a competing firm boasts. . . . A mop and a full bucket of hot soapy water would not only get a floor cleaner but would be a lot more dignified for the person who does the cleaning. But it is this primal posture of submission—and of what is ultimately anal accessibility—that seems to gratify the consumers of maid services.
>
> I don't know, but Mrs. W.'s floor is hard—stone, I think, or at least a stone-like substance—and we have no knee pads with us today. . . . So here I am on my knees, working my way around the room like some fanatical penitent crawling . . . , when I realize that Mrs. W. is staring at me fixedly. . . . She's . . . watching that I don't leave out some stray square inch, and when I rise painfully to my feet again, blinking through the sweat, she says, 'Could you just scrub the floor in the entryway while you're at it?'"

Source: Barbara Ehrenreich, *Nickel and Dimed: On (Not) Getting By in America*. New York: Metropolitan Books, 2001, pp. 83–85.

---

face a structurally in-built handicap in managing social and emotional information and this handicap may, in turn, contribute to existential fear, anxiety and neuro-physiological perturbation."

Stressful Social Interactions

Because dramaturgical stress is linked with structural factors, especially social status, it is likely to be a feature of regular social interaction in which social stratification and power are embedded in social relationships.

Work   In corporate and bureaucratic jobs, a great deal of control over the presentation of self is an important part of a person's work skills. Manners and po-liteness become tools for the efficient and effective accomplishment of work (Mum-ford, 1963: 139). In postindustrial economies, the proportion of jobs providing ser-vice has increased. Occupations involving selling (salesclerk, stockbroker, for instance) or providing emotional services such as friendliness or reassurance (nurse, flight attendant) have increased dramatically (Hochschild, 1983). These service jobs demand elaborate skills in self-presentation and in managing one's emotions (both of which entail emotion work).

According to Hochschild (1983), **emotional labor** is the active effort to change one's emotional expression and experience, required as a part of one's work in order to interact with clients, customers, or others within the work hierarchy. Psychologist Eric Fromm (1965: 268) observed:

> If you do not smile you are judged lacking in a "pleasing personality" and you need to have a pleasing personality if you want to sell your services whether as a waitress, a salesman or a physician. Only those at the bottom of the social pyramid, who sell nothing but their physical labor, and those at the very top do not need to be particularly pleasant.

In his description of bureaucratic white-collar workers, Mills (1956: xvii) noted that the management of one's personality had increasingly become an essential work skill "of commercial relevance and required for the more efficient and profitable distribution of goods and services." Demand for pleasing personalities, particularly in the face of job conditions that are anything but pleasing, can be highly stressful and often require workers to deny their emotional responses. A study of bank employees found that when the emotional and physical appearances demanded of workers conflicted with their own sense of self, they began to experience self-artificiality. Bureaucratized structures, particularly those with commercial goals, are most likely to produce this tension between the public face and private self (Karasek and Theorell, 1990: 33). The rude customer who "is always right," the demand for geniality in the face of social isolation within the office, the interpersonal competitiveness, and the hierarchical pressures all produce dramaturgical stress in the workplace (Freund, 1982, 1998). Box 5.2 illustrates how emotional labor is linked with dramaturgical stress.

Much of the burden of emotional labor falls on women. Women increasingly do "second shifts" of emotional labor, at work *and* at home (Hochschild, 1989). Emotional "second shifts" can result in overload. Research shows that women's well-being at work can be influenced by the demands of stressful emotion work at home (Wharton, 1999).

Emotion work entails more than merely assuming a smiling mask, because that might appear insincere. Rather one must convince oneself, to some extent, that one's angry reaction is not valid. Hochschild (1983) describes how flight attendants are taught to see the nasty customer as a victim and one's own angry response as unnecessary. They were expected to convince themselves that they felt something other than what they were feeling. Such invalidation of one's emotions may have long-term health consequences, especially as the split between what one feels and what one shows may become automatic, no longer a temporary mask that one assumes voluntarily (see Williams, 2000). Emotional labor need not be very stressful or alienating; in fact, sometimes, it can be a source of job satisfaction.

Box 5.2

Emotional Labor and Dramaturgical Stress—Problems for Paralegals

"'I was trying to be pleasant, pay attention and take notes [while the witness was talking]. Not an easy feat, [because] I felt like I was next to a human time bomb [the attorney].'

Whenever a lawyer is angry about something, the paralegal is liable to be the recipient of that anger—even when the fault lies elsewhere. . . . Law firms recognize this aspect of the job; they specifically seek to hire legal assistants who can deal gracefully with irate attorneys. . . . Being pleasant or cheerful is an attitude paralegals are expected to convey while trying to accomplish other aspects of their jobs.

'Sometimes I think she [the law firm's personnel director] thinks smiling is supposed to be part of my job.'"

Source: Jennifer L. Pierce, "Emotional labor among paralegals," *Annals, AAPSS,* 561 (January), 1999, pp. 130–131.

This is *not* the case, however, when workers lack autonomy or control over their work (Wharton, 1999).

Race and Ethnicity   Over 30 years ago, Franz Fanon, the Algerian psychiatrist, wrote about the connections between racial and colonial domination and psychological and physical well-being. In the following passage, he linked muscular tension and illness in Algerians to their powerlessness in the face of French colonial authority:

> This particular form of pathology (generalized muscular contraction) had already called forth attention before the revolution began. But the doctors described it by portraying it as a congenital stigma of the native, an original part of his nervous system where it was stated, it was possible to find the proof of a predominance of the extra-pyramidal system in the native. The contracture is in fact simply the postural accompaniment to the native's reticence and the expression in muscular form of his rigidity and his refusal with regard to colonial authority. (Fanon, 1963: 293)

Because it was not possible for the colonized Algerians to express anger openly toward colonial authority, it was held in, but manifested itself in the form of muscular tension. Note also that the effects of a social problem (colonial rule) were viewed by the colonial doctors as an inherited, individual problem. The individual could not leave the social space of a racist encounter and thus expressed somatically the resistance that could not be shown openly. The particular form and distribution of muscular tensions throughout the body represented how the body was used to create an impermeable boundary between self and other. This muscular armoring keeps the other and their claims on one out of one's psychological space.

Geographical variations in levels of disrespect, prejudice, and racism have been linked to high mortality rates in African Americans (Kennedy et al., 1999). Racism may promote illnesses, such as hypertension, which is prevalent among African Americans. Their elevated rates of hypertension cannot be explained simply by diet or genetics (Johnson and Gant, 1996). One study of African American women concluded that face-to-face encounters with racist provocation can affect cardiovascular reactivity (for example, heart rate, blood pressure). Cardiovascular reactivity increased more among those individuals who were able to speak during a racist provocation compared to those who were simply listening, but support from another person in responding to the provocation helped reduce reactivity (McNeilly et al., 1995). Another study showed that black women who responded actively to unfair treatment were less likely to have high blood pressure than women who held their responses "inside" themselves (Krieger and Fee, 1994).

Similarly, African American males may be exposed to more anger-provoking encounters with arbitrary authority (in regard to housing, employment, and the law, for instance) than other groups, but they cannot express their anger. The suppression of their emotional responses might well contribute to their greater incidence of hypertension (Johnson and Gant, 1996). Socialization to suppress hostility may be especially high among upwardly mobile, upper-lower-class persons, who emphasize the importance of politeness and respect higher-status people (Harburg et al., 1973). One study, comparing hypertensive African Americans with those with normal blood pressure, described those with hypertension as humble, docile, sober, serious, and controlled (Johnson and Gant, 1996: 98). The demand that one always be polite and civil—no matter how rude someone else may be—represents a form of social control. Strict control over anger is a norm in our society (Elias, 1994; Stearns and Stearns, 1986).

Sexual Orientation Those who must cope with a social stigma by concealing their identity under a cloak of normal appearances face special stresses. For example, in our society widespread homophobia (fear of homosexuality) pressures homosexuals to hide their true selves in order to perform according to social expectations; however, trying to pass as heterosexuals may cause considerable dramaturgical stress. In addition to the self-hatred that comes from internalizing society's antihomosexual values and the repressed anger from discrimination, they may suffer from the constant fear of disclosure:

> Visible lesbians are treated as outcasts or queers. They are ignored, fantasized about, and played with. Lesbians are subject to verbal and physical harassment. Closeted lesbians live in fear of being found out. A lesbian's family may be a source of stress for her as coming out to one's family can often mean risking anger, pain or exile. Drifting apart from one's family may be the result of not coming out. (O'Donnel, 1978: 14)

"Closets" are the refuge of the powerless, but the use of this refuge has its price. "Closets are a health hazard" was a slogan first used by the physicians marching in the 1981 Gay Freedom Day Parade in San Francisco.

Family   Not all situations that demand a split between self-presentation and feelings are equally stressful. One may more easily distance oneself from work relationships than from intimate, primary group relationships (such as family or loved ones). Pearlin (1983: 6) observed:

> [T]he family does have a dimension to its place in the stress process that sets it apart from occupations, however. It is, of course, a major reservoir of problems and tribulations. Multiple facets of marital relations, parent-child encounters, and the transitional points along the family life cycle have been viewed as fertile ground out of which stress can grow. It is likely, too, to be an arena in which problems generated elsewhere are transplanted. But the family domain, unlike occupation, is also the place where the wounds that people incur outside are most likely to be healed. The family is truly many things to its members: it is commonly an active and rich source of pain, and it is just as commonly where people turn to find relief from pain. In the stress process, it stands in a uniquely pivotal position.

Several studies suggest that persons whose families make them feel powerless, force them to surrender their autonomy, or inhibit their displays of anger in response to arbitrary authority will experience subsequent health problems (Doherty and Campbell, 1988; Sagan, 1987; Seligman, 1992).

Noting the high incidence of somatic symptoms among people who live in totalitarian societies, Griffith and Griffith (1994: 55) observe:

> In non-totalitarian, Western societies, we find remarkably similar examples of somatic symptoms that have been fostered within micropolitical systems of abusive families, where a child sexually abused at home hides the abuse at school and church, even defending her father as if he were a wonderful parent; or where a wife is physically beaten at home by her husband but hides the abuse even from friends or coworkers, believing that she cannot or should not escape and will only suffer more if she were to disclose.

Thus, micropolitical circumstances (such as marriage and family), like oppressive macropolitical contexts (such as a totalitarian state), may require a distressful containment of feeling that can be expressed only somatically.

Situations in which sexual abuse or gendered violence occur are intensely stressful interactions. Griffith and Griffith (1994: 55–56) present a case of a woman who was sexually abused but had to contain her distress while routinely encountering her abuser in the micropolitical context of the home:

> In meeting with Jana alone, however, the story widened. With specific questioning about possible abuse, she told how during the summer, while out of school, she stayed at home with her stepfather on days that her mother worked. When they were alone, the stepfather had sexually fondled her and warned her not to tell anyone. She had not spoken out of fear that she would not be believed, that she would be punished by him, or that the revelation would threaten her mother's new marriage. She was terrified that he would touch her again but spoke to no one. Instead her body began jerking violently out of control.

Such situations create what the authors describe as "unspeakable dilemmas," because these women must live with their abuser and dramaturgically conceal their distress. Women with young children, few job skills, and no alternative place to live often feel trapped in abusive situations. Children who are victims of sexual abuse, when seen in emergency rooms, often show symptoms of seizures that are nonepileptic in origin (Griffith and Griffith, 1994: 55). Gendered violence (sexual abuse, rape, domestic violence, or the threat of abuse) attacks the victim's psychophysical boundaries, sense of self, and security in their world. The threatened person's feelings often cannot be acknowledged or expressed; they must be dramaturgically hidden.

Dramaturgical Stress and Health

As discussed in Chapter 4, certain kinds of prolonged or acute stress can lead to physiological responses and, ultimately, sickness. Dramaturgical stress, affecting body and emotions, may promote illness in a number of ways. Contradictory psychosomatic states are responses to dramaturgical demands and the result of dramaturgical stress. Interviews of patients with "somatoform symptoms" showed the following:

> [T]he bodily experience of such a dilemma is that of mobilizing the body for action (e.g., an aggressive emotional posture), while expressing a contradictory emotional posture (e.g., a warm welcoming with smiles and attentive listening, belying privately held seething). In essence, the body receives two conflicting directions for organizing its physiological readiness to act. (Griffith and Griffith, 1994: 61)

These physical symptoms are one way of responding to social situations in which a profound disjuncture exists between how one desires to present oneself and a contrary self-presentation, demanded by a social situation in which the actor cannot leave the field. Thus, the body may cope with such a "push me-pull you" situation by expressing somatic symptoms.

Several studies have examined the relationship between the expression of such emotions as anger and physiological responses. In one early experiment some subjects responded to provocative situations by expressing overt hostility ("anger out"). Persons displaying "anger in" responses were more likely to blame themselves and not express overt hostility. "Anger in" respondents exhibited more extended physical stress reactions than the "anger out" group (Funkenstein et al., 1957). In another experimental situation, anger was induced experimentally by having a colleague arbitrarily harass and insult subjects while they were trying to solve a problem. The subjects' anger resulted in increases in their blood pressure, but those who could express their hostility by giving the harasser what they believed was a mild electric shock returned to normal blood pressure levels more rapidly. Those who were not allowed to express anger in this fashion continued to show signs of elevated blood pressure long after the harassment had stopped (Hokanson and Burgess, 1962). Such experiments point to how emotion work might influence us physically.

Some evidence links the denial of feelings to coronary heart disease (Karasek and Theorell, 1990: 114). Yet this evidence is by no means unproblematic: Some studies find the *inhibition* of anger expression to be linked to coronary heart disease; others find the *expression* of anger to be the link (Engebretson and Stoney, 1995). A study of airline pilots concluded that both those who inhibit their anger a lot *and* those who often express their anger are prone to have higher levels of cholesterol in their blood than their more moderate colleagues (Engebretson and Stoney, 1995); this finding may account for the apparently conflicting prior evidence. Such studies are suggestive of how one's presentation of self, emotion work, social interaction, and the body might be linked.

Individuals develop coping strategies in distressful situations, particularly those situations of heightened dramaturgical stress in which a sincere performance that belies distress is demanded. This coping is accomplished by compartmentalizing, by dissociating feelings (separating "gut" feelings from conscious feelings), thereby convincing oneself that "all's well." Such dissociation may separate bodily activities of expression and internal functions such as blood pressure—akin to what has been called "schizokinesis." A person whose demeanor appears "cool" on the exterior, but whose internal response to stress involves such dramatic bodily changes as sharp increase in blood pressure, exemplifies this dissociation (Lynch, 1985). How do social and cultural factors encourage such compartmentalization? A consequence of such splits is *emotional false consciousness* (Freund, 1990), which occurs when emotion work disrupts the body's equilibrium and our ability to interpret embodied feelings. Such false consciousness involves a split between bodily expressions and an awareness of internal psychosomatic sensations, on the one hand, and continued heightened physiological reactivity to distressful situations, on the other (Freund, 1990, 1998; Williams and Bendelow, 1996). It is as if the levels of consciousness come to be more or less permanently split between bodily appraisals and cognitive appraisals of situations.

An effective social performance (that is, one that appears sincere) may be accomplished through subjectively redefining relationships and emotional responses to them (Hochschild, 1983, 1989). For example, a flight attendant dealing with a rude customer who refused to abide by smoking rules tried subjectively to convince herself, "I shouldn't be angry, because it's not his fault; he may have had a miserable business trip." Problems arise, however, if feelings are reworked on only one level as consciousness and not also on the level of somatic or body consciousness; this emotion management thus short-circuits the signal function of emotion (Hochschild, 1983). Emotions "lie at the juncture between mind, body, culture and biology and are often considered crucial to our survival by their signal function in relation to danger" (Bendelow and Williams, 1995: 151). Emotion work strategies may seem effective for the short term, but on another level of consciousness continue to produce feelings of insecurity. These feelings are apprehended as free floating because one has redefined the source of the threat out of one's wide awake consciousness.

In social interaction, people may *collectively reproduce* emotionally oppressive and distressing situations (Newton, 1995). Indeed, oppressive situations produce individuals who collude in their own social control to reproduce distressing arrangements. The splitting of emotional consciousness facilitates the smooth functioning of hierarchical relationships, even while they produce distress. Furthermore, chronically disavowing one's feelings may also blur the boundaries between self and other. By affecting one's ability to experience social situations clearly, this process makes it harder for the victim of oppressive situations to identify accurately those situations as oppressive.

SUMMARY

In this chapter we continued our discussion of mind, body, and society relationships, emphasizing the role of emotions in social interaction. Some research on social support was critically reviewed. The distribution of power is an important factor in influencing the availability and quality of supportive social relationships. We then looked at some of the stressful aspects of interaction that come from role playing. Those in subordinate social statuses may be more vulnerable to dramaturgical stress and more likely to lack resources to cope with such stress. The chapter concluded with a discussion of dramaturgical stress and health.

THE SOCIAL MEANINGS OF SICKNESS

✳ ✳

"... [P]olitical and entrepreneurial interests are, above all, driving what is to be defined as abnormal today.... We are no longer in a mood where normal means average; we are in an era of amelioration, enhancement, and progress through increasing intervention into the 'mistakes' of nature. However, in this climate, the environmental, social, and political factors that, rather than genes, contribute to so much disease, are eclipsed, and tend to be removed from professional and public attention. Research in connection with these factors remains relatively underfunded.... [W]hen, under the guise of health promotion, individual bodies and individual responsibility for health are made the cornerstone of health care, *moral responsibility for the occurrence of illness and pathology is often diverted from where it belongs* (on perennial problems of inequality, exploitation, poverty, sexism, and racism) *and inappropriately placed at the feet of individuals designated as abnormal* or at risk of being so because of their biological makeup" [emphasis added].

> *Source:* Margaret Lock, "Accounting for Disease and Distress: Morals of the Normal and Abnormal," p. 273 in G. L. Albrecht et al., eds., *Handbook of Social Studies in Health and Medicine.* London: Sage, 2000.

W hat does it mean to be sick? In some ways a tree's disease is similar to a human's disease: Trees can recover or they can die of disease; branches become lifeless, leaves wither, and roots and trunks function poorly. Unlike trees, however, humans must also grapple with the experiential aspects of sickness. Humans are capable of reflecting on themselves, their bodily conditions, and their self-perceptions. This capacity to reflect means that humans typically suffer not merely from disease but also from their experience of illness and the meanings that they and others attach to it.

Sickness is upsetting to the social group too. Because it is a breach of the ideals or norms of the society, it can be disruptive. Illness represents a threat to the order and meanings by which people make sense of their lives and organize the routines of their everyday existence. Sickness also raises moral questions, such as, "Who (or what) is responsible for this misfortune?"

ILLNESS AS DEVIANCE

The very notion of health is a social ideal that varies widely from culture to culture or from one historical period to another. For example, in the nineteenth century the ideal upper-class woman was pale, frail, and delicate. A woman with robust health was considered to lack refinement (Ehrenreich and English, 1978). In other periods, cultures, or subcultures, however, the ideal of health might be identified with traits such as strength, fertility, spirituality, righteousness, the absence of pain, the presence of certain pain, fatness, thinness, or youthfulness. The ideal of health thus embodies a particular culture's notions of well-being and desired human qualities. Standards of health in any culture reflect that culture's core values. Through ritual action and symbols (especially language), the social group continually reproduces these central, shared meanings (Durkheim, [1915] 1965).

Durkheim ([1895] 1938: 68–69) observed that deviance serves to remind the entire social group of the importance of certain collective values. Like crime, sickness is a form of **deviance,** or departure from group-established norms. Society typically imputes different kinds of responsibility for crime than for sickness. Durkheim asserted that the very existence of social norms—however defined—means there will be deviance in all societies. The way a society reacts to sickness and crime reaffirms its core values. Furthermore, the practices for sanctioning deviance (such as punishing the criminal or treating the sick person) reaffirm and revitalize the collective sentiments and maintain social solidarity. Durkheim ([1893] 1964: 108) argued that societal reaction against deviance "is above all designed to act upon upright [non-deviant] people." This function suggests that the treatment of the sick in all healing systems serves to reaffirm cultural norms and ideals for the sick and the well alike.

Thus, deviance is more a description of the social group that defines it than a quality of the individual considered deviant. Labeling of an attribute or behavior as deviant is, in fact, a social product (Becker, 1963; Waxler, 1980). Cultures vary widely as to whether they consider deviant such bodily conditions as facial scars, obesity, shortness, and paleness. One cultural standard, for example, considers a certain amount of hair on a man's chest to be desirable, representing fortitude, robustness, and manliness. Much less hair on the chest is treated as too effeminate; much more is considered coarse and animal-like. Other cultures (and subcultures), however, have different definitions of desirable body hair and different connotations of deviance from those norms.

As Chapter 9 illustrates, defining deviance is a social process involving factors such as power and stratification. Power in a society includes having significant influence in setting social norms and labeling deviance. It also involves having control over the social mechanisms by which these norms are taught and enforced. Indeed, one function of social control is to perpetuate the dominance of those in power in the establishment of norms. Socially established norms are *imposed* on people, regardless of their own beliefs. Power is a factor in both the creation of a deviance label and its application to some individual persons.

The Sick Role

Like all social roles, the sick role is primarily a description of social expectations (including those of the sick person). Although these expectations strongly influence behavior, the sick role does not describe how sick persons actually behave (see, for example, Twaddle, 1981: 56–58).

According to Parsons (1951: 428–447), the sick role entails certain responsibilities as well as certain privileges:

1. The individual's incapacity is a form of deviance from social norms, but because it is not deliberate, the individual is not held responsible;
2. The sickness is legitimate grounds for being exempted from normal obligations, such as work or school attendance;
3. The legitimacy of this exemption is, however, predicated on the sick person's intent to get well;
4. The attempt to get well implies also seeking and cooperating with competent help to treat the illness.

The sick role of someone with pneumonia exemplifies Parsons's use of this concept. A person with serious pneumonia would not be expected to report to work, to do housework, or to keep an appointment. Failure to perform such basic social obligations is a form of deviance that is typically sanctioned, for example, by firing an employee. Having pneumonia, however, is usually considered an acceptable, but temporary, excuse for not meeting these obligations. The employer does not hold the sick person immediately responsible. How society responds to an instance of perceived deviance depends largely on its determination of the individual's responsibility for the deviant behavior. This part of the sick role concept is thus connected with Parsons's larger concern with how societies maintain their equilibrium in the face of deviance and disruptions such as sickness.

Although having pneumonia is a legitimate excuse for not reporting to work, the sick person is expected to act sick and try to get well. The employer would be less than happy to see the supposedly sick employee at a baseball game later that day, for example. According to Parsons, part of trying to get well involves seeking competent health care from a trained physician. The social expectations for a person with pneumonia thus include going to a doctor, obtaining and taking the doctor's prescription, and otherwise conforming to whatever regimen the doctor ordered. Thus, he tied the sick role inevitably with the role of medical professionals. (Parsons was especially interested in the development of professionalism as a feature of modern society.) In his usage, the sick role directly implies the patient role; by contrast, we explore the patient role as a separate role, which sick persons may or may not enter, depending on whether their sickness is brought to the attention of medical professionals (see Chapter 10).

Parsons's concept of the sick role is valuable in that it highlights the social control functions of how society treats sickness. It also emphasizes the extent to which social definitions of sickness reflect larger cultural values of modern Western societies (Parsons, 1972: 124). The cultural narrowness of this concept is partly due to Parsons's explicit focus on mid-twentieth-century American values (for example, individual achievement and responsibility). The sick role, however, is not as clear cut as Parsons's model suggests. Four problems with his approach are discussed next.

The Sick Role Is Not Necessarily Temporary   Parsons's conception of the sick role is based on only one, relatively narrow class of health problems. The obligations and exemptions described in his model appear to fit serious, acute illnesses reasonably well. **Acute illnesses** characteristically occur suddenly, peak rapidly, and run their course (that is, result in death or recovery) in a relatively short time. Examples include influenza, measles, and scarlet fever.

Chronic illnesses, by contrast, are of long duration—typically as long as the sufferer lives. They often result in the steady deterioration of bodily functioning. Examples include emphysema, diabetes, multiple sclerosis, epilepsy, and heart disease. Furthermore, some acute illnesses are considered chronic when they become a continuing pattern in an individual's life; examples include chronic bronchitis, asthma, and ulcers. Additionally, a number of chronic, disabling conditions (such as paraplegia from a car accident) do not involve any ongoing disease, but may result in an ambiguous, lifelong sick role.

Although many acute conditions can be cured (or are self-limiting), most chronic conditions are permanent. Treatment of chronic illness is aimed at best at controlling the deterioration caused by the disease and at *managing* the illness. Many of the most dangerous acute (usually infectious) diseases of earlier generations have been brought under control in developed countries through improved sanitation, nutrition, housing, and the like. Inoculations, antibiotics, and other medical treatments have also had some effect in curing infectious diseases (although, as Chapter 2 shows, their role has been somewhat overstated). The proportion of persons suffering chronic illnesses has greatly increased, however; modern medical intervention does not appear so potent in the face of such conditions.

The nature of chronic illness does not fit Parsons's sick role pattern (Radley, 1994). Obviously, his assumption of the necessity of an "intent to get well" is irrelevant if the illness is, by definition, permanent. His sick role conception presumed that the benefits were conditional, but chronic illnesses make most of the conditions meaningless (Alexander, 1982). Unlike acute infectious disease, chronic ailments are more likely to be considered partly the fault or the responsibility of the sufferer. Whereas few people consider a case of chicken pox, for example, to be the sick person's fault, lay and medical conceptions of many chronic conditions, such as lung cancer, high blood pressure, and cirrhosis of the liver, are believed to be brought on—at least partially—by the sufferer's own lifestyle.

Feelings about whether a chronic illness is sufficient grounds for exemption from normal responsibilities are also ambiguous. Because the condition is not temporary, the exemptions are all the more problematic for both the sufferer and those who would grant the exemptions. Just how disabling is the condition? Often persons suffering chronic illnesses do not want total exemption from normal responsibilities, but the illness prevents them from fulfilling some usual duties. As Chapter 7 shows, due to societal values enforced by the sick role, persons with chronic illness have considerable difficulty negotiating such concessions. As a means for maintaining stability and social control, the sick role allows temporary exemptions from normal role requirements *without changing those requirements*.

Similarly, many other "deviant" health conditions do not fit the sick role model of acute diseases and thereby lead to ambiguities about expectations. Should a person born with a physical handicap be treated as sick? What about accident victims or the mentally ill? Should such normal conditions as pregnancy or menopause be treated as sickness? Considerable ambiguity surrounds the role expectations of those whose health conditions are treated as somehow "deviant" yet do not fit the (acute) sick role.

The Sick Role Is Not Always Voluntary   Parsons's model holds that the sick person, in exchange for the advantages of the sick role, is motivated to assume that role and voluntarily cooperate with the agents of social control in the appropriate therapy for the deviant condition. In the preceding example of the worker with pneumonia, for example, the person's discomfort and fear of complications would presumably motivate the individual to see a doctor, have blood tests and X-rays, get bed rest at home or in a hospital, and take medications. Parsons thus assumed that, in contrast to criminal deviance, the sick person voluntarily enters the socially prescribed role.

Not all persons, however, want to enter the sick role, even when they feel ill. Many people resist the expected childlike dependency the role often entails; many others have strong aversion to medical treatments, especially in the hospital. A Scottish study of lower-class women found considerable negative moral evaluation of persons who give in, or "lie down," to illness (Blaxter and Paterson, 1982). Some people, furthermore, simply cannot afford to withdraw from normal obligations; the sick role is a threat to their subsistence (Kasl and Cobb, 1966).

Some sicknesses carry a negative connotation or stigma. Although the sick person would obtain some benefits (such as exemption from work or other duties) from the sick role, the stigma of that illness could be worse than the condition itself. For example, a person suffering epilepsy may actively avoid being socially identified with it because of the repulsion and often outright discrimination associated with the illness (Schneider and Conrad, 1980).

Many persons are placed into the sick role by others, regardless of their own wishes. Children and the dependent aged are generally not considered competent to decide for themselves whether to assume the role; instead, their caretakers make the decision for them. Likewise, some conditions (for example, loss of consciousness) force an involuntary entrance into the sick role. Other ambiguous situations arise when someone's family (or unrelated caretakers, such as doctors, social workers, or police) decide that an individual is too sick to have good judgment and then place the person into the sick role. Because many people thus do not enter the sick role voluntarily, their cooperation with the medical regimen cannot be assumed. In many such cases, the social control functions of the sick role are more coercive and less benign than portrayed by the model.

By contrast, some persons seek to enter the sick role and are denied access. A process of subtle social negotiation occurs when an individual claims the sick role. This claim must then be accepted as legitimate by others, especially authoritative others. Often medical personnel such as the school nurse and the company doctor are the critical *gatekeepers* who have the power to determine who will be admitted to the sick role in their institutional setting. Informal negotiation also typically takes place as the person claiming the sick role attempts to convince family and others of the legitimacy of the claim, and the others judge—and sometimes test—that legitimacy. Entry into the sick role is thus essentially a social and political process. This link between social control and medical personnel's gatekeeping roles is developed further in Chapter 9.

Variability in Sick Role Legitimacy   Parsons's conception of the sick role also presumes that a single, stable value system is operative for all persons in a society. Historically, however, the legitimate exemption of sick persons from various obligations has been highly variable. The criteria for such an exemption may also differ according to gender, social class, and subcultural expectations.

Legitimate exemptions from work obligations, for example, vary enormously, typically according to social class. Unskilled workers, for example, often have no paid sick days, whereas many white-collar workers are given an annual allowance of such days of absence proportionate to their rank or seniority. Indeed, the idea that absence due to sickness should not be a basis for dismissal is relatively recent; even today sickness is not a legitimate exemption for many workers, and they have no legal protection of their jobs.

The meaning of the sick role itself varies considerably according to social class. The same sickness has different connotations according to the class or gender of the sufferer. For example, in the nineteenth century, consumption (tuberculosis) was a romanticized illness among the middle and upper classes. This sick role implied a "consuming" passion as expressed in artistic sensitivity and creativity. Some of the physical effects of tuberculosis were considered beautiful: slenderness, fever-bright eyes, pallor, and a transparent complexion accompanied by pink cheeks. One young woman with consumption wrote in her diary:

> Since yesterday I am white and fresh and amazingly pretty. My eyes are spirited and shining, and even the contours of my face seem prettier and more delicate. It's too bad that this is happening at a time when I am not seeing anyone. It's foolish to tell, but I spent a half-hour looking at myself in the mirror with pleasure; this had not happened to me for some time. (Marie Bashkirtseff's Journal of 1883, quoted in Herzlich and Pierret, 1987: 81)

The well-to-do sufferer was "'apart,' threatened but all the more precious for it" (Herzlich and Pierret, 1987: 25). Although the disease was more prevalent and devastating among the lower classes, no such privileged or positive sick role was available to them.

The sick role was considered especially appropriate for women of that era because it was thought to reflect ladies' refinement and delicacy. It was expected and even stylish for well-to-do women to faint frequently and to retire to bed for "nerves," "sick headaches," "female troubles," and "neurasthenia." Lower-class women, by contrast, were considered to be more robust, as evidence of their coarseness and less civilized nature (Ehrenreich and English, 1978).

Upper-class Victorians could obtain exemption from normal obligations by claiming the sick roles of neurasthenia or hysteria, illnesses of the "nerves" believed to afflict particularly intellectual or sensitive persons. The label of neurasthenia appears to have been especially useful for men, whose normal role expectations of fortitude and active participation in the world outside of the home made it difficult for them to exhibit dependency or weakness. The vague symptoms identified as neurasthenia, however, were a legitimate basis for men to assume the sick role (Sicherman, 1978; see also Drinka, 1984).

Cultural expectations of the sick role also vary, perhaps widely. Some evidence indicates that cultures differ in the degree of legitimacy they accord various illnesses and their resulting claims to exemption from responsibilities (see Morris, 1998). For example, neurasthenia is a legitimate basis of the sick role among contemporary Taiwanese, whereas in the United States it is a far less common diagnosis or culturally recognized reason for assuming the sick role (see, for example, Kleinman, 1980). Similarly, persons of Hispanic background would be more likely than those of Anglo-Saxon heritage to consider a certain "fright" (*susto*), such as being startled by an animal or a possible assailant, to be a legitimate basis for the sick role (Baer et al., 1998). Because cultures vary in how they understand various illnesses, they also have different expectations for the behavior of persons occupying the sick role, such as the amount of pain and disability they may experience (see, for example, Angel and Thoits, 1987). These examples illustrate that the expectations identified as a sick role change; problems that were identified in the past as a legitimate basis for claiming the role are no longer appropriate, whereas other problems—formerly unrecognized or discounted—are now accepted as legitimate.

Responsibility for Sickness   Parsons's model of the sick role held that, unlike crime, sickness was not the responsibility of the deviant person. Furthermore, he considered the professional diagnosis and treatment of medical deviance to be purely technical, neutral, and unbiased. As Chapter 9 illustrates, however, the very definition of illness is socially constructed, and social groups often impute responsibility for illness to the sick person.

Freidson (1970) observed that certain conditions are typically viewed as the responsibility of the sick individual and thus are treated relatively punitively, like crimes. Examples include various sexually transmitted diseases as well as substance abuse and conditions derived from such abuse. Freidson noted that the attitudes of both the society and the medical profession, although greatly expanding the range of conditions considered to be properly "medical" problems, do not necessarily abolish the negative moral connotations attached to these conditions. He also described another category of sicknesses that, although not technically considered the fault of the sick person, are nonetheless stigmatized (Freidson, 1970: 234–237). **Stigma** is a powerful discrediting and tainting social label that radically changes the way an individual is viewed as a person (Goffman, 1963: 2–5). For example, being an illegitimate child was (in the past more than now) an enormous barrier to presenting oneself as a "normal," upright citizen.

Many sicknesses carry a stigma. Leprosy, epilepsy, and AIDS, for example, all carry connotations of disreputability and even evil. The sick role for someone with a stigmatized illness is clearly different than that for a person with a neutral sickness. Stigmas can result in various forms of discrimination: Persons with epilepsy, for instance, have experienced job discrimination, difficulty in obtaining insurance, and prohibitions against marrying (Schneider and Conrad, 1980). Even after someone has been treated and pronounced cured of such a condition, the stigma often remains on that person. Furthermore, the stigma frequently spreads to the family and close friends of the sick person in what Goffman (1963: 30–31) calls a "courtesy stigma." For example, families and friends of persons with epilepsy, cancer, or AIDS sometimes find themselves shunned or harassed (Conrad, 1986).

The source of stigma is not the disease itself but rather the social imputation of a negative connotation. Leprosy is highly stigmatized in India, but far less so in neighboring Sri Lanka. Lepers in India are treated as outcasts, whereas many lepers in Nigeria remain in the village and carry on normal social lives (Waxler, 1981). Because cultures vary in the stigma imputed to different sicknesses, the sick role for those illnesses varies accordingly.

The degree of stigma and responsibility attached to a sickness may also change over time, often as notions about an illness change. In the nineteenth century, when tuberculosis was considered to be a somewhat romantic sickness resulting from an inherent disposition of passion and creativity, the illness had relatively little stigma. Later, however, when tuberculosis was considered infectious, those with the disease were seen as carriers to be avoided, isolated, and feared (Herzlich and Pierret, 1987).

Specific social and historical conditions lead to the stigmatizing of a sickness. Before the middle of the nineteenth century, leprosy in Hawaii was of minor importance and not stigmatized. As international trade and colonialism began to change the islands' social and economic situation, however, many outsiders came to the islands. Large numbers of Chinese immigrants arrived to work on the plantations, and the Hawaiians believed they had brought leprosy. Although the Chinese immigrants were hard working and frugal, they were viewed as an inferior ethnic-racial group that threatened the jobs of other working-class persons. In 1880, Hawaii enacted laws to exclude the Chinese, partly based on the belief that they carried disease. Health data suggest that the Chinese were not, however, an important source of leprosy, which more likely came to the islands through the ethnically mixed crews of ships from countries where the disease was prevalent. The Chinese were stigmatized in part because they were thought to be the source of leprosy, which at the same time became stigmatized because it was identified with the Chinese. A relatively unknown and unimportant disease was thus transformed into a morally threatening sickness (Waxler, 1981).

The stigma attached to AIDS in recent years is a parallel situation. The widespread imputation of responsibility and stigma to sick persons suggests that Parsons's sick role model understates the moral judgment and social control aspects of sickness.

The Medicalization of Deviance

Religious, legal, and medical institutions have all contributed to the definition of deviance in society. For example, "Thou shalt not steal" is a religious norm: Stealing is a sin. Legal systems define similar norms of behavior, and violation of the norms is a crime. In a process called the **medicalization of deviance,** medical systems increasingly also define what is normal or desirable behavior: Badness becomes sickness (Conrad, 1996).

The relative influence of religious, legal, and medical institutions in defining deviance has shifted in Western societies. As the Middle Ages waned and these three institutions became increasingly differentiated from each other, the religious organizations still had the greatest weight in defining deviance. This preeminence continued into the eighteenth century, but in America and France (and later in other European countries), the legal mode of defining deviance gained ascendancy (see Freidson, 1970: 247–252). In America, the increasing preeminence of the legal definitions was promoted by religious pluralism and by the increasingly rational organization of the nation-state (see, for example, Hammond, 1974).

The significance of legal definitions of deviance has diminished somewhat in the twentieth century, and medical definitions have gained in importance. This shifting balance is clearly reflected in the 1954 precedent-setting case *Durham* v. *United States* (214 F.2d 863), in which the court ruled that "an accused is not criminally responsible if his unlawful act was the product of a mental disease or mental defect." The shift in balance favoring medical definitions of deviance corresponds chronologically with a period of the rapid professionalization of medicine, when medical discoveries and technology proceeded quickly, and public faith in science and medicine was increasing.

Part of the reason for the declining importance of religious definitions is that they appear too nonrational and, in a religiously pluralistic country, lack society-wide acceptance. Legal definitions, although more rational, seem to hinge too greatly on human decisions, such as the judgment of 12 ordinary citizens on a jury. Medical definitions, by contrast, *appear* to be more rational and scientific, and based on technical expertise rather than human judgment.

The concept of sickness, however, far from being a neutral scientific concept, is ultimately a moral one, establishing an evaluation of normality or desirability (Freidson, 1970: 208). The medical profession (especially its psychiatric branch) has defined a wide range of disapproved behavior as "sick": alcoholism, homosexuality, promiscuity, drug addiction, arson, suicide, child abuse, and civil disobedience (Conrad and Schneider, 1992; Peele, 1989). Social stigma adheres to many sicknesses, such as leprosy, AIDS, pelvic inflammatory disease, and cirrhosis of the liver.[1] Moral judgment is also applied in the evaluation of good patient behavior, defined as acknowledging the necessity of medical care and following doctors' orders for various conditions, which may include receiving prenatal care, accepting blood transfusions, obtaining inoculations for one's children, and following prescribed drug and dietary regimens. Issues of moral judgment and responsibility are at stake.

Zola (1983: 261) argued that "if anything can be shown in some way to affect the workings of the body and to a lesser extent the mind, then it can be labelled an 'illness' itself or jurisdictionally 'a medical problem.'" Thus, even normal and healthy physical conditions or processes, such as menstruation, pregnancy and childbirth, body and facial shape and size, and aging, have been brought under medicine's jurisdiction (Dull and West, 1991).

The Medicalization of Moral Authority

The same historical processes that brought about the preeminence of medical definitions of deviance also led to a much stronger role for medical authority in moral issues, such as what is good or bad?, and whose good should prevail? Sometimes court events involve a clash of several sources of authority.[2]

---

[1] Cultures vary, however, as to which sicknesses are stigmatized. For example, in China, diseases attributed to socially unapproved emotions such as anger are more stigmatized than those attributed to purely physical causes (Ots, 1990).

[2] This section is adapted with permission of the publisher from *Religion: The Social Context* (5th ed.) by Meredith B. McGuire, 2002, by Wadsworth/ITP.

In one representative court case, claims were made from legal, medical, parental, and religious bases of authority. A young person had been comatose for months, and was as good as dead in the commonsense view. Her body was being kept alive by technological intervention, and eventually her parents sought legal permission to terminate these extraordinary measures. Because no single authority held uncontested legitimacy, the case was complicated. Medical experts gave their opinions on the medical definitions of death. Legal experts raised issues of the legal rights and guardianship of comatose patients. Theological experts offered briefs on the borderlines of life and death, and the girl's father made a thoughtful personal statement about his request. The relevant issue is not merely the uncertainty of the outcome, but also that it was the court in which medical, legal, religious, and parental figures vied to have their statements taken seriously (Fenn, 1982; Willen, 1983).

The growing legitimacy of medical authority, relative to other sources of judgment, is further illustrated by contemporary court decisions upholding medical judgments to perform Caesarian sections. Caesarian sections are increasingly common, now accounting for about one in four births in the United States. They involve major abdominal surgery, with its concomitant risks and complications. An investigation of court cases between 1979 and 1986 showed that courts often accept physicians' decisions to operate over the objections of patients, their families, or religious persuasion, even though subsequent medical developments suggest that many of these operations were not necessary (Irwin and Jordan, 1987).

Nevertheless, nontechnical judgments are often involved in decisions to impose medical treatment, even a serious breach of the bodily integrity of the unwilling patient. Court-ordered surgical delivery was disproportionately used on women of color, poor, and non-English-speaking women. These factors appear to be linked with doctors' moral evaluation of some women as incompetent, ignorant, or "bad" mothers, who cannot take the interests of their child into account (Daniels, 1993: 31–55). Such a paternalistic stance was also evident in a Canadian study of aggressive medical intervention in childbirth; the physicians viewed themselves as "fetal champions," looking out for the best interests of the fetus (Bassett et al., 2000). Similarly, medical authority has legitimated the legal prosecution of women charged with "prenatal endangerment," for example by engaging in childbirth without medical assistance or failing to follow doctors' orders to stop smoking or drinking (Tsing, 1990).

Medical dominance has effectively reduced the legitimacy of actions of other "encroaching" institutional areas such as religion and the family. Several courts have overruled religious or moral objections to various medical procedures. Jehovah's Witnesses, for example, believe that blood transfusions are forbidden by scripture, but the courts have generally upheld the medical authorization of such treatments, even for unwilling recipients (*United States* v. *George*, 239 F. Supp. 752, 1964). Medical authority was also ruled to supersede parental authority in decisions presumed to determine life or death (precedent cases in 1952, 1962, and 1964 are cited in Burkholder, 1974: 41). In 1990, a lower court denied the parents' request to terminate artificial nutrition and hydration for a patient in a vegetative state, while upholding hospital employees' refusal to cooperate with their wishes (*Cruzan* v. *Missouri, Department of Health,* 497 U.S. 261, 110 S.Ct. 2841, 1990). Although this case was essentially about whether the parents' judgment was adequate substitution for the patient's own decision, the cultural authority attached to hospital-administered medical technology took the decision out of the parents' area of legitimate authority.

Even in instances in which the medical ability to prevent death is more doubtful, greater legitimacy is given to medical rather than parental authority. In 1994, for example, a California court ordered that a Hmong Laotian child suffering from leukemia be removed from her parents' custody because they refused medically prescribed chemotherapy for her; more than 200 Hmong demonstrated against the decision, which overruled the parents' ethnic and religious objections to Western medical treatment (*New York Times,* 1994c).

Social Control and Power

The labeling of deviance is an issue of legitimacy on another level as well, for the power to define sickness and to label someone as sick is also the power to discredit that person (Zola, 1983: 276–278). If a person's mental health is called into question, the rest of society does not have to take that person seriously. The individual then becomes the locus of the so-called problem. During the Vietnam War, a physician refused to train medical personnel for the army, claiming that his religious conscience compelled him to refuse this service. The army insisted that his compulsions were psychological rather than religious (Fenn, 1978: 57). By thus raising doubt about his psychological health, the army was able to evade his religious dissent as well as his legal claim to protection under the First Amendment of the Constitution.

Medical control in defining deviance also produces medical power in certifying deviance, which is another aspect of social control. The societal acceptance of medical definitions of deviance gives the medical profession unique power to certify individuals as sick or well. If a back disorder is a legitimate basis for taking the sick role (and thus to be excused from work or to claim insurance), a physician is considered the appropriate agency for certifying a valid claim. Sick persons typically use "feeling" terms to describe internal states that they experience as illness; they say, for example, "I don't feel good" or "I feel too dizzy to stand." When the bodily source of feeling sick is not obvious to their audiences, they need doctors' substantiation to legitimate their claims (Telles and Pollack, 1981). Putting a medical label on an illness can be beneficial when it validates and demonstrates serious concern about patients' symptoms and gives some meaning or coherence to their distressing experience, thereby supporting their efforts to manage the illness (Broom and Woodward, 1996; Lorber, 1997). Doctors, however, often resist diagnosing ambiguous illnesses (especially contested categories such as chronic fatigue syndrome) because they do not want to encourage patients to take the sick role. They are thus caught between conflicting roles for themselves: physician as patient advocate and patient-claimant versus physician as agent of social control.

One of the social control functions of physicians is the role of gatekeeper (Stone, 1979), making them responsible for separating the "deserving" from the "undeserving" claims for sympathy and social support, sick leave, disability pay, health insurance, hospitalization, and so on. Physicians became the chief arbiters of claims for workers' compensation for repetitive strain injuries; not surprisingly, company doctors selected by manufacturers or insurers typically were less likely to certify the injury or provide sympathetic care than were personal physicians (Reid et al., 1991). Similarly, from 1952 to 1979, when homosexuality was considered a legitimate basis for denying a person U.S. citizenship, psychiatrists were given the power to certify that a homosexual should be thus denied (see Szasz, 1970).

When a person is certified as deviant, the agency of social control must then deal with this offender. Religious responses to deviance include counseling, moral indignation, confession, repentance, penance, and forgiveness. Legal responses include parallel actions, such as legal allegations, confession, punishments, rehabilitation, and release with or without the stigma of a record. In the medical model, the responses entail other parallels: diagnosis, therapy, and counseling.

The process of reintegrating the deviant individual into the social group is therapy, which for even relatively minor deviance involves a form of social control (such as getting a young mother "back on her feet" so she can resume her family responsibilities). The social control functions of therapy are most clearly evident in such situations as the kidnapping and forcible "deprogramming" of persons with deviant religious or political views (Robbins and Anthony, 1982) and the mental hospitalization of political dissidents (Freidson, 1970: 246; see also Turner, 1977; Medvedev and Medvedev, 1971).

The use of psychoactive drugs for social control is one area of particular concern. Several U.S. and Canadian studies have documented the very large proportion of the elderly receiving drugs that affect the central nervous system, such as tranquilizers, analgesics, antidepressants, sedatives, hypnotics, and anticonvulsants. One function, deliberate or not, of the use of these drugs is the management of elderly persons. For example, older persons need shorter but more frequent periods of sleep than younger adults, but sedatives are often prescribed in many institutions to try to keep the elderly in an eight-hour sleeping pattern, so the staff can better supervise them at night (Harding, 1981; see also Harding, 1986).

Similarly, difficult-to-manage school children are often prescribed Ritalin (or its competitors, Adderal, Concerta, Metadate CD, and so on) to calm their excess activity and get them to pay attention to their learning tasks. U.S. patients use 90 percent of the world's production of Ritalin, prescribed to up to 6 percent of elementary and pre-teen schoolchildren for a variety of behavioral disorders (Environment News Service, 2001). In 2000, doctors wrote almost 20 million monthly prescriptions for these stimulants; most were written for children, especially boys. Sales for Ritalin and related stimulants were $758 million, an increase of 13 percent since the preceding year (Zernike and Petersen, 2001). Other childhood behavioral disorders (for example, Oppositional and Defiant Disorder, Anxiety Disorder) are increasingly treated pharmacologically, as well.

Social control is also involved in the use of drugs to make it possible for persons to accommodate themselves to an unsatisfactory social role. When workers experience severe stress in the workplace, treating their stress-related health conditions with drugs keeps them performing their roles without challenging the work conditions or the appropriateness of those roles. One pharmaceutical company was investigated in 1987 by the U.S. Food and Drug Administration for sending doctors an advertising brochure depicting on the cover a very tense air traffic controller at the computer monitor in a hectic control tower. The caption read, "He needs anxiolytic [tranquilizer] therapy . . . but alertness is part of his job." Inside the folder, the worker is portrayed as cheery and smiling, and the text reads, in part, "BuSpar. . . . For a different kind of calm." Although the ad was criticized as misleading in its downplaying of negative side effects of the drug, the more serious sociological issue is that a tranquilizer is being promoted as a solution to workplace stress brought on by specific policy decisions. According to a U.S. Government Accounting Office study, air traffic controllers suffered low morale, extreme overwork, and other pressures due to chronic and serious understaffing—a major problem since President Reagan had fired 11,000 striking air traffic controllers in 1981 (*Health Letter*, 1987).

Research in the United States, Canada, and Europe shows that women have been the overwhelming majority of recipients of prescriptions for tranquilizers and sedatives (Ashton, 1991; Harding, 1986). Pharmaceutical company advertising to doctors specifically recommended such psychoactive drugs to deal with women's dissatisfaction with their social roles. An advertisement for Valium (diazepam) showed a troubled young woman sitting at a table in a school gymnasium; the photo was labeled as follows:

> Symbols in a life of psychic tension: M.A. (Fine Arts), PTA (President-elect), GYN repeated examinations, normal (persistent complaints). . . . Rx: Valium . . . representations of a life currently centered around home and children, with too little time to pursue a vocation for which she has spent many years in training . . . a situation that may bespeak continuous frustration and stress: a perfect framework for her to translate the functional symptoms of psychic tension into major problems. For this kind of patient—with no demonstrable pathology yet with repeated complaints—consider the distinctive properties of Valium (diazepam). Valium possesses a pronounced calming action that usually relieves psychic tension promptly, helping to attenuate the related somatic signs and symptoms.

Like the air traffic controller, this young woman is identified as suffering from the stress and frustration of her social role. The solution of prescribing psychotropic drugs—as advocated by physicians, as well as the pharmaceutical industry (Raskin, 1997)—serves the social control function of keeping people in their roles without questioning the role demands themselves (for a review of the literature on prescription of psychotropic drugs for women, see Ettorre and Riska, 1995).

In the 1990s a newer form of medicalized social control became evident in the United States, Canada, and several European countries. In the name of improving health, the medical establishment (in the form of national health services, public health programs, corporate wellness programs, and managed care organizations) promoted *moral* judgments attached to "lifestyle" decisions. These lifestyle expectations were highly individualized: It became solely the individual's responsibility to maintain a "healthy" lifestyle, for example by getting lots of exercise, eating "right," ceasing smoking and drinking alcohol, reducing stress, maintaining the "right" weight, and so on. Although the promotion of behaviors that might help prevent diseases is an appropriate part of public health measures, by individualizing the concept of "lifestyle" these programs had the effect of distracting from the *social* and *public* causes of disease, such as environmental pollution, illness-producing work and workplaces, and socioeconomic constraints that prevent individuals from achieving a healthy "lifestyle" (Bunton et al., 1995; Mechanic, 1999). Notice the moral connotations of such notions as eating "right," with little or no recognition of the difficulties of obtaining a good diet on a poverty-level income. These moral judgments are readily medicalized because biomedicine treats disease as a feature of the individual.

Social control may seem more pleasant or humane when the deviance is treated as sickness rather than as crime or sin, but the potency of the control agencies is just as great. Certain medically defined deviance can permanently spoil the individual's identity (see Goffman, 1963). Even when the condition is considered medically cured or under control, stigma still adheres to such illnesses as alcoholism, drug abuse, mental disorders, syphilis, and cancer. This problem of stigma is especially evident in the case of illnesses involving deviance from one very important cultural norm: self-control. Chapter 7 further examines the problems of stigma and control in chronic illness and disabilities.

Sickness and Social Dissent

The social control functions of the sick role and of some medical interventions demonstrate that society's constraints on individual behavior are real, even when individuals do not agree with the norms for behavior. Although social control measures may be objectively powerful in a society, their effect is never total. Society's members are never fully socialized and compliant. Thus, deviance such as sickness can also be a form of social dissent—usually unorganized, but sometimes organized—against existing social arrangements.

Sickness is, as the sick role concept shows, an act of refusal that is potentially threatening to the established order. In effect, the sick person is saying, "I will not . . . any longer." By claiming the sick role, the individual may refuse to go to school or work, to be responsible for dependents, to serve in the armed forces, and to participate in everyday social obligations. Indeed, in its extreme form, sickness is a refusal to cope, to struggle, and to endure. As such, claiming the sick role resembles the political activist strategy of passive resistance (Lock and Scheper-Hughes, 1990; Scheper-Hughes and Lock, 1991; see also Herzlich and Pierret, 1987: 183–184; Kleinman, 1992). Taking the sick role is thus often a way of expressing dissent from other social roles. Many social historians consider the epidemic of hysteria among Victorian women to be an expression of their dissent against the constraints of their social roles (Sicherman, 1978). Similarly, workers' job dissatisfaction is often expressed by high rates of absenteeism for sickness.

Sickness is not necessarily an effective form of dissent, however. Waitzkin (1971) suggested the sick role has latent (that is, not recognized or intended) functions that maintain the status quo in society and reduce conflict and change. For example, if disgruntled workers take sick leave to relieve the tensions of their job satisfaction, the sick role reduces the likelihood that those tensions will be addressed politically, such as in a confrontation with management. The sick role instead provides only a *temporary* safety valve to reduce pressure in various institutional settings, such as the family, prisons, and the military.

Although the sickness may not be able to change social arrangements, such as social class or gender hierarchies, it may be effective in obtaining actual advantages or relief for the sick person. Some secondary gains of sickness, such as receiving extra attention in the family, may be such a result. For example, many African societies have special healing cults for women, such as the *zar* cult of the predominantly Muslim peoples in Ethiopia, Egypt, Sudan, and Somalia. Some anthropologists have interpreted the *zar* affliction, in which the sick person is believed to be possessed by spirits, as women's assertion of dissatisfaction with their lack of social and economic power (Lewis, 1971). Taking the sick role can be a relatively successful (albeit manipulative) assertion of power of the subordinate members of the society. It poignantly expresses women's dissent, but does not fundamentally alter the social arrangements.

Similarly, sickness is sometimes the attempt to cope (although not always constructively) with an intolerable social situation, as discussed in Chapter 4. Sickness expresses frustration, dissatisfaction, and anger turned against oneself. Alcoholism and other substance abuse, depression, and suicide exemplify this potentially self-defeating attempt. To interpret, for example, the alcoholism of a middle-aged, unemployed, impoverished Native American on a reservation as a purely individual sickness is thus to miss the likelihood that it is the expression of his frustration and hostility in the face of his utterly marginalized social condition (Scheper-Hughes and Lock, 1991; see also Kleinman, 1997).

Likewise, to interpret an immigrant woman's severe case of "nerves" as a quaint relic of old-country folk beliefs misses the meaning of nerves (or "*nervios*," "*nevra*," and so on) as a physical expression of real distress (Finkler, 1989; see also Guarnaccia et al., 1989). Her distress, expressed in the physical symptoms of "nerves," may be produced by the perceived disorder of daily life in a society where she experiences exploitation as a worker and discrimination as a member of an ethnic minority. Her "nerves" may be a reaction to a lack of meaning and perceived assault on self-esteem from living in a culture that lacks the values by which she would have been honored in her native culture (Lock, 1990).

Scheper-Hughes and Lock (1991) argued that modern medicine has so thoroughly individualized its image of sickness that it has lost sight of the extent to which sickness may be the expression of social dissent about frustrated and unmet human needs. They stated:

> In summary, we wish to stress that while illness symptoms are biological entities they are also coded metaphors that speak to the contradictory aspects of social life, expressing sentiments, feelings, and ideas that must otherwise be kept hidden. As patients—all of us—we can be open and responsive to the hidden language of pain and protest, rage and resistance, or we can silence it, cut it off by relegating our complaints to the ever expanding domains of medicine ("It" is in the body) or psychiatry ("It" is in the mind). Once safely medicalized, however, the social issues are short-circuited and the message in the bottle—the desperate plea for help and the scream of protest—is forever lost. (Scheper-Hughes and Lock, 1991: 422–423)

Metaphorical aspects of sicknesses are linked with meaning and order.

PROBLEMS OF MEANING AND ORDER

Illness is upsetting because it is experienced as a threat to the order and meanings by which people make sense of their lives. Suffering and death create problems of meaning not simply because they are unpleasant, but also because they threaten the fundamental assumptions of order underlying society itself (see, for example, Berger, 1967: 24). For the individual, illness and affliction can likewise be experienced as assaults on the identity, and on the ability to predict and control central aspects of one's own and one's loved ones' lives. Healing, in all cultures, represents an attempt to restore order and to reassert meaning.

Illness disrupts the order of everyday life. It threatens our ability to plan for the immediate or distant future, to control, and to organize. Even a relatively minor malady, such as a head cold, can disturb the order of daily life; how much more so can serious, potentially fatal, or debilitating illnesses, such as cancer or diabetes, throw our lives into disorder! A study of the impact of childhood leukemia found two characteristic experiences of sufferers and their families: uncertainty and the search for meaning (Comaroff and Maguire, 1981).

Medical systems in all cultures restore order in the face of illness in a number of ways. Diagnostic action, whether accomplished by divination or computer tomography scan, divine revelation or physical examination, is a means of naming the problem and giving it a culturally recognizable form. Naming the illness imposes order on a previously chaotic set of experiences, thereby giving the sick person a set of expectations and some basis for acting. Etiologies likewise contribute to restoring a sense of order, because they identify a causal relationship between sickness and socially prescribed normal or ideal social relationships. In applying particular etiologies to a given illness episode, the medical process ritually reaffirms these values (Young, 1976).

The healing process in many cultures (including our own) addresses not only individual disruption but also disordered *social* relations. The individual

Box 6.1

Sickness and the Disordered Social Realm

The phrase "*hais cuaj txub kaum txub*" (to speak of all kinds of things) aptly describes the worldview of the Hmong culture: Everything in the world is connected, no event occurs in isolation from others, and "you can miss a lot by sticking to the point."

Lia Lee was born in 1981, in a U.S. hospital, to recent immigrant Hmong parents from Laos. Lia had epilepsy, which the Hmong describe as "the spirit catches you and you fall down." For five years, she was treated by American doctors who attempted to control her seizures without taking into account the parents' understanding of their causes and best treatment. It was clear to her parents, Foua and Nao Kao Lee, that Lia's soul was lost; presumably, her sister Yer had slammed the door and frightened Lia's soul out of her body. The seizures were caused by a spirit *dab* that caught Lia. It was also clear to the Lees that the medicine should be taken only for a week and should be complemented by *neeb,* Hmong medicine, and sacrificing pigs and chickens. Yer's carelessness had caused Lia's seizures, and the Lee family "knew" that the return of Lia's soul to her body was the remedy. The restoration of order, wellness, would not be attained by Western medicine alone.

Source: Anne Fadiman, *The Spirit Catches You and You Fall Down,* 1996, pp. 21–23, 100–109.

---

disordered body is only an expression of the disordered *social* relations. For instance, in some Christian groups, healing a troubled marriage involves bringing the "body" (wife and children) into proper relationship (namely, submission) with the "head" (husband and father). Healing in these groups restores order through healing the metaphorical body (McGuire, 1982, 1988). In Western culture, the importance of the body as a natural symbol suggests that illness and healing may be ways of symbolizing order and meaning on several levels.

The Body as a Symbol

The human body is a natural symbol. The meanings of the symbol are not intrinsic in it, but are socially constructed and attached to it. As Douglas (1970: 93) stated:

> The social body constrains the way the physical body is perceived. The physical experience of the body, always modified by the social categories through which it is known, sustains a particular view of society. There is a continual exchange of meanings between the two kinds of bodily experience so that each reinforces the categories of the other. As a result of this interaction the body itself is a highly restricted medium of expression.

Thus, she argued that bodily control is social control, and attitudes toward the body reflect the social concerns of the group (Douglas, 1970: 11–18).

Body symbolism works on several levels; often the body and its parts are used as metaphors. For example, when we say a person is upright, we are referring to both a moral evaluation and a physical posture. Similar body metaphors are applied when we evaluate people as spineless, underhanded, open-eyed, heartless, cold-blooded, brown-nosed, blue-blooded, sinister, thick-skinned, or gutless. Social relations are likewise reflected in body metaphors, such as, "He is a pain in the ass," or "They are thicker than blood."

Consider all the symbolic meanings we give to various body parts and body products, including hands, heart, womb, hair, eyes, milk, blood, spit, feces, and sweat. These meanings are not inherent in the physical properties but are applied by a social group. In socialization, we learn our society's meanings. A baby is not born with an aversion to the sight of blood. A young child must learn to be disgusted by the feel of feces (usually only after having played with them and receiving several reprimands).

Through the meanings attached to the body, social structure shapes individual bodily expression. At the same time, bodily expression reflects the social structure. Numerous studies of various cultures, including Western industrialized societies, have shown how core values are revealed in body-related beliefs and practices, such as eating (Banks, 1992; Lupton, 1996a; Turner, 1982); beauty and adornment (Kunzle, 1981); birth and death (Comaroff, 1984; Davis-Floyd, 1992); sex (Foucault, 1978; Turner, 1984); pollution and cleanliness (Classen, 1994; Douglas, 1966; Elias, 1994 [1978]); fitness and healthy "lifestyle" (Bordo, 1993; Lupton, 1995; O'Brien, 1995); and health and healing (Comaroff, 1985; Crawford, 1984; McGuire, 1988).

The Meaning of Affliction

Illness is also upsetting because it raises the questions of meaning: Why is this happening to me? Why now? Who's responsible? How could God allow this to happen? Why do the good suffer and the evil prosper? In many cultures, the medical system and the religious system are inextricably interwoven. Religious meaning is thereby connected with illness explanations.

In his analysis of religious systems, Weber noted the importance of **theodicies,** or religious explanations of meaning-threatening experiences, for sickness, suffering, and death ([1922] 1963: 138–150). Theodicies tell the individual or group that the experience is not meaningless but is rather part of a larger system of order, a religious cosmology (see also Berger, 1967: 24). Some successful theodicies are in fact nothing but assertions of order. A woman discussing her personal meaning crisis after her husband's premature death said, "I finally came to understand that it didn't matter whether *I* understood why he died when he did, but that God had a reason for it, and that was all that mattered." For this believer, knowing that an order exists behind events was more important than knowing what that order was (McGuire, 1982). Theodicies do not necessarily make the believer happy or even promise future happiness; they simply answer the question, Why do I suffer?

At the same time that Western societies are experiencing the increasing medicalization of authority, Western medicine is having difficulty dealing with sufferers' problems of meaning. Anthropologists remind us that however well Western medicine deals with the symptoms the sick person suffers, it fails to address the problem of "who sent the louse" (Comaroff, 1978). Illness etiologies in Western medicine typically deal with such proximate causes as germs, viruses, and genetic defects, but these notions are not adequate explanations for many people, because questions of meaning frequently beg for ultimate causes.

A foremost characteristic of the institution of medicine in modern Western societies is its differentiation from other institutions that provide meaning and belonging. **Institutional differentiation** is the process by which the various institutional spheres in society become separated from each other (see Parsons, 1966). For example, religious functions are focused in special religious institutions, which are separate from other institutions, such as the educational, political, and economic. The medical institution has limited itself to the cure of disease, as a biophysical entity, and to the physical tending of the diseased individual. Provision of meaning and belonging is treated as relatively unimportant for healing and relegated to the private-sphere institutions of family and religion. These private-sphere institutions are allowed, even encouraged, to handle the meaning problems of the sick, but only so long as their beliefs and actions do not interfere with the medical management of the disease (McGuire, 1985).

Just as the physical body is a potent symbol of one's selfhood, so too are experiences of suffering linked with one's identity. Practically, being unwell implies being disabled, in the sense of being made unable to do what one wants or needs to do; it implies reduced agency. It means losing some control (an especially important quality in this society), and it involves losing one's routines—the very patterns by which daily existence is ordered (Cassell, 1982; see also Comaroff, 1982).

Suffering is not connected with disease or pain in any precise causal or proportionate way. The pain of childbirth, for example, may be more severe than the pain of angina, but it generally causes less suffering because it is perceived as temporary and associated with a desired outcome. A disease may be incurable yet cause little suffering if it does little damage to the person's sense of self and ability to engage in everyday life. For example, a chronic fungal infection may cause less suffering than a temporary but disfiguring episode of Bell's palsy. Many people may seek help and healing less for disease itself than for suffering and affliction.

Cassell (1982: 639) has suggested that suffering poses difficulty for the biomedical system because it is "experienced by persons, not merely by bodies, and has its sources in challenges that threaten the intactness of the person as a complex social and psychological entity." He observed that medical personnel can unknowingly cause suffering when they do not validate the patient's affliction, and when they fail to acknowledge or deal with the personal meanings the patient attaches to the illness. Cassell (1982: 642) noted that "people suffer from what they have lost of themselves in relation to the world of objects, events and relationships." One woman still suffered greatly from a hysterectomy she had undergone six years earlier. As she explained, "It meant losing a huge part of my future." Unmarried, childless, and only 29 years old, she lost hopes and dreams for the future. She expressed enormous anger at the insensitivity of physicians and hospital staff who had treated her "like an ungrateful child, crying over spilt milk" (quoted in McGuire, 1988). The medical personnel, even if thoroughly well intentioned, probably felt their sole duty was the correct treatment of her specific uterine problem; the woman's suffering was not their problem, nor relevant to their tasks.

Whether brought on by a physical problem or not, affliction often results from a threat to the *coherence* of a person's world. As noted in Chapter 4, a sense of coherence itself is related to health and healing. People suffer from a loss of connectedness—links with loved ones, valued social roles, and groups that are important to them. As Chapter 7 shows, the illness experience often involves such losses. In the face of affliction, people seek meaning and order to address this essential coherence (Cassell, 1982; see also Antonovsky, 1984).

SUMMARY

Sickness is not merely the condition of an individual, but is also related to the larger social order. It is connected with moral issues and the imputation of responsibility for deviance from social norms. Society deals with such deviance through social control mechanisms, including the sick role. Sick role expectations, however, vary historically and cross culturally. The discrepancies between the ideal image of the sick role (based on certain forms of acute illness) and chronic and other nonacute conditions result in ambiguous expectations for those whom society defines as sick. The medicalization of deviance and the social stigma of illness highlight the social control functions of medicine, which are yet another connection between power and health. The medical profession has successfully asserted primacy in the defining deviance and the corollary function of certifying deviance, thereby becoming a primary moral authority in modern societies.

A related issue is the problem of meaning created by illness, suffering, and death. Because of the importance of the human body as a natural symbol, bodily control and healing practices reflect social relationships and concerns. The problems of meaning brought on by illness are particularly difficult in modern Western medical settings, due to the differentiation of medical institutions from meaning-providing institutions such as religion and family. The biomedical model, with its nearly exclusive focus on physical conditions, does not deal adequately with suffering and the subjective experience of affliction.

EXPERIENCING CHRONIC ILLNESS, PAIN, AND DISABILITY

❋ ❋

"Any person reading the words on this page is at best momentarily able-bodied. But nearly everyone reading them will, at some point, suffer from one or more chronic diseases and be disabled, temporarily or permanently, for a significant part of their lives."

Source: Irving Zola, *Missing Pieces: A Chronicle of Living with a Disability.* Philadelphia: Temple University Press, 1982, p. 242.

Illness, pain, and disability are profoundly human experiences that call into question "normal" expectations about our bodies and capacities. We tend to take the relationship between our bodies and our selves for granted, especially when illness, pain, and disability are not part of our life. Indeed, we are not likely to think about our bodies or be particularly conscious of many bodily sensations. In health, we expect our bodies to be able to function and to sustain a presentation of our selves as normal, reliable participants in social interaction (Dingwall, 2001: 99). But *all* of us will be disabled, sick, or in pain for some or much of our lives.

How does the ongoing experience of chronic pain or disability change that taken-for-granted set of "normal" expectations? Box 7.1 describes one woman's experience.

ILLNESS AND SELF

Although even the most minor illness can be problematic for the sufferer, we emphasize those illnesses most likely to have a strong effect on the person's identity and sense of self. Most everyday illnesses are not profoundly disruptive, although they too remind the sufferer of personal limits and dependencies. Many accidents wounding the body and many acute illnesses, although temporarily very discomforting or even seriously threatening, do not damage the ill person's sense of self. If I suffer acute pneumonia, the condition may be life threatening and require dramatic medical intervention—hospitalization, antibiotics, and intense nursing care—but I emerge to retain my essential relationships and identity. Other illnesses, however, are deeply disruptive, threatening the ill person's important relationships and very sense of self (Bury, 1991; Kelly and Field, 1996; Radley, 1994).

The experience of illness, even if only temporary, reminds us of our limitations, of our dependencies—present and potential—and of our ultimate mortality. When ill, our bodies inform us that they cannot always be counted on to be able for what we want them to do. Because our very sense of who we are and our important social relationships are intimately connected with our bodies and their routine functioning, being ill is disruptive and disordering. We identify our selves with our bodies, as evidenced by one physician's introspective account of his own accident and gradual recovery. He exclaimed, "What seemed, at first, to be no more than a local peripheral breakage and breakdown now showed itself in a different, and quite terrible, light—as a breakdown of memory, of thinking, of will—*not just a lesion in my muscle, but a lesion in me*" (Sacks, 1984: 67).

Thus, the illness experience is much more than a biophysical event; it has far-reaching social, emotional, moral, and spiritual implications. Kleinman's (1978, 1988) distinction between disease and illness is useful. According to his definitions, **disease** refers to the biophysical condition—the problem as seen from the biomedical practitioner's perspective. The physician transforms the patient's and the family's expressions of illness into terms that fit the theoretical models of disease. By contrast, **illness** refers to "how the sick person and the members of the

BOX 7.1

One Voice on Disability

I have an "invisible" disability. Judging from the surprised reactions when I explain my problem ("but you look fine"), I appear healthy, vigorous and energetic. Yet I am nonetheless "disabled" because of a common invisible disability, chronic low back pain.

The problem began in my early twenties, resulting in two spinal disk surgeries, compounded when I was hit by a car several years later. I did not work for almost 15 years, was in bed for extended periods, and was repeatedly hospitalized.

My day is punctuated by pauses and breaks, not flowing in a smooth stream. I can't sustain activity from when I wake up until bedtime, but only for eight or nine hours. I must build in lying down periods, and go straight home from work. Sitting and standing are only tolerated for limited periods, continuously alternating positions. There is constant planning, mapping out the next step, anticipating likely consequences if I "deviate" from the constraints of a rhythm of sitting/standing/lying down that has allowed me to manage the pain, to function and to work. I have a constant fear of the "unexpected." If I can't sit/stand/rest as needed and planned, this can trigger incapacitating pain, lasting days, weeks or months. If I continue activity while in pain, I "pay" for it with relapses and flare-ups. There is little room for slack or spontaneity. My day revolves around back pain and is compartmentalized: sit/stand/rest. A preset inner alarm monitors my activity so I can continue to function. My invisible disability has determined the contours of my life, career choice, and social life.

My workday as a teacher presents endless difficulties. I partly chose teaching as a career as it allows some flexibility in sitting and standing, and I teach on a modified schedule.

"But I see you are able to sit. Why can't you type your own reports?" But typing involves prolonged, lengthy sitting. The fact that sitting time must be planned and restricted is not visible to others at work. If I "have" to sit for extended periods, I eat dinner lying down.

My social life with friends is affected by these kinds of limits. I cannot go for *both* a dinner and a movie, because it involves extended sitting. Sometimes I stand during the movie, but it's often uncomfortable and not enjoyable.

"Lets go out after work." "No, I can't." I am on my feet from 6:30 a.m. when I wake up; I have to go straight home, lie down, before I can resume activity.

I love to travel, a new found life after years of confinements. But travel and airports pose obstacles, and have sometimes ended in unpleasant incidents. I am unable to lift my luggage (and I travel *very* light) from my rolling cart to the x-ray security trolley. Some airport staff have refused to assist. I have been asked mockingly, "Are you an invalid?"

I cannot sit through the long hours of trans- or intercontinental airline flights. I place myself so as not to interfere with anyone's movement, standing only when the seatbelt sign is off. "You can't keep standing there. You shouldn't fly, you shouldn't travel."

An "outsider's" lens through which an invisible disability is viewed is a snapshot, a still life, frozen in time, out of context, not seeing the flow of the movie, the before and after. Unseen are the planning, the calculating, the preparation for activity, and the physical consequences of missteps, which may make me immobilized, limping, unable to stand straight. "But you look so healthy. Surely you can. . . ."

Miriam Fisher, Learning Disabilities Specialist

family or wider social network perceive, live with, and respond to symptoms and disability" (Kleinman, 1988: 3–6).

Because doctors of Western medicine have been trained to focus almost exclusively on disease, they have difficulty dealing with the illness experience (Kleinman, 1978). With the rise of scientific biomedicine, the importance of the patient's experience has declined. The biomedical model views disease as located in the body, separated from the individual and the contexts in which each lives. This model considers disease as something to be understood only by experts, with the patient reduced to a passive informant (Bury, 2001).

Loss is one factor that can make an illness experience profoundly disruptive. People actively grieve because the loss of body parts (for example, amputation of an arm) or functions (such as partial blindness) represent loss of integrity–the wholeness of the person (Cassell, 1982). People suffer not only from the loss of present capacities and roles, but also from feeling robbed of their future: the teenager who has paraplegia after a car accident, the middle-aged lawyer who loses her eyesight, the elderly musician whose arthritis makes playing a beloved instrument impossible. One woman with breast cancer said, "The loss of being able to dream for the future is the most significant effect of cancer. This makes me feel like I'm left out and on a separate track from others" (quoted in Fife, 1994: 313).

Chronic illness and pain in particular force the sufferer to come to new terms with the experience of time. Sometimes a life-threatening acute illness or a serious accident has such impact, but an acute condition is–by definition–temporary. Chronic illness, by contrast, often leads to a radical reassessment, in light of changed and yet-changing capacities, of one's self in relationship to one's past and future. The experience of chronic illness thus involves both a sense of loss and a heightened self-consciousness (Charmaz, 1987, 1991). Chronic illness often demands complex strategies for managing symptoms. Adhering to drug regimens must be balanced against the side effects of drugs; symptoms may be concealed from other people; life must be scheduled around symptom flare-ups or to avoid flare-ups (Bury, 1991). These strategies break up taken-for-granted rhythms and activities of daily life and heighten self-consciousness.

Illness is especially damaging to the self when it is experienced as overwhelming, unpredictable, and uncontrollable because it paralyzes the person's ability to manage life, to plan, and to act. Enormous attention must be given not merely to actual crisis periods in the illness but also to minute, mundane worries such as these: Can I visit my friend's apartment without having an asthma attack? Can I make it to the bathroom quickly enough? If I attempt sexual intercourse, will my back pain flare up? Do I risk a heart attack if I take on this interesting project at work? (see, for example, Kleinman, 1988: 44). Unpredictability and uncontrollability result in a disjunction between the person and the body; the functioning that was once taken for granted is gone, and the person in effect feels, "I cannot count on my body. *It* fails *me.*" The body becomes an "other"–at best an unpredictable ally.

Illness that results in ongoing social marginality is also particularly damaging to the self. Much of our web of social relationships is predicated on the assumptions that members will be able to reciprocate, that one member will not be utterly dependent on others, and that all give and receive. Some illnesses undermine the assumption of reciprocity and thus make social relationships precarious. Losing independence is threatening to one's sense of self not just because of pride in self-sufficiency (a related value in our culture), but more because it impairs one's ability to participate as an equal in important social relationships. Valued friendships and social roles become strained or lost altogether. Often the individual lives in a deliberately collapsed world because the larger world becomes unmanageable or threatening. One woman commented,

> What is really so awful is that illness, I believe, really makes you very lonely. . . . One is really out of the world. *When there is illness one is, and one stays, alone.* It's very hard to get help. . . . It destroys what one would like to do, it isolates you. . . . If I got into very poor health, I could no longer take care of them as I do. . . . I would be cut off from my family, life would have to be organized without me, I would not play the role that I play now. I believe that one who is sick is outside of normal life. (quoted in Herzlich and Pierret, 1987: 178)

Pain and treatment often become a focus for the chronically ill, forcing them to withdraw into themselves. Lack of access to everyday activities also fosters isolation. Others, unable to deal with chronic problems, socially withdraw, and thus a spiral of increasing isolation is set into motion: The less one can or wants to do, the less one socializes; but the less one socializes, the more others withdraw, and in turn the more the person with a chronic illness withdraws (Radley, 1994). One man with severe rheumatoid arthritis said,

> Now the only place I go now is down to the local club. Everybody knows me sort of thing. They might say it's a shame for him, but nobody bothers me, they accept me as I am. But if I go anywhere else . . . people are embarrassed. People say "bloody hell, is that . . . ? Dear me, what's the matter with him?" And they try not to catch your eye, if you will. People tend to stay away from you. I don't know, they just don't want to be involved. You tend to do the same then. (quoted in Bury, 1982: 176)

All the more marginalizing are illness experiences involving stigma, which by definition have the potential to discredit the self that the individual is trying to present to others. For example, one young woman had undergone a colostomy in which a large part of her colon was surgically removed, necessitating the perpetual wearing and cleaning of a device that collected and held the contents of her bowels. She exclaimed,

> I feel so embarrassed by this—this thing. It seems so unnatural, so dirty. I can't get used to the smell to it. I'm scared of soiling myself. Then I'd be so ashamed I couldn't look at anyone else. . . . Who would want a wife like this? How can I go out and not

feel unable to look people in the eyes and tell them the truth? Once I do, who would want to develop a friendship, I mean a close one? How can I even consider showing my body to someone else, having sex? (quoted in Kleinman, 1988: 163)

Because control is so strongly valued in our culture, loss of control is especially problematic. People experience an assault on their sense of self when their illnesses involve losses of control, such as incontinence, loss of bowel control, flatulence, seizures, stumbling and falling, tics and tremors, and drooling. We rely on relative control of our bodies to present ourselves in socially valued ways (Goffman, 1963), but chronic illness and disability disrupt that control (Radley, 1994; Schneider and Conrad, 1983). Furthermore, in a culture in which productivity, vigor, beauty, and youth are very important values, disability and aging are especially threatening. Disability and chronic illness may remind people of their vulnerability (Livneh, 1991; Murphy, 1987). Thus, certain chronic illnesses and disabilities are especially likely to threaten the individual's sense of self and connectedness with others.

There may be gender differences in response to chronic illness and disability. Men whose identities are invested in being autonomous, independent, dominant, problem solvers, and having personal power may experience narrow options for preserving their sense of self and social relationships in the face of chronic illness. Women can be more flexible and resourceful (Charmaz, 1995).

Even with nonfatal chronic illnesses, such as arthritis, the illness experience requires individuals, families, and personal networks continually to confront problems of uncertainty, dependency, and understanding. It also necessitates the negotiation of new role relationships with others. Sometimes a chronic illness results in outright conflict or rejection (Bury, 1988). A retired lawyer described the effects of his wife's ten years of decline with Alzheimer's disease:

> Our children come and they cry. And I cry. We reminisce about old times. We try to recall what Anna was like before this happened. But I can see it wears them out just being here for a day or two. They've got their own troubles. I can't ask them to help out any more than they do already. Me? It's made a different person out of me. I expect you wouldn't have recognized me if you had met me ten years ago. I feel at least ten years older than I am. I'm afraid what will happen if I go first. I haven't had a half hour free of worry and hurt for ten years. This illness didn't just destroy Anna's mind, it has killed something in me, in the family, too. If anyone asks about Alzheimer's, tell them it is a disease of the whole family. (quoted in Kleinman, 1988: 183)

Illness is not experienced merely by the individual in whose body the symptoms are located; often the family and other close members of the sufferer's social network also feel the disruptiveness of illness. For example, the husband of a woman with cancer said,

> I keep saying we felt, like I guess I feel like this is my disease, too. That's because it's so drastic. It's a fight that she has to undertake, so it's partly mine, too. It's a

psychological thing, the helplessness for the husband. This is not just her disease, it is my disease, too. (quoted in Wilson, 1991)

Chronic illness is, by definition, ongoing, recurrent, and often degenerative. Chronic illnesses and pain pose special problems that stable, predictable conditions (such as paraplegia caused by an accidental fall) do not (Pinder, 1995). Living with chronic illness requires coping with the very uncertainty of the course of the illness itself (Royer, 1995). People with disabilities or chronic illnesses in our society face a number of common problems regarding the social organization of their environments, the attitudes of others, and their sense of self.

The human response to illness is to give it meaning, to interpret it, to reorder the disordering experience. To make sense of what is happening to us, we draw on socially available categories from a large cultural repertoire and from personal and family stories and meanings absorbed from our particular ethnic and religious backgrounds (see Fife, 1994). In the case of minor illnesses, the interpretations might include our underlying definitions of health and illness, and our notions about why we got sick and how to get well. Seriously disruptive illnesses are likely to evoke further interpretations about the meaning of life, moral responsibility, suffering, relationships, and death.

PAIN AND ITS PSYCHOSOCIAL DIMENSIONS

The sociocultural and psychological dimensions of pain demonstrate how profoundly greater the illness experience is compared to its mere biophysical aspect. Because the medical model does not adequately encompass these dimensions, it often fails to meet the needs of pain sufferers. Pain is a form of biofeedback essential to our survival. Occasionally someone is born without the capacity to feel pain. In one such case, the person was deformed by the age of 25 because he had severely burned his hand and suffered other injuries without feeling them. Further, the ulceration and wearing down of bodily extremities characteristic of leprosy were once thought to be symptoms of the disease, until it was discovered that they were produced by its deadening of the victim's ability to feel pain (Neal, 1978: 47–50). Although pain is an essential warning system for the body, it can also be a scourge and a terrible existential reality, a source of fear and anxiety that in some cases becomes all-consuming and overwhelming.

Pain is the symptom that people report most frequently when they see a doctor. Musculoskeletal problems (lower back pain, joint pain, or arthritis, for example) are the leading causes of disability among people in their working years; back pain is second only to respiratory problems as a reason for missing work (Osterweis et al., 1987). Approximately 7 million Americans have serious back problems (Bogin, 1982). A nationwide sample of 1,254 adults revealed that about 75 percent of Americans suffer from occasional headaches and more than 50 percent from back and muscular pain. People who reported high levels of stress also reported high levels of all kinds of pain (Schmeck, 1985). Pain seems to be a very individual and personal matter. As a physical sensation, it does not seem to be subject to socio-cultural influences, yet there are many ways in which the private world of pain interacts with the sociocultural world.

The clinical reality of pain is complex, however, and involves three compo-nents: a person's actual *sensation of pain;* a person's *tolerance threshold for pain;* and a person's *expression of pain.* Pain is unique as a medical phenomenon because its mea-surement relies on individuals' accounts of what they are feeling as well as the doctors' observations of pain-related behavior. The doctor can observe a person's gait or flex limbs to see if pain is inhibiting movement, but all indicators are based on what the patient says or does. In other words, pain measurement depends on patients' intended or unintended expressions of the pain they are feeling. Although of limited reliability, several laboratory techniques (such as thermography and positron emission tomography, or PET, scans) attempt to measure organic signs of pain without relying on patients' reports, but these are only indirect measures of the manifestations of pain, such as the degree of sympathetic nervous system ac-tivity (Osterweis et al., 1987: 141–142). Thus, clinicians must rely heavily on the individual sufferers to describe or show what they feel.

Pain Experience and Tolerance: Biosocial Aspects

Pain is obviously a **sensation;** a cut finger produces a "simple" physical sen-sation. Pain generally involves more than simply a physical sensation, however, because it is imbued with meaning. For some ballet students or athletes, the pain that comes with a workout is "good pain," or a normal, acceptable consequence of well-done exercise, whereas a sharp, sudden new pain of unknown origin would signal that something fundamental has gone wrong. One doctor observed that the wounded soldiers he was treating during World War II complained of less pain and requested less pain medication than civilians who had suffered equally serious wounds. The soldiers, for whom the wounds meant leaving the battlefield and further danger of death, apparently experienced and tolerated pain differently (Beecher, 1956).

Although **pain experience** obviously involves physical sensations, it is often more than just sensations. As something that accompanies disease or a serious in-jury, pain takes on meaning as a form of suffering. "People in pain report suffering from pain when they feel out of control—when the pain is overwhelming, when the source of pain is unknown, when the meaning of the pain is dire or when the pain is chronic" (Cassell, 1982: 641). In short, when pain threatens one's integrity as a person and one's physical existence, it becomes suffering (Cassell, 1982). These negative meanings of pain may in turn amplify the physical sensations the person experiences (Kleinman, 1988).

In Chapter 4, we argued that the mind and the body should be seen as an interrelated whole. Placebos, for example, do not merely relieve pain "in the mind" but can also generate physical changes by stimulating the release of pain-relieving endorphins. The spinal-gate control theory of pain suggests another mind-body-society thoroughfare by proposing that activity in the nervous system affects the opening and closing of gates in the spinal cord that modulates the flow of pain messages. Most theories of pain hold that a specific pain stimulus produces an input in the form of a pain message that travels upward along the spinal cord to a pain center in the brain, where an alarm is set off. In contrast, the spinal-gate control theory argues that pain messages from the frontal cortex (a higher brain center), from the limbic system (a midbrain area that controls emotions), and from other parts of the body can affect the opening and closing of these spinal gates, and thus modify incoming pain messages (Melzack and Wall, 1983).

The experience of pain is more than an incoming sensation, however, because it is affected by emotional states and higher-order cognitive mental functions (Bendelow, 1993; Osterweis et al., 1987). Indeed, pain does have important biopsychosocial and cultural dimensions (Bates, 1987; Freund, 1982). There may be important variations in the *pain experience*–by sex, ethnicity, and race. But, if these variations *do* exist, are they biological, cultural, or biocultural? (Bates, 1987; Overfield, 1985).

Sociocultural Variations in Pain Expression

Pain expression refers to how a person shows and behaviorally responds to pain. Pain expression is clearly influenced by sociocultural factors. Cultures in which emotional control is valued encourage stoicism about pain. "Big boys don't cry!" reveals a cultural expectation that adult males should repress the expression of pain. The ability to control the social presentation of pain even under conditions that inflict a great deal of pain may be a sign of one's moral status (that is, one's "manhood," moral uprightness, or reliability). An elder of the Kuranko society of Sierra Leone in Africa, for example, describes the circumcision of an adolescent going through a puberty rite:

> Even when they are cutting the foreskin you must not flinch. You have to stand stone still. You must not make a sound from the mouth. Better to die than to wince or blink or cry out. (quoted in Jackson, 1983)

In the Kuranko society, control over pain expression symbolizes the ability to assume an adult male role. Painful procedures such as tatooing and scarification are endured by adolescents partly because the expression of pain is negatively sanctioned, and perhaps because the meaning and honor of the procedure affects the experience of pain itself. Many athletes endure pain that most other people would not. On the whole, however, our culture teaches that pain can and should be avoided, and we tend to medicate it extensively (Bogin, 1982; Kleinman, 1988).

Under some situations, persons suffer excruciating pain, yet must quickly learn to manage their expression in order not to threaten a group's morale or its ability to function. Medical settings are an excellent example of this. Were one to scream hysterically in a dentist's chair, what influence would this have on waiting patients, especially small children? In hospitals the treatment for severe burns, which includes scrubbing the wounds, scraping away dead tissue, and applying new dressings and medication, inflicts a lot of pain in addition to the extreme pain of the burns themselves. However, burn victims are socialized into enduring the pain by the "coaching" of staff as well as of other patients who have been through similar experiences (Fagerhaugh and Strauss, 1977).

Responses to other people's pain expressions are influenced by cultural assumptions about what those expressions mean. An African woman's response to stomach pain due to infection is reasonable given her fears about infertility, a source of shame in her culture. The same woman, however, may handle the pain of childbirth without complaints (Susser et al., 1985: 136). One study of burn patients found Samoans (in contrast to, for instance, American burn patients) were calmer, more "stoic," accepting of the situation, and less complaining (Ablon, 1986). Zborowski (1952) found that because Italians expressed their pain so dramatically, non-Italian doctors tended to question the credibility of their Italian patients, interpreting their problems as "psychiatric." Such differences in the social and cultural backgrounds of doctor and patient can thus lead to very different interpretations of pain. One study reported the following:

> [T]he pain of women was treated later and less directly than the pain of men. Women suffered longer before being referred to the Pain Unit. They were less often treated with procedures specifically intended to cure the pain. The men in a shorter period since pain onset were operated upon twice as often as the women. Paradoxically, women reported twice as many surgical procedures unrelated to pain. (Lack, 1982: 62)

Women were also given more minor tranquilizers, antidepressants, and analgesics, and fewer narcotics than men. This difference implies that the doctors took women's pain less seriously, interpreting it as of psychological origin; however, they accepted men's pain as "real" and prescribed painkillers. Was this difference due to variation in how men and women showed pain, or because of how male doctors interpreted women's presentations of pain? Other studies (such as Bendelow, 1993) suggest that health workers were more likely to believe that women's pain was psychogenic. For instance, in a study of how doctors evaluate patients' presenting symptoms of chest pain (an important symptom of coronary heart disease), women's symptoms were more likely than men's to be treated as psychogenic and not as evidence of heart troubles (Emslie et al., 2001).

The visibility of the source of pain is another significant factor in determining how seriously people take another's pain symptoms. It is often hard to see the cause of pain. Patients with chronic back pain may, for example, learn to conceal signs of pain, such as masking a limp caused by sciatic nerve pain. Because they look healthy, their pain may not always be taken seriously (Fagerhaugh and Strauss, 1977). By contrast, a bloody gash—even on a part of the body with relatively little nerve sensitivity—is taken seriously as a source of pain.

Chronic Pain

Approximately 17 percent of U.S. adults have suffered chronic pain lasting at least six months (Kolata, 1994). By definition, chronic pain is recurring or ongoing. It is not simply continuous but is experienced qualitatively differently from acute pain episodes. Because it is ongoing, chronic pain often has profound implications for a sufferer's life and very identity. People with chronic pain face continuing problems in symptom management (Strauss, 1975). How does one deal with pain and live life as normally as possible? People in chronic pain may not be able to tolerate regular employment, to follow schedules, or even to meet the demands of home life. Chronic pain is not always constant, but is often intermittent and unpredictable, flaring up unexpectedly (Bogin, 1982). Each day sufferers must manage a host of problems associated with activities that are taken for granted by others: They must pace their activities in order to tolerate or not aggravate the pain, and they must balance the undesired side effects of medication against the benefits of pain reduction.

Chronic pain also poses basic problems for the sufferer's sense of self. One person explained,

> Our personalities have been shaken to the core, and what we most counted on—our close relationships, our marriages, our jobs—may well have fallen by the wayside. Our whole sense of life has radically changed since pain became a part of it, yet no one seems to understand our listlessness, our loss of hope, our lack of optimism. Other people can't see our pain, so how can they imagine what it's done to us? Only someone who has lived with chronic pain knows how insidious the process is. (Bogin, 1982: 4)

Acute pain goes away and does not become an ongoing, major focus of everyday existence. Chronic pain, by contrast, is a "somatic reminder that things are not right and may never be right. This reminder, phenomenally situated in one's own body, is inescapable" (Hilbert, 1984: 370; see also Good, 1994). The body as subjectively experienced is transformed into an object with pain. One "moment one is one's body, the next one has a body" (Bergsma, 1982: 111). Chronic pain demands constant attention and can become all-consuming. Indeed, it can alter one's consciousness of the world, changing one's sense of time and state of alertness. Chronic pain alters one's relationship with one's own body and bodily experience; "it" cannot be trusted and is experienced as acting unpredictably (Good, 1994). The phenomenon of pain highlights how inextricably mind and body are meshed; it is simultaneously sensation and emotion (Jackson, 1994; see also Bendelow and Williams, 1995).

People in chronic pain often face invalidating responses from others, particularly if their pain is not believable or if an organic basis of pain is not apparent. One sufferer stated that she had considered unneeded surgery so she would have a scar to show (Hilbert, 1984: 373). Another believed his several surgical treatments had worsened the pain but at least gave him scars that symbolized the physical reality of the pain (Kleinman, 1988: 68). Core values in American culture may contribute to the invalidation experienced by chronic pain sufferers. Some anthropologists (Good et al., 1992: 205), writing on chronic pain, observed,

> A number of our subjects complained of something akin to a North American *tyranny of health*. The dominant images in the popular culture extol physical vitality and deny anything short of robust health. Blemishes, illnesses that cannot be rapidly cured, and especially grave infirmities that suggest disability or death are banished from everyday life. A strong will, we are told, can influence the body, so infirmity is often associated with a lack of individual strength. The chronically ill feel great discomfit in this ethos. They are discredited as burdensome, anomalous, and, in some unspoken but definite way, responsible for their condition. Suffering is accorded no positive value. . . . Thus, the chronically ill—especially those with conditions that are at the borderline of respectability—feel that they are culturally illegitimate, unaccepted in the wider society.

Invalidating responses often come from doctors (Hilbert, 1984: 368), particularly when they are frustrated by their inability to treat effectively or find an organic cause for the pain (Bogin, 1982; Kleinman, 1988). Chronic pain challenges doctors' sense of competence and control. More significantly, chronic pain raises issues about mind-body relationships that threaten sharp distinctions between "real" versus "imagined," "psychological" versus "physical" pain (Good, 1994; Williams and Bendelow, 1996). "Physical" experiences of pain may be influenced by "perturbed" neuroendocrinological rhythms (Weiner, 1992). Physicians are unlikely to look for those factors and, given their assumptions about the nature of pain, would not "notice" them.

Invalidation of the reality of the experience of pain is particularly disconcerting because sufferers are being told that what their bodies are telling them is not real. Because our bodies and physical sensations are primary sources of our sense of reality, this invalidation is especially devastating (Kleinman, 1992; Ware, 1992). Chronic pain sufferers find themselves in a bind. On the one hand, concealing signs of their pain reduces the likelihood that their claims to being in pain will be taken seriously. On the other hand, persons who regularly display and dramatize their pain risk wearing down other people's sympathy, placing a strain on their social support networks.

Somatization

In *all* cultures, the body serves as a means of expressing and communicating cultural, as well as personal, messages. No tidy distinction exists, however, between physical and emotional pain (see Jackson, 1994); a person in pain or distress may be simultaneously expressing and experiencing *both* physical and emotional pain inseparably. Like language, pain and illness are *idioms* in which people sometimes "encode" their distress (Good, 1977; see also Blair, 1993). For example, a young adult's parents may be stifling her autonomy, but to leave home means to alienate them and to face an uncertain, perhaps hostile, existence away from home. Pain may be both a way of delaying the difficult decision and a means of communicating something about the conflicts she is experiencing (Kleinman, 1988).

Somatization is "the communication of personal and interpersonal problems in a physical idiom of distress and a pattern of behavior that emphasizes seeking of medical help" (Kleinman, 1988: 57). To understand pain as "somatization" does not mean it is inauthentic. Pain may be physical in origin but sustained and amplified by sociopsychological factors. Social distress may create the physiological changes that amplify existing pain or create an experience of pain (Kleinman, 1988). In her study of Mexican women's sickness and pain, Finkler (1994) refers to the damaging effects of women's distresses, social situation (especially gender roles), and cultural beliefs as "life's lesions." Kleinman (1995) reminds us that somatized pain, as well as psychological suffering such as depression, may be the traumatic products of political violence such as war or repression and oppressive cultural forms, for example, abusive family structures.

Each person's particular idiom of distress is drawn from a cultural repertoire. For example, in Iran "heart distress" is a meaningful expression linking an entire set of social concerns: infertility, attractiveness, sexual intercourse, pollution, and old age. Thus, when an Iranian complains of a "pressed heart," that complaint must be understood in terms of its cultural meanings (Good, 1977; see also Guarnaccia and Farias, 1988). Similarly, just as there are class and gender differences in how people encode their meanings in language, so too does somatized distress differ according to social class and gender (Blair, 1993).

Even when it has sociopsychological sources, however, pain is not simply "in the mind" but also is a bodily phenomenon.[1] Labeling an illness "psychosomatic" or "psychogenic" delegitimates people's real suffering. Because their pain is expressed in body idioms, it is too easily medicalized and, thereby, distorted or trivialized. For example, to label the suffering of a Salvadoran refugee as posttraumatic stress disorder is to isolate and euphemize the consequences of pervasive political violence (Kleinman, 1995, 1997; Kleinman and Kleinman, 1991; Kleinman et al., 1997).

DISABILITY: THE POLITICS OF IMPAIRMENT AND DIFFERENCE

One definition used in the United States considers disability to be "an inability to engage in gainful employment"; more broadly, it refers to a reduction of activity, a "restricted activity day" (Mausner and Bahn, 1985: 113). In 1997, 52.6 million

---

[1]Although pain always involves sociopsychological aspects, this should not detract from the reality of the physical aspects. A doctor who cannot discern organic sources of pain should not assume there are none; biomechanical causes, for example, that were not detectible by earlier technologies (for example, X-rays or myelograms) may appear through newer imaging technologies. Is it possible that painful social experiences at one point in one's life (for example, sexual abuse in childhood) may alter a person's physiological reactivity to pain later in life? Can socially distressing life circumstances increase pain sensitivity or amplify the painful effects of physical trauma? Perspectives such as Kleinman's (1988) that stress the biopsychosocial aspects of pain recognize the relationship between social life and pain, including the subjective reality of somatized pain.

Americans (19.7 percent of the population) had some level of disability, and 33 million (12.3 percent of the population) had a severe disability (*Ragged Edge,* 2001: 11). Fifteen percent (37.7 million people) of the noninstitutionalized U.S. population have a limitation of activity caused by chronic illness or impairment. The most prevalent sources of activity limitation are musculoskeletal impairments that affect walking, climbing, and lifting (La Plante, 1996). These figures suggest that disabilities are not as uncommon as many believe. Our perceptions are based partly on the fact that Western society, especially the United States, tends to deny and to segregate disability, old age, and death. Furthermore, the likelihood of having a disability is socially distributed, as are individual resources for coping with disability.

Categorizing people as disabled has implications for social policy, as Zola (1982: 242) pointed out:

> By trying to find strict measures of disability or focusing on "severe," "visible" handicaps we draw dividing lines and make distinctions where matters are very blurry and constantly changing. By agreeing that there are 20 million disabled or 36 million, or even that half the population are in some way affected by disability, we delude ourselves into thinking there is some finite, no matter how large, number of people.

Treating disability as a status obscures the fact that as more and more people live to very old ages, proportionately more people will have to deal with significant impairments (Williams and Busby, 2000). Being disabled is thus a normal condition of humanity, and categorizing people by disability status can create misleading distinctions. Such definitions are social and political constructions, as illustrated by the fact that the boundaries are historically shifting and cross-culturally variable (Brzuzy, 1997; Shakespeare, 1999).

What then is a disability? Disability can be defined from a biomedical perspective or as a social status. It may also be viewed from the perspective of the *social model,* an important approach in disability studies (especially in the United Kingdom). The social model emphasizes addressing disabling attitudes and social organizations of space, time, and practices (Freund, 2001). This approach contrasts with the biomedical model which emphasizes cure, rehabilitation, and the normalization of people with impairments, rather than changing people's disabling social and cultural contexts.

An **impairment** is the loss of some physiological or anatomical function, whereas a **disability** is the consequence of such an impairment, such as the inability to walk, climb stairs, or travel (Barton, 1996; Oliver, 1996). Many people with disabilities object to the term handicap because of its negative connotations, especially when it implies that the whole person is handicapped. We therefore speak of persons with disabilities rather than "disabled persons" (Zola, 1993). Although some people with chronic illnesses experience both impairment and disability, chronic illness does not inevitably lead to disability. For example, diabetes may interfere only minimally with some people's functioning. While some people with an impairment (for example, from an automobile accident) are not sick and object to being defined as such, nonetheless, many people with chronic illnesses share problems with those who have an impairment at birth or from an accident.

An impairment is relatively verifiable in "objective" medical terms, in degrees of reduced "normal" bodily functioning. Although impairment can be biomedically measured, there is still the important question: What is a normal body? "Impairment" is thus a socially constructed category which carries a negative connotation and primarily biomedical meanings. As such, it excludes variation and *differences* which while not impairments may nonetheless be disabling in particular contexts (Shakespeare, 1999). Being very tall or short, very small or large, for instance, can be disabling in a "one-size-fits-all" society.

Disability, thus, is not easily defined apart from the social and cultural context of impairment or differences. Disability is not a bodily or mental attribute but results from the interaction between person and environment: "Disability is something imposed on top of our impairments by the way we are unnecessarily isolated and excluded from full participation in society" (Oliver, 1996: 22). In a small Egyptian village, for example, trachoma (an infection that affects the eyelids) is widespread, but the "Western" standards of blindness do not apply to those who are afflicted. Instead, the social and cultural arrangements make it possible for many villagers with severely impaired vision to function without disability:

> Most visually impaired adults are illiterate, so they do not need signs to read. There are no street signs or house numbers to read in the hamlet. The structure of the village changes very slowly. If a new house is built every five years the visually impaired can learn to find their way around it. . . . Plowing, sowing seed and harvesting ripe produce do not require much vision. If there is some small task they are unable to do, their extended family does it for them. Thus, they do not perceive themselves as disabled. (quoted in Cockburn, 1988: 13)

There, this social organization of space and time keeps visual impairments from becoming disabilities; things change slowly and the pace of life is slower. Rather than view the sociomaterial arrangements of everyday life as simply "natural," we could interpret them as social constructions that favor some bodies but not others (Freund, 2001).

Whether an "objective" impairment or difference becomes a disability depends on the person's environment, expected daily activities, and the attitudes of others. For example, until the 1940s, many inhabitants of Martha's Vineyard (an island community in Massachusetts) were deaf. The whole community knew sign language, and hearing people used it even among themselves as a natural and ordinary form of communication. People with impaired hearing worked, married, and were not thought of as significantly different (Whyte and Ingstad, 1995). Impairment is universal, found among people in all societies; however, social and cultural responses and the "design" of social environments vary (Oliver, 1996). The sociological focus, therefore, is not on disabled people but on disabling attitudes, practices, and environments.

Disability and the Social Organization of Space and Time

The organization of the spaces in which people move and the time arrangements of their practices are related to the quality of life and health. Building codes, government ordinances, financial considerations, and many other factors structure the qualities of the buildings in which we work, live, and play (Hahn, 1988). Social and political considerations influence the quality and accessibility of transportation. Zola (1982: 208) described the inhospitable nature of many environments for a person wearing a leg brace:

> Chairs without arms to push myself up from; unpadded seats which all too quickly produce sores; showers and toilets without handrails to maintain my balance; surfaces too slippery to walk on; staircases without bannisters to help me hoist myself; buildings without ramps, making ascent exhausting if not dangerous; every curbstone a precipice; car, plane, and theatre seats too cramped for my braced leg; and trousers too narrow for my leg brace to pass through. With such trivia is my life plagued. Even though I am relatively well off, mobility is a daily challenge.

Imagine trying to walk about in a physical space designed only for those in wheelchairs. The doors would be too low, the floors would be too slippery for walking, and no chairs would be provided for sitting. People with physical impairments simply have more specialized or individual physical needs than those without impairments. The failure of social environments to account for individual rhythms and patterns for comfortable movement contributes to problems in health and the quality of life for all people, but to a greater degree for people with impairments.

Although technological advances have made it possible for many people with impairments to survive and potentially to function, such advances have not generally been applied to the design of public, work, and living environments. We live in human-made, artificial spaces that are not currently adapted to a wide spectrum of bodies but could be so modified. There have been some alternative movements toward "emancipatory architecture" (Imrie, 1998), based on designing freedom into our life spaces and structures. One U.S. architect with a disability advocated a movement in architecture toward "universal design." "Universal design" is a *technical* solution to designing the built environment such that it can be comfortably used by the widest possible range of bodies. It involves designing environments that are safe, aesthetic, comfortable, and usable, not only by full-grown, fit adults, but also by small children and elderly persons whose strength or range of motion may be reduced (Fleischer and Zames, 2001; Freund, 2001; Imrie, 1998). Although no environment can accommodate everyone's needs, "universally" designed spaces make it possible for people with a wider range of abilities to function independently. One example is a park built for accessibility, with its tennis courts, pool, and swings designed for use by people in wheelchairs (Brown, 1988).

There has been misplaced research emphasis on whether persons with chronic illness and impairment are malingering and on whether government social welfare benefits motivate people with disabilities not to work. Rather, research should examine how work and economic conditions themselves discourage people experiencing physical difficulties from maintaining their jobs. During World War II, people with disabilities who had been defined as unemployable were placed into full-time employment. The need for labor, *not* the impairment, defined employability (Oliver, 1996). For all workers during that time, there were lower rates of absenteeism, work-related accidents, and turnover, and higher rates of production. After the war, workers with disabilities were replaced by returning "able-bodied" veterans (Struck, 1981: 26). The nature of the job, such as the pace of work and the physical design of the workplace, is an important determinant of work disability (Yelin, 1986). Shorter, more flexible work schedules, opportunities for breaks, and general social-temporal arrangements that accommodate slower or differently paced rhythms would allow individuals with impairments to function more effectively.

People with chronic impairments do not usually challenge disabling time limitations and pressures. They do not generally question the arrangements of work and living spaces in which they must function; rather, they typically assume such arrangements to be natural and given (Charmaz, 1983). People come to believe that their inability to squeeze their bodies and rhythms of movement into inadequate social-spatial arrangements are signs of their *personal* inadequacy. Disabling environments and attitudes thus contribute to a loss of sense of self and to suffering among those who have chronic physical impairments (Charmaz, 1991).

Disabling Attitudes and Sense of Self

Our society often places people who violate somatic norms into institutions or segregates them behind the scenes of everyday life (Baird, 1992). One woman with multiple sclerosis commented,

> I once asked a local advertiser why he didn't include disabled people in his spots. His response seemed direct enough. "We don't want to give people the idea that our product is just for the handicapped," he said. . . . If you saw my blind niece ordering a Coke, would you switch to Pepsi lest you be struck sightless? No, I think the advertiser's excuse masked a deeper and more anxious rationale: to depict disabled people in the ordinary activities of daily life is to admit that there is something ordinary about disability itself, that it might enter anybody's life. If it is effaced completely or at least isolated as a separate "problem," so that it remains at a safe distance from other human issues, then the viewer won't feel threatened by her or his own physical vulnerability. (Mairs, 1987: C2)

The stigmatizing opinions of others have a strong impact on one's sense of self. A stigma is a deeply discrediting attribute that, when visible, can brand a person as less than human, as pitiable, horrible, and publicly discreditable. The degree to which an attribute is stigmatizing depends on its sociohistorical context and the status of the person who possesses such an attribute:

> Conjure in your mind a military man with an eye patch. Is there not something romantic and heroic about the injury? Doesn't it suggest a dark and complex past, a will of uncommon strength, perhaps a capability for just enough brutality to add a trace of virile unpredictability to the man? Now replace the image of the mysterious man who wears an eye patch with the image of a 7-year-old girl who wears one. For most people, something strange happens. The romance and mystery disappear; what we see is a handicapped child. There is something sad and even pitiful about her; we fear for her future and worry about her present. We think: this poor kid is going to have a hard time growing up and making it in this world. (Gliedman and Roth, 1980: 29)

In all societies, certain deviations from somatic norms are considered stigmatizing, but there are no inherently stigmatizing attributes. Rather, stigma is a social construction that depends on person and context (Susman, 1993).

In our society, those with "severe" impairments are sometimes viewed as "visually repulsive; helpless; pathetic; dependent; too independent; plucky, brave and courageous; bitter with chips on our shoulders; evil (the 'twisted mind in a twisted body'); mentally retarded; endowed with mystical powers and much else" (Sutherland, 1981: 58). People with disabilities may be targets of hate crimes. One woman recalled a man who grabbed her cane, threw it down an escalator, spat on her, and told her "move, blind lady ... you people belong in concentration camps" (cited in Wolfe, 1995). Given the cultural obsession with health and bodily control, people with disabilities may be experienced as threatening (Norden, 1995; Susman, 1993). Some of these attitudes are changing. The mass media, however, still perpetuate stereotypes that associate disability with evil and criminality (recall Frankenstein's hunchbacked assistant), a loss of self-control, an attempt to compensate for their impairment, and a tendency to either be asexual or deviantly sexual (Longmore, 1987; Shakespeare, 1996).

Media images project some heroic role models: the blind skier, the one-legged pitcher who made it to the major leagues, and Helen Keller and her many achievements.[2] These examples show people's ability to transcend the most limiting of conditions, and in that respect they are inspiring. They may, however, imply another message: "that if a Franklin Delano Roosevelt and a Wilma Rudolph could *overcome* their handicap, so could and should all the disabled. And if we fail, it is our problem, our personality, our weakness" (Zola, 1982: 204–205). Many media success stories similarly communicate a message in tune with the American ethos of rugged individualism and responsibility for oneself. This imagery, however, deflects from an understanding of the mundane problems faced by those with impairments and the many barriers that most humans simply cannot overcome.

---

[2] Very few people know that Helen Keller was displayed for a while as an exhibit, like the Elephant Man, in a vaudeville show.

Sexual expression is an important source of pleasure, tension release, and sense of self. Until recently, however, the prevalent attitude, even among many professionals working with people with disabilities, was to deny or avoid recognition of their sexuality (Lonsdale, 1990). The deviation of persons with disabilities from somatic norms often arouses an aesthetic anxiety in others, particularly in Western societies, which put a high premium on "supernormal standards of bodily perfection" (Baird, 1992; Hahn, 1994). Media-driven standards of sexual attractiveness, particularly for women, result in even greater disadvantages for people whose bodies deviate from the ideal (Sutherland, 1987: 27). In one Swedish experiment counselors acted as sex surrogates with their clients who had disabilities; the experiment was stopped, however, because the counselors began to enjoy their contacts (Zola, 1982). The fear that "deviant" bodies may be "deviant" only in the eyes of the beholder made this experiment a threat. Some societies have begun to accept sexual pleasure as a *right* for the disabled. In 1992, a government agency in the Netherlands ruled that a municipality must pay a person with a disability a monthly stipend to cover the services of a sex surrogate (Stalk, 1992).

People with disabilities also face special problems in the management of such emotions as anger. The impairment itself may inhibit anger expression. Being physically weak or on crutches may make the direct, motoric, dramatic expression of emotions difficult. Furthermore, disabling attitudes and environments force people into a dependency beyond the biological consequences of their impairments.

People with disabilities are also socialized out of their anger. They are expected to be grateful for what help they receive and cannot "afford" the luxury of overt anger expression for fear of risking the alienation of the people on whom they depend (Zola, 1982). Like fat people, people with disabilities are expected to tolerate their situation quietly and to be cheerful and jolly (Charmaz, 1991: 201). When people regularly and vocally respond to frustrating or disempowering conditions, they further risk having their anger treated as a by-product of their impairment rather than as an appropriate response to their social environment or living conditions. The docudrama "Captives of Care" depicted a resident of an institution who was angry with the staff for the arbitrary limits imposed by institutional life. In one encounter, he lashed out at a nurse for invading his privacy. The nurse did not understand his reaction, and a colleague explained to her that "that's the way he is because he is twisted." Because his physical impairment was thus seen as explaining his behavior, his protest over institutional conditions was invalidated.

The constant emotional work involved in managing anger often results in repressing the anger, and turning it inward and against oneself. Zola (1982: 222) argued that depression among those with disabilities is partly due to constraints against getting angry. This depression is often viewed as the individual's problem rather than a normal response to social pressures. Turning socially provoked anger inward is thus socially functional, but individually repressive. Another destructive emotional response to lack of privacy and autonomy, to stigma, and to the "threatened integrity of the body" is dissociating and "switching off" oneself from one's body (Shakespeare, 1996: 207).

One strategy for avoiding the potential stigma of some disabilities is *passing,* or concealing a discrediting social status or stigmatizing attributes. In some cases, disclosure or "selective telling" can act as a means of forestalling a negative reaction from another person. For example, people with epilepsy weigh the stigma potential of their condition against positive consequences (for example, having someone to help in case of seizure) of revealing the fact (Schneider and Conrad, 1983). Concealing one's condition is sometimes a way of avoiding stigmatizing attitudes. *Because* people with impaired vision may consider a cane to be a stigma symbol or an overt sign of disability, they may prefer a less obtrusive folding cane, even though it may not be as effective an instrument. Charmaz (1991: 151) observes, "An appliance that simplifies logistical problems and arduous tasks can confound self-image and social identity. Hence some ill people prefer to stay at home or risk heart failure, a fall or exhaustion rather than use a walker, wheelchair or a handicapped parking space." The refusal to use highly visible prosthetic devices, however, is not necessarily irrational, but may be based on well-founded fears of being viewed as a "cripple."

Disability as a Minority Status

Some people with disabilities consider themselves to be members of a minority group because of their relative powerlessness and their identifiability, both of which promote discrimination and stigmatization (Fleischer and Zanes, 2001). Unlike other minority groups, however, the disabled do not usually share a subculture, a geographical location, or history. Their cultural status is ambiguous: They are "betwixt and between," neither healthy nor sick. Murphy (1987) argues that because such ambiguity is threatening to normals, the isolation and discrimination faced by those with disabilities may come from their anomalous and ambiguous status in our system of cultural classification. Nevertheless, like other minority groups, such as women, blacks, Hispanics, and gays, they *do* experience similar problems of being powerless objects of stereotypes and discrimination.

One survey found that some three quarters of all persons with disabilities *do* identify with one another, and that close to half consider themselves a minority in the same sense as African Americans or Hispanics (Fine and Asch, 1998). Some people who are deaf, for instance, are resistant to "technical fixes," such as cochlear implants (in which the inner ear is wired to a receiver), precisely because the technology denies people who are deaf their identity in a deaf culture, such as participating in the use of sign language (Barringer, 1993). Some studies suggest that physically "normal" people view those with impairments, such as blindness, as inferior to members of ethnic minority groups (Susser et al., 1985). One study found a hierarchy of attitudes toward persons with disabilities, with those who were blind ranked below those with cerebral palsy, total paralysis, or epilepsy. Other studies show that blacks as a group were ranked close to the blind in terms of social preference. Such biases develop as early as the age of six (Gliedman, 1979).

Perhaps the most important feature that people with disabilities share with racial and ethnic minorities is the tendency for others to attribute their perceived inferiority and "differentness" to biological factors alone, rather than to social conditions. Disabling attitudes and environments create a self-fulfilling prophecy that legitimates individualistic and biologistic assumptions about the disabled. Because such environments and attitudes exclude people with disabilities from the community and from workplaces, the nondisabled conclude that this exclusion is evidence that the disabled cannot function in such settings. "Like racists, able-bodied people often confuse the results of social oppression with the effects of biology" (Gliedman and Roth, 1980: 28).

Disability Civil Rights Movements: Recapturing Self and Access

Stimulated by the 1960s civil rights movement, people with disabilities became politically active, working from the assumption that they constituted a minority group deprived of their civil rights. Shifting their focus from individual problems to attacking unfair social structures, they began demanding equal access to housing, jobs, transportation, and health care. The activism of the 1960s had widened the definition of political issues to include the personal, everyday problems faced by various groups. Disability rights activists realized that definitions of disability were sociopolitical (Scotch, 1988).

Groups like the Center for Independent Living in California and Disabled in Action on the East Coast, staffed largely by people with disabilities, sought to define issues such as access not as charity or welfare, but as basic civil rights. The disability rights movement emphasizes the involvement of citizens with disabilities in shaping their own fate (Shapiro, 1993).

Such activist movements remind us that socially created environments are designed for a narrow range of bodies. Humanly authored landscapes, cities, workplaces, and transport systems favor healthy young bodies. Furthermore, the disability rights movement has highlighted the pervasiveness of disabling attitudes in our society, calling attention to the social, political, and economic contexts of such attitudes and environments (Oliver, 1996; Paterson and Hughes, 2000).

In the United States, the disability rights movement contributed to the passage of the 1990 Americans with Disabilities Act (ADA), the first comprehensive civil rights legislation for people with disabilities (Shapiro, 1993). This law prohibits employers from discriminating against people with disabilities; it requires businesses to provide reasonable accommodations to workers and customers with disabilities, and it orders accessible public transportation and other reasonable public accommodations for persons with disabilities. The United Kingdom passed similar legislation, the Disability Discrimination Act (Hendriks, 1999).

In the United States, the efficacy of ADA legal protection is decreasing as a number of court decisions narrowly interpret the criteria for disability rights. Whereas the 1990 ADA defined a disability as a "physical or mental impairment that substantially limits one or more of a person's major life activities," in 1999, the Supreme Court held that the determination of whether an impairment substantially limits a major life activity must take into consideration the effect of mitigating measures. United Air Lines had rejected two job applicants with myopia because they could not pass the vision test without corrective lenses. They were denied protection under the ADA; the Supreme Court held that they were not disabled because their vision could be corrected with glasses (*Sutton* v. *United Air Lines,* Inc., 527 U.S. 471, 1999).

SUMMARY

Illness is the complex set of ways in which the sick person (and family and friends) perceive, manage, and respond to symptoms and disability. The experience of illness reminds us of our limitations, dependencies, and ultimate mortality. Although ordinary, even minor illnesses disrupt one's life, certain illness experiences are likely to have a serious effect on the sick person's identity and sense of self. Certain disabling conditions and chronic pain and illnesses are especially problematic, because they involve a sense of loss; they are overwhelming, unpredictable, and uncontrollable; and they produce social marginality for the sufferer. The chronic illness experience is not limited to the sick person but often involves family and friends as well. People interpret their illness, giving it meaning, form, and order. These meanings in turn shape their perception of their symptoms and pain.

Both the experience and expression of pain are linked with sociocultural factors. Suffering is often increased, however, when others invalidate the reality of the pain. Because the majority of serious illnesses today are chronic, in contrast to the acute illnesses predominant in the recent past, we need to appreciate their powerful impact on the person's daily life, social relationships, and very self.

Social and political factors are involved in both the definition and management of disability. Disabling social and physical environments and attitudes are responsible for many of the problems suffered by persons with chronic illnesses, impairments, or even differences. Biomedical, individual-focused approaches produce very different understandings of disability from the perspective of the *social model.* From this social model perspective, our focus should not be on impairment and difference but rather on analyzing discriminatory and disabling attitudes, as well as the social organizations of space, time, and practices.

Chapter

8

SEEKING HEALTH
AND HELP

A Navajo healer described the traditional healing ceremony:

"The songs tell us about our history, tell us about our creation. To be able to do that is trying to restore, to cure the patient, for him or her to become part of harmony again . . . . During the night you have to talk about these songs, what they mean, so everybody, everybody is protected. And in the morning they give thanks."

Source: Quoted in Lewton and Bydone, *Identity and healing in three Navajo religious traditions*, 2000, p. 483.

- **Lay Conceptions of Health and Illness**

- **Noticing Illness, Self-Treatment, and the Decision to Get Help**

- **The Hidden Health Care System**
  Home and Family Care
  Women's Roles
  Mutual Aid

- **Alternative Healing Systems**
  Nonallopathic Practitioners
  Indigenous Healers and Religious Healing Groups
  The Effectiveness of Indigenous Healing

- **Adherence to Therapeutic Recommendations**

How do people conclude that they are ill, and what actions do they choose to take in response? There are a number of implicit and often utterly incorrect assumptions about how people seek health and respond to health problems. Probably each one of us can think of instances in our own experiences when these assumptions did not hold:

> People know for sure when they are ill.
>
> As soon as they realize they are ill, they seek competent help, specifically a medical doctor (or dentist, psychiatrist, or other appropriate professional).
>
> When they consult the professional, they give an explanation of the problem that is as medically correct as possible.
>
> The doctor understands what they are saying about their problem.
>
> The doctor's explanation of the problem makes sense to them.
>
> When the doctor prescribes therapeutic action, they follow that advice carefully until it takes effect or until the doctor changes the instructions.
>
> People know for sure when they are well, and they are satisfied when this state of health is restored.

The fact that these assumptions are rarely accurate is a source of considerable tension and outright dissatisfaction on the part of both medical professionals and patients. One key reason for this tension is the enormous, and generally unrecognized, chasm between the medical models of illness and the conceptions used by laypersons in understanding and making decisions about their own health and illnesses. This gap is built into the structure of professionalized medicine, where—by definition—the layperson does not share the specialized body of knowledge used by the professional (Freidson, 1970: 278–279).

Most modern societies tend to treat professional interpretations as vastly superior to lay understandings. Medical professionals often demean lay conceptions, labeling them as superstition, ignorance, foolishness, or instances of persons being unwilling to take proper care of themselves. From this perspective, the doctor is viewed as the expert whose rational pronouncements are the result of legitimate authority, whereas the patient should be passive and obedient, deferring all judgment to the expert.

By contrast, West (1979: 162) argues that attention should be directed to "the person as a conscious, reflective actor engaged in the process of making sense of various kinds of body changes within the framework of his own 'lay' knowledge." Women's perceptions of illness and appropriate treatment are particularly likely to be shaped by pragmatic motives. People accept, reject, or treat with indifference their doctors' recommendations for their treatment, depending on the "fit" with their own priorities and values (Lock and Kaufert, 1998; Steinberg and Baxter, 1998).We examine the vast range of interpretations and decisions the ordinary person makes in seeking health.

Contrary to the common misconception, health seeking is largely *not* a process of getting professional medical care. Most health-enhancing or preventive measures are nonmedical, and only a very small portion of ailments are ever brought to a physician's attention. As Zola (1983: 111) commented,

> Virtually every day of our lives we are subject to a vast array of bodily discomforts. Only an infinitesimal amount of these get to a physician. Neither the mere presence nor the obviousness of symptoms seems to differentiate those episodes which do and do not get professional treatment.

This observation is corroborated by studies documenting the "iceberg of morbidity"–the vast majority of physical problems that are never brought to medical (or formal health statistics) attention (Verbrugge, 1986). The Health in Detroit Study found, on the basis of health diaries, that persons over 18 experienced an average of 23 health problems in 16 days within a six–week period (Verbrugge and Ascione, 1987). This means that people experienced discomfort sufficient to be considered a health problem more than one-third of the days of the study (which itself was scheduled to avoid the height of hay fever and winter colds seasons, so this figure is probably conservative). The *least* commonly mentioned action in response to these problems was medical care; on only 5 percent of days on which they experienced problematic symptoms did respondents have medical contact of any kind (office visit, appointment scheduling, medical advice by telephone, or hospital visit). The study found that people typically responded promptly to symptoms, but that "for most symptoms of daily life, people opt to do something on their own without medical help" (Verbrugge and Ascione, 1987: 549).

This society generally and medical professionals in particular hold an ambiguous norm: Responsible persons *should* get professional medical care for all serious, medically treatable ailments and, at the same time, *should not* bother doctors or use medical facilities for unimportant or nontreatable ailments. This norm furthermore assumes that people share the professional definition of which ailments are serious or treatable and are able to assess their own situations adequately to determine into which category they fit. Although physicians strongly urge professional attention for health problems, they simultaneously dislike being bothered with trivial problems or problems they do not know how to treat effectively (Klein et al., 1982). One emergency room doctor who objected to dealing with worried mothers of young children who were not "real" emergency cases commented, "Anxious mothers, I sometimes think that they haven't got the sense that they were born with" (quoted in Roberts, 1992: 119). The contradictory or ambiguous norm is that laypersons should be actively expert in judging correctly which ailments to refer to the professional, and then assume a humbly passive role when under the care of the professional.

LAY CONCEPTIONS OF HEALTH AND ILLNESS

How do you know you are sick? How do you know if your condition is potentially serious enough to warrant doing something about the illness? Long before they seek any outside help (medical or otherwise), individuals interpret their own condition. Underlying all such evaluations is a set of ideas about health and illness. The concepts and logic of these ideas are not those of science or medicine, although they may be borrowed, accurately or inaccurately, from those formal systems of knowledge. Rather, they are the concepts and logic of ordinary people whose experiences, socialization, cultural background, and immediate social network shape and continually develop their notions of health and illness. There is considerable cultural variability in people's understandings of health.

Many people think of health as simply the absence of illness. For example, a Scottish study of older persons found that key dimensions of health mentioned were an absence of illness, a reserve of strength, and a feeling of being generally fit or capable of accomplishing daily tasks (Williams, 1990). Corroborating evidence came from a study of middle-aged French subjects, who described health in terms of an absence of illness, an equilibrium in daily life, and a capacity to work (Herzlich, 1973; Herzlich and Pierret, 1987).

Other research found that although both working-class and middle-class persons shared the notion that health meant the absence of illness, working-class people tended to emphasize health as a tool in their everyday lives: It enabled them to carry out their tasks, especially job and family duties (Blaxter and Paterson, 1982). Middle-class persons were more likely to mention broader, positive conceptions of health that included such factors as energy, positive attitudes, and the ability to cope well and be in control of one's life (Calnan, 1987; Saltonstall, 1993).

The sense of being in control may be particularly important to the middle class, for it meshes with their experiences of making decisions and having a degree of control in their work and daily life. By contrast, because working-class persons have control over far fewer areas of their lives, this value may be remote or inconceivable to them. Crawford (1984: 78) argued that middle-class values have expanded the notion of health to something that must be actively achieved, because "to be healthy [in this culture] means to demonstrate to self and others appropriate concern for the virtues of self-control, self-discipline, self-denial, and will power." Embedded in lay conceptions of "being healthy" is a moral code by which one is judged (Litva and Eyles, 1994). One U.S. study found that people included wide-ranging criteria when rating their health, including such nonphysical factors as their emotional well-being, their social relationships, and their ability to perform valued activities (Idler, 1995).

Various subcultures differ in lay conceptions of health and illness as well. Persons raised in different ethnic subcultures—Chicano, Irish, Appalachian, or Polish, for example—typically learn their group's ideas about health and illness, including: What is health? What can cause illness? What does a given illness mean? How can I protect myself and loved ones from illness? How can I counteract illness when it occurs? What can I expect to experience with different illnesses? What resources can I turn to for help in the face of illness?

Religious subcultures likewise influence not only their members' responses to illness but also their very definitions of health and illness. One member of a Christian healing group stated, "Health, wholeness—all these words to me are Scripture and salvation. It all goes together. A healthy person to me would be one that was whole in spirit, soul, mind, and body" (quoted in McGuire, 1988: 39). A study of middle-class spiritual healing groups found that, as persons became more actively involved, they expanded their notions of what needed healing in their lives. Because health was an ideal encompassing all their religious ideals, healing was part of an ongoing process of striving for those goals (McGuire and Kantor, 1987).

Although few studies have been done about other kinds of subcultural groups, it is probable that they too influence members' conceptions of health, illness, and healing. For example, to what extent is an adolescent subculture (and not just chronological age) a factor in the health notions of teenagers? Are there health belief systems communicated by other subcultures, such as homosexuals or the military? We have only begun to explore the diversity of lay conceptions of health and illness. The sketches we have thus far, however, illustrate the importance of lay conceptions for understanding people's behavior in the face of illness.

People seek to comprehend what is wrong with them: What is the nature of this illness? Where did it come from? Why me? Why now? What can be done about this illness? What can be done to protect myself from other illness? Individual belief systems about illness are typically drawn from, but not necessarily rigidly determined by, larger cultural belief systems, which give shape to the illness experience, help the individual interpret what is happening, and offer a number of choices about how to respond (see Bury, 2001).

Lay images of various diseases reveal why certain responses make sense. A study of middle-class New Yorkers found that people regularly refer to disease and diseased body parts as "its"—as objects separate from the person. This image allows ill persons to distance themselves from their problems. The concept of disease as an "it" also meshed with notions that the problem had its source in some external agent that invaded the body (Cassell, 1976). Because lay images of illness reflect people's diverse experiences, they vary by such factors as social class, gender, ethnicity, and religion. For example, some religious subcultures promote fatalist interpretations of disease causation and others tend to be activist (Mullen, 1994).

A study of Scottish women showed the predominance of the image of disease as a thing that one "has," "gets," or "catches." Accordingly, "it" attacks, strikes, or sets in. One respondent said, "My family wis never bothered wi' their chest . . . it wis always their throats. It always went for their throat, not their chest" (quoted in Blaxter, 1983: 61). The regional idiom of "taking" a disease distinguishes temporary (typically infectious) illnesses from chronic illnesses or a clear physical abnormality. One might "take" pneumonia, measles, bronchitis, or scarlet fever, but not a tumor, cyst, arthritis, or cancer (Blaxter, 1983).

People employ their lay conceptions to explain the nature and causes of specific maladies. In one English community, respondents tended to think of their illnesses in terms of hot or cold and wet or dry; for example, a chest cold fit the wet-cold image, whereas a fever was depicted as hot-dry. By extension, then, certain maladies were linked especially with damp, cold weather or house environment (Helman, 1978). The causal categories used by laypersons may not be correct in bioscientific terms but are generally rational and based on the kinds of empirical evidence available to laypersons (see Blaxter, 1993).

The interpretation of illness is an ongoing process. People reinterpret their situation at various stages of their illness. They look back at earlier experiences and actions and reinterpret them to make sense of subsequent events and new beliefs. Interaction with physicians is only one source, among many, of people's reinterpretations (Hunt et al., 1989). Interaction with important others is another source of new interpretations. One purpose for this ongoing reconstruction is to make sense of a whole sequence of events, rather than viewing each part as an episode that just "happened." Thus, for example, cardiac patients retrospectively noticed the symptoms that had built up to their heart attack. Their reconstruction of the meaning of the sequence of events made the heart attack seem less threatening and more understandable (Cowie, 1976).

Cross-cultural research suggests that several explanatory logics are used by laypersons, including those in modern Western cultures. One category of logic is that of invasion, in which an outside agent is believed to come into the body to cause the illness. Examples include notions of possession, germ theory, or object intrusions. Another logic involves degeneration, in which the illness is explained as due to the breakdown of the body or its parts from such causes as exhaustion or the accumulation of toxic substances. Mechanical models provide another logic, explaining illness as the result of misalignment of body structures, or blockages of digestive or nervous channels, for example. A fourth logic commonly used is the notion of equilibrium, which attributes illness to the failure to maintain harmony (individual or social), balance, and order (Chrisman, 1977).

Lay understandings of illness typically address the broader issues of meaning, such as those discussed in Chapter 6: Why must I suffer? Why me and not someone else? Why now? Have I done something bad to bring this on myself? Indeed, in much lay thinking, cause and meaning are not separate interpretive categories. Serious illnesses in particular evoke broader causal interpretations that are often used in combination with medical interpretations. For example, one young woman accepted the medical etiology of her vision problems, but simultaneously employed a broader causal meaning to her illness: "With my eye problem, there was something that I didn't want to see. I couldn't get well until I opened my eyes to that something" (quoted in McGuire, 1988).

NOTICING ILLNESS, SELF-TREATMENT, AND THE DECISION TO GET HELP

How do people know they are ill? In addition to these underlying ideas about health and illness, a number of other social factors influence whether an individual will perceive a particular disturbance and come to define it as distressing enough to warrant further attention. People react to the meaning of a symptom, not merely the symptom itself. The significance of symptoms is not self-evident; the person must actively give attention and interpretation to them. Sometimes a bodily disturbance is sufficiently acute and obvious to merit certain treatment. A person with a gaping and painful wound that is bleeding profusely is not likely to ignore the bodily disturbance. Other disturbances, however, are more open to varying interpretations, including those that make the person less likely even to notice them. Mechanic (1976) suggested that the ordinary response to such disturbances involves testing hypotheses by observing the situation over time. Part of this process involves assuming a wait-and-see stance to test such hypotheses as these: This is something minor, the body will heal itself, and further symptoms may develop to give a better idea of what this could be.

Typically, people try to normalize their symptoms. They interpret disturbances as within the range of "okay," or at least understandable. A man who was hospitalized for a heart attack stated,

> I just felt rotten and I had a pain in my chest and I thought it was indigestion. I'd been rushing in the lunch hour and lifted a heavy box and all this sort of thing, and it was, oh three quarters of an hour after the actual rush that I felt the pain. (quoted in Cowie, 1976)

Normalizing a disturbance, however, does not necessarily make it unimportant or less real. For example, a person might normalize an excruciating abdominal pain by interpreting it as a bout of recurring gallbladder problems. For this reason, the response to acute illnesses is typically different from the response to chronic illnesses. One U.S. study found that for acute problems, people focus on the symptoms. The amount of effort the individual puts into some form of treatment often depends on the severity of the symptoms themselves. For chronic problems, by contrast, people develop strategies of management over the long term. When problems flare up, the response is routinized and not necessarily directly related to the severity of symptoms of that single episode (Verbrugge and Ascione, 1987).

The vast majority of actions people take to prevent illness or to treat everyday health problems are done without expert help, either medical or nonmedical. A British study found that women respondents most frequently listed the following ways of keeping healthy: good diet, exercise and fitness, no smoking, sufficient sleep and rest, and fresh air. Very few respondents (less than 10 percent) mentioned medical checkups or screening (Calnan, 1987: 101–130).

Likewise, the individual or family typically responds directly, without lay or professional help, to ordinary health problems (see Dill et al., 1995). The Health in Detroit Study found that self-dosing with prescription or nonprescription drugs was the most common response, used during 58 percent of the days on which people experienced symptoms. Self-imposed restriction of activities (such as cutting down on errands and chores) was also common, used on nearly 24 percent of the days on which symptoms were noticed (Verbrugge and Ascione, 1987).

British researchers found that although 91 percent of adults studied reported symptoms during the two weeks prior to the interview, only 16 percent had consulted a physician. Indeed, only 28 percent had consulted their doctor at all during the previous 12-month period, even though, under the British National Health Service, the cost of consulting a doctor is not a deterrent, as it is for many in the United States. A far more frequent action in response to symptoms was taking medicine. In the 24 hours before the interview, 55 percent of adults had used some medicine; in the two weeks before the interview, they had taken an average of 2.2 different items of medication. Most were taken in response to specific symptoms: a temperature, headaches, indigestion, and sore throats. Self-medication also includes the decision to take medicines prescribed and often kept for long periods, to be taken "as needed." In a sample of households in England, Wales, and Scotland, 99 percent of homes kept one or more medicines; the average number was 7.3 nonprescribed and 3.0 prescribed. Two-fifths of households kept some medication that the respondent could not even identify (Dunnell and Cartwright, 1972).

Some responses to illness are not merely physical. If the person's belief system attributes illness to nonphysical causes, such as emotions or spiritual factors, then it is logical for a sick person to choose nonphysical approaches to treating the illness. If, for example, a person believes that she is especially vulnerable to infections when she is "blue," she might choose to treat an ailment by doing things that cheer her up. Similarly, if someone believes that God will intervene to heal his illness, then prayer for healing constitutes a therapeutic action.

Such nonphysical responses are rarely done to the complete exclusion of physical treatments, and often they are meshed in interesting combinations. For example, when a person chooses to treat a bad case of the flu by consuming a bowl of steaming chicken soup or a concoction of milk toast, is the treatment merely the ingestion of a therapeutic substance or the soothing emotional connotations of the food, or both? Likewise, when a sick person says a blessing prayer over a bottle of prescription pills, is the treatment purely a physical response to illness?

The Health in Detroit Study found that about half the time people responded to their health problems by talking with family or friends (Verbrugge and Ascione, 1987). This response is both therapeutic in itself and also a way of consulting with other laypersons about what to do. Laypeople rely on their own networks of contact for advice, including suggestions about where to seek further help. Family, friends, neighbors, and colleagues at work, school, a religious group, or a social club all constitute potential sources of advice. The sick individual, however, must decide whose advice is sought and whose advice is heeded. For example, your grandmother might be a valued source of home remedies, and her burn ointment may be more effective than any commercial salve you have tried, but you might not want her advice on what might be a sexually transmitted disease because the advice is likely to come with a lecture on sin. Individuals are typically selective in their choices of lay advice.

Some evidence indicates that these lay advice networks rely especially on women as knowledgeable sources of referrals and as the seekers of health advice both for themselves and for members of their families (Graham, 1985). The division of labor in many households allocates to women more than to men such duties as caring for sick family members or selecting and arranging for appointments with medical and/or nonmedical practitioners.

Not all lay advice comes from existing networks, however. Sometimes people seek out new sources of advice or create a new network of lay advisers. A person with Parkinson's disease, for example, may look for a group of fellow sufferers, whose advice on some matters may be more valued than that of longtime friends or even doctors who have not experienced the disease themselves. One specific form of advice is the lay referral to a source of help (Freidson, 1970: 290). Through lay referrals, the individual learns of many treatment options, including a favorite (or least favorite) doctor; the type of specialist to try; alternative practitioners, such as an herbalist or acupuncturist; self-help health groups; and alternative healing groups, such as a prayer group or meditation center.

A study of Puerto Ricans in a small northeastern city, for example, found that sick persons with effective networks of kin and fictive kin (*compadrazgo*) received much concrete assistance in selecting and negotiating entry to both institutional health resources (for example, prenatal care programs) and noninstitutional help (such as *espiritistas*–spiritual healers). The study concluded that such kin networks should be viewed as health educators because of their role in teaching members how to find and select among available help resources, and how to deal with bureaucratic and other roadblocks to getting help (Schensul and Schensul, 1982).

Social interaction with family, friends, and acquaintances often plays an important part in the decision to seek help. One study of the decision to take a health problem to a clinic found that the individual rarely sought help at the physically sickest point. Rather, the nature of symptoms themselves appeared to be less significant than social interaction in prompting the decision to see a doctor:

> For our patients the symptoms were "really" there, but their perception differed considerably. There is a sense in which they sought help because they could not stand it any longer. But what they could not stand was more likely to be a situation or a perceived implication of a symptom rather than any worsening of the symptom *per se.* (Zola, 1983: 118)

For example, a person might be motivated to seek help after a friend's description of some serious disease that could possibly be related to her symptoms; symptoms that were formerly not worrisome then became significant, even though she had experienced no change in the symptoms themselves. Similar factors are probably involved in the decision to seek nonmedical forms of help. Thus, the motivation to do something about a health problem often results from social interaction that heightens the significance imputed to the symptoms.

People do not always seek help mainly to *cure* a health problem. For example, a person might go to a *shiatsu* (Japanese acupressure) therapist for pain relief but not accept the diagnostic interpretations the therapist gives. Some people consult medical doctors for diagnoses more to rule out feared serious outcomes than actually to treat the symptoms. Similarly, some people want the medical diagnosis but distrust the medical treatment (especially certain drugs or surgery). One middle-class American woman said, "I still think they give you too much medication, which I accept gratefully and then don't take" (quoted in McGuire, 1988). We have too little data on what patients actually hope to accomplish by consulting medical and nonmedical health experts, but probably much of what professionals call noncompliance (discussed further in this chapter) is due to the fact that the doctors' orders are not necessarily what laypeople want when they seek professional help.

THE HIDDEN HEALTH CARE SYSTEM

Too often, when people speak of the health care system, they refer only to the professionalized, institution-oriented *illness care* system of health care professionals, hospitals, clinics, insurance companies, pharmaceutical companies, and government agencies. There is, however, another highly important system of health care.

Home and Family Care

The **hidden health care system** refers to all the laypersons who are often the real *primary* health care providers (Levin and Idler, 1981).[1] The vast majority of efforts to maintain health takes place in the home and other private spheres of action, including diet, rest, recreational exercise and relaxation, hygiene, adequate shelter, avoidance of dangerous substances, and prevention of accidents and injuries.[2]

Likewise, most health care takes place in the home and is either self-administered or given by members of the family. Virtually all care of minor illnesses occurs outside the formal health care system. Imagine how many people in any given day may be taking care of themselves or someone else who is miserable with such illnesses as chicken pox, a bad head cold, or stomach flu! Even for health problems that have been treated in the formal system, most of the actual care is done at home: giving medications, tending a person restricted to bed, changing dressings, and monitoring symptoms.

Furthermore, throughout the society enormous amounts of energy and time are also required to care for persons with chronic illnesses, disabilities, and mental

---

[1]This usage differs from the common one in the literature, where "primary providers" refers to general practitioners, pediatricians, and other medical doctors or nurse practitioners who, in contrast to specialists, are supposed to be the first to evaluate patients' needs.

[2]As Chapter 2 shows, much of the great reduction in mortality between the 1870s and 1950s was due to improved living standards (especially better nutrition and hygiene) rather than medical measures. One important factor in this improvement was increased domestic labor created by the consolidated role of "full-time housewife and mother." The domestic labor required to cook meals, wash clothing, and so on (with few "modern" conveniences such as running water) was a *key social practice* producing health for the family, even though the women *doing* the domestic labor themselves often experienced chronic ill health due to childbearing and overwork (Thomas, 1995).

retardation, and those who are dying. In the United States there were 5.14 million elderly patients, discharged from hospital care, who received home health care services from 1992 to 1996 (Munson, 1999). Many more persons (for example, nonelderly with disabilities or retardation) also received some form of paid health care help in their homes. The majority of these persons were living with their families, also receiving family help with everyday activities such as walking, bathing, dressing, preparing meals, and eating. Note that these figures do *not* include persons receiving only unpaid care. Older adults accounted for the vast majority of persons needing home care, and the rates of persons needing assistance increased dramatically for those over age 85. The graying of modern societies, described in Chapter 2, results in a larger proportion of members surviving to an age at which they need long-term care for chronic health problems.

Even in nations with large government expenditures for health care, the *formal health care system is predicated on the expectation that most care will be given at home.* Indeed, the transfer of even part of these services (for example, complete care of all victims of Alzheimer's disease or AIDS) to the public sphere would probably swamp the system. In 1997, 25.8 million Americans worked an average of 18 hours a week caring for sick loved ones (Arno et al., 1999). If they were all paid an hourly wage commensurate with their duties (for example, changing bed linens and administering intravenous medications), their economic value would come to $196 billion, about six times the $32 billion formally spent on home care that year (Zuger, 1999). Informal health care, which provides care at little or no cost to the government or insurers, has thus remained a part of the domestic economy.

There are several health-related benefits to self-treatment and home treatment, especially compared with treatment in a formal, usually institutional, setting. Those who participate in the care of their own illness are more likely to experience a sense of independence, mastery, self-confidence, and control than those who are the passive recipients of care. A number of studies show the benefits of self-care, especially in treatment of chronic illnesses such as diabetes, hemophilia, and kidney disease (see Levin and Idler, 1981: 79–80).

Home care of illness and injury is typically more personal than formal or institutional care, although personal ties can be problematic because care givers can have negative as well as positive feelings for the sick person. Home care is also likely to involve more nurturance than perfunctory tending, although the actual care also varies from home to home. Another advantage of home care is greater continuity; the patient will not have to face an unfamiliar shift of nurses or a new specialist. Finally, home care is usually not as isolating as institutional care.

Just as persons with disabilities need special enabling environments, so too is the optimum setting for recuperation or the management of chronic illness one that is enabling. For example, a person with a debilitating chronic illness may require assistance with treatments (such as injections), the management of routine activities (like bathing), and ambulation (for instance, climbing stairs). Much home care, like many institutional settings, is disabling. Like institutional care, home care given by families, volunteers, or paid workers sometimes subordinates the sick person's needs to other household goals, such as keeping to a certain schedule. Home care sometimes increases sick people's dependency rather than enabling them to manage on their own as much as possible.

For most of us, the idea of home care raises cozy images of our comfortable room, surrounded by our favorite home entertainments, with Mom bringing us whatever we want for comfort: home-cooked special foods, a hot-water bottle, or a soothing drink. This image is, however, not the reality for many sick persons. For instance, what is the reality of home care for the widowed elderly person living alone in a bare furnished room, or the single mother who is seriously ill?

Nor are all families loving sources of nurturing care. Many families offer their members—especially children and elderly dependents—daily lives of negligence or outright abuse (Steinmetz, 1988). Indeed, the very health-related problems for which they need care may exacerbate these victims' abuse by other family members. Constant demand for help might drive a tired care giver over the edge to abuse or neglect. Some long-term or demanding tasks can strain the emotional and physical resources of even the most caring family.

The expectation that most health-related care will be given at home also fails to take into account that poverty prevents many people from maintaining a healthful home; a growing proportion of U.S. families are utterly homeless, and many more live in seriously substandard housing. Unlike previous patterns, the period of the 1980s and 1990s saw a dramatic number of women and children and entire families become homeless (Link et al., 1994). Children constitute about 15 percent of the officially recognized homeless population, and that proportion is growing rapidly (Burt, 1992), especially in the wake of 1996 changes in welfare legislation that made many families ineligible for public assistance.

Homeless children tend to have particularly great health problems: low birth weights, poor nutrition, generally poor health and poor access to regular health care and preventive medicine, high rates of preventable infectious diseases and lead poisoning, and more developmental, cognitive, and emotional problems (NIAA and NIMH, 1992). Without decent shelter and basic means to make a home, family care givers find it impossible to maintain their family's health or to care for the sick. For example, a homeless mother living without utilities or sanitation in an abandoned tenement would lack control over her family's living conditions necessary to maintain a therapeutic regimen of serving a sick child prescribed foods or giving perishable medications at specified hours daily. Given such absolute lack of control in their lives, many poor patients give up trying to adhere to therapeutic recommendations (Hilfiker, 1994).

U.S. health care policies have barely begun to explore (much less fund) a vast range of physical and social arrangements that would support such enabling environments as noninstitutional collective living situations, copatienting, adequate services to sick persons living independently, barrier-free physical settings for chronically ill persons, and well-trained and well-paid institutional and home health workers. Adequate funding must address the full range of help needed to meet the home-care needs of persons who are chronically ill or have disabilities, or are recuperating from accidents, surgery, or acute illnesses (Soldo, 1985). Few families can afford many of the time- or labor-saving arrangements that might relieve care givers' burdens; domestic help and hydraulic lifts, for example, are expensive. Where they exist, some community nursing and social service agencies and volunteer groups do help some families with certain of these needed resources. In the United States, however, very few of the costs of home health care are provided under the terms of health insurance or government medical programs.

Women's Roles

When people speak of home care, they mean care by a *woman* (typically a wife, mother, or daughter), an assumption that becomes particularly problematic in light of women's changing roles within the larger society. It is estimated that three-quarters of care given in the home is provided by unpaid relatives, of whom 70 percent are women (Shapiro, 1993: 252). Approximately one in four U.S. workers—mostly women—are providing unpaid health services to at least one disabled elderly person (Brody, 1994). Family members care for the vast majority (96 percent) of terminally ill patients, and most of these caregivers (more than 72 percent) are women (Emanuel et al., 1999).

The assumption that it is the wife-mother who should care for the family's sick results in real restrictions on women's opportunities in the public sphere, especially the world of work. Mothers, far more often than fathers, nurse sick children. Missing work to care for a child who has a throat infection is not a mere inconvenience; it may also seriously reduce a woman's job opportunities. The world of work assumes key participants will not be taking off time to care for dependents; anyone (female or male) who takes home responsibilities more seriously than work risks losing promotion opportunities or even the job itself. Ironically, it is often hospital nurses who suffer the double conflict between "good worker" and "good mother" (Garey, 1995). Working through the night allows them to be routinely available to care for their children during the day, yet be conscientious night shift workers—literally a "second shift" of care-giving.

Furthermore, the care-giving role requires many women to forgo paid jobs to care for a chronically disabled relative. Although there may also be some rewards for such duties, caring for some homebound sick persons can be a 24-hour-a-day responsibility, leaving little time for personal needs. One study found that, in order to care for their elderly disabled parents, 11.6 percent of caregiving daughters had to leave their jobs, 23 percent had to reduce their hours of paid work, and 35 percent had to rearrange their work schedules (cited in Brody, 1994). A report issued by the Older Women's League noted that women spend an average of 17 years caring for children and 18 years assisting aged parents (cited in *New York Times,* May 13, 1989; see also Abel, 1991; Hooyman and Gonyea, 1995).

The view that the health and illness care role belongs to the wife-mother is so pervasive that media and health education programs assume women will rearrange their lives to provide for the health of their families. One British health education project published a pamphlet urging measures women should take to prevent their husbands from having heart attacks. It recommended, for example, the following:

> The sensible wife will first decide whether her husband should lose weight, and then plan his menu accordingly. Pressure and pace at work, family responsibilities and general worries can be controlled to some extent by the man himself. . . . But perhaps more important is the tolerance and understanding of his wife. Let your husband talk about his worries, and whenever possible take the work from him—draft letters, pay bills, arrange for the plumber to come yourself. (quoted in Graham, 1985)

In efforts to reduce medical costs, insurers (including Medicare) and hospitals have emphasized outpatient surgery and other treatments while reducing the length of hospital stays (discussed further in Chapters 11 and 12). The result of these policies is that recuperating patients return home needing more extensive lay nursing care for longer periods. New technologies make possible the home administration of some fairly sophisticated therapies, such as kidney dialysis and intravenous feeding and medicating. The cost savings of performing these procedures at home is considerable. In 1997, the hospitalization cost associated with feeding by tube was about $39,204 a month, but only about $9,600 at home (Reddy and Malone, 1998). These procedures usually cannot be done by the sick person without help, however. In addition to requiring visits from skilled nurses who teach the procedures, supervise home treatment, and monitor the sick person's condition, much home care involves the extensive commitment of family members. Their unpaid labor increasingly includes providing complex nursing medical care previously done only by physicians, registered nurses, or therapeutic specialists (Glazer, 1990).

In recent years, policy changes by government, private insurers, and hospitals have resulted in considerable **work transfer** for women providing health care, paid and unpaid. Economists and public policy analysts typically conceptualize domestic production (that is, work done in the home) as separate from the larger (public) economy, but the ability of these public-sphere institutions to extract cost savings or profits by transferring labor "costs" to unpaid women workers in the home shows how inaccurate such an idea is. Indeed, it suggests that public-sphere institutions use the notion of duty to one's family as an ideological legitimation for extracting unpaid labor (Glazer, 1993; Hooyman and Gonyea, 1995).

This cost-cutting policy shift toward home care is developing precisely at a time when women are beginning to achieve somewhat greater equity in educational and occupational opportunities. The larger proportion of women in the work force also results in fewer (women) volunteers available for neighborhood assistance to those who need help at home. The policy shift also comes as nurses and other health care workers are struggling to achieve greater recognition (and pay) for the work they do (Brown, 1983).

Although moving more care of the sick to the home superficially appears to be demedicalization, note that it is not mainly the *doctors'* tasks or fees that are being reduced by earlier release from the hospital, but rather the more so-called menial tasks of care, which are being transferred to the family or family-paid workers. Whereas previously these tasks would have been done in the hospital or nursing home by low-paid nurses' aides and licensed practical nurses (LPNs), they are now transferred to unpaid relatives, who are sometimes assisted by very low-paid home health workers; nearly all are women (see Fine, 1988). It is no coincidence that this "caring labor" is seriously underpaid, because it is considered "women's work." Cultural sexism prevents recognizing the value of the work of caring. Thus, women suffer a "care penalty," both in the low pay and the low prestige for their nurturing roles (England and Folbre, 1999).

The nature of (paid) professional home nursing does appear to be a move away from a highly medicalized model because ideally the nurse treats the patient as a whole person in the emotional and social context of home and family relationships. Home nursing also emphasizes teaching sick persons and their families to care for themselves.[3] Home nursing is part of a larger class of occupations that are not fully commodified; many home nurses and other professional caretakers who work in the context of the home also care about values that are not purely monetary. Many paid caretakers feel a strong sense of responsibility for the welfare of their clients and often take on tasks beyond their job requirements (Himmelweit, 1999).

The trend to community-based health care has *not* usually reduced medical control, however. The home birth movement, for example, has been vigorously suppressed. In the United States, although some physicians have supported the practice of out-of-hospital births, professional organizations such as the American College of Obstetricians and Gynecologists have vigorously opposed it. Certification for trained midwives is available only to registered nurses who have taken extra training, but even these certified nurse-midwives have been severely restricted in their attempts to practice independent of physician control and have had great difficulty obtaining malpractice insurance. The virtual monopoly of obstetricians and hospitals has thus been protected (see Rooks, 1997).

Mutual Aid

Self-help and mutual aid groups are another form of hidden health care. These voluntary associations offer *reciprocal* help, usually among persons with similar health needs. The mutual quality of this aid is the key feature distinguishing these groups from professional health care. Members exchange roles as provider and receiver of health and illness care (see Katz et al., 1992; Levin and Idler,

---

[3]The work of community health nurses (including many nurse-practitioners and nurse-midwives) is comparable to that of their predecessors, public health nurses, who since the 1920s enjoyed greater professional autonomy and respect in their work than did hospital- or office-based nurses (see Melosh, 1982: 113–157). Physicians, however, have perceived them as professional competitors and have often fought to prevent laws that would permit these nurses to work independently. Because nurse-practitioners can provide primary care, comparable to physicians, for about 80 percent of the patients in ambulatory clinics, there are many possibilities for status and role conflicts between the two gender-stratified occupations (Little, 1982).

1981). Examples include support groups such as those for persons with certain diseases (such as epilepsy and Parkinson's disease) or disabling conditions (chronic pain, for example), or who have undergone certain operations (like mastectomies or colostomies) or other traumatic experiences (for instance, the suicide of a loved one, or a rape).

Self-help groups typically offer their members much mutual social support, concrete suggestions about how to manage the many day-to-day problems, information about their condition and various therapeutic possibilities, and advice about dealing with family, friends, and medical professionals (see Droge et al., 1986). One aim is to break the isolation of those whose regular networks may not include anyone in a similar situation. As one member explained, "In the beginning one is truly cut off, one feels completely different from everyone else. . . . The healthy cannot understand the sick, one really belongs to a world apart" (quoted in Herzlich and Pierret, 1987: 220).

Mutual help groups appear to be a feature of lay health care especially in the United States, where they mesh with cultural values and historical experience of mutual and self-reliance (see Risse et al., 1977). Due to their lack of access to professional health care, many uninsured families in the United States have devised highly creative self-care strategies, including social networks that serve as sources of medication and information (Vuckovic, 2000). Immigrant communities, similarly, provide mutual health help and advice to their members, many of whom are not adequately served by the medical system in the United States (Ell and Casteñeda, 1998). Interestingly, in recent years, long-distance telephone connections and the Internet have provided lay mutual help networks a way of communicating beyond their immediate communities to exchange experiences with their disease and ideas about how to deal with it.

Considerable diversity characterizes the social organization of these groups, with many of the long-term groups imitating professional, bureaucratic health care organizations, yet many others remaining adamantly loosely organized lay groups. Some are formed at lay initiative; others have been created by helping professions for their clients. Thus, there is a difference in the degree of independence of power experienced, for example, by a group of chronically ill persons who organize to do something for themselves and each other, as compared with a therapy group organized by the outreach staff of a hospital.

Mutual help groups also vary greatly in the degree to which they address any of the political issues implicit in self-care or mutual aid. The Independent Living Movement for persons with disabilities and chronic illnesses and the Women's Health Movement have taken a politically activist stance (see Crewe and Zola, 1983; Tudiver, 1986). Out of one such women's support group emerged the now famous "handbook" for women's health: *Our Bodies, Ourselves* (Boston Women's Health Collective, new edition, 1998).

Assuming self-care and mutual responsibility in the face of illness, however, also has *implicit* political consequences because the sick persons take an active and often knowledgeable role in the treatment of their own sickness. They often consider their proficiency in treating their particular illness to be superior to that of the professionals (see, for example, Herzlich and Pierret, 1987: 217–218). For example, diabetics who must give themselves frequent injections and persons with renal (kidney) failure who may perform their dialysis at home often distrust having those services performed in the hospital. People who have had long experience managing their chronic illness or disability often gain considerable expertise about their condition and are more likely to expect medical personnel to share power with them.

Our recognition of this hidden health care system helps us to understand better the full range of activities people engage in to keep well or to treat illnesses. Not all outside help is professional medical care. Beyond the lay help of home, neighborhood, and mutual aid groups are a number of nonmedical healing alternatives that people may seek.

ALTERNATIVE HEALING SYSTEMS

People's belief systems inform their decisions as to when they need help and which kinds of help are appropriate. Even in modern Western societies, where biomedicine is the dominant medical paradigm, people may use several healing systems simultaneously with biomedicine. A study (McGuire, 1988) of middle-class Americans who used various alternative, spiritual healing approaches (such as Christian faith healing, psychic healing, and Eastern or occult healing) found that virtually all adherents used both biomedical *and* alternative systems. Furthermore, their beliefs shaped how they combined these various approaches. For example, one man had his broken arm X-rayed and set in a cast by medical professionals at the hospital, but followed this treatment with frequent prayers at home and in his religious group. He believed that the prayers resulted in faster and more effective healing. Adherents of the various alternative healing approaches felt that medical doctors were not necessarily the best source of help for such problems as chronic pain and illness, because they "treat the symptoms, not the cause." These adherents believed that the "real" causes of such illnesses were spiritual (or the socio-emotional by-products of spiritual problems). Thus, by definition, modern medicine alone was not a sufficient source of help (McGuire, 1988).

Even people who are not consciously using alternative belief systems seek different sources of healing help, depending on how they understand or express their problems. Someone with back pain, for example, might consult a pharmacist, massage therapist, orthopedist, physiatrist, or chiropractor, depending on how the person interpreted the pain, its seriousness, and its possible causes. For many people, seeking help for health or illness includes several options in addition to orthodox medical care.

Nonallopathic Practitioners

One long-standing alternative source of health-related help is a professional practitioner from a formal healing system other than allopathy. Although allopathy is only one approach to doctoring, as described in Chapter 10, it has attained a virtual monopoly of medical education, licensing, and practice in the United States and Canada. It is also the dominant form of medicine practiced in most of Europe, although several nonallopathic approaches have greater legitimacy and freedom there than in North America. Medical systems that dissent from the dominant one have often been called sects, perceived as analogous to religious sects that dissent from the established church (see Jones, 1985). These medical systems are based on completely different, competing paradigms of illness causation and cure.

Probably the best known alternatives in the United States are two nineteenth-century challenges to allopathy: chiropractic and osteopathy, therapeutic systems based on the idea that malalignments of the musculoskeletal system also produce problems in the neuroendocrine system. Osteopathy has become largely subordinated within regular (allopathic) medical practice and licensing. Until the 1980s, chiropractic was actively suppressed by the AMA and licensing legislation, and it had to fight several court battles to force the AMA to change its prohibition against MDs referring patients to chiropractors. Chiropractic treatment has since gained greater legitimacy and is now covered for limited services by much health insurance (Wardwell, 1994; see also Singer and Baer, 1995).

There are few studies on how patients combine the use of both chiropractic and medical doctors. In Canada (where chiropractic has been officially recognized and is reimbursable by the national health insurance), one study found that, although all the low-back pain sufferers in the study had gone initially to medical doctors, those who subsequently sought help from chiropractors were part of lay referral networks (family, friends) that informed them of a wider range of alternative healing approaches (Wellman, 1995). Although chiropractors appear to be widely used alternative practitioners in the United States as well, patients seem to seek their services only for narrowly focused problems, especially back-related complaints, rather than general health or preventive care (Coulter et al., 1996). Early chiropractic was far broader in scope, but chiropractors today appear to have sacrificed that role to acquire legitimacy (Moore, 1993).

Homeopathy, a holistic form of pharmacological therapeutics developed in the early nineteenth century (Kaufman, 1971), is now more common in Europe and Latin America than in the United States. In England, for example, homeopathic physicians are licensed to practice and are reimbursed under the National Health Service. Homeopathy is the most popular alternative medical approach in France and Norway, too (*British Medical Journal,* 1996). The homeopathic movement also encourages laypersons to self-treat certain illnesses and to learn to use some of the homeopathic medicines (Coulter, 1984).

Like homeopathy, naturopathy utilizes presumably milder medicines, primarily herbs. One form of naturopathy, Thompsonism, was influential in the United States in the eighteenth and nineteenth centuries because it was linked with the rising tide of political populism and the needs for lay modes of healing in frontier and other rural communities (Cassedy, 1977; Numbers, 1977). The various natural health movements were generally suppressed in the United States, but in several European countries these practices have long been more acceptable as a complement to biomedicine (Maretzki and Seidler, 1985). Contemporary versions of naturopathy as well as homeopathy appear to be used increasingly in the United States and Britain, perhaps as a result of dissatisfaction with the dominant, allopathic medical system (Baer, 1992; Goldstein, 2000; Sharma, 1992; Thomas et al., 1991).

Another extant nineteenth-century alternative to allopathy is hydrotherapy, which utilizes water (in the form of baths, mineral water, and mud) for treatments. So-called New Age alternative healing practices include some indigenous and religious healing approaches (described further in this chapter), but also include such alternative techniques as reflexology, iridology, aromatherapy, colonic irrigation, and radionics.

Some traditional Asian medical practices have recently been introduced into Western societies.[4] The paradigms of illness and healing of such therapies as acupressure, acupuncture, *qigong,* and Asian herbal medicine are very different from those of Western biomedicine. Acupressure, or shiatsu, is generally administered like a massage, so it is not in direct competition with licensed medicine, but neither is it typically covered by medical insurance. Acupuncture, which involves the insertion of needles, is under tighter legal control. In most of the United States nonphysician acupuncturists are required to work under the supervision of licensed doctors, although some states have made allowances for licensing nonphysician acupuncturists (who, ironically, are often better trained as acupuncturists than physicians who took relatively brief training in the method). Patients who utilize acupuncture alongside regular medical treatment often do not tell their own physicians for fear of alienating them (Wolpe, 1985).

Surveys indicate that in Europe roughly one of every five persons has used alternative healing approaches, and their popularity is growing (*British Journal of Medicine,* 1996; Fulder, 1993; Menges, 1994). In Germany, a 1998 law gave alternative health treatments the same status as conventional medicine. It required insurance to cover approved alternative treatments, such as herbal remedies and acupuncture, and changed standards for review of research on alternative therapies (Hinman, 1998). Some two-thirds of Japanese patients use nonmedical alternatives (many of which were derived from their Asian traditional approaches to healing) in combination with Western biomedicine (*British Journal of Medicine,* 1996).

These nonallopathic therapeutic systems are used widely in the United States, too (see Goldstein, 1999; Jonas and Levin, 1999; McGuire, 1988). A 1997 study in Oregon found that about half of the patients interviewed used some type of alternative medical therapy, the most popular of which were chiropractic (42 percent), massage (32 percent), herbal medicines (30 percent), megavitamins (24 percent), meditation (21 percent), and homeopathy, naturopathy, and acupuncture (each used by 10 percent of the patients). More than a third were also seeing a medical doctor for the condition, but only 53 percent of those who used alternative

---

[4]Professionalized practice is also a feature of other Asian medical traditions, such as Ayurvedic and Yunami medicine, but these have not been extensively "borrowed" by Westerners (see Leslie, 1976).

treatments told their family physician that they were doing so (Minz, 1997). There is evidence of a sharp increase in the use of alternative medicine since 1990, as well. By 1997, an estimated 83 million Americans had used some form of it (Eisenberg et al., 1998).

In response to the rapid expansion of alternative medicine, government agencies in Europe and North America became involved in trying to regulate a diversifying health care market. In the United States, Congress instructed the National Institutes of Health to open the Office of Alternative Medicine (OAM), providing some funds for research. Only certain therapies, however, have attracted government support—those that have altered their organizational structure and limited their medical claims, thus reducing their competition with approved medical approaches to health care (Cant and Sharma, 2000).

Because these nonallopathic professional healers are in direct competition with allopathic medicine, political and legal maneuvers regarding their practice have concrete economic effects. Like allopathic medicine, these alternatives are organized as professional practices, with their own body of knowledge, training and certification standards, code of ethics, and organizations (see the review of literature in Cassidy et al., 1985; see also Budd and Sharma, 1994; Jonas and Levin, 1999; Saks, 1992; Sharma, 1992). They also rely largely on learned diagnostic and therapeutic techniques, which do not require the patient to understand or agree with the underlying paradigm in order to be treated effectively. Like biomedicine, many nonallopathic therapeutic approaches tend—despite their more holistic ideals—to locate illness in the *individual* (separate from social context) and to treat patient's bodies as reified objects (Sharma, 1995).

Indigenous Healers and Religious Healing Groups

The acceptance of an underlying belief system is more likely to be a feature of **indigenous healing,** or native, folk, or popular practices for health and healing. Anthropologists have documented a vast array of such systems around the globe. The early literature, however, generally assumed that as societies became modernized and Westernized, they would shed these "primitive" beliefs and practices and substitute the biomedical system, but this expectation has not been borne out (Kleinman, 1984). Furthermore, indigenous healing has remained widespread in modern industrialized societies. Social scientists once interpreted these beliefs and practices as remnants of peasant, old-country traditions or as characteristic of uneducated, lower-class persons who could not afford modern medical treatment.

By contrast, some anthropologists argue that—rather than a negative reflection on lower-class persons who use indigenous healing approaches—this persistence may be a form of resistance to the "racist and class features of the American dominative medical system" (Singer and Baer, 1995: 196). Furthermore, indigenous and other nonprofessional alternative healing beliefs and practices are in fact relatively widespread also among educated, fully acculturated, and economically secure persons (McGuire, 1988).

The sheer diversity of indigenous health and healing beliefs and practices makes it very difficult to generalize about these alternative options. Some indigenous practices are conducted by healers—lay specialists who have particular knowledge and/or spiritual or natural "gifts" for healing. Other indigenous healing is done by the sick person or nonspecialists in the group. In the United States, for example, indigenous healing approaches include those of spiritual healers, mediums, shamans, herbalists, lay midwives, fire doctors (for burn pain), bone setters, and occult healers. Indigenous healing also includes a wide variety of meditation approaches, prayer, spiritual exercises, massage and other body work, exercise disciplines, and martial arts. These nonprofessionalized forms of healing alternatives are more likely than professionalized forms (such as chiropractics and homeopathy) to be integrative—not only linking the patient's body to a wider social context, but also addressing both body and emotions in therapeutic practices (see Csordas, 1994; Csordas and Kleinman, 1996; McGuire, 1996).

Although most indigenous healing occurs outside orthodox medical practice and is generally denigrated by the medical establishment, a number of medical doctors are open to some of these alternative practices. One study of these physicians found that their personal web of experiences, including religion and spirituality or their own illness or pain experiences, led them to integrate alternative approaches with mainstream medical practices. It concluded that many mainstream physicians hold views about health and healing and deviate from norms promulgated by their professional organizations (Goldstein et al., 1987).

Because indigenous and other nonprofessional alternative healing is loosely organized, there are no clear-cut boundaries for acceptable practice. To the extent that indigenous healers are members of an established community in which they work, however, ordinary social control is operative. Someone who is believed to be pretending to heal and exploiting neighbors' needs in time of trouble would almost certainly be punished. When indigenous healing occurs more anonymously (for example, by a traveling healer or advertised nostrums), there is greater potential for deliberately fake healing. Most indigenous healing, however, is sincere; it is practiced by people—healers and patients alike—who, to some degree, share a belief system in which that approach to healing is plausible and indeed advisable (see Box 8.1).

Some of these alternative approaches are systematized by recognized movements; others are developed by independent healers, often drawing eclectically from a wide range of Western and non-Western traditions. The various spiritual healing approaches are generally based on a larger religious belief system. For example, healing done in a prayer group is not an isolated activity but an expression of the group's larger belief that God acts directly in believers' everyday lives in response to their prayer and faith.

Spiritual healing is rather widespread, even in modern Western societies. Obvious examples include Christian healing, Christian Science and other New Thought healing, psychic healing, and healing approaches imported from various Eastern

Box 8.1

One American Healer[5]

"Marge is a 48-year-old pediatric nurse employed full-time in a large hospital in a suburban community. She is successful in her career, with the appropriate advanced degrees and experience for high level positions, although she has not chosen to leave active nursing for administration. Her husband is a senior partner in a law firm in a nearby city. The couple has four grown children. . . .

Marge is involved . . . in several groups using alternative healing. She personally utilizes some Eastern methods . . . but she does not teach these methods nor is she affiliated with a group in which Eastern spirituality is a focus. As a nurse, she has used Therapeutic Touch for about three years. She uses her psychic healing methods to "get in touch with" the pain and suffering of the children in her ward; patients do not need to know that she is "sending" them healing energies. Privately, she has been practicing psychic healing for about six years; her methods are eclectic and she tries new "modalities" as she learns about them, discarding some approaches, keeping others. Her main support group is a psychic healing circle that meets each week in members' homes. . . . When she seeks healing for herself, she usually turns to the members of this group. In addition, she attends the monthly or weekly meetings of three regional holistic health and metaphysical societies. These meetings are important sources of new ideas and techniques. She has also taken numerous workshops and short courses on various alternative methods: foot reflexology, rebirthing, and crystal and color healing.

Marge does healing almost any time, any place and with anyone—including many people who do not know she is "sending" them healing energy. Marge described working on healing herself and others even while doing the dishes or in the elevator at work. Sometimes she engaged in it deliberately; other times, she felt, it was simply a part of her being. She stated: "I believe that in every moment of my life I release energy to those around me. I think everybody needs it every moment. . . . I feel that whoever makes connection with me or I make connection with them, I'm using my energy to heal."

She is also a good example of the general lack of clear financial motivation on the part of many "expert" alternative healers. She charges private clients only a nominal fee (depending upon ability to pay). These services are, however, minor sources of income for Marge. Her professional salary, combined with that of her husband, supports a high standard of living; Marge views her paid work as healer as a sideline, done mainly as a service."

[5]This is a composite portrait to protect the identity of the actual healers studied.

Source: From *Ritual Healing in Suburban America* by Meredith B. McGuire with the assistance of Debra Kantor. Copyright 1988, by Rutgers, The State University. Reprinted with permission of Rutgers University Press.

spiritual traditions such as Zen and Tibetan Buddhism and Jainism (Csordas, 1994; English-Lueck, 1990; McGuire, 1988, 1982; Tipton, 1982; Wagner, 1983; Westley, 1983).

Ethnic and other subcultural belief systems inform the indigenous healing practices of most ethnic groups in the United States (and elsewhere). The healing actions of such persons as the Mexican American *curanderos,* Navaho singers, Puerto Rican *espiritistas,* Hawaiian *kahunas,* or Haitian vodou healers are based on complex systems of ideas about illness and power (Brown, 1991; Fontenot, 1994; Harwood, 1977; Lewton and Bydone, 2000; Roeder, 1988; Snow, 1993; Trotter and Chavira, 1981; Watson, 1984).

The Effectiveness of Indigenous Healing

The foremost reason why people use indigenous healing is that *it makes sense* to them. Indigenous healing beliefs are plausible, especially to people who grew up in a culture or subculture in which they were common. Indigenous healing "works" partly by fitting into people's understandings of their world and how it operates. Young (1976: 8) pointed out that therapies are considered efficacious not merely when they are a means of curing sickness, but "equally important, [when] they are a means by which specific, named kinds of sickness are defined and given culturally recognizable forms."

Indigenous systems are also frequently open, adaptive systems that incorporate new ideas and beliefs (such as from contact cultures) and rework them to mesh with existing beliefs (Green, 1998). This adaptive quality means that indigenous healing done in a new context (for example, an African immigrant living in the Bronx) can be more than "merely" persistence of an old-country tradition. In Chinese healing traditions, illnesses attributed to demons were traditionally viewed as a religious category of illness, but in an American setting, they have become psychological illnesses. Demon-provoked illnesses are re-interpreted as "blockages" that need to be unblocked. This innovative synthesis is simultaneously religious and psychotherapeutic (Barnes, 1998).

Indigenous healing forms and transforms the illness experience. It utilizes symbols and ritual action, meaningful to believers or members of that culture, that can produce change on several levels: social, bodily, and emotional.[6] A number of studies of symbolic healing suggest that just as mind, body, and society are linked in illness causation, so too are they (potentially at least) part of the healing process (Csordas, 1994; Csordas and Kleinman, 1996; Dow, 1986; Kelaher

---

[6]Biomedicine also uses symbols of power to enhance its effectiveness. For example, a pill may symbolize medical power to cure inside the body (Pellegrino, 1976). Surgery, lab tests, and diet regimens may likewise be used as ritual practices (see, for example, Posner, 1977). Medical costumes and settings (for example, stethoscopes and white uniforms) symbolize professional expertise. Such symbols increase trust and expectancy and, indirectly, may increase healing effectiveness (Frank, 1973). Much of what is called the "placebo effect" may in fact be related to symbolic healing (Moerman, 1997).

et al., 1998; Laderman and Roseman, 1995; Lyon, 1990; McGuire, 1983, 1996; Waldram, 2000).

The therapeutic practices themselves also make sense to members of the subcultural group. To an outsider, the Vermont folk remedy of a honey-vinegar mixture may seem nonsensical and repulsive. To persons raised in that rural New England subculture, however, it may be a plausible and appealing way of conceptualizing problems of health and illness; the remedy invokes images of benign nature, living "near to the soil," and being in harmony with the laws of nature by which health is maintained and produced (Atkinson, 1978).

In summarizing several outcome studies, which generally evaluate the results of healing efforts in terms of Western medical as well as indigenous standards, Kleinman (1984: 150) observed, "These studies document three things: that folk healers are frequently effective, that there are limits to their efficacy, and that, while toxicities of folk healing are infrequent, they do occur."[7] This summary probably also applies not only to folk healers but to the full range of healing practices in modern Western societies—including biomedicine, which some anthropologists refer to as our culture's "ethnomedicine."

ADHERENCE TO THERAPEUTIC RECOMMENDATIONS

Part of the health-seeking process is whether and how the sick person follows the recommended therapeutic procedures. For example, is a recommended diet followed? Are prescriptions filled and medicines taken? A medical doctor's recommendations may not be the only course of action to which a sick person would adhere. The advice of a lay consultant, a massage therapist, or spiritual healer might also be considered. Some sick persons deliberately seek several opinions—medical or otherwise—and therefore obtain several therapeutic recommendations. Adherence thus implies actively choosing which advice to follow.

Some formulations of the sick role have included following the doctor's orders as a role expectation (see Chapter 6). Many doctors, likewise, consider it a patient's duty to comply with their therapeutic regimen. The very notion of patient compliance implies a power relationship: The doctor is treated as authoritative and

---

[7] We need to keep in mind that the *exact* same generalizations could be made about healing by medical doctors: They are frequently effective, their efficacy is limited, and some treatments are dangerous. This evaluation does not mean, however, that one should not consult a doctor, but it does imply we should be cautious about naive assumptions that medical treatment is necessarily beneficial or safe just because it is more scientific than other healing approaches. Likewise, we should avoid romantic notions that indigenous healing is necessarily beneficial or safe. The effort to evaluate or compare the effectiveness of indigenous or religious healing with medical healing is greatly complicated by the fact that, because they operate with totally different paradigms, their notions of what constitutes a "successful" healing are very different. Although there is much overlap in what problems they consider to need healing, indigenous or religious healing usually have very different goals from those of medicine.

powerful, the patient as powerless and appropriately obedient (Chrisman, 1977). The idea that the patient should comply thus may have ideological functions for the physician (Trostle, 1988).

A number of studies show that health care professionals greatly underestimate the amount of patients' nonadherence to medical regimens (see the review of literature in DiMatteo and Friedman, 1982: 35–57). One study demonstrated dramatic discrepancies between prescribed and actual use of medications. More than half (51 percent) of the patients took medications about which they did not tell their doctor, 29 percent did not take prescribed medications, and 20 percent took a different dosage than the one prescribed (Bedell et al., 2000). When doctors' orders involve major lifestyle changes (such as changing eating or exercise patterns), compliance is even less common. Doctors often experience patient nonadherence to their recommendations as an affront to their authority; they blame patients as irresponsible.

Often, however, there are many other reasons why patients do not adhere to recommended therapies. Because patients do not want to alienate their doctors, they often hide their nonadherence to the doctors' recommendations and the extent of their search for other opinions. For example, because pregnant women do not typically think of themselves as sick, often they do not take their doctor's advice as seriously as they would if acutely ill. One study found that pregnant women continually juggled their prenatal health practices, sometimes resisting and sometimes complying with their doctor's advice (Root and Browner, 2001). Similarly, many patients dealing with chronic illnesses develop their own strategies for managing their illness. Such strategies include the selective use of biomedical approaches, but often also involve other therapeutic approaches, advice from more than one doctor, and/or their tailoring of the doctor's advice. From the patients' point of view, such noncompliant health-seeking behavior is rational, and it preserves for them some element of control (Herzlich and Pierret, 1987; see also Alexander, 1982).

Rather than conceptualizing the sick person's role in terms of degree of compliance with doctors' orders, it is useful to understand the meaning of medications and other therapies from the perspective of the sick person. One study found that many people with epilepsy modify and self-regulate their use of prescribed medications in an attempt to assert a degree of control over their condition (Conrad, 1985; see also Donovan and Blake, 1992; Trostle et al., 1983).

Noting the extent of nonadherence to doctor's recommendations, Zola (1983: 217) argued that "to 'take one's medicine' is in no sense the 'natural thing' for patients to do. If anything, a safer working assumption is that most patients regard much of their medical treatment as unwanted, intrusive, disruptive, and the manner in which it is given presumptuous." The patient is engaged in an ongoing process of evaluation of recommended therapies; whether the recommendation is medically correct is only one, sometimes minor criterion in this evaluation. Other criteria include such matters as these: Does the doctor appear to understand my illness correctly? Do the doctor's methods of diagnosis, interpersonal style, and treatment meet my expectations of competent? Is there a safer, more pleasant, or less drastic alternative (especially to surgery and powerful medications)? Does it feel like this therapy is working? When dissatisfied, patients may try to modify the treatment either by negotiating with their doctor or by modifying the plan by themselves (known as noncompliance). Both approaches represent patients' attempt to assert some control (Donovan and Blake, 1992).

Much patient nonadherence can be traced to difficulties of understanding and communication in the doctor-patient interaction (see Clark, 2001), as described further in Chapter 10. Part of the problem, however, is due to important differences in the perspectives and goals of doctors and their patients. The doctor's focus is typically on curing or managing the specific disease presented by the patient. Laypersons, by contrast, are more likely to have a broader notion of health and illness and to be concerned with all aspects of their life, not merely one health problem, no matter how serious. For example, a patient may feel that the depression experienced as a side effect of blood pressure medicine is so debilitating that continuing the medication is not worth the struggle (see Twaddle, 1981).

Often the decision not to follow the doctor's recommended course of action (or not to seek professional help in the first place) is due to a discrepancy between the layperson's and the professional's understandings of the sickness. For example, a Louisiana study of black women with hypertension (high blood pressure) found that their cultural beliefs and folk-illness models affected their adherence to the medical regimen prescribed. Many of these women conceptualized their sickness as "high blood," a subcultural term implying the blood is too rich, thick, and hot, and total blood volume is too great; this conceptualization is not what doctors mean by high blood pressure. When health professionals failed to understand that medical diagnostic terms invoked a whole different set of cultural meanings for these patients, they inadvertently contributed to patient noncompliance (Heurtin-Roberts and Reisin, 1990).

One study of sufferers of specific chronic illnesses found that primary care physicians and nurse practitioners showed very limited knowledge of their patients' conceptions of these illnesses. Although professionals were more likely to know the beliefs of college-educated patients than those of less educated patients, overall they understood the lay explanatory models used by less than half of the patients in the study (Helman, 1985). This lack of shared understanding of the nature of the illness is likely to lead to considerable nonadherence to doctors' orders and to dissatisfaction on the part of both medical professionals and their patients.

Adherence to any therapeutic regimen is likely to require some effort. The sheer logistics of putting all recommendations into effect are enormous, especially for chronic illness, for which the therapeutic regimen must last a lifetime and may become more demanding as the condition deteriorates. Health seeking is an active process throughout, but the active participation of the sick person is especially evident when it comes to putting some or all therapeutic advice into effect.

SUMMARY

The process by which people seek health is an active one. Both preventive care and the treatment of problems involve numerous decisions about the body and its needs. Self-treatment is far more common than treatment by professionals, medical or nonmedical. In addition to professional medical care, a vast hidden health care system provides advice, preventive and therapeutic care, emotional and practical support, and guidance in the search for professional care.

Orthodox Western biomedicine is only one of several healing systems available in most societies. Other options include nonallopathic practitioners and various indigenous healers and healing groups. The individual, then, has a range of health-seeking options. Even after consulting outside help, the individual also chooses which advice or therapeutic regimens to accept and put into practice.

THE SOCIAL CONSTRUCTION OF MEDICAL KNOWLEDGE

O ur culture and social structure shape the way we understand and interpret our bodies, illness, and disease as well as whether or how we perceive illness. This chapter examines how what we know about illnesses is socially constructed, used, and changed.

A sociological approach to knowledge about illness differs from the biomedical approach in that it does not assume the objective existence of what medicine categorizes as disease. The sociologist does not take for granted that disease entities exist in nature and await discovery. This perspective does not mean that people's health conditions have no objective foundation. People do experience real pain, sickness, and death. But this approach does mean that both laypersons' and professionals' ideas about illness are **social constructions,** or the result of human activity. Therefore, no matter how empirically precise these ideas are, they are always open to the influence of social factors in their production, transmission, and development. Medical ideas are bound by assumptions implicit in the language and cultural rules for producing knowledge (that is, epistemology). Thus, they are always delimited in their representation of the real world (see Young, 1978).

MEDICAL IDEAS AND SOCIAL FORCES

These ideas about body, health, and disease are nonetheless very powerful in shaping a society's medical reality. Any society's knowledge is the product of its social history. Western medicine's knowledge of its disease categories is a social-cultural product, as is the knowledge of diseases in other medical systems, such as Ayurvedic medicine in Asia and *curanderismo* in Latin America.

In Chapter 8 we described lay conceptions of health, illness, and the body. By contrast, formal medical knowledge in Western societies is typically highly specialized and based on bioscientific theories and categories of thought. The contemporary medical paradigm represents a major historical change in how the body is viewed (see Davis-Floyd and St. John, 1998). Scientific **paradigms** are frameworks of formal knowledge that members of a given scientific community share, mainly due to having undergone similar educations and professional initiations, to sharing a common professional language, rules of evidence, and conceptual schemes, and to relying on the same professional literature and communication of the same scientific community (Kuhn, 1970: 176). Paradigms are rather like lenses; the world viewed through one paradigm looks very different from the world viewed through another. We examine briefly the recent history of current medical paradigms and how they have come to have such a powerful impact on the practice of medicine and the development of the medical profession.

Although Western medical practice is based on scientific knowledge, the practitioners themselves are not typically scientists. The scientist's objective is to gather empirical data, and to analyze, interpret, and generalize from these findings. Scientists are not necessarily concerned with the practical application of scientific knowledge. By contrast, the practitioner's goal is more pragmatic: to deal with the specific conditions of individual patients or clients. What the practitioner needs to know is likewise more practical. The only portion of medical knowledge relevant to doctors is that which relates to conditions they are most likely to encounter in clinical practice. Much medical knowledge is thus often "recipe knowledge," or "knowledge limited to pragmatic competence in routine performances" (Berger and Luckmann, 1967: 42). For example, pediatricians' use of immunizations does not require their detailed understanding of the latest scientific theories about the operations of the body's immune system (although their medical education typically introduced this subject). Rather, they rely on recipe knowledge of which immunizations are recommended for children, at which ages, and with what common side effects and contraindications. They also rely on knowledge of where to turn when a situation is no longer routine.

A person's possession of a valued form of knowledge can be an important factor in determining his or her power and prestige in any society. For example, if the knowledge of how to make a valued ritual potion is held only by the women of a particular family, then their knowledge is the basis of some power or honor. Knowledge is unevenly distributed in a society, often along lines of gender, social class, age, ethnicity, and the division of labor (Berger and Luckmann, 1967: 76–81). Access to and possession of specialized, formal knowledge, such as medical knowledge, is particularly uneven. Because very few people in modern societies possess advanced medical knowledge or technical skills, being able to control such knowledge is the basis of rewards (such as high fees), power, and privilege. People who control specialized knowledge are thus in a position to limit the access of others to that knowledge (for instance, by controlling professional school admissions and discouraging laypersons from gaining knowledge). The social distribution of knowledge both reflects and shapes social distinctions of power and prestige.

"Discovering" Disease: A Historical Example

Many diseases that were diagnosed frequently in the past either are not commonly found today or are no longer recognized as diseases. Similarly, some conditions diagnosed as disease nowadays may very well cease to fit any disease category in the future. The forces shaping the so-called discovery of disease categories are not purely objective, scientific factors; rather, value judgments, economic considerations, and other social concerns frequently enter the process. For instance, a famous physician during the American Revolution identified a disease he called "revolutiona," which was characterized by presumably irrational opposition to the "natural rule" of the English monarch (Conrad and Schneider, 1992: 49). In the 1850s, the classification of "diseases of the Negro race" included "drapetomania," which caused slaves to run away from their masters, and "dysaethesia aethiopis," which accounted for laggard work habits among slaves (see Cartwright, 1851). Disease categories thus have political uses, and those on whom they are imposed may suffer serious consequences.

A prime example of changing medical definitions is a disease prevalent in the latter half of the nineteenth century and the first part of the twentieth century that had the following characteristics:

> It retards the growth, impairs the mental faculties and reduces the victim to a lamentable state. The person afflicted seeks solitude, and does not wish to enjoy the society of his friends; he is troubled with headache, wakefulness and restlessness at night, pain in various parts of the body, indolence, melancholy, loss of memory, weakness in the back and generative organs, variable appetite, cowardice, inability to look a person in the face, lack of confidence in his own abilities.
>
> When the evil has been pursued for several years, there will be an irritable condition of the system; sudden flushes of heat over the face; the countenance becomes pale and clammy; the eyes have a dull, sheepish look; the hair becomes dry and split at the ends; sometimes there is a pain over the region of the heart; shortness of breath; palpitation of the heart . . . ; the sleep is disturbed; there is constipation; cough; irritation of the throat; finally, the whole man becomes a wreck, physically, morally and mentally.
>
> Some of the consequences of [this disease] are epilepsy, apoplexy, paralysis, premature old age, involuntary discharge of seminal fluid, which generally occurs during sleep, or after urinating, or when evacuating the bowels. Among females, besides these other consequences, we have hysteria, menstrual derangement, catalepsy and strange nervous symptoms. (Stout, 1885: 333–334)

This serious disease was onanism, better known as masturbation. The fact that the doctor writing this description of symptoms slips easily into referring to it as an "evil" alerts us to the strong moral connotations that this disease label carried. This supposedly scientific medical category thus clearly reflected the moral and social judgments of the doctors who applied it (see, for example, Engelhardt, 1978).

What functions did the identification of masturbation as a disease serve? For the distraught parents of a moody teenager, the label explained a wide range of behaviors. It is less likely that the young person experienced much relief at having this diagnosis applied to symptoms such as poor appetite, headaches, or split ends. Another important function was to establish this "disease" within the proper jurisdiction of the medical profession. The author of the preceding description concluded emphatically that "the treatment of this disease should be undertaken only by a skillful physician" (Stout, 1885: 334).

Applying the category of disease to masturbation implied etiological explanations. The **etiology** of an illness is a set of ideas about its causality in general or about the origins of a particular illness episode. Like all ideas, they are human constructions that change over time. Early etiological theories of masturbation implicated the loss of seminal fluid, whereas later theories emphasized the overstimulation of the nerves, which led to general debility. Several authorities held that all sexual activity was potentially debilitating, but that masturbation was especially injurious because it was "unnatural" and thus more likely to disturb the nerve tone (Engelhardt, 1978: 15–17). The diagnosis of masturbation as a disease syndrome is no longer common; indeed, in many medical and lay conceptions it is now considered to be quite normal and healthy.

Identifying a person's problems as the disease of masturbation subsequently implied a particular course of therapy in accordance with etiological ideas about the disease. Therapies were supposed to first, eliminate the practice, and second, calm the nerves and rebuild the person's sapped strength. Some of the more tolerant therapies included hard work, a simple diet, tonics, cold baths, sedatives and narcotics such as opium, and alternative sexual outlets such as prostitutes or mistresses (Engelhardt, 1978: 19). If these therapies were not successful, more drastic measures were often recommended, such as restraining devices, acid burns and rings inserted in the foreskin to make masturbation painful, circumcision (of males and females), clitoridectomy (surgical removal of the clitoris), vasectomy, acupuncture of the prostate or testicles, and even castration (Barker-Benfield, 1975; Engelhardt, 1978; Groneman, 1995). Such a seriously debilitating disease required serious measures, including drastic surgery. Those symptoms once clustered and classified as signs of the insidious disease of masturbation may still exist (for example, some teenagers still have variable appetites, split ends, and dull, sheepish looks), but the characteristics are no longer classified as a disease.

Conversely, new classifications, such as premenstrual syndrome (PMS), have been defined into existence as a disease. The diagnostic category of PMS is a social construction which, like the diagnosis of onanism, embodies a set of cultural ideas and values. The considerable controversy within the American Psychiatric Association over whether to include the diagnosis (called "Late Luteal Phase Dysphoric Disorder") in the revised *Diagnostic and Statistical Manual* (DSM-III-R, 1987) illustrates the political and social value considerations implicit in the definition and diagnosis of PMS, or LLPDD (Figert, 1995; John Richardson, 1995). The attempts by medical doctors to define PMS are similarly problematic; some definitions are so broad that they classify as PMS the normal variance during as much as 17 days of the 28-day cycle in virtually all women with menstrual cycles. Accordingly, they define almost all adult women as having a medical problem (and presumably needing medical treatment).[1] Despite lack of strong empirical evidence, doctors, lawyers, psychologists, journalists, and laypersons have used the notion of PMS and other hormonal cycle variance to purportedly explain women's violent crimes, automobile driving patterns, accident proneness, suicidal impulses, and quarrelsomeness. Thus, like the nineteenth-century diagnosis of hysteria, a "modern" medical diagnosis—seemingly factual and empirically based—comes to embody old cultural assumptions that women's reproductive systems cause irrationality and "sick" behavior (Rodin, 1992; Swann, 1997).

Such new categories both justify medical control and legitimate the expense of medical care for that disease. For example, in the United States socially

---

[1]Clinical diagnoses of PMS are similarly problematic, because more than 150 symptoms have been associated with PMS and no confirming laboratory test exists. One study found that few doctors making the diagnosis of PMS confirmed it by use of a daily symptom report—the only reliable way to link the individual's menstrual cycle with reported symptoms (Frye and Silverman, 2000). When the patent on Prozac expired, its manufacturer aggressively marketed Prozac packaged as a treatment for PMS; the ambiguity of (150!) PMS symptoms was turned into a marketing advantage to persuade women that they needed the product.

constructed disease categories are the only basis for most insurance reimbursement. These categories, accepted as legitimate by the medical establishment, become the basis for funding research, treating patients, and institutionally establishing treatment programs. By putting these ideas into practice, medicine gives the disease categories a reality of their own. The process by which symptoms are selectively clustered and defined as disease is a social process and reflects cultural assumptions and power relationships (see Johnson, 1987).

Science as a Social Product

With its emphasis on a scientific model, biomedicine has developed increasingly complex **nosologies** (typologies of diseases). The medical model held that each particular disease could be characterized by a specific pathological configuration and attributed to a definite, unique cause. Thus, medicine has emphasized the classification and description of all diseases. The movement toward ever more precise differentiations of medical nosologies and etiologies is based on the assumption of **disease specificity**–the medical belief that each disease or syndrome has characteristic qualities and causes specific to that category of disease. This assumption has led to a focus on the individual rather than the social and contextual locus of sickness (Cassell, 1986; see also Dingwall, 2001: 50).

Medical ideas are the product of social processes and are continually changing. All scientific work involves the social construction of facts and interpretive schemes (Berger and Luckmann, 1967: 60–72; Latour and Woolgar, 1979: 243). Modern medical science strives to be as empirically neutral as possible, for example, by conducting blind experiments in which neither administrator nor subject knows whether a substance being given is the experimental substance or an inert control substance. Nevertheless, much medical research cannot be readily conducted neutrally, because–among other reasons–live human bodies are not readily detached from the persons who inhabit them. Thus, neither the scientific observers nor the objects of scientific observation can have their influential social characteristics and attitudes eradicated (see Lantz and Booth, 1998).

Social, economic, and political factors greatly influence the scientific discovery of new diagnostic categories. Funding for research largely depends on what is socially defined as a serious problem at the moment. For example, a disease syndrome known as GRID (Gay-Related Immune Deficiency) received relatively little medical attention or research funding, but when the same syndrome was later considered to be a national threat to the heterosexual population and redefined as AIDS (acquired immune deficiency syndrome), enormous increases in research funding enabled scientists to identify variants of the syndrome and to describe some of the complex ways it can damage the body (see Shilts, 1987). Funding for research on what is now a serious international health problem was thus significantly delayed due to the politics surrounding a stigmatized illness.

Similarly, research on women's problems has been funded at a much lower rate than men's. In 1988, only 13.5 percent of the National Institute of Health's budget was used to research women's health problems, such as heart disease, cancers, and osteoporosis (Rosser, 1994). In response to public outcry, in 1990 Congress increased funding for women's health issues and spurred the creation of the NIH Office of Research on Women's Health (Haseltine and Jacobson, 1997). Furthermore, most clinical studies (for example, tests of the effectiveness of pharmaceutical and surgical therapies) have been done almost exclusively on males. Although this testing bias may protect some women (and offspring) from harmful effects of drug testing, it also results in potentially harmful misdiagnosis and treatment when symptoms, course of the disease, and response to drugs and surgery are different in women's bodies than in men's (Inhorn and Whittle, 2001; Mastroianni et al., 1994).

Coronary heart disease (CHD) is the foremost cause of death among women, accounting for approximately half of their deaths, yet physicians learn to diagnose CHD using symptoms and methods of testing derived from studies of *men's* heart disease. Thus, doctors are more likely to misdiagnose and undertreat women's heart disease, not recognizing that the disease has different manifestations: For example, in men the most common initial manifestation is myocardial infarction—an acute symptom, whereas for women it is angina pectoris—serious pain but often continuing for years before a more acute symptom occurs (Mastroianni et al., 1994). One study showed 192 randomly sampled male internists videotapes in which "patients" (actors) with different characteristics (age, gender, race, socioeconomic status) presented the exact identical clinical information, and physicians were asked what they would do for their own patients in similar circumstances. Despite the fact that all tests and symptoms were identical, for the heart "cases" doctors were much less likely to diagnose cardiac disease in younger women compared to men, to consider medical treatment for (younger and older) women to be necessary, or even to recommend therapeutic lifestyle changes involving diet and exercise for women (McKinlay, 1996). The lack of solid research about heart disease in women may produce a vicious circle: Doctors fail to diagnose women's CHD because they do not expect to find it, but they do not expect to find it because the morbidity statistics showing low rates of CHD in younger women may be faulty due to failure to recognize the disease in women.

Thus, bias in scientific research is not merely a matter of levels of funding. Both scientific knowledge and medical practice are shaped by *social, cultural,* and *political* factors. These determine which research tasks are considered worth pursuing, how research questions are framed, and how the research is connected to a larger body of knowledge. Biomedical science is clearly a social product.

Often the development of new disease categories is connected with the emergence of a new occupational specialization. Considerable professional prestige is attached to "discovering" and describing a "new" disease or syndrome. In psychiatry, for example, the 1987 *Diagnostic and Statistical Manual* (DSM-III-R; APA, 1987) recognized 292 disorders and appended many "Proposed Diagnostic Categories Needing Further Study." Subsequently, nearly 100 new diagnoses were proposed for the next edition (Pincus et al., 1992). The process of proposing and gaining acceptance of new categories of diagnosis is partly political and often based on cultural assumptions rather than "pure" empirical evidence (Gaines, 1992). Corporate interests also promote "discovering" legitimation for new disease categories, especially when they purport to have a marketable "treatment" for the newly labeled condition (Conrad and Schneider, 1992). Finding new diseases is thus an active process; medicine is consciously oriented to creating disease categories where previously there were none (Freidson, 1970: 252). The case of menopause as a medical syndrome illustrates this process.

Creation of Medical "Problems": The Case of Menopause

Social and economic considerations promote the search for new diseases. For example, menopause, the period of women's lives in which menstruation naturally ceases, is now indexed in the *International Classification of Diseases* (USDHHS, 1989: 524–525). Although menopause is a normal biological process, in the last 50 years, it has come to be seen as a medical problem in the United States and many other Western societies. Medicalization of women's lives has not proceeded unchallenged, however, and often women actively resisted it (Lock and Kaufert, 1998). The Western biomedical literature generally treats menopause as an estrogen deficiency disease or ovarian dysfunction that produces various physical and emotional problems (see Ball, 1990; McCrea, 1983). Considerable cross-cultural variation is noted in its biophysical, social, and emotional concomitants, however (see Hunter and O'Dea, 1997; also, Goldstein, 2000).

In our culture, symptoms such as hot flashes, headaches, dizziness, fatigue, anxiety, insomnia, irritability, depression, and general emotional problems are typically associated with menopause. Cross-cultural data suggest, however, that women's responses to the cessation of menstruation may be connected to the structure of society and its cultural expectations for women (see Bowles, 1990; Lock, 1991, 1993b). For example, in Islamic and many African societies, menopause brings relative freedom from many of the restrictions of women's lives: They are no longer required to be secluded, veiled, and restricted in male company. These women experience few of the physiological and psychological symptoms attributed to menopause in Western societies (Townsend and Carbone, 1980). Interestingly, immigrant women experienced a change of symptoms, reflecting the influence of their new culture, as well as the old (Im et al., 1999). Menopause is thus a good example of how social meanings influence individuals' physical experiences and perceptions of their own bodies.

The Western medical construction of menopause, however, ignores these social meanings, reducing the experience to a set of biochemical processes presumed to characterize all female bodies, regardless of cultural or socioeconomic factors. Medical knowledge often becomes detached and independent of the research on which it is based. Thus, limitations in the original research are not taken into account in the accumulated stock of knowledge. For example, the medical construction of menopause is based in part on clinical studies with small numbers of subjects, typically drawn from patient populations—women whose menopause was surgically induced (as through oophorectomy) or whose problems with menopause had already been medically defined as severe enough to warrant treatment. There are severe methodological limitations to such studies, and cautious researchers know not to generalize too extensively from them to the general populace. Unfortunately, once in the medical literature, these ideas are treated as facts that are presumably generalizable to all women (Kaufert, 1988).

More recent studies of a wider population of middle-aged women have found relatively little evidence of pathology or medical problems due to menopause. One U.S. study followed the self-reported experiences of 8,050 women over several years before and after menopause; the majority of women did not seek help for menopause-related problems, and those who did experience significant "symptoms" were disproportionately those who reported prior poor health, independent of menopause. The researchers concluded with concern that physicians may be too quickly assuming that these women's problems were due to menopause and, thus, failing to diagnose or treat other, more probable causes such as chronic illnesses, stressful social situations, or preexisting psychological problems like depression (McKinlay et al., 1991). Part of the reason for doctors' acceptance of the methodologically flawed studies is that the medical construction of menopause meshes with physicians' assumptions about bodies and diseases. Thus, to define and treat a normal process as a disease fits the medical model, and the idea that menopause is a disease implies a concrete medical course of action.

In the United States, the definition of menopause as a deficiency disease resulted from the professional efforts of a small elite segment of the American medical profession during the 1930s and 1940s. A study of the medical literature during this transition shows that this process involved both the "discovery" of a theory of etiology of this "disease" and the development of pharmacologic methods of treatment. Using the paradigms of sex endocrinology, doctors attributed menopause to the deficiency of hormones (in particular, estrogen) regularly produced by the woman's body before cessation of menstruation. The development of a relatively inexpensive synthetic estrogen replacement subsequently made the medical management of this "disease" possible (Bell, 1990).

Although these specialists acknowledged that most menopausal women (a common estimate was 85 percent) experienced few or no problems, the efficacy of hormone "replacement therapy" (HRT) created the possibility of treating *all* menopausal women. Indeed, despite growing criticism and concern over the safety of HRT (some studies had linked it to cancer and some other serious conditions), by 1975 estrogens had become the fifth most frequently prescribed drug in the United States. In 1975, one gynecologist stated,

> I think of the menopause as a deficiency disease like diabetes. Most women develop some symptoms *whether they are aware of them or not,* so I prescribe estrogens for virtually all menopausal women for an indefinite period. (quoted in Brody, 1975: 55 [emphasis added])

In the mid-1970s the scientific literature began to implicate HRT in iatrogenic diseases (that is, those caused by medical treatment). Debates over the curbing of HRT involved conflicts between the pharmaceutical companies and the Food and Drug Administration, which ruled in 1976 that the industry must prepare a warning on the risks of estrogen for insertion in packages. The FDA originally approved HRT for temporary relief of hot flashes and other unpleasant symptoms experienced by a small proportion of women during the period immediately surrounding menopause. By 2002, however, pharmaceutical corporations were aggressively promoting HRT to doctors and consumers as appropriate for *all* menopausal and postmenopausal women as *lifelong* "preventive" treatment for a large range of postmenopausal ills, such as heart disease, Alzheimer's disease, depression, urinary incontinence, and osteoporosis. Many doctors accepted their claims without questioning the data on which they were based. The marketing strategy worked: U.S. sales in 2001 were $2,750 million (see Grady, 2002b).

Subsequently, a panel of international experts made a systematic review of all prior scientific studies of the effects of HRT and concluded that there was no good evidence that HRT would adequately treat or prevent any of these ills. The experts saw, in the evidence, reason for concern about serious or fatal health problems (such as stroke) with long-term use of these pharmaceuticals (see Grady, 2002b). Further evidence from experimental (rather than observational) studies also found that HRT creates serious risks for some women—not of cancer (as earlier feared) but of heart attacks, blood clots in legs and lungs, and gallbladder disease (see Grady, 2002a). After those research reports in 2002, HRT remained on the market and prescribed for hundreds of thousands of women, but many medical authorities quickly withdrew their support for HRT as a long-term or preventive treatment for post-menopausal women. The heavy involvement of the drug industry in the writing and publication of medical literature itself (see Foster, 1995: 83) made it difficult for physicians, as well as laypersons, to judge competing claims.

Denial of Medical "Problems": Tardive Dyskinesia

Despite the general disposition to find new diseases and syndromes, the medical profession sometimes *resists* accepting new disease categories. Social and political factors also account for some constraints against medical "discovery." Tardive dyskinesia is a seriously debilitating, often irreversible disorder of the central nervous system, characterized by a variety of involuntary movements, most notably of the lips, jaw, and tongue. It is a seemingly new disorder partly because it is a pervasive, iatrogenic side effect of antipsychotic (neuroleptic) drugs, such as chlorpromazine, which came onto the market in the 1950s. In the 1960s and 1970s, the prevalence of tardive dyskinesia increased because neuroleptic drugs were being prescribed more frequently and in higher doses. Even after the syndrome had been identified and named in 1960, many clinicians did not accept or use the diagnostic category (Brown and Funk, 1986: 116–124).

One significant factor in this resistance was that acknowledging the existence and pervasiveness of tardive dyskinesia hurt the economic and political interests of many clinicians. The institutional and professional mandate to control the deviant behaviors of patients often superseded concerns for the drugs' physical risks for patients. The researchers and others who called attention to tardive dyskinesia were generally identified with the National Institute of Mental Health, medical schools, and research institutes, whereas the clinicians who dealt with patients with the syndrome were working in mental hospitals and private psychiatric practice.

Many clinicians simply did not *observe* the disease, even in patients with obvious symptoms. The professional self-interest of these psychiatrists was involved; they relied heavily on pharmacological methods in their claims for efficacy in the treatment of psychoses, and their claims for recognition and remuneration as medical professionals were linked with their emphasis on biopsychiatry and psychopharmacology. Because the patients were generally already defined as mentally ill, their complaints could be readily discounted and their overt symptoms attributed to other problems, such as brain disorders (Brown and Funk, 1986). The economic and political interests of these physicians prevented them from recognizing the disease they were creating.

IDEAS AND IDEOLOGIES

Despite the supposed value-neutrality and objectivity of so-called scientific medicine, the knowledge produced, held, and used by its practitioners is, with considerable regularity, connected to their personal social location and the larger social situation of medical institutions in that society. In particular, social stratification (by criteria such as social class, age, political power, gender, and race) appears to be closely correlated with ideas about the body, health, illness, and healing. Thus, medical ideas often reflect or serve as ideology.

Ideology is a system of ideas that explains and legitimates the actions and interests of a specific sector (class) of society. For example, when the coal mining industry was in conflict with coal miners' representatives over black lung disease, the medical ideology of the industry promoted a very narrow definition of the disease, thereby diminishing the industry's legal responsibility toward the victims and its social responsibility for prevention of the syndrome (see Smith, 1981, 1987).

Ideas about health and illness frequently serve as legitimations for the interests of one group over another. A **legitimation** is any form of socially established explanation that is given to justify a course of action (see Berger and Luckmann, 1967: 92–128). In Chapter 6, we examined how ideas of health and illness legitimate the larger social order. Here we focus on legitimations for the interests of certain social groups in the stratification system.

In Western industrialized societies, the medical profession has organized itself, as we describe further later, specifically to promote its interests. Different professional interests pertain to other health-related occupations, such as nurses, pharmacists, X-ray technicians, midwives, and physical therapists. Incorporated into their ideas about health and healing are legitimations for their occupational statuses and income.

The 1975 so-called discovery of Lyme disease, a tick-borne spirochetal infection, illustrates how American rheumatologists successfully claimed the "discovery" and right to define treatment for the disease, superseding the "turf" claims of European dermatologists, who had "discovered" the same (or closely related) condition decades earlier and identified it as ECM (erythema chronicum migrans). By presenting Lyme disease as new and threatening, the mass media enhanced public attention to the disease, and commercial interests fanned public fears to promote a growing range of antitick products for people, pets, and property. Rather than being a discrete, objective entity that was simply medically "discovered," Lyme disease exemplifies the complex process by which a legitimized diagnosis is socially negotiated and developed (Aronowitz, 1991).

Other interests served by medical legitimation include those of the health-related industries: pharmaceutical industries, biotechnological industries, hospitals, nursing homes, and the medical, life, and disability insurance companies. Medical legitimations are especially important for various agencies of social control, such as the courts, mental hospitals, and schools. Ideas about health and illness are also used to legitimate the interests of such parties as employers, workers, producers, consumers, polluters, environmentalists, and the military.

Ideology influences actions subtly, most often without the actors' awareness. It is incorporated in the language and rituals of everyday interaction, and thus comes to be taken for granted and unnoticed or unexamined (Fisher, 1986). For example, the language used in referring to a patient as "the broken hip in room 305" depersonalizes the ill person, transforming her into a case that can be managed more readily by a professional team. Even matters of professional dress (such as a uniform, clipboard, and stethoscope) subtly symbolize status differences.

Ideological aspects of thought and practice often go unnoticed because they are often self-confirming. Ideology shapes our awareness of medical problems and our willingness to address them. For instance, the World Health Organization estimates that 3.2 million children under five years old die every year of diarrheal disease. Yet, we do not perceive this obvious medical danger as an "epidemic" that requires our attention (Moeller, 1999). Similarly, viruses that emerge from remote parts of the globe and assail the indigenous population are not worthy of attention unless or until they kill wealthy people or foreigners, especially Americans (McCormick and Fisher-Hoch, 1996). Clearly, the perceived social value of the victims of the virus influences the definition of the condition as an epidemic worthy of research and resources.[2]

Material interests are not the only motivating force for individuals; for example, spiritual or altruistic motives might lead people to work for conditions that

---

[2]In 2001, several U.S. postal workers contracted fatal anthrax infections while handling mail destined for important political and media figures. The first government disease control efforts focused on inspecting and decontaminating the federal office buildings and court chambers, but gave no thought to the working-class postal workers until some had already become seriously ill. Ideology was subtly involved in this oversight.

are not in their personal interest. Nevertheless, in general, people tend to hold ideas and engage in practices that serve or at least do not conflict with their own interests. The following examples illustrate some ways that interests influence ideas of health and illness, medical research, and individual diagnosis and treatments in Western bioscientific medicine.

Medicalization, Demedicalization, and Professional Interests

Medicalization is the process of legitimating medical control over an area of life, typically by asserting and establishing the primacy of a medical interpretation of that area (see Conrad and Schneider, 1992; Illich, 1992; Zola, 1983). The process of medicalization is illustrated by the medical treatment of pregnancy and childbirth, as doctors took over a business previously done primarily by midwives.

With the medicalization of childbirth, aspects of women's reproductive lives that are not pathological were brought under the canopy definition of illness (Davis-Floyd, 1992, 1994; Foster, 1995). Medical education for the new specialization of obstetrics and gynecology fostered the notion that the events of childbearing—pregnancy, labor and delivery, and puerperium (the period immediately following childbirth)—could best be understood in purely physical and pathological terms (Hahn, 1995: 209–233). More recently, sexuality, potency, fertility, and the process of conception have also become increasingly medicalized (Becker and Nachtigall, 1992; Lock, 2000a; Ragoné and Willis, 2000; Tiefer, 1992, 1994).

The medical profession persuaded the public and the regulators of health care that women needed doctors to manage their pregnancies and childbirth; however, that initial medicalization was linked more with doctors' professional interests than with patients' well-being. Indeed, when medical control over childbirth was first being consolidated, doctors and hospitals had abysmal records, especially for spreading infection to both mothers and babies (Oakley, 1984; Wertz and Wertz, 1979).

Artificial insemination has similarly been medicalized for reasons unrelated to health per se; the actual process of artificial insemination can be safely and effectively done without advanced technology or medical procedures. Rather, medicalization serves social control functions, for example, by screening applicants (and denying insemination to many). Physicians medicalize the process by representing it as a response to a husband's fertility problems, rather than as a response to a woman's wish to become pregnant. By medicalizing the artificial insemination, physicians retain a monopoly over the market and their control is protected by law in several states (Wikler and Wikler, 1991).

Just as medicalization is a largely political process, so too are efforts to undo previously medicalized conditions. For example, after considerable politicking in the American Psychiatric Association, homosexuality was removed from its earlier classification as a disease. Patients' interests are rarely the foremost political force for demedicalization; often more powerful interests such as competing professionals, insurers, pharmaceutical companies, and government agencies engage in the effort to medicalize or demedicalize a category. For example, if normal childbirth were redefined as a nonmedical event, insurers would be less likely to pay for physicians and hospitals for delivery. In general, medical institutions and medical professionals still retain vast and culturally respected authority over anything they have defined as "disease."

As Chapter 6 shows, some medicalization results from redefining "badness" as "sickness" and bringing the treatment of deviance under medical control. In this process, too, the medicalized ideas about the problem serve professional interests. When sicknesses thus labeled are defined as "bad," the doctors who join or organize efforts to eradicate or control them function as "moral entrepreneurs" (Becker, 1963: 147–163), or those who make an enterprise out of moral concerns.

The "discovery" of an illness category called hyperkinesis (more recently subsumed under the label ADHD "attention deficit hyperactive disorder") involved such entrepreneurial action. Virtually all of the persons labeled with this syndrome have been children; most are boys. Behaviors identified as characteristic of ADHD include excess of motor activity, short attention span, restlessness, impulsivity, and inability to sit still in school and comply with rules. These behaviors, however, have been frequently observed among schoolchildren, probably since the invention of the institution of the school. Although no organic basis was identified, the medical category of hyperkinesis resulted in part from social factors, such as the development and vigorous promotion of psychoactive drugs (specifically, Ritalin [methylphenidate]) for controlling hyperkinetic behavior and the crusading efforts of moral entrepreneurs, including doctors, educators, and parents. Hyperkinesis rapidly became an attractive diagnosis, and the drug Ritalin accounted for significant proportions of the pharmaceutical industry's profits (Conrad and Schneider, 1992: 156–158).

The promotion of ideas about a disease category is thus a political effort, by which professionals are promoting their own interests. *Ideas function as ideologies.* The attempt to define participation in religious cults as a medical problem illustrates how the illness label is a product of specific political efforts (Robbins and Anthony, 1982). The 1980 and 1987 editions of the American Psychiatric Association's *Diagnostic and Statistical Manual of Mental Disorders* (DSM-III and DSM-III-R) contained several changes from previous editions in order to characterize participation in new religious movements or in non-Western religions in the United States as characteristic of mental disorder (Post, 1992). For example, in the definition of paranoid personality disorder, the revised manual stated that "individuals with this disorder are over-represented among leaders of mystical or esoteric religions and/or pseudoscientific and quasipolitical groups" (American Psychiatric Association, 1987: 308). Thus, an evaluation of someone's mental health includes a judgment as to whether the individual's religious, scientific, or political persuasion is deviant (Lukoff et al., 1992). Interestingly, the efforts to define participation in new religious movements as sick were primarily those of a relatively small number of therapists who made their living "deprogramming" former members or testifying as expert witnesses in court cases involving the very religious movements they were "diagnosing." These moral entrepreneurs established professional territory for themselves by creating illness labels (Richardson, 1993).[3] Medicalization is selective; it is not likely to occur when it does not promote the self-interest of medical practitioners or industries (Saks, 1995).

Similar political processes are often involved in classifying physical ailments. Ideas about the etiology of an illness (and, by extension, responsibility for it) are often debated politically. For example, a syndrome called miners' nystagmus has been the subject of continual political negotiation as a medical category. In the nineteenth century, this syndrome was a recognized diagnostic category (characterized by such symptoms as oscillation of the eyes and spasms of eyelids, dizziness, headaches, and sensitivity to light). Later, however, it had become an expensive item of compensation, so the British mining industry engaged in continual medical-legal debates as to whether it was a legitimate illness. The incidence of nystagmus complaints was often related directly to changes in conditions of work (such as production schedules) in the mines. As the result of complex social interactions involving doctors, management, labor, and government agencies, this illness was eventually psychologized, and thereby both recognized as a problem yet invalidated as a compensable illness (Figlio, 1982).

By trying to define the issues as mere medical problems with purely technical responses, some researchers and their commercial sponsors are evading profound social and moral issues. For example, in justifying experiments involving injections of healthy children with the genetically engineered human growth hormone, researchers framed short stature as a deficiency disease with a purely technical solution. It is a debatable ethical issue whether an inherited characteristic previously considered to be within the range of normal should be redefined as a "medical problem" needing medical treatment (Hotz, 1993).

Corporate Interests

A good example of how ideology figures into the definition of, diagnosis of, and response to illness can be seen in ideas about occupational health hazards. In recent years, manufacturers, unions, workers' rights groups, medical authorities, and several government agencies have been involved in a growing confrontation over issues of the genetic protection of workers and their offspring. One episode occurred in 1979, when the Department of Labor cited and fined American Cyanamid for requiring women to be sterilized to keep their jobs at the company's lead pigments manufacturing operations in West Virginia. Numerous chemicals used to manufacture paints, pesticides, herbicides, plastics, and heavy metals are

---

[3]The 1994 edition (DSM-IV) reduced some bias, dropping reference to "terrorists and cultists" in its definition of dissociative disorder; however, it added a new code (V62.89) to legitimate psychiatric treatment for persons with spiritual distress (James Richardson, 1995).

strongly implicated in reproductive damage. Sterility, miscarriages, and birth defects have been identified with workers' exposure to these chemicals.

In 1984, the United Automobile Workers union sued Johnson Controls, the nation's largest producer of batteries, over its exclusionary policies for workers' exposure to lead, the basic raw material of batteries. One worker had undergone sterilization to keep her job; another worker was transferred to a nonexposed job at loss of pay, despite very low probability of becoming pregnant; but a male employee's request to transfer to a nonexposed job to avoid reproductive risk was denied. This case resulted in a 1991 landmark decision by the U.S. Supreme Court that personnel practices limiting the employment of fertile women in jobs posing reproductive health hazards constituted sex discrimination and thus were illegal under the 1964 Civil Rights Act. This court decision has long-term policy implications related to several health issues: Are women more at risk than men (who also contribute genetic material to their offspring)? Is the risk to the fetus the most important concern, or should there be concern for male and female workers as well? Are these reproductive problems only one manifestation of health threats (such as cancer) that might affect all workers? (see Daniels, 1993; Draper, 2000).

Captive Professionals

The company doctor is a good example of what Daniels (1969) called **"captive professionals,"** or those whose presumed professional autonomy is compromised by organizational pressures from the bureaucracies that employ them. Daniels's study noted that psychiatrists practicing in the armed services accommodated their professional judgments to the military's manpower needs and values. Whereas psychiatrists working for mental hospitals tended to diagnose patients as mentally ill (in accordance with the expectations of the employer institutions), psychiatrists working for the military (where sickness reduced active manpower) tended to deny soldiers' claims of illness (Daniels, 1969, 1972; Rosenhan, 1973). The diagnoses made by both of these "captive professionals" served to legitimate administrative decisions of the bureaucracies that employed them.

Similarly, many medical personnel employed by industry are "captive professionals." One Canadian study found that company doctors exhibited a "lack of sympathy with or intolerance of workers' attitudes towards health and safety in the workplace," and often perceived workers' health concerns as "fashions" or unreasonable fears. Rather than press the company to engineer changes in the production process or to initiate expensive monitoring programs, these doctors often emphasized workers' use of protective equipment and the screening and exclusion of supposedly "hyper-susceptible" workers (Walters, 1982). Although the corporate physician is potentially in a position to influence improved occupational health for employees, the professional's employer—not the individual worker—is still the "client," so ethical ambiguity and conflicting pressures are inherent in the structure of the job (Walsh, 1987; see also Brown and Kelley, 2000).

Although some professionals' organizational situation makes them clearly vulnerable or "captive" to their employers' interests, all professionals are likely to be influenced by their identification with certain class or status interests. Source of income indirectly affects medical decisions and doctor-patient relationships. For example, doctors employed by industry tend not to diagnose occupational diseases, whereas doctors employed by unions or workers' health clinics frequently do (Lewin, 1987). Doctors who profit from patient fees-for-service are likewise more likely to urge patients to undergo Caesarian sections, whereas those working at public hospitals are much less likely to perform such operations (Stafford, 1991).

Whose Interests Are Served?

Although ideologies legitimate certain interests over others, they are often accepted by people whose interests are not necessarily served by those ideas. Ideological elements are often subtly diffused in a society through popular culture, educational institutions, mass media, and commercial advertising. For example, whose interests were served by the turn-of-the-century glorification of women's domesticity? Throughout the first half of this century, this ideal was meshed with popular ideas and fears of bacterial contagion to create much more work for housewives, who were taught in school and in women's magazines that they should be occupied with "scientific cleaning" and buying numerous products to protect their families from these dangerous invisible agents (Ehrenreich and English, 1978: 127–164). Interest groups exert power to shape ideology and to have it accepted and disseminated through channels such as the mass media and public education (Berger and Luckmann, 1967: 119–124).

Ideologies are not peculiar to medicine under capitalism and absent under other social and economic arrangements. *All* medical systems embody ideologies, but the nature of these ideologies varies according to the structure of that society. In capitalist societies, the treatment of health and healing as **commodities** to be bought and sold under market conditions produces certain economic benefits for various individual and corporate interests. Medical systems in noncapitalist societies, however, also utilize ideologies to legitimate and promote the interests of certain groups, such as state bureaucracies, dominant ethnic or tribal groups, or patriarchal powers (Donahue and McGuire, 1995).

Reification: Diseases and Bodies as Objects

Ideas that serve as ideologies often come into use subtly, frequently without explicit intention or awareness that the ideas have ideological uses. One such set of ideas are contemporary medical conceptions of the nature of disease and of the body. The product of this development is the notion that diseases are discrete, identifiable (or potentially identifiable) entities—in short, objects. The body is likewise treated as an object, separate from the person who inhabits it.

This conception illustrates the process of reification and its ideological functions. **Reification** is the "apprehension of human phenomena as if they were things," or something other than human products (Berger and Luckmann, 1967: 89). Reified reality confronts people as something outside themselves, as a nonhuman object. Institutions, social roles, norms, and other social processes are often reified; they come to assume a greater-than-human authority and inevitability. Reification thus entails a certain amount of mystification, as the human roots of phenomena are veiled (see Taussig, 1980).

Reification of disease means conveniently forgetting the social processes by which the concept of disease is produced. It means denying the social meanings embodied in symptoms, diagnoses, and therapy, and in the very experience of illness itself. Reification of the body results in an even greater dehumanization because of the close connection between the body and the identity of the individual. For example, an anesthetized body lying on a gurney before surgery on its testicles is medically no more than an object with a pathological entity (disease) in its tissues (things) that must therefore be surgically removed. To the person himself, however, that body and those testicles are an important part of who he is—his very self.

Reification creeps pervasively into the practice of bioscientific medicine because the guise of the scientific process masks the human factors involved in the creation of medical knowledge, as illustrated earlier in this chapter. It also occurs when any individual practitioner fails to acknowledge that a diagnosis or medical disposition is a human creation. The diagnostician constructs a disease identification from an assortment of ambiguous signs and symptoms elicited by human processes, and interpreted in the context of a human evaluation of the patient's social and psychological—as well as physical—condition.

Diagnoses are the product of social interaction, yet rarely does a physician accept authorship of a disease identification. Rather, the disease comes to be seen as a feature or property of the patient (Taussig, 1980). For example, the complex process by which a physician applies the diagnostic label "diabetes" to a patient's condition is forgotten, and the diabetes is treated as an objective thing that the patient "has." The reified disease identification often assumes primacy; if it conflicts with the patient's subjective illness experience, the objectified disease-thing is often treated as more real than the sick person's feelings. To the extent that patients internalize this image of their bodies and diseases, the reified reality shapes even their self-perception and experience.

One of the ideological functions of the reification of disease and the body is an emphasis on individualistic rather than social or political responses to disease. In the example of workers' health risks in a chemical factory, the location of disease as a property of individual bodies led to an emphasis on finding which individuals were more likely to be susceptible to workplace toxins. It promoted the idea that those who were identified at risk should be counseled to change jobs, rather than reducing the exposure of all workers or eliminating the industrial processes that required the use of toxic substances. Reification transforms occupational disease into a thing that befalls some individuals instead of the result of specific human decisions affecting workers' health.

The emphasis on disease as an object that occurs within an individual also produces a tendency to locate responsibility for illness in the individual. It is thus one form of **blaming the victim** (Ryan, 1971), a type of legitimation which argues that the victim rather than the agent of a misfortune (such as rape, homelessness, or family abuse) was actually responsible for the occurrence. In the case of battered women, for instance, medical personnel often respond by minimizing the abuse, labeling, and victim-blaming. One study of medical responses to battering incidents found that health care providers wrote in medical charts that women had been "hit with ashtray" or "kicked with foot." Note how the use of passive voice in the records omits the *agent* of abuse and euphemizes the violence, as though the woman were injured when a flying ashtray or loose foot just "happened" to strike her. Only in one in forty episodes did the medical record refer clearly to domestic violence (Stark and Flitcraft, 1996). Blaming the victim results in medical neglect that compounds the trauma of abuse victims.

Such attention to the individual as the locus of disease often results in inattention to the sick person's whole situation. Even extremely caring physicians can lose sight of the sociostructural roots of patients' suffering by focusing on an utterly individualized image of disease. For example, one study of doctor-patient communication noted the extent to which the patient's larger social predicament (for example, an extremely stressful workplace) was generally ignored or reduced to individualistic treatments, such as recommendation of tranquilizers (Waitzkin, 1984). *Medical ideas about disease thus serve subtle ideological functions, legitimating an individualistic—rather than social—approach to prevention and healing.*

THE DEVELOPMENT OF MODERN BIOMEDICINE

We sometimes view the present nature of medical practice as a cultural given. When we think of medical care, our ready mental images include doctors, hospitals, nurses, medical laboratories, operating rooms, X-rays, hypodermic needles, and pills. But the institutions, occupations, and technologies we identify with medical care are the peculiar result of specific political, economic, and social interactions. The history of modern medicine shows that many alternative courses were possible, and the particular form that medical knowledge and practice have taken in this society made certain medical advances possible but also limited the field by cutting off other potentially fruitful approaches to health and healing.

The paradigm of modern scientific medicine incorporates a number of assumptions about the nature of the body and disease. Ideas do not just happen; rather they are produced, accepted, and transmitted in a political and social context. The elevation of this particular paradigm to become the medical model for understanding human bodies occurred through the political process by which the medical profession gained dominance relative to other social authorities and healers.

Professional Dominance

In the nineteenth century, most medical doctors were barely considered professionals. Their credentials were relatively easy to achieve (or fake), their body of medical knowledge was skimpy, their tools for diagnosis and therapy were primitive and often dangerous, and their abilities to heal were not particularly impressive. Several kinds of physicians, each having very different ideas about the causes and treatments of sickness, competed for patients and social legitimacy. Furthermore, physicians were only a small percentage of the total number of persons practicing various healing arts, who included, among others, midwives, bone setters, nurses, pharmacists, barbers (who performed minor surgery), herbalists, and folk and religious healers.

In the early part of the twentieth century, medical doctors achieved, within just a few decades, virtually total professional dominance. Subsequently, they successfully eliminated, coopted, or subordinated all competing health professionals and acquired a state-legitimated monopoly over the health care market in the United States. The authority of medical knowledge became so great that any other framework was literally unthinkable (Jordan, 1997). Although medicine enjoyed similar professional preeminence in other nations, it lacked the degree of state-legitimated dominance over the entire health care system that characterized the American situation during most of the twentieth century (Freidson, 1970; see also Coburn et al., 1983; Herzlich and Pierret, 1987). By the beginning of the twenty-first century, however, this exclusive dominance of the medical profession was seriously challenged, but the profession retained much public confidence (Pescosolido et al., 2001). This shift is evident in the popular media, which sometimes present modern medicine as a savior, but just as often portray it as the site of malpractice, despair, greed, and human error (Lupton, 1998).

A profession is a service occupation characterized by legitimate control over the market for its services and over a body of specialized knowledge or expertise. The **professionalization** of medicine as an occupation is thus a sociopolitical movement organized to achieve a "monopoly of opportunities in a market of services or labor and, inseparably, monopoly of status and work privileges" (Larson, 1979: 609). For medicine to achieve professional status, three main developments were necessary: (1) achieving standardization and cohesion within the profession; (2) convincing the state at various levels to grant a monopoly, for example, by requiring medical licenses to engage in healing practices; and (3) gaining public respect and persuading the public to accept the profession's definitions of what problems properly should be brought to it for service.

One definitive characteristic of a developed profession is its autonomy, which is an organizational product of its ability to dominate its area of expertise in the division of labor. In the case of the medical profession, autonomy is evidenced by doctors' legal protection from encroachment by other occupations. A second factor in medical autonomy is the profession's control over the production and application of medical knowledge and skill, especially the training and licensing of physicians. A third indication of medicine's status as a developed profession is its presumed self-regulation with a code of ethics (Freidson, 1970).

In 1847, the American Medical Association (AMA) was established as a professional organization for physicians from the medical belief system dubbed **allopathy,** which was characterized by "heroic" and invasive treatments such as bloodletting, purging, blistering, vomiting, and medicating with powerful drugs (such as opium) and poisons (like mercury and arsenic). Allopathic physicians called themselves "regular" or orthodox physicians, but the public was, understandably, attracted to some of the less dangerous forms of medicine practiced by competing approaches such as homeopathy, naturopathy, and hydropathy.

The initial program of the AMA was relatively straightforward: to create internal professional cohesion and standardization by controlling the requirements for medical degrees and by enacting a code of ethics that would exclude "irregular" practitioners from the ranks. These efforts were aimed primarily at reducing the influence of the chief competitors, homeopathic physicians, who had organized the American Institute for Homeopathy in 1844. Between 1850 and 1880, the two camps became increasingly polarized, as the AMA censured members who continued to have dealings with the "enemy." For example, in 1878 the local medical society expelled a Connecticut doctor for having consulted with a homeopathic physician—his wife. "Regular" physicians lost considerable ground in the latter half of the nineteenth century while homeopathy gained as much public respect and legal considerations as allopathy. So-called regular practitioners accounted for nearly 90 percent of all doctors, but the proportion of irregular physicians increased in the mid-1800s. For the latter half of the century, irregulars commanded approximately one-fifth of the market (Starr, 1982: 88–99).

The AMA and the irregular physicians cooperated, however, in their political efforts to have states enact licensing laws, because they shared a common interest in eliminating competition from persons who had not attended any form of medical school, such as midwives, ministers, pharmacists, and folk healers. From its outset, the AMA has been especially interested in exposing and prosecuting what it calls "quackery," which is practically defined as all forms of medicating or healing outside the profession's control. A related campaign successfully eliminated much competition from patent medicine manufacturers and eventually subordinated the practice of pharmacy to medical control. Licensing legislation began to specify the quality of the medical education required, and some states set up boards of medical examiners, initially making allowances for various irregular forms of professional training alongside the regular. The courts and legislatures had begun to grant professional prerogatives to thus-approved doctors. Gradually, regular medicine coopted and absorbed most irregular physicians, but rejected and actively opposed later organized alternatives such as chiropractic (Starr, 1982: 99–112; Wolpe, 1990).

Scientization of Medicine and Medical Training

The most dramatic change in the medical profession's dominance occurred after the turn of the century. The adoption of scientific medicine and the insistence on standards of rigorous medical education were central strategies in the professionalization process. Science and education did not, however, characterize the actual practice of regular medicine at that time. In fact, scientific training was available to only a small elite of physicians, mainly researchers and educators, who had the money to study in Europe (Berliner, 1976).

Control of medical education was critical to a monopoly in the market. In the early 1900s, practicing physicians made relatively poor incomes; one comparison suggests that they earned less than an ordinary mechanic of the day (Berliner, 1976: 584). There appeared to be a growing oversupply of physicians relative to the market of paying clients. Licensing laws had not resulted in fewer physicians but merely more medical schools. The national population grew between 1870 and 1910 by 138 percent; the number of physicians increased by 153 percent. Many professional leaders objected not only to the numbers of new physicians these medical schools were graduating but also to the fact that they had recruited "undesirable" students: women, blacks, immigrants, and working-class persons. Advocates of reforming medical education believed that medicine could not become a respected profession if its ranks included such lowly elements. Shortly after the turn of the century, the AMA underwent a major internal organization and subsequently made such "reform" its primary focus (Starr, 1982: 112–117).

After a preliminary review of medical colleges, the AMA invited an outside group, the Carnegie Foundation, to conduct a thorough investigation of the approximately 160 medical colleges in the United States and Canada. The resulting report in 1910 was devastating to many medical education programs (Flexner, 1910). The report's foremost objection was to the lack of medical science in the curriculum and training experiences.[4] It recommended that the great majority of medical schools should be closed; the first-rate schools should be strengthened on the model of Johns Hopkins, which had a singularly science-oriented program; and a few medium-quality schools should be greatly improved to meet the upper standard. With the support of state legislatures and many universities themselves,

---

[4]One review of the history of medicine (Ludmerer, 1999) posits that the curricular emphasis on medical science resulting from the Flexner Report has been systematically dismantled by the competitive, market-driven organization of corporate "managed care" in the second half of the twentieth century. In this corporate context (where even teaching hospitals are owned by for-profit corporations), the training of doctors has little to do with the ideals of science, caring, or even professionalism.

the governing body of the AMA subsequently became the de facto national accrediting agency for medical schools (Berliner, 1975).[5]

These reforms of medical education had exactly the kind of effects the AMA wanted: increased internal cohesion of the profession and increased control of the market. Not only had the supply of licensed physicians been dramatically cut, but the homogeneity of the profession had also been assured by greatly limiting access to medical education for women, blacks, Jews, and all who could not afford the newly required four years of college and four full-time years of medical school. The declining numbers of new physicians adversely affected poor and rural areas. Flexner had expected that the new highly trained graduates would disperse throughout the country, but in practice they gravitated to the wealthiest regions.

The increased cost of their medical education reduced the likelihood that they would accept the modest incomes of practices in small towns and rural areas (Starr, 1982: 123–127). There were likewise fewer doctors for blacks. Due to widespread discrimination and segregation, blacks received treatment mainly from black physicians, but the reforms dramatically reduced their numbers (Starr, 1982: 124). Only two of the seven medical schools for blacks survived the reforms. Because the medical colleges run by irregular physicians had been somewhat more open to interracial admissions, their disproportionate demise also reduced opportunities for blacks to become doctors.

In the latter part of the nineteenth century, considerable numbers of women had entered medical practice. In the decade from 1880 to 1890, women doubled their proportional representation of all doctors in the United States (from 2.8 to 5.6 percent); 17 medical colleges for women were founded in that period. After considerable struggle, women began to be admitted to elite medical schools after 1890, and by 1893–1894, women constituted 10 percent or more of the student body at 19 of the coeducational schools (Starr, 1982: 117).

Women's acceptance into coeducational settings was far from smooth, however; they experienced considerable harassment from male professors and students (Morantz-Sanchez, 1985). Many physicians believed that women's menstrual cycles made them incapable of professional work. For example, one doctor declared, "periodical infirmity of their sex . . . in every case . . . unfits them for any responsible effort of mind . . . [and that during their menstrual] condition, neither life nor limb submitted to them would be as safe as at other times" (quoted in Wertz and Wertz, 1979: 57). After the Flexner Report, all but three of the 17 women's medical colleges closed, and coeducational medical colleges maintained quotas that, until the 1960s, limited women to about 5 percent of admissions (Starr, 1982: 124).

---

[5]The conspicuous role of the capitalist philanthropies, notably the Rockefeller Foundation (which gave some $66 million to just nine medical schools in the aftermath of Flexner's report), has led some to suggest a direct affinity between capitalist classes and the type of medicine they chose to support (see Brown, 1979; and the critique in Starr, 1982: 228). Even if there were no deliberate collusion, it is true that the outcome was a version of medicine that necessitated extensive expenditures on pharmaceuticals, medical technology, and capital-intensive hospitals, as described further in Chapters 11 and 12.

Because they were excluded from mainstream medicine, some women turned to the less prestigious area of public health, such as campaigns for better hygiene, nutrition, and mother-and-child health care. The medical profession often opposed these efforts, which it perceived as threats to its dominance and as competition for health expenditures. For example, female public health advocates campaigned for the Sheppard-Towner Act of 1921, which provided health care for mothers and infants until 1929, when the AMA pressured Congress not to renew funding (Morantz-Sanchez, 1985).

Professional Autonomy and Control

By the 1930s, the medical profession had achieved significant autonomy. It controlled the recruitment and training of new physicians, including the length and content of medical education, as well as the examination and licensing by which new doctors could be admitted to practice. The profession defined (and regularly expanded) the scope of its work, specified its own standards of practice, and maintained the right to enforce them (Freidson, 1970).

The prerogative to define the scope of medical work is connected with the process of *medicalization* by which increasing numbers of areas of life were brought under medicine's purview and control. Childbirth, alcoholism, obesity, infant feeding formulas, and menopause are just a few of the areas that previously were not defined as properly "medical" matters but, through the medical profession's influence, were redefined as issues needing doctors' attention, regardless of whether the medical approach was more effective than nonmedical (see Barker, 1998). Other efforts to expand their markets included the campaign to persuade well persons to get an annual checkup.

In defining the scope of its work, the medical profession also eliminated much of its competition. Some professional competitors, such as homeopaths and osteopaths, were coopted; others, such as pharmacists, nurses, anesthetists, and X-ray technicians, were subordinated; whereas still others, such as midwives, clergy, and barber-surgeons, were driven from legitimate practice outright (Gritzer, 1981). The AMA also worked to limit public health authorities severely; medical professional interests campaigned (usually successfully) against public dispensaries, the compulsory reporting of tuberculosis, municipal laboratories and vaccination programs, the provision of health services in the public schools, and national public health programs, which were all viewed as competitors in the provision of services and as threats to the profession's autonomous authority over its domain. By controlling licensing, the access to facilities (such as hospitals and labs), access to other physicians as backups, and the legitimacy of third-party reimbursement, the medical profession greatly reduced its competition (Dolan, 1980).

The medical profession rapidly consolidated its control over the conditions of its work as the organization of hospitals specifically reflects. In recent years, however, the profession has lost some of its control under "managed care," as described in Chapters 11 and 12. Because of its market monopoly, the medical profession also asserted its control over the terms of its remuneration. The profession's model of the ideal economic relationship was one of direct payment by the patient-receiver to the health care provider. The rise in importance of third-party payment from the government, insurance companies, labor unions, or fraternal organizations, who paid part or all of some patients' medical fees, represented an intrusion and danger to medical dominance. As Starr (1982: 235) observed, "to be the intermediary in the costs of sickness is a strategic role that confers social and political as well as strictly economic gains." Over the years the medical profession has vehemently asserted its interests in campaigns against national health insurance, Social Security health benefits, Blue Cross and Blue Shield, prepaid health plans, Medicare, and Medicaid. As shown in Chapters 11 and 12, the role of third parties has nevertheless increased, resulting in some regulation and limitation of medical practice and payments.

Modernization and Medical Practice

The features of modern medicine are in many ways the products of the broader process of modernization, which has similarly shaped other institutional spheres, such as industry, education, and communications. The specific historical development of the medical profession also contributed to certain structural features of modern medicine.

Several aspects of modernization apply to the development of medicine. One is the trend toward **institutional differentiation,** in which various institutional spheres in society become separated from each other, as each comes to perform specialized functions. Differentiation resulted in the separation of healing functions from the institutions of religion and the family. A second aspect of modernization is **rationalization,** the application of criteria of functional rationality to many aspects of social and economic life. When applied to the division of labor, rationalization promoted bureaucratic forms of organization and an emphasis on efficiency, standardization, and instrumental criteria for decision making. The structure of the modern hospital reflects this rational principle of organization.

Rational ways of knowing emphasized the use of empirical evidence to explain natural phenomena without reference to nonnatural categories of thought. Weber ([1904] 1958: 139) observed that this led to the "disenchantment" of the world, meaning that phenomena once held in awe or reverence were stripped of their special qualities and became ordinary. The human body itself has been thus disenchanted. For example, the modern view of the body contrasts strongly with the medieval notion that the body should not be dissected lest it be unfit for reuniting with the soul in resurrection. Bodies that are considered spiritual temples must be respected; bodies that are disenchanted entities require no special reverence. The key feature of the rationalization process is not so much the particular explanations of phenomena but the belief that all phenomena can be rationally explained. A by-product of this belief is an increased emphasis on technology and technique by which rational knowledge can presumably be translated into control.

Modern societies particularly value rational mastery. For example, we believe that if we can explain what causes a disease, then it is only a matter of time before we can develop a technology or technique for healing or even preventing the disease.

Although the process of rationalization occurred in all modernizing medical systems, an additional feature in capitalist societies was **commodification,** or the process by which such qualities as health, beauty, and fitness are transformed into objects that can be bought and sold in the marketplace. Not only material objects such as pharmaceuticals and prosthetic devices but also the entire range of health services become commodities to be bought and sold.[6] Commodification encourages both the sick and the well to become avid consumers of the nebulous product known as health (Featherstone, 1991).

Although these aspects of contemporary Western medical systems are linked with the larger process of modernization, many of the specific characteristics of modern medicine are the products of the historical-political struggle for professional dominance and the assumptions implicit in the biomedical belief system described next. Indeed, it is entirely likely that if different factions and competitors had won those early battles for legitimacy and a share of the medical market, we would today have an entirely different model of medical knowledge, of what constitutes health and health care, and of what it means to be a doctor.

Assumptions of the Biomedical Model

The present system of medical knowledge is based on a number of assumptions about the body, disease, and ways of knowing. Although many of these assumptions have a long history, they do not necessarily produce better medical care. They also deflect attention from nonmedical measures for promoting health, such as nutrition and public health, and as the last part of this chapter illustrates, contribute to serious problems in doctor-patient communication.

Mind-Body Dualism   The medical model assumes a clear dichotomy between the mind and the body; physical diseases are presumed to be located within the body (Engel, 1977; Gordon, 1988; Kirmayer, 1988; Leder, 1984). The medical model also holds that the body can be understood and treated in isolation from other aspects of the person inhabiting it (Hahn and Kleinman, 1983).

The philosophical foundations for this split may go back to Descartes's division of the person into mind and body. The practical foundations, however,

---

[6]The organ-trafficking market is one of the more vulgar contemporary examples of commodification. To raise money for an operation that would save his son's life, a father in Istanbul, Turkey sold one of his kidneys for $10,000 to a broker who then sold it to a man in Israel who had scraped together $145,000 to buy the kidney (Finkel, 2001). Some politicians in the United States are proposing legislation to legalize monetary exchange or reimbursement for transplant organs. Unlike most other economically advanced countries, the United States already allows the sale of blood. Some social scientists are questioning both the *process* by which such moral issues are decided politically on ideological grounds and the *assumptions* about human bodies and persons that are implicit in the terms of debate (Scheper-Hughes, 2000).

probably lie in medicine's shift to an emphasis on clinical observation toward the end of the eighteenth century and pathological anatomy beginning in the nineteenth century. Foucault (1973) demonstrated that medicine shifted its ways of viewing the body and developed a "clinical gaze." Previously, physicians saw the body indirectly, mainly through patients' descriptions of their experience of a malady. By contrast, the clinical gaze emphasized direct clinical observation and physical examinations; technological developments, such as the invention of the stethoscope in 1819, gave physicians access to direct (and presumably more objective) clinical knowledge than previously could be gained only indirectly. Foucault noted that the way the body is viewed has profound political implications. The ascending medical perspective saw the body as docile—something physicians could observe, manipulate, transform, and improve (see also Armstrong, 1983). Increasingly sophisticated pathological anatomy meant that diseases were conceptualized in terms of alterations in tissues that were visible upon opening the body, such as during autopsy. This mode of conceptualizing disease had a profound effect in splitting body from mind in the practice of clinical medicine (Sullivan, 1986: 344–345).

Physical Reductionism   The medical model not only dichotomizes body and mind, but also assumes that illness can be reduced to disordered bodily (biochemical or neurophysiological) functions. This physical reductionism, however, excludes social, psychological, and behavioral dimensions of illness (Engel, 1977). The result of this reductionism, together with medicine's mind-body dualism, is that disease is localized in the *individual* body. Such conceptions prevent the medical model from conceiving of the *social* body, or how aspects of the individual's social or emotional life might impinge on physical health. Another result is medicine's general inattention to social conditions (as described in Chapters 3–5) that contribute to illness or could aid in healing (Bologh, 1981).

Specific Etiology   A related assumption of the biomedical model is what Dubos (1959: 130–135) called the "doctrine of specific etiology," or the belief that each disease is caused by a specific, potentially identifiable agent. It developed from the nineteenth-century work of Pasteur and Koch, who demonstrated that the introduction of specific virulent microorganisms (germs) into the body produced specific diseases. One primary focus of scientific medicine became the identification of these specific agents and their causal link to specific diseases. The doctrine of specific etiology was later extended beyond infectious diseases to other diseases, such as deficiency diseases in which the etiology was not an infectious agent, but the lack of a necessary element, such as a vitamin or hormone.

Although the doctrine of specific etiology has led to important theoretical and practical achievements, Dubos noted that it has rarely provided a complete account of the causation of disease. He asked why, although infectious agents are nearly ubiquitous, only some people get sick some of the time. Accordingly, an adequate understanding of an illness etiology must include broader factors, such as nutrition, stress, and metabolic states, that affect the individual's susceptibility to infection. As noted in Chapter 2, the search for specific illness-producing agents worked relatively well in dealing with infectious diseases but is too simplistic to explain the causes of complex, chronic illnesses. Also, as Dubos (1959) observed, this approach often results in a quest for a medicinal "magic bullet" to "shoot and kill" the disease, producing an overreliance on pharmaceuticals in the "armamentarium" (stock of weapons) of the modern physician.

The Machine Metaphor One of the oldest Western images for understanding the body is a comparison with the functioning of a machine. Accordingly, disease is the malfunctioning of some constituent mechanism (such as a "breakdown" of the heart). Other cultures use other metaphors; for example, ancient Egyptian societies used the image of a river, and Chinese tradition refers to the balance of elemental forces (yin and yang) of the earth (Osherson and AmaraSingham, 1981). Modern medicine has not only retained the metaphor of the machine but also extended it by developing specializations along the lines of machine parts, emphasizing individual systems or organs to the exclusion of an image of the totality of the body. The machine metaphor further encouraged an instrumentalist approach to the body; the physician could "repair" one part in isolation from the rest (Berliner, 1975). Such mechanical metaphors further justify, as a medical procedure, the replacement of nonworking parts by organ transplants, pacemakers, and artificial joints, for example.

Regimen and Control Partly as a product of the machine metaphor and the quest for mastery, the Western medical model also conceptualizes the body as the proper object of regimen and control, again emphasizing the responsibility of the individual to exercise this control in order to maintain or restore health. Modernizing trends toward rationalization have further encouraged the standardization of body disciplines, such as diets, exercise programs, etiquette, routines of hygiene, and even sexual activity (Foucault, 1979; Turner, 1995).

This brief history shows that the knowledge and practice we know as medicine have their roots in sociopolitical processes. The ideas and assumptions of biomedicine forcefully influence economic and power relationships—interpersonal (for example, doctor and patient), as well as institutional (for example, law). We must remember that these medical realities are socially produced.

SUMMARY

What we know about health, illness, and the body is socially constructed. Both lay and professional medical knowledge are influenced by social, economic, and political factors. The categories and even the very language for describing and understanding diseases are likewise subject to powerful social influences. Diseases and disease syndromes are discovered and professionally accepted through concrete social processes; other disease categories are similarly denied, dropped, or disavowed by social processes. These socially constructed ideas also influence the experiences of our own and others' bodies and bodily conditions.

The nature of modern medicine is partly determined by the larger process of modernization, especially the extension of rationalization to the body and ways of knowing about and treating the body. In capitalist societies, the additional societal process of the commodification of health and health care has altered the economic meaning of medical services, as health has become an ambiguous product to be bought and consumed.

Medical knowledge sometimes serves ideological purposes, legitimating the interests of certain persons or groups. Ideological aspects of thought and practice are typically very subtle, and often go unnoticed by people who believe and use them. The medicalization of various areas of life and the uses of medicine in service of various institutional goals illustrate some of the ways ideology influences medical ideas and practice. The tendency of bioscientific medicine to treat diseases and bodies as objects masks the social history of ideas of disease and the social processes of finding disease. Reification also leads to a view of disease as a property of the sick person, thus reducing the significance of the social and environmental causes of the disease and the social context of the person's illness.

Many characteristics of the contemporary medical establishment can be traced to political developments in the recent history of the profession. Certain features of modern medicine are the results of the assumptions of the biomedical approach itself, which is characterized by its dichotomization of mind and body, physical reductionism, the doctrine of specific etiology, the machine metaphor for the body, and an emphasis on bodily regimen and control. These assumptions have concrete implications for the delivery of health care.

MODERN BIOMEDICINE: KNOWLEDGE AND PRACTICE

❀ ❀

Dr. Ogle reflects on an encounter with a dying patient years earlier when she was an oncology fellow and a junior member of a medical team that, in retrospect, failed to treat the person:

"Maybe the white coats blind us. They are a costume, and in costume we play a role. Do doctors learn to see only what the role requires? Perhaps that is why we looked at a patient ravaged by cancer and recited a litany of facts— surgery dates, complications endured, disease statistics—but failed to see her humanity. . . .

We've begun to change, but the old costume binds us. Modern medicine, despite miraculous ways of illuminating the body's secrets, can still be blind to the spirit of the human who inhabits that body. . . ."

Source: Kathleen M. Ogle, "Sometimes the doctor is blind," *New York Times*, November 6, 2001.

- **Professional Dominance**
  Information Control
  Uncertainty and Control
  The Micropolitics of Professional Dominance

- **The Doctor-Patient Relationship**
  Rationalization and the Medical Model
  Labeling Patients

- **Transforming the Sick Person into a Case**
  Social Influences on Medical Judgments
  Depersonalization of the Patient

- **The Ends of Modern Medicine: Moral Dilemmas and Social Policies**
  The Medical Model and the Conquest of Death
  The Technological Imperative
  Policy Implications

S ocial constructions enter the practice of Western medicine not only through the ideas and professional organization of biomedicine, but also through routine so-cial practices, such as interactions between medical personnel and their patients. Detailed analyses of doctor-patient interactions show how professional dominance affects the interpersonal level of health care. Many problems of doctor-patient rela-tionships are due to social-structural aspects of medical training and practice. Other very important factors are embedded assumptions of the medical model of disease and treatment. Some of these medical assumptions also make it difficult for physi-cians and society as a whole to deal effectively with emerging dilemmas in modern health care: the proper ends of medical treatment and the limits of medicine.

When people turn to medical professionals for help, they typically enter the patient role. Unlike the sick role, which is defined by broader social expectations (see Chapter 6), the patient role involves primarily the *reciprocal* expectations and norms held by the doctor and patient.[1] These expectations are emotionally charged; doctors and patients alike are often deeply dissatisfied with the actual situation.

Although each patient negotiates a different relationship with each particular doctor, a number of general social-structural factors shape the doctor-patient re-lationship. Two factors in particular are at the root of many of the problems in Western medical practice: (1) professional dominance, and (2) rationalization of the body in the medical model. Professional dominance creates and exacerbates social chasms between doctor and patient, and the medical model's rationalization of the body creates enormous discontinuities between medicine's paradigm of disease and curing, on the one hand, and patients' experience and understanding of their illness and their needs, on the other.

Although individual doctors could do much to overcome these problems in their own work with patients, these two characteristics are thoroughly embedded in the *structure* of the profession, medical education, hospital and other medical in-stitutional structures, and the organization of medical practice. Without structural change, they will continue to limit the potential for individual change in the doctor-patient relationship. Although the issue of patient (or consumer) dissatisfaction is a genuine concern, a more serious problem is that inadequacies in the doctor-patient relationship may gravely impede the very process of healing. The following discus-sion suggests some of the ways these social-structural factors may diminish the healing effectiveness of medical practitioners.

PROFESSIONAL DOMINANCE

The professionalization of medicine produced social distance between the practi-tioner and the sick person. The doctor is assumed to be the knowledgeable expert; the patient, the relatively ignorant recipient of the doctor's professional services.

---

[1]The role of patient is qualitatively different relative to other professional and nonprofessional workers (such as nurses, technicians, or hospital aides), and varies dramatically according to institu-tional context (such as doctor's office, hospital, patient's home, clinic).

Indeed, typically the patient is limited in ability to judge whether the doctor is using adequate medical knowledge, making competent treatment recommendations, and providing good service.

The greater the social distance between two people, the less sensitivity either is likely to have toward the other's problems. **Social distance** refers to a sense of separation, difference, and inability to identify with each other produced by a myriad of social characteristics and experiences (see, for example, social class or gender differences). Doctors who themselves have had extensive experience in the patient role may be more empathetic toward their own patients (see, for example, Hahn, 1995: 234–261). Considerable social distance is inherent in the expert-layperson dichotomy.

Social distance produced by divergence in *ascribed* statuses (such as race or gender) appears to be more important than other status differences in causing doctor-patient miscommunication. One study found that (female) nurse-practitioners interacted with women patients with far less social distance than did male medical doctors. Although promoting better communication with their patients, however, the nurse-practitioners did not succeed in overcoming social distance based on barriers of social class and expertise (Fisher, 1995).

The sick person who wants medical help is in an intrinsically weak position. As medicine and other professional domains become increasingly specialized, mediated by high technology, and based on a growing, complex body of knowledge, the gap between laypersons and various experts grows wider. The gap is further exaggerated when a position of professional power is used to legitimate physicians' economic rewards and professional autonomy. When patients are in awe of doctors' knowledge and skill, they are more likely to defer to physicians' judgment and to consider high fees reasonable. Although this awe and deference to doctors' expertise may promote healing by raising patients' confidence, hope, and cooperation in the therapeutic process, they may also be a source of unrealistic expectations and anger, such as that leading to malpractice lawsuits (see, for example, Fielding, 1999).

Professional power protects physicians from potentially damaging problems such as therapeutic failure. If a diagnosis is incorrect or a treatment does not work, the distance in knowledge between doctor and patient reduces the likelihood that the patient would be able to evaluate whether the failure was due to the doctor's lack of knowledge or skill. Professional dominance also legitimates the power and prestige of some health care professionals over others. For example, there is an ongoing "turf war" (with profound implications for the well-being of birthing mothers) among obstetricians, family practitioners, nurse-midwives, and lay-midwives (Good, 1995).

Information Control

One of the foremost ways doctors protect their professional power is by controlling the flow of information to the patient. On the one hand, the doctor cannot possibly, even in a long-term relationship, communicate to the patient everything the expert knows relevant to the limited actual circumstances of the patient's condition. On the other hand, patients need information about their condition: What is wrong with me? How serious is it? What is the expected outcome? What are my treatment options?

The more information patients have, the better able they are to understand their situation, evaluate options, and participate in treatment decisions. But such evaluation and decision making is often threatening to the physician's control of the case. As a result, some physicians consider the "good" patient to be one who trustingly accepts the doctor's judgment and complies with doctor's orders, full of unquestioning appreciation of the doctor's ministrations. Especially in hospital settings, professionals use control of information as a protective device in managing medical mistakes (Millman, 1976). Withholding information after treatment may, however, have the opposite effect of increasing patient anger and litigiousness (Fielding, 1999). Sometimes keeping patients ignorant of their condition enables the doctor to manage them more effectively by preventing emotional responses that the physician might find disruptive or unpleasant. Although individual doctors do not necessarily engage consciously in these protective legitimations, the very structure of the profession promotes them.

Although the doctor-patient relationship is based on reciprocal role expectations, many doctors cast patients in stereotypical roles that serve to justify information control and doctors' dominant position relative to patients. One such expectation is the notion that patients are generally medically ignorant and childlike, unable to comprehend explanations of the causes, alternative treatments, and the expected outcome of their conditions (Segall and Roberts, 1980). Several studies have found that patients want to be informed of treatment alternatives and to be involved in treatment decisions when there is more than one treatment alternative (Guadagnoli and Ward, 1998). Despite these findings, relatively few doctors adequately involve their patients. One study of hospitalized patients found that physicians discussed test or treatment rationale in only 43 percent of cases and treatment alternatives in a mere 12 percent of cases (Wu and Pearlman, 1988). Another study reviewed the making and discussion of treatment decisions in routine office visits. Analysis of 1,057 taped transcripts of these doctor-patient encounters found that some important involvement of the patient was missing in 91 percent of the discussions (Braddock et al., 1999).

Information control involves both information gathering and information giving. The doctor controls the medical interaction, deciding how much and which information to seek, and how much and which information to impart to the patient. The rationale and method for this model of a medical encounter are discussed further later. The medical interview and clinical examination consist of many such information-gathering and -giving decisions. Doctors control the information-gathering aspect by framing questions, cutting off patients' statements, ignoring certain patient input as irrelevant, and actively eliciting other input. The doctor decides whether and how extensively to conduct a physical examination, which tests to have done, and what follow-up study is needed; these aspects of a consultation are highly variable, a matter of the doctor's discretion (Fisher, 1983).

The medical interview is a constrained, prestructured form of talk. West (1983) found that patient-initiated questions are "dispreferred." Her detailed analysis of 21 medical exchanges showed that only 9 percent of the 773 questions were initiated by patients. Patient assertiveness often resulted in less response from doctors, whose pervasive dislike of patient-initiated questions was linked with the physicians' reluctance to answer "too many" such questions (West, 1984: 156). Patients sensed that their questioning was not the preferred pattern for the interaction; when they did pose questions, nearly half (46 percent) exhibited some anxiety, such as stutters or nervous giggles.

How patients express themselves and certain of their personal characteristics are also important factors influencing the amount and quality of information that physicians give them. One study of a hospital family practice clinic found that doctors gave more information to their patients who appeared to be better educated, younger, or more anxious about their health problems. Patients with communicative styles that were more active and affectively expressive tended to receive more information; patients who were more passive, asked few questions, and exhibited few worries or emotions about their conditions received less information about their conditions and treatments. Because well-educated patients were also disproportionately represented among those with active communicative styles, these findings suggest that some patients are doubly disadvantaged in doctor-patient communication (Street, 1991; see also Lupton, 1996b; Street, 1992).

Information-giving and question-asking exchanges between doctor and patient vary significantly according to social class. A British study of general practitioners' consultations found that patients' social class differences accounted for a significant proportion of the variance in both the information doctors gave in answer to questions and in the explanations volunteered by the doctors. Doctors may misinterpret working-class patients' reticence to ask questions as due to their lack of interest, but this study suggested that such patients' diffidence may be due more to the social distance between them and the doctor, and perhaps also to learned patterns of deference to higher social classes (Pendleton and Bochner, 1980).

Social distance between doctor and patient affects not only the quality of the medical interview and information giving, but also the likelihood that the patient will cooperate with the doctor's therapeutic recommendations. Men physicians typically couched their treatment recommendations as explicit commands, resulting in compliant responses among patients less than half the time. By contrast, women physicians' communicative style was more collaborative, reducing some social distance from the patient. By giving directives in a characteristically "feminine" mitigated form (for instance, "Now that we've got your blood pressure stable, let's make our plan about the next steps in treatment"), women physicians achieved a more symmetrical doctor-patient relationship, which produced a far higher rate (67 percent) of patient "compliance" (West, 1993; see also Ong et al., 1995, for a review of the literature on doctor-patient communication).

Uncertainty and Control

Uncertainty and fallibility are built-in features of medical practice, and the boundaries between an "avoidable" versus "unavoidable" mistake are themselves uncertain (Paget, 1988; Rosenthal, 1995, 1999). One physician, describing his experience with medical mistakes, commented,

> Many situations do not lend themselves to a simple determination of whether a mistake has been made. Seriously ill, hospitalized patients, for instance, require of doctors almost continuous decision-making. . . . there always seem to be things that could have been done differently or better: administering more of this medication, starting that treatment a little sooner. . . . The fact is that when a patient dies, the physician is left wondering whether the care he provided was inadequate. . . . Medicine is not an exact science; errors are always possible, even in the midst of the humdrum routine of daily care. Was that baby I just sent home with a diagnosis of mild viral fever actually in the early stages of serious meningitis? . . . A doctor has to confront the possibility of a mistake with every patient visit. (Hilfiker, 1984)

Medical uncertainty is an inherent difficulty for both doctor and patient. Although precision, certainty, and control are goals of bioscientific medicine, clinical practice rarely comes close to meeting such goals. Real patients' problems are often complex, and even highly trained physicians cannot know everything about every possible problem. Diagnoses have, at best, only a certain probability of accuracy; straightforward diagnoses of well-known diseases have only a higher probability of accuracy than those of complex, poorly understood diseases. Pressures for certainty in diagnosis may lead to excessive medical testing (Kassirer, 1989). Control in treatment is likewise often elusive; much therapy is a matter of trial and error. Rather than resolve ambiguity, technological medicine often produces greater expectations at the same time as more arenas for uncertainty. For example, technological capabilities for keeping alive premature infants who would otherwise have died shortly after birth but now may survive with serious debilities increase the range of medical uncertainty for doctors who must decide whether to use these technologies for a particular infant (Beresford, 1991).

Medical training provides some preparation for dealing with clinical uncertainty (Fox, 1957, 2000), but routine medical practice often involves judgments whose accuracy and effects are uncertain and, in some cases, unknowable. Although practicing physicians do acknowledge a number of areas of uncertainty (Gerrity et al., 1992), they are uncomfortable with uncertainty as an indicator of personal inadequacy, failure, error, or lack of knowledge.

The patient's situation in the face of uncertainty is even more anxiety producing because the patient lacks medical expertise. Doctors sometimes prolong patients' uncertainty, even after their own uncertainty about the disease or therapy has been reduced or resolved. Physicians may use their control over patient uncertainty to preserve their power and keep their options open (Waitzkin and Stoeckle, 1972). For example, the head of one pediatric ward had a policy of aggressively treating children with leukemia up to the moment of death; no child was ever labeled terminal, no matter how unsuccessful the treatment. The mother of a child who was obviously succumbing asked this doctor, "Is my child critical?," to which the doctor replied, "No." Another member of the staff asked him privately, "Why did you tell her the child is not critical, when we know he has only a few weeks to live?" The doctor's answer: "He is not technically critical until he is on some life-support system." To control information about the child's status further, he ordered that the records not be shown or otherwise divulged to the distraught mother. He believed that if the mother knew how near to death her child was, she might refuse the course of chemotherapy he had ordered for the boy.

By contrast, many physicians consider informing patients a necessary part of involving patients in their treatment. One surgical oncologist said,

> If it's malignant, I want them to have enough information so that they have the truth, but also so that they have some hope. They know that there are things that can be done that will help them. I think the hardest thing is uncertainty, and also I think it's extremely hard if you begin to think that your doctors are not telling you things. Then you don't know if you can ever believe them. . . . When patients start out being involved from the beginning and being in control from the beginning, it's much better. (quoted in Good, 1995: 177)

Doctor-patient negotiations over information vary according to the type of illness. In the course of the long-term treatment of chronic illness, the balance of power is often altered, requiring renegotiation of the doctor-patient relationship. Patients are likely to become increasingly expert about their specific condition and thus more assertive in challenging their doctors (Herzlich and Pierret, 1987: 212).

Doctor-patient communication is especially problematic in the face of the uncertainty related to diseases such as multiple sclerosis (MS), a gradually debilitating, incurable disease of the nervous system. Because many MS victims are in young adulthood, when serious chronic illness is least expected, doctors at first may not consider the diagnosis. MS creates uncertainty for both the doctor and patient partly because its early symptoms are unclear or elusive. Another reason is that the diagnosis is fearsome to both the sufferer and the doctor because MS is incurable and potentially severely debilitating. Physicians thus frequently fail to diagnose MS correctly or postpone telling their patients of the diagnosis until it is inevitable.

One study suggested that this protective strategy for the doctor can create significant problems for the patient, perhaps leading to iatrogenic emotional difficulties (Stewart and Sullivan, 1982). Lacking physician confirmation that their symptoms were indeed related to a "real" illness, many MS patients were viewed by family, friends, and doctors as hypochondriacs or as "imagining things." As a result many sufferers experienced symptoms of stress that were actually more troublesome than the MS-related symptoms themselves. They lost faith in their doctors, shopped around for others, challenged physicians' diagnoses, and self-diagnosed (actions that typically elicited very negative reactions from physicians).

Similarly, a study of interactions in a clinic for chronic illness sufferers showed that a major concern of the patients was to convince others—especially doctors—of the reality of their diseases. This was done by elaborating their illness behavior, but the sicker they behaved, the less likely doctors were to believe them. Their "doctor shopping" to confirm the fact of their illnesses also increased the likelihood that doctors would label them as "crocks" (Alexander, 1982).

Especially when medical knowledge about repetitive strain injuries was in the early stages of development, sufferers engaged in a similar search for doctor-patient communication in which their expression of pain would be taken seriously, as a legitimate problem. The medical consultation thus became a situation in which patients needed to convince the doctor of the reality of their symptoms, especially pain and disability (see also Hydén and Sachs, 1998). They feared being labeled as "neurotic," "crocks," or "malingerers." When physicians must serve as both curers and gatekeepers (in determining whether workers' compensation or disability leaves are legitimate), doctor-patient communication can be even more strained or adversarial (Reid et al., 1991).

One researcher analyzed in detail the transcripts of three problematic doctor-patient encounters that were marked by tension, ambiguity, and no apparent resolution (Paget, 1983). Without much background about the patient, the reader sees in the transcript an apparently neurotic woman, overly preoccupied with little details of her body's functioning. After these three meetings, her doctor's assessment was that the patient's health was good and that her problem was "nerves." The transcript takes on an entirely different meaning, however, when we realize that the woman had recently had an operation for cancer. Her primary agenda in each of these encounters was clearly to address her fears that her cancer would metastasize or was not fully excised, but those fears never once became a topic of discourse. The doctor did not acknowledge that her fears existed or might be legitimate; he only heard her seemingly minor complaints about her teeth and her scalp. Indeed, an analysis of the doctor's responses to her input shows that he was not really listening to any of her expressions, perhaps because he had already defined them as the product of her "nerves," and therefore medically unreal or unimportant. She too contributed to the ongoing misunderstanding between them by referring only indirectly to the operation in the first encounter and not at all thereafter. She was afraid to express her fears and yet afraid to ignore them. The doctor's treating her fears as unreal made them worse.

Often such patients come to view physicians as evasive, nonsupportive, insensitive, uncaring, or dishonest. One MS patient said,

> I went to seven or eight doctors in less than two years. I'd tell them about my pins-and-needles feelings, or my numbness, or my weak arms and they'd all do the same thing—nothing. I really got upset with those doctors. They'd usually just say that my problems were normal for a woman my age (25) and things like that. And I'd get really uptight because they would just give me a Valium and not try to find out what was really wrong. Some of them thought I was going off my rocker. They thought I was imagining the problems. . . . One of them just threw up his arms and said he

didn't know what was wrong with me. Now isn't that some way for a doctor to act! I got so I didn't believe any of them. I knew something was wrong and felt they could find out if they would just try. (quoted in Stewart and Sullivan, 1982: 1401)

In such situations the doctors' unwillingness to communicate a diagnosis resulted in the patient's suffering and loss of trust in the doctor-patient relationship.

At the same time, however, total disclosure of all information is neither possible nor helpful for the patient. For instance, too great a barrage of information about a diagnosis and multiple treatment options can overwhelm the patient and, in effect, make patient participation in decision making impossible. Similarly, if a doctor discloses all of the remotely possible diagnoses, it would unnecessarily raise the patient's anxiety.

Information control includes basic communication about diagnosis and treatment. Sometimes, even long after a doctor has a working diagnosis, the patient is not told what the problem may be. Before the enactment of a series of laws in the United States in the 1970s, it was possible for doctors to perform surgery, put patients on medication, and order other treatments without the patients' informed consent.

The issue of informed consent is particularly problematic in medical experimentation and clinical trials of treatments not yet proven safe or effective. One notorious instance of medical science misconduct was the Tuskegee syphilis study, begun in 1932 and continued until 1972, when a Public Health Service worker blew the whistle to the press. The U.S. Public Health Service had recruited in Alabama some 400 black men who had syphilis at the time they were enrolled in the project; it also monitored 200 uninfected control subjects. The research was supposed to document the course of untreated syphilis, including autopsy after the subject died. Research subjects were recruited with misleading promises of "special free treatment" (actually spinal taps done without anesthesia—lab tests, not treatments), and they were denied antibiotic therapy in the 1940s when it became the effective treatment for syphilis (Jones, 1981; King, 1992). Outrage over the Tuskegee study led directly to the 1974 National Research Act, which established procedures to guard the rights of human subjects of research.

The central principle of protection for research subjects also applies to medical treatments: informed consent. This principle means that researchers and physicians should give enough information about the procedures, their risks, and benefits so that the subject or patient can decide whether to consent to the treatment. Just what kind and how much information is necessary or desirable, however, is still debated. Unfortunately, the requirement of informed consent has been routinized (especially in institutional settings) into one more procedure that is performed on the patient. For example, a senior surgeon may ask an assistant, "Did you consent the patient yet?"—implying the patient is a passive recipient of a purely bureaucratic procedure.

In the treatment of potentially fatal or particularly fearsome diseases, such as cancer, many doctors prefer to tell their patients as little as possible. As recently as the 1960s, most physicians routinely withheld from patients diagnosis of feared diseases and prognosis of impending death. One 1960s study found that 95 percent of physicians did not disclose a diagnosis of cancer to patients (Oken, 1961; see also Glaser and Strauss, 1968). The same questionnaire, distributed nearly two decades later, found a complete reversal: 90 percent of the physicians claimed they disclosed all information (Novack et al., 1979). But although physicians believe they are giving their patients all relevant information, many patients are dissatisfied with both the amount and the quality of information they receive. One explanation for this dissatisfaction is that although doctors now usually disclose even unpleasant diagnoses such as cancer or AIDS, their information giving is still selective. For example, a physician may give considerable information about treatment options while downplaying or withholding information about prognosis (that is, prospects for recovery or probable course of the disease). Thus, the physician retains considerable control, especially over the patient's willingness to accept the recommended treatment (Miyaji, 1993).

Even for nonfatal illnesses, many doctors do not communicate their full diagnosis or prognosis. Doctors may want to protect patients from unpleasant information. This paternalistic approach may simultaneously protect the doctor from dealing with the unpleasant reactions such knowledge might evoke. Giving bad news is very uncomfortable for physicians, as one surgeon explained:

> I really hate this part of the work. I feel terrible . . . always . . . it never seems to get easier. . . . I know it's not my fault . . . I didn't give the patient the disease . . . but I always somehow feel that it is . . . and besides . . . I never really know what to say. They sure never had a course on this part of medicine when I went to school, but let me tell you, I could sure use it now . . . and I usually don't ever get to know these patients who think their lives are in my hands. How am I supposed to deal with it? I hate doing it . . . but I can't avoid it! (quoted in Taylor, 1988)

In response to this stress, physicians adopt complex strategies to routinize the painful task: telling the truth, professing uncertainty, evading the issue, and dissimulation. One study found that the majority viewed their role as selecting and interpreting information for patients. In deciding how much to tell, they considered such factors as the certainty of the diagnosis, whether medical science understands the disease's natural course, whether there are potentially effective therapeutic options, and whether the patient is competent to understand information and make decisions on the basis of that information (Drickamer and Lachs, 1992).

Brody (1992) argues for a new ethic for doctor-patient relationships in which most power is shared with patients, without eschewing the beneficial aspects of the doctor's power as expert. He suggests the following:

> [P]hysicians most effectively empower patients neither by reflexively disclosing nor by reflexively withholding any particular sort of information. They empower patients by creating an atmosphere that encourages participation and dialogue. (Brody, 1992: 136)

The Micropolitics of Professional Dominance

When a patient interacts with a doctor, the relationship is not symmetrical. In addition to the physician's presumed medical expertise, a number of microstructural factors increase the relative power of the doctor in the medical encounter. The professional dominance of doctors is enhanced by their control over minute parts of their interaction with patients.

Language Use Doctors control even seemingly medically irrelevant aspects of the doctor-patient interaction, such as humorous exchanges and other sociability (West, 1984: 152; see also Todd, 1983). Several patterns of language use reflect the subtle ways in which dominance is asserted. For example, interrupting is an assertion of whose input to the interaction is more important. Doctors frequently interrupted their patients, whereas they were seldom interrupted by their patients.

Doctors' unilateral use of false-familiar terms increases the gap between doctor and patient. For example, many doctors expect to be addressed deferentially by their title ("Dr. Jones"), but regularly address patients—regardless of age or other status—by their first names. Likewise, the use of diminutives is a subtle assertion of doctors' dominance and condescension. One study of doctor-patient interactions in gynecological practice found that doctors frequently used diminutives in talking to patients. For example, a doctor teaching women to perform breast self-examinations said, "Just march your little fingers . . ." (Todd, 1983).

The Dossier The doctor typically has far more information about the patient than the patient has about the doctor. Such one-sided familiarity serves to remind the patient that the doctor is dominant (Stimson and Webb, 1975). The medical record functions as a third agent, introducing the patient (and personal details about the patient, such as marital status and age) even before the face-to-face interaction. One researcher observed that doctors often appear to be more oriented to the patient's objectified record or chart than to the patient (West, 1984: 132–133). Records can indeed take on a reality greater than that expressed by patients themselves. Patients' narratives of their illness experiences often bear little resemblance to the case record (see Berg, 1996; Kleinman, 1988).

Patients typically lack access to or control over these records. They are prevented from seeing their charts, reading their records, or challenging items of information in their files. Particularly in institutional settings such as hospitals, control over medical records is a form of social control over inmates (Goffman, 1961). In ordinary office practice too, patient records often contain discrediting information. For example, a doctor in a group practice may read a colleague's comment that a patient is a constant complainer and accordingly decide not to give that person's current problem serious attention.

Social Organization of Space The physical setting of most medical encounters is likewise supportive of the physician's dominance. Medical staff have the uniforms and props of authority—white coats, stethoscopes, framed certificates, and complicated equipment. Office and hospital consultations are on doctors' home field, which is organized to their specifications. For example, rarely is the doctor's office arranged so that doctor and patient are seated on a par; much of the interaction may in fact occur in the examining room with the patient undressed and in an awkward posture. Studies of the uses of space, posture, and gesture demonstrate that such differences are related to power and stratification (Henley, 1977).

Social Control of Time   Significantly, doctors exert considerable control over the time spent with patients. One useful indicator of relative power in a dyad (that is, a two-person interrelationship, such as teacher-student) is which party is in a position to make the other wait for access to his or her presumably more precious time. Typically, the patient waits to see the doctor rather than the reverse. In private practice, physicians often overbook patients to assure that every block of office consultation time is filled, but they are more sensitive to the need for customer satisfaction than doctors in clinic or institutional settings, where patients are not free to take their business elsewhere.

The allocation of time spent with patients depends partly on the expectations and rewards for doctors in a particular institutional setting. One study found that prenatal clinic patients experienced different waiting times and received very different amounts of doctor time depending on whether they were being seen in the obstetrics or the family practice clinic. Residents in obstetrics spent an average of five to ten minutes with a prenatal patient, and expected clinic nurses to do the job of communicating information about pregnancy and delivery. By contrast, family practice residents spent up to 45 minutes with patients. Family practice residents were encouraged and rewarded for the time spent with patients, whereas obstetric residents were discouraged from devoting time to "normal" pregnancies and were informally sanctioned if they failed to process their share of the patient workload fast enough (Lazarus, 1988).

Doctors spend an estimated 13 to 18 minutes in office visits with patients, and only a small part of the visit involves communication with the patient (see Lawrence and McLemore, 1983; Mechanic et al., 2001; Waitzkin, 1985, 2000). Because doctors' goals include the efficient, task-oriented use of this brief time, the interview and examination are directed to gathering information that they believe is directly relevant to fairly routinized diagnostic decision rules. A British study corroborated the impact of a sense of time constraints on doctor-patient communication. Even when time is actually available for more medical work, doctors narrow the objectives of their routine (and typically uninteresting) practice by thinking not "What can I do for this patient?" but "What can I do for this patient in the next six minutes?" (Horobin and McIntosh, 1983: 328). One physician commented on his tight control of patient interactions:

> The doctor's primary task is to manage his time. If he allows patients to rabbit on about their conditions then the doctor will lose control of time and will spend all his time sitting in a surgery [office consultation] listening to irrelevant rubbish. Effective doctoring is characterized by a "quick, clean job." (quoted in Byrne and Long, 1976: 93)

Patients are unlikely to know the criteria by which doctors are judging their input, and often doctors interrupt or discard information about problems that patients want to communicate. One study found that, on average, doctors cut off patients' descriptions of their complaints within the first 18 seconds (Beckman and Frankl, 1984). This practice is particularly problematic because patients only rarely readily reveal the important reasons that triggered their visit (Good and Good, 1982). For example, a patient may start out by presenting a "simple" problem such as a persistent rash, but may have really come to the doctor mainly to obtain reassurance that he does not have heart disease like his brother who recently had a heart attack. If given the time to present all their concerns, patients frequently identify three or four problems, of which the first mentioned is often not the most serious.

THE DOCTOR-PATIENT RELATIONSHIP

Broader structural factors also shape the pattern of miscommunication between doctors and their patients. As described in Chapter 8, patients come to the medical encounter with fundamentally separate (and often irreconcilable) expectations and goals from those of their doctor: What am I doing and why? What are the central facts about my situation? How should we proceed to make sense of this? What is my expected outcome?

Rationalization and the Medical Model

Modern biomedicine has developed a conception of disease as separate from the person experiencing it. Rationalized medicine views the body as an object; the body is incidentally inhabited by a person who can potentially help or hinder the task of treating diseases of the body. But people cannot simply leave their bodies at the repair shop. Although individual doctors may choose to relate to their patients as persons and not just bodies, such an approach is not essential in the biomedical model. In many ways, the training and socialization of medical personnel actively discourages them from understanding their patients as whole persons with social, emotional, aesthetic, spiritual, and other health-related facets to their lives.

Medical training emphasizes technical skills in diagnosing and treating pathologies (physiological deviations that constitute or characterize disease). Thus, doctors are trained to approach a medical encounter with a patient with the goal of efficient diagnosis of a pathology and active treatment intervention. By contrast, the patient comes to the doctor with a broader, and more often vague, set of goals. The patient's needs may be related to a range of problems, some of which are unrelated or only indirectly related to an identifiable pathology or bodily condition. The patient may be experiencing illness but lack a clinically detectible pathology. The illness may also be a chronic condition in the face of which the doctor's active intervention is not very effective, although the patient may suffer from certain socio-emotional aspects of the illness and its management. With a narrow disease-oriented training, doctors are likely to misunderstand completely what these patients need.

Most persons seeking medical help do not need the kind of medical intervention that physicians have been trained to appreciate. In medical school, internships, and residencies, the emphasis is on the interesting cases, which are typically acute and dramatic, and thus challenging—but not impossibly so—for the doctors' diagnostic skills. Cases often are defined as interesting if they offer the chance to practice new surgical techniques; once the doctor has mastered these procedures, such cases become less interesting (Scully, 1980: 166–171). In ordinary office practice, however, such interesting cases are proportionately very rare, and doctors are likely to be bored and impatient with the majority of patients' health problems.

One hospital's head midwife, who trained obstetric residents, noted:

> It is a rare medical student who wants to sit with a woman in labor. Residents will even pass on watching normal deliveries. They see people as pathology, as a uterus. I rarely see the art of medicine, the understanding of seeing a patient as a total entity—where she is going, where she has been. I heard a resident say that "If I never do another normal vaginal delivery, it won't be too soon." They train for pathology but go into private practice with normal patients. There is more money in it, and it is the least amount of time for the most amount of money. (quoted in Lazarus, 1988: 39)

In general practice, which includes most of the work done by general practitioners, pediatricians, family practitioners, internists, and obstetrician-gynecologists, only about 15 percent of consultations are for the kind of acute, major, or life-threatening conditions that are likely to be interesting. By far the largest proportion of office visits are for seemingly minor, self-limiting conditions or for well-person preventive care; chronic illnesses are the second largest category. Physicians whose medical training was oriented toward interesting cases find such routine work far less rewarding. One doctor exclaimed,

> Our skills are absolutely wasted . . . frustration and boredom set in. There are days when you go home and think, "Have I got to do this for another twenty years?" You've done a lot of work but you really haven't done anything for anybody. . . . There's no stimulation at all. (quoted in Horobin and McIntosh, 1983: 321)

As an antidote to overrationalized medical practice, one physician (Epstein, 1999) recommends what he calls "mindful practice," meaning that the doctor should not only view the patient as a whole person (getting beyond the mind-body dualism implicit in Western biomedicine), but also *practice* medicine as a whole person. Accordingly, mindful practitioners would be fully present while listening to and observing the patient, would self-monitor to be aware of their own biases and preconceptions, and would bring to consciousness their tacit personal knowledge and values. Such mindfulness would prevent medical errors, such as "treating the chart" (that is, the medical record) rather than the patient (that is, a real human being who may be mistakenly misrepresented in the chart). It requires a reflectiveness and centered self-awareness that are not encouraged (much less taught) in most medical training.

Labeling Patients

Another feature of doctors' socialization can be very detrimental: Informally, they often acquire negative stereotypes of patients. The use of such stereotypes does vary according to the institutional setting; doctors in private practice are less likely than doctors on hospital staff to use pejoratives openly to refer to patients, although they may hold some of the same negative attitudes (see, for example, Hahn, 1995: 173–208). Nevertheless, the values reflected in these attitudes toward patients are encouraged in both the self-selection of doctors and their medical education. Doctors learn that real medicine is about pathologies, not patients.

In a U.S. study, 439 family physicians anonymously answered a questionnaire about those patient characteristics to which they responded negatively (Klein et al., 1982). The doctors reacted negatively not only to various social and personal traits of their patients but also to certain medical conditions, especially those for which medical treatment offered little or no likelihood of cure or clear alleviation. The authors suggested that physicians particularly dislike certain situations, such as emphysema, senility, diabetes, arthritis, psychiatric conditions, and obesity, that challenge their faith in the potency of bioscientific medicine. Although they may find a challenging case with a high probability of a dramatic cure "interesting," they dislike conditions such as back pain, chronic vague pains, headaches, and chronic fatigue that offer little probability of cure while bringing their competence or diagnostic skills into question. Furthermore, they dislike conditions for which they believe the patient or others are responsible, such as sexual behavior, auto accidents, suicide attempts, and other self-inflicted injuries (Klein et al., 1982; see also Hahn, 1995; Smith and Zimmy, 1988).

One study found the leading common characteristics of patients that doctors label as "gomers" ("*get outta my emergency room*") were illnesses and/or personal characteristics that created management difficulties for the hospital staff (Leiderman and Grisso, 1985). Many patients were identified as gomers because their conditions defied solution by medical intervention. Their deterioration under treatment was thus a source of frustration and ideological doubts for doctors, especially the beginning doctors who typically staff hospital emergency rooms and clinics.

Many of the other derogatory terms used for patients reflect similar values. A widespread distinction in doctors' stereotyping of patients is between "sick people" and "trolls." The latter term is applied to patients whom doctors believe lack a "real" disease and to those held culpable for the cause of and/or the failure to control their condition. Other derogatory terms for undesirable patients include "albatross," "turkey," and "crock." Medical education encourages compassion for "sick people" but contempt for "trolls." Such negative stereotypes often supersede even the medical model itself in informing the doctor's understanding of a case, thus leading to failed empathy (Stein, 1986).

Medical students, interns, and residents learn and use extensive slang terms for their patients, patients' conditions and bodies, hospital situations, and working conditions (see Khipple, 2001). Although use of slang serves other psychosocial functions, such as a safety valve for stressful working conditions and emotionally charged work, it also serves to distance doctors from their patients and confirm negative stereotypes (see Coombs et al., 1993; Yoels and Clair, 1995). Even though patients generally do not understand the meanings of insider talk among the medical staff, the terms reflect and produce problems of doctors' empathy. Consider, for example, the effect on interns' attitudes of routinely referring to patients under their care by such terms as: "BW" (*b*eached *w*hale, meaning obese), "slug" (not motivated to move around out of bed), "dud" (not an interesting case), "supratentorial" (patient's problem is considered to be psychological, not physical), or "HOWDY" (*h*ypertensive, *o*bese, *w*hite, *d*iabetic, *y*ahoo). Medical professors' routine use of vulgar or derogatory humor about patients and their conditions to make lectures more entertaining may encourage such stereotyping and failed empathy among medical students (Konner, 1987).

Contempt for "trolls" is particularly encouraged in the United States by the use of student doctors to staff emergency rooms and clinics that serve a disproportionate number of these "undesirable" patients compared to private practice. The characteristic contempt is exemplified by a junior resident in an emergency room, who said:

> At least 40–50 percent are gomers. Some weeks there is nothing but alcohol-induced diseases. The other night on call I met only three people with genuine diseases—having nothing to do with anything they ever did to themselves. I spend hours [with them] and check them everyday, but some guy who comes in with alcoholic pancreatitis—I'll tune him up and fire him out the door, and not give two shakes about him. (quoted in Mizrahi, 1986: 102)

Hospital staff generally admitted that they often treated undesirable patients less thoroughly. Sometimes the stereotypes led to misdiagnoses and other medical mistakes (Mizrahi, 1986). For example, a homeless person brought unconscious to the emergency room may be treated as a gomer under the assumption that the condition was alcohol induced, whereas a thorough treatment might discover that the symptoms resulted from a serious neurological problem.

Doctors' negative stereotypes of patients are also based on social and personal characteristics. Doctors tended to consider "undesirable" those patients whose behavior violated the physicians' personal norms, even norms with little or no relevance to health. The largest category of social characteristics (33 percent) eliciting negative responses from doctors included such violations as being dirty, smelly, vulgar, chronically unemployed, promiscuous, homosexual, malingering, or on welfare, Medicaid, or workers' compensation. Doctors' expectations of patients are based largely on white, middle-class values that are accentuated by the self-selection and professional training processes. Social class differences also appear to figure into some negative stereotypes (Klein et al., 1982).

Doctors' often unrecognized value judgments of patients can result in failed empathy and less adequate care (Stein, 1986), as illustrated by one resident who admitted that he had detested patients who demanded Vistaril (an antianxiety drug often used in pain control). He had viewed them as not legitimately sick but rather as weak, irresponsible, and dependent. Coming from a religious, rural, self-sufficient background, he valued patients who were self-sufficient in their health care and who rarely complained. Until he himself experienced considerable pain from minor surgery (and quickly wrote himself a prescription for Vistaril), he had a strong negative stereotype of patients whose requests for pain medication did not mesh with his personal values.

A study of the medical education process showed how both the structure of medical training and professional ideology work against the development of humanistic doctor-patient relationships.[2] New physicians are taught to avoid interaction with patients, to restrict the time spent with them, and to limit the patient input they listen to in medical interviews (Mizrahi, 1986: 118–119). This study concluded that the very structure of internship and residency teaches doctors to get rid of noninteresting patients. Reflecting both the attitudes of his supervisors and his personal experience with enormous time pressures, one junior resident said, "There are different kinds of ideal patients. When you're an intern, the ideal patient is someone you can get out and get out quickly" (quoted in Mizrahi, 1986: 74–75). Interns and residents, for example, were informally rewarded for quickly and efficiently taking patient histories, and they learned not to bother with inquiring about social aspects of the cases because nobody noticed or appreciated if that were done.

Medical students learned, formally and informally, that what their supervisors really wanted them to do was to narrow their clinical findings efficiently to biophysical data relevant to possible pathology. One senior resident explained,

> I guess I could use the excuse that I don't have the time to do that [deal with patient's social problems]. . . . It would be nice to bullshit with your patients for an hour or so and get a feel for their social situation. . . . It may affect the complaints they present with, . . . If I was Marcus Welby [a former TV physician] and saw one patient per week, maybe I would be more concerned. I doubt it though, because it's really not appealing to me. . . . What appeals to me is treatment of sick people by diagnosing their diseases and giving medications. *I like good hard facts and physical findings*–things I can deal with on a tangible basis–not some intangible nebulous feeling of what their social situation is. (quoted in Mizrahi, 1986: 95 [emphasis added])

This attitude reflects the medical model's separation of the disease from the socioemotional aspects of the patient's illness; doctors are socialized to view the nonbiophysical aspects as "soft" facts that are ultimately irrelevant to their essential task.

---

[2]For a more detailed and textured description of the medical education process and its impact on treatment of patients, see Cassell, 1991; Davis-Floyd, 1987; Epstein, 1999; Good, 1995; Groopman, 1987; Konner, 1987; Mizrahi, 1986.

TRANSFORMING THE SICK PERSON INTO A CASE

Just as the medical paradigm views the body as separate from the person, so too does the interaction between doctor and patient often involve isolating salient information about the sick body from the sick person. One effect of most medical encounters is to transform the sick person into a medical case. Drawing from their medical training and the biomedical paradigm for interpreting disease and pathology, physicians use the medical encounter for relatively narrow goals: the efficient eliciting and honing of facts relevant to a medical diagnosis, the precise application of a set of decision rules for proceeding, and active therapeutic intervention. Although their understanding of the medical encounter is informed by rational biomedicine, it is also the product of situational factors, cultural biases, and subjective influences that are often subtly embedded in the doctors' practice of medicine itself (Stein, 1986; see also Good, 1995; Mishler, 1984).

Social Influences on Medical Judgments

The process of locating and interpreting medical evidence is always socially mediated. Such medical judgments as the factors the diagnostician considers relevant, the clues that are thought worth seeking and thus are elicited in conversation and testing, and those that should be overlooked or discarded often entail *social* attributes. For example, doctors treating elderly persons sometimes do not carry out routine tests in physical examinations, because they assume patient problems are due to senility or old age (Glassman, 1980).

Both the patient and the doctor often treat the diagnosis as a conclusion rather than a working hypothesis. Even before the diagnosis is reached, the physician's expectations and hunches may limit the clues examined. A study of medical thinking showed that doctors tended to develop hypotheses very early in an intake interview, often basing their hunches on only the patient's general appearance and one or two presenting complaints (Kassircr and Gorry, 1978). The physician's expectations are often subsequently self-confirming; contradictory clues are neither noticed nor sought (Jones, 1982: 156–161).

Medical evidence is typically ambiguous and multifaceted. In both scientific and other medical systems, the process of reaching a diagnosis is one of pattern forming (Brown, 1995a). Despite extensive diagnostic technologies, the art of diagnosis in modern medicine is highly imprecise and seldom matches the reality of human experience (Davis-Floyd and Davis, 1997). A study of diagnostic failures in myocardial infarction (heart attacks) showed that physicians who relied on technological assessment, in place of their own observation and clinical skills, were likely to make a mistaken diagnosis (Zarling et al., 1983). U.S. data on autopsies show that in biomedical terms, at least one out of five diagnoses were mistaken, and that in half these cases the correct diagnosis could have saved or prolonged the patient's life (Landefeld and Goldman, 1989; Landefeld et al., 1988; see also Rosenthal, 1995). To form a pattern, one must actively select pieces of evidence to cluster into an understanding. This process necessarily entails deciding which pieces of information to include and which to exclude.

Similarly, in the interpretation of evidence and treatment decisions, non-physical elements, such as the emotional or social situation of the ill person, become part of the pattern.[3] Often the person creating the pattern is not aware of these elements; instead, moral judgments and ideological assumptions enter the process under the guise of objective physical observations. For example, in examining X-rays of workers' lungs for symptoms of asbestosis, company physicians saw very different patterns than did doctors not connected with the industry (Brodeur, 1974: 174).

No necessary connection exists between the many diagnoses and possible treatments. Numerous, sometimes contradictory treatment options exist in any single medical system, and social factors influence which one the doctor recommends. Individual practitioners differ in the *decision rules* they follow in choosing certain treatments for the same condition. (Decision rules are a form of knowledge that provides a set of minimally acceptable criteria for selecting a treatment, such as surgery or medication.) A British study of ear, nose, and throat specialists revealed that widely varying decision rules determine whether an adenotonsillectomy should be performed. Some relied heavily on a physical examination; others attached no significance to examination findings and relied instead on the case history. Some recommended surgery only when several signs were present; others considered the existence of only one sign sufficient (Bloor, 1976).

Social judgments also enter into physicians' decision rules. Often the therapy proposed by a doctor varies greatly from patient to patient, even when the same biophysical conditions are present. When recommending hysterectomies (surgical removal of the uterus, resulting in sterility), physicians often included in their decision rules such factors as the woman's age, ethnicity, poverty, marital status, and whether she was on welfare, had had multiple abortions, and had already had children (Fisher, 1986). A more serious biophysical condition in a 25-year-old white woman with no children thus might be less likely to be treated with a hysterectomy than a less serious condition in a 35-year-old black woman with four children.

Similarly, studies show that the social attitudes, beliefs, and personal characteristics of physicians influence the treatment options they offer their patients with breast cancer. For instance, although breast-conserving surgery is medically recommended for the majority of women whose cancer is in an early stage, older women (the vast majority of cancer patients) are significantly less likely to be offered this treatment option than younger women (Ganz, 1992).

Judgments of social worth also enter into medical decisions. Studies of treatment decisions and other actions in hospital emergency services show that the

---

[3]This is not a criticism; effective treatment probably takes the sick person's entire situation into consideration. The issue here is the extent to which uncritical assumptions and ideological biases often enter the process and are treated as part of so-called objective reality, without the participants' awareness.

young are treated as more valuable than the old, and welfare cases are treated as less worthy than those not on welfare. Especially disvalued persons, such as those labeled "drunks" and "PIDs" (women with pelvic inflammatory disease, often assumed to be due to promiscuity), are given even less prompt and considerate treatment (Roth, 1972; see also Sudnow, 1967).

Considerable evidence suggests that prejudice, stereotyping, and racial/ethnic biases on the part of health care providers contribute to persistent disparities in care. The Institute of Medicine (IOM) commissioned a report on the continued unequal treatment of racial and ethnic minorities in the United States, noting that disparities are serious and widespread even when minority patients have insurance coverage. Prejudice may be a factor in treatment decisions. The IOM report (Smedley et al., 2002) stated, for example, that minorities are less likely than whites to be given the appropriate cardiac medications or to undergo bypass surgery for heart diseases. There are significant racial differences in who receives the appropriate cancer diagnostic tests and treatments, and in which HIV-infected patients received antiretroviral therapy to forestall the onset of AIDS. Particularly troubling was the finding that, for diseases that disproportionately affected minority patients (such as stroke and diabetes), they had a much lower rate of receiving key diagnostic and therapeutic interventions. Minorities are also more likely than whites to receive undesirable treatments, such as lower limb amputations for diabetes and other conditions. While some of the disparities can be explained by lower quality health insurance, language barriers, and lack of health care providers for minority neighborhoods, the report cited several studies that found disturbing amounts of outright prejudice on the part of health care providers.

An appreciation of the social construction of ideas of illness helps explain how cases are constructed. Medical decision making is powerfully influenced by social assumptions that are often implicit and unacknowledged. The creation of a medical case shows that medical practice, likewise, is a social construction.

Depersonalization of the Patient

Patients also bring an understanding—sometimes fragmented and contradictory—of the nature of their illness. They enter the medical encounter with an array of important social, emotional, and situational concerns. Drawing from cultural models, the patients have some interpretation of their own illness. Furthermore, they are likely to be struggling with problems of meaning, at least in the instance of feared, serious illness, including these concerns: Why me? Who is responsible? Why this disease? What will this do to my identity and my future?

Serious miscommunication and depersonalization occur when the doctor disconfirms or ignores patient concerns and understandings. Box 10.1 illustrates a gravely flawed exchange between doctor and patient. The doctor, intent only on his biophysical assessment, has failed to hear the person, ignoring or interrupting her attempts to explain her illness. In conducting the interview and writing his report, the doctor is using the technically correct forms he learned in his training.

Box 10.1

The Creation of a Medical Case

Background: Mrs. Flowers is returning to the clinic, where she had previously been treated for her hypertension. She is 39 years old, black, the mother of five children. She lives with four of her children, her mother, and two grandchildren in an inner-city ghetto. She works as a waitress in a restaurant, but periodically she has been unemployed and on welfare. She has been married twice, but both of her husbands have deserted her. As a result, she is a single head of household. Mrs. Flowers is active in the community, especially in the local Baptist church, which has been an important source of support to her and her family for many years.

In the household of eight, she is the only wage earner. Her mother is 59 and partially paralyzed owing to a stroke that was the result of poorly controlled hypertension. Her oldest daughter, the unmarried 19-year-old mother of two small children, is at present unemployed and pregnant. Mrs. Flowers's 15-year-old daughter is also pregnant. Their 18-year-old brother is in prison. The 12-year-old brother has had problems with truancy and minor delinquency. The baby of the family (11) is said by her mother to be an angel.

A year ago, Mrs. Flowers's long-time male companion, Eddie Johnson, was killed in a barroom brawl. Recently, Mrs. Flowers has been increasingly upset by memories of Eddie Johnson, and by worries about her sons. She is also concerned about her mother's worsening disability, which includes what she fears may be early signs of dementia.

"DR. RICHARDS:	Hello, Mrs. Flowers.
MRS. FLOWERS:	I ain't feelin' too well today, Doc Richards.
DR. RICHARDS:	What seems to be wrong?
MRS. FLOWERS:	Um, I don't know. Maybe it's that pressure of mine. I been gettin' headaches and havin' trouble sleeping.
DR. RICHARDS:	Your hypertension is a bit worse, but not all that bad, considering what it's been in the past. You been taking your medicines as you ought to?
MRS. FLOWERS:	Sometimes I do. But sometimes when I don't have no pressure, I don't take it.
DR. RICHARDS:	Gee whiz, Mrs. Flowers, I told you if you don't take it regularly you could get real sick like your Mom. You got to take the pills every day. And what about salt? You been eating salt again?
MRS. FLOWERS:	It's hard to cook for the family without salt. I don't have time to cook just for me. At lunch, I'm in the restaurant and Charlie, he's the chef, he puts lotsa salt in everythin'.
DR. RICHARDS:	Well, now this is a real problem. Salt restriction, I mean a low-salt diet, is essential for your problem.
MRS. FLOWERS:	I know, I know. I mean to do all these things, but I just plain forget sometimes. I got so much else goin' on and it all seems to affect the pressure. I got two pregnant daughters at home and my mother is doin' much worse. I think she may be senile. And then I worries about J.D., and here comes Teddy with the same problems startin' up. I–
DR. RICHARDS:	Have you any shortness of breath?

MRS. FLOWERS:	No.
DR. RICHARDS:	Any chest pain?
MRS. FLOWERS:	No.
DR. RICHARDS:	Swelling in your feet?
MRS. FLOWERS:	The feet do get a little swollen, but then I'm on them all day long at the restaurant—
DR. RICHARDS:	You said you had headaches?
MRS. FLOWERS:	Sometimes I think my life is one big headache. These here ain't too bad. I've had 'em for a long time, years. But in recent weeks they been badder than before. You see, a year ago last Sunday, Eddie Johnson, my friend, you know. Uh huh, well, he died. And—
DR. RICHARDS:	Are the headaches in the same place as before?
MRS. FLOWERS:	Yeah, same place, same feelin', on'y more often. But, you see, Eddie Johnson had always told me not to bother about—
DR. RICHARDS:	Have you had any difficulty with your vision?
MRS. FLOWERS:	No.
DR. RICHARDS:	Any nausea?
MRS. FLOWERS:	No. Well when I drank the pickle juice, there was some.
DR. RICHARDS:	Pickle juice? You've been drinking pickle juice? That's got a great deal of salt. It's a real danger for you, for your hypertension.
MRS. FLOWERS:	But I have felt pressure this week and my mother told me maybe I need it because I got high blood and—
DR. RICHARDS:	Oh, no. Not pickle juice. Mrs. Flowers, you can't drink that for any reason. It just isn't good. Don't you understand? It's got lots of salt, and salt is bad for your hypertension.
MRS. FLOWERS:	Uh huh. Ok.
DR. RICHARDS:	Any other problems?
MRS. FLOWERS:	My sleep ain't been too good, doc. I think it's because—
DR. RICHARDS:	Is it trouble getting to sleep?
MRS. FLOWERS:	Yeah, and gettin' up real early in the mornin'. I been dreamin' about Eddie Johnson. Doin' a lot of rememberin' and cryin'. I been feelin' real lonely. I don't know—
DR. RICHARDS:	Any other problems? I mean bodily problems?
MRS. FLOWERS:	No, 'cept for tired feelin', but that's been there for years. Dr. Richards, you think worryin' and missin' somebody can give you headaches?
DR. RICHARDS:	I don't know. If they are tension headaches, it might. But you haven't had other problems like dizziness, weakness, fatigue?
MRS. FLOWERS:	That's what I'm sayin'! The tired feelin', it's been there some time. And the pressure makes it worse. But I wanted to ask you about worries. I got me a mess o' worries. And I been feelin' all down, as if I just couldn't handle it anymore. The money is a real problem now.
DR. RICHARDS:	Well, I will have to ask Mrs. Ma, the social worker to talk to you about the financial aspect. She might be able to help. Right now why don't we do a physical exam and see how you're doing?

Box 10.1 (*continued*)

MRS. FLOWERS: I ain't doin' well. Even I can tell you that. There's too much pressure and it's makin' *my pressure* bad. And I been feelin' real sad for myself.

DR. RICHARDS: Well, we'll soon see how things are going."

After completing the physical examination, Dr. Richards wrote the following note in the medical record:

"April 14, 1980

39-year-old Black female with hypertension on hydrochlorothiazide 100 mgs. daily and aldomet 2 grams daily. Blood pressure now 160/105, has been 170/80–110/120 for several months alternating with 150–/95 when taking meds regularly. Has evidence of mild congestive heart failure. No other problems.

Impression: (1) Hypertension, poorly controlled
               (2) Noncompliance contributing to (1)
               (3) Congestive heart failure—mild
               (1) Change aldomet to apresoline
               (2) Send to dietician to enforce lower salt diet
               (3) Social work consult because of financial questions
               (4) See in 3 days, regularly until blood pressure has come down and stabilized

Signed: Dr. Staunton Richards"

Dr. Richards sent a note to the dietician: "39 year old Black woman with poorly controlled hypertension who does not comply with low salt diet. Please help plan 2 gram sodium diet, and explain to her again relationship of salt intake to her disease and that she must stop eating high salt foods and cooking with salt."

Source: *The Illness Narratives: Suffering, Healing, and the Human Condition,* by Arthur Kleinman, M.D. Copyright 1988 by Basic Books, Inc. Reprinted by permission of Basic Books, Inc., Publishers.

However, in the medical record he produces, the patient is dehumanized and transformed into a reified, thing-like case, very unlike the person who, as revealed in the transcript, speaks eloquently of her commitments, fears, stresses, and economic and social problems.

In transforming Mrs. Flowers into a medical case, the doctor reduces the person to her hypertension, her noncompliance with the medical regimen, her early signs of heart failure, and her medications. The doctor, following the technically correct approach to interviewing and treating, has completely missed the person with her complex social, psychological, and economic problems. His control of the interview consistently constrains Mrs. Flowers's presentation of her concerns; she is frequently ignored or interrupted when talking about the very matters that brought her to see the doctor. The doctor permits her to speak about her physical complaints, but disallows her psychological or social problems. The interview elicits only facts about her biophysical diseases and medical treatment. Even though Mrs. Flowers's human suffering is very much a part of her chronic illness, it is relegated to a perfunctory referral to a social worker (Kleinman, 1988: 134–136).

The disease orientation of the medical model and the doctor's professional distance from the patient combine to turn the complex person into a rationalized case with its biophysical parts neatly separated from its social, emotional, spiritual, and economic elements. In this situation, the doctor is also so culturally distant from the patient, he is ignorant of the ideas and social practices that inform her own understanding of her situation. For example, she refers to her "high blood"—a folk illness in lower-class black American subculture. Because "high blood" is believed to result from blood rising to the head, her consumption of pickle juice makes sense as a folk remedy because it is believed to thin or "cut" the blood. Cultural and social factors, such as the limitations posed by her job, make it unlikely that the sick woman would actually follow the difficult instructions for managing her serious illnesses. Rather than understanding these factors, the doctor views what he labels her "noncompliance" as a moral failing. She is not a "good" patient because she does not do what he tells her to do to control her biophysical condition (Kleinman, 1988: 135–136).

An interesting contrast is the inner-city clinic experience of a young black internist from a middle-class background; her understanding of a patient like Mrs. Flowers is remarkably different:

> The more I see, the more appalled I am at how ignorant I have been, insensitive to the social, economic, and political causes of disease. . . . Today I saw an obese hypertensive mother of six. No husband. No family support. No job. Nothing. A world of brutalizing violence and poverty and drugs and teenage pregnancies and–and just plain mind-numbing crises, one after another after another. What can I do? What good is it to recommend a low salt diet, to admonish her about control of her pressure? She is under such real outer pressure, what does the inner pressure matter? What is killing her is her world, not her body. In fact, her body is the product of her world. She is a hugely overweight, misshapen hulk who is a survivor of circumstances and lack of resources and cruel messages to consume and get ahead impossible for her to hear and not feel rage at the limits of her world. Hey, what she needs is not medicine but a social revolution. (quoted in Kleinman, 1988: 216–217)

In learning the medical model and the specific techniques of clinical practice, doctors are trained to transform the patient into a case. A study of case presentations–a standard training method in which interns, residents, and fellows in a teaching hospital present formal case studies to their superiors–found that the standard discourse depersonalized patients, referring to them as objects: their disease, their treatment procedure, or a shorthand term for their health status (Anspach, 1988). For example, a pregnant woman is transformed into a "Gravida III, Para I, AbI, black female at 32 weeks gestation" (Anspach, 1988: 363). Furthermore, by using the passive voice and referring to technological procedures, doctors' case presentations also failed to acknowledge the *human agency* in observing or treating. For example, they state, "He was put on phenobarb," rather than "I decided to put him on phenobarb," or "The arteriogram showed that this AVM was fed . . . ," instead of "I requested an arteriogram and interpreted its findings to mean . . ." (Anspach, 1988: 366–368).

Learning to present cases according to these norms affects doctors' interactions with patients; student doctors describe editing out patients' own stories and structuring their conversations with patients around the categories considered relevant for a case presentation. One study of medical education noted, "Case presentations are a genre of stories, through which persons are formulated as patients and as medical problems" (Good, 1994: 79). Case presentations and other professional discussions are as much "about" the physician's presentation of self to colleagues and the negotiation of responsibility and authority for medical decisions as "about" the patient's illness per se (Ericksen, 1999; Atkinson, 1999).

The very language and interviewing techniques of the standard doctor-patient interaction result in losing sight of the patient as person and the patient's concerns. For example, physicians recode the patients' expressions into medical terminology, which becomes a shorthand for their medical condition and glosses over possibly relevant nonphysical aspects of the patients' description of their problems (Mishler, 1984; Waitzkin, 1991). In the preceding example, Mrs. Flowers's expressions are transformed into "hypertension, poorly controlled," "noncompliance," and "mild congestive heart failure." In recoding the language for conceptualizing the problem, the patient's perspective is obscured (Cicourel, 1983: 238).

Likewise, the structure of the medical interview leads to inadequate doctor-patient communication and truncated, distorted understandings of the patient's problem. Doctors are trained to use a set of formulas for conducting interviews with patients. One such formula is a "decision tree," a sequence of small decisions that culminates in a diagnosis and treatment plan. Accordingly, doctors elicit information from patients that enables them to narrow the range of possible medical problems down to smaller and smaller "branches." While they are talking with patients, doctors are simultaneously mentally testing hypotheses. Thus, doctors experience patient input not immediately relevant to the part of the decision tree they are considering as disruptive to their line of thought. Similarly, doctors are trained to proceed in the interview by reviewing each of the bodily systems (respiratory system, circulatory system, and so on), often in a verbal checklist format. This routine device guarantees a certain thoroughness, but doctors often become irritated by the "disruption" of a patient who introduces a question or a point relevant to some area of concern other than the immediate item on the checklist (West, 1984; see also Waitzkin, 1989).

Furthermore, the process by which the medical record (that is, the institutional, written medical file for each patient) is constructed reflects the construction of the patient as an *object* of medical practice. This medical record also transforms subsequent doctor-patient interaction, affecting the content of further medical decision making. The medical record does not contain *all* potentially relevant information for all the patient's problems; rather, it is a highly selective, abstract representation focused on a problem that is manageable in the doctor's (and/or hospital's) routines (Berg, 1996). Although this selective representation is efficient for the expert's decision making and routine practice, it both depersonalizes and distances the patient nonexpert from the physician expert.

Thus, the typical patterns of doctor-patient communication produce a case, a reified representation of a sickness in which the sick *person* is remote or absent. Often subsequent interaction between the patient and doctor as well as other medical staff is based on this representation, rather than on any fresh input from the sick person. Such depersonalization results when the focal object of doctors' work is the medical case.

THE ENDS OF MODERN MEDICINE: MORAL DILEMMAS AND SOCIAL POLICIES

Implicit in the medical model of disease and curing are a number of assumptions about life and death and the proper ends of medical intervention. These assumptions are so deeply embedded that rarely are they acknowledged, much less examined. They have contributed to major contemporary problems for medical personnel and for society as a whole about how to deal with death and dying, life and potential life, and "normal" and "abnormal" life (see Begley, 2001; Lock, 2000b; Stolberg, 2001). In short, should the foremost goal of medicine be preserving and extending life for all patients?

The Medical Model and the Conquest of Death

Comaroff (1984) suggested that the biomedical model's interventionist stance against disease, which is defined as the disruption of the body's organic functioning, led to the acceptance of the conquest of death as a major goal of medicine. Although acknowledging that ultimately all persons will die, the medical model makes it difficult and sometimes impossible to *decide* that any given person shall be allowed to die (see, for example, Muller and Koenig, 1988). The focus on the conquest of death also reduces medicine's attention to other needs, such as ameliorating suffering or making mundane improvements in the sick (or dying) person's quality of life.

Contemporary medical dilemmas are in part the result of biomedicine's very successes. Modern technologies enable doctors to prolong lives, even though often they cannot actually cure the disease. For example, the technology of dialysis allows persons with otherwise fatal kidney failure to live three or more years longer. Technological developments enable neonatal intensive care units to reduce the rate of respiratory distress syndrome among undersized infants who would have surely died soon after birth in earlier decades. Other technologies simulate virtually every organic function, artificially supplying the body with breath, food, water, immune responses, heartbeat, excretion, and blood cleansing. Similarly, the extremely expensive technology of organ transplantation extends some lives, often for many years.

Whereas in the recent past, people expected that death was inevitable and would occur at its appointed time, now they expect medicine to intervene to prevent death and to prolong life. In modern societies, we have come to view potentially fatal heart attacks, strokes, and accidents as treatable events for which we expect cures. An entire industry has grown up around cardiopulmonary resuscitation (CPR) despite the fact that it is rarely successful (fewer than 1 to 3 percent of out-of-hospital cardiac arrest victims live to be discharged from the hospital). Modern society builds and supports this extensive resuscitation system that defies death and medicalizes the dying process (Timmermans, 1999). Medicine—especially the promise of its technical efficacy—offers a nonreligious version of "salvation" from human sickness, death, and finitude (Good, 1994). Indeed, in promulgating the successes of scientific medicine, the profession itself may have raised people's expectations unrealistically high.

The idea that medicine can and should intervene to prolong life is consonant with both the medical model and physicians' professional ideologies. Doctors want to assert their control over sickness and the loss of life; many physicians view the death of a patient as a failure. The expectation that the goal of medicine is to prevent death has many negative consequences, however.

Our culture is profoundly uncomfortable with death and dying. It does little to prepare people for their own and others' deaths. Ariès (1974) documented the historical development of modern taboos about death. Accordingly, as society failed to provide a consensus about how to die a "good death," it segregated sickness and death from normal social interaction. Medical institutions perform the latent function of segregating the unpleasantness of sickness and dying while aspiring to the manifest function of curing (Kearl, 1993). As recently as 40 years ago, more than half of American deaths occurred in people's homes; by the mid-1990s, 80 percent took place in health care institutions under medical care (Stryker, 1996).

Death and dying have become medicalized partly because of expectations that medicine will be able to intervene in the process, and partly because many people are relieved to have their family members' dying supervised by medical personnel in a hospital setting. Death is perhaps less threatening if it is thus removed, sterilized, and routinized. At the same time, however, the dying process is partly cut off from the very institutions of society most likely to be able to provide meaning in the face of death: religion and the family. Some alternative arrangements for dying, such as the hospice movement, encourage demedicalizing and rehumanizing the process.

Nevertheless, to choose an alternative arrangement for dying requires that alternatives be available, affordable, and legally allowed; that doctors and family members be aware and consciously accept the patient is dying; and that mechanisms are in place to help dying persons consider their options and express their intentions regarding death. Many social structures and attitudes in our society make it difficult for people to die with dignity (see Rosenthal, 1997b). The specter of an unavoidable, overmedicalized end is not unrealistic: Medical technology makes possible keeping the body "alive" with respirators, feeding tubes, intravenous hydration and antibiotics, heart resuscitators, and the like, long after the person in the body has lost the ability to consider or express a desire to live or die (see Lock, 1996).

The Technological Imperative

Another cultural value that makes it difficult to decide to let nature take its course and allow death to happen is the **technological imperative,** a prevalent idea in most Western societies (especially the United States) urging us that if we have the technological capability to do something, we should do it. The technological imperative implies that action in the form of the use of an available technology is always preferable to inaction. Indeed, once a technology becomes available, its use becomes almost inexorably routinized and considered standard. The failure to apply this standard care—no matter how inappropriate for the individual patient—would be reprehensible (Koenig, 1988).

The technological imperative is deeply embedded in many institutional responses to health crises. Institutional decisions to invest in technology are often driven by financial incentives, such as government subsidies (see, for example, Anspach, 1993). For example, most hospitals have created (and thus need to use in order to pay for) several high-technology wards, such as coronary and neonatal intensive care units, equipped and staffed to provide maximum multiple technological responses to patients' conditions. Similarly, many health insurance plans cover hospital care and high-tech medicine (such as treatment in a coronary care unit) but not low-tech or nontechnological responses (such as therapeutic massage or nursing home care). One study of therapeutic escalation (that is, the physician's decision to order more extensive and expensive treatments after prior therapy failed) found that the source of payment (such as private insurance) and the organizational setting (hospitals' internal incentives, for example) significantly affected doctors' decisions about whether to increase, maintain, or withdraw treatments (Ross and Albrecht, 1995).

In arguing that the proper goal of medicine should not be the unquestioned prolongation of life, the ethicist Callahan (1987: 173) wrote, "The existence of medical technologies capable of extending the lives of the elderly who have lived out a natural life span creates no presumption whatever that the technologies must be used for that purpose." Similar but perhaps more difficult questions need to be posed about the uses of technology for prolonging the lives of persons who have not lived out a natural life span (see Hilfiker, 1983). What medical intervention should be used, for example, for an accident victim left in a persistent vegetative state, for a medically unsalvageable patient (for instance, a person with cancer of the esophagus who subsequently has a heart attack), or for an irreparably damaged newborn (with anencephaly—congenital lack of a brain)?

There are also serious ethical questions about the use of medical responses that themselves cause pain or other suffering. For example, under what conditions should a patient or a patient's family be allowed to refuse a prescribed treatment, such as chemotherapy or surgery? The technological imperative has considerable legal support in many states; patients and their families must go to court to assert (and sometimes lose) the right to decide to refuse treatment or life supports. Other legal and ethical rights are also uncertain. Does a person have the right to obtain a particular treatment, even if it will not provide certain benefits for that individual? For example, does every person with kidney failure have the right to a transplant?

Because they underlie legal and social policies, such ethical issues are matters for the entire society as well as individual doctors, patients, and families to consider. These issues are difficult for the courts, in part because the courts have deferred to the medical profession itself as the proper authority on matters of defining life and death. As Chapter 6 notes, the medicalization of moral authority has undermined the authority of other institutions, such as religion and the family.

On issues such as these, however, there is no technical, purely medical answer. The boundaries of life and death are blurred, and biomedicine is incapable of clearly delineating them for the courts in purely technical terms, as illustrated by the ambiguities of court cases involving the abortion of second trimester fetuses and the passive euthanasia of patients in a persistent vegetative state. As Callahan (1987: 179) observed, "The 'sanctity of life' has to be the sanctity of personhood, not merely the possession of a body." Moral and legal rights adhere to *persons,* but there are no neat biomedical criteria to distinguish when or whether a body is a person. The choice of such criteria must come from outside scientific medicine, although they may include medically measurable determinants, such as brain death.

Policy Implications

Our society must come to terms with these issues in order to develop sensible social policies: How shall we pay for the care needed by the sick and dying? Toward what ends shall we train doctors and other medical personnel? How shall we allocate our society's research funding? What kinds of institutional support are required to fulfill our health care goals; for example, should society's focus be on high-tech hospital care, or is more societal support needed for other institutional settings, such as public health programs, real homes for the aged, or home health aides? Such policy decisions regularly require difficult choices because no society can possibly meet every need of all citizens and thus must set its priorities.

These policy decisions have been thrust on us by the burgeoning costs of high-tech medicine; by the medicalization of birthing, dying, and other areas of life; and by the increasing numbers and proportions of the population who are old and very old. Medicare expenditures to physicians and hospitals are rising dramatically and threaten to deplete those funds. About 25 percent of annual Medicare expenditures pay for the medical costs of only approximately 5 percent of the enrollees—those in their last year of life (Hogan et al., 2001).

Furthermore, as recently as 15 years ago, babies born very prematurely died shortly after birth. Now many of these babies live, although a substantial proportion suffer serious physical and mental disabilities and chronic illnesses. The main factors in their survival are the new technologies in neonatal wards and intensive nursing. In many hospitals, the technological resuscitation of very premature babies is done automatically, without consulting the parents about their wishes; this process then necessitates considerable later agonizing over whether to sustain the infants on life supports and whether to perform invasive, sometimes painful procedures to keep them alive (see Anspach, 1993).

Neonatal intensive care requires extremely expensive services; the necessary three or four months of hospitalization may cost $90,000 or more. In many parts of the United States, the rates of premature birth are rising. Furthermore, the rates of severely disabled survivors is also increasing, ironically at a time that the U.S. government is decreasing its support for disabled persons (Anspach, 1993). Because of the burgeoning cost of such care, even though it is medically effective for some babies, society must examine whether this expenditure is the best use for its moneys (see Rhodes, 1992; Young and Stevenson, 1990). Might it not be better to spend health care dollars on public health programs that could prevent premature births, such as prenatal care and nutrition programs for women of childbearing age?

Similar allocation questions also apply to decisions about who shall receive high-priced organ transplants and other expensive surgery. What proportion of the nation's health care resources should go to care for the elderly and the dying? What priorities should be given to heroic interventions (such as bypass surgery) compared to palliative efforts (such as pain relief) or to simple care and nursing? If we have limited resources, should children get priority over the very old? Should preventive efforts take precedence over treatments for the dying? Should the amount of care that the ill receive depend on how much they can afford to buy? One survey showed that many Americans place priority on allocating resources to severely ill patients, even when they would benefit less from that treatment than would others who also need those resources for health (Ubel, 1999). There are serious ethical issues involved in many such policy decisions.

The United States operates with a de facto system of rationing health care. Accordingly, the wealthy buy whatever they want; however, the upper middle classes (that is, those whose income is roughly between the fiftieth and ninetieth percentiles) buy what their insurance allows and have the option to deplete their other resources to buy more. The very poor get whatever the state and Medicaid systems, public hospitals, and Medicare offer—often a very inadequate patchwork of health care services. And the working poor (the lower middle classes) are likely to have few or no resources for access to needed health care. This form of rationing results in enormous and growing inequities (Fein, 1986; Smedley et al., 2002). The nation needs to confront the ethical issues that have been only implicit in its health care system and must examine its priorities.

SUMMARY

Modern biomedical forms of knowledge and practice are the particular result of social, political, and economic processes. The accomplishment of professional dominance by medical doctors in this century gives them both preeminence in the medical division of labor and control over the definitions of health, illness, and healing practices.

Medical professional dominance also creates problems for the treatment of the sick. The layperson-expert gap and other sources of social distance often result in poor communication and failed empathy. Doctor-patient relationships may reflect other social distance, such as that produced by gender and class stratification. Much interaction between doctor and patient serves to protect the power of the physician, which often directly disempowers the patient. Both the socialization of physicians and the social structure of medical practice promote patterns of doctor-patient interaction that disrupt real communication and lead to unsatisfactory treatment.

Assumptions implicit in the medical model have made it difficult for doctors and laypersons to admit to the limits of modern medicine and to consider setting different goals for its practice. By focusing on the conquest of death, medicine overemphasizes an interventionist approach to treatment and has difficulty coming to terms with death and dying. Not only do doctors and their patients need to reconsider the proper ends of medicine, but society as a whole is also confronted with massive ethical, legal, and policy issues about health care and medical treatment.

Chapter 11

STRATIFICATION AND POWER IN HEALTH CARE SYSTEMS

� ✶

The Convention on the Rights of the Child has become the most widely accepted human rights treaty ever. Approved by the United Nations General Assembly in 1989, it has been ratified by 191 countries. Only two member countries have not ratified—the United States (the only economically developed country that has failed to make this legal commitment) and Somalia. The Convention guarantees (among others) the following Human Rights of children:

"States Parties recognize the right of the child to the enjoyment of the highest attainable standard of health and to facilities for the treatment of illness and rehabilitation of health. States Parties shall strive to ensure that no child is deprived of his or her right of access to such health care services. [*Article 24*]. . . .

States Parties recognize the right of every child to a standard of living adequate for the child's physical, mental, spiritual, moral and social development. [*Article 27*]. . . . "

Source: United Nations, *Convention on the Rights of the Child,* (1989) retrieved from the World Wide Web at www.unicef.org.

- **U.S. Problems in Comparative Perspective**

- **Recipients**

- **Physician-Providers**
    Corporatization of Medical Production
    Fee-for-Service Payment and Capitation
    Clinical Decisions and Economic Considerations
    Malpractice: Economic Burdens and Regulation

- **Nurse-Providers and Other Helping Professionals**
    The Development of Nursing
    Stratification and Predominantly Female Health Professions

- **Nonprofessional Health Care Workers**

Enormous variety characterizes how societies respond to the health needs of their members. Economic and social-structural arrangements determine how a society cares for members' sick bodies, frail elderly bodies, disabled bodies, infant bodies—the well-being of all its members. This chapter explains the importance of social power in shaping these economic and social-structural arrangements. Each society's political economy creates its health care system's goals and the policies for achieving those goals.

A health care system is the "aggregate of commitments or resources which any national society 'invests' in the health concern" (Field, 1973: 763). As a system, all parts mutually influence each other, for better or for worse. Changes in one part of the system result in changes in another part. For example, cutbacks in government reimbursements for hospital patients under Medicare may drive up costs of health insurance premiums paid by workers and their employers, as hospitals compensate for lost revenues.

U.S. PROBLEMS IN COMPARATIVE PERSPECTIVE

In U.S. social policy, health care has been equated with medical care, and most data in Chapters 11 and 12 refer only to medical care, its organization, and its costs. U.S. social policies have not conceptualized—much less accommodated—a *total* health care system. The development and possible effectiveness of social policy are ultimately a political process in which powerful interest groups vie to define the agenda. The present emphasis on medical care of disease (rather than, for example, preventive medicine or public health) is itself the political product of the relative muscle of various interest groups (see Light, 1993). Attempts to set a broader agenda for the health of the nation are contested by powerful interest groups benefiting from the present pattern of spending for medical care.

It is useful to compare the health care systems of nations because they show alternative ways of arranging the parts of the system. For example, the Swedish system regulates and controls doctors and hospitals more extensively than the U.S. system. It is more holistic in its concern for health-related issues like nutrition, child care, environmental pollution, and occupational health and safety. The Swedish system has also achieved a healthier nation by all international standards.

The United States could learn from developing nations as well as industrialized ones because our health care system is having to face real limits in the nation's human and financial resources for dealing with health needs. We need to find ways to maximize the health-producing results of how we use our resources. For example, Cuba has achieved levels of health and longevity for its people comparable, on average, to those of the United States. Despite the nation's low per capita GDP (about one-eighth that of the U.S.), Cubans enjoy one of the highest per capita food supplies in the world, and their health care delivery system emphasizes public health and preventive care measures. There is universal access to hospital-based care and far less disparity in the quality of health care between the wealthy and the poor than in the United States (Chomsky, 2000). The health-outcomes success of such a relatively poor developing country from redirecting resources toward food, public health efforts (such as an effective campaign to eradicate dengue fever), and preventive medicine (such as inoculation campaigns) is an instructive lesson for the United States and other developed countries. It suggests that if we directed health care expenditures toward "refocusing upstream" (as described in Chapter 2) to prevent illness, rather than on high-tech medical care of those already sick, the American people would experience long-term gains in health without such a grave drain on the economy as health care expenditures are now.

In the United States, the power of competing interest groups, together with the ideology of free-market competition, has resulted in an amazingly complex, unwieldy, and expensive health care system that is now in crisis. The ideology of a laissez-faire market has obscured the fact that relatively few parts of the health care system are amenable to real market conditions; thus, the notion that competition governs this type of health care system is a fiction. Nor has the United States maintained pure private enterprise, implied in its rejection of national health plans like Canada's. Indeed, nearly half of all U.S. health care expenditures are directly from public monies, collected by city, state, or federal taxes, and much more is indirectly subsidized by government agencies (such as by tax writeoffs to employers who pay employee health insurance). The U.S. system fits the ideal type of a laissez-faire health care system only in that health care has become *highly commodified,* and the *drive for profits* is, indeed, a central dynamic, making it even more difficult to control or plan to meet the entire society's needs.

The contradictions implicit in the U.S. health care system have driven it to the brink of crisis. U.S. health care expenditures have grown dramatically—much faster than other expenses in the consumer price index. Figure 11.1 shows how greatly the proportion of the total U.S. gross national product (GNP) consumed by health care costs increased between 1940 and 2000. These figures include only expenditures for *formal* health care (including doctors, hospitals, pharmaceuticals, and medical supplies); they do not include most costs of informal care (for example, assistance with daily living for persons with chronic illnesses) or most health maintenance and sickness prevention expenses (such as nutrition, pollution control, and accident prevention). Runaway health care costs have eroded the nation's ability to address other public needs, such as education and scientific research.

The United States spends a larger share of the gross domestic product (GDP) on health than any other developed country (Eberhardt et al., 2001: 11).[1] Figure 11.2 shows comparisons of health spending, both per capita and as a percent of the GDP. This figure shows that in 1998, the United States spent 13.0 percent of its GDP and $4,164 per capita. Total health expenditures in the United States, as a percentage of the gross domestic product, grew from 5.1 percent in 1960 to 14 percent in 2000—a 41 percent increase (Jarvis, 2001). By contrast, Canada's expenditures grew from 5.4 percent in 1960 to only 9.5 percent of its GDP in 1998; for the same time period, the United Kingdom's grew from 3.9 to

---

[1]The GDP (rather than GNP) is regularly used for international comparisons.

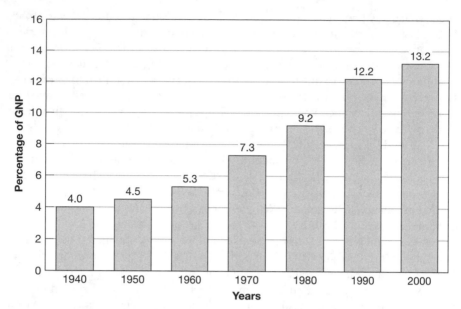

FIG 11.1 **U.S. Health Care Expenditures as a Percentage of Gross National Product.** *(Source: U.S. Department of Health and Human Services, Health, United States, Hyattsville, MD: National Center for Health Statistics. Note: These data differ from those given in previous editions of this publication, due to Department of Commerce revisions of the gross national product (GNP).)*

6.7 percent. From 1970 to 1998, Germany's expenditures grew from 6.3 to 10.6 percent. (Eberhardt et al., 2001: 327). The staggering growth of the U.S. trend is not likely to wane. By 2010, health care is expected to account for at least 16 percent of the U.S. GDP, and economists predict that even 30 percent would not be unlikely in 2040 (Leonhardt, 2001).

U.S. health care spending also consumes a larger amount per capita—roughly twice as much as that in the economically advanced countries of Europe, as illustrated in Figure 11.2. If these enormous expenditures produced proportionately better health outcomes for Americans, they might be justified. On the contrary, by virtually every measure, Americans enjoy less health and longevity, on average, than citizens of some 30 other economically developed countries. This figure, using male life expectancy as an indicator, illustrates that American males have life expectancy roughly comparable to that of Irish males, despite the fact that Irish per capita health care expenditures are about one-third the amount of the U.S. level. Furthermore, the two countries with the highest rankings of male life expectancy (Japan and Sweden) spend less than half the U.S. per capita rate and less than three-fourths the proportion of the GDP, compared to the United States.

The U.S. cost increases are particularly troubling, because unlike Canada or European countries, the U.S. health care system is not accessible to many of its

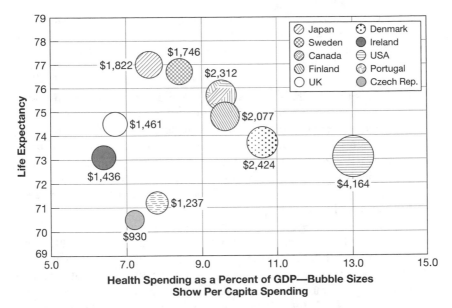

FIG 11.2 **Male Life Expectancy and Health Spending for Selected Developed Countries.** Countries listed in decreasing order of life expectancy. *(Source: Organisation for Economic Cooperation and Development (OECD). OECD Health Data 1998: A Comparative Analysis of 29 Countries. Washington, DC: OECD CD-ROM, 1999.)*

citizens who are uninsured or underinsured. Although the United States has been less successful in controlling costs, it shares with other developed nations the growing problem of meeting citizens' needs for basic social well-being–health, education, affordable housing, nutrition, old age security, basic support for children–while participating in a globalized economic system in which paying for citizen well-being reduces corporate profit and international competitiveness. Thus, all nations are struggling to find a way to provide for their citizens' well-being, but the U.S. system is in a worse crisis, because it has *never* had an adequate safety net to protect its citizens in times of economic troubles.

Americans worry about premium and health care costs, as well as whether they will be denied needed care due to inadequate insurance or lack of money for out-of-pocket health expenses (Blendon and Kim, 2001; Gallup, 2001; Smith, 1992). International comparisons suggest that their fears are well founded. U.S. spending, for every category of health expenditure, is the highest of all nations, but the rate of utilization (calculated by number of doctor visits per person or average number of and length of hospital stays) is well below the average of other industrialized nations (Anderson and Poullier, 1999).

Because of inadequate cost controls, even those Americans who are fully covered (that is, older persons covered by Medicare) receive considerably less needed health care service than do Canadians, whose system pays far less per person for their care (Welch et al., 1996).[2] These figures suggest that many Americans who experience the kinds of health problems that would be treated by the medical care system in other countries are not getting treatment in the United States. Extremely high costs in the United States may be one important reason why many Americans cannot obtain needed services.

By contrast with the United States, in the three decades since the inception of Canadian national health insurance, substantial gains have been made in making medical services accessible to all Canadians, regardless of ability to pay, and greatly reducing mortality disparities between wealthier and poorer, and urban and rural regions (Charles and Badgely, 1999; Gorey, 1999). Although some economic barriers still exist, the poor are far less at risk of being denied needed health care, and the middle classes are not in fear of being made poor by health care expenses (Marmor and Mashaw, 1997).

In 1993, a U.S. presidential commission urged a system guaranteeing coverage for all citizens. One alternative set of bills proposed a national health insurance program, comparable to Canada's. At the time, surveys showed that the majority of Americans preferred the Canadian arrangement of national health insurance financed by tax money to the present form of public and private health insurance (*New York Times*, 1992). The various interest groups, especially the insurance industry whose profits in this sector would be eliminated were the country to adopt a system similar to Canada's, spent enormous amounts of money on media campaigns, lobbying Congress and other influential politicians and jockeying for a favorable position relative to other interest groups in the resulting program.[3] No significant program developed, and the problems in the U.S. system have grown worse.

America's lack of adequate health policies is related to its historical failure to develop *social* security protection for all citizens. Most developed countries try to secure their citizens' health and well-being by using tax funds to support education, public health, affordable housing, and infrastructure (such as safe water systems). They develop government regulatory agencies that monitor and control a wide range of health-related problems, such as environmental purity, safety of food and water, workplace health and safety, and pharmaceutical safety and effectiveness. Other governmental policies address citizens' health and well-being by establishing labor laws that mandate minimum wages capable of maintaining workers' families securely above the level of poverty and that protect workers

---

[2] Canadian elderly received 44 percent *more* evaluation (doctor visits) and management services (such as physical therapists) but 25 percent *fewer* surgical procedures. Canadian surgery rates for procedures known to be medically beneficial (hip replacement, for example) were the same as the United States, but much lower for procedures (such as knee replacement) about which there was low consensus as to medical benefit (Welch et al., 1996).

[3] During the 1993–1994 debate over national health care policy, campaign contributions from the health and insurance industries reached $37.9 million, an increase of 51 percent over the same time period in the previous election cycle (Podhorzer, 1995). Total special interest spending (including paid lobbyists, mass media advertising, and so on) may have totaled over $100 million, making health care reform the most heavily lobbied legislative initiative in recent U.S. history (Center for Public Integrity, 1995).

from crushing stress and overwork. Although the United States has, in the not-too-distant past, legislated some measures along these lines, since the 1980s these policies of protection have been reduced, unenforced, or eliminated. Table 11.1 illustrates how the United States compares with nine other developed countries. It shows how U.S. social policies have failed to protect too many of its weakest citizens—children—from poverty, sickness, and death.

The U.S. rate of child (under five) mortality is abysmal compared with all other wealthy developed countries. Worldwide, the United States ranks 31st (with first being best). Ironically, the United States is tied for 31st with Cuba, which has

TABLE 11.1 **Comparative Social Policies and Outcomes: United States and Nine Other Developed Countries**

Country	Child (0–5) Mortality Rank[i] (1 = Best in World)	Child Poverty Rate[ii] (% Children Living in Poverty)	Inequality Ratio[iii] (90th %ile : 10th %ile, Low # = Low Inequality)	Private Health Care Spending as % of Total Health Care Spending[iv]	Percentage Covered By Govt.-Assured Health Care[v]	Percentage with no Coverage from any Source[vi]
Sweden	1	3.7	2.78	n.a.	100	0
Norway	1	4.5	2.80	24	100	0
Denmark	4	5.9	2.18	n.a.	100	0
Netherlands	4	8.4	2.59	31	72	>0.5
France	4	9.8	3.06	22	99.5	0
Germany	4	11.6	2.32	24	92.2	>0.5
Czech Rep.	18	1.8	n.a.	8	100	0
Canada	18	16.0	3.90	30	100	0
U.K.	18	21.3	4.67	17	100	0
U.S.A.	31	26.3	5.78	55	33.3	14–30

[i] *Source:* UNICEF, *State of the World's Children, 2000.* Using data for 1998, UNICEF's ranking is from worst (Sierra Leone) to best (Sweden, Norway, Japan). To focus on developed countries, the above ranking is reversed, with best ranked 1. The OECD median falls in the large group of countries tied for 4th rank. The U.S. U5MR is below most other developed countries and tied for 31st place with a developing country, Cuba.

[ii] *Source:* UNICEF, *State of the World's Children, 2000.*

[iii] *Source:* Navarro, "The political economy of the welfare state in developed capitalist countries," 2002b, pp. 160–161. Navarro's calculations are based on 1990–91 data; in the 1990s, the rate of inequality in the United States has grown more rapidly than in European countries.

[iv] Calculated from *OECD Health Data 2001,* based on data for 1998. Private spending includes voluntary insurance premiums (paid by employer and/or employee), as well as out-of-pocket spending, such as co-pays or direct purchase or payment for expenditures not covered by insurance or government program.

[v] *Source:* Anderson and Poullier, 1999: 181. Government-assured health care in the United States would include, for example, Medicare, CHAMPUS (for military personnel and families), and Medicaid.

[vi] *Source:* Anderson and Poullier, 1999: 181 (for Europe); USDHHS, *Health United States, 2001;* and Bennefield, 1998. The low figure in the range is the percentage uninsured at any one time in a good year (that is, low unemployment and low job turnover); the high figure is the percentage who had been uninsured any time during a three-year period.

achieved remarkable levels of nutrition and health for all citizens, despite a very low per capita income. As Chapter 2 suggests, inequality may be a key factor in sickness and death. Table 11.1 shows a strong connection between countries' health outcomes and their levels of inequality (here measured as a ratio between the average income of the 90th percentile to that of the 10th percentile). The United States has the highest inequality—more than double that of many advanced European societies. This inequality is embedded in the structure of the society, affecting health through such related factors as the proportion of children living in poverty (and thus without nutritious and sufficient food, in substandard housing, exposed to lead poisoning and high levels of air pollution, and so on). In the United States, more than one-quarter of all children live in poverty and, due to structural inequalities (for example, deficient schools), will not get out of poverty in their lifetimes.

Lack of accessible, affordable health care is *not* the main reason for a high under-five mortality rate in the United States, but the inadequacies of the nation's health insurance "system" do reduce the chances that sick children will get timely diagnoses and good care. The United States is the *only* advanced economically developed country that has *no* comprehensive health care system for all citizens. As a result, between 14 and 30 percent of all Americans—disproportionately working poor, minorities, and women—have no health insurance from any source. Roughly 33 percent have insurance that is government-provided (such as Medicare and Medicaid). These programs are described further in Chapter 12.

Lacking a distributive system that uses tax monies to secure equal access to needed health care, America's "system" requires much private spending. More than half of the enormous U.S. health care expenditure comes from private funds—mainly premiums for employment-provided insurance and out-of-pocket expenditures for everything not covered by insurance. This arrangement for paying out-of-control health care costs is devastating to anyone with many health problems and to the poor and near-poor.

The U.S. health care system is the product of a long history of considerable political maneuvering, haggling, and contesting. This system places a particularly heavy emphasis on medical treatment rather than on health care. As a corollary, its focus is on institutional and professional forms of care. Furthermore, the U.S. system—even more so than other capitalist systems—emphasizes the **commodification** of health and health care; making money is one important driving force in the system. The interplay of numerous conflicting interests created the existing system, and the same interests are exerted vigorously whenever change to the system is proposed. To understand this complex system, we must first appreciate the relative power among these interest groups and how they use their resources to further their interests.

The following is a greatly simplified sketch of the various economic interests represented in the U.S. health care system. In this chapter we consider the social organization and interests of some of the people involved in receiving or providing health care, especially those whose income is derived from providing such care. With the development of high-technology and specialized medicine, work within the medical care system has become heavily reliant on large bureaucratic organizations. The structure and functions of these medical organizations reflect the structure of the larger society. Workers in the medical care system are stratified largely according to the class, gender, ethnic, and other divisions in the whole society.

In Chapter 12 we describe the economic interests of large-scale organizations involved in the system, especially hospitals, medical industries, insurance companies, and government agencies. These interest groups vary dramatically in their relative power at various historical moments. The development of economically powerful interest groups as major institutional actors in the U.S. health care policy debates was a nearly inevitable result of the combination of the laissez-faire ideology of the system and the expansion of health care profits and markets.

In order to think critically about a better future, we need to understand the structural sources of the present crises and the systemic problems that make the existing health care system so ineffective in providing good, affordable health care to all citizens. There appears to be a general consensus that the U.S. health care system requires significant changes, but there is less consensus on what parts to change and what the long-range objectives should be.

If we could build the system anew, what might it include? It is useful to imagine alternatives that might better address some of the health needs poorly met by the existing system. We need to consider many criteria—not merely cost—for a better system. Our nation could try to provide better access to care for rural and inner-city communities and more preventive measures for all age groups. We could reshape medical education to discourage overspecialization and encourage better doctor-patient relationships. Our country could restructure payments to providers to promote better decision making about use of surgery, medications, and medical technology, as well as to create hospitals that emphasize caring and skilled service, rather than cost-effective tending of patients.

At root are also some fundamentally moral issues, which we rarely acknowledge or discuss in a public forum. For instance, *what kind of nation do we want to be?* Do we want to consider health as a commodity that the wealthy can buy in abundance, that the middle classes can afford occasionally in limited measure, and that the poor cannot have at all? Or do we, as a nation, want to consider health, like education, as something we should try to provide for all in order to promote the good of all?

RECIPIENTS

Decades ago, the prospect of catastrophic medical costs was remote, even for poor persons, because the level of medical knowledge and technology did not command high prices. Hospitals were relatively low-tech, generally not-for-profit organizations that subsidized costs of care for those who could not afford to pay. Doctors, who lived in the very neighborhoods they served, charged for their services according to what people there could afford to pay. The implicit contract that protected the recipients of medical services also protected the doctor: affordable service for patients, even at inconvenient times, in exchange for community respect, deference to professional judgment, and a good standard of living for the physician. That kind of social contract, based on long-term communitywide commitments and loyalties, no longer pertains in most modern life (see Rubin, 1996). In its place have come impersonal, short-term commitments.

Recipients of health care now fear catastrophic medical costs, because they sense that their interests are not being protected in a laissez-faire system of powerful corporate interests. Health care costs have taken much larger portions of the family budget (in premiums, taxes, and out-of-pocket expenses), but the families themselves have little or no say over these expenditures.

The U.S. system has been portrayed in political rhetoric as an open market of competing providers that (in theory) would lower prices if only patients would be more savvy consumers. In reality, however, the patient is in an inherently weak position as a consumer, primarily because medicine has become so sophisticated that the patient typically lacks the expertise to evaluate services (from doctor or hospital) and products (pharmaceuticals or technological devices, for example). Unlike standardized products, medical services are highly variable. Although an individual can do much to become an informed consumer of medical services, the enormous disparity in expertise between professional and patient places the consumer in a relatively weak position.

The market model also assumes the consumer is the one making the choices in the marketplace, but in medical care the recipient rarely makes such decisions. Ideologically the U.S. system emphasizes the patient's freedom to choose doctors, but actual choice may be severely constrained by the limited availability of doctors in a region, by insurance that is limited to certain providers, or by the assignment of a patient without private insurance to a clinic, military, or other institutional doctor. Before the 1980s, most employees' health insurance allowed the open choice of a provider, but in less than a decade nearly all employees lost this choice. Furthermore, most insured individuals do not even choose their own health insurance program; insurance plans are typically marketed to *employers,* rather than to the health care consumers themselves. Insurers compete only to insure the most profitable pools of employees—those who need the least health care—so market principles do not help reduce prices overall (Bodenheimer and Grumbach, 1997).

The recipient's doctor or insurance plan determines in which hospital to place the patient. Unlike most other industrialized countries, U.S. doctors do not relinquish care of (or income from) their hospitalized patients. Doctors maintain "admitting privileges" with certain local hospitals, and they bill their hospitalized patients separately from the hospital bill. This arrangement makes the hospital and private practitioner mutually dependent. Patients insured through managed care plans are further limited to hospitals connected with the managed care organizations. The patient thus rarely actually chooses a hospital, and hospitals do not compete for customers in an open market. Like insurance companies, hospitals give admitting privileges to doctors who will bring in only the most desirable pools of customers—those with ample insurance and whose care is most likely to result in net income for the hospital.

The doctor also guides the patient's decisions about health services, selects pharmaceuticals and treatment procedures, and refers the patient to specific other doctors for specialized care. The doctor refers the patient to specific outpatient labs and clinics for diagnostic or therapeutic services. Lacking significant decision-making power, the patient is hardly a consumer in an open, competitive marketplace.

Another feature of health care decisions that makes them difficult to weigh rationally as in a market situation is the high value our culture places on health and life. When we say our health is priceless, we imply that we cannot imagine what limit we would pay to preserve that health. The consumer's medical treatment decisions are even more complicated because they often must be made quickly and under stress. Unlike buying a house, the consumer may have to decide to commit several hundred thousand dollars with no opportunity to shop around or even consider other options.

Recipients of medical care are among the least powerful interest groups in the U.S. system. Collectively, some groups of potential patients have wrested benefits from the system, but their successes are related to their political clout (as is the case with senior citizens protecting funding of Medicare benefits) and/or their powerful socioeconomic position (for instance, upper-middle-class workers achieving substantial health care benefits from their employers). Less powerful groups of recipients, such as the working poor, have little or no influence against the interests of other parties in the system.

PHYSICIAN-PROVIDERS

As a profession, physicians collectively constitute one of several "countervailing powers" contending for economic advantages and control of the organization of health care delivery (Light, 1993). Historically, medical doctors' achievement of professional dominance (described in Chapter 10) accomplished both their preeminence over other medical occupations and their extraordinarily high level of income. Other occupational groups also have asserted their interests: to define their domains of expertise, to achieve recognition and pay as professionals, and to have more control over the structure of their jobs. The resulting hierarchy of specialized health care occupations is fluid and changing, but all occupational interest groups utilize whatever resources of power they have to protect their interests. The prestige, power, financial success, and professional autonomy of medical doctors is a standard against which other occupational groups measure themselves.

Just as the long-term social contract binding a community with its physician(s) is a relic of the past, so too is doctors' high degree of autonomy and control of their own incomes, treatment of their patients, and the terms and structure of their work. The prior system of medical work was vulnerable to the pressure of countervailing powers, in large part because of excesses or inconsistencies within that system itself, but the emerging arrangements are creating new problems for health care workers and for recipients of their services. In the last two decades, U.S. medicine has come to be practiced largely in the context of large-scale corporations, most of which *operate for profit*–hospital corporations, insurance corporations, managed care organizations, and so on (Salmon, 1995; Starr, 1982: 420–449). Technocratic control of the labor process has transformed work in many professional fields including medicine (Burris, 1993: 120ff.). Although still prestigious and high-paying work, all medical fields are increasingly constrained, either by external regulations or by direct control of a corporate employer.

Corporatization of Medical Production

Whereas at mid-century, most U.S. doctors were in private, entrepreneurial practice, by the end of the twentieth century, more than half of all licensed physicians were salaried employees (Weiss, 1997). Even when not directly employed by corporations, few doctors practicing in urban or suburban settings are independent of the corporate reach of insurers, hospital corporations, and managed care organizations. These developments are discussed further in Chapter 12.

As a result of these new structural arrangements, health care providers are losing some of the autonomy they gained in their ascent to professional dominance (Light, 2000; McKinlay and Stoeckle, 1988). The same development of technologically advanced, hospital-based medical practices that enhanced the prestige and authority of the medical profession in the first half of the century has, in the second half, also produced conditions of the profession's corporate dependence. Modern medicine is capital intensive. So practitioners turn to corporate sponsors–medical groups, hospitals, and managed care corporations–to provide the necessary equipment and support services (Rodwin, 1993).

Physicians' relations with their economic sponsors are hardly as disempowering as those faced by nonprofessional workers because the medical profession retains near-monopoly control over much needed, complex skill and knowledge (Light, 2000; Navarro, 1988). In the context of institutional cost cutting, however, even such highly expert employees as physicians may experience their jobs and entire incomes as vulnerable. For example, when two hospitals merge, much of the professional staff could become redundant; doctors, therapists, and nurses–especially the experienced ones with larger paychecks–may be dismissed (Rosenthal, 1997a).

Government agencies and private insurance companies (that is, "third-party payers" of medical bills) also increasingly monitor and regulate doctors' work. In an effort to curb rising costs and overuse of hospitals, diagnostic tests, surgery, and so on, these organizations have added new layers of bureaucratic management of health care, increasing standardization, surveillance, and sometimes countermanding physicians' professional judgment (see White et al., 1994). Loss of autonomy and increase of hassle connected with regulations and monitoring are major sources of dissatisfaction among doctors. One study found that British cardiologists were dissatisfied mainly with their heavy workloads and the health system's lack of resources; by contrast, American cardiologists were dissatisfied at being forced into a bureaucratic system of rules and regulations, hierarchical authority, and rationalized procedures, which reduces their autonomy (Gross, 1994). Another comparative survey found serious dissatisfaction with the nation's health care system among 77 percent of U.S. physicians, compared to only 33 percent of Canadian and 48 percent of German doctors (Blendon et al., 1993).

The corporate interests of hospitals and insurers have thrust considerations of cost effectiveness and profit maximization into the fore. *Who speaks for the interests of the patient-recipient?* In the former model, the doctor was supposed to be the advocate for the patient's interests (White et al., 1994). If a doctor said, "This patient needs to be hospitalized," that decision was once accepted as authoritative by third-party insurers and hospitals. Physicians' sponsors today, however, are more likely to discourage, question, and even override their professional opinions. Although not all physicians are trustworthy guardians of their patients' best interests, for-profit corporations may be even less trustworthy because they are remote, impersonal, and their profitability depends on minimizing the costs of patient care (Davies and Rundall, 2000; Iglehart, 1998; Mechanic, 2000).

Doctors' loss of total autonomy and control of patients' care was, however, largely the result of several countervailing powers—especially insurers and government—that developed policies and procedures to counteract abuses and excesses in the former system of provider reimbursement and incentives. One problem was the system of *fee-for-service billing,* which made it difficult to control escalating health care costs. A related problem was the extent of *perverse incentives* for a doctor to order unnecessary tests or perform extra procedures. *Conflicts of interest* due to sources of secondary income were another systemic problem. Unresolved problems with the system's response to *medical malpractice* created further cost escalation.

Fee-for-Service Payment and Capitation

As noted in Chapter 10, physicians achieved a legally recognized monopoly over the provision of most paid medical care, as well as the training and admission of new personnel. Historically, the economic basis of physicians' service has been a fee-for-service system in which the doctor typically charges the patient for each service provided at each visit. In principle, this system establishes an economic link between physician-provider and patient-recipient, but few contemporary doctor-patient relationships are so simple because the vast majority of physicians' services are paid through third parties, such as the government or insurance companies. The idea that the mode of payment itself forges a direct link between provider and consumer is thus more a myth, harking back to an era of more personal doctor-patient relationships. This ideology supports the interests of physicians because the fee-for-service arrangement has allowed them great freedom to set their own terms of remuneration.

Many doctors themselves have been dissatisfied with how the fee-for-service arrangement has affected their everyday practice of medicine. One thoughtful physician described his realization of how detrimental these economic considerations had become:

> An aged patient had come in to the office and was talking about her aching feet. She not only had several very real physical problems but she was also very lonely and quite hypochondriacal. . . . As she continued to tell me how tired she was, I realized I wasn't listening. I was angry. What she needed was someone to sympathize with her, gently encourage her, and to make some simple suggestions that might alleviate her suffering. I knew from past experience that that kind of listening and empathetic presence would require at least half an hour, but I would only be able to charge $20 for an intermediate call, Medicare would discount the charge significantly, and my half after overhead, would be, maybe, $8. I also knew that if I just stood up, cut the woman off by giving her a prescription for a pain medicine and scheduled her for next month, I could charge the same $20 and move into the next room where another patient was waiting with a small laceration from which I would earn about $30 in perhaps 10 minutes.
>
> As soon as I recognized what I was angry about, I was ashamed. But the truth of my feelings was nonetheless real. . . . I was looking at my interactions with patients more and more as business transactions. (Hilfiker, 1986)

These problems show how unsatisfactory for both patient and provider is a system of highly commodified health service, in which each aspect of care is delivered as a discrete entity.

In the face of escalating medical costs, critics have questioned how doctors who receive fee-for-service payments set their fees. The practice of medicine in the United States has been essentially entrepreneurial (that is, incomes are made in the business of selling of goods and especially services). What, then, are these services worth? Considerable evidence indicates that the level of fees is governed primarily by physicians' desired standard of living (Reinhardt, 1987). Overall, the profession is exceptionally well paid—in the top 3 percent of all earners in the United States (Altman and Rosenthal, 1990). In the last decade the median income of physicians has increased only moderately, compared to prior decades, and payments to health care providers accounted for a small proportion of the dramatic increases in health care spending. Nevertheless, the average physician income (about $200,000 in 1997)[4] increased more than the median, suggesting that some doctors employed in certain types of specialties and practices are commanding significantly increased incomes (*New York Times*, 1998).

Specialists, particularly surgeons, earn far more than general practitioners and other doctors engaged in the more labor-intensive primary care. Physician services accounted for 22 percent of the $1.2 trillion health care expenditures in the United States in 1999 (Eberhardt et al., 2001: 11). Anesthesiologists and radiologists enjoyed increases as high as 22 percent in 2001, bringing the average radiologist salary to $355,065. In 2001, the two specialties with the lowest average annual

---

[4]For comparison, note that the mean for all full-time workers in 1997 was $38,500.

salary were primary care physicians: pediatricians, $138,000, and family practitioners, $145,000 (Romano, 2001).

Because the U.S. health care system has no centralized planning or effective controls over the numbers of doctors in the various branches of medicine, there continue to be dramatic imbalances in the supply of specialists. Most of the surplus consists of surgical specialists; the supply of family practitioners and pediatricians is about the same as the amount needed, but there are nearly twice as many neurosurgeons and cardiologists as needed (Bencomo et al., 1995). These imbalances are expected to continue to grow because only about 20 percent of medical graduates want to practice in primary care (such as family practice) rather than medical specialties (Gamliel et al., 1995).

Interestingly, the oversupply of specialists has not led to competitive pricing. Indeed, rather than competition driving physicians' fees down, the existence of an oversupply of physicians in an area generally increases health care costs because the doctors compensate for the fact that each has fewer patients by raising their fees for each procedure and by recommending more procedures for each patient they treat. For example, the dramatic increase in the number of prostatectomies (for nonmalignant enlargement of the prostate gland) performed in the United States is not due to any disproportionate increase in prostate disease (compared to other countries). Only a small fraction of the increase is explained by the existence of Medicare coverage for men over 65. Rather, the oversupply of competing specialists has made this surgery a financial mainstay of urologists' practices, motivating them to convince patients that prostate enlargement is a health problem and the surgery is necessary, effective, and acceptable (McDade, 1996).

The medical profession never has been effective in policing itself for illegal and unethical fiduciary practices, such as fee splitting, kickbacks, and self-referral (Rodwin, 1993). There is a fine and imprecise line between uniform pricing among doctors in a community and illegal price fixing. Nevertheless, doctors who set fees according to what the market will bear rarely undercut the going rate; rates are thus seldom competitive within a single community. No matter how honest the fee schedule, the patient typically is not able to evaluate its appropriateness.[5]

Between 1980 and 1989, when physician costs were soaring, the components of doctors' income that accounted for those increases were the volume of procedures performed (calculated by the number of surgical procedures and diagnostic tests per physician) and increased price per service. On average, doctors had not increased the amount of time spent with patients and other medical work. Rather, insurance and Medicare reimbursement policies made these fees for service *less* sensitive to market forces (Pope and Schneider, 1992). These excesses of the 1980s may have seriously undermined physicians' autonomy in the long run,

---

[5]This analysis focuses on economic pressures experienced by all physicians, honest and dishonest alike; illegal behavior is one response to the opportunities for gain. Initially, it was only individual unscrupulous physicians who profited from illegal kickbacks and fraudulent billing (Rodwin, 1993).

because they brought into question whether the surgery, testing, and other increased utilization of medical services were really necessary for the patient's health.

In an effort to cut costs, many managed care organizations (discussed further in Chapter 12) negotiated contracts with physicians to pay for their services by a different method. **Capitation** means the doctor is paid a fixed rate per month per patient (the amount varies according to age and sex of the patient), regardless of how much physician service is actually needed. About 70 percent of health maintenance organizations pay their primary care physicians by capitation (Friedman, 1996). Capitation is advantageous to the doctor because it simplifies billing and ascertains a regular flow of income. At the same time, however, because these doctors are not on a salary, they must fill their patient load with enough patients—often a mixture of capitated and fee-for-service clients—to bring in enough income. The third-party insurers have thus transferred some of the risk of their business to the doctors. It is the doctor—not the insurer—who must compensate when patients have serious, medical service-consuming illnesses.

This risk shifting has several deleterious effects on their patients. Embedded in capitation is the *perverse incentive* to deny care to patients, because the physician is rewarded for taking on more patients and doing less for them (Gray, 1997; Rodwin, 1993; Weiss, 1997). A related problem is that it creates incentives to avoid serving the needs of high-use patients, such as persons with diabetes or asthma. Precisely those patients who most need to utilize doctors' care are those most likely to be avoided by doctors paid by capitation.

Clinical Decisions and Economic Considerations

The fee-for-service arrangement is riddled with **perverse incentives**—built-in financial encouragements to treat the patient inappropriately by increasing services, overprescribing medications and diagnostic tests, or to choose treatment sites according to physician rather than patient interests. When doctors can increase their own income by having their patients get medical services from which they personally profit, there is a significant conflict of interest often resulting in questionable medical treatment (see Frazier and Mosteller, 1995).[6] Furthermore, many unneeded tests are ordered as part of "defensive" medicine to protect against malpractice suits. Some estimates suggest that between 20 and 60 percent

---

[6] In an effort to find a "neutral" way to evaluate treatment options, unbiased by the perverse incentives of either physicians' or corporate interests, some critics are calling for a turn to evidence-based medicine. Evidence-based medicine is the application and standardization of patient treatment practices based on scientific research and professional consensus judgment. This involves adoption of national standards of care and accountability for medical decisions. Accordingly, the individual physician's loss of autonomy may result in better quality of care and better medical outcomes (Ferlie and Shortell, 2001). Good scientific evidence is more expensive and time-consuming to achieve than clinical (observational) evidence. If the policy change toward requiring sound evidence for the effectiveness of new drugs and surgical procedures results in more funding for independent research, it may result in improved treatment standards.

of these tests are unnecessary, adding nothing to the patient's diagnosis or treatment (Califano, 1989).

Likewise, the fee-for-service system gives incentives to doctors to use surgery rather than less invasive treatments. The decision to operate is based on a number of discretionary choices, perceptions, evaluations, and decision rules that vary considerably among physicians and medical situations. *All* surgery involves assessing the probability that the operation will improve function, reduce pain, or increase the quality of life as balanced against the risks of complications from the surgery itself. The fee-for-service system complicates the medical decision-making process with the added criterion of financial gain for doctor and hospital (see Bunton, 1998). For example, if a woman in labor does not give birth quickly, the physician experiences considerable incentive to perform a Caesarian section, a serious abdominal operation for which fee-for-service reimbursement is high and time required is relatively short, rather than work with the mother for a normal vaginal delivery for which the reimbursement is far lower proportionate to the time required. One study of rates of Caesarian sections for women whose previous deliveries had been Caesarians found that financial considerations were a significant predictor of the decision to operate (Stafford, 1991).

Especially for new and unproven procedures, there is considerable potential for physicians to conduct surgery for inappropriate reasons relative to the patient's health and needs. Critics assert that the U.S. rates of coronary bypasses, hysterectomies, and Caesarean sections are at least double the appropriate level (see, for example, Angier, 1997; McDade, 1996). Compared to other industrialized countries, the United States has exceptionally high rates of surgery without concomitant lower rates of mortality. We cannot infer that the difference is due only to unnecessary surgery (see Schwartz, 1984), but the socioeconomic incentive of fee for service is certainly one factor promoting high rates of surgery.

In principle, the physician is an advocate for the patient, representing the patient's interests to insurers, hospitals, and other specialists on the case. An inherent conflict of interest exists, however, even for physicians who take their role as advocate seriously, when they are in a position to order for their patients certain procedures that also happen to be an important source of their own income (Gray, 1991; Rodwin, 1993). For example, some for-profit hospital corporations made such financial incentives explicit by asking doctors who practice at their facilities to buy shares in the hospital itself. A 1997 study found that physicians who had invested in a Columbia/HCA-owned hospital in Miami increased their referrals to that hospital by 13.4 percent, and their referrals to other hospitals dropped by 22.4 percent in the first two years after the chain took control of the hospital (Gottlieb and Eichenwald, 1997).[7]

---

[7]This kind of hospital investment scheme is aimed at areas in which a large proportion of patients have Medicare or other kinds of insurance that does not limit doctors' selection of hospital. A reverse of this perverse incentive is characteristic of HMOs and other managed care programs, which reward physicians for *not* recommending hospitalization or other services (see Chapter 12).

Financial incentives have even more impact on the kinds of physician services performed in response to patient demand rather than because of clear-cut medical need. Medical services for fertility or potency problems, sterilizations or abortions, obesity, or chronic pain exemplify these financial interests. A cosmetic surgeon is not likely to counsel a prospective patient that her nose is lovely without surgery.[8] So long as the U.S. health care system continues to provide economic incentives for inappropriate surgery and other medical procedures, both doctors and hospitals will continue to be subject to the influence of economic considerations in deciding on patient treatment.

Even greater potential for conflict of interest is involved when the physician can receive **secondary income** from the treatment. When physicians own a joint venture, such as a free-standing diagnostic imaging facility, nursing home, or psychiatric hospital, they benefit financially by referring their patients, while evading antikickback laws (Mitchell and Scott, 1992). A California study of patients covered by workers' compensation found that physicians who referred patients to physical therapy, psychiatric, or magnetic resonance imaging (MRI) facilities of which they were owners tended to order significantly more services, including more medically inappropriate services, than did a control group of doctors with no financial interest in those facilities (Swedlow et al., 1992).

By 1991, more than 10 percent of U.S. doctors had invested in businesses to which they refer their patients; in some states, such as Florida, more than 40 percent of all doctors have such investments (Pear, 1991; Pear and Eckholm, 1991). Contrary to claims of proponents of joint ventures, such facilities do not increase access to needed medical services for underserved populations. One study of joint ventures in radiation therapy in Florida found that none of the facilities were located in inner-city neighborhoods or rural areas, compared to 11 percent of nonjoint-venture facilities. Joint ventures received 39 percent of their revenues from patients with good insurance coverage, in contrast to 31 percent for nonjoint-venture facilities. Furthermore, the principal personnel at joint-venture facilities spent 18 percent less time with each patient than those at nonjoint-venture facilities. Both the frequency and costs of radiation therapy at free-standing investor-owned facilities were 40 to 60 percent higher in Florida than the rest of the United States, despite the absence of other factors that might explain the difference in use and costs (Mitchell and Sunshine, 1992).

The program for end-stage renal disease (ESRD), a chronic, debilitating, and often fatal disease of the kidneys, illustrates the murky causal link between physician-investors' conflicts of interest, medical judgments, and escalating U.S. health care costs. One treatment for ESRD is hemodialysis. When it was first developed, hemodialysis was such an expensive technology that it was systematically rationed. In response to a concerted political campaign by well-organized

---

[8]Because cosmetic surgery, fertility treatments, and many of these other elective physician services are done outside hospital contexts and are not reimbursable by insurance, they are particularly poorly regulated for cost, safety, effectiveness, malpractice, or fraud (Sullivan, 1993).

groups of patients and providers, however, in 1972 the U.S. government passed an amendment to Medicare legislation that provided federal reimbursement for ESRD treatments, even though most ESRD patients were not old enough to qualify for Medicare.[9]

The actual costs were many times the projected costs, and subsequently national expenditures for ESRD treatments escalated dramatically. By 1994, the ESRD program annual per-patient cost ($33,745) was eight times higher than the average Medicare per-patient cost (U.S. Congress, 1997). The enormous cost escalation occurred because the legislation created incentives to put all sufferers of ESRD on dialysis, even though it is not an appropriate or even beneficial treatment for many (Simmons and Marine, 1984). Ironically, the United States, a nation with no program for equitable distribution of health care, became the most liberal subsidizer of dialysis for all. In 1989, the U.S. rate of treatment for renal failure was 2.2 times that of Canada and 3.8 times that of all European countries (Iglehart, 1993).[10]

After the passage of the ESRD program in 1973, in-center dialysis became a booming business; the number of for-profit dialysis facilities more than tripled in the 1980s alone. To curb runaway costs, in 1983 Medicare greatly reduced the reimbursement rate, but for-profit dialysis facilities continued to proliferate and earn profits, compensating for lower reimbursement rates by increasing billable services (for instance, by giving more injections), giving dialysis to more and more patients, including a much larger proportion of patients for whom the treatment was of questionable benefit. The dialysis centers also maintained profits by reducing their operating costs; they substituted less skilled staff for registered nurses, used dangerously obsolete dialysis equipment, and reused dialyzer fluids on multiple patients. Such changes raise questions about the quality of their care (Eichenwald, 1995a, 1995b, 1995c, 1996; Iglehart, 1993). Although many sick people have been helped by the ESRD program, the drive for profits by many participating physicians and dialysis centers have propelled the costs (more than $6 billion in 1996) and influenced professional judgments.

The potential for physician profits on such secondary gains has dramatically increased in recent years with the expansion of high-tech medicine. Government attempts to curb abuses have been limited, because both Medicare and Medicaid use mainly fee-for-service reimbursement, which is hard to monitor. Although outright fraud is illegal, the system has too few controls to prevent it (Sparrow, 1996). Many other secondary income schemes are not illegal, merely unethical. In 1991, the AMA adopted a policy discouraging physician referral to businesses in which

---

[9]The existence of a single organ-specific program of government provision medical services illustrates the inefficiency of the U.S. health care system. If, instead, the system guaranteed that all Americans received care for hypertension and diabetes, before kidney complications developed, far fewer people would need ESRD treatment (Adams, 1995).

[10]The overutilization of dialysis (that is, using it for patients who have a low probability of benefiting from it) may be a significant factor in why the rate of death of persons on dialysis in the United States is extremely high (23.6 percent in 1992) compared to other developed nations such as France (11 percent) and Japan (9.7 percent). Another significant factor may be the cost-cutting measures used in the U.S. dialysis centers to turn a profit (Eichenwald, 1995a).

they have an interest, but the policy is only advisory and voluntary, so it carries little weight and no sanctions. The organized American medical profession has been historically very ambivalent about ethical problems tied to financial interests; it did not seriously address financial conflicts of interest as a professional ethical issue until the 1980s. Even though fee splitting, kickbacks, and other questionable commercial practices have been a problem in professional practice since the turn of the century, in the second half of this century, the AMA steadily weakened its stance against abuses to placate its members and reflect their economic interests (Rodwin, 1993).

Regardless of whether physicians are conscious of their economic interests in clinical decisions, the profit connection in the United States results in a very different pattern of patient care than in countries where doctors cannot profit from the treatments they recommend. The ESRD program illustrates the necessity of restructuring physician payment programs such that conflicts of interest cannot affect physicians' decisions about whether or how to treat their patients.

Malpractice: Economic Burdens and Regulation

The issue of malpractice is related to the socioeconomic basis of provider-recipient relationships. Around the turn of the century, medical societies provided for the mutual defense of members against malpractice suits. Courts deferred to local doctors' judgment as expert witnesses, which made it virtually impossible for aggrieved patients to get one doctor to testify against another. Furthermore, medical societies were so successful in protecting members from suit that they were able to obtain very favorable insurance rates, whereas nonmembers were often unable to obtain insurance at all (Starr, 1982: 111).

In the latter half of the twentieth century, however, the legal and cultural climate changed. Patients became more willing to take doctors to court, partly because of the growing impersonality of all economic relationships. Rising expectations of the wonders of medical science may also have both enhanced doctors' prestige and remuneration while creating unrealistic public beliefs about what doctors could accomplish. Simultaneously, courts allowed the wider use of outside experts and cosmopolitan rather than local standards of care, and legislation—especially since the 1970s—clarified patients' rights, such as the right to informed consent for procedures. The result has been a dramatic increase in malpractice litigation, increasingly large awards to patient-plaintiffs, and increased malpractice insurance premiums, the cost of which is generally passed on to the consumer (Hay, 1992; Horwitz and Brennan, 1995). Although the costs of malpractice insurance and litigation (probably only 1 percent of total health care spending) have been exaggerated by state legislators calling for reform, the system of handling malpractice in the United States is particularly ineffective and inefficient in protecting the recipient of medical services (Horwitz and Brennan, 1995).

The expansion of malpractice litigation has created a number of additional powerful interest groups in the health care arena. Malpractice insurance is typically offered as part of a for-profit insurance industry. Lawyers, courts, and layers of legal paper-processing organizations have likewise become major recipients of the health care dollar. An estimated 60 percent of the billions paid annually for malpractice insurance goes not to aggrieved patients but to the insurance and litigation industries (Califano, 1989). At the same time, however, the expense of litigation prevents the vast majority of injured patients from going to court to obtain any compensation (see, for example, Rosenthal, 1988). Indeed, well-to-do and privately insured patients (that is, those who could most afford to litigate for malpractice) are those least likely to be injured by medical negligence. Negligent and substandard care is disproportionately given to the elderly, the poor, and the uninsured (Weiss, 1997: 46–48).

Most cases that reach the courts are reasonable claims. The National Institute of Medicine reported that medical mistakes kill somewhere between 44,000 and 98,000 people in U.S. hospitals each year. One study described in this report found that medical mistakes were significant factors in the medical problems of some 36 percent of patients in one university hospital. Of these iatrogenic conditions, 9 percent were life threatening or produced considerable disability and another 2 percent were believed to have contributed to the patient's death. (Kohn et al., 2000). Another study of over 30,000 patients who had been hospitalized found that 3.7 percent had suffered some injury as a result of medical care; of those, 28 percent were injured due to doctor negligence or substandard care. Although 14 percent of the injuries were fatal and nearly 3 percent were permanently disabling, only one out of every 9.6 cases of injury due to negligence resulted in a lawsuit (Brennan et al., 1991). Another study found that most malpractice cases won by patients were, in fact, well-founded cases of substandard care and the amount of payment awarded closely correlated with the severity of the injury (Taragin et al., 1992).

Furthermore, the fear of malpractice suits encourages doctors to practice defensive medicine in which clinical decisions are made with an eye to protecting themselves from lawsuits. By practicing defensive medicine, hospital staff often construct a patient's chart as a case record designed more to stand up in court than to describe the patient's actual situation. Communication about the patient then takes place informally, off the record, such as by one specialist writing notes to another (Millman, 1976: 145). Defensive medicine also results in unnecessary tests and procedures (Califano, 1989). For example, fearing lawsuits if they deliver imperfect babies, obstetricians are more likely to order fetal monitoring during labor and are more likely to perform possibly unnecessary Caesarian sections if the monitor indicates any signs of fetal distress.

The problems of malpractice are due to two unmet needs in the U.S. health care system. First, the system has had no adequate method of identifying, controlling, or punishing physicians who were incompetent, negligent, or otherwise detrimental to the health of their patients. One of the prerogatives achieved by medical dominance was the right to peer review: Only doctors could identify and punish malpractice. Historically, however, once a physician passed the credentialing process and obtained a license to practice, fellow doctors were highly unlikely to constrain that practice, much less to take it away. The United States has only a loose system of state medical boards with authority to discipline malpractice, and no coordinated national monitoring is in place to prevent negligent or incompetent physicians from simply obtaining a license to practice in another state. Fewer than a third of the doctors disciplined for serious incompetence or misconduct lose their license to practice medicine (Hilts, 1996). Furthermore, the U.S. practice of dealing with medical negligence through lawsuits fails to deter doctors from negligent behavior (Horwitz and Brennan, 1995).

A second reason for the rise in importance of malpractice suits is that the nation provides few other avenues for a family to obtain recompense for the actual costs created by medical mistakes. Iatrogenic medical practices often create years of additional medical expenses as well as the loss of income due to disability, yet the U.S. health care system offers little assistance with such costs. Most patients have no safety net of economic help for serious medical problems. Thus, malpractice suits become the last-chance effort to obtain economic relief. Litigation is a highly unsatisfactory way to provide recompense for medical mistakes, however, because few people with legitimate claims can afford the long and expensive courtroom route. In the United States, the vast majority of persons injured by medical mistakes ultimately receive no financial help whatsoever.

By contrast, in Sweden, where equitable access to health care is a citizen's right, these functions are addressed by the nation's health system. Their Patient Compensation Fund is publicly financed no-fault insurance that compensates both economic and noneconomic aspects of injury, and settles claims rapidly according to a predetermined schedule. The mere fact of injury is sufficient for compensation; claimants do not have to prove that anyone was at fault. Relatively very few claims are arbitrated beyond this point, and patients are generally satisfied that compensation is fair. A completely separate mechanism, the Medical Responsibility Board—a free-standing national governmental body—deals with malpractice complaints against physicians. It investigates reported incidents and can employ a range of sanctions, from a reprimand to a recommendation that the National Board of Health and Welfare revoke a physician's license to practice. The Responsibility Board's rate of disciplinary actions was significantly higher than the rate by U.S. disciplinary boards (Rosenthal, 1988).

NURSE-PROVIDERS AND OTHER HELPING PROFESSIONALS

As noted in Chapter 10, the rise of the medical profession was achieved by a legal monopoly over the labor market for its services. By the 1990s, however, the countervailing powers of managed care and government insurers had encouraged labor market competition for medical work by allowing other professions (for example, nurse-practitioners, chiropractors, and nurse-midwives) to do previously monopolized work (see Hartley, 1999). At the same time, they also opened some professional employment to paraprofessional and nonprofessional workers, resulting in their substitution for workers with higher credentials (Hughes, 1996).

The historic professionalization of medicine also entailed the subordination, cooptation, or elimination of virtually all competing health care professions. For example, as early as 1906, the AMA's campaign against patent medicines (that is, proprietary drugs) produced laws granting doctors monopoly over the prescription of powerful medicines. Commercial medicine companies had to market their products to doctors rather than to customers (Starr, 1982: 127–134). The nascent profession of pharmacy was subordinated to the medical profession by requiring patients to consult doctors to obtain prescriptions for medicine.

Nonphysician practitioners in the predominantly male professions of dentistry, podiatry, optometry, pharmacy, and chiropractic were able to retain relatively independent practices, even while the medical profession exerted its organizational control. Traditionally female health care professions did not fare so well; they were kept subordinate in pay, working conditions, educational programs, and bureaucratic organization. The development of nursing and various allied health professions, such as laboratory technology, physical therapy, and radiological technology, is a result of *nearly total gender stratification of medical work.*[11]

The Development of Nursing

Early nursing was typically private care by an unpaid member of the family or a paid family helper. It was part of the domestic economy and inextricably linked with women's roles. One of the founders of professional nursing, Florence Nightingale, wrote, "Every woman is a nurse" (1860: 3). She also argued that women should not aspire to be doctors because nursing meshed with their "natural" abilities. Nightingale's hospital reforms envisioned genteel nurses competently running hospitals as domestic managers, completely supportive of and dependent on doctors, who were analogous to the male heads of household.

Even today, nursing is a predominantly female occupation; in 1999, 93 percent of all registered nurses (RNs) were women, but only 24.5 percent of physicians were women. Table 11.2 shows the distribution of women among several health occupations. The gender segregation of these two jobs means that gender-role expectations figure prominently in the working relationships between doctor and nurse (Brown, 1983). Traditionally, the nurse has been expected to be deferential, nurturing, and submissive, even while taking an active role in the patient's care. In the 1960s, researchers observed a series of strategies by which nurses communicated their recommendations without appearing to make a recommending statement; physicians asked for nurses' recommendations without appearing to be asking for help (Hughes, 1988; Stein, 1967). Although recent studies show nurses to be less deferential and more assertive than in the 1960s, changes in the doctor-nurse interaction occurred more in the behavior of nurses than in the

---

[11]Even when women practice medicine, they have been generally segregated in the lower paid primary care specialties such as pediatrics. Studies find that male physicians earn significantly more than female physicians, even after differences in the number of hours worked, speciality, type of practice, and other work characteristics are taken into account (Bird, 1996).

TABLE 11.2   **Selected Health Occupations by Total Employment (1999)**

Occupation	Total Employed (in Thousands)	Black (%)	Hispanic (%)	Female (%)
Physicians	720	5.7	4.8	24.5
Dentists	173	1.9	3.1	16.5
Registered nurses	3,019	9.1	3.4	93.0
Laboratory technicians and technologists	338	19.4	5.6	78.5
Dental hygienists	106	2.8	1.5	99.1
Licensed practical nurses	357	18.4	5.8	95.1
Nursing aides and orderlies	1,970	35.6	9.8	89.9

Source: U.S. Bureau of the Census, *Statistical Abstract of the United States, 2000.* Washington, D.C., 2000.

reciprocal roles or expectations of doctors (Porter, 1992; Stein et al., 1990). Societies with less hierarchical medical work roles have developed different patterns of interaction (Svensson, 1996). Nevertheless, the historical emphasis on "womanly" qualities in nursing has been simultaneously an ideological hindrance to professional recognition and a basis for nurses to seek a distinctive, caring way of relating to patients in contrast to the impersonality of the bioscientific medical model (Reverby, 1987).

In the early twentieth century, two major developments in medical care shaped the direction of nursing: the shift to hospital-based care and the growing emphasis on scientific medicine. The latter, together with many technological developments, created the need for highly trained assistance for doctors; the knowledge and skills required of nurses expanded rapidly. Previously hospitals had been little more than sick wards of the poorhouse, staffed by minimally qualified nurses drawn from the lowest social classes. Male attendants worked in men's wards and female attendants in women's wards. Only those who had no family or means of private care were nursed in hospital settings. As middle- and upper-class persons began to use hospitals for sickness, surgery, and childbirth, and as medical and nursing education became hospital centered, hospitals became more prestigious and profitable rather than totally charitable institutions. Their new fee-paying clientele accordingly expected a much higher standard of care (Melosh, 1982: 15–35; Rosenberg, 1987: 212–236).

Hospitals were expanding rapidly and needed the very kind of disciplined, trained workers they found in nurses; however, the profession was further subordinated as it lost control over nursing education. Hospital administrators established nursing schools so that the student nurses would serve the hospital. Student nurses put in 60- and 70-hour workweeks for two or three years of ward service in exchange for their subsistence and a small sum (typically $10 a year) for uniforms and books (Rosenberg, 1987: 220–221). The economic disincentives and the structural subordination of nurses made the occupation increasingly unattractive to men. For women, however, nursing was one of the few occupations deemed respectable and was considered an appropriate preparation for marriage as well as a source of income.

In the early decades of the twentieth century, many voices within nursing urged greater professionalization and standardization of training. By mid-century, there was considerable division between those nurses advocating hospital training and those urging higher education (Melosh, 1982: 67–76). At stake was the relatively greater professional independence of nursing as well as ideas about the proper role of the nurse.

Technological developments in medicine, especially in the second half of the century, further increased specialization in hospital nursing. After World War II, when hospital-based medical care expanded rapidly, nursing was organized according to stratified functions, with routine bedside tasks and lower-skill nursing tasks relegated to LPNs (licensed practical nurses), aides, and orderlies, under the direction of RNs (registered nurses). Although this practice resulted in cost savings in hospital payrolls and some organizational prestige for RNs, it also resulted in RNs serving as managers more than as nurses. Greater prestige and pay were incentives for some upper-echelon nurses to specialize for work in the intensive care unit, cardiac unit, or operating room.

During the 1970s and 1980s, many hospitals reorganized the nursing labor process in a system called primary nursing, in which a single professional nurse (RN) was responsible for completion of all physicians' orders for a set of patients. Although primary nursing emphasized the professional role of nurses, few hospitals were willing to pay for sufficient nursing staff to enable workers to do both the professional work and the work of nonprofessionals who were displaced. Combined with the fact that hospital patients were increasingly seriously ill, the restructuring greatly intensified nurses' workload, increased time pressures, stress, and the likelihood of dangerous errors (see Furlong and Wilken, 1998; Norrish and Rundall, 2001). This reorganization also significantly tightened the hospital management's control by unambiguously identifying a single employee responsible for all nursing tasks for each patient (Brannon, 1994). Such structural changes in nursing work have caused considerable worker turnover. Two particularly important causes of nurse turnover are loss of autonomy over work and emotional burnout (Lake, 1998; see also Oleson, 2000).

In the 1990s, however, the "restructuring" of nursing work was more a matter of "downsizing" entire hospital work forces—laying off expensive employees and replacing them with cheaper, lower-skilled workers, or not replacing them at all (Furlong and Wilken, 1998). Between 1981 and 1993, nursing personnel as a percentage of the hospital work force decreased from 45 percent to 37 percent (Aiken et al., 1996). Some hospital corporations justified these job cuts by arguing that they are responsible for medical treatment, but not for care during patients' convalescence, recovery, and learning to cope—labor intensive medical work central to nursing (Gordon, 2000). Recent restructuring of nursing work appears to be designed, not only to cut costs (and raise corporate profits), but also to increase managerial control:

> [I]n addition to an emphasis on cost containment rather than quality improvement, work redesign is being applied in a manner that, rather than empower workers, is designed to reduce the level of professional staffing and destroy work jurisdictions that interfere with the further rationalization of the labor process. (Brannon, 1996: 649)

Ironically, although nurses are the health care provider most respected and supported by the public (Hart, 1990: 10), they are also the health care profession structurally most vulnerable to the power of other countervailing powers.

Stratification and Predominantly Female Health Professions

The structural subordination of nursing relative to both physicians and hospital bureaucracies has worked severely against the economic interests of nurses. Nurses' wages have historically been low, and for most years in the last three decades of the twentieth century their pay raises failed to keep apace of increases in the cost of living. In 2000, the mean annual salary for full-time nurses was $37,980 (Mee and Carey, 2001), or about one-fourth of the average primary care physician's net income.

Patients and their insurance companies are not generally billed separately for nursing services, as they are for the services of MDs, such as surgeons, radiologists, and anesthesiologists. Thus, employers of nurses try to keep wages low and to maximize the labor they can extract for those wages. Relative to other professions with comparable years of training, hospital nurses experience several other important occupational disadvantages: unfavorable hours and shift work (sometimes with forced overtime), high stress, and little opportunity for advancement in status or pay. As hospitals and corporations reorganized nursing work, they pitted RNs against less well paid LPNs and nursing aides (Hughes, 1996).

In the health care industry, most occupations are gender segregated (that is, one gender accounts for 70 percent or more of those employed). Table 11.2 shows that the health-related occupations of greatest power, prestige, and income are concentrated mainly among white men. Women make up at least 75 percent of all health industry workers, although constituting only about 42 percent of the national work force. Not only are predominantly female occupations generally low paid, but women also earn less than men in the same job categories (U.S. Bureau of the Census, 2000d).

Predominantly female health care occupations are also characterized by relatively low amounts of professional autonomy. Nurses, medical technologists, dental hygienists, and other auxiliary workers frequently assume many of the less interesting and more time-consuming tasks of hospitals and doctors' offices.

These "physician extenders" are able to do as much as 80 percent of the routine tasks of office medical practice; similarly, dental assistants can assume tasks such as cleaning, patient education, and X-ray work that would otherwise account for most of the dentist's time. The amount the doctor or dentist can charge for these services is roughly the same, regardless of whether they are done by the doctor or dentist or delegated to a relatively low-paid assistant. Masculine behavioral norms are deeply embedded in the organizational life of hospitals and clinics and, indeed, the very definition of a profession (Davies, 1995).

The medical profession has used its regulatory and educational controls to prevent serious competition from these auxiliary professions (Brown, 1978, 1983). Their control also enables them to suppress the wages paid to other health care professionals. For example, by using the states' Medical Practice Acts to abolish private X-ray laboratories, radiologists (MDs) were able to control the terms of employment of X-ray technicians and technologists, and to prevent them from competing with radiologists' own labs and those of hospitals.

Similarly, the independent practice of medicine by physicians' assistants was made illegal in all states where the licensing boards are controlled by doctors. Since 1971, however, a majority of states have amended their Medical Practice Acts to allow nurses to diagnose some conditions, prescribe some drugs, and perform other medical duties under certain conditions; similarly, since 1978, federal guidelines have allowed direct reimbursement to nurse-practitioners for Medicare patients. Home health care is one area in which nurse-practitioners have been particularly active; they have also served extensively in locations (such as the inner city and remote rural areas) considered undesirable by many physicians. The growing surplus of physicians (particularly of specialists such as obstetricians) puts nurse-practitioners in direct conflict with physicians for health care employment.

The tension between physicians and other health care professionals is best illustrated by the competition posed by a recent professional classification, the nurse-midwife. Obstetricians vehemently opposed allowing them to deliver babies and lobbied for legislation limiting the conditions under which nurse-midwives could practice (see Good, 1995). Nurse-midwives' inability to obtain independent insurance also prevented their practice in many states (Rooks, 1997). There is a marked oversupply of obstetricians (Bencomo et al., 1995). As a surgical specialty, obstetrics initially responded to its market condition by greatly increasing the number of Caesarian sections and other procedures; the rate of Caesarian sections soared from 10.4 percent in 1975 to 22.7 percent in 1985 (Rosenblatt et al., 1997). Another strategy was to turn investment in hospital corporations into privileged control of deliveries in those hospitals, thus edging out nonspecialist MDs and midwives.

By contrast, nurse-midwives are trained to help the mother to have her baby naturally; they emphasize a more holistic approach to the mother and child, including both prenatal and early infancy care and education. Their market strategy has been to offer comprehensive services at a much lower cost while appealing to consumers looking for a more satisfying birth experience (Little, 1982; see also Good, 1995). A study of healthy low-risk patients found that nurse-midwives' patients had fewer Caesarian sections, received less anesthesia, and had lower rates of episiotomies and induced labor than physicians' patients (Rosenblatt et al., 1997). Vulnerable populations stand to benefit from the accessible and attentive care offered by nurse-midwives; however, in the United States, the distribution of nurse-midwives varies, not by need or demand, but rather by state regulatory and reimbursement policies (Declercq et al., 1998).

For patients, there is no obvious immediate benefit of these conflicts among health care professionals. For example, giving nurses greater professional recognition, autonomy, and pay may create a more satisfied work force, which may or may not result in better patient care. It may also increase the professional distance between the nurse and patient. Greater emphasis on nonphysician providers should be more cost effective, but the patient will not necessarily realize any financial benefits if the savings go to a hospital corporation, insurance company, or group medical practice. Although many of the predominantly female health care professions hold ideals of providing greater caring and patient service compared to the medical profession (Fisher, 1994), trends toward their specialization and professionalization may promote the further disempowerment of the patient.

NONPROFESSIONAL HEALTH CARE WORKERS

The health industry employs a vast number of nonprofessional workers, such as orderlies, clerks, receptionists, kitchen help, and housekeeping staff. Employment in the health industry reflects patterns of stratification in the larger society, especially occupational segregation by gender, class, and race. White men from well-to-do families disproportionately occupy the jobs at the top of the health industry; health care work at the bottom of the stratification heap is typically done by black women. Black workers are overrepresented in the menial and low-status occupations, such as practical nurse or home health aide, as shown in Table 11.2. Black women are particularly concentrated in the nursing home and home care labor markets, and are far more likely than white women working in such nonhospital services to have earnings below the poverty level (Feldman et al., 1990).

Furthermore, women and blacks are concentrated in occupations with the least opportunity for advancement. Especially in hospital settings, there is almost total lack of job mobility, even though various workers can and do perform tasks appropriate to higher echelon workers. The resulting structural inequality promotes conflict, with the technical and managerial elite (doctors and administrators) separated from and opposing the interests of the lower-status workers (Sacks, 1988).

The interests of nonprofessional health workers, like those of nurses and doctors, do not necessarily coincide with the interests of patients. At the same time, however, the health care system's failure to compensate, regulate, and educate its lower-level care givers adequately has been seriously detrimental to patients. As shown in Chapter 12, for-profit nursing homes tend to hire socially marginal, poorly educated, and poorly trained workers, giving them little or no incentive to be committed to their work or caring toward their patients. Such low-paid, low-prestige custodial care of a powerless population of elderly patients promotes neglect and abuse. Furthermore, the gross understaffing of nursing homes—91 percent of all U.S. nursing homes were found to be understaffed, 40 percent of them dangerously so (Pear, 2002c)—pits the professional nursing staff against the lowly nonprofessional workers. For example, rather than provide whatever care patients need, professional nurses typically refuse to do the work of cleaning patients, especially their excreta, vomit, or drool (Jervis, 2001).

Similarly, the U.S. health care system's recent emphasis on home care has resulted in a new cadre of underpaid, undervalued aides who help the infirm with cooking, cleaning, bathing, dressing, and moving about their homes. Although some home health aides work for nonprofit agencies, many are employed by commercial agencies contracted by Medicare, state or city agencies, or insurance companies. According to the U.S. General Accounting Office (2001), the median wage of all nursing home aides and home care aides in 1999 was just $7.97 per hour. The median annual wage for nursing aides was $13,287, and for home care aides, $12,265. Their pay is so low that approximately 46 percent, working full-time, are sufficiently poor to qualify their families for Food Stamps and CHIP, and 18 to 19 percent are unable to lift their families above the poverty level. Because of their poor remuneration, few of these women had health insurance for their own health problems (see, for example, Feldman et al., 1990).

Thus, while federal, state, and private insurers enjoy the cost savings of home care compared with hospitalization, their savings are subsidized by a large number of poor working women. Home health aides are even more disadvantaged than similarly unskilled workers in hospitals because they have none of the social interaction, reassurance, job stability, economic rewards, or prestige associated with working in a medical setting. Further incentives to exploit home health aides exist when the agency employing them operates as a for-profit health industry (Fine, 1988).

SUMMARY

The social organization of health care services in any health system reflects the stratification and power of various interest groups in that society. Because of the commodified, laissez-faire system in the United States, these interests are particularly obvious as they compete for available resources and control. Social stratification and power are important considerations for understanding the quality of health services. Stratification is related to the social distance between patient and providers and between various levels of health service workers; it is also related to imbalances in the socioeconomic power of recipients and providers.

The stratification and power of these interest groups are also linked to structural incentives and disincentives that affect the quality of health services. Some of the rapid changes in the nature of medical work, such as the corporatization of doctors' and nurses' work roles, are the result of changes in these structural incentives. Many of the problems of the U.S. health care system can be best understood in light of these powerful socioeconomic structural features, which any attempt to solve the problems of quality, access, and cost must address. In Chapter 12 we continue examining the socioeconomic interests in U.S. health care with a discussion of the large-scale organizations that are increasingly powerful in this system.

ECONOMIC INTERESTS AND POWER IN HEALTH CARE

The health care system in the United States has changed dramatically and rapidly; it has undergone major shifts even in the last five years. As noted in Chapter 11, considerable evidence indicates that the American health care system is in crisis. Many Americans are hard pressed to afford the health care available. A large number are simply not served by the system at all, and many of those who are served receive insufficient and inferior care. Despite many cost-cutting efforts, the amount spent on health care consumes an enormous proportion of the nation's gross national product, and the costs of most medical treatment continue to spiral upward.

Yet, as a nation, we are not getting as satisfactory health care as other nations spending far less. The cost-cutting efforts of the 1990s, however, often failed to make health care more affordable to the ordinary family because employers, hospitals, and other agencies shifted more of their costs to the recipients themselves. As the weakest of the interest groups, the recipients of health care have little control over and little understanding of their predicament.

The medical care system is a major part of the larger system of economic production and consumption. It is structured to allow various interest groups to make significant profits and to control considerable resources in medical production. In the U.S. system most medical care is *big business*. The powerful economic interests involved in medical businesses—insurance companies, hospital corporations, pharmaceutical companies, medical technology corporations, and so on—often supersede the interests of both sick people and health care workers. These same powerful interests have also been successful in getting their products and services defined as *primary* expenditures in the health care system. As a result, much-needed expenditures on public health, preventive care, and palliative care (for example, long-term care for infirm elderly persons) are underfunded.

The dramatically increased scale of profits and power commanded by medical businesses has been itself a factor in the crisis of the U.S. health care system. Cost-accelerating profits that in the 1950s seemed like merely deplorable inconsistencies in the system escalated by the 1990s to an unsustainable burden, depriving many people of their sense of security in matters of health and illness, and threatening to tear apart a minimally integrated health care system. Well-financed interest groups have poured resources into influencing government attempts to rethink health care policies; each is vying to protect and enhance its power and profits. In this chapter we offer an overview of some of these large-scale medical care organizations.

In addition to examining the structural power of health care businesses, we hold the U.S. system up to three criteria for evaluation: quality, cost, and access. We identify some of the structural changes that are necessary for the health care system to meet the needs of the American people.

ECONOMIC INTERESTS AND THIRD-PARTY PAYMENT

The inherent inadequacies of the *system of payment* for health care in the United States are probably the foremost causes of the crisis. This unwieldy system, as it has developed, fails to provide access to health care for tens of millions of Americans, makes the guarantee of quality difficult to monitor or regulate, and drives up costs. The very complexity of the system itself makes it more costly than other nations' systems.

Ultimately, the *American people pay all health care costs,* but health care dollars are directed from the people to the providers via three main patterns: by direct payment by the consumer; from government taxation at various levels; and through private insurance. Other countries have different arrangements, nearly all of them less complex and expensive to administer. Canada, the nation with the system most similar in other respects to that of the United States, has abolished private insurance and all persons are insured through a single payer, thus covering everyone in each province equally.

The U.S. method of financing health care is highly *regressive;* low-income families pay more than twice the share of income paid by high-income families. Out-of-pocket expenditures and payments for private insurance premiums are the most regressive because they are not priced according to the families' ability to pay. Expenditures financed by corporate or household income taxes are generally progressive. A more equitable health care system would eliminate or greatly decrease reliance on expenditures made out of pocket and on premiums (Rasell et al., 1994).

Despite our national rhetoric regarding private enterprise, *public* funding is the single largest source of payments for health care, and reliance on public funding has steadily increased. In 1965, public funds (from federal, state, and local governments) covered only 25 percent of all health care expenditures, but by 2000, public funds accounted for 45 percent of all health care expenditures (USHCFA, 2002). Indeed, if payments made by all level governments for health insurance premiums and Medicare for their own employees are included in the total, the public sector paid more than 50 percent of all U.S. health care (see Rasell et al., 1994).

The existence of insurance for *some* citizens encouraged the inflation of costs for *all,* thus increasing the disparity in the affordability of health care for those with ample coverage and those with insufficient or no coverage. In the health care marketplace, *demand is not a function of need.* Many people need health care but cannot demand it because they lack the means to pay. Insurance functions to create the demand for goods and services among persons not wealthy enough to afford them otherwise. For example, when Medicare and some private insurance began to cover home health care services, the new demand created a profitable market, so prices for home health care rose far faster than other consumer prices.

The sense of crisis is largely due to the perception—especially on the part of ordinary citizens and payers of private health insurance—that the present arrangement of health care insurance does not *secure* their health care. Americans have become afraid they will be denied good medical care when they and their loved ones need it, afraid they will lose their health insurance coverage, afraid their insurance will not cover important medical needs, afraid they could be thrown into poverty by uninsured costs of catastrophic illness or long-term nursing care. The following discussion documents the extent to which many Americans' fears are well founded. Until the health care system in the United States provides the security that all citizens will obtain good quality health care when they need it, the crisis will not have been resolved.

C. Wright Mills (1959) reminds us that we are often trapped in our private "troubles" and fail to realize they are the result of public issues. The private struggles for health care and health insurance experienced by families across the United States are, indeed, the product of government and corporate policies that need to be reevaluated and changed. Boxes 12.1, 12.2, and 12.3 use a composite portrait of one family's private troubles to illustrate the larger systemic source of the U.S. crisis in health security.

Private Insurance

Less than one-third of U.S. health care costs are paid through private insurance (USHCFA, 2002), but premiums to buy it are a big portion of family and business budgets. The very idea of and need for health insurance is a relatively recent development. Early in the twentieth century, medical services consumed a small proportion of a family's budget. Doctors and other healers charged comparatively modest fees, which often were adjusted according to a person's ability to pay. Pharmaceuticals were simple and inexpensive. The family itself provided most of the nursing care.

Historical Roots of Today's Problems   With the rapid expansion of technologically sophisticated, hospital-centered medicine, costs quickly began to climb, increasing the risk that treatment expenses would exceed the family's ability to pay. The Great Depression of the 1930s created another major impetus for insurance as voluntary hospitals experienced massive income reductions due to patients' inability to pay. Hospitals financially underwrote health insurance as a *way to stabilize their incomes* (Feigenbaum, 1987; Fein, 1986; Starr, 1982). The idea of using health insurance to spread the financial risks over time and across a population of insured thus came to fruition.

In industrialized countries of Europe such as Sweden, Denmark, and Switzerland, national programs of compulsory health insurance were developed as early as 1883. These state-subsidized programs were not instituted mainly for medical costs (which were as yet small proportions of people's expenses) but rather for income maintenance—"sick pay." Nevertheless, their existence later enabled European nations to expand national coverage to include medical costs not just for workers but for all citizens (Starr, 1982: 237–240).

Blue Cross, created in the 1930s, was the foremost early form of health insurance in the United States. Actively encouraged by the American Hospital Association, Blue Cross was a not-for-profit hospital insurance plan based on noncompeting territorial divisions in which participants paid premiums according to communitywide ratings. Typically, employers paid most or all of these premiums, not only as a benefit for employees, but also to sustain the community's hospital. The hospitals benefited by insurance because their incomes were stabilized; however, the system sowed the seeds of its later crisis, because *having health insurance became linked with having a specific job*. It also resulted in the hospitals (and later, physicians and other "covered" services) being paid "off the top"; thus, in times of economic downturns, employers and workers were committed to pay regular premiums even when their incomes were reduced. Because initially medical care costs were low, employers and workers did not realize this structural disadvantage. Subsequently, when costs spiralled out of control, neither employers nor employees had the leverage to restructure the payment system.

Blue Cross later developed its companion plan, Blue Shield, for nonhospital services, such as doctors' services and lab tests. At first, the AMA (American Medical Association) opposed Blue Cross and other forms of third-party payment on the ideological grounds that they came between the doctor and patients, and restricted doctors' decisions about treatment. The AMA also lobbied to prevent Congress from creating national compulsory health insurance. Eventually, the AMA agreed to accept Blue Shield, because the profession was given some control over the program, thus greatly increasing its income (Starr, 1982: 290–334).

Blue Cross had been conceived as a plan for an entire community, and premium rates were based on local experience with participants' hospital utilization and costs. Risks were thus widely spread. The initial institutional goal was to stabilize hospital use and income; income from insurance itself was not important. Blue Cross began to lose its competitive edge in the 1950s. Commercial insurers, explicitly seeking to maximize profits, began to approach employers of low-risk groups and offer them much lower premiums than possible by the community-rating method of Blue Cross. Commercial insurers, rather than spreading risk widely in a large pool of insured, made their profits by insuring only the low-risk groups.

Eventually, Blue Cross had to abandon its communitywide risk rating (Feigenbaum, 1987). Indeed, in the 1990s many formerly nonprofit Blue Cross/Blue Shield programs were completely taken over by for-profit corporations (Bond and Weissman, 1997). The shift to for-profit health insurance produced a system in which profit was based on *denying coverage to those who needed health care the most* (Light, 1992).

The enduring effect of this "risk-based" method of setting premium rates has been that only certain employers (such as very large corporations and those with mainly young, healthy workers) can obtain reasonably priced insurance coverage for employees. Other workers are likely to receive little or no employment-related health insurance because commercial insurers price premiums too high for employers to absorb. Furthermore, because the federal government subsidizes employer-arranged private insurance with a tax writeoff (Barer, 1995), large and profitable companies have further advantages over small companies and nonprofit organizations (like universities, churches, and social service agencies).

One of the most serious problems with the U.S. insurance system, as it has thus developed, is that most private insurance is employment related. Americans

Box 12.1

An Insurance Nightmare*

Barbara was 40 when her husband divorced her, changed jobs, and moved out of state, leaving her and her two daughters without health insurance. Although she had been trained as a cosmetologist, workers in that field are often not able to obtain affordable health insurance. With little previous clerical experience, she considered herself lucky to find a job as a clerk-typist at a small university. The job had low pay—only $820 per month when she began in 1989, but at least it had a good benefits package—or so Barbara thought.

As the university struggled with soaring premium costs for employee health care, it made employees pay a greater and greater share. The university announced that it would pay only a fixed amount per employee annually for all insurance premiums; the employees who wanted to be covered under the plan would have to pay the balance. In the first year of this so-called flexible benefits plan, the university paid a total of $110 per month toward Barbara's insurance coverage (life, disability, medical, and dental), but the premiums for family medical insurance alone cost $220 each month. The next year, the university's health insurer significantly increased the premiums (to $320 per month) because two employees had incurred significant medical expenses the preceding year. Although health costs had increased nationally by over 10 percent, the university increased its "contribution" by 4 percent. The cost to Barbara amounted to nearly 30 percent of her after-tax income!

For a look at the larger picture, statistics show the following:

- At least 5 million women between 40 and 65 have no insurance as a result of divorce, death, or retirement of their spouse (Bodenheimer, 1990).
- Health insurance companies "redline" (that is, do not offer coverage to) workers in entire industries, such as barber and beauty shops, convenience stores, hotels, restaurants, and construction (Light, 1992).
- Many insurers also engage in "policy churning," a practice that deliberately creates a regular turnover each year. By offering employers attractively low first-year prices, they sign on new group accounts but pay out very little because they build in a 12-month waiting period for most expensive health needs. The next year, they increase the premiums dramatically for all but the lowest-risk groups, knowing that those companies will change to cheaper insurance elsewhere. Small companies are particularly vulnerable because risk cannot be spread over many employees. (Light, 1992)

*This story is a hypothetical composite of three persons' actual problems; features have been changed to protect their anonymity.

---

have relied since the 1920s on a largely private welfare system—available particularly to corporate employees—to provide health care benefits, old age pensions, job security, and vacations. The public welfare system, which encompasses Social Security, Medicare, and Medicaid, was loosely constructed to fill gaps in the private, employment-based system and to regulate benefits (for instance, by controls on corporate pension plans). Beginning in the 1970s and accelerating in the 1980s and 1990s, dramatic changes in the social contract have resulted in job insecurity (through "downsizing," "outsourcing," involuntary retirements, and increased use of part-time and temporary employees), producing haphazard and uncertain social welfare (Morone, 1995; see also Rubin, 1996).

A growing problem is the lack of regulation of the insurance and managed care industries. Like the savings and loan industry in the 1980s, some health insurance providers in the 1990s have been severely undercapitalized. When they become insolvent, persons who thought they were insured are left unprotected. Other health insurers are downright fraudulent (Tillman, 1998). State and federal regulatory legislation and oversight of the industry has not adequately protected consumers (Akula, 1997). For-profit health insurance companies and their managed care subsidiaries make money primarily in two ways: by paying out less in benefits than they receive in premiums, and by investing premium funds before disbursing them as benefits. Thus, for-profit insurance programs involve strong incentives[1] for insurers to *deny* coverage of claims and to *delay* paying claims (Freudenheim, 1997b).

Furthermore, insurance companies' portfolios frequently include investments in other for-profit health care ventures, such as hospitals, nursing homes, home health care agencies, and medical supply companies. Control over such large sums for investment is a significant source of economic and political power for major insurance corporations (Salmon, 1995). Many HMOs are subsidiaries of insurance companies. The scale of their financial interests and power is indicated by the fact that insurance lobbyists to state legislatures outnumber lobbyists representing other interests (Bodenheimer, 1990). As health care reform became an issue in the 1992 national elections, the industry spent $18.6 million in congressional campaign contributions (Podhorzer, 1995; see also Center for Public Integrity, 1995). Although health care reform was a relatively minor issue in 1999–2000 (also a presidential election campaign), according to Federal Election Commission figures, health industry Political Action Committees (PACs) contributed nearly $22 million to candidates for national offices (Center for Responsive Politics, 2002). In 1999, when Congress was considering legislation to regulate managed care and the health insurance industry, the Health Insurance Association of America (HIAA) spent $4.8 million and the American Association of Health Plans (AAHP) spent $2.5 million to lobby against the reform measures, especially the "Patients' Bill of Rights" (Center for Responsive Politics, 2001). Clearly, for-profit health insurance has become a big business, exceeding in power (and often taking over) the hospitals that originated the idea of health insurance.

---

[1]As HMO and for-profit insurers' stock values and profit margins soared, the company executives received cash and stock awards greater than those in *any* industry, making them among the best-paid CEOs in the country. In 1996, the 25 highest paid executives of large HMOs received more than $6.2 million, on average, not including unexercised stock options (that is, valuable opportunities for future additional earnings) averaging $13.5 million each. The highest paid HMO executive that year was the Oxford Health Plan's CEO, who received $29.1 million in compensation and held an additional $82.8 million in unexercised stock options (Families USA, 1998).

Box 12.2

The Insurance Nightmare Continues

Barbara began to look for a better job, but she was trapped by her insurance needs. Because her younger daughter had a history of asthma, no insurer would offer affordable individual coverage for the family. Barbara needed a job with group insurance, but many employers offered no health insurance whatsoever; others had inadequate group policies. So Barbara kept her job at the university and began to work a second job (with no benefits) at night.

Meanwhile, the insurer again steeply increased the premiums, so the university changed insurers. Barbara was relieved that her new premiums were only $235 per month. Her relief was short lived, however, because eight months later the insurance company declared bankruptcy, leaving employees struggling with mountains of claims paperwork and negotiations with unpaid providers. Eventually the state covered the employees' insured health expenses for the remainder of their contract year.

The larger picture shows the following:

- Some 6 percent of Americans have been denied coverage because of conditions such as diabetes, asthma, birth defects, or other problems indicating the potential for needing expensive care (Himmelstein et al., 1992).
- With very little federal regulation and uneven regulation by the states, insurers can become precipitously undercapitalized. When health insurance companies and prepaid health care programs declare bankruptcy, the persons they were supposed to cover lose not only the health care for which they have prepaid but also their protection for coverage of preexisting conditions and other excludable health problems (Weiss, 1997).

Private Insurance and "Perverse Incentives"   Each of the different forms of private health insurance instituted in the United States has embedded "perverse incentives" that prevent the health care system from meeting the needs of the American people. What they all have in common is the *insurmountable contradiction between maximizing profit for the insurance companies and optimizing the quality, affordability, and accessibility of needed health care for all Americans.* Like the perverse incentives described in Chapter 11 that reward health care providers at the expense of their patients' care, these perverse incentives are built into the very structure of private health insurance.

The earliest form of for-profit private health insurance was the **indemnity plan.** Unlike Blue Shield's original *service* coverage, most *indemnity plans* today specify limits to the costs borne by the insurer by imposing deductibles, limits on per-service payments, and annual and/or lifetime ceilings on payments for various types of service (Feigenbaum, 1987). Indemnity plans involve no incentive for the insurer to keep costs down because the excess is borne by the insured. Indemnity plans pay health care providers on a fee-for-service basis, according to the "going rates" in the area. Because individual health care recipients often have little choice or leverage over hospitals and other providers, many persons covered by limited indemnity plans find themselves underinsured.

Indemnity plans have accounted for a decreasing proportion of the group insurance market since the mid-1980s, as employers and insurers shifted to some form of managed care for cost savings. Whereas in 1988, 71 percent of employer-arranged insurance was indemnity insurance, by 2000, less than 10 percent was that type (Jensen et al., 1997; Harris, 2001). The most serious perverse incentive (which was retained by many managed care companies) is that this form of insurance makes its profits mainly by *denying care* to those who need it.[2] Another serious perverse incentive of indemnity plans is that they have little or no brake on costs. Doctors and hospitals have incentives to do more tests and procedures than necessary, because they can bill more for each additional service. A further perverse incentive, built into indemnity plans, is for the insurer to deny or delay paying claims in order to use the accumulated premiums for investment longer. This type of plan has no positive incentives for the insurer, providers, or patients to "invest" in preventive measures.

Managed care forms of insurance control what they spend on health care by intensely screening prospective utilization of insured medical care. They also manage expenditures by limiting coverage to care provided by providers who have accepted their discounted payment rates or are directly operated or employed by the managed care corporation. Thus, managed care severely limits, either directly or indirectly, patients' choice of physician and hospital. By 1990, various forms of managed care accounted for 25.3 percent of group health insurance premiums, compared to less than 1 percent in 1984 (Hoy et al., 1991). By 2000, more than 90 percent of workers were in managed care plans (Harris, 2001).

Managed care organizations (MCOs) try to control costs by using physicians as gatekeepers to reduce use of expensive specialists and hospitalization. Some further cut costs by paying contracted physicians on the basis of capitation rather than fee for service. As explained in Chapter 11, **capitation** means physicians are paid a preset amount per patient per month, regardless of how much medical service those patients actually need. This method of payment forces health care *providers* to assume much of the risk that insurance is supposed to assume. If the patient pool is large and not very sick, physicians could earn as much as under fee-for-service plans and would (presumably) save on some costs of billing.

---

[2] A looming problem is the possible use of genetic testing for denying insurance coverage to persons who do not actually have a medical condition but carry the genes that greatly increase the likelihood of developing a disease. As the Human Genome Project identifies specific genes that cause propensity to specific diseases, insurers will try to use genetic testing to deny coverage or to limit the coverage of each individual so that they do not have to pay claims for precisely the diseases for which that individual is most likely to need health care. Such uses of genetic testing are not only *not* medically beneficial for the persons tested, but are also morally reprehensible as a way to discriminate against the sick (see Lock, 2000a).

Two serious problems with capitation are now evident. It creates perverse incentives for doctors to provide *too little* service because they earn the same regardless of whether they do little or much for each patient. Similarly, it encourages doctors to refuse to accept patients, such as those with diabetes, whose need for medical services is predictably high (Gray, 1997; Poplin, 1996).

Since the 1970s the federal government has encouraged managed care, hoping it would contain health care costs better than other forms of insurance, but the anticipated efficiency gains and cost containment have not resulted. Indeed, several studies have shown that most MCOs are not more cost efficient than other insurance plans, yet cost more in employee contributions, contributed to overall inflation of premium costs for all types of private insurance, and were sometimes engaged in outright fraudulent practices (Morone, 1990; see also Gold, 1999; Weiss, 1997).

By 1990 most MCOs were owned by commercial insurers (Bodenheimer, 1990). Patient dissatisfaction was due largely to the limitations imposed to increase profitability. For example, some MCOs imposed "gag" rules on physicians, forbidding them from telling patients about treatment alternatives that might be more expensive for the insurer (*New York Times,* 1996b). Despite some relaxation of these constraints, more than half of respondents in surveys criticize HMOs (Health Maintenance Organizations) and other MCOs for such constraints on service as decreased time that doctors spend with patients and preventing access to specialists. The approval rating of managed care companies dropped from 51 percent (saying the industry is doing a good job of serving customers) in 1997, to 29 percent in 2000 (cited in Martinez, 2001).

Many HMOs and other prepaid plans create a conflict of interest for doctors whom they employ or contract because they base their remuneration on expectations of low rates of referral to specialists and hospital utilization. With these incentives, doctors can maximize their earnings by *decreasing* medical services for their patients. This conflict of interest, which is the reverse of the conflict of interest under fee-for-service payments, can have adverse effects on the quality of care (Rodwin, 1993; see also Mechanic, 2000).

Like indemnity plans, *for-profit managed care* plans are severely compromised in their ability to provide the health care Americans need, due to the perverse incentives built into the very structure of their programs. The most serious perverse incentive is to cut costs by denying needed care. A related structural contradiction is the drive for corporate profits at the expense of health care providers and patients. For-profit health insurers, whose objectives are high profits and higher stock price increases have every incentive to skimp on service, quality, access, and coverage.

Since the early 2000s, several insurance companies have marketed a new type of health coverage that costs employers less in premiums, because it shifts most health care expenses to the insured employees. Euphemistically called a **"health care savings account,"** this type of pseudo-insurance allows each family a fixed amount (for example, $2,000 per year) to spend on all medical expenses, including drugs. The family pays the basic annual premium (for example, $1,200). After the annual allowance is spent, the family must pay *every* cost over that amount up to a preset cap (for example, $5,000). Above that cap, the employer's "major medical" part of the coverage would pay a large proportion of the costs (for example, 90 percent). If the family does not spend the entire allowance, it may carry over the "savings" to cover future years' expenses. This kind of coverage is not really insurance, because it does not pool the risk of expenses over the entire group. Rather, it makes the families who need health care the most even less likely to be able to afford the care they need. It is particularly likely to discourage all but the highest income workers from getting preventive care for themselves and their families (Freudenheim, 2001b). If this type of employment-related "coverage" becomes widespread, it will lead to many families experiencing financially devastating expenses or risking deterioration of their health because they can no longer afford to buy the care they need.

Cost Shifting and the Underinsured One of the biggest problems for persons counting on private health insurance is that, as health costs have escalated rapidly, insurance companies and employers have passed on a significant part of that burden to the insured. Some companies have dramatically raised the deductibles, copayments, and out-of-pocket expenses to be paid by the employee. Whereas in 1987, 43 percent of workers with single coverage and 36 percent of those with family coverage had employers who paid their full premiums, by 1994, these proportions had dropped to 34 and 26 percent, respectively (Holahan et al., 1995). Between 1980 and 1991, the premium cost for an employee and family increased by 241 percent; employee out-of-pocket expenses increased by over 500 percent (Rasell, 1993). These cost-shifting measures hurt the working poor disproportionately, causing many workers to forgo insurance because they simply could not afford the employee share of the premiums (Seccombe, 1996).

This cost shifting has put employer-offered insurance out of reach of many persons previously insured through their jobs. Nearly one-fifth of working Americans are not offered health insurance by their employer (Reinhardt, 1999). More than three-quarters of the drop in persons covered by employment-related private insurance is due to greatly increased premium contributions required of employees (Sheils et al., 1999). Many dependent children and their mothers lost health insurance coverage due to cost shifting by employers. In 1999, less than 60 percent of all U.S. children under age six were covered by parents' employment-related private health insurance (USDHHS, 2001a). One of every six mothers of children under age 19 (about 6 million women) lacked health insurance of any kind; nearly all of them were in working families with no access to affordable insurance coverage for dependent members of the family (Center on Budget and Policy Priorities, 2001).

Many retirees were also severely hurt. In 2000, only 31 percent of companies with 500 or more employees provided any health insurance coverage to retirees under 65, compared to 46 percent in 1993 (Cusac, 2001). Thus, cost shifting

Box 12.3

An Unending Nightmare?

Subsequently, Barbara's employer decided to self-insure. The university collected employees' premiums, added its own contributions, chose a Preferred Provider Organization (PPO) to negotiate discounts, and contracted an outside agency to screen claims. Thus, the employer saved some of the expense of commercial insurance, especially marketing costs and profit margin, and simultaneously controlled the assets, while briefly collecting earnings on the insurance pool. The self-insured plan retained the terms (including deductibles and copayments) of the prior commercial plan, but added "managed care" PPO regulations. If Barbara's family used doctors and hospitals not on the preferred provider list, she had to pay considerably larger deductibles and copayments each visit. So Barbara had to find completely new doctors, selected from the ones covered by the PPO.

Although the self-insured plan is more stable, Barbara's worries are not over. Her daughter had to give up dreams of attending an out-of-state college, because the health plan did not cover doctors or hospitals there. Barbara's younger daughter suffered a serious anxiety disorder in her senior year of high school, but the university had dropped all coverage for mental health; Barbara paid close to $4,500 out of pocket for therapy and medications for that problem alone. And soaring health care costs in the late 1990s and early 2000s resulted in double-digit increases in health insurance premiums paid by the university employees. Despite a promotion and 13 years of salary increments, Barbara's real take-home pay has actually decreased—due largely to the uncontrolled problem of health insurance.

---

has produced considerable increases in the numbers of middle-class persons who become underinsured or uninsured.

Underinsured persons are those who have some health insurance coverage, but it is inadequate to protect them from financial disaster or from having to forgo needed care because their insurance coverage is inadequate to pay for it. Underinsured families' disastrous medical bills accounted for about 40 percent of personal bankruptcy filings in 1999 (Associated Press, 2000).[3] Exact figures are not available on the number of persons who are underinsured due to seriously limited health plans; often employees do not discover how poorly they are insured until they are denied benefits during an actual health crisis. Although hospital care costs may be largely covered by insurance, consumers typically must pay most or all of outpatient medical services, prescription drugs, dental care, and long-term nursing

---

[3]Because that study pertained to a year in which overall employment and pay levels were unusually high, a similar study in 2002, after recession layoffs and dramatic health care cost increases in 2001 and 2002, would likely find far more U.S. families dangerously underinsured. In 2001, many employees faced huge increases in their costs for health insurance premiums; some families' premiums more than doubled (see Freudenheim, 2001a).

care, as well as a large proportion of physicians' services (Knickman and Thorpe, 1995).

Some policy analysts argue that patients should have to pay, in the form of copayments, a substantial share of the costs of each use of health care services in order to make them more selective and cost conscious. The Rand Health Experiment (1974–1982) found, however, that although cost sharing did reduce the demands for health services, it did not result in good decisions about those demands. In fact, financial barriers reduced the use of health services *even when those services were needed and appropriate* (Lohr et al., 1986). Greater cost sharing likewise does not lead to more competitive pricing and consumer "shopping" (Marquis, 1984). One survey found that 26 percent of persons insured by Medicaid, 8 percent of persons insured by Medicare, and 8 percent of persons covered by employment-related insurance could not afford to fill some of their prescriptions in the last year (Pear, 2002a). Consumers have little or no leverage over the costs of lab tests, doctors' services, or pharmaceuticals. Their only choice may be *not* to see physicians when they are sick, *not* to buy medicines doctors have prescribed, and *not* to get the lab tests they need. In the United States, lack of adequate insurance essentially means severely limited access to health care.

The U.S. system of private insurance is structurally inefficient and expensive to administer because it is based on the exclusion and discrimination of *denying coverage* to precisely those who need the most health care. In order to maximize profits, insurance companies compete to *avoid* insuring higher-risk persons—those likely to actually need health care (Light, 1992). They issue complex policies with elaborate exclusions (for instance refusing to pay for care for any conditions that patients had before becoming covered by that insurance policy) and different terms of coverage for different groups of employees. To screen all claims by insured patients to enforce these exclusions and other restrictive terms, commercial insurance companies spend 33.5 cents for each dollar of benefits provided. These administrative costs are many times higher than those of Canadian health insurance, where all persons have the same coverage and terms (Evans and Roos, 1999).

This estimate of insurers' administrative inefficiency does not include the cost of paperwork on the part of the providers and claimants, which further adds to the costliness of the U.S. health care system. The administrative, overhead, and marketing costs of commercial insurance companies have increased faster than the costs of providing health care. Administrative/bureaucratic costs consume about one-fourth of U.S. total health care spending. Some analysts have suggested that a public program of universal coverage would save enough on these costs that efficiency savings alone would pay for insurance for tens of millions of Americans who are presently without adequate coverage (Hellander et al., 1994).

Although employer-based insurance covers about two-thirds of the U.S. population, it accounts for less than one-third of total national health spending. Essentially, public insurance programs are supporting the profitability of the private insurance programs by covering the (higher costing) health care of those most likely to be denied affordable care by private insurance—the elderly, poor, and disabled (Reinhardt, 1999; Shi, 2001).

Public Programs

The number, type, and quality of health care programs financed from tax revenues by various levels of government demonstrate the complexity and inadequacy of the U.S. health care system. The federal government, for example, directly provides care for large numbers of persons in the military and their dependents, veterans' hospitals, and federal prisons. The largest federal health insurance programs subsidize some care for the poor (Medicaid) and elderly (Medicare). The federal government also finances much health-related research, and has at times supported medical education and other training programs. State, county, and municipal governments also fund health care, by maintaining, for example, public hospitals, nursing homes, community health services, and public health programs. State governments are also cosponsors of Medicaid, Children's Health Insurance Program (CHIP), and other health services for the poor. They pay directly for health care in state institutions, such as prisons and mental hospitals. The quality of and access to medical care provided by these many programs vary widely across the nation, but no national organization or central planning coordinates or regulates even the public efforts, much less connects public and private programs.

Medicare Medicare was enacted in 1965 to finance acute medical care mainly for elderly Americans. It quickly accomplished one of its objectives—to protect elderly persons unable to obtain private insurance from impoverishment due to health costs; the proportion of persons over 65 living in poverty dropped dramatically in the first few years of Medicare (Tynes, 1996). Medicare coverage was expanded in 1972 to include people of all ages with chronic kidney disease or long-term disabilities. By 1999, Medicare covered 39 million Americans. The program has two parts: Part A is hospital insurance, funded by a portion of the Social Security payroll tax. Part B is supplementary medical insurance (SMI) for physicians' services, outpatient care, laboratory fees, and home health care. Because Part B is funded through general federal revenues, its growth as a budget item pits health care financing against other expenses, such as defense. From the outset Medicare was aimed at the acute medical care of the elderly. Chronic illness and long-term care were not part of the plan, even though they affect the health status and economic well-being of the elderly as much or even more than acute illness. Thus, as Box 12.4 illustrates, Medicare does not cover many needed health services and products.

Before Medicare, only about one-third of the elderly had health insurance; private insurance rates were outside the means of most older Americans, and employers benefitted when Medicare took over the costs of insuring retirees over 65. The enactment of Medicare immediately increased the average health care utilization

Box 12.4

Regressive Impact of Health Care Expenditures
on Family Budgets: The Elderly

Dorothy and Frank are in their mid-70s and rely on their Social Security income of $1,465 per month (just above the poverty level) for all their living expenses. They have Medicare coverage, but noncovered health care expenditures consume more than 50 percent of their entire family budget, leaving them scrimping to pay for food, utilities, and other basic needs. Their monthly costs include a modest Medigap insurance policy, $255; Medicare premiums, $100; prescriptions and other medicine, $350; and deductibles and other charges not covered by Medicare or Medigap, $50. They have become too poor to maintain long-term care insurance, so they dropped it after paying $8,000.

Clarissa is an 85-year-old widow, living alone on Social Security payments of $650 per month. Her health care expenses not covered by Medicare consume 50 percent of her fixed income. They include a Medicare premium, $50; prescription and other medicine, $200; Medigap insurance, $120 (for a minimal policy); and other charges not covered, $20. Her state does not have generous Medicaid benefits for low-income elderly, so she fears she will be sent to a third-rate nursing home when she can no longer manage to cope in her own apartment.

The figures show the following:

- An increasing proportion (in 1992, nearly one-third) of aged persons rely on Social Security for 80 percent or more of their income (Davis and Burner, 1995). In 1997, Social Security benefits kept about one-third of U.S. elderly persons from slipping below the poverty line (*New York Times*, 1999).

- Elderly families in all income brackets pay a *higher* proportion than nonelderly families of their total income on health care premiums (8.3 percent, compared to 4.9 percent) and on out-of-pocket expenditures (8.3 percent, compared to 3.2 percent)(Rasell et al., 1994). Medicare beneficiaries in poor health whose incomes are below the poverty line are estimated to spend, on average, about 44 percent of their meager incomes on out-of-pocket health care expenditures (Maxwell et al., 2000).

- Elderly Americans who are at risk for higher out-of-pocket costs have a greater chance of dying within five years than those at risk for lower out-of-pocket costs; financial barriers (such as co-payments and high premiums) to needed health care lead to poor health outcomes and death (Doescher et al., 2000).

- Elderly women are more likely than elderly men to have long-term, chronic disabling diseases. Assistance with tasks of daily living is required by 30.2 percent of women aged 75 and older, compared to 17.2 percent of men that age. Women constitute three-quarters of all nursing home residents; half the costs of U.S. long-term care are paid by Medicaid (see Barringer, 1992; Butler, 1996).

- The median annual income of older low-income women in poor health is only $10,029, compared with the $14,494 median individual income of all elderly Medicare beneficiaries. Low-income single women over age 85 who are in poor health spend, on average, about 52 percent of their incomes on out-of-pocket health care expenses (Maxwell et al., 2000).

rate among the elderly by more than 30 percent (Sorkin, 1986). Whereas in 1964, 21 percent of elderly had not seen a doctor in the last two or more years, by 1993 that rate was down to 7.4 percent (Davis and Burner, 1995). Although it dramatically increased access to health care, Medicare failed to protect beneficiaries from destitution in the face of health care costs, because its cost-sharing provisions did not limit liabilities in the event of catastrophic illness and did not cover most long-term (for example, nursing home) care or prescriptions (which increased in cost at a rate many times the rate of inflation most years since 1970).

The financing of Medicare has been problematic from the outset (see Marmor, 1999). Medicare legislation created less of a public health care program and more of an *infusion of public money into private channels* (Fein, 1986: 69–92). Initially, there were few cost-control regulations in the program. Primarily due to increasing charges by various providers, the expenditures were far more than anticipated. A limited cost-control measure was introduced in 1972, but it was largely ineffective. Between 1979 and 1982, Medicare expenditures grew much faster than general inflation (Sorkin, 1986). Part of the costliness was due to high-tech medicine and labor-intensive medical care. And part was due simply to overexpansion, greed, and in some cases outright fraud on the part of providers, hospitals, and insurance administrators (Sparrow, 1996).

At first, the AMA fought against the creation of Medicare, but the medical profession has been among its prime beneficiaries and now generally supports the program and its expansion. To secure the cooperation of physicians, the initial Medicare legislation allowed reimbursement of doctors' "usual and customary fees," so long as those fees were "reasonable." Such vague language, especially in the context of a seldom competitive fee-setting process, led to rapid inflation. Fees increased disproportionate to other rates of inflation; the number of elderly treated increased, and the number of medical services ordered by doctors for their Medicare patients rose markedly. After Medicare began, doctors who had previously reduced their fees for the needy elderly could receive their "customary" full payments. Physicians who had previously been frustrated by their inability to treat their pensioner-patients with the best available methods could, under Medicare, prescribe therapies without prejudice of ability to pay. Medicare funding provided stability for both physician and hospital income, much as private health insurance had done three decades earlier (Fein, 1986: 80–92).

Administration of Medicare regulations and reimbursement paperwork, however, add to the cost of the program. The waste of resources on administrative costs in the United States is particularly highlighted by contrasts with Canada and Great Britain, where insurance company intermediaries are eliminated and providers deal directly with the government rather than struggle with billing and collections (Evans and Roos, 1999; see also Fein, 1986: 157).

A major ongoing problem has been that some providers do not accept Medicare rates of reimbursement, so patients must bear the cost of the difference either out of pocket or by buying a relatively expensive ("Medigap") insurance policy (Davis and Burner, 1995). The government itself shifted significant costs to the elderly by increasing the monthly premiums, beginning in 2001 (Carter, 2001). Because most Medicare reimbursement is still based on fee-for-service rates, there is no incentive for physicians to reduce the number of services or recommend less costly services. New Medicare regulations are regularly being proposed to try to contain costs, to ascertain greater physician cooperation, and to get better care for the monies spent. The process is a political one, however, in which providers and insurers have disproportionately powerful voices (see Marmor, 1999).

In fee-for-service Medicare, higher per capita expenditures do not produce better quality care or better health results. For example, Texas and Louisiana are among 17 states with the highest per capita Medicare spending, but they rank 45th and 49th, respectively, in quality of care. Often, Medicare is charged more, simply because doctors and hospitals in high-cost areas are performing more intensive and expensive procedures in the last months of life; a smaller proportion of Medicare spending in those states is used for preventive care or quality assurance (see *Harper's Magazine,* 2001).

In the 1990s the government encouraged (again, in concert with corporate interest groups) special Medicare HMOs, with the hopes that managed care corporations could contain costs. Policy analysts remind us, however, that ". . . HMOs provide 'managed money, not managed care' and at a higher cost than does Medicare," because they take a much higher proportion of monies paid by Medicare for administrative costs than does fee-for-service Medicare (Estes and Linkins, 2000: 167). However, studies show that elderly (Medicare) and low-income (Medicaid) patients have generally done worse in health status in HMOs than in fee-for-service programs (Ware et al., 1996). Medicare HMOs often engage in "cream-skimming"—recruiting only younger, healthier senior citizens, whose care under traditional Medicare payment would have cost the government only 89.3 percent of the average.

In 2001, Medicare HMOs forced enrollees to bear increased out-of-pocket expenses, dropping prescription medicine coverage, increasing co-pays for services, and reducing availability of services. The average Medicare HMO enrollee paid nearly 50 percent more out of pocket in 2001 than three years earlier (Freudenheim, 2002b). Many Medicare HMOs had attracted subscribers away from the regular Medicare plan, offering free prescription drugs that are not covered at all by Medicare itself. Then, as pharmaceutical prices soared and HMOs pressed Congress to pay a higher premium for Medicare enrollees, the HMOs began squeezing the elderly by reducing or abolishing drug coverage. Several HMOs stopped Medicare coverage altogether; between 1998 and 2002, about 2.2 million Medicare beneficiaries were dropped by HMOs and forced to return to regular Medicare (Freudenheim, 2002a).

The proposal of "medical savings accounts" is another "cream-skimming" measure. These would allow participants to pocket a portion of the unused Medicare-paid premiums if their medical expenditures are very low, but they must accept the risk of much higher deductibles and co-payments when they do need medical care, thus encouraging postponing needed care. Only very healthy and financially comfortable elderly persons could afford to take this risk, so others would remain in traditional Medicare. And as they aged and developed serious illnesses, those with "medical savings accounts" would drop such a risk-laden program. Because the government still has to cover the needs of the older, sicker elderly not in HMOs and other cream-skimming plans, its share of costs for the elderly is actually *increased* (Lynch and Minkler, 1997).

Although Medicare has been an important contribution to the health of covered citizens, it is less and less sufficient for their needs, and less able than ever to cover the increasing proportion of the eligible population. Most of the changes to Medicare that have been approved or proposed in the last decade have had the effect (intended or not) of pouring more tax money into corporate coffers, while leaving many more older citizens *seriously underinsured* for their health care needs. Proposals to raise the age of eligibility for Medicare would leave hundreds of thousands completely uninsured. Inadequacies of Medicare have made many elderly beneficiaries so poor that they have been thrust into reliance on Medicaid—an even less adequate and underfunded public program.

Medicaid Medicaid was created at the same time as Medicare, but was organized very differently. Because Medicaid is funded through general revenues rather than a trust fund and is perceived as charity rather than deserved aid, the program is particularly vulnerable to cutbacks at every funding level. Each state operates its own program, with federal contributions varying according to the scope of the state's program, relative level of income, and certain features of providers and recipients. The federal program includes health care for persons covered by federal Supplemental Security Income (SSI), which assists blind, disabled, and elderly persons; members of families eligible for Aid to Families with Dependent Children (AFDC); and pregnant women in certain income brackets. Many states have defined the criteria for Medicaid so stringently that they exclude more than half the people who could be covered under federal guidelines (Fein, 1986: 108–112).

Due to deficiencies in Medicare coverage, Medicaid has become a significant source of funding for health care for the elderly. Some states use Medicaid to pay Medicare premiums, deductibles, and co-payments that poor elderly persons cannot afford. Medicaid also covers services, such as long-term care, not provided by Medicare. More than 65 percent of U.S. nursing home residents are supported by Medicaid (Levit et al., 1996), and public spending (mainly Medicaid) paid for more than 60 percent of all nursing home expenditures (USHCFA, 2002). The House Select Committee on Aging reported that 90 percent of single elderly patients "spend down" to the poverty level after paying one year of nursing home charges; half of the couples with one spouse in a nursing home reach poverty level within six months, and unless Medicaid helps pay for the nursing home, the well spouse could be left destitute, often with many years of life ahead. Thus, Medicaid has become the de facto long-term care supplement to Medicare.

Children constitute 47 percent of Medicaid recipients, but consume only about 16 percent of Medicaid funds; elderly, blind, and disabled persons account for 26 percent of Medicaid recipients and 71 percent of expenditures (Eberhardt et al., 2001: 12). Thus, Medicaid has *not* functioned primarily as a source of health care for lower-class persons, especially children, among whom poverty rates are continuing to climb.

The administrative costs of Medicaid are higher than for Medicare. Many states parcel out portions of the program to various local agencies, including for-profit administration; the several layers multiply administrative costs. Furthermore, unlike Medicare, Medicaid eligibility must be determined by complex formulas and continually reviewed because agencies have a state-directed imperative to trim rolls and discourage coverage.[4] A substantial portion of the funds that Americans believe are used for health care is actually going to the mere administration of public insurance programs (Fein, 1986).

Ironically, the greatest documented abuses of Medicaid funding have been on the part of unscrupulous providers, often abetted by the politically motivated purchasing policies of state and local agencies. For example, in 1971 the California legislature arranged to have Medicaid recipients assigned to HMOs contracting with the state. The legislature had reasoned that these large health care contractors would be more efficient and cost effective than previous arrangements. Compared to other HMOs, which spent about 10 percent of the premium dollar on administration and profits, welfare HMOs used 52 percent of state payments for administration and profits (Lewis, 1976). Subsequent investigations also showed that the Medicaid HMOs had denied access to the poor (for example, by contracting with proprietary hospitals 30 to 50 miles from the client population) (Gabel and Redisch, 1979). Later research found that persons enrolled in Medicaid-paid HMOs suffered considerably worse health outcomes than those whose Medicaid paid for conventional fee-for-service visits (Ware et al., 1996).

The structure of Medicaid has thus encouraged a two-tiered system of medical care, with the service to those covered by Medicaid being distinctly inferior. Medicaid has, however, increased the access of the poor to some medical assistance; after the implementation of the program, poor families used significantly more physician services and hospitalization. Likewise, in the 1980s when government cutbacks reduced Medicaid rolls, the poor with no insurance had significantly less access and utilization than those with Medicaid (Davis, 1991). In the 1990s, as the proportion of children covered by employer-based private insurance dropped dramatically, Medicaid coverage was again expanded.

Medicaid has further failed to meet the health needs of the poor due to changes in other policies, particularly the so-called welfare reform of the late

---

[4]For example, New York State rapidly enacted legislation for disaster-relief Medicaid after the September 11, 2001, attack on the World Trade Center. This new program reduced the application form from eight pages to one; in the six weeks following the attack, there were 75,000 applicants, a dramatic upsurge from the typical 8,000 applications each month (Finkelstein, 2001).

1990s. Many states had granted Medicaid eligibility to families on welfare, so when low-income families went off welfare rolls, many became uninsured even though they were no better able to obtain private insurance than before. Children accounted for two-thirds of those who lost Medicaid coverage due to welfare reform, but some of them were subsequently covered by a new federally financed program, Children's Health Insurance Program (CHIP), discussed further in this chapter. Few of the parents who were dropped from Medicaid when they were forced off welfare were subsequently covered by insurance from employment or any other source. Although states could receive federal funds for at least half of the cost of using Medicaid to cover parents in low-income families, very few states have been willing to commit their share of funds to match the federal monies (Families USA, 1999, 2000).

Changes in the labor market and an economic recession adversely affected Medicaid coverage in 2001 and 2002. In the preceding two years, there was a high employment rate and the tight labor market had prevented employers from further reducing insurance coverage for their privately insured workers. Thus, for two years at the turn of the century there was a slight decrease in the proportion of Americans who were uninsured, from 14.3 to 14.0 percent. Despite that decrease, *nearly 30 percent of the poor lacked health insurance from any source* (Pear, 2001). Unfortunately, as medical costs continued to escalate dramatically, the recession that began in 2001 resulted in widespread layoffs (thus making workers and their families uninsured) and, simultaneously, in greatly reduced tax revenues for Medicaid (Pear and Toner, 2002).

The ongoing failure of private insurance and Medicaid to meet the health care needs of America's low-income families is reflected in the high rates of people who are uninsured or underinsured. Ever since Medicare alleviated the needs of many low-income elderly persons in the 1960s, the U.S. health care system's greatest failure is lack of coverage for all children. At the end of the twentieth century, the federal government authorized the Children's Health Insurance Program to provide health insurance for more children.

Children's Health Insurance Program (CHIP) Many children are uninsured because their families are working poor. Holding full-time, low-wage jobs, these workers cannot lift their families out of poverty, but they earn too much to qualify for Medicaid according to many states' stringent eligibility requirements. States receive, under the CHIP program, a higher proportion of their costs from the federal government than under Medicaid. To utilize this additional money, the states must enroll children whose families earn up to 200 percent of the poverty line. Unlike Medicaid, however, CHIP is not an entitlement program, so meeting the eligibility criteria is not enough to guarantee that a child will become covered. Like Medicaid, CHIP is organized differently in each state, so some states have not funded the program adequately to reach many uninsured families. Some states used CHIP to expand Medicaid coverage, while others created separate programs with means-adjusted co-pays and other contributions that families must pay. In

12 states, CHIP and Medicaid have been particularly ineffective in insuring poor children, because their programs make it very difficult for people to enroll (for example, requiring parents to fill out lengthy applications with documentation). Nevertheless, by 2000, 3.3 million children were receiving health insurance through CHIP-supported programs (USHCFA, 2001).

The Uninsured and Underinsured

In 1999, an estimated 40 million Americans had *no private or public coverage* for their medical expenses. Furthermore, more than 60 million—more than one-quarter of the entire U.S. population—were estimated to have gone without coverage for part of the year (USDHHS, 2001a; Bennefield, 1998). These figures are indicators of widespread failure of the patchwork public and private health insurance in the United States. Lack of health insurance and inadequate health insurance coverage are significant barriers to access to needed health services and medications. Combined with other serious deficiencies in U.S. health policy—such as inadequate provisions for all citizens' basic needs for food, shelter, sanitation, and other public health protection—this failure results in many preventable deaths and incapacitating diseases.

Health insurance alone would not bring the United States up to the health standard of other developed countries, as discussed in Chapter 11. The reasons for the failure of U.S. health insurance in meeting people's needs, however, do explain why the United States is paying so much more than other developed countries without achieving such favorable results. The failures of health insurance policies are closely linked with other policy failures, such as lack of minimum wage laws that require employers to pay a living wage; lack of public health and safety regulation and enforcement to protect food, water, and air for all; and lack of an adequate "safety net" for senior citizens, children, unemployed, and disabled citizens, who could not reasonably be expected to support themselves adequately in this economy. Because the policy failures of certain public programs vary by state, Box 12.5 provides an illustration of one populous state's complex policy failures.

Despite large, steady increases in government health spending for Medicaid and Medicare, the number of persons uninsured increased significantly throughout the 1980s and 1990s (Rowland et al., 1994). Between 1989 and 1997, the proportion of Americans covered by private (mainly employer-provided) health insurance dropped steadily from 74.6 percent to 70.0 percent. In the same period, Medicaid coverage grew from covering 8.6 percent to 10.8 percent, and the proportion of Americans who were uninsured grew from 13.6 percent to 16.1 percent (USDHHS, 2001a). Many of the persons covered in 1999 by employment-related health insurance subsequently lost their coverage when jobs were cut in the economic recession that began in early 2001 (Toner, 2001).

Who Are the Underinsured and Uninsured? Only those Americans in the top income brackets are likely to be able to obtain adequate health insurance

Box 12.5

Public Insurance and the Uninsured in Texas:
A Case Study

Texas is an example of a state with a very large proportion of the population that is uninsured, mainly because they are among the working poor. Texas has no state income tax and relies heavily upon regressive taxes for much of its state budget. Texas has also had very stringent eligibility requirements for public insurance programs, such that only the desperately poor could qualify. A Medicaid reform act, which would have liberalized these requirements for poor children, was vetoed by then-governor, George W. Bush. Because of its high poverty rate, Texas is required to provide a smaller-than-average proportion of Medicaid (40 percent) and CHIP (24 percent) expenditures; the federal government would cover the rest, but Texas does not accept enough Medicaid enrollees to receive the full amount of federal matching funds. Texas was very slow to implement CHIP (not until May 2000) and set discouraging barriers to prevent CHIP monies from being used for entitlement programs for the very poor. The following facts help us understand why so many Texans have no health insurance.

- Texas ranking among states on percentage of uninsured population in 1999: 2nd
- Texans without health insurance in 1999: 23 percent
- Texas Medicaid recipients in 1999 who were children: 62 percent
- Percentage of Texas Medicaid budget spent on children in 1999: 22 percent
- Annual income limit for eligibility for family of three in 2000: $2,406 (that is, 17 percent of federal poverty level for family of three in 2000)
- Texas ranking among states on percentage drop in children's enrollment in Medicaid and CHIP, 1996–1999 (that is, after welfare reform): 1st (14.2 percent drop)
- Percentage of Texas children in families at or below 200 percent of poverty line in 2000: 44.5 percent
- Texas ranking among states on percentage of poor children uninsured in 2000: 2nd
- Percentage of low-income mothers uninsured in 2000: 45 percent
- Percentage of the uninsured population employed in 1997: 70 percent
- Percentage of uninsured adults below 200 percent of poverty line in 1999: 51 percent
- Texas ranking among states on percentage of hungry families: 2nd
- Texas ranking among states on income inequality in the late 1990s, between the richest 20 percent and the middle 20 percent: 5th

Sources: Texas Health and Human Services Commission, 2001; also, Center for Public Policy Priorities, 1998; Center on Budget and Policy Priorities, 2000, 2001; Families USA, 1999, 2000; Selby, 2002; Texas HHSC, 1999; U.S. Bureau of the Census, 2000c; USHCFA, 2001; U.S. Bureau of Labor Statistics, 2001.

within their means. Many (indeed, most) Americans are **underinsured;** they have some health insurance but it is insufficient to protect them from inadequate care or financial disaster in case of serious or prolonged illness. Due to all of the adequacies of both public and private forms of health insurance, the main factor that the underinsured have in common is *need* for extensive health care. If they happen to be healthy and need little health care, then their insurance is adequate. It is precisely those who need health care the most—those with serious illnesses, those with chronic illnesses, those born with medical problems—who are likely to be inadequately protected by private or public insurance.

Underinsured persons covered by employment-related insurance are disproportionately those who are self-employed or work for small businesses, not-for-profit organizations like churches and schools, or other employers who cannot or will not pay premiums to provide adequate group insurance coverage. Many of those who are underinsured in such private plans subsequently become completely uninsured when they can no longer afford the costs shifted to them by employers (see Carrasquillo et al., 1999). Underinsured persons covered by Medicare are disproportionately those who cannot afford to buy expensive Medigap and long-term-care insurance policies to cover expenses, like home nursing care, not covered by Medicare. General characteristics of underinsured persons covered by Medicaid vary from state to state, but people who are poor enough to qualify for Medicaid can rarely afford basic subsistence (like food and shelter), so in the case of serious or chronic illness, *any expense not covered* by insurance would constitute a hardship.

The working poor, as well as many self-employed workers, are particularly likely to be **uninsured altogether.** *Employed persons and their dependents account for approximately 80 percent of the uninsured population* (National Academy of Sciences, 2001a). The uninsured Americans also include a large number of persons who are temporarily without health insurance. One study found that over a three-year period (1993–1996) close to 30 percent of all Americans were uninsured for some of that time (Bennefield, 1998). Interestingly, the largest increase in the number and proportion of uninsured was among the middle-income families. The fact that loss of employment-related insurance continued to increase steadily during the 1990s (a period of economic expansion nationally) shows that the United States should not count on employment-related insurance for its health care system (Carrasquillo et al., 1999).

Women, minorities, children, and young adults are particularly likely to be uninsured altogether. Women are extremely disadvantaged in access to health insurance. One study found that women's chances of being covered by employer-arranged insurance were lower than men's, even when factors such as hours worked, years tenure on the job, and company size were taken into account (Institute for Women's Policy Research, 1994). Only 9 percent of all poor women under 65 are insured by employer-provided insurance (Lyons et al., 1996). Mothers of dependent children are also particularly vulnerable unless they can obtain affordable coverage through their spouse's employment. As employers shifted costs to employees, many workers had to drop coverage for their nonworking spouses—typically women (USGAO, 1997). Divorce and widowhood also leave many women without a source of private health insurance (Meyer and Pavalko, 1996). Furthermore, many women who went off welfare into low-paying jobs lost their Medicaid coverage but were not offered employment-related coverage. In the 15 states with the most uninsured low-income adults, so-called welfare reform resulted in a 27 percent decline in the number of low-income parents enrolled in Medicaid (Families USA, 2000).

Particularly troubling is the high proportion of children and young adults who are without any form of health insurance. Despite expansion of Medicaid and the introduction of CHIP, the numbers of uninsured children remain stubbornly high. The proportion of U.S. children covered through employment-related insurance has been steadily dropping, and children's health care is particularly vulnerable to even short-term interruptions in insurance. Young adults are increasingly unlikely to have any form of health insurance, as they become ineligible for coverage as dependents and yet cannot get employment that includes insurance benefits.

Blacks and Hispanics are especially likely to be uninsured because they are disproportionately represented among the working poor, in jobs paying no insurance benefits, and in regions of the United States where labor is less commonly unionized and Medicaid insurance is least available (see Ginzberg, 1991). For example, the percentage of Mexican Americans under the age of 65 who are uninsured (38 percent) is more than three times that of white, non-Hispanics (12.1 percent) (Eberhardt et al., 2001). Furthermore, in the 1990s, when rates of uninsured persons were growing steadily, the rates of lack of insurance increased among Black and Hispanic Americans more steeply than among white, non-Hispanic Americans, largely because of their geographical and labor-market segregation in uninsured sectors of the economy (see Carrasquillo et al., 1999).

Some Americans believe that immigrants and noncitizens account for much of the uninsured population, but this is a mistaken idea. While recent immigrants do have high rates of uninsurance (46 percent), they and their children (many of whom are U.S. citizens) account for only about 6 percent of the total uninsured population (Holahan et al., 2001; Ku and Matani, 2001).

Consequences of Underinsurance and Uninsurance   Having such a large proportion of the people of the United States uninsured or underinsured has serious negative consequences for *the entire society*—not just for those who are inadequately protected for their health care needs. According to surveys, most Americans mistakenly believe that the uninsured will get health care when they really need it, but the reality is that lack of insurance results in very real barriers to much needed care. A comprehensive study by the Institute of Medicine found that the uninsured are more likely to be denied medically necessary treatments, regular care for chronic conditions, and care for problems that are symptomatic of serious illnesses (National Academy of Sciences, 2001a). Numerous studies have documented the higher morbidity and mortality rates of the uninsured, who are limited in or denied access to physician, hospitals, medicines, and other treatments (Callahan and David, 1995; Lyons et al., 1996; National Academy of Sciences, 2001a).

Without insurance, many Americans go without a regular source of care (for example, a family physician), such that they are likely to miss necessary preventive care (like immunizations) and receive fragmented care from doctors unfamiliar with their condition when they do get treatment. For example, while less than 10 percent of poor children who are covered by insurance lack a regular source of health care, nearly 40 percent of poor uninsured children and more than 20 percent of all nonpoor uninsured children have no regular source (USDHHS, 2001a). Lacking a physician as their usual source of care, sick children are less likely to be taken to a physician when they need care. Their care is more likely to be delayed and they end up in the emergency room, where their treatment costs more than if they had been able to see a doctor in the first place (National Academy of Sciences, 2001a).

Lack of health insurance prevents women from getting prenatal care, and their newborns are disproportionately likely to have serious health problems (see Long and Marquis, 1998). The uninsured are less likely to be able to get preventive health services, such as Pap smears, and they have higher rates of preventable hospitalization. Most seriously, the uninsured have higher (adjusted) mortality rates.

The underinsured are also likely to have to forgo needed care, due to their inability to pay. A survey in spring 2001 (before the steep economic downturn in the second half of the year), found that 21 percent of the insured and 54 percent of the uninsured went without needed care because of cost; fully 40 percent of those uninsured had experienced in the preceding year a time when they could not pay for their basic living costs (Commonwealth Fund, 2001).

Furthermore, public insurance programs rarely cover all needed expenses. Elderly families pay, on average, nearly 17 percent of their incomes for noncovered health expenses. Medicaid coverage is less adequate than that of Medicare, so many poor persons are simply denied access to care and go without needed medicine. Even after the contribution of public assistance, poor families pay, on average, an estimated 14 to 15 percent of their meager incomes, compared to roughly 8 percent for middle-income families and less than 3 percent for wealthy families (Rasell et al., 1994). Even seemingly small medical expenditures become financially catastrophic for families with low incomes and inadequate health insurance (Berki, 1986). Box 12.5 illustrates the impact of inadequate public insurance for the working poor.

Thus, the financial barriers to decent medical care for the underinsured and uninsured result in higher rates of sickness, disabling disease, and death. Uninsurance and underinsurance also result in personal bankruptcy, crippling amounts of debt, and agonizing decisions over whether to forgo needed care or to forgo food and other subsistence expenditures. Occupational instability and uncontrolled

Box 12.5

Regressive Impact of Health Care Expenditures on Family Budgets: The Working Poor

Esperanza and Roberto both work, but their combined incomes cannot raise them out of poverty. Esperanza's job offers no health insurance and Roberto's offers only minimal coverage for which he must pay much of the premium. They rely on public clinics and emergency rooms for most care for themselves and their two children, but earn too much to be eligible for Medicaid in Texas. Even by doing without needed doctor visits and medications, their health care expenses consume 15 percent of their combined take-home pay of about $1,500 per month. They pay Roberto's insurance premium, $85; clinic fees, $35; hospital bills being paid back a little each month, $65; and prescriptions and other medicine, $40.

Connie is the divorced mother of two school-aged children. She works full time as a home health aide, with take-home pay of less than $1,000 per month. She has no employer-provided insurance for herself or the children, one of whom has been diagnosed with sickle-cell anemia (a hereditary chronic disease affecting mainly African Americans). The child is not yet sick enough to qualify for public insurance for the disabled, but does have frequent infections and needs far more medical attention than non-anemic children. Connie's family health expenditures consume nearly 30 percent of her income. They include doctor and clinic fees, $80; hospital bills being paid back, $100; prescriptions and other medicine, $50; and taxis to doctors, hospitals, and clinics not located near public transportation, $35.

Not only do these families lack adequate access to health care, but also they must forgo spending on food, clothing, and shelter, in order to pay such a high percentage of their income on health care. They are not alone. The figures show the following:

- Low-income families pay a much higher proportion of their incomes for health care than do high-income families. Families in the top fifth spend 9 percent for out-of-pocket expenses, compared to middle-income families' 16 percent, and low-income families' (bottom fifth) 13 percent (USFIFA, 2000).
- Minority families are particularly unlikely to be able to obtain affordable private health insurance (Carrasquillo et al., 1999). Due mainly to the exclusion of working poor families from Medicaid insurance, the rates of minority persons with *no* private *or* public insurance coverage are two to three times the rates for white, non-Hispanic-origin Americans (USDHHS, 2001a).
- Only 9 percent of all poor women under 65 are insured by employer-provided insurance (Lyons et al., 1996).
- Chronic illnesses (such as hypertension, diabetes, sickle-cell anemia) that disproportionately afflict certain minority groups are particularly likely to be inadequately treated among the working poor due to lack of adequate insurance (Hill, 1995).

costs for health care expenditures undermine the security of middle-class, as well as poorer, families.

Ironically, lack of adequate insurance coverage for all Americans results in expensive inefficiencies that also affect those who are insured. Insured people pay indirectly (in higher rates) for emergency room use that could have been precluded by insuring regular sources of medical care for all. Taxpayers must pay indirectly (for example, for staffs who screen Medicaid eligibility) for the costs of *excluding* persons from needed care, and then pay again for the costs (for example, intensive care for low-birth-weight infants) caused by the system's failure to provide preventive care to all who need it. Health care providers also pay indirectly, because they must pay staff to screen patients for ability to pay and to process enormous amounts of paperwork to get reimbursed by the many diverse sources of insurance.

Because of rising proportions of uninsured and underinsured Americans, together with the inadequacies of existing programs of public insurance, the health care crisis now affects all but the wealthiest citizens. In place of the fragmented for-profit health insurance industry, some policy experts have called for a nationwide program guaranteeing universal access to health care.

National Health Insurance: The Canadian Model

National health insurance is a perennial issue in the United States. As early as 1914 and with increasing fervor in the 1930s and 1940s, some American health reformers were urging social insurance legislation comparable to that in Europe. Insurance companies and the AMA vigorously fought these proposals (Starr, 1982: 240–289). The idea of a national health insurance has been raised in Congress many times since, but America has not yet enacted any comprehensive health care program for its citizens.

In light of the large numbers of uninsured and underinsured Americans and the rapidly escalating burden of health care expenditures, policymakers need to look again at the merits of the Canadian national health insurance as a model for the United States. Since 1972, a national program has covered all Canadian citizens for hospitalization, physician care, and many ancillary services. Each province maintains its own insurance plan, but federal approval and funding require the following minimal criteria: (1) universal coverage (all citizens must be covered); (2) comprehensive coverage (it must pay for all conventional hospital and medical care); (3) access (for instance, no extra charges that make the insurance regressive); (4) portability (each citizen's insurance must be accepted throughout the country); and (5) nonprofit, public administration. Private insurers are legally excluded from the health care arena. Doctors and other health care providers are mostly in the private sector, but the government controls expenses by an annually negotiated, binding fee schedule. Incentives for excessive surgery and other costly procedures have been eliminated (Marmor, 1993).

Canadian doctors have many incentives to work in primary care and to locate their practices in the kinds of communities, such as rural or inner-city areas, that are seriously underserved in the United States. The Canadian government maintains a smaller proportion of specialists (about one for every four primary care physicians, compared to one to one in the United States). Canadian doctors are paid far less than U.S. doctors, but they remain the best paid professionals in Canada. Doctors are paid according to a fixed, annually negotiated schedule, with professionwide spending caps to prevent overruns. No evidence indicates that Canadian doctors are sufficiently dissatisfied with their system to leave to practice elsewhere. Canada has a higher proportion of applicants for medical training than the United States, although cost-containment has made it necessary to reduce the oversupply of new physicians (Adams, 1993; Charles and Badgley, 1999; Fooks, 1999).

Patients are free to choose their own doctor, although they must be referred by a primary care physician to use services of many specialists. When Canadians consult the doctor or go to the hospital, they simply show their medical card; they are not billed at all. Health care providers may not add on any charges, such as co-payments, over those covered by the national insurance program. Canada's program covers most medical services, including many (such as long-term home care and nursing home care) not covered by medical insurance in the United States. The provinces are allowed but not required to cover additional services, such as physiotherapy, eyeglasses, and adult dental care (Fooks, 1999; Kane, 1993).

Control over the hospital sector also keeps costs down. Hospitals are run by each province on an annual budget basis, with no incentives to overbuild or invest in duplicates of expensive technological devices. Authorization for purchase of new technology is more conservative in Canada than in the United States. The policy in Canada is to wait until there is strong evidence of the medical effectiveness, safety, and usefulness of expensive technology, and then to purchase gradually while gauging the actual rate of use of facilities. These controls have enabled the Canadian system to keep its health care expenditures to a much smaller portion of the country's GNP while providing very high rates of access to health care for all citizens (Marmor, 1993). Because all citizens are covered by the same level and kind of insurance, administrative costs in Canada are far lower than in the United States; for instance, U.S. hospital administrative costs average 24.8 percent of overall spending—about 2.5 times the rate of Canadian hospitals (Woolhandler et al., 1993). Nevertheless, while dramatically lower than the United States, Canadian health care expenditures are greater than most other developed countries, so the system has engaged in cost-containment, including reducing the services covered (Fooks, 1999).

The Canadian system does have some drawbacks, compared to health care services afforded by upper-class Americans. Provincial facilities for some high-tech procedures and testing may not be located conveniently. The system also has an operative form of rationing, especially of very expensive services such as organ transplants. For example, a person with unfavorable prospects for long-term health benefits from a kidney transplant would be less likely than in the United States to be able to obtain one.

Canadians are generally satisfied with their system—although less so than before the cost cutting of the 1990s. A cross-national survey showed that 23 percent of Canadians affirmed, "Our health care system has so much wrong with it that we need to completely rebuild it." By contrast, 33 percent of Americans affirmed that they were so strongly dissatisfied (Blendon and Kim, 2001).

The Canadian health care system has achieved many of its objectives. All citizens are insured, and the system is very good at delivering care to those who need it, regardless of their socioeconomic status. The difference in health outcomes for the poor is demonstrable in cross-border studies. For example, a study of cancer survival rates for the most common treatable cancers (breast, prostate, colon) found that treatments available in the Canadian system produced far superior survival rates among the poor (differentials between American and Canadian rates ranged between 20 and 50 percent). If the U.S. health care system were to achieve survival rates comparable to those among the Canadian poor, an estimated 1 million years of people's lives each year could be saved (Gorey, 1999).

Had the United States enacted a national health program such as Canada's several decades ago, it might have realized similar cost controls and universal health care access. Now, however, vested interests profiting from the laissez-faire American system have become so entrenched, economically centralized, and powerful that it has become extremely difficult to establish any economical national health plan, even one as limited as national health insurance. A few decades ago, U.S. hospitals could have been organized as public facilities, but now many are organized as enormous for-profit businesses with major investments to protect. Likewise, health insurance is big business; without eliminating the profit and paper-work of third-party payments, a national health plan could not realize the kinds of savings achieved in the Canadian system. Stringent government controls could prevent national health insurance from creating yet another inflationary spiral of health costs, but is there sufficient political will to take such a strong stand?

A national insurance program would probably resolve one major aspect of the current crisis in the U.S. health care system: the access of poor and middle-class people to adequate physician and hospital care. National health insurance also has the potential, if implemented with certain regulatory safeguards, of improving the quality of care received by nonwealthy citizens. Absent major structural changes to eliminate or greatly restrict profit taking, however, a national health insurance program would probably not be able to reduce or even control costs.

The American people could decide that affordable health care for all is a sufficiently important value to warrant such structural changes. The enormous political and economic power of the vested interests of hospital corporations, insurance companies, medical industries, and health care providers would almost certainly be utilized to fight those changes.

HEALTH CARE INSTITUTIONS

We tend to think that institutions have always been run pretty much as they are now; however, health care institutions have changed dramatically even in the last two decades. When we think about changes that need to be made to improve health care delivery, it is useful to remember that these institutions have been *socially constructed* and are thus amenable to human efforts for improvement and reconstruction for the future.

The provision of health care in large-scale institutions, such as hospitals, is a relatively recent phenomenon. In the nineteenth century, most sick people were treated and nursed in their homes. Almshouse wards were the main form of hospital, nursing home, and insane asylum, offering a modicum of care and custody to indigent persons lacking family members to provide care. They were run as charitable institutions, with little real curative function (Rosenberg, 1987).

The Development of the Modern Hospital

By the time of the early twentieth-century reformation of the medical profession (described in Chapter 9), hospitals too had changed dramatically. Both hospitals and medicine were becoming more rationalized: science oriented, specialized, and bureaucratized. Many towns established community hospitals, which lacked the stigma of the poorhouse wards. The rapid development of new medical "tools," such as antiseptic conditions for surgery, X-rays, and clinical laboratories, provided an important rationale for centering care in hospitals, which could capitalize these facilities and provide the necessary support staff. Hospitals' prestige and growth hinged on the practice of surgery (Rosenberg, 1987: 337–352).

One reason for the increase of middle- and upper-class hospital patients was the growing faith in the efficacy of medicine; another was the concerted advertising by hospitals, depicting well-appointed private rooms and immaculate conditions. Income from private patients made community hospitals economically viable. Hospital-admitting privileges became crucial to physicians' careers; hospitals in turn became dependent on doctors to bring in private patients (Rosenberg, 1987: 237–261).

Nursing too was changed from an untrained domestic task to a hospital-oriented and -trained occupation, bringing discipline and efficiency to the care of paying patients. By the 1920s American hospitals were, therefore, being transformed from charitable enterprises to bureaucratic organizations selling medical commodities in an impersonal marketplace. The very technology and specialization of tasks that made hospitals plausible sites for the centralized practice of medicine were subsequently major sources of the spiraling costs leading to the present U.S. health care crisis.

Hospital Ownership and Control

One of the biggest changes in the last 40 years has been in how hospitals are owned and controlled. Before the 1970s most hospitals were operated primarily as not-for-profit enterprises. Some not-for-profit hospitals are public institutions, funded mainly from tax revenues of a city, county, state, or national government; this includes many teaching hospitals, where the training of new doctors is combined with the care of indigent patients. Private not-for-profit institutions include community hospitals run by local boards as well as hospitals run by various religious and charitable organizations. Since the early years of private patient hospitalization, there have been private, for-profit hospitals, typically proprietary hospitals set up by several doctors in a community, but small groups of investors could not readily capitalize modern high-tech hospitals. Since about 1980, increasingly, for-profit hospitals are owned by large business corporations with investor-stockholders.

The numbers of public and not-for-profit hospitals are dwindling, and they are increasingly operating with considerable financial losses, because they have been left caring for a disproportionate number of the sickest and poorest patients, who are turned away from for-profit hospitals (Freudenheim, 1997c; Preston, 1996). Closures and downsizing of not-for-profit community hospitals resulted in the loss of 31,000 beds from 1989–1994 and 72,000 beds through 1999 (Heffler et al., 2001).

The failure of the U.S. health care system to provide adequate insurance coverage for all citizens has wreaked havoc on the budgets of hospitals. A growing proportion of Americans—about one-fifth of the nation—lack health insurance, and government cost cutting has reduced the levels of funding of care for many poor, disabled, and elderly previously provided by Medicaid and Medicare. Only hospitals whose patients have good private insurance coverage can "break even" in operating costs; indeed, they can make sizable profits. As the private for-profit hospitals increasingly control this desirable market, other not-for-profit hospitals suffer financial losses and bankruptcies.

A rapidly growing trend in the United States is toward the proprietarization and corporatization of health care facilities, such as hospitals, nursing homes, psychiatric hospitals, and free-standing clinics and outpatient surgery centers. **Proprietarization** is the process by which a greater proportion of health care institutions are operated explicitly for profit. **Corporatization** is the process by which a relatively small number of investor-owned corporations control a greater concentration of proprietary interests.

For example, Columbia Healthcare Corporation bought a number of small failing hospitals to get a market toehold in cities such as Houston and Miami; then it acquired Galen Health Care, a 73-hospital chain. In 1993, Columbia merged with the HCA (Hospital Corporation of America), making it the world's largest investor-owned hospital group (Jones, 1993; see also Bond and Weissman, 1997). Although it was unsuccessful in its attempt to take over Blue Cross-Blue Shield of Ohio, by 1997 Columbia/HCA owned 343 hospitals, 136 outpatient surgery centers, 550 home-care agencies, and numerous other medical services (Freudenheim, 1997a).

By 2000, the vast majority of all nonfederal hospitals belonged to for-profit corporations. For-profit hospitals have been highly profitable for investors. Interestingly, studies have found that for-profit acute-care hospitals are not more cost efficient than their not-for-profit counterparts, but rather are more expensive to operate. For-profit hospitals spend much less of their income on patient care than the national average for all kinds of hospitals, and they spend much more on administrative costs and profits (Woolhandler and Himmelstein, 1997).

Rather than cost efficiency, their profitability appears to depend on controlling patient-mix (that is, limiting the served population to the well insured), as well as dominating or monopolizing specific markets. For-profit takeovers of nonprofit health organizations have resulted in several instances of plunder of publicly created assets. For example, several Blue Cross insurance funds, as well as numerous community or religiously supported hospitals, have been acquired by for-profit chains with little or no return of the real value of the assets of the institution that community had created or supported with its donations of time and money (Bond and Weissman, 1997; Lewin and Gottlieb, 1997; Young et al., 2000).

Although initially, after a corporate buyout of a hospital, for-profit hospitals may realize some economies of scale (for example, better prices on supplies bought through the united purchasing power of the chain), they cannot in the long run further reduce costs and maintain the same quality without seriously diminishing their profits. Indeed, if they eventually buy out or drive their nonprofit competitors to bankruptcy, they may be in a position to increase their profits by driving up prices (Jones, 1993). Because profits are their foremost reason for existence, investor-owned hospitals have no incentive to return cost savings to the payers of medical costs. The unprecedented power and potential for market monopoly of for-profit hospitals is a significant problem that any viable U.S. health care policy must address.

Hospital Costs and Financing

Any effort to address the U.S. health system crisis must confront the costs of hospital care. Payments to hospitals account for the largest single category of national health expenditures. Not only have costs of hospital care risen far faster than the cost of living in the United States, they have also consumed an ever greater proportion of total national health expenditures. Whereas in 1929, the costs of hospital care amounted to 18 percent of all U.S. health spending, they were 30 percent by 1950, 37 percent by 1970, and in the low-to-mid-40 percent range in the 1990s (Gibson, 1982; Letsch, 1993; Anderson and Poullier, 1999). In the early 2000s, despite decreases in the nation's economic productivity, hospital spending increased dramatically, surpassing drugs as the main cause of health care inflation (Strunk et al., 2001).

One source of spiraling hospital costs has been the proliferation of sophisticated and expensive technologies. Many of these expensive investments are, however, not fully utilized in the community; many services are duplicated (see Glaser, 1991). For example, all five hospitals in one city may have purchased and staffed an expensive magnetic resonance imaging (MRI) unit, but none of them had real use for more than one-fourth of the MRI's capacity, so the costs for each use were high. Then in order to recoup more of the expense of the unit, the hospitals encouraged their physicians to order more MRI scans for their fee-for-service insured patients. The proliferation of technologies from the minor (such as blood tests) to the massive (neonatal intensive care units, for example) has driven up hospital costs not only because they are expensive to acquire and house but also because they require costly specialized support workers. Whereas modernizing capital expenditures in industrial production usually decrease labor costs, technological investments in hospital production generally increase labor expenditures.

U.S. hospitals are far more expensive than their counterparts in other developed countries with health outcomes as good as or better than those of the United States. In 1996, U.S. spending on hospitals was $1,646 per capita, compared to $902 in France, $796 in Germany, and $521 in the United Kingdom. One major factor in the difference is that U.S. hospitals employ more personnel per bed (3.9 in the U.S., 1.1 in France, 1.5 in Germany, and 3.5 in the U.K.). Unfortunately, in the United States, a large proportion of those employees do not engage in patient care but rather work in fiscal and bureaucratic operations, for example, screening patient insurance coverage and billing various insurers. Another factor in the difference is the extensive investment in high-tech equipment and the personnel to run it. For example, in 1996, the United States had 16.0 expensive MRI units per million population, compared to the 2.8 median for developed countries. A further factor is profit margins, because very few other developed countries have for-profit hospitals. As a result, the very high per capita U.S. spending on hospitals, is based on *less service* to *fewer patients* than in most other developed countries. Patients were admitted to U.S. hospitals at lower rates than in most other developed countries (for example, 12.2 percent in the United States, compared to 22.5 percent in France), and their average length of stay was much lower (7.8 days, compared to 11.2 for France). Thus, the U.S. hospital expenditure per day of service was $1,128—about double the rate of the next most expensive (Denmark, $632) and many times greater than the median, $227, for developed countries (Anderson and Poullier, 1999).

Hospital Reimbursements In 1983, in an effort to contain spiraling hospital costs, the federal government adopted DRGs (Diagnosis Related Groups) as a basis for Medicare reimbursement (Ruggie, 1992; Smith, 1992).[5] In this system, each procedure or service that can be provided to a hospital patient is placed in a diagnosis-related category, each with a price fixed by computing what similar hospitals had been charging for like cases. The hospital is not paid more if the actual services cost more; if the actual services cost less, the hospital keeps the difference. Before DRGs, hospitals had strong financial incentives to use many procedures and services for each patient, because they could charge for each and every item in the patient's treatment. There were unforeseen negative effects of DRGs, however. Doctors were pressured not to request services that may have been beneficial

---

[5]Several states also had statewide DRG controls, but by the mid-1990s their programs were abandoned in failure.

to their patients, and many patients were discharged early—"quicker and sicker." Many of those patients were subsequently readmitted, because they had been discharged before they were well, but the hospitals could then bill Medicare anew for another admission.

Rather than contain costs, the DRG system actually increased them (Reinhardt, 1996). Hospitals shifted the costs of patient care, for example by sending postoperative patients home to be cared for by the family, sometimes aided by visiting nurses or home health aides (not at the hospitals' expense). The costs of subacute care (such as in a convalescent facility) and home health care (which Medicare and other insurers paid separately, even when delivered by a subsidiary of the very hospital corporation that discharged the patient) rapidly escalated, more than equaling what had previously been paid for in-hospital care. The system was also vulnerable to outright fraud in hospital billing. For example, in 1997, a federal probe indicted the nation's largest hospital chain, Columbia/HCA Healthcare Corp., for systematically "upcoding" patient diagnoses in order to increase the bill to Medicare. By claiming a more serious condition (bleeding ulcer with complications rather than bleeding ulcer, for instance), the corporation more than doubled its charges (Lagnado, 1997).

The DRG system of Medicare payment, together with cost controls instituted by private managed care corporations, may have also financially weakened many hospitals leading to acquisitions by for-profit chains or to closure. Shorter hospital stays left many hospitals underutilized. Between 1980 and 1993 there was a 36 percent cut in hospital inpatient days per thousand population, but the per capita spending on health services rose by 65 percent. In the name of cost controls, many hospitals were gutted, but their actual care of patients was diminished and, ironically, cost more overall (Reinhardt, 1996).

Hospitals can remain financially stable—and in some cases even highly profitable—if they can control the mixture of payers of their patients' bills. Thus, the system of hospital reimbursements promotes perverse incentives. Hospitals run by HMOs (especially Medicare and Medicaid HMOs) have every incentive to discourage hospital admissions and procedures. Hospitals that are reimbursed through insurance have perverse incentives to accept as few as possible of patients with highly restrictive insurance (for example, Medicaid), to manipulate DRGs for Medicare-insured patients, and to reject patients without adequate insurance or other means of paying. Hospital competition for high-paying patients has led to serious problems of access to needed care.

Problems of Access Most inner-city and rural hospitals, however, do not have the luxury of controlling the mixture of payers because they are often the only hospital available to a population. Many of them end up in dire financial straits, and their patients experience serious problems of access to needed health care. Many rural hospitals serve a relatively small, widely dispersed population; rural poor or uninsured persons including many farm families who cannot afford private insurance must rely on these hospitals to partially subsidize their care.

Rural hospitals accounted for a disproportionately large number of the more than 500 hospitals that closed between 1980 and 1987 (DeFriese et al., 1992). Some failed hospitals were outmoded and/or substandard, but many were the *only* ones available to the populace (Reinhold, 1987). Many rural areas have difficulty attracting physicians to practice in their areas, and losing a local hospital to which physicians can admit patients may further disadvantage the community. Closure of rural hospitals also decreases access to emergency medical care. Although the vast majority of the U.S. population lives in urban areas, some 70 percent of trauma fatalities occur in rural areas. There are workable substitutes for small rural community hospitals (outpatient satellite clinics and paraprofessional emergency teams, for example), but these require national or statewide policymaking and funding for restoring access to health facilities in rural areas (Rutledge et al., 1992; Straub, 1990).

Another problem of access is the use of the hospital emergency room (see Albrecht et al., 1996). All communities need access to some trauma center, open 24 hours a day, staffed and equipped to handle a vast range of possible medical emergencies. But emergency rooms are rarely profitable; indeed, they are unlikely to generate enough income to cover costs, because emergency rooms are used disproportionately by uninsured and underinsured patients who lack any other source of medical care. In predominantly poor areas, emergency rooms create massive losses to hospitals. Unable to afford primary care, poor persons appear at emergency rooms when they are extremely sick, requiring extensive medical attention. Hospitals have responded by eliminating their emergency room services. In Los Angeles, where 27 percent of all nonelderly adults and 30 percent of all children have no health insurance, 15 hospitals closed or downgraded their emergency rooms between 1986 and 1988 (Reinhold, 1988). As a result, people with serious injuries or critical illnesses must be transported farther and wait longer before reaching a trauma center.

In the inner cities, public hospitals, operated by city or other government bodies, are where most of the urban poor, the underinsured, and the uninsured go for treatment. These hospitals are gravely underfunded because of their inability to control their patient mix. They receive only about 12 percent of their revenues from private insurance, and nearly one-third of their patients, on average, have no insurance—public or private—and cannot afford to pay for their care (Kassirer, 1995). In the early 1990s, nationally, hospitals averaged profit margins in the range of 4 to 6 percent (while investor-owned hospitals earned considerably more). By contrast, inner-city hospitals operated at huge losses. For example, not-for-profit Presbyterian Hospital (New York City) suffered a 3.1 percent loss in 1993, and New York City's 13 municipal hospitals sustained an 8.5 percent loss (Freudenheim, 1995c). Underfunded, many public hospitals have been forced to close. In the early 1980s there were more than 1,800 public hospitals, but by 1993 only 1,390 remained open, leaving the poor and uninsured even more vulnerable (Kassirer, 1995).

For-profit hospitals frequently refuse to serve patients who cannot pay. Often they transfer uninsured patients in medically unstable conditions to public hospitals or those nonprofit hospitals willing to accept indigent patients. This extensive "*dumping*" of undesirable patients puts an added burden on inner-city hospitals, especially the publicly financed hospitals that become the poor's last resort. In Chicago in 1983, after the governor had placed a ceiling on state payments for hospital services to the poor, transfers of patients from private hospitals to the county public hospital increased from an average of 100 per month to 450 per month. A subsequent study found that of 467 patients transferred to Cook County Hospital from private hospitals, 89 percent were black or Hispanic, 81 percent were unemployed, and nearly a fourth were medically endangered by the transfer (Schiff et al., 1986). In outrage over this and similar instances, Congress outlawed the "dumping" of patients in April 1987. A 2001 review of government investigations found that the federal government cited more than 500 hospitals (about 10 percent of all U.S. hospitals) for dumping patients during a three-year period (1997–1999). In the 15 years since the law was enacted, about one in five hospitals had been cited for violations and more than 100 had been cited over and over. Because the government's fines for violations were so low that it was cheaper to pay the fine than to provide care, hospitals had no incentive to obey the law (Rohrlich and Riccardi, 2001).

Hospitals and managed care organizations vie to avoid the unreimbursable expenses of treating emergency patients, even when patients are dangerously ill. For example, an ambulance took an 18-month-old child in critical condition (due to a massive bacterial infection) to Los Angeles County's Martin Luther King Jr./ Drew Medical Center. Her HMO refused to cover a blood test at the non-HMO hospital. The doctor at King treated the child's dehydration and subsequent seizure, but did not administer the blood test or antibiotics. The doctor knew what was medically needed, but the child did not get that treatment because of her insurance status. Four hours after she arrived at King, she was transferred to her HMO hospital—*not* in stable condition—and she died 20 minutes after arrival (Dolan, 1999).

Another problem for emergency care is that many hospitals avoid having staff and beds underutilized at any time, so there are not enough places in critical care units to handle emergency patients. This staffing policy results in ambulances being diverted to other hospitals, increasing the time before the patient is treated. One survey found that one-third of all hospitals (and more than half of urban hospitals) had emergency departments operating over capacity; many more were operating fully at capacity. One-third of all hospitals and two-thirds of urban hospitals had diverted ambulances (some for multiple periods) during the month of the study (*New York Times*, 2002; see also Kelley, 1999).

Ironically, in the wake of the September 11, 2001, attacks on the World Trade Center and the Pentagon, many public health experts are calling attention to how unprepared the nation's hospitals had become for facing any kind of disaster with widespread serious injuries. To trim their operations, hospitals reduced the number of intensive care unit beds by 17 percent in the 1990s alone, and eliminated about 12 percent of all hospital beds. A large medical emergency could swamp not only the emergency rooms, but also a city's supply of emergency medications, supplies, and equipment (Bernstein, 2001a).

The trend toward for-profit health care and corporate control in the United States is closely linked with this underfunding of accessible care for the poor and underinsured (Whiteis and Salmon, 1987), especially when for-profit hospitals displace previously not-for-profit hospitals (see Gray, 1991). For-profit hospitals (and some not-for-profit hospitals that emulate big businesses) engage in marketing and demarketing strategies to maximize their revenues. *Demarketing* is a euphemism for the practice of actively discouraging "undesirable" patients who seek their services.

For example, economically depressed Brownsville, Texas, is served by two hospitals, both owned by for-profit chains. They regularly turn away all but the most critical emergency cases if patients cannot pay. The administrator of one Brownsville hospital said, "We ask all the patients for money. . . . We work with the poor patients and tell them we'd be happy to set up a payment program" (quoted in Tolchin, 1988b). Critics charge that the hospitals aggressively intimidate patients into leaving without health care service (Tolchin, 1988a). One survey of physicians found that those practicing at for-profit hospitals were two to three times as likely to report their hospital discouraged admissions of uninsured, Medicaid, and Medicare patients (Schlesinger et al., 1987). Nonpaying or low-paying patients also may be subjected to long waits and inferior facilities compared to full-paying patients. Underinsured patients are routinely asked to pay, in advance, for the difference between what the hospital and its doctors charge and what their insurance will pay. For example, women covered by Medi-Cal (California Medicaid) were told by Northridge Medical Center that they had to pay cash in advance for the $400 difference between what Medi-Cal paid for anesthesia in childbirth and what the hospital anesthesiologists demanded (Bernstein, 1998).

A more subtle marketing strategy of profit-oriented hospitals is *cream skimming*, or the targeting of a market of highly desirable patients, typically middle- and upper-class persons with good insurance who need treatments that cost the hospital relatively little. Frills, such as cozy birth centers that provide champagne for the new parents, are advertised to attract well-insured patients. To the extent that some hospitals are successful in attracting the cream of patients, others are worse off, because their patient mix no longer includes those who are least expensive to treat.

A related form of cream skimming is the investment in specialty hospitals. For-profit corporations own the vast majority of specialty hospitals, such as those offering psychiatric care, substance abuse treatment, and physical rehabilitation. Specialized care is not subject to much federal cost-containment pressure; nearly all patients are privately insured, are younger than Medicare recipients, and tend to stay about three times as long as patients in acute care hospitals. Another feature that yields higher profits is that little expensive technology is required. Although the long-term profitability of specialty hospitals may be greatly reduced by insurer cost-containment measures, the early impact has been to siphon desirable patients away from not-for-profit hospitals (Freudenheim, 1987b).

The nursing home industry—more than 75 percent of which is controlled by for-profit companies—has become less profitable than other specialty hospitals, because it relies very heavily on government payments through Medicare and Medicaid. These two programs support more than 75 percent of all U.S. nursing home residents. Medicare pays about 10 percent of nursing home expenditures nationally, while Medicaid pays about 48 percent (USHCFA, 2000). When Medicare payments were liberal, nursing home chains made huge profits and expanded rapidly. For example, in California the average nursing home made a profit of 41 percent on net equity in 1978–1979. In those boom years, for-profit chains grew as much as 900 percent in just four years (see Harrington, 1984). Government funding became more restrictive in the 1990s; however, profit margins still outranked those in other industry groups, and corporate executives continued to make handsome seven-figure incomes (Harrington, 1996).

Medicare payments to nursing homes increased by at least 30 percent every year from 1990 to 1997, with the per day payments from Medicare reaching some $400 per day for short-term care. Medicare payments became more restrictive in 1998, however. Also, under the Clinton administration, the Justice Department began prosecuting cases of outright fraud by nursing home chains. Virtually all of the largest for-profit nursing home corporations were charged with Medicare fraud and false claims—a total of several billion dollars of illegal use of Medicare money. For example, Vencor, a large chain with nursing homes in 31 states, was charged with over $1 billion for overcharging, keeping fake financial records, and charging for unnecessary medical tests (Imse, 2000).

The profit motive in specialty hospitals, especially those such as nursing homes and psychiatric hospitals where patients are relatively isolated and powerless raises serious questions about the quality of care. The nursing home industry has had a long and continual history of patient neglect and abuse, physical danger, filthy conditions, and inadequate nursing care (see Harrington, 1996). Indeed, the proportion of nursing homes cited for physically abusing their residents doubled between 1996 and 2000. Nearly 10 percent of these abuses resulted in serious injury or death (Trapps, 2001). Such institutions have a very high proportion of unskilled workers, barely earning the minimum wage, with an annual turnover rate of 70 to 100 percent, leading to frequent understaffing. A 2002 study by the Department of Health and Human Services concluded that more than 91 percent of U.S. nursing homes have too few workers to adequately care for patients. More than 40 percent were dangerously understaffed. Patients in understaffed homes were more likely to experience bedsores, malnutrition, dehydration, pneumonia, and serious blood-borne infections (Pear, 2002c). For-profit nursing homes make less money for their stockholders/owners when they hire sufficient numbers of well-trained nursing aides at a level of pay that enables workers to support their own families.

Understaffed nursing homes relied heavily on psychotropic drugs and physical restraints to control patients. Changed federal regulations in 1987 and 1991 significantly reduced the rate of restraint, but many nursing homes still use improper restraints. One study of preventable adverse drug events in nursing homes found that psychotropic drugs (specifically sedatives, antidepressants, antipsychotics, and hypnotics), were the main causes of these drug-related injuries and deaths. More than 60 percent of nursing home residents are medicated with antidepressants and sedatives. The study estimated that overmedication of nursing home residents accounts for about 175,000 preventable adverse drug events annually (Gurwitz et al., 2000).

The profit motive has also made specialty hospitals particularly prone to fraud, unethical marketing, and overcharging. For example, in 1991, Psychiatric Institutes of America, the nation's largest and most profitable chain of private psychiatric hospitals with 73 psychiatric hospitals nationwide, was implicated in systematic fraudulent practices. Investigators identified such abuses as inflating bills for medications and services, billing for services never rendered, altering diagnoses and treatments to match insurance coverage, admitting insured patients who did not need hospitalization, keeping patients against their will, and releasing patients—regardless of their condition—as soon as their insurance was exhausted (Kerr, 1991; Vandenburgh, 1999).

Overcharging and outright fraud contribute to the rapidly rising costs of medical care both directly, as when fraudulent Medicare claims are paid, and indirectly, as insurance companies pass on inflated costs by increases in premiums (Sparrow, 1996). Although many hospitals do not engage in such unscrupulous business practices, the added costs created by those that do are enormous. Federal, state, and local government regulatory agencies must then spend additional monies trying to detect and control abuses of the system, adding yet more to the actual costs of the health care system. The trends toward proprietarization and corporatization are not inevitable; the government could, for example, decide to redirect funds into public health care programs or public or not-for-profit hospitals for all. These growing hospital corporations, however, wield massive political and economic force that they use to influence government policymaking to keep the hospital industry and their position in it as profitable as possible.

MEDICAL INDUSTRIES

Vast and profitable industries have developed to supply products and processes for medical care. They manufacture, distribute, and market known products while continuously researching and developing new ones. The most obvious example is the pharmaceutical industry, which markets large numbers of both prescription and over-the-counter drugs. Other industries supply everything from the simplest devices to the most complex, including monitors for various organ functions, radiological equipment, laboratory equipment, prosthetic devices, surgical equipment, medical office and hospital supplies and equipment, and intravenous solutions.

Costs

Changing medical technologies involve not only innovations in material objects (such as drugs, equipment, and devices), but also the development of new procedures and scientific and technical knowledge bases. Rapidly changing medical technology has been a major source of the increases in hospital and physician-related costs to pay for new technological equipment, to build and adapt spaces to use it, and to hire and supervise the specialized workers to operate it. Between one-third and three-quarters of increased expenditures for medical care is due to the costs of medical technology (Lassey et al., 1997).

Expenditures for prescription drugs also contributed a disproportionate amount to the rapid increase in U.S. health care expenditures. Prescription drug spending in the United States increased in 1999 by 19.2 percent, 17.3 percent in 2000, and 17.1 percent in 2001, the seventh consecutive year of double-digit growth—many times the rate of overall growth in incomes. In the decade between 1990 and 2000, total national spending on prescription drugs tripled (Pear, 2002d).

About one-third of these dramatic increases is due to price hikes (see White, 2002). In 1999, for example, prescription drugs posted a 5.7 percent price hike, one of the highest rates of increase in the Consumer Price Index (USDHHS, 2001a: 11). Prescription drug use is not very price-sensitive, because when doctors and their patients find a drug that works well with few side-effects, they are loath to experiment with cheaper alternatives when the price is raised. Prices for many generic drugs have also increased dramatically, especially when the manufacturers have an effective monopoly for a needed pharmaceutical. For example, only one company (Aventis Pasteur) now produces tetanus vaccine, a critical inoculation for children. When the manufacturer quadrupled the price (from $14.50 per ten-dose vial to $60.40) in 2000, state public health programs could not afford to purchase enough vaccine to protect unvaccinated schoolchildren (Bernstein, 2001b). A considerable portion of these price increases went to corporate profits. Pharmaceutical industry profits grew throughout the 1990s and early 2000s annually by double-digit increments—many times the profit levels of other U.S. industries (see Bettleheim, 1999; Freudenheim and Petersen, 2001).

Price-setting for pharmaceutical products in the United States is unlike that in all other developed countries, where the governments have significant roles in controlling costs. For example, in Australia, where the government pays for 80 percent of prescription drug expenditures, the government sets prices by examining nine factors, including what is charged in other countries and evidence of the drug's therapeutic value. As a result of the U.S. political failure to exert any controls on drug prices,[6] Americans pay many times more for prescription medicines than people in other countries. For example, in 1999, a dose of the top-selling prescription drug Prilosec (for heartburn and ulcers) cost $3.31 in the United States, compared to $1.67 in Britain, $1.47 in Canada, $1.29 in Australia, and $0.99 in Mexico (Cauchon, 1999).

---

[6]The pharmaceutical industry's pseudonymous organization, "Citizens for Better Medicare" contributed more than $20 million in PAC, soft money, and individual contributions to federal candidates in 1999–2000 to try to prevent a Medicare prescription drug benefit that included any government price controls. Overall, the pharmaceutical industry contributed about four times as much to the Bush campaign as to the Gore campaign (Center for Responsive Politics, 2001, 2002).

New drugs are often extremely costly because they involve expensive research and development processes, including the costs of clinical trials required for federal approval, marketing, product liability insurance, as well as corporate profits. Drug manufacturers estimate that 16.7 percent of their revenues are used for research. The majority of that research is *not* devoted to finding remarkable cures, however. Much research is in order to find patentable alternatives to drugs made by rival companies or to drugs whose patent is soon to run out. Only about 40 percent of new drugs represent significant medical advancement (Rosenthal, 1993). For example, the drug Sarafem, marketed as a treatment for a severe premenstrual disorder,[7] is not a new drug but an older one that is patented, repackaged, and targeted toward a different market. Many doctors and insurers contend that Sarafem is a cleverly timed marketing ploy, merely a renamed version of the antidepressant drug, Prozac. Critics argue that it is no coincidence that the pharmaceutical company is now marketing Prozac as a "new" drug, precisely when the patent on Prozac expired and doctors could prescribe much less expensive generic drugs instead (Silverman, 2001; Vedantam, 2001).

A more important component of the cost of pharmaceuticals in the United States is the cost of marketing, particularly because drugs are now marketed *both* directly to consumers and indirectly to physicians who must prescribe them (Wolfe, 1996). Before the 1990s, when the Food and Drug Administration (FDA) relaxed restrictions, prescription medicines could not be marketed directly to consumers. Marketing expenditures were directed to persuading doctors to prescribe patented drugs by name. Drug companies spend tens of billions of dollars each year on promotion and marketing, of which more than $5 billion is spent on sales representatives who go to doctors' offices and professional conventions to promote their companies' brand-name prescription drugs. These "detail men" (sic) and other promoters offer gifts, samples, meals, travel, and other incentives, to doctors and medical students, hoping to induce them to prescribe specific drugs. An extensive review of some 538 studies found that such interactions between physicians and the pharmaceutical marketing personnel did, indeed, affect doctors' prescribing and professional behavior for the worse (Wazana, 2000).

Some pharmaceutical sales representatives also offer physicians incentives of making significant secondary income by prescribing their company's drug or drug-related treatment. This practice, while fraudulent and illegal, has been widespread over the last 20 years and has cost insurance programs, especially Medicare, billions of dollars. For example, Centocor's marketing of the new drug Remicade, an expensive treatment for rheumatoid arthritis, suggested that doctors could make more revenue by prescribing it compared to oral medications for the same disease,

---

[7]The advertising for Sarafem may be very misleading, however, because it suggests that many—perhaps most—women "need" the drug for their "symptoms." The disorder exists in no more than 5 to 10 percent of premenopausal women and it cannot be diagnosed correctly without six months of daily monitoring of the correlation between the woman's ovulation cycle and her moods. Thus, many women are not being diagnosed properly.

because they could charge Medicare for intravenous drug treatments administered in doctors' offices (Petersen, 2002).

Pharmaceutical companies have little reason to price their products competitively, because marketing to physicians, rather than to those who pay for the medicines, makes affordability less relevant. Although many physicians are concerned to prescribe the most affordable drugs for their patients (especially those lacking drug coverage by third-party payers), they are generally ignorant of the actual costs of prescription drugs. They tend to seriously underestimate the cost of the more expensive drugs and overestimate the cost of less expensive drugs (Glickman et al., 1994).

Some managed care programs have tried to negotiate deep discounts for pharmaceuticals in exchange for restricting covered drugs to one manufacturer's product. Unfortunately, this practice indirectly hurts persons whose insurance does not cover pharmaceuticals, who must pay full drugstore prices and have no leverage.

For example, in 1998, large purchasers such as HMOs paid $1.75 for a supply of Synthroid, a treatment for thyroid deficiency (common especially among elderly persons), whereas the undiscounted price was $27.05. Zocor (for high cholesterol) was $42.95 for favored customers, compared to the undiscounted price of $104.80. Thus, persons without prescription coverage under their health insurance paid significantly more out of pocket, resulting in unaffordable prescriptions (Bettleheim, 1999).

After the FDA relaxed controls over direct consumer advertising of prescription drugs in 1997, the amount spent on such ads on television and in magazines soared to $2.5 billion in 2000 (Pear, 2002b). Such advertising is clearly effective in increasing sales revenue to pharmaceutical companies. The increase in sales for the 50 most advertised prescription medicines accounted for about half of the $21 billion increase in prescription drug spending in 1999–2000; the other half of the increase involved spending on the 9,850 other drugs (see White, 2002).

Drug advertising directly to consumers contributes to increased U.S. health care expenditures in at least four ways. First, the costs of expensive mass media advertising must be recouped from sales before profits are realized, so drugs are priced much higher. Second, the advertising raises customer "demand" for brand-name drugs, regardless of whether a less expensive generic drug might be an appropriate treatment. For example, many patients who ask for prescriptions for Prilosec or Prevacid (heavily advertised, expensive treatments that account for nearly 75 percent of prescriptions for heartburn) could deal with their problems safely and effectively by changing their diets and using inexpensive over-the-counter medications (Connolly, 2002). An FDA study found that nearly one-quarter of people seeing a doctor asked for a specific brand of medicine, and 69 percent subsequently got a prescription for the brand they requested (O'Connell, 2002).

A third way such advertising raises health care spending is by increasing the number of patients' visits to doctors. Pharmaceutical advertising accounted for a significant portion of the 22 percent increase, between the first half of 1997 and the first half of 1998, in new patients seen by doctors for the seven heavily advertised groups of drug treatments—cholesterol reduction, smoking cessation, osteoporosis, hair loss, ulcers, postmenopausal problems, and depression (Freudenheim, 1998). Some of these advertising-stimulated doctor visits result in an unforeseen benefit when patients get needed care for other conditions they did not realize they suffered, but many more are just to get the prescription (and later, refills) authorized. Because drug company advertising emphasizes treating "*symptoms*"—rather than causes—of people's maladies, a fourth way it increases health care spending is by reducing the likelihood that people will address the actual *causes* of their problems. For example, people with serious depression or anxiety need much more than just mood-altering medications, so getting prescriptions too easily may prevent them from seeking psychotherapeutic help. At the same time, people with mild depression or anxiety might benefit from lifestyle changes (like exercise and learning better coping skills) far more than reliance on drugs.[8]

One reason that many medical technologies and drugs are so expensive over the course of a patient's lifetime is that they are *"halfway" technologies,* that is, not resolutions of a problem but merely partial responses to it. For example, the iron lung was a response to some needs of polio victims but did not resolve the problem of the disease itself; a resolution came with the development of the polio vaccine. Although they may prolong some people's lives, improve some people's functioning, or hold some people's dangerous symptoms in abeyance, even impressive technological developments often do not fully resolve the medical problem for which they were invented. Such medical costs, thus, continue to mount so long as patients live.

Modern medicine is struggling to respond to many chronic illnesses that are not so amenable to a "technological fix" as were the acute infectious diseases prominent a few decades ago. For example, in 2000, six of the seven most-advertised prescription drugs were for chronic conditions like arthritis, ulcers, and high cholesterol (see White, 2002). Patients must typically take such medications for many years, often for the rest of their lives. Because these medications are taken predominantly by older persons, the aging of the "baby boom" generation will cause dramatic increases in their use and expense for the next several decades.

Some new drugs and technologies do save money, however. For example, some new vaccines can prevent outbreaks of serious diseases. Some new screening devices can detect illnesses earlier when they are more readily cured. New inventions can make surgery safer or simpler. New drugs for conditions such as ulcers can make costly surgery unnecessary; however, whether this substitution

---

[8]The direct-to-consumer advertising of mood-altering medications is particularly pernicious when it tries to convince people not to cope with normal emotions, such as anxiety. For example, GlaxoSmithKline spent more than $16.5 million to promote Paxil (for anxiety) in October, 2001, after the attacks on the World Trade Center, although the company had planned a media blitz for that fall as soon as they got FDA approval to market the drug for generalized anxiety disorder (O'Connell and Zimmerman, 2002). Many Paxil ads were targeted toward women to encourage use of the drug for "symptoms" as minor as shyness and social reticence (Cottle, 1999).

saves money depends on whether the course of drugs is less expensive than the operation.

Another major reason for the increased costs of drugs and medical technologies has been the medicalization of problems not previously treated as medical issues (as described in Chapter 9). The medicalization of menopause, childbirth, old age, hyperactivity, alcoholism and other substance abuse, emotional troubles, and the like, has resulted in the prescription of a number of technological medical responses—drugs, devices, and procedures—that have all contributed to the greatly increased cost of treating these "conditions."

Regulation

Many interest groups are involved in the creation and utilization of new medical technologies. Three obvious parties are the manufacturers who profit from their sales, the physicians and hospitals who may choose to employ them, and the regulatory agencies that have varying degrees of power and responsibility over them. Other groups, including research scientists, political figures, media representatives, consumer groups, insurers, and patients, are also involved, sometimes in complex ways. Because of the rapid pace of technological development in medicine and the enormous economic, social, and health stakes involved, ongoing critical analysis of medical products and technologies is important (see Giacomini, 1999). The complexity and sheer quantity of new developments, however, make it difficult for even well-endowed and powerful nations to monitor them adequately. Developing countries are far less able to evaluate and control the use of new products and technologies, so the regulation of medical products marketed by transnational corporations has become a worldwide problem.

In the United States, the Food and Drug Administration (FDA) regulates pharmaceuticals and has the power to allow or ban their sale and control their labeling; the Federal Trade Commission (FTC) has some additional regulatory authority over the content of advertising claims made for health-related products. In 1938 Congress authorized the FDA controls, but a "grandfather" clause exempted preexisting drugs from scrutiny. Drug regulations required evidence of safety and truth in labeling and, since 1962, proof of efficacy (regarding the politics of FDA regulation, see Abraham, 1995; Silverman et al., 1992).

Because of political pressures on behalf of medical industries, the FDA often relaxes its regulatory control (Collins, 1995). For example, the FDA allowed a nonsteroidal anti-inflammatory drug (such as is used for relief in chronic arthritis) to be marketed, despite the evaluation that its testing for long-term effects (especially cancer-causing effects) was seriously inadequate. In response to political pressure, the FDA further allowed the manufacturer to reword the printed warnings (to patients and their doctors) such that these possible effects—especially for chronic users—were downplayed. The drug subsequently proved seriously harmful, but the FDA did not remove it right away, because the regulatory agency gave benefit of doubt to the drug company rather than to consumers. The degree of trust that regulatory authorities invest in pharmaceutical companies and their research processes leads to inadequate protection to patients/consumers (Abraham, 1995).

Initially, only pharmaceuticals and cosmetics were regulated; in 1976 after tragedies such as the deaths from the Dalkon Shield (intrauterine device used for contraception), the FDA was given authority to regulate medical *devices*. Medical *procedures* such as new forms of surgery are not regulated or even systematically evaluated. Many technologies have not been independently evaluated for safety or effectiveness whatsoever, or they were employed widely prior to systematic evaluation and many continue to be used long after studies resulted in negative assessments. Products and technologies that have been poorly, belatedly, or negatively evaluated include electronic fetal monitors, prenatal ultrasound screening, intrauterine devices, silicon gel breast implants, oral contraceptives, an artificial heart valve, and coronary care units (Foster, 1995; Palley, 1995).

Often use of a medical technology is related to a complex web of changes that are not carefully evaluated because of the influence of the *technological imperative* (that is, the belief that if we have the technological capability to do something, then we should do it). Electronic fetal monitor (EFM) technology was introduced in the late 1960s and aggressively marketed in the 1970s. EFM involves placing monitors (usually external) on the woman in labor to provide machine-recorded measures of fetal heart rate and strength of contractions. Many physicians were sold on the prospect of using EFM to detect early signs of "problem" deliveries, and hospitals invested in the technology as an efficient way to monitor several women in labor simultaneously (Kunisch, 1989).

Thus, long before adequate research on the effectiveness, accuracy, and side effects of EFM technology had been done, the devices had already been widely sold to hospitals throughout the United States and accepted in medical training as "good" obstetrical care. High-tech deliveries also enhanced physicians' professional prestige, legitimated obstetricians' control over the childbirth process, and justified hospital childbirth in an era in which both were being challenged (see Jordan, 1997). Likewise, hospitals considered themselves up to date if their labor and delivery rooms were equipped with the monitoring machines. The cost of the equipment could be passed on to patients and their insurers, and often hospitals could realize profits through increased use of testing and monitoring technologies.

The decision to *buy* the monitors led almost inexorably to the decision to *use* them for all laboring women, not merely the 10 to 15 percent who might be at risk of problem deliveries. By 1994, EFM was used in 80 percent of all live births (USDHHS, 1996b). Probably the foremost reason that EFM technology became a standard for medical intervention in labor and deliveries is that machine readouts were accepted in courts as evidence against malpractice suits (Kunisch, 1989). The decision to use monitors for all births combined with the fear of malpractice suits led to a rapid increase in the rate of delivery by Caesarian section, which involves major abdominal surgery on the mother. In the first decade of EFM use, the rate of surgical deliveries more than tripled. Although the rates dropped and then leveled off, the 1997 Caesarian section rate was 21.5 percent of all deliveries, compared to 16.5 percent in 1980 before widespread use of EFM (Curtin et al., 2000).

Because 98.9 percent of EFM alarms are false, much of this surgery is medically unnecessary and potentially harmful to the mother (Nelson et al., 1996). Research on the accuracy and effectiveness of EFM technology, as well as the appropriateness of Caesarian sections as medical intervention, came *after* the technologies and standard procedures were already in place. Indeed, the first large-scale trial of EFM came more than 15 years after monitors had first been marketed. Despite research assessments of EFM that concluded the technology provided little benefit in low-risk labors and greatly increased rates of costly and dangerous surgery (Kunisch, 1989; Leary, 1995b), rates of utilization of EFM continued to increase (USDHHS, 1996b),[9] because its use is motivated by complex and unexamined *non*medical factors (Banta, 1995).

Medical technologies often have harmful or undesirable side effects. They may even cause illness (iatrogenesis) and death. The evaluation of their safety is difficult, however, partly because it may take years for harmful effects to become evident. For example, in the 1940s and 1950s, unaware of the dangers of radiation, many physicians and dentists used X-rays and other radiological imaging frequently and indiscriminately, thus delivering relatively large doses of radiation to their patients. Because the effects of such radiation are cumulative and may take many years to culminate in disease, which even then may be attributable to multiple causes, the safety of early radioactive technologies was not readily questioned.

Unfortunately, serious adverse effects from drugs often are not observed until after the drugs are already on the market. Unlike many other countries, the United States does not have systematic or mandatory *postmarketing surveillance* for risks of adverse effects. The FDA relies mainly on voluntary reporting by doctors and hospitals. Only about 10 percent of such negative reactions are thus reported. One extensive study reviewed the 548 drugs approved by the FDA between 1975 and 1999, finding that more than 10 percent had been withdrawn or labeled with serious cautions due to serious adverse reactions discovered after approval. The evidence reported in the study suggests that, for some dangerous drugs, the adverse effects were known *before* approval and the FDA should not have allowed the drugs to be marketed (Grady, 2002c).

Safety is also always relative. The risks of dangerous side effects of a drug or procedure must be weighed against the probabilities and risks of the condition itself as well as of alternative therapies (Banta, 1995). For example, oral contraceptives carry the risk of unpleasant, dangerous, and even fatal side effects, but pregnancy and childbirth create serious health risks too. Regulators have not yet figured how to deal with the fact that safety is also relative to certain characteristics

---

[9]Later studies suggest that EFM-provoked Caesarian sections were not even preventing birth defects, as doctors hoped; babies delivered by EFM-triggered surgery were just as likely as those delivered vaginally to have cerebral palsy (Nelson et al., 1996).

of the patient population. Regulations often restrict drugs that are unsafe for children, for example, but fail to limit those that are unsafe for the elderly (Avorn, 1995). Risks must also be weighed against the potential health benefits. Dangerous side effects might be more acceptable in a drug for potentially fatal AIDS than in one for baldness, weight loss, or acne.

The importance of the powerful regulation of these new products and technologies is amply illustrated by the tragedies created by several dangerous products. Between 1958 and 1962, some 10,000 children were born with severe birth defects as a result of thalidomide, a sedative prescribed for their mothers to reduce nausea in pregnancy. The drug was not approved in the United States due to the tenacious efforts of a single medical officer with the FDA. The thalidomide disaster in Europe spurred the passage of the U.S. Drug Act of 1962 (and similar regulatory reform in the United Kingdom, where the drug had been approved) and changed the criteria for testing drug safety (Abraham, 1995; Silverman et al., 1992).

A similar tragedy occurred in the United States and elsewhere for children whose mothers took prescribed diethylstilbestrol (DES) during pregnancy. Between 1943 and 1970, DES, a synthetic estrogen, was widely prescribed for women in the United States, despite early and growing evidence that it was cancer causing and ineffective for preventing miscarriages. It was advertised in medical journals in the mid-1950s as "recommended as routine prophylaxis in *all* pregnancies" (quoted in Brody, 1997, emphasis in original ad). Subsequently, researchers found that DES caused iatrogenic disease in the children born to pregnant recipients and several million sons and daughters may have been thus affected (Weiss, 1983). Thus far, DES has been responsible for several hundred cases of cancers of the vagina, cervix, or testicles, but researchers are now discovering more insidious side effects, including immune system defects, urological and genital defects, and reproductive problems (Brody, 1997; Mastroiani et al., 1994).

The case of DES children illustrates the effects of poor scientific analysis and shoddy clinical trials, lack of regulatory control over doctor experimentation with unapproved drugs, and the readiness of a portion of the medical community to prescribe a potent substance that was not fully understood or proven safe and effective (Dutton et al., 1988; see also Bale, 1990; Bell, 1986, 1994; Direcks and Hoen, 1986). It also illustrates the difficult problem of how regulate and control adequately an industry capable of producing dire iatrogenic effects.

Rather than increase regulatory control and requirements for careful trials, Congress weakened U.S. drug regulation in 1997 (passing the FDA Modernization Act). This legislation made the FDA dependent upon industry money for its regulatory reviews, greatly lowering the threshold standards of evidence for drug approval and granting the industry benefit of doubt when evidence points to health risks. For example, in 1999, based on merely two clinical trials, the FDA recommended approval of Lotronex for treatment of women with irritable bowel syndrome, a nonlife-threatening condition that affects as many as one in five adults. The drug went on the market in February 2000, with lavish advertising claims of safety and effectiveness, but already by August there were several cases in which Lotronex had caused severe complications, some requiring surgery. The FDA could have responded by ordering Lotronex withdrawn from the market, but in August it merely issued a "medication guide" to clarify to doctors the drug's known risks. By November, however, five people had died from Lotronex, and the company finally withdrew the deadly drug from the market (Horton, 2001).

The tragedies caused by the Dalkon Shield illustrate the need for greater regulation of medical devices, as well as pharmaceuticals. In 1968 the shield was entrepreneurially promoted for birth control by a respected gynecologist, who later sold the patent to Robins, a large pharmaceutical company. At the time, the government had no effective regulation for medical devices. No agency checked the doctor's claims of safety and effectiveness, and the manufacturer had no legal accountability for using those inaccurate claims in its advertising. Several million women in the United States and overseas had the device inserted. Despite numerous reports of health- and life-threatening side effects due to the IUDs, massive infections, and dangerous abnormal pregnancies, the company did not issue physicians any warnings about its dangers until after the first documented death (Perry and Dawson, 1985; see also LaCheen, 1986).

Robins continued international sales of the device for two years after lawsuits and deaths forced them to cease U.S. sales. The company offered the U.S.-sponsored development agency, AID, a 48 percent discount on bulk packages of unsterilized shields. Dalkon Shields were still being inserted in new patients in developing nations through 1980 (Hartmann, 1987). In the face of extensive U.S. lawsuits (by about 200,000 eligible claimants), Robins filed for bankruptcy, limited its liability by paying $2.3 billion to a trust, and simultaneously provided its shareholders the highest rate of appreciation of any security on the New York Stock Exchange. The terms of the trust provided that some injured women would receive some payment with the amount depending, not on degree of injury, but on the number of eventual claims sharing the trust and whether the trust funds were depleted. However, there was virtually no provision for foreign women injured by the product (Sobol, 1991).

Although some evidence pertaining to safety (and effectiveness) can be deduced from the chemical properties of substances and devices, and further data can be gained from experiments on animals, medical industries and the FDA need to test innovations on human subjects. Early procedures for drug approval allowed clinical trials done under uncontrolled circumstances to be used as evidence of safety and effectiveness. Any licensed physician was permitted to experiment on patients with drugs before FDA approval, and pharmaceutical companies provided large quantities of free samples for so-called clinical trials. Only in the 1970s, however, were experimenters required to obtain the informed consent of patients; previously many subjects did not even know that they were taking experimental drugs. Because of the great medical and commercial interest in the many aspects of women's reproductive lives, women—especially poor and Third World women—have been disproportionately used as guinea pigs in medical research (Ward, 1986).

Profits and Products

The free enterprise model of technological development and marketing in the United States means the profit motive is a particularly important influence in the creation and marketing of new drugs and technologies. One critic argued that the proliferation of technological innovation is inevitable because "expansion is an absolute necessity for capitalist enterprises" (Waitzkin, 1979: 1263).

On the one hand, the quest for profits has motivated some impressive research; many technological advances of bioscientific medicine might not have occurred were it not for the investment of much research time and money. Private enterprise is not the only way a society could organize its research incentive, however. We gain much—perhaps most—of our medical advances from *government-*supported research in universities and government research centers.

On the other hand, the profit orientation has greatly *limited* the scope of research and development; the medical industries are understandably interested only in new developments that will produce marketable commodities. In recent years, the profit incentive has influenced even university and medical school research centers, which are licensing patents, becoming partners with corporate interests that manufacture and market new devices and procedures, and seeking to develop "technology parks" on their campuses. Thus, academic research centers jeopardize their ability to evaluate new technologies objectively (Wright, 1987).

Even when scientists and clinicians are not directly employed by medical industries, these corporations indirectly control their work or compromise their scientific neutrality. For example, the researcher who published an article on Retin-A (an acne medication), claiming it could reverse skin wrinkles, had received over $1 million in research and honoraria monies from Ortho Pharmaceuticals' parent company (Bell, 1992; Crossen, 1994).

Medical journals are a critical vehicle for practicing physicians to keep abreast of the latest medical research findings. They have become significant sources of revenues for the medical societies that publish them, however, with annual profits in the tens of millions of dollars primarily from pharmaceutical company advertisements. This commercial incentive sometimes results in biased reporting of the properties of new drugs (Altman, 1999). For instance, the British pharmaceutical manufacturer of Synthroid (taken daily by some 8 million Americans for hypothyroidism) paid University of California at San Francisco researchers to do a study that could demonstrate its superiority to similar, less expensive drugs. But when the study found that the rival drugs were just as effective, the corporation suppressed for several years the publication of the researchers' findings, which had been accepted by the *Journal of the American Medical Association* (Altman, 1997a, 1997b; King, 1996).

Another problem is that drugs to meet people's *actual* health needs are often of limited commercial interest. The industry is not likely to fund research on a cheap, readily available remedy, even when it may be the best treatment for a condition. For a drug to be profitable, it must be patentable; natural substances and shelf chemicals are not, so they are not researched, even if they may be highly effective.

Marketability increasingly depends on whether the cost of the drug or technology will be reimbursed by third-party payment. If HMOs and Medicare are not likely to pay for a new treatment, then companies are not likely to invest in its development (Pear, 1988). Drugs for developing nations are likewise of little commercial interest; although large numbers of people need some of these medications, researching and producing them would not be profitable. There is a worldwide surge in tuberculosis that is resistant to previously effective cures, but pharmaceutical corporations are unwilling to invest in developing new drugs, because only a tiny portion of the 8 million persons who get tuberculosis each year live in developed nations and could afford to pay for expensive drugs (Altman, 1995).

This general profit orientation does not mean that individual companies always gauge all policies to maximize profits. For example, when a drug developed by Merck for parasitic worms in livestock turned out to be a safe and effective treatment for a human parasitic infection causing river blindness among more than 18 million people in Africa, Merck made the drug available without charge through the World Health Organization (Leary, 1991).

Pharmaceutical companies avoid investing in new drugs for small markets; government research institutes do most of what research is done. The federal government also heavily subsidizes and gives private industry special incentives for the production of needed pharmaceuticals for small markets, called "orphan drugs" (Asbury, 1981). Unfortunately, these government incentives led to high drug prices and windfall profits by eliminating competition without controlling prices. The 1983 Orphan Drug Act granted seven-year market monopolies to companies developing treatment for relatively rare diseases. For example, Genentech was granted orphan-drug status for its version of the human growth hormone. Its research and development costs were $45 million, but sales in the first six years of its monopoly were an estimated $580 million. Some orphan drugs, like Ceredase (the only treatment for a rare hereditary disease), are actually discovered and initially tested by nonprofit researchers rather than drug companies. Nevertheless, a monopoly for their production is protected by the Orphan Drug Act, so the producer is allowed to set whatever price it chooses (Arno et al., 1995).

The U.S. government uses tax monies (more than $10 billion annually) to subsidize the research and development of drugs. For example, 34 of the 37 cancer drugs approved between 1955 and 1994 were developed with government research support. In 1995, however, the government relinquished the rights to require "reasonable pricing" on drugs thus researched, so taxpayers are not benefiting from government subsidization (Leary, 1995a; *New York Times,* 1994b).

In the United States, much medical research and new medical technological developments have been directed toward maximizing profits. Sometimes the interests of these corporations coincide with the needs of the sick, but there is no structural reason for this to occur. A market-oriented, profit-maximizing industry does not give first priority to the actual needs of the citizenry.

SOCIAL POLICY AND HUMAN RIGHTS

The United Nations' Universal Declaration of Human Rights states:

> Everyone has the right to a standard of living adequate for the health and well-being of himself and of his family, including food, clothing, housing and medical care and necessary social services, and the right to security in the event of unemployment, sickness, disability, widowhood, old age or other lack of livelihood in circumstances beyond his control. Motherhood and childhood are entitled to special care and assistance. . . . [Article 25 of the Universal Declaration of Human Rights, adopted and proclaimed by the General Assembly of the United Nations on 10 December 1948]

By all these standards, the United States has shown serious disregard for the basic human rights of its own citizens.

Our society needs to consider the means to health as a basic human right that a government should provide for its citizens, just as it protects citizens' human rights to freedom of religion and freedom from political repression. To how much and what kind of health care or medical care do people have a right? Does a country not have obligations to provide universal health care, comparable to universal education? What priority should health care expenditures have, relative to other national spending on the military, education, highways, and the environment? How do we balance citizens' rights to affordable health—both the maintenance of health and the treatment of illness—against the interests of the many corporations and individuals who profit from the health care system?

Our society's health policy reflects the larger values of the nation: What kind of a people do we want to be? Perhaps the current crisis in the American health system will encourage public discourse on these broader moral and political issues.

Throughout this book, we have outlined numerous ideas about how society affects the body, health, and illness. These ideas, however, are not mere abstractions, removed from people's actual lives. Real people get sick, experience afflictions, and try to find help; real people also enjoy health, and successfully use their bodies to enrich their lives and to fulfill their goals. Even seemingly abstract social factors, such as social control, economic organization and cultural practices, are—for individuals—very real in their consequences.

The issues we raise in this text suggest the diverse points at which social arrangements might be changed to help reach the goal of a healthier society. We hope we have stimulated readers to consider many ways to promote health in this society and globally. It is necessary to have a genuinely holistic understanding of the connections between the mind, body, and society to envision the far-ranging possibilities for enhancing health. We need to go way beyond narrow medical conceptions of health and to appreciate the entire web of socioenvironmental contexts that promote health. From such a holistic perspective, we might not only imagine changes in obvious problem areas, such as nutrition, water pollution, occupational health, and health care financing, but also consider possible health-promoting alterations in areas such as urban landscapes, automobile design, dependent care programs, media messages, and uses of leisure. A broad, holistic perspective to health transforms our ways of thinking about what is relevant to health and to illness prevention.

Similarly, we have suggested points of influence for improvements in the prevention and treatment of illness. Because power is such a pivotal factor in both illness causation and treatment, when we envision healthier alternative social arrangements, we should give special attention to considering changes in the exercise of power and to social arrangements that encourage the *empowerment* of individuals. Likewise, we have noted the importance of access to resources to stay healthy or to get well. Alternative scenarios for a healthier society need to pay close attention to *social inequalities* and the way we choose to distribute the resources necessary to be well or to be alive.

Although the social arrangements that influence our health may seem remote and objectlike, they are human products and as such can be humanly changed. It is necessary, however, for us to move beyond the boundaries of our individual lives to effect many measures that potentially have a wide-ranging ability to prevent illness and death. Our purpose in examining the institutional sources of illness and problems in health care is not to blame but rather to suggest some of the points at which social structure and social policy can be changed. Understanding the complex interrelationships of these arrangements prevents naïve notions that an isolated new program, policy change, or medical innovation will alone produce dramatic changes in people's health. Although most envisioned changes are matters of policy and social organization, some needed changes are embedded in cultural values and stubbornly change-resistant social structures; while still human products, they often change more slowly. Nevertheless, becoming aware of the human sources of the social arrangements that shape our lives is a first step in making effective efforts to change those forces.

SUMMARY

As American medicine has become increasingly specialized and reliant on advanced technology, large-scale organizations such as hospitals, insurance companies, health maintenance organizations, and medical industries have consolidated their power and economic interests. The corporatization of hospitals has changed the economic situation for patients and affected the autonomy of physicians and other health care professionals. Insurance companies and managed care corporations have become powerful agents in the health care system, creating regulations and controlling access to health services. In an array of poorly articulated programs, government agencies are also significant third-party payers and direct providers of health services. Medical industries, especially those researching and developing new pharmaceuticals and technologies, have substantial economic interests in health-related markets. Always a loosely regulated, relatively unplanned, laissez-faire arrangement, the American health system is now powerfully dominated by large for-profit industries.

This system has resulted in major problems of access and cost. The quality of care available under the system is mixed; much is outstanding, but much is terrible. Although the poor receive generally lower-quality medical care, spending lots of money on medical services does not guarantee good quality. Structural incentives, which are related to profitability, are responsible for both the achievements and failures of the American medical system. The problems of the American system clearly illustrate a key theme emphasized throughout this volume: Health and illness are socially produced, especially by structural features of power and stratification.

Appendix A
Bibliographic and
Internet Resources

Students launching research—whether a term paper project or a doctoral dissertation—in the sociology of health and illness face a bewildering mountain of information. The Internet has made entire books, data sets, and scholarly journals accessible to scholars. At the same time, however, the World Wide Web is full of misinformation, because the vast majority of sites are self-published and their content is unverifiable. Thus, you will get better references by narrowing your searches to:

- Indexes (electronic or print) of scholarly journals
- Catalogues of university libraries (available on-line)
- Government documents and statistics (on the Web and in print)
- Critically selected academically oriented Web sites and nongovernmental organization Web sites
- Web subject directories sponsored by academic institutions

This Appendix is a guide to getting the best research documentation from these resources. An annually updated version of this Appendix will be available on-line with links at http://www.trinity.edu/mmcguire.

Always start your preliminary search of resources early—as soon as you are clear about your research topic. In the preliminary search, you do not need to read the articles or books yet, but you do need to *identify potential information sources* and find out how to obtain them. Many databases have abstracts or additional catalogue information to help you weed out irrelevant references before you try to obtain them. If you start promptly, you will increase your chances of getting ample good references, even from remote libraries.

RECOMMENDED SCHOLARLY JOURNALS

Scholars rely primarily on refereed journals, because these journals are highly selective in what they publish. Each article has been screened for its scholarly merit by several professionals in that subdiscipline. Articles in scholarly journals are expected to be unbiased, documented by data and references to the scholarly literature, and based on sound research methods appropriate to that subdiscipline. Most of the following journals are indexed in both print and electronic indexes, such as *Social Sciences Abstracts*, *Sociological Abstracts*, *Academic Search Premier*, *MEDLINE*, *Contemporary Women's Issues* (in order of usefulness for subjects in this text). Some indexes are searchable on CD-ROM instead of on-line. Be sure to check the "search tips" to streamline your search process. Each index has somewhat different search terms and different ways to search for phrases and for "wild card" terms; some also have useful guides for narrowing or expanding your search. Do not waste your time on indexes (such as Infotrac) that include many popular periodicals and journals of opinion—sources that do not have refereed scholarly articles.

Do not limit your bibliography only to articles you can retrieve on-line, because very few university libraries can afford to make available on-line to their students, all years of all good journals. Expect to supplement your on-line literature search by finding print copies, either on the shelves of the university library or through interlibrary loan services. *Spend time with the relevant journals and books in a good university library,* because the research process is stimulated by serendipitous connections you can make there.

    I. Social science journals in health and illness
        Anthropology and Medicine
        Culture, Medicine, and Psychiatry
        Health: An Interdisciplinary Journal for the Social Study of Health, Illness, and Medicine
        International Journal of Health Services
        Journal of Health and Social Behavior
        Medical Anthropology Quarterly (new series)
        Qualitative Health Research
        Social Science & Medicine
        Sociology of Health and Illness: A Journal of Medical Sociology

    II. Sources on current issues, social policy, and health ethics
        Critical Public Health
        Disability Studies Quarterly
        Hastings Center Reports
        Health/PAC Bulletin
        Health Affairs
        Health, Risk & Society
        Journal of Health Care for the Poor
        Journal of Health Politics, Policy, and Law
        Journal of Immigrant Health
        Journal of Public Health Policy
        Milbank Quarterly
        Women and Health

    III. Medical and public health journals
        American Journal of Public Health
        Journal of Alternative and Complementary Medicine
        Journal of the American Medical Association
        Journal of American Women's Medical Association
        The Lancet
        Medical Care
        New England Journal of Medicine

ACADEMIC BOOKS

Books are less likely than journals to have the most current information because they take longer to write and are not published (or revised) frequently. Books do allow for more depth of coverage, however. Thus, they are particularly useful for getting a sense of the scope of an issue, for understanding complex interdisciplinary connections, and for thinking about interpretations of the data presented. For some topics, book sources become out-of-date rapidly, but others have enduring relevance. For example, a 1982 book on how social control and domination affect health may be relevant and highly useful in 2002, whereas a 1982 book on the social distribution of what is now called HIV/AIDS has probably been completely superseded by more current works.

The Bibliography of this text is a good place to start your research, because each source cited is listed there. Then, if an author cited in this text has particularly interesting ideas, do an "author search" in both book and journal search databases; it is likely that author has written further articles or books more recently. Check the references to books in bibliographies of good recent journal articles.

Also, use an electronic database search (keyword searches are usually best to start, but each good "hit" will give clickable subject headings, from which one can easily do a subject search as well). Unless your university library has limited collections of books, your university's catalogue is a good place to start an electronic search, because you can have ready access to the books in that catalogue. If you must rely on interlibrary loan for most of your book sources, try searching a good university library source, such as Harvard University's catalogue at http://hollisweb.harvard.edu.

For a more comprehensive search, you may sometimes want to try:

The Library of Congress at http://catalog.loc.gov
The British Library Public Catalogue at http://blpc.uk

The disadvantage to these enormous general catalogues is that they include too many non-scholarly books that are thus not appropriate for your research. If your literature search has already identified the relevant scholarly experts on the topic, then focus your use of the national public catalogues only on those authors.

STATISTICS AND RESEARCH REPORTS

Try to obtain the most current facts to support your assertions, especially if your topic is a rapidly changing or newly discovered issue. In addition to research data published in scholarly journals and books, the following are generally reliable sources[1] of data:

I. United States Government Sources
   U.S. Government statistics are now available on-line, as well as in print. Many university libraries hold print copies of important government documents, and each

---

[1] Even when using reliable sources, you should use data critically. For example, the U.S. Census Bureau publishes annual updates about incomes, and these data report both the range and the median incomes for each quintile (20 percent) of households, from the rich to the poor. Although these data are generally reliable, they are misleading because of how the incomes of the highest earners are measured. In order to promise anonymity, the Census reports the incomes of all households earning *over* $999,999 per year as earning *exactly* that sum. Thus, the mean income for the top quintile is completely inaccurate, because it does not include some incomes of many million dollars. Better government data are produced by the Congressional Budget Office (see Center on Budget and Policy Priorities for 2001).

region has a designated Federal Depository Library that holds copies of all Government Printing Office (GPO) documents. In preparing this text, we have consulted the following Web sites for rapid access to the most recent U.S. statistics:

Bureau of the Census—http://www.census.gov—includes Census 2000, *Current Population Reports, Current Population Survey, Statistical Abstract of the United States*

Bureau of Labor Statistics—http://www.bls.gov/

Center for Disease Control—http://www.cdc.gov/—includes National Center for Health Statistics, National Institute for Occupational Safety and Health, Health Topics (such as Women's Health, Minority Health, Chronic Disease Prevention)

Center for Medicare and Medicaid Services—http://www.cms.hhs.gov—new Web site for the Health Care Finance Administration (which covers Medicare, Medicaid, and S-CHIP); also includes annual reports, such as National Health Expenditures, and the *Health Care Finance Review*

Department of Health and Human Services—http://www.hhs.gov/—includes *Health United States, 2001* (pdf format), Health United States chartbooks (for example, 2001, on Urban and Rural Health; 1998, on Socioeconomic Status and Health), Initiative to Eliminate Racial and Ethnic Disparities in Health, Surgeon General's reports, as well as *Vital and Health Statistics Reports: Advance Data; Monthly Vital Statistics Report; Morbidity and Mortality Weekly Report; Vital Statistics of the United States*

Federal Interagency Forum on Aging-Related Statistics—www.agingstats.gov—annual status report, "Older Americans" (with seven health indicators)

Forum on Child and Family Statistics—http://www.childstats.gov—annual status report, "America's Children"

National Institutes of Health—www.nih.gov—includes

- National Center for Complementary and Alternative Medicine (www.nccam.nih.gov),
- National Center on Minority Health and Health Disparities (www.ncmhd.nih.gov),
- National Institute on Aging (www.nia.nih.gov), and
- National Library of Medicine (www.nlm.nih.gov).

II. International Sources, Country Profiles, and Other Governments' Statistics

Health statistics for most developed countries are comparable in quality, if not also quantity, to those of the United States, but their publication on the Web is variable. Comparative statistics and data about health-related issues in developing countries are locatable through an excellent cyber-portal, ELDIS (found at http://www.ids.ac.uk/eldis), maintained by the Institute of Development Studies in Sussex, England.

Canadian Institute of Health Information—www.cihi.ca

Organization for Economic Cooperation and Development—comparative data for developed countries—www.oecdwash.org/DATA/online.htm

United Nations includes

- United Nations Programme on HIV/AIDS—www.unaids.org,
- United Nations Development Program—www.undp.org.np—includes annual Human Development Report,
- United Nations Food and Agricultural Organization—www.fao.org, and
- United Nations International Children's Emergency Fund—www.unicef.org.

World Bank Group—www.worldbank.org—includes World Development Report (annual)

- Poverty Net (at www.worldbank.org/poverty/) includes country-by-country profiles on poverty rates, health, and other social indicators.

World Health Organization—www.who.int—includes

- Annual *World Health Report* (www.who.int/whr/),
- World Health Statistical Information Service (www.who.int/whosis/), and
- Women's Health and Development Programme (www.who.int/frh-whd/).

III. Research Organizations, Advocacy Groups, and Other Recommended Nongovernmental Agency Sources

Center for Public Policy Priorities—www.cppp.org

Center for Responsive Politics—www.opensecrets.org

Center on Budget and Policy Priorities—www.cbpp.org

Center on Hunger, Poverty and Nutrition Policy, Tufts University—http://hunger.tufts.edu/us.html

Doctors Without Borders—www.doctorswithoutborders.org—the U.S. Web site of Médecins Sans Frontières)—www.msf.org—Nobel prize-winning NGO

Families USA—www.familiesusa.org—advocacy group

Hunger Web—http://www.brown.edu/Departments/World_Hunger_Program—data and links by The World Hunger Program of the Watson Institute of International Studies at Brown University

Kaiser Family Foundation—www.kff.org—foundation that supports research and pilot projects on health care

Rand Corporation—www.rand.org—a policy research organization with many studies on health care issues

Schneider Institute for Health Policy—www.sihp.brandeis.edu—university policy institute

Appendix B
Visual Resources

We have found visual resources, such as films and videos, to be invaluable in teaching the sociology of health and illness. New recommendations are highlighted with an asterisk (*). A more extensive list of reviewed visual resources for teaching will be posted and updated annually at http://www.trinity.edu/mmcguire.

RECOMMENDED FOR USE WITH CHAPTERS 1–5

The Angry Heart.* Fanlight Productions, 2001, 57 minutes. A compelling illustration of how racism and discrimination contribute to the disproportionate rate of heart disease among African Americans.

The Brain. WNET, 1984, each episode 60 minutes. "Stress and Emotion" describes the physiology of stress and coping.

Breath Taken.* Fanlight Productions, 1990, 33 minutes. Documentary on environmental and occupational contamination from asbestos, as well as the toll of sickness and death due to asbestos-related diseases.

Clockwork. California Newsreel, 1982, 25 minutes. Work organization and time, from early Taylorism to contemporary computer-assisted regulation.

Ending Hunger in the Garden State: Recommendations and Reform. New Jersey Commission on Hunger, 1987, 35 minutes. Hunger in one of the wealthiest states.

Famine Within. Direct Cinema, Ltd., 1990, 50 minutes. Women, food, body image, and eating disorders.

Life: A Series about Globalization.* Bullfrog Films, 2000, each episode 24 minutes. A compelling portrayal of the human toll of a globalized economy. Particularly relevant: "From Docklands to Dhaka" shows a British doctor who works London's poverty-stricken Docklands district as he visits health workers in Dhaka, Bangladesh, a desperately poor country; "India Inhales," about the effects of global tobacco companies' advertising campaigns in developing countries; "The Cost of Living," about the struggle to make antiretroviral drugs for HIV/AIDS accessible to people of developing countries; "Lost Generations," on maternal poverty and ill health, leading to low-birth-weight babies with ill health.

Plagued: A Series on Disease and Society. Film Australia (distributed by Filmakers Library), 1994, four 52-minute episodes. A historical and cross-cultural analysis of plagues and new diseases. Part 4: AIDS and syphilis in a comparative perspective.

The Politics of Food. Yorkshire Television, 1988, two hours. Political sources of hunger.

Song of the Canary. New Day Films, 1978, 57 minutes. Occupational health issues.

Trade Secrets.* PBS, 2001, 150 minutes. Bill Moyers probes the issue of chemical hazards in the workplace and industries' concealment of these dangers for their workers.

RECOMMENDED FOR USE WITH CHAPTERS 6–9

Community Voices: Exploring Cross-Cultural Care through Cancer.* Fanlight Productions, 2001, 69 minutes. Explores how cultural differences (such as language and communication styles, religion and cultural values, ethnic patterns, and ideas about health and illness) affect health and health care services.

The Deadly Deception: The Tuskegee Study of Untreated Syphilis in the Negro Male. WGBH/Films for the Humanities and Sciences, 1993, 56 minutes. Ethically questionable biomedical research.

Healing and the Mind. PBS/Ambrose Video, 1993. Five-part series. Bill Moyers explores Chinese healing approaches, research on mind-body connections, nonmedical therapies.

Inventing Reality. PBS/Millennium series, #8, 1992, 60 minutes. Compares nonbiomedical healing systems.

Medicine at the Crossroads. WNET and BBE Productions, 1993. Relevant episodes: "The Code of Silence," on doctor-patient communication; and "Life Support," on the ethics of death and aging in various countries.

The Mind. WNET, 1988. Relevant episodes: "Aging" and "Pain and Healing."

On Our Own Terms.* PBS/Films for the Humanities & Sciences, 2000, four-part series, each episode nearly 90 minutes. Bill Moyers shows extraordinary empathy and profound insight in this examination of death and dying in America. Episodes 2 (on hospice and other forms of alternative settings for dying) and 4 (on changing the health system to improve end-of-life care) are particularly relevant.

The Skin Horse. Central Independent Television PIC, 1983. Sexuality and disability.

To Taste a Hundred Herbs. New Day Films, 1986, 58 minutes. Traditional Chinese medicine, religion, Chinese village life, and the role of the doctor.

Titticut Follies. Zipporah Films, 1967, 16 mm., 89 minutes, black and white. Frederick Wiseman's controversial cinéma verité documentary (no narration) about a hospital for the criminally insane.

When Billy Broke His Head and Other Tales of Wonder. Fanlight Productions, 1994, 57 minutes. Narrated/directed by Billy Golfus who was brain-injured, this video looks at disabilities, and issues of accessibility and social inclusion.

Without Pity.* HBO/Films for the Humanities and Sciences, 1996, 56 minutes. Narrated by Christopher Reeve, this fine documentary humanizes people with disabilities and emphasizes their resilient efforts to live full, productive lives.

RECOMMENDED FOR USE WITH CHAPTERS 10–12

Borderline Medicine. Baxley Media, 1991, 58 minutes. Canadian National Health Insurance as a model for the United States.

Can't Afford to Grow Old. Filmakers Library, 1990, 55 minutes. Social policy issues surrounding long-term care, Medicare and Medicaid, and a medicalized old age and death.

Critical Condition.* (with Hedrick Smith). SCET/Films for the Humanities and Sciences, 2000, four 50-minute episodes. A series addressing the crisis in the U.S. health care system. The fourth episode on "The Uninsured" is the strongest.

Doctors and Dollars. PBS, 1993, 57 minutes. Depicts the issues involved in doctors' self-referral and conflicts of interest.

Health Care Rationing. PBS, 1991, 58 minutes. Oregon's efforts to devise a fair system for rationing health care for the poor compared with the situation of Chicago's de facto system of rationing according to who can pay.

Nurses: Code Blue.* Films for the Humanities & Sciences, 2001, two episodes, each 29 minutes. The nursing shortage and dissatisfaction with working conditions in the profession.

Pharmaceuticals: For Export Only. Richter Productions, English and Spanish editions, 57 minutes. Pharmaceuticals banned or highly restricted in the United States are still produced here for export to Third World countries, where they harm public health.

Prescriptions for Profit. PBS, 1989, 60 minutes. Questions the marketing practices of the pharmaceutical industry.

Setting Limits. Medical University of South Carolina, 1988, 47 minutes. Ethicist Daniel Callahan discusses the proper ends of medicine, appropriate medical care for the aged and dying.

Who Lives, Who Dies. Public Policy Productions, 1987, 60 minutes. The U.S. health care crisis, issues of health care spending, equity, rationing.

Appendix C
Bibliography

ABEL, EMILY K.
    1991   *Who Cares for the Elderly? Public Policy and the Experiences of Adult Daughters.*
                Philadelphia: Temple University Press.

ABLON, JOAN
    1986   "Reactions of Samoan burn patients and families to severe burns," pp. 163–180
                in C. Currer and M. Stacey, eds., *Concepts of Health, Illness and Disease.*
                Leamington Spa, England: Berg.

ABRAHAM, JOHN
    1995   *Science, Politics and the Pharmaceutical Industry: Controversy and Bias in Drug Regulation.*
                London: UCL Press.

ADAMS, MIRIAM E.
    1995   "Kidney transplantation," pp. 79–91 in H. S. Frazier and F. Mosteller, eds.,
                Medicine Worth Paying For: Assessing Medical Innovations. Cambridge, MA: Harvard
                University Press.

ADAMS, ORVILL
    1993   "Understanding the health care system that works," pp. 113–141 in A. Bennett
                and O. Adams, eds., *Looking North for Health: What We Can Learn from Canada's
                Health Care System.* San Francisco: Jossey-Bass.

ADLER, NANCY, THOMAS BOYCE, MARGARET A. CHESNEY, SHELDON COHEN, SUSAN
FOLKMAN, ROBERT L. KAHN, and S. LEONARD SYME
    1999   "Socioeconomic status and health: The challenge of the gradient," pp. 181–200
                in J. Mann, S. Gruskin, M. A. Grodin, and G. J. Annas, eds., *Health and Human
                Rights.* New York: Routledge.

AIKEN, LINDA H., JULIE SOCHALSKI, AND GERARD F. ANDERSON
    1996   "Downsizing the hospital nursing workforce," *Health Affairs* 15(4): 88–92.

ÅKERSTEDT, TORBJÖRN
    1990   "Psychological and psychophysiological effects of shift work," *Scandinavian
                Journal of Work, Environment and Health* 16 (supplement): 67–73.

AKULA, JOHN L.
    1997   "Insolvency risk in health carriers: Innovation, competition, and public protec-
                tion," *Health Affairs* 16(1): 9–33.

ALBRECHT, GARY L., DAVID SLOBODKIN, AND ROBERT J. RYDMAN
    1996   "The role of emergency departments in American health care," *Research in the
                Sociology of Health Care* 13B: 289–316.

ALEXANDER, JACQUI
    1988   "The ideological construction of risk: An analysis of corporate health pro-
                grams in the 1980s," *Social Science and Medicine* 26(5): 559–567.

ALEXANDER, LINDA
  1982   "Illness maintenance and the new American sick role," pp. 351–367 in N. J. Chrisman and T. W. Maretzki, eds., *Clinically Applied Anthropology*. Dordrecht, Netherlands: D. Reidel.

ALTMAN, LAWRENCE K.
  1988   "U.S. moves to improve death certificate," *New York Times*, October 18.
  1995   "As TB surges, drug producers face criticism," *New York Times*, September 18.
  1997a "Drug firm, relenting, allows unflattering study to appear," *New York Times*, April 16.
  1997b "Experts see bias in drug data," *New York Times*, April 29.
  1999   "Inside medical journals, a rising quest for profits," *New York Times*, August 24.
  2001   "Swift rise seen in H.I.V. cases for gay blacks," *New York Times*, June 1.

ALTMAN, LAWRENCE K., AND ELISABETH ROSENTHAL
  1990   "Changes in medicine bring pain to healing profession," *New York Times*, February 18.

AMERICAN CANCER SOCIETY
  2001   "Cigarette use among teens inches downward," November 2001, retrieved from the World Wide Web at www.cancer.org on 1 April, 2002.

AMERICAN PSYCHIATRIC ASSOCIATION
  1987   *Diagnostic and Statistical Manual of Mental Disorders* (3rd ed., rev.). Washington, DC: American Psychiatric Association.

ANDERSON, GERARD F., AND JEAN-PIERRE POULLIER
  1999   "Health spending, access, and outcomes: Trends in industrialized countries," *Health Affairs* 18(3): 178–192.

ANDERSON, RONALD, MEEI-SHIA CHEN, LU ANNE ADAY, AND LLEWELLYN CORNELIUS
  1987   "Health status and medical care utilization," *Health Affairs* 6(1): 136–156.

ANDREWS, AHMED, AND NICK JEWSON
  1993   "Ethnicity and infant deaths: The implications of recent statistical evidence for materialist explanations," *Sociology of Health and Illness* 15(2): 137–156.

ANGEL, RONALD, AND PEGGY THOITS
  1987   "The impact of culture on the cognitive structure of illness," *Culture, Medicine, and Psychiatry* 11(4): 465–494.

ANGIER, NATALIE
  1997   "In a culture of hysterectomies, many question their necessity," *New York Times*, February 17.

ANSPACH, RENEE
  1988   "Notes on the sociology of medical discourse: The language of case presentation," *Journal of Health and Social Behavior* 29: 357–375.
  1993   *Deciding Who Lives: Fateful Choices in the Intensive-Care Nursery*. Berkeley: University of California Press.

ANTONOVSKY, AARON
  1979   *Health, Stress and Coping*. San Francisco: Jossey-Bass.
  1984   "The sense of coherence as a determinant of health," *Advances* 1(3): 37–50.
  1987   *Unraveling the Mystery of Health: How People Manage Stress and Stay Well*. San Francisco: Jossey-Bass.
  1990   "Personality and health: Testing the sense of coherence model," pp. 155–177 in H. S. Friedman, ed., *Personality and Disease*. New York: Wiley.

ARAGHI, FARSHAD
    2000   "The great global enclosure of our times: Peasants and the agrarian question at the end of the twentieth century," pp. 145–160 in F. Magdoff, J. B. Fostern, and F. H. Buttel, eds., *Hungry for Profit*. New York: Monthly Review Press.

ARIÈS, PHILIPPE
    1974   *Western Attitudes Toward Death: From the Middle Ages to the Present*. Baltimore: Johns Hopkins University Press.

ARMSTRONG, DAVID
    1983   *Political Anatomy of the Body: Medical Knowledge in Britain in the Twentieth Century*. Cambridge, England: Cambridge University Press.

ARNO, PETER S., KAREN BONUCK, AND MICHAEL DAVIS
    1995   "Rare diseases, drug development, and AIDS: The impact of the Orphan Drug Act," *The Milbank Quarterly* 73(2): 231–251.

ARNO, PETER S., C. LEVINE, AND M. M. MEMMOTT
    1999   "The economic value of informal caregiving," *Health Affairs* 18(2): 182–188.

ARONOWITZ, ROBERT A.
    1991   "Lyme disease: The social construction of a new disease and its social consequences," *The Milbank Quarterly* 69(1): 79–112.

ASBURY, CAROLYN H.
    1981   "Medical drugs of limited commercial interest: Profit alone is a bitter pill," *International Journal of Health Services* 11(3): 451–462.

ASHTON, HEATHER
    1991   "Psychotropic drug prescribing for women," *British Journal of Psychiatry* 158(S10): 30–35.

ASSOCIATED PRESS
    2000   "Study: Medical bills bankrupting Americans," news-service posting, April 26.

ATEKA, GIVENS K.
    2001   "Factors in HIV/AIDS transmission in Sub-Saharan Africa," *Bulletin of the World Health Organization* 79(12), retrieved from the World Wide Web at www.who.int on 30 January, 2002.

ATKINSON, PAUL
    1978   "From honey to vinegar: Lévi-Strauss in Vermont," pp. 168–188 in P. Morley and R. Wallis, eds., *Culture and Curing*. Pittsburgh, PA: University of Pittsburgh Press.
    1999   "Medical discourse, evidentiality and the construction of professional responsibility," pp. 75–107 in S. Sarangi and C. Roberts, eds., *Talk, Work and Institutional Order: Discourse in Medical, Mediation and Management Settings*. New York: Mouton de Gruyter.

ATKINSON, THOMAS, RAMSAY LIEM, AND JOAN LIEM
    1986   "The social costs of unemployment: Implications for social support," *Journal of Health and Social Behavior* 27: 317–331.

ATTIE, ILANA, AND J. BROOKS-GUNN
    1987   "Weight concerns as chronic stressors in women," pp. 218–254 in R. Barnett, L. Biener, and G. K. Baruch, eds., *Gender and Stress*. New York: Free Press.

AVORN, JERRY
    1995   "Medication use and the elderly," *Health Affairs* 14(1): 276–287.

BACK, AARON
    1981   *Occupational Stress: The Inside Story*. Oakland, CA: Institute for Labor and Mental Health.

BAER, HANS A.
  1992   "The potential rejuvenation of American naturopathy as a consequence of the holistic health movement," *Medical Anthropology* 13: 369–383.
BAER, HANS A., MERRILL SINGER, AND IDA SUSSER
  1997   *Medical Anthropology and the World System.* Westport, CT: Bergin and Garvey.
BAER, ROBERTA D., LAUREN CLARK, AND CAROLINE PETERSON
  1998   "Folk illnesses," pp. 183–202 in S. Loue, ed., *Handbook of Immigrant Health.* New York: Plenum.
BAIRD, VANESSA
  1992   "Difference and defiance," *New Internationalist* 233 (July): 4–7.
BAKAL, DONALD A.
  1979   *Psychology and Medicine.* New York: Springer.
BAKER, DEAN
  1981   "The use and health consequences of shift work," pp. 107–122 in V. Navarro and D. M. Berman, eds., *Health and Work Under Capitalism: An International Perspective.* Farmingdale, NY: Baywood.
BAKER, SUSAN B., STEPHEN TERET, AND ERICH M. DAUB
  1987   "Injuries," pp. 177–206 in S. R. Levine and A. Lilienfeld, eds., *Epidemiology and Health Policy.* New York: Tavistock.
BALE, ANTHONY
  1990   "Women's toxic experience," pp. 411–439 in R. D. Apple, ed., *Women, Health, and Medicine in America: A Historical Handbook.* New York: Garland.
BANKS, CAROLINE GILES
  1992   "'Culture' in culture-bound syndromes: The case of anorexia nervosa," *Social Science and Medicine* 34(8): 867–884.
BANTA, H. DAVID
  1995   "Technology assessment in health care," pp. 401–421 in A. R. Kovner, ed., *Jonas's Health Care Delivery in the United States.* New York: Springer.
BARER, MORRIS L.
  1995   "So near, and yet so far: A Canadian perspective on U.S. health care reform," *Journal of Health Politics, Policy and Law* 20(2): 463–476.
BARKER, K. K.
  1998   "A ship upon a stormy sea: The medicalization of pregnancy," *Social Science and Medicine* 47(8): 1067–1076.
BARKER-BENFIELD, BEN
  1975   "Sexual surgery in late nineteenth-century America," *International Journal of Health Services* 5(2): 279–298.
BARNES, LINDA L.
  1998   "The psychologizing of Chinese healing practices in the United States," *Culture, Medicine and Psychiatry* 22(4): 413–443.
BARNOUW, ERIK
  1978   *The Sponsor: Notes on a Modern Potentate.* New York: Oxford University Press.
BARRINGER, FELICITY
  1992   "Among elderly, men's prospects are the brighter," *New York Times,* November 10.
  1993   "Pride in a soundless world: Deaf oppose a hearing aid," *New York Times,* May 16.
BARTON, L., ED.
  1996   *Disability and Society.* London: Longman.
BARTROP, R. W., L. LAZARUS, L. LUCKHURST, L. KILOH, AND R. PENNY
  1977   "Depressed lymphocyte function after bereavement," *Lancet* 1(8,016): 834–836.

BASSET, MARY T., AND MARVELLOUS MHLOY
  2001   "Women and AIDS in Zimbabwe: The making of an epidemic," pp. 76–87 in
          D. A. Matcha, ed., *Readings in Medical Sociology*. Boston: Allyn and Bacon.
BASSETT, KEN L., N. IYER, AND A. KAZANJIAN
  2000   "Defensive medicine during hospital obstetrical care: A by-product of the
          technological age," *Social Science and Medicine* 51(4): 523–537.
BATES, MARYANN S.
  1987   "Ethnicity and pain: A biocultural model," *Social Science and Medicine* 24(1):
          47–50.
BAXBY, DERRICK
  1995   "Myths in medicine: Surveillance-containment is key to eradication of
          smallpox," *British Medical Journal* 310(6971): 62.
BEARAK, BARRY
  2001   "U.S. raids kill 4 U.N. aides outside Kabul," *New York Times,* October 10.
BECKER, E. LOVELL
  1986   *International Dictionary of Medicine and Biology*. New York: Wiley.
BECKER, GAY, AND ROBERT D. NACHTIGALL
  1992   "Eager for medicalisation: The social production of infertility as a disease,"
          Sociology of Health and Illness 14(4): 456–471.
BECKER, HOWARD
  1963   *Outsiders: Studies in the Sociology of Deviance*. New York: Free Press.
  1967   "History, culture, and subjective experience: An exploration of the social
          bases of drug-induced experiences," *Journal of Health and Social Behavior* 8(3):
          163–176.
BECKMAN, HOWARD, AND R. M. FRANKL
  1984   "The effects of physician's behavior on the collection of data," *Annals of Internal
          Medicine* 101(5): 692–696.
BEDELL, S. E., S. JABBOUR, R. GOLDBERG, H. GLASER, S. GOBBLE, Y. YOUNG-XU, T. B.
GRABOYS, AND S. RAVID
  2000   "Discrepancies in the use of medications–Their extent and predictors in an
          out-patient practice," *Archives of Internal Medicine* 160(14): 2129–2134.
BEECHER, HENRY K.
  1956   "Relationship of the significance of wound to the pain experience," *Journal of
          the American Medical Association* 161: 1604–1613.
  1959   *Measurement of Subjective Responses: Quantitative Effects of Drugs*. New York: Oxford
          University Press.
BEGLEY, SHARON
  2001   "Cellular divide," *Newsweek,* July 9: 23–27.
BELL, ROBERT
  1992   *Impure Science: Fraud, Compromise and Political Influence in Scientific Research*. New
          York: Wiley.
BELL, SUSAN E.
  1986   "A new model of medical technology development: A case study of DES,"
          Research in the Sociology of Health Care 4: 1–32.
  1990   "Changing ideas: The medicalization of menopause," pp. 43–63 in R.
          Formanek, ed., *The Meanings of Menopause: Historical, Medical and Clinical
          Perspectives*. Hillsdale, NJ: The Analytic Press.
  1994   "From local to global: Resolving uncertainty about the safety of DES in
          menopause," *Research in Sociology of Health Care* 11: 41–56.

BELLABY, PAUL
   1999   *Sick from Work: The Body in Employment.* Aldershot, England: Ashgate.
BENCOMO, CHRISTOPHER, CARLOS TREJO, AND DAVID CALKINS
   1995   "Physicians," pp. 12–39 in D. Calkins, R. J. Fernandopulle, and B. S. Marino, eds., *Health Care Policy.* Cambridge, MA: Blackwell Science.
BENDELOW, GILLIAN A.
   1993   "Pain perceptions, emotions and gender," *Sociology of Health and Illness* 15(3): 273–294.
BENDELOW, GILLIAN A., AND SIMON J. WILLIAMS
   1995   "Transcending the dualisms: Towards a sociology of pain," *Sociology of Health and Illness* 17(2): 139–165.
BENNEFIELD, ROBERT L.
   1998   "Dynamics of economic well being: Health insurance 1993–1995, who loses coverage and for how long?" *Current Population Reports* (August): 70–64.
BERESFORD, ERIC B.
   1991   "Uncertainty and the shaping of medical decisions," *Hastings Center Report* (July–August): 6–11.
BERG, MARC
   1996   "Practices of reading and writing: The constitutive role of the patient record in medical work," *Sociology of Health & Illness* 18(4): 499–524.
BERGER, PETER
   1967   *The Sacred Canopy: Elements of a Sociological Theory of Religion.* Garden City, NY: Doubleday.
BERGER, PETER, AND THOMAS LUCKMANN
   1967   *The Social Construction of Reality.* Garden City, NY: Doubleday.
BERKI, SYLVESTER E.
   1986   "A look at catastrophic medical expenses and the poor," *Health Affairs* 5(4): 138–145.
BERKMAN, LISA F., AND THOMAS GLASS
   2000   "Social integration, social networks, social support, and health," pp. 137–173 in L. F. Berkman and I. Kawachi, eds., *Social Epidemiology.* New York: Oxford University Press.
BERKMAN, LISA F., THOMAS GLASS, I. BRISSETTE, AND T. E. SEEMAN
   2000   "From social integration to health: Durkheim in the new millennium," *Social Science and Medicine* 51(6): 843–857.
BERKMAN, LISA F., AND ICHIRO KAWACHI
   2000   "A historical framework for social epidemiology," pp. 3–12 in L. F. Berkman and I. Kawachi, eds., *Social Epidemiology.* New York: Oxford University Press.
BERKMAN, LISA F., AND S. LEONARD SYME
   1979   "Social networks, host resistance, and mortality: A nine-year follow-up study of Alameda County residents," *American Journal of Epidemiology* 109: 186–204.
BERLANT, JEFFREY L.
   1975   *Profession and Monopoly: A Study of Medicine in Great Britain and the United States.* Berkeley: University of California Press.
BERLINER, HOWARD S.
   1975   "A larger perspective on the Flexner Report," *International Journal of Health Services* 5(4): 573–592.
   1976   "Starr wars," *International Journal of Health Services* 13(4): 671–675.

BERMAN, DANIEL M.
1978   *Death on the Job: Occupational Health and Safety Struggles in the United States.*
New York: Monthly Review Press.

BERNSTEIN, SHARON
1998   "Inquiry into childbirth practices is expanded," *Los Angeles Times,* June 17.
2001a   "Few resources are available for massive disaster," *Los Angeles Times,*
November 19.
2001b   "Soaring prices curb availability of tetanus vaccine," *Los Angeles Times,* March 13.

BETTLEHEIM, ADRIEL
1999   "Do medications cost too much and are they safe?" *Congressional Quarterly
Researcher* 9 (September): 753–770.

BIELIAUSKAS, LINAS
1982   *Stress and Its Relationship to Health and Illness.* Boulder, CO: Westview.

BIRD, CHLOE I.
1996   "An analysis of gender differences in income among dentists, physicians, and
veterinarians in 1987," *Research in the Sociology of Health Care* 13A: 31–61.

BIRD, CHLOE I., AND ALLEN M. FREMONT
1991   "Gender, time use, and health," *Journal of Health and Social Behavior* 32(2):
114–129.

BIRD, CHLOE E., AND PATRICIA P. RIEKER
1999   "Gender matters: An integrated model for understanding men's and women's
health," *Social Science and Medicine* 48(6): 745–755.

BIRKE, LYNDA
1986   *Women, Feminism and Biology: The Feminist Challenge.* New York: Methuen.

BLACK, DOUGLAS
1980   *Inequalities in Health: Report of a Research Working Group.* London: Department of
Health and Social Services.

BLAIR, ALAN
1993   "Social class and the contextualization of illness experience," pp. 27–48 in
A. Radley, ed., *Worlds of Illness.* New York: Routledge.

BLANE, DAVID
1986   "Inequality and social class," pp. 119–124 in D. L. Patrick and G. Scambler,
eds., *Sociology as Applied to Medicine.* London: Bailliere Tindall.

BLAXTER, MILDRED
1983   "The causes of disease: Women talking," *Social Science and Medicine* 17: 59–69.
1990   *Health and Lifestyles.* New York: Tavistock/Routledge.
1993   "Why do the victims blame themselves?" pp. 124–142 in A. Radley, ed., *Worlds
of Illness.* New York: Routledge.
2000   "Class, time and biography," pp. 27–50 in S. J. Williams, J. Gabe, and
M. Calnan, eds., *Health Medicine and Society.* London: Routledge.

BLAXTER, MILDRED, AND ELIZABETH PATERSON
1982   *Mothers and Daughters: A Three-Generational Study of Health Attitudes and Behavior.*
London: Heinemann.

BLENDON, ROBERT J., KAREN DONELAN, ROBERT LEITMAN, ARNOLD EPSTEIN, JOEL
CANTOR, ALAN COHEN, IAN MORRISON, THOMAS MOLONEY, CHRISTIAN KOECK, AND
SAMUEL LEVITT
1993   "Physician perspectives on caring for patients in the United States, Canada,
and West Germany," *New England Journal of Medicine* 328(14): 1011–1016.

BLENDON, ROBERT J., AND MINAH KIM
    2001   "When it comes to health policy, Americans are not British," *Harvard Health Policy Review* 2(1), retrieved from the World Wide Web at http://hcs.harvard. edu/~epihc/currentissue/spring2001/blendon.html on 21 March, 2002.

BLOOR, MICHAEL
    1976   "Bishop Berkeley and the adenotonsillectomy enigma: An exploration of variation in the social construction of medical disposals," *Sociology: The Journal of the British Sociological Association* 10(1): 43–61.
    1991   "A minor office: The variable and socially constructed character of death certification in a Scottish city," *Journal of Health and Social Behavior* 32(3): 273–287.
    1995   *The Sociology of HIV Transmission.* Thousand Oaks, CA: Sage.

BLOOR, MICHAEL, M. SAMPHIER, AND L. PRIOR
    1987   "Artefact explanations of inequalities in health: An assessment of the evidence," *Sociology of Health and Illness* 9(3): 231–263.

BODENHEIMER, THOMAS, AND KEVIN GRUMBACH
    1997   "Paying for health care," pp. 273–281 in P. Conrad, ed., *The Sociology of Health and Illness.* New York: St. Martin's Press.

BOGIN, MEG
    1982   *The Path to Pain Control.* Boston: Houghton Mifflin.

BOHUS, B., J. M. KOOLHAAS, AND S. M. KORTE
    1991   "Psychosocial stress, anxiety and depression: Physiological and neuroendocrine correlates in animal models," pp. 120–138 in A. R. Genazzani, G. Nappi, F. Petraglia, and E. Martignoni, eds., *Stress and Related Disorders: From Adaptation to Dysfunction.* Park Ridge, NJ: Parthenon.

BOLOGH, ROSLYN
    1981   "Grounding the alienation of self and body: A critical, phenomenological analysis of the patient in western medicine," *Sociology of Health and Illness* 3(2): 188–206.

BOND, PATRICK, AND ROBERT WEISSMAN
    1997   "The costs of mergers and acquisitions in the U.S. health care sector," *International Journal of Health Services* 27(1): 77–87.

BOOKCHIN, MURRAY
    1962   *Our Synthetic Environment.* New York: Harper & Row.

BOOKER, SALIH, AND WILLIAM MINTER
    2001   "Global apartheid," *The Nation,* July 9: 11–17.

BORDO, SUSAN
    1990   "Reading the slender body," pp. 83–112 in M. Jacobus, E. F. Keller, and S. Shuttleworth, eds., *Body/Politics: Women and the Discourses of Science.* New York: Routledge.
    1993   *Unbearable Weight: Feminism, Western Culture, and the Body.* Berkeley: University of California Press.

BOSTON WOMEN'S HEALTH COLLECTIVE
    1998   *Our Bodies, Our Selves for the New Century* (rev. ed.). New York: Simon & Schuster.

BOTKIN, DANIEL B., AND EDWARD A. KELLER
    1982   *Environmental Studies.* Columbus, OH: Charles E. Merrill.

BOWLES, CHERYL L.
    1990   "The menopausal experience: Sociocultural influences and theoretical models," pp. 157–175 in R. Formanek, *The Meanings of Menopause: Historical, Medical and Clinical Perspectives.* Hillsdale, NJ: Analytic Press.

BRADDOCK, CLARENCE H., KELLY A. EDWARDS, NICOLE M. HASENBERG, TRACY L. LAIDLEY, AND WENDY LEVINSON
  1999 "Informed decision-making in outpatient practice," *Journal of the American Medical Association* 282(24): 2313–2321.

BRANNON, ROBERT L.
  1994 *Intensifying Care: The Hospital Industry, Professionalization, and the Reorganization of the Nursing Labor Process.* Amityville, NY: Baywood.
  1996 "Restructuring hospital nursing: Reversing the trend toward a professional work force," *International Journal of Health Services* 26(4): 643–654.

BRAUDEL, FERNAND
  1973 *Capitalism and Material Life: 1400–1800.* New York: Harper & Row.

BRAVERMAN, HARRY
  1974 *Labor and Monopoly Capital.* New York: Monthly Review Press.

BRENNAN, TROYEN A., LUCIAN L. LEAPE, NAN M. LAIRD, LIESI HEBERT, A. RUSSELL LOCALIO, ANN G. LAWTHERS, JOS. P. NEWHOUSE, PAUL C. WILDER, AND HOWARD LIBIT
  1991 "Incidence of adverse events and negligence in hospitalized patients–Results of the Harvard Medical Practice Study I," *New England Journal of Medicine* 324(6): 370–376.

BRENNER, JOEL, JENNIFER ROSS, JANIE SIMMONS, AND SARAH ZAIDI
  2000 "Neoliberal trade and investment and the health of *maquiladora* workers on the U.S.-Mexico border," pp. 261–290 in J. Y. Kim et al., eds., *Dying for Growth: Global Inequality and the Health of the Poor.* Monroe, ME: Common Courage Press.

BRITISH MEDICAL JOURNAL
  1996 "Complementary medicine is booming worldwide," 313: 131–133.

BRODEUR, PAUL
  1974 *Expendable Americans.* New York: Viking.

BRODY, ELAINE M.
  1994 "Women as unpaid caregivers: The price they pay," pp. 67–86 in E. Friedman, *An Unfinished Revolution: Women and Health Care in America.* New York: United Hospital Fund.

BRODY, HOWARD
  1992 *The Healer's Power.* New Haven, CN: Yale University Press.

BRODY, JANE E.
  1975 "Physicians' views unchanged on use of estrogen therapy," *New York Times,* December 5.
  1983 "Research lifts blame from many of the obese," *New York Times,* March 24.
  1995 "Despite reductions in exposure, lead remains a danger to children," *New York Times,* March 21.
  1997 "Prenatal exposure to DES can also hurt men, and they should be vigilant," *New York Times,* July 30.
  2001 "A price to pay as autopsies lose favor," *New York Times,* January 9.

BROOKER, ANN-SYLVIA, AND JOAN M. EAKIN
  2001 "Gender, class, work-related stress and health: Toward a power-centered approach," *Journal of Community and Applied Social Psychology* 11: 97–109.

BROOM, DOROTHY H., AND ROSLYN V. WOODWARD
  1996 "Medicalisation reconsidered: Toward a collaborative approach to care," *Sociology of Health and Illness* 18(3): 357–378.

BROWN, CAROL A.
1978   "The division of laborers: Allied health professions," pp. 73–82 in S. Wolfe, ed., *Organization of Health Workers and Labor Conflict.* Farmingdale, NY: Baywood.
1983   "Women workers in the health service industry," pp. 105–116 in E. Fee, ed., *Women and Health: The Politics of Sex in Medicine.* Farmingdale, NY: Baywood.

BROWN, E. RICHARD
1979   *Rockefeller Medicine Men: Medicine and Capitalism in America.* Berkeley: University of California Press.

BROWN, KAREN MCCARTHY
1991   *Mama Lola: A Vodou Priestess in Brooklyn.* Berkeley: University of California Press.

BROWN, LEIGH PATRICIA
1988   "Designs take heed of human frailty," *New York Times,* April 14.

BROWN, PETER J., AND MARCIA C. INHORN
1990   "Disease, ecology and human behavior," pp. 187–214 in T. M. Johnson and C. F. Sargent, eds., *Medical Anthropology: A Handbook of Theory and Method.* New York: Greenwood.

BROWN, PHIL
1995a   "Naming and framing: The social construction of diagnosis and illness," *Journal of Health and Social Behavior* 33: 267–281.
1995b   "Popular epidemiology, toxic waste and social movements," pp. 91–112 in J. Gabe, ed., *Medicine, Health and Risk.* Oxford, England: Blackwell.
2000a   "Environment and health," pp. 143–158 in C. E. Bird, P. Conrad, and A. M. Fremont, eds., *Handbook of Medical Sociology.* Upper Saddle River, NJ: Prentice-Hall.
2000b   "Popular epidemiology and toxic waste contamination," pp. 46–71 in S. Kroll-Smith, P. Brown, and V. J. Gunter, eds., *Illness and the Environment: A Reader in Contested Medicine.* New York: New York University Press.

BROWN, PHIL, AND STEVEN C. FUNK
1986   "Tardive dyskinesia: Barriers to the professional recognition of an iatrogenic disease," *Journal of Health and Social Behavior* 27: 116–132.

BROWN, PHIL, AND JUDITH K. KELLEY
2000   "Physicians' knowledge, attitudes and practice regarding environmental health hazards," pp. 46–71 in S. Kroll-Smith, P. Brown, and V. J. Gunter, eds., *Illness and the Environment: A Reader in Contested Medicine.* New York: New York University Press.

BROWN, PHIL, AND EDWIN J. MIKKELSEN
1990   *No Safe Place: Toxic Waste, Leukemia and Community Action.* Berkeley: University of California Press.

BRUMBERG, JOAN
1988   *Fasting Girls: The Emergence of Anorexia Nervosa as a Modern Disease.* Cambridge, MA: Harvard University Press.

BRUNNER, ERIC
1996   "The social and biological basis of cardiovascular disease in office workers," pp. 272–299 in G. Blane, E. Brunner and E. Wilkinson, eds., *Health and Social Organization.* London: Routledge.

BRZUZY, STEPHANIE
1997   "Deconstructing disability: The impact of definition," *Journal of Poverty* 1(1): 81–91.

BUDD, SUSAN, AND URSULA SHARMA, EDS.
1994   *The Healing Bond: The Patient-Practitioner Relationship and Therapeutic Responsibility.* New York: Routledge.

BULLINGER, MONIKA
1990   "Environmental stress: Effect of air pollution on mood, neuropsychological function and physical style," pp. 244–250 in S. P. Allegra and A. Oliverio, eds., *Psychobiology of Stress.* Boston: Kluwer Academic.

BUNKER, JOHN P., AND HOWARD S. FRAZIER
1994   "Improving health: Measuring effects of medical care," *The Milbank Quarterly* 72(2): 225–258.

BUNTON, ROBIN
1998   "Inequalities in late-modern health care," pp. 23–41 in A. Petersen and C. Waddell, eds., *Health Matters: A Sociology of Illness, Prevention and Care.* Buckingham, England: Open University Press.

BUNTON, ROBIN, SARAH NETTLETON, AND ROGER BURROWS
1995   *The Sociology of Health Promotion: Critical Analyses of Consumption, Lifestyle and Risk.* London: Routledge.

BURKHOLDER, JOHN R.
1974   "The law knows no heresy: Marginal religious movements and the courts," pp. 27–52 in I. Zaretsky and M. Leone, eds., *Religious Movements in Contemporary America.* Princeton, NJ: Princeton University Press.

BURRIS, BEVERLY H.
1993   *Technocracy at Work.* Albany: State University of New York.

BURT, MARTHA R.
1992   *Over the Edge: The Growth of Homelessness in the 1980s.* New York: Russell Sage Foundation.

BURY, MICHAEL
1982   "Chronic illness as biographical disruption," *Sociology of Health and Illness* 4(2): 167–182.
1988   "Meanings at risk: The experience of arthritis," pp. 89–116 in R. Anderson and M. Bury, eds., *Living with Chronic Illness: The Experience of Patients and Their Families.* London: Unwin Hyman.
1991   "The sociology of chronic illness: A review of research and prospects," *Sociology of Health and Illness* 13(4): 451–467.
2000   "Health, aging and the life course," pp. 87–105 in S. J. Williams, J. Gabe, and M. Calnan, eds., *Health, Medicine and Society.* London: Routledge.
2001   "Illness narratives: Fact or fiction?," *Sociology of Health and Illness* 23(3): 263–285.

BUSHNELL, OSWALD A.
1993   *The Gifts of Civilization: Germs and Genocide in Hawaii.* Honolulu: University of Hawaii Press.

BUTLER, ROBERT N.
1996   "On behalf of older women: Another reason to protect Medicare and Medicaid," *New England Journal of Medicine* 334(12): 794–796.

BUTTEL, FREDERICK H.
2000   "Ending hunger in developing countries," *Contemporary Sociology* 29(1): 13–27.

BUYTENDIJK, JACOBUS
1974   *Prolegomena to an Anthropological Physiology.* Pittsburgh, PA: Duquesne University Press.

BYRNE, PATRICK S., AND BARRIE E. LONG
    1976   *Doctors Talking to Patients.* London: Her Majesty's Stationery Office.

CAHILL, JANET, AND PAUL A. LANDSBERGIS
    1996   "Job strain among post office mailhandlers," *International Journal of Health Services* 26(4): 731–750.

CALIFANO, JOSEPH A.
    1989   "Billions blown on health," *New York Times,* April 12.

CALLAHAN, DANIEL
    1987   *Setting Limits: Medical Goals in an Aging Society.* New York: Simon & Schuster.

CALLAHAN, TAMARA L., AND RONALD DAVID
    1995   "Access," pp. 173–193 in D. Calkins, R. J. Fernandopulle, and B. S. Marino, eds., *Health Care Policy.* Cambridge, MA: Blackwell Science.

CALNAN, MICHAEL
    1987   *Health and Illness: The Lay Perspective.* New York: Tavistock.

CANNON, WALTER B.
    1929   *Bodily Changes in Pain, Hunger, Fear, and Rage.* New York: Harper & Row.
    1942   "'Voodoo' death," *American Anthropologist* 44: 169–181.

CANT, SARAH L., AND URSULA SHARMA
    2000   "Alternative health practices and systems," pp. 426–437 in G. L. Albrecht et al., eds., *Handbook of Social Studies in Health and Medicine.* London: Sage.

CAPLAN, ROBERT D.
    1972   "Organizational stress and individual strain: A sociopsychological study of risk factors in coronary heart disease among administrators, engineers, and scientists." Unpublished Ph.D. dissertation, University of Michigan.

CARPENTER, MICK
    2000   "Reinforcing the pillars: Rethinking gender, social divisions and health," pp. 36–63 in E. Annandale and K. Hunt, eds., *Gender Inequalities in Health.* Philadelphia: Open University Press.

CARRASQUILLO, OLVEEN, DAVID U. HIMMELSTEIN, STEFFIE WOOLDHANDLER, AND DAVID H. BOR
    1999   "Trends in health insurance coverage, 1989–1997," *International Journal of Health Services* 29(3): 467–483.

CARTER, JANELLE
    2001   "Medicare spending increases 10 percent," Associated Press, October 31, retrieved from the World Wide Web at www.nlm.nih.gov on 1 November, 2001.

CARTWRIGHT, SAMUEL A.
    1851   "Report on the diseases and physical pecularities of the Negro race," *New Orleans Medical and Surgical Journal* 7: 691–715.

CASH, THOMAS F., BARBARA WINSTEAD, AND LOUIS JANDA
    1986   "The great American shape-up," *Psychology Today* 20(4): 30–37.

CASSEDY, JAMES H.
    1977   "Why self-help? Americans alone with their diseases, 1800–1850," pp. 31–48 in G. Risse, R. L. Numbers, and J. W. Leavitt, eds., *Medicine Without Doctors: Home Health Care in American History.* New York: Science History.

CASSELL, ERIC J.
    1976   "Disease as an 'it': Concepts of disease revealed by patients' presentation of symptoms," *Social Science and Medicine* 10: 143–146.

1982 "The nature of suffering and the goals of medicine," *New England Journal of Medicine* 306: 639–645.

1986 "Ideas in conflict: The rise and fall (and rise and fall) of new views of disease," *Daedalus: Journal of the American Academy of Arts and Sciences* 115(2): 19–41.

CASSELL, JOAN

1991 *Expected Miracles: Surgeons at Work*. Philadelphia: Temple University Press.

CASSIDY, CLAIRE M., HANS BAER, AND BARBARA BECKER

1985 "Selected references on professionalized heterodox health systems in English-speaking countries," *Medical Anthropology Quarterly* 17(1): 10–18.

CAUCHON, DENNIS

1999 "Americans pay more; here's why," *USA Today,* November 10.

CENTER FOR PHILOSOPHY AND PUBLIC POLICY

1985 "Air pollution: The role and limits of consent," *Report from the Center for Philosophy and Public Policy,* Vol. 5, No. 5. Hyattsville, MD: University of Maryland.

CENTER FOR PUBLIC INTEGRITY

1995 "Well-healed: Inside lobbying for health care reform, part II," *International Journal of Health Services* 25(4): 593–632.

CENTER FOR PUBLIC POLICY PRIORITIES

1998 "Food and hunger fast facts: Texas," retrieved from the World Wide Web at www.cppp.org on 29 March, 2002.

CENTER FOR RESPONSIVE POLITICS

2001 "Managed care," and "Tracking the payback: Health care, patients' bill of rights," 28 August, 2001, and "Tracking the payback: Prescription drugs," 4 June, 2001, retrieved from the World Wide Web at www.opensecrets.org on 24 March, 2002.

2002 "Health: PAC contributions to federal candidates, 1999–2000," 1 February, 2002, retrieved from the World Wide Web at www.opensecrets.org on 24 March, 2002.

CENTER FOR STUDY OF RESPONSIVE LAW

1982 *Eating Clean: Food Safety and the Chemical Harvest*. Washington, DC: Center for Study of Responsive Law.

CENTER ON BUDGET AND POLICY PRIORITIES

2000 "Texas: Income inequality among families," retrieved from the World Wide Web at www.cbpp.org on 23 March, 2002.

2001a "Mother's Day 2001 finds six million mothers lack health insurance," retrieved from the World Wide Web at www.cbpp.org on 1 November, 2001.

2001b "Pathbreaking CBO study shows dramatic increases in both 1980s and 1990s in income gaps between the very wealthy and other Americans," 31 May, retrieved from the World Wide Web at www.cbpp.org on 18 June, 2002.

CHAPMAN, SIMON, RON BORLAND, DAVID HILL, NEVILLE OWEN, AND STEPHEN WOODARD

1990 "Why the tobacco industry fears the passive smoking issue," *International Journal of Health Services* 20(3): 417–427.

CHARLES, CATHERINE A., AND ROBIN F. BADGLEY

1999 "Canadian National Health Insurance: Evolution and unresolved policy issues," pp. 115–150 in F. D. Powell and A. F. Wessen, eds., *Health Care Systems in Transition: An International Perspective*. Thousand Oaks, CA: Sage.

CHARLES, NICKE, AND MARION KERR
    1987   "Food for feminist thought," *Sociological Review* 34(3): 537–572.

CHARMAZ, KATHY
    1983   "Loss of self: A fundamental form of suffering of the chronically ill," *Sociology of Health and Illness* 5(2): 168–195.
    1987   "Struggling for a self: Identity levels of the chronically ill," *Research in the Sociology of Health Care* 4: 167–182.
    1991   *Good Days, Bad Days: The Self in Chronic Illness and Time.* New Brunswick, NJ: Rutgers University Press.
    1995   "Identity dilemmas of chronically ill men," pp. 266–291 in D. Sabo and D. F. Gordon, eds., *Men's Health and Illness.* Thousand Oaks, CA: Sage.

CHERFAS, JEREMY, AND ROGER LEWIN, EDS.
    1980   *Not Work Alone: A Cross-Cultural View of Activities Superfluous to Survival.* Beverly Hills, CA: Sage.

CHERNIN, KIM
    1981   *The Obsession: Reflections on the Tyranny of Slenderness.* New York: Harper & Row.

CHOMSKY, AVIVA
    2000   "'The threat of a good example': Health and revolution in Cuba," pp. 331–357 in J. Y. Kim et al., eds., *Dying for Growth: Global Inequality and the Health of the Poor.* Monroe, ME: Common Courage Press.

CHRISLER, JOAN C.
    1994   "Reframing women's weight: Does thin equal healthy?", pp. 330–338 in A. J. Dan, ed., *Reframing Women's Health.* Westport, CT: Auburn House.

CHRISMAN, NOEL J.
    1977   "The health-seeking process: An approach to the natural history of illness," *Culture, Medicine and Psychiatry* 1: 351–377.

CICOUREL, AARON V.
    1983   "Hearing is not believing: Language and the structure of belief in medical communication," pp. 221–239 in S. Fisher and A. Todd, eds., *The Social Organization of Doctor-Patient Communication.* Norwood, NJ: Ablex.

CLARK, L. R.
    2001   "'Will the pill make me sterile?' Addressing reproductive health concerns and strategies to improve adherence to hormonal contraceptive regimens in adolescent girls," *Journal of Pediatric and Adolescent Gynecology* 14(4): 153–162.

CLASSEN, CONSTANCE
    1994   *Aroma: The Cultural History of Smell.* London: Routledge.

COBB, LEONARD A., GEORGE THOMAS, DAVID H. DILLARD, K. ALVIN MERENDINO, AND ROBERT A. BRUCE
    1959   "An evaluation of internal mammary artery ligation by a double-blind technic," *New England Journal of Medicine* 260: 1115–1118.

COBURN, DAVID, AND C. LESLEY BIGGS
    1986   "Limits to medical dominance: The case of chiropractic," *Social Science and Medicine* 22: 1035–1046.

COBURN, DAVID, GEORGE M. TORRANCE, AND JOSEPH M. KAUFERT
    1983   "Medical dominance in Canada in historical perspective: The rise and fall of medicine?" *International Journal of Health Services* 13(3): 407–432.

COCKBURN, ALEXANDER
    1988   "Live souls," *Zeta Magazine* 1(2): 5–15.

COCKERHAM, WILLIAM C.
　1978　*Medical Sociology.* Englewood Cliffs, NJ: Prentice-Hall.
　1999　*Health and Social Change in Russia and Eastern Europe.* New York: Routledge.

COHEN, MARC J., AND RICHARD J. HOEHN
　1991　*Hunger.* Washington, DC: Bread for the World Institute on Hunger and Development.

COHEN, STANLEY, AND LAURIE TAYLOR
　1976　*Escape Attempts: The Theory and Practise of Resistance to Everyday Life.* London: Allen Lane.

COLLINS, CATHERINE FISHER
　1996　"Commentary on the health and social status of African-American women," pp. 1–10 in C. F. Collins, ed. *African-American Women's Health and Social Issues.* Westport, CT: Auburn House.

COLLINS, GLENN
　1995　"Making gains on the winds from Washington," *New York Times,* March 26.

COMAROFF, JEAN
　1978　"Medicine and culture: Some anthropological perspectives," *Social Science and Medicine* 12B: 247–254.
　1982　"Medicine: Symbol and ideology," pp. 49–68 in P. Wright and A. Treacher, eds., *The Problem of Medical Knowledge: Examining the Social Construction of Medicine.* Edinburgh, Scotland: Edinburgh University Press.
　1984　"Medicine, time, and the perception of death," *Listening* 19(2): 155–169.
　1985　*Body of Power, Spirit of Resistance: The Culture and History of a South African People.* Chicago: University of Chicago Press.

COMAROFF, JEAN, AND PETER MAGUIRE
　1981　"Ambiguity and the search for meaning: Childhood leukaemia in the modern clinical context," *Social Science and Medicine* 15B(2): 115–123.

COMMONWEALTH FUND, THE
　2001　*2001 National Survey of Health Insurance,* December 12, 2001, retrieved from the World Wide Web at www.cmwf.org on 24 December, 2001.

CONGRESSIONAL BUDGET OFFICE
　2001　"Historical effective tax rates, 1979–1997," May 2001, retrieved from the World Wide Web at www.cbo.gov on 28 August, 2001.

CONNOLLY, CECI
　2002　"Pharmaceutical spending continues steady increase: A few heavily advertised and high-priced 'blockbuster' medications drive 17 percent increase," *Washington Post,* March 29.

CONRAD, PETER
　1985　"The meaning of medications: Another look at compliance," *Social Science and Medicine* 20: 29–37.
　1986　"The social meaning of AIDS," *Social Policy* 17(1): 51–56.
　1988　"Worksite health promotion: The social context," *Social Science and Medicine* 26(5): 485–489.
　1996　"Medicalization and social control," pp. 137–162 in P. Brown, ed., *Perspectives in Medical Sociology.* Prospect Heights, IL: Waveland Press.

CONRAD, PETER, AND JOSEPH W. SCHNEIDER
　1992　*Deviance and Medicalization: From Badness to Sickness.* Philadelphia: Temple University Press.

CONRAD, PETER, AND DIANA WALSH
1992 "The new corporate health ethic: Lifestyle and the social control of work," *International Journal of Health Services* 22(1): 89–111.

COOMBS, ROBERT H., SANGEETA CHOPRA, DEBRA R. SCHENK, AND ELAINE YUTAN
1993 "Medical slang and its functions," *Social Science and Medicine* 36(8): 987–998.

COOPER, MARC
1997 "The heartland's raw deal," *The Nation* 264(4): 11–17.

CORIN, E.
1994 "The social and cultural matrix of health and disease," pp. 93–132 in R. G. Evans, M. L. Barer, and T. R. Marmor, eds., *Why Are Some People Healthy and Others Not?: The Determinants of Health of Populations*. New York: Aldine de Gruyter.

COTTLE, MICHELLE
1999 "Selling shyness," *The New Republic* 221(5): 24–30.

COUCH STEPHEN R., AND STEVE KROLL-SMITH
2000 "Environmental movements and expert knowledge," pp. 384–404 in S. Kroll-Smith, P. Brown, and V. J. Gunter, eds., *Illness and the Environment: A Reader in Contested Medicine*. New York: New York University Press.

COULTER, HARRIS L.
1984 "Homoeopathy," pp. 57–79 in J. W. Salmon, ed., *Alternative Medicines: Popular and Policy Perspectives*. New York: Tavistock.

COULTER, IAN D., RON D. HAYS, AND CLARK D. DANIELSON
1996 "The role of the chiropractor in the changing health care system," *Research in the Sociology of Health Care* 13A: 95–117.

COUSINS, NORMAN
1989 *Headfirst: The Biology of Hope*. New York: Dutton.

COWIE, BILL
1976 "The cardiac patient's perception of his heart attack," *Social Science and Medicine* 10: 87–96.

CRAWFORD, ROBERT
1984 "A cultural account of 'health': Control, release, and the social body," pp. 60–103 in J. B. McKinlay, ed., *Issues in the Political Economy of Health Care*. New York: Tavistock.

CREWE, NANCY M., AND IRVING K. ZOLA, EDS.
1983 *Independent Living in America*. San Francisco: Jossey-Bass.

CRIMMINS, EILEEN M., AND YASUHIKO SAITO
2001 "Trends in healthy life expectancy in the United States, 1970–1990: Gender, racial, and educational differences," *Social Science and Medicine* 52(11): 1629–1641.

CRITSER, GREG
2000 "Let them eat fat," *Harpers Magazine*, March: 41–47.

CROSSEN, CYNTHIA
1994 *Tainted Truth: The Manipulation of Fact in America*. New York: Simon & Schuster.

CROSSETTE, BARBARA
2001 "In India and Africa women's low status worsens their risk of AIDS," *New York Times*, February 26.

CSIKSZENTMIHALYI, MIHALY
1990 *Flow: The Psychology of Optimal Experience*. New York: HarperCollins.

CSORDAS, THOMAS J.
1994   *The Sacred Self: A Cultural Phenomenology of Charismatic Healing.* Berkeley: University of California Press.

CSORDAS, THOMAS J., AND ARTHUR KLEINMAN
1996   "The therapeutic process," pp. 3–20 in C. F. Sargent and T. M. Johnson, eds., *Medical Anthropology: Contemporary Theory and Method.* Westport, CT: Praeger.

CURTIN, SALLY C., L. J. KOZAK, AND K. D. GREGORY
2000   "U.S. cesarean and VBAC rates stalled in the mid-1990s," *Birth* 27(1): 54–57.

CUSAC, ANNE-MARIE
2001   "Cut loose: Companies trick retirees out of health benefits," *The Progressive* 65(April): 21–25.

DANIELS, ARLENE K.
1969   "The captive professional: Bureaucratic limitations in the practice of military psychiatry," *Journal of Health and Social Behavior* 10(4): 255–265.
1972   "Military psychiatry: The emergence of a subspecialty," pp. 145–162 in E. Freidson and J. Lorber, eds., *Medical Men and Their Work.* Chicago: Aldine Atherton.

DANIELS, CYNTHIA R.
1993   *At Women's Expense: State Power and the Politics of Fetal Rights.* Cambridge, MA: Harvard University Press.

DANZINGER, RENÉE
2000   "The social impact of HIV/AIDS in developing countries," pp. 41–55 in A. Lemelle, C. Harrington, and A. LeBlanc, eds., *Readings in the Sociology of AIDS.* Upper Saddle River, NJ: Prentice-Hall.

DAVIES, CELIA
1995   *Gender and the Professional Predicament in Nursing.* Buckingham, England: Open University Press.

DAVIES, HUW, AND THOMAS G. RUNDALL
2000   "Managing patient trust in managed care," *The Milbank Quarterly,* 78(4): 609–624.

DAVIS, JOEL
1984   *Endorphins: New Waves in Brain Chemistry.* Garden City, NY: Doubleday.

DAVIS, KAREN
1991   "Inequality and access to health care," *The Milbank Quarterly* 69(2): 253–273.

DAVIS, MARGARET H., AND SALLY T. BURNER
1995   "Three decades of Medicare: What the numbers tell us," *Health Affairs* 14(4): 231–242.

DAVIS-FLOYD, ROBBIE
1987   "Obstetric training as a rite of passage," *Medical Anthropology Quarterly* 1(3): 288–318.
1992   *Birth as an American Rite of Passage.* Berkeley: University of California Press.
1994   "The technocratic body: American childbirth as cultural expression," *Social Science and Medicine* 38(8): 1125–1140.

DAVIS-FLOYD, ROBBIE, AND E. DAVIS
1997   "Intuition as authoritative knowledge in midwifery and homebirth," pp. 145–176 in R. Davis-Floyd and P. S. Arvidson, eds., *Intuition: The Inside Story.* London: Routledge.

DAVIS-FLOYD, ROBBIE, AND GLORIA ST. JOHN
1998   *From Doctor to Healer.* New Brunswick, NJ: Rutgers University Press.

DEATON, ANGUS
    2002   "Policy implications of the gradient of health and wealth," *Health Affairs* 21(2): 13–30.

DECLERCQ, E. R., L. L. PAINE, D. R. SIMMES, AND J. F. DEJOSEPH
    1998   "State regulations, payment policies and nurse-midwife services," *Health Affairs* 17(2): 190–201.

DEFRIESE, GORDON H., GLENN WILSON, THOMAS C. RICKETTS, AND LYNN WHITENER
    1992   "Consumer choice and the national rural hospital crisis," pp. 206–225 in W. M. Gesler and T. C. Ricketts, eds., *Health in Rural North America.* New Brunswick, NJ: Rutgers University Press.

DEMBE, ALLARD E.
    1996   *Occupation and Disease.* New Haven, CT: Yale University Press.

DIAMOND, MARIAN CLEEVES
    1988   *Enriching Heredity: The Impact of the Environment on the Anatomy of the Brain.* New York: Free Press.

DILL, ANN, PHIL BROWN, DESIRÉE CIAMBRONE, AND WILLIAM RAKOWSKI
    1995   "The meaning and practice of self-care by older adults," *Research on Aging* 7(1): 8–41.

DIMATTEO, M. ROBIN, AND HOWARD S. FRIEDMAN
    1982   *Social Psychology and Medicine.* Cambridge, MA: Oelgeschlager, Gunn, and Hain.

DINGWALL, ROBERT
    2001   *Aspects of Illness.* Burlington, VT: Ashgate.

DIRECKS, ANITA, AND ELLEN'T HOEN
    1986   "DES: The crime continues," pp. 41–49 in K. McDonnell, ed., *Adverse Effects: Women and the Pharmaceutical Industry.* Toronto: Women's Educational Press.

DOESCHER, MARK P., PETER FRANKS, J. S. BANTHIN, AND C. M. CLANCY
    2000   "Supplemental insurance and mortality in elderly Americans," *Archives of Family Medicine* 9: 251–257.

DOHERTY, WILLIAM J., AND THOMAS L. CAMPBELL
    1988   *Families and Health.* Beverly Hills, CA: Sage.

DOHRENWEND, BARBARA, AND LEONARD PEARLIN
    1982   "Report on stress and life events," pp. 55–88 in G. R. Elliott and C. Eisdorfer, eds., *Stress and Human Health.* New York: Springer.

DOLAN, ANDREW K.
    1980   "Antitrust law and physician dominance of other practitioners," *Journal of Health, Politics, and Law* 4: 675–689.

DOLAN, MAURA
    1999   "Court: Violation of federal patient dumping law was alleged," *Los Angeles Times,* March 26.

DONOVAN, JENNY L., AND DAVID R. BLAKE
    1992   "Patient compliance: Deviance or reasoned decision-making?" *Social Science and Medicine* 34(5): 507–513.

DOUGLAS, MARY
    1966   *Purity and Danger: An Analysis of Concepts of Pollution and Taboo.* London: Routledge and Kegan Paul.
    1970   *Natural Symbols: Explorations in Cosmology.* London: Barrie and Jenkins.

DOW, JAMES
    1986   "Universal aspects of symbolic healing: A theoretical synthesis," *American Anthropologist* 88(1): 56–69.

DOYAL, LESLEY
    1995   *What Makes Women Sick.* New Brunswick, NJ: Rutgers University Press.
DRAPER, ELAINE
    2000   "Competing conceptions of safety," pp. 193–214 in S. Kroll-Smith, P. Brown,
            and V. J. Gunter, eds., *Illness and the Environment: A Reader in Contested Medicine.*
            New York: New York University Press.
DRESSLER, WILIAM W., AND JAMES BINDON
    2000   "The health consequences of cultural consonance: Cultural dimensions of
            lifestyle, social support, and arterial blood pressure in an African American
            community," *American Anthropologist* 102(2): 244–260.
DREW, CHRISTOPHER
    1995   "In the productivity push, how much is too much?" *New York Times,*
            December 17.
DRICKAMER, MARGARET A., AND MARK S. LACHS
    1992   "Should patients with Alzheimer's disease be told their diagnosis?" *New
            England Journal of Medicine* 326(18): 947–951.
DRINKA, GEORGE FREDERICK
    1984   *The Birth of Neurosis: Myth, Malady, and the Victorians.* New York: Simon &
            Schuster.
DROGE, DAVID, PAUL ARNTSON, AND ROBERT NORTON
    1986   "The social support function in epilepsy self-help groups," *Small Group Behavior*
            17(2): 139–163.
DUBOS, RENÉ
    1959   *The Mirage of Health.* Garden City, NY: Doubleday.
    1968   *Man, Medicine and Environment.* Baltimore: Penguin.
DUFFIE, MARY K.
    1996   "Intrapsychic autonomy and the emotional construction of biocultural illness:
            A question of balance," pp. 47–71 in J. Subedi and E. B. Gallagher, eds.,
            Society, Health and Disease. Upper Saddle River, NJ: Prentice-Hall.
DuGUERNY, JAQUES, AND ELISABETH SJOBERG
    1999   "Interrelationship between gender relations and the HIV/AIDS epidemic:
            Some possible considerations for policies and programs," pp. 202–215 in
            J. Mann, S. Gruskin, M. A. Grodin, and G. J. Annas, eds., *Health and Human
            Rights.* New York: Routledge.
DULL, DIANA, AND CANDACE WEST
    1991   "Accounting for cosmetic surgery: The accomplishment of gender," *Social
            Problems* 38(3): 54–70.
DUNNELL, KAREN, AND ANN CARTWRIGHT
    1972   *Medicine Takers, Prescribers, and Hoarders.* London: Routledge and Kegan Paul.
DURKHEIM, EMILE
    [1893] 1964   *The Division of Labor in Society.* New York: The Free Press.
    [1895] 1938   *Rules of the Sociological Method.* New York: The Free Press.
    [1897] 1951   *Suicide: A Study in Sociology.* New York: The Free Press.
    [1915] 1965   *The Elementary Forms of the Religious Life.* New York: Collier/Macmillan.
DUTTON, DIANA
    1986   "Social class, health and illness," pp. 31–62 in L. Aiken and D. Mechanic, eds.,
            Applications of Social Science to Clinical Medicine and Health Policy. New Brunswick,
            NJ: Rutgers University Press.

DUTTON, DIANA, THOMAS A. PRESTON, AND NANCY E. PFUND
1988   *Worse Than the Disease: Pitfalls of Medical Progress.* New York: Cambridge University Press.

DYE, JAMES W.
1981   "Man a machine: A philosophical critique," *Journal of Biological Experience: Studies in the Life of the Body* 3(2): 44–60.

EASTWELL, HARRY D.
1982   "Voodoo death and the mechanism for dispatch of the dying in East Arnheim, Australia," *American Anthropologist* 84(1): 5–18.

EBERHARDT, MARK S., D. D. INGRAM, D. M. MAKUC, ET AL.
2001   "Urban and rural health chartbook," *Health United States, 2001.* Hyattsville, MD: National Center for Health Statistics.

ECKHOLM, ERIK
1977   *The Picture of Health: Environmental Sources of Disease.* New York: W. W. Norton.
1989   "River blindness: Conquering an ancient scourge," *New York Times Magazine,* January 8.

EHRENREICH, BARBARA
2001   *Nickel and Dimed: On (Not) Getting By in America.* New York: Metropolitan Books.

EHRENREICH, BARBARA, AND JOHN EHRENREICH
1978   "Hospital workers: Class conflicts in the making," pp. 41–49 in S. Wolfe, ed., *Organization of Health Workers and Labor Conflict.* Farmingdale, NY: Baywood.

EHRENREICH, BARBARA, AND DEIRDRE ENGLISH
1973   *Witches, Midwives, and Nurses: A History of Women Healers.* Old Westbury, NY: The Feminist Press.
1978   *For Her Own Good: 150 Years of the Experts' Advice to Women.* Garden City, NY: Doubleday.

EICHENWALD, KURT
1995a   "Death and deficiency in kidney treatment," *New York Times,* December 4.
1995b   "Doctors' highest-paid skill: Steering in kidney patients," *New York Times,* December 5.
1995c   "Making incentives work in kidney patients' favor," *New York Times,* December 6.
1996   "Long neglected, the quality of kidney dialysis now may get U.S. guidelines," *New York Times,* January 14.

EISENBERG, DAVID M., R. B. DAVIS, S. L. ETTNER, S. APEL, S. WILKEY, M. VAN ROMPAY, ET AL.
1998   "Trends in alternative medicine use in the United States, 1990–1997: Results of a follow-up national survey," *Journal of the American Medical Association* 280(18): 1569–1575.

EISENBERG, DAVID M., THOMAS L. DELBANCO, CATHERINE S. BERKEY, TED J. KAPTCHUK, BRUCE KUPELNICK, JACKIE KUHL, AND THOMAS C. CHALMERS
1993   "Cognitive behavioral techniques for hypertension: Are they effective?" *Annals of Internal Medicine* 118: 964–972.

ELIAS, NORBERT
[1978] 1994 *The Civilizing Process,* Vols. 1 and 2. Oxford, England: Basil Blackwell.

ELL, KATHLEEN, AND IRMA CASTAÑEDA
1998   "Health care seeking behavior," pp. 125–143 in S. Loue, ed., *Handbook of Immigrant Health.* New York: Plenum.

ELLING, RAY H.
  1986   *The Struggle for Workers' Health: A Study of Six Industrialized Countries.* Farmingdale,
          NY: Baywood.

EMANUEL, EZEKIEL J., D. L. FAIRCLOUGH, J. SLUTSMAN, H. ALPERT, D. BALDWIN, AND
L. L. EMANUEL
  1999   "Assistance from family members, friends, paid care givers, and volunteers in
          the care of terminally ill patients," *New England Journal of Medicine* 341(13):
          956–963.

EMSLIE, CAROL, KATE HUNT, AND GRAHAM WATT
  2001   "Invisible women? The importance of gender in lay beliefs about heart prob-
          lems." *Sociology of Health and Illness* 23(2): 203–233.

ENGEBRETSON, TILMER O., AND CATHERINE M. STONEY
  1995   "Anger expression and lipid concentrations," *International Journal of Behavioral
          Medicine* 2(4): 281–298.

ENGEL, GEORGE L.
  1971   "Sudden and rapid death during psychological stress: Folklore or folk wisdom?"
          Annals of Internal Medicine 74: 771–782.
  1977   "The need for a new medical model: A challenge for biomedicine," *Science* 196:
          129–136.

ENGELS, FRIEDRICH
  [1845] 1973   *The Conditions of the Working Class in England in 1844.* Moscow: Universal.

ENGLAND, PAULA, AND NANCY FOLBRE
  1999   "The cost of caring," *Annals of the American Academy PPS,* 561(January):
          39–51.

ENGLEHARDT, H. TRISTAM
  1978   "The disease of masturbation: Values and the concept of disease," pp. 15–24 in
          J. W. Leavitt and R. L. Numbers, eds., *Sickness and Health in America.* Madison:
          University of Wisconsin Press.

ENGLISH-LUECK, JUNE ANNE
  1990   *Health in the New Age: A Study in California Holistic Practices.* Albuquerque: Univer-
          sity of New Mexico.

ENVIRONMENT NEWS SERVICE
  2001   "Reading, writing and Ritalin–TV program overlooks evidence on cancer
          risks in children," April 10.

EPSTEIN, PAUL, AND RANDALL PACKARD
  1987   "Ecology and immunity," *Science for the People* 19(1): 10–20.

EPSTEIN, RONALD M.
  1999   "Mindful practice," *Journal of the American Medical Association* 282(9): 833–839.

EPSTEIN, SAMUEL S.
  1990a   "Losing the war against cancer: Who's to blame and what to do about it,"
          International Journal of Health Services 20(1): 53–71.
  1990b   "Corporate crime: Why we cannot trust industry-derived safety studies,"
          International Journal of Health Services 20(3): 443–458.

ERICKSON, FREDERICK
  1999   "Appropriation of voice and presentation of self as a fellow physician: Aspects
          of a discourse of apprenticeship in medicine," pp. 109–143 in S. Sarangi and
          C. Roberts, eds., *Talk, Work and Institutional Order: Discourse in Medical, Mediation
          and Management Settings.* New York: Mouton de Gruyter.

ESTES, CARROLL L., AND KAREN W. LINKINS
2000 "Critical perspectives on health and aging," pp. 154–172 in G. L. Albrecht et al., eds., *Handbook of Social Studies in Health and Medicine.* London: Sage.

ETTORRE, ELIZABETH, AND ELIANNE RISKA
1995 *Gendered Moods: Psychotropics and Society.* London: Routledge.

EVANS, ROBERT G., M. HODGE, AND I. B. PLESS
1994 "If not genetics then what? Biological pathways and population health," pp. 161–189 in R. G. Evans, M. L. Barer, and T. R. Marmor, eds., *Why Are Some People Healthy and Others Not?: The Determinants of Health of Populations.* New York: Aldine de Gruyter.

EVANS, ROBERT, AND NORALOU P. ROOS
1999 "What is right about the Canadian health care system?" *The Milbank Quarterly* 77(3): 393–399.

EYER, JOSEPH
1984 "Capitalism, health and illness," pp. 23–58 in J. B. McKinlay, ed., *Issues in the Political Economy of Health Care.* New York: Tavistock.

EYER, JOSEPH, AND PETER STERLING
1977 "Stress-related mortality and social organization," *Review of Radical Political Economics* 9(1): 1–44.

FADIMAN, ANNE
1997 *The Spirit Catches You and You Fall Down.* New York: Farrar, Straus and Giroux, LLC.

FAGERHAUGH, SHIZUKO, AND ANSELM STRAUSS
1977 *Politics of Pain Management: Staff-Patient Interaction.* Reading, MA: Addison-Wesley.

FAMILIES USA
1998 "Premium pay: Corporate compensation in America's HMOs," 1 April, 1998, retrieved from the World Wide Web at www.familiesusa.org on 24 March, 2002.
1999 "One step forward, one step back: Children's health coverage after CHIP and welfare reform," October 1999, retrieved from the World Wide Web at www.familiesusa.org on 8 December, 1999.
2000 "Go directly to work, do not collect health insurance: Low income parents lose Medicaid," retrieved from the World Wide Web at www.familiesusa.org on 29 March, 2002.

FANON, FRANZ
1963 *The Wretched of the Earth.* New York: Grove.

FARB, PETER, AND GEORGE ARMELAGOS
1980 *Consuming Passions: The Anthropology of Eating.* Boston: Houghton Mifflin.

FAUST, MARLENE, JAMES C. SPILSBURY, AND SANA LOUE
1998 "African health," pp. 329–348 in S. Loue, ed., *Handbook of Immigrant Health.* New York: Plenum.

FEATHERSTONE, MIKE
1991 "The body in consumer culture," pp. 170–196 in M. Featherstone, M. Hepworth, and B. S. Turner, eds., *The Body: Social Process and Cultural Theory.* London: Sage.

FEDER, BARNABY
1996 "Increase in teen-age smoking sharpest among black males," *New York Times,* May 24.

FEIGENBAUM, SUSAN
    1987   "Risk bearing in health care finance," pp. 105–144 in C. J. Schramm, ed., *Health Care and Its Costs.* New York: Norton.

FEIN, RASHI
    1986   *Medical Care, Medical Costs: The Search for a Health Insurance Policy.* Cambridge, MA: Harvard University Press.

FELDMAN, PENNY HOLLANDER, WITH ALICE M. SAPIENZA AND NANCY M. KANE
    1990   *Who Cares for Them? Workers in the Home Care Industry.* New York: Greenwood Press.

FENN, RICHARD
    1978   *Toward a Theory of Secularization. SSSR Monograph Series, No. 1.* Storrs, CT: Society for the Scientific Study of Religion.
    1982   *Liturgies and Trials: The Secularization of Religious Language.* Oxford, England: Basil Blackwell.

FENTON, STEVE, AND KATHARINE CHARSLEY
    2000   "Epidemiology and sociology as incommensurate games: Accounts from the study of health and ethnicity," *Health* 4(4): 403–425.

FERLIE, EWAN B., AND S. M. SHORTELL
    2001   "Improving the quality of health care in the United Kingdom and the United States: A framework for change," *The Milbank Quarterly* 79(2): 281–315.

FIELD, MARK G.
    1973   "The concept of the 'health system' at the macrosociological level," *Social Science and Medicine* 7: 763–785.

FIELD, MARK G., DAVID M. KOTZ, AND GENE BUKHMAN
    2000   "Neoliberal economic policy, 'state desertion,' and the Russian health crisis," pp. 155–173 in J. Y. Kim, J. V. Millen, A. Irwin, and J. Gershman, eds., *Dying for Growth: Global Inequality and the Health of the Poor.* Monroe, ME: Common Courage Press.

FIELDING, STEPHEN L.
    1999   *The Practice of Uncertainty: Voice of Physicians and Patients in Medical Malpractice Claims.* Westport, CT: Auburn House.

FIFE, BETSY L.
    1994   "The conceptualization of meaning in illness," *Social Science and Medicine* 38(2): 309–316.

FIGERT, ANNE E.
    1995   "The three faces of PMS: The professional, gendered, and scientific structuring of a psychiatric disorder," *Social Problems* 42(1): 56–73.

FIGLIO, KARL
    1982   "How does illness mediate social relations?: Workmen's compensation and medico-legal practices, 1890–1940," pp. 174–217 in P. Wright and A. Treacher, eds., *The Problem of Medical Knowledge: Examining the Social Construction of Medicine.* Edinburgh, Scotland: Edinburgh University Press.

FINE, DORIS R.
    1988   "Women caregivers and home health workers: Prejudice and inequity in home health care," *Research in the Sociology of Health Care* 7: 105–117.

FINE, MICHELLE, AND ADRIENNE ASCH
    1988   "Disability beyond stigma: Social interaction, discrimination and activism," *Journal of Social Issues* 44(1): 3–21.

FINKEL, MICHAEL
  2001 "Complications," *New York Times Magazine,* May 27: 26–33, 40, 52.
FINKELSTEIN, KATHERINE E.
  2001 "Disaster gives the uninsured wider access to Medicaid," *New York Times,* November 23.
FINKLER, KAJA
  1989 "The universality of nerves," pp. 171–179 in D. Davis and S. Low, eds., *Gender, Health, and Illness: The Case of Nerves.* New York: Hemisphere.
  1994 *Women in Pain: Gender and Morbidity in Mexico.* Philadelphia: University of Pennsylvania Press.
FISCHER, CLAUDE
  1983 "The friendship cure-all," *Psychology Today* 17(1): 74–78.
FISHER, SUE
  1983 "Doctor talk/Patient talk: How treatment decisions are negotiated in doctor-patient communication," pp. 135–157 in S. Fisher and A. Todd, eds., *The Social Organization of Doctor-Patient Communication.* Norwood, NJ: Ablex.
  1986 *In the Patient's Best Interest: Women and the Politics of Medical Decisions.* New Brunswick, NJ: Rutgers University Press.
  1994 "Is care a remedy? The case of nurse practitioners," pp. 301–329 in A. J. Dan, ed., *Reframing Women's Health.* Thousand Oaks, CA: Sage.
  1995 *Nursing Wounds: Nurse Practitioners, Doctors, Women Patients and the Negotiation of Meaning.* New Brunswick, NJ: Rutgers University Press.
FLEISCHER, DORIS Z., AND FRIEDA ZAMES
  2001 *The Disability Rights Movement: From Charity to Confrontation.* Philadelphia: Temple University Press.
FLEXNER, ABRAHAM
  1910 *Medical Education in the United States and Canada. Bulletin, Number 4.* New York: Carnegie Foundation for the Advancement of Teaching.
FONAGY, PETER
  1996 "Patterns of attachment, interpersonal relationships and health," pp. 125–151 in D. Blane, E. Brunner, and R. Wilkinson, eds., *Health and Social Organization.* London: Routledge
FONTENOT, WONDA L.
  1994 *Secret Doctors: Ethnomedicine of African Americans.* Westport, CT: Bergin & Garvey.
FOOD RESEARCH AND ACTION CENTER
  2000 "State of the states" (Reports on food insecurity by state, December 2000) retrieved from the World Wide Web at www.frac.org on 22 December, 2001.
FOOKS, CATHERINE
  1999 "Will power, cost control and health reform in Canada, 1987–1992," pp. 151–172 in F. D. Powell and A. F. Wessen, eds., *Health Care Systems in Transition: An International Perspective.* Thousand Oaks, CA: Sage.
FOSTER, PEGGY
  1995 *Women and the Health Care Industry: An Unhealthy Relationship?* Buckingham, England: Open University Press.
FOUCAULT, MICHEL
  1973 *The Birth of the Clinic: An Archaeology of Medical Perception.* New York: Tavistock.
  1978 *The History of Sexuality: An Introduction.* New York: Pantheon.
  1979 *Discipline and Punish: The Birth of the Prison.* Harmondsworth, England: Penguin.

FOX, RENÉE C.
    1957   "Training for uncertainty," pp. 207–241 in R. K. Merton, G. C. Reader, and P. L. Kendall, eds., *The Student Physician*. Cambridge, MA: Harvard University Press.
    2000   "Medical uncertainty revisited," pp. 409–425 in G. L. Albrecht et al., eds., *Handbook of Social Studies in Health and Medicine*. London: Sage.

FRANK, JEROME D.
    1973   *Persuasion and Healing*. New York: Shocken.

FRANKE, RICHARD W., AND BARBARA H. CHASIN
    1994   *Kerala: Radical reform as development in an Indian state* (2nd ed.). Oakland, CA: Food First Books.

FRANKEL, GLENN
    1986   "Even the diseases are segregated," *International Herald Tribune,* July 17.

FRANKENHAEUSER, MARIANNE
    1981   "Coping with stress at work," *International Journal of Health Services* 11(4): 491–510.
    1991   "The psychophysiology of sex differences as related to occupational status," pp. 39–61 in M. Frankenhaeuser, U. Lundberg, and M. Chesney, eds., *Women, Work and Health*. New York: Plenum Press.

FRANKENHAEUSER, MARIANNE, AND BERTIL GARDELL
    1976   "Underload and overload in working life: Outline of a multidisciplinary approach," *Journal of Human Stress* 2(3): 35–46.

FRASER, JILL ANDRESKY
    2001   *White Collar Sweatshop*. New York: W. W. Norton and Company.

FRAZIER, HOWARD S., AND FREDERICK MOSTELLER, EDS.
    1995   *Medicine Worth Paying For: Assessing Medical Innovations*. Cambridge, MA: Harvard University Press.

FREIDSON, ELIOT
    1970   *Profession of Medicine: A Study of the Sociology of Applied Knowledge*. New York: Dodd, Mead.

FREUDENHEIM, MILT
    1987   "Specialty health care booms," *New York Times,* November 24.
    1995   "Profit levels stagnating at hospitals," *New York Times,* February, 6.
    1997a   "Columbia/HCA makes new, cash offer for Value Health," *New York Times,* April 16.
    1997b   "Dragging out HMO payments," *New York Times,* April 17.
    1997c   "For teaching hospitals, multiple complications," *New York Times,* May 20.
    1998   "Influencing doctor's orders," *New York Times,* November 17.
    2001a   "High cost of being well: Benefits at a premium, employees will pay a sharp increase for insurance plans," *New York Times,* October 16.
    2001b   "New health plan may raise expenses for sickest workers," *New York Times,* December 5.
    2002a   "Many H.M.O.'s for the elderly cut or abolish drug coverage," *New York Times,* January 25.
    2002b   "Personal costs for Medicare H.M.O.'s rise," *New York Times,* February 14.

FREUDENHEIM, MILT, AND MELODY PETERSEN
    2001   "The drug-price express runs into a wall," *New York Times,* December 23.

FREUND, PETER E. S.
    1982   *The Civilized Body: Social Domination, Control and Health*. Philadelphia: Temple University Press.

1990 "The expressive body: A common ground for the sociology of emotions and health and illness," *Sociology of Health and Illness* 12(4): 452–477.

1998 "Social performances and their discontents: Reflections on the biosocial psychology of role playing," pp. 393–430 in G. A. Bendelow and S. J. Williams, eds., *Emotions in Social Life: Social Theories and Contemporary Issues*. London: Routledge.

2001 "Bodies, disability and spaces: The social model and disabling spatial organisations," *Disability and Society* 16(5): 689–706.

FREUND, PETER E. S., AND GEORGE T. MARTIN
1993 *The Ecology of the Automobile*. Montreal, Canada: Black Rose.
1997 "The automobile and transport policy." *Policy Studies* 18: 269–283.
2001 "Moving bodies: Injury, disease and the social organization of space." *Critical Public Health* 11(3): 1–12.
2002 "Risky vehicles–risky agents: Mobility and the politics of space, movement and consciousness," forthcoming in J. P. Rothe, ed., *Driving Lessons: Exploring Systems That Make Traffic Safer*. Edmonton, Canada: University of Alberta Press.

FRIEDMAN, EMILY
1996 "Capitation, integration, and managed care," *Journal of the American Medical Association* 275(12): 957–962.

FRIEDMAN, GARY D.
1987 *Primer of Epidemiology* (3rd ed.). New York: McGraw-Hill.

FRIEDMANN, GEORGES
1961 *The Anatomy of Work*. Glencoe, IL: The Free Press.

FRIES, JAMES F.
1990 "An introduction to the compression of morbidity," pp. 35–41 in P. R. Lee and C. L. Estes, eds., *The Nation's Health*. Boston: Jones and Bartlett.

FROMM, ERIC
1965 *Escape from Freedom*. New York: Avon Books.

FRYE, GLADYS M., AND STEPHANIE D. SILVERMAN
2000 "Is it premenstrual syndrome?" *Postgraduate Medicine* 107(5): 151–158.

FULDER, STEPHEN
1993 "The impact of non-orthodox medicine on our concepts of health," pp. 105–117 in R. Lafaille and S. Fulder, eds., *Towards a New Science of Health*. London: Routledge.

FUNKENSTEIN, DANIEL, S. H. KING, AND M. E. DROLETTE
1957 *Mastery of Stress*. Cambridge, MA: Harvard University Press.

FURLONG, BETH, AND MARLENE WILKEN
1998 "Managed care and the nursing profession," *Research in the Sociology of Health Care* 15: 173–185.

GABEL, JOHN R., AND MICHAEL A. REDISCH
1979 "Alternative physician payment methods: Incentives, efficiency, and National Health Insurance," *Milbank Memorial Fund Quarterly* 57(1): 38–59.

GAINES, ATWOOD D.
1992 "From DSM-I to III-R: Voices of self, mastery and the other: A cultural constructivist reading of U.S. psychiatric classification," *Social Science and Medicine* 35(1): 3–24.

GALLUP ORGANIZATION
    2001   "Healthcare system," November 8–11, retrieved from the World Wide Web at www.gallup.com/poll/topics/healthcare.asp on 30 December, 2001.

GAMLIEL, SANDY, ROBERT M. POLITZER, MARC L. RIVO, AND FITZHUGH MULLAN
    1995   "Managed care on the march: Will physicians meet the challenge?" *Health Affairs* 14(2): 131–145.

GANZ, PATRICIA A.
    1992   "Treatment options for breast cancer—Beyond survival," *New England Journal of Medicine* 326(17): 1147–1149.

GAREY, ANITA ILTA
    1995   "Constructing motherhood on the night shift: 'Working mothers as 'stay-at-home moms,'" *Qualitative Sociology* 18(4): 415–437.

GARRETT, LAURIE
    2000   *Betrayal of Trust: The Collapse of Global Public Health.* New York: Hyperion.

GARSON, BARBARA
    1988   *The Electronic Sweatshop.* New York: Simon & Schuster.

GEBREMEDHIN, TESFA G.
    1997   "A critical analysis of the causes of world food insecurity," *Land Reform, Land Settlement, and Cooperatives* (Journal of the U.N.F.A.O.), 1997(1): 19–29, retrieved from the World Wide Web at www.fao.org.

GELLHORN, ERIC
    1969   "The consequences of the suppression of overt movements in emotional stress: A neurophysiological interpretation," *Confinia Neurologica* 32: 289–299.

GEOGHEGAN, THOMAS
    1999   "Tampering with the time clock: How bosses take a free hour here, a free hour there," *New York Times,* January 24.

GEORGE, SUSAN
    1982   *How the Other Half Dies.* Montclair, NJ: Allanheld, Osmun.

GERRITY, MARTHA S., JO ANNE L. EARP, ROBERT F. DEVELLIS, AND DONALD W. LIGHT
    1992   "Uncertainty and professional work: Perceptions of physicians in clinical practice," *American Journal of Sociology* 97(4): 1022–1051.

GERSHMAN, JOHN, AND ALEC IRWIN
    2000   "Getting a grip on the global economy," pp. 11–43 in J. Y. Kim, J. V. Millen, A. Irwin, and J. Gershman, eds., *Dying for Growth: Global Inequality and the Health of the Poor.* Monroe, ME: Common Courage Press.

GIACOMINI, MITA K.
    1999   "The which-hunt: Assembling health technology for assessment and rationing," *Journal of Health Politics, Policy and Law* 24(4): 715–758.

GIBSON, ROBERT
    1980   "National Health Expenditures, 1979," *Health Care Financing Review* 2(1): 1–36.
    1982   "National Health Expenditures," *Health Care Financing Trends* 2(5): 1–9.

GILBERT, EVELYN
    1997   "Achoo, baby!" *Village Voice* (January 28): 42–43.

GINZBERG, ELI
    1991   "Access to health care for Hispanics," *Journal of the American Medical Association* 165(2): 238–241.

GLASER, BARNEY, AND ANSELM STRAUSS
    1968   *Time for Dying.* Chicago: Aldine.

GLASER, WILLIAM A.
    1991   "Paying the hospital: American problems and foreign solutions," *International Journal of Health Services* 21(3): 389–399.

GLASSMAN, MARJORIE
    1980   "Misdiagnosis of senile dementia: Denial of care to the elderly," *Social Work* 25(4): 288–292.

GLASSNER, BARRY
    1989   "Fitness and the postmodern self," *Journal of Health and Social Behavior* 30: 180–191.

GLAZER, NONA Y.
    1990   "The home as workshop: Women as amateur nurses and medical care providers," *Gender and Society* 4(4): 479–499.
    1993   *Women's Paid and Unpaid Labor: The Work Transfer in Health Care and Retailing.* Philadelphia: Temple University Press.

GLICKMAN, L., E. A. BRUCE, F. G. CARO, AND J. AVORN
    1994   "Physicians' knowledge of drug costs for the elderly," *Journal of the American Geriatrics Society* 42(9): 992–996.

GLIEDMAN, JOHN
    1979   "The wheelchair rebellion," *Psychology Today* 13(3): 59–64, 99–101.

GLIEDMAN, JOHN, AND WILLIAM ROTH
    1980   "The unexpected minority: Why society is so mystified by handicap," *New Republic* 182(5): 26–30.

GOFFMAN, ERVING
    1959   *The Presentation of Self in Everyday Life.* Garden City, NY: Doubleday.
    1961   *Asylums.* Garden City, NY: Doubleday.
    1963   *Stigma: Notes on the Management of Spoiled Identity.* Englewood Cliffs, NJ: Spectrum/Prentice-Hall.

GOLD, MARSHA
    1999   "The changing U.S. health care system: Challenges for responsible public policy," *The Milbank Quarterly* 77(1): 3–37.

GOLDOFTAS, BARBARA
    1991   "Hands that hurt," *Technology Review* 94(1): 42–50.

GOLDSMITH, FRANK, AND LORIN E. KERR
    1982   *Occupational Safety and Health.* New York: Human Sciences Press.

GOLDSTEIN, MICHAEL S.
    1992   *The Health Movement: Promoting Fitness in America.* New York: Twayne.
    1999   *Alternative Health Care: Medicine, Miracle, or Mirage?* Philadelphia: Temple University Press.
    2000   "The growing acceptance of complementary and alternative medicine," pp. 284–297 in C. E. Bird et al., eds., *Handbook of Medical Sociology.* Upper Saddle River, NJ: Prentice-Hall.

GOLDSTEIN, MICHAEL S., DENNIS JAFFE, CAROL SUTHERLAND, AND JOSIE WILSON
    1987   "Holistic physicians: Implications for the study of the medical profession," *Journal of Health and Social Behavior* 28(2): 103–119.

GOOD, BYRON J.
    1977   "The heart of what's the matter: The semantics of illness in Iran," *Culture, Medicine, and Psychiatry* 1: 25–58.
    1994   *Medicine, Rationality, and Experience.* Cambridge, England: Cambridge University Press.

GOOD, BYRON J., AND MARY-JO DELVECCHIO GOOD
    1981   "The meaning of symptoms: A cultural hermeneutic model for clinical practice," pp. 165–196 in A. Kleinman and L. Eisenberg, eds., *The Relevance of Social Science for Medicine*. Dordrecht, Netherlands: D. Reidel.
    1993   "'Learning Medicine': The constructing of medical knowledge at Harvard Medical School," pp. 81–107 in S. Lindenbaum and M. Lock, eds., *Knowledge, Power, and Practice*. Berkeley: University of California Press.

GOOD, MARY-JO DELVECCHIO
    1995   *American Medicine: The Quest for Competence*. Berkeley: University of California Press.

GOOD, MARY-JO DELVECCHIO, AND BYRON J. GOOD
    1982   "Patient requests in primary care clinics," pp. 275–295 in N. J. Chrisman and T. W. Maretzki, eds., *Clinically Applied Anthropology*. Dordrecht, Netherlands: D. Reidel.

GOOD, MARY-JO DELVECCHIO, BYRON J. GOOD, ARTHUR KLEINMAN, AND PAUL E. BRODWIN
    1992   "Epilogue," pp. 198–207 in M.-J. Delvecchio Good, B. J. Good, A. Kleinman, and P. E. Brodwin, eds., *Pain as Human Experience: An Anthropological Perspective*. Berkeley: University of California Press.

GORDON, DEBORAH
    1988   "Tenacious assumptions in Western medicine," pp. 19–56 in M. Lock and D. R. Gordon, eds., *Biomedicine Examined*. Dordrecht, Netherlands: Kluwer.

GORDON, SUZANNE
    2000   "Profits and prejudice: The undervalued work of nursing," *Dollars and Sense* 231(September/October): 16–30.

GORE, SUSAN
    1978   "The effect of social support in moderating the health consequences of unemployment," *Journal of Health and Social Behavior* 19: 157–165.

GOREY, KEVIN M.
    1999   "What is wrong with the U.S. health care system?: It does not effectively exist for one of every five Americans," *The Milbank Quarterly* 77(3): 401–407.

GOTTLIEB, MARTIN, AND KURT EICHENWALD
    1997   "A hospital chain's brass knuckles, and the backlash," *New York Times*, May 11.

GOULD-MARTIN, KATHERINE, AND CHORSWANG NGIN
    1981   "Chinese Americans," pp. 130–171 in A. Harwood, ed., *Ethnicity and Medical Care*. Cambridge, MA: Harvard University Press.

GRADY, DENISE
    2002a   "Hormone therapy study finds risk for some," *New York Times*, July 3.
    2002b   "Scientists question hormone therapies for menopause ills," *New York Times*, April 18.
    2002c   "Study finds new drugs may carry extra hazards," *New York Times*, May 1.

GRAHAM, HILARY
    1985   "Providers, negotiators, and mediators: Women as the hidden carers," pp. 25–52 in E. Lewin and V. Oleson, eds., *Women, Health, and Healing: Toward a New Perspective*. New York: Tavistock.
    2000   "The challenge of health inequalities," pp. 3–21 in H. Graham, ed., *Understanding Health Inequalities*. Philadelphia: Open University Press.

GRAY, ALASTAIR MCINTOSH
    1982   "Inequalities in health, The Black Report: A summary and comment," *International Journal of Health Services* 12(3): 349–380.

GRAY, BRADFORD H.
    1991   *The Profit Motive and Patient Care: The Changing Accountability of Doctors and Hospitals.* Cambridge, MA: Harvard University Press.
    1997   "Trust and trustworthy care in the managed care era," *Health Affairs* 16(1): 34–48.

GREEN, EDWARD C.
    1999   *Indigenous Theories of Contagious Disease.* Walnut Creek, CA: Altamira Press.

GREEN, JEREMY
    1983   "Detecting the hypersusceptible worker: Genetics and politics in industrial medicine," *International Journal of Health Services* 13(2): 247–264.

GRIFFITH, JAMES L., AND MELISSA E. GRIFFITH
    1994   *The Body Speaks.* New York: Basic Books.

GRITZER, GLENN
    1981   "Occupational specialization in medicine: Knowledge and market explanations," *Research in the Sociology of Health Care* 2: 251–283.

GRONEMAN, CAROL
    1995   "Nymphomania: The historical construction of female sexuality," pp. 219–249 in J. Terry and J. Urla, eds., *Deviant Bodies.* Bloomington: Indiana University Press.

GROOPMAN, LEONARD C.
    1987   "Medical internship as moral education: An essay on the system of training physicians," *Culture, Medicine, and Psychiatry* 11: 207–227.

GROSS, EDITH B.
    1994   "Health care rationing: Its effects on cardiologists in the United States and Britain," *Sociology of Health and Illness* 16(1): 19–37.

GROSSINGER, RICHARD
    1990   *Planet Medicine.* Berkeley, CA: North Atlantic Books.

GRUCHOW, WILLIAM
    1979   "Catecholamine activity and infectious disease episodes," *Journal of Human Stress* 5(3): 11–17.

GUADAGNOLI, EDWARD, AND PATRICIA WARD
    1998   "Patient participation in decision-making," *Social Science and Medicine* 47(3): 329–339.

GUARASCI, RICHARD
    1987   "Death by cotton dust," pp. 76–92 in S. L. Hills, ed., *Corporate Violence.* Totowa, NJ: Rowman and Littlefield.

GUARNACCIA, PETER J., AND PABLO FARIAS
    1988   "The social meaning of nervios: A case study of a Central American woman," *Social Science and Medicine* 26(12): 1223–1231.

GUARNACCIA, PETER J., VICTOR DELACANCELA, AND EMILIO CARRILLO
    1989   "The multiple meanings of *ataques de nervios* in the Latino community," *Medical Anthropology* 11: 47–62.

GUENDELMAN, SYLVIA
    1998   "Health and disease among Hispanics," pp. 277–301 in S. Loue, ed., *Handbook of Immigrant Health.* New York: Plenum.

GURALNIK, JAMES M., AND EDWARD L. SCHNEIDER
1990 "The compression of morbidity: A dream which may come true, someday!" pp. 42–53 in P. R. Lee and C. L. Estes, eds., *The Nation's Health.* Boston: Jones and Bartlett.

GURWITZ, JERRY H., T. S. FIELD, J. AVORN, D. MCCORMICK, S. JAIN, M. ECKLER, M. BENSER, A. C. EDMONDSON, AND D. W. BATES
2000 "Incidence and preventability of adverse drug events in nursing homes," *The American Journal of Medicine* 109(2): 87–94.

GUSFIELD, JOSEPH R.
1981 *The Culture of Public Problems: Drinking-Driving and the Symbolic Order.* Chicago: University of Chicago Press.

GUSSOW, JOAN DYE, ED.
1978 *The Feeding Web: Issues in Nutritional Ecology.* Palo Alto, CA: Bull.

HABER, SUZANNE N., AND PATRICIA BARCHAS
1984 "The regulatory effect of social rank on behavior after amphetamine administration," pp. 119–132 in P. Barchas and S. P. Mendoza, eds., *Social Hierarchies: Essays Toward a Sociophysiological Perspective.* Westport, CT: Greenwood.

HAHN, HARLAN
1988 "The politics of physical differences: Disability and discrimination," *Journal of Social Issues* 44(1): 39–47.
1994 "The minority group model of disability: Implications for medical sociology," *Research in the Sociology of Health Care* 11: 3–24.

HAHN, ROBERT A.
1995 *Sickness and Healing: An Anthropological Perspective.* New Haven, CT: Yale University Press.

HAHN, ROBERT A., AND ARTHUR KLEINMAN
1983 "Biomedical practice and anthropological theory: Frameworks and directions," *American Review of Anthropology* 12: 305–333.

HAMMOND, PHILLIP E.
1974 "Religion, pluralism, and Durkheim's integration thesis," pp. 115–142 in A. Eister, ed., *Changing Perspectives in the Scientific Study of Religion.* New York: Wiley.

HARASZTI, MIKLOS
1978 *A Worker in a Worker's State.* New York: Universe.

HARBURG, ERNEST, JOHN C. ERFURT, LOUISE HAUNSTEIN, CATHERINE CHAPE, WILLIAM SCHULL, AND M. A. SCHORK
1973 "Socio-ecological stress, suppressed hostility, skin color, and black-white male blood pressure, Detroit," *Psychosomatic Medicine* 35: 276–296.

HARDING, JIM
1981 "The pharmaceutical industry as a public-health hazard and as an institution of social control," pp. 274–291 in D. Coburn, C. D'Arcy, P. Ness, and G. M. Torrance, *Health and Canadian Society: Sociological Perspective.* Pickering, Canada: Fitzhenry and Whiteside.
1986 "Mood-modifiers and elderly women in Canada: The medicalization of poverty," pp. 51–86 in K. McDonnell, ed., *Adverse Effects: Women and the Pharmaceutical Industry.* Toronto, Canada: Women's Educational Press.

HARPER'S MAGAZINE
2001 "Medicare: Too little, too late," May: 84.

HARRINGTON, CHARLENE
  1984   "The nursing home industry," pp. 144–154 in M. Minkler and C. L. Estes, eds., *Readings in the Political Economy of Aging*. Farmingdale, NY: Baywood.
  1996   "The nursing home industry: Public policy in the 1990s," pp. 515–534 in P. Brown, ed., *Perspectives in Medical Sociology*. Prospect Heights, IL: Waveland Press.

HARRIS, GARDINER
  2001   "The Medicine Maze," *Wall Street Journal*, February 21.

HARRISON, JAMES, JAMES CHIN, AND THOMAS FICARROTTO
  1992   "Warning, masculinity may be dangerous to your health," pp. 271–285 in M. S. Kimmel and M. A. Mesner, eds., *Men's Lives*. New York: Macmillan.

HART, PETER
  1990   *A Nationwide Survey of Attitudes on Health Care and Nurses*. Washington, DC: Peter Hart Organization.

HARTLEY, HEATHER
  1999   "The influence of managed care on supply of certified nurse-midwives: An evaluation of the physician-dominance thesis," *Journal of Health and Social Behavior* 40(1): 87–101.

HARTMANN, BETSY
  1987   *Reproductive Rights and Wrongs: The Global Politics of Population Control and Contraceptive Choice*. New York: Harper & Row.

HARWOOD, ALAN
  1977   *Rx: Spiritist as Needed: A Study of a Puerto Rican Community Mental Health Resource*. New York: Wiley.

HASELTINE, FLORENCE, AND BEVERLY GREENBERG JACOBSON, EDS.
  1997   *Women's Health Research: A Medical and Policy Primer*. Washington, DC: American Psychiatric Press.

HATFIELD, ELAINE, AND SUSAN SPRECHER
  1986   *Mirror, Mirror . . . : The Importance of Looks in Everyday Life*. Albany: State University of New York Press.

HAY, IAIN
  1992   *Money, Medicine and Malpractice in American Society*. New York: Praeger.

HAYES, DENNIS
  1989   *Behind the Silicon Curtain: The Seductions of Work in a Lonely Era*. Boston: South End Press.

HAYNES, SUZANNE G.
  1991   "The effect of job demands, job control and new technologies on the health of employed women," pp. 157–169 in M. Frankenhaeuser, U. Lundberg, and M. Chesney, eds., *Women, Work and Health*. New York: Plenum Press.

HEALTH LETTER
  1987   "Tranquilizing air traffic controllers," 3(12): 11–12.

HEFFLER, STEPHEN, K. LEVIT, S. SMITH, C. SMITH, C. COWAN, H. LAZENBY, AND M. FREELAND
  2001   "Health spending growth up in 1999: Faster growth expected in the future," *Health Affairs* 20(2): 193–203.

HEIM, CHRISTINE, D. JEFFREY NEWPORT, STACEY HEIT, YOLANDA P. GRAHAM, MOLLY WILCOX, ROBERT BONSALL, ANDREW H. MILLER, AND CHARLES B. NEMEROFT
  2000   "Pituitary-adrenal and autonomic responses to stress in women after sexual and physical abuse in childhood," *Journal of the American Medical Association* 284(5): 592–597.

HELLANDER, IDA, DAVID U. HIMMELSTEIN, STEFFIE WOOLHANDLER, AND SIDNEY WOLFE
    1994   "Health care paper chase, 1993: The cost to the nation, the states, and the District of Columbia," *International Journal of Health Services* 24(1): 1–9.

HELMAN, CECIL
    1978   "'Feed a cold, starve a fever'–Folk models of infection in an English suburban community and their relation to medical treatment," *Culture, Medicine, and Psychiatry* 2: 107–137.
    1985   "Communication in primary care: The role of patient and practitioner explanatory models," *Social Science and Medicine* 20(9): 923–931.

HENDRICKS, ART
    1999   "Disabled persons and their right to equal treatment: Allowing differentiation while ending discrimination," pp. 113–129 in J. Mann, S. Gruskin, M. A. Grodin, and G. J. Annas, eds., *Health and Human Rights*. New York: Routledge.

HENLEY, NANCY M.
    1977   *Body Politics*. Englewood Cliffs, NJ: Prentice-Hall.

HERZLICH, CLAUDINE
    1973   "Health and illness: A social-psychological analysis," *European Monographs in Social Psychology, Vol. 5*. London: Academic Press.

HERZLICH, CLAUDINE, AND JANINE PIERRET
    1987   *Illness and Self in Society*. Baltimore: Johns Hopkins University Press.

HESS, JOHN L.
    1987   "Malthus then and now," *Nation,* 244(15): 496–500.

HEURTIN-ROBERTS, SUZANNE, AND EFRAIN REISIN
    1990   "Folk models of hypertension among black women: Problems in illness management," pp. 222–250 in J. Coreil and J. D. Mull, eds., *Anthropology and Primary Health Care*. Boulder, CO: Westview Press.

HIBBARD, JUDITH H., AND CLYDE R. POPE
    1993   "The equality of social roles as predictors of morbidity and mortality," *Social Science and Medicine* 36(3): 217–225.

HILBERT, RICHARD A.
    1984   "The acultural dimensions of chronic pain: Flawed reality construction and the problem of meaning," *Social Problems* 31(4): 365–378.

HILFIKER, DAVID
    1983   "Allowing the debilitated to die: Facing our ethical choices," *New England Journal of Medicine* 308: 718.
    1984   "Making medical mistakes," *Harper's Magazine* 268(1606): 59–65.
    1986   "A doctor's view of modern medicine," *New York Times Magazine,* February 23.
    1994   *Not All of Us Are Saints: A Doctor's Journey with the Poor*. New York: Hill and Wang.

HILL, ROLLA B., AND ROBERT ANDERSON
    1988   *The Autopsy: Medical Practice and Public Policy*. Boston: Butterworth.
    1991   "The autopsy crisis reexamined: The case for a national autopsy policy," *The Milbank Quarterly* 69(1): 51–78.

HILL, SHIRLEY A.
    1995   "Taking charge and making do: Childhood chronic illness in low-income black families," *Research in the Sociology of Health Care* 12: 141–156.

HILLMAN, MAYER, JOHN ADAMS, AND JOHN WHITELEGG
    1990   *One False Move–A Study of Children's Independent Mobility*. London: Policy Studies Institute.

HILTS, PHILIP J.
  1996   "Most doctors with violations keep their license," *New York Times,* March 29.
HIMMELSTEIN, DAVID, STEFFIE WOOLHANDLER, AND SIDNEY M. WOLFE
  1992   "The vanishing health care safety net: New data on uninsured Americans," *International Journal of Health Services* 22(3): 381–396.
HIMMELWEIT, SUSAN
  1999   "Caring labor," *Annals of the American Academy PPS* 561(January): 27–38.
HINMAN, AL
  1998   "Study: More doctors learning alternative medicine, but safety still questioned," CNN Interactive, September 1, retrieved from the World Wide Web at www.cnn.com/HEALTH/ on 12 November, 2001.
HOCHSCHILD, ARLIE
  1983   *The Managed Heart: Commercialization of Human Feeling.* Berkeley: University of California Press.
  1989   *The Second Shift.* New York: Viking Penguin.
HOGAN, CHRISTOPHER, JUNE LUNNEY, JON GABEL, AND JOANNE LYNN
  2001   "Medicare beneficiaries' costs of care in the last year of life," *Health Affairs* 20(4): 188–195.
HOGUE, CAROL J. R., MARTHA A. HARGRAVES, AND KAREN SCOTT COLLINS, EDS.
  2000   *Minority Health in America: Findings and Policy Implications from the Commonwealth Fund Minority Health Survey.* Baltimore: The Johns Hopkins University Press.
HOKANSON, J. E., AND M. BURGESS
  1962   "The effects of three types of aggression on vascular processes," *Journal of Abnormal and Social Psychology* 648: 446–449.
HOLAHAN, JOHN, LEIGHTON KU, AND MARY POHL
  2001   "Is immigration responsible for the growth in the number of the uninsured?" The Henry J. Kaiser Family Foundation Issue Paper, February 2001, retrieved from the World Wide Web at http://www.kff.org on 18 January, 2002.
HOLAHAN, JOHN, COLIN WINTERBOTTOM, AND SHRUTI RAJAN
  1995   "A shifting picture of health insurance coverage," *Health Affairs* 14(4): 253–264.
HOLTZ KAY, JANE
  1997   *Asphalt Nation.* New York: Crown.
HOMOLA, SAMUEL
  1968   *Backache: Home Treatment and Prevention.* West Nyack, NY: Parker.
HOOYMAN, NANCY R., AND JUDITH GONYEA
  1995   *Feminist Perspectives on Family Care.* Thousand Oaks, CA: Sage.
HOROBIN, GORDON, AND JIM MCINTOSH
  1983   "Time, risk, and routine in general practice," *Sociology of Health and Illness* 5(3): 312–331.
HORTON, ELIZABETH
  1985a   "Unfriendly persuasion," *Science Digest* 93(12): 214.
  1985b   "Why don't we buckle up?" *Science Digest* 93(2): 22.
HORTON, RICHARD
  2001   "Thalidomide comes back," *The New York Review,* May 17: 12–15.
HORWITZ, JILL, AND TROYEN BRENNAN
  1995   "Medical malpractice," pp. 307–327 in D. Calkins, R. J. Fernandopulle, B. S. Marino, eds., *Health Care Policy.* Cambridge, MA: Blackwell Science.

HORWITZ, RALPH I., CATHERINE M. VISCOLI, LISA BERKMAN, ROBERT M. DONALDSON, SARAH M. HORWITZ, CAROLYN J. MURRARY, DAVID F. RANSOHOFF, AND JODY SINDELAR
  1990   "Treatment adherence and risk of death after a myocardial infarction," *The Lancet* 136(September 1): 542–545.

HOTZ, ROBERT LEE
  1993   "Experiment to aid growth of short children resumes," *Los Angeles Times,* June 29.

HOUBEN, GERARD J.
  1991   "Production control and chronic stress in work organizations," *International Journal of Health Services* 21(2): 309–327.

HOUSE, JAMES S.
  1981   *Work Stress and Social Support.* Reading, MA: Addison-Wesley.

HOUSE, JAMES S., KARL R. LANDIS, AND DEBRA UMBERSON
  1988   "Social relationships and health," *Science* 214(July): 540–545.

HOWARD, GEORGE, ROGER T. ANDERSON, GREGORY RUSSELL, VIRGINIA J. HOWARD, AND GREGORY L. BURKE
  2000   "Race, socioeconomic status and cause specific mortality," *Annals of Epidemiology* 10: 214–223.

HOWARD, ROBERT
  1985   *Brave New Workplace.* New York: Penguin.

HOY, ELIZABETH W., RICHARD E. CURTIS, AND THOMAS RICE
  1991   "Change and growth in managed care," *Health Affairs* 10(4): 18–36.

HUGHES, DAVID
  1988   "When nurse knows best: Some aspects of nurse/doctor interaction in a casualty department," *Sociology of Health and Illness* 10(1): 1–22.

HUGHES, JAMES J.
  1996   "Managed care, university hospitals, and the doctor-nurse division of labor," *Research in the Sociology of Health Care* 13A: 63–92.

HUNT, LINDA M., BRIGITTE JORDAN, AND SUSAN IRWIN
  1989   "Views of what's wrong: Diagnosis and patients' concepts of illness," *Social Science and Medicine* 28(9): 945–956.

HUNT, LINDA M., ROLANDO TINOCO OJANGUREN, NORAH SCHWARTZ, AND DAVID HALPERIN
  1999   "Balancing risks and resources: Applying pesticides without using protective equipment in southern Mexico," pp. 235–254 in R. A. Hahn, ed., *Anthropology in Public Health: Bridging Differences in Culture and Society.* New York: Oxford University Press.

HUNTER, MYRA S., AND IRENE O'DEA
  1997   "Menopause," pp. 199–222 in J. M. Ussher, ed., *Body Talk: The Material and Discursive Regulation of Sexuality, Madness and Reproduction.* London: Routledge.

HUROWITZ, JAMES C.
  1993   "Toward a social policy for health," *New England Journal of Medicine* 329(2): 130–133.

HYDÉN, LARS-CHRISTER, AND LISBETH SACHS
  1998   "Suffering, hope and diagnosis: On the negotiation of chronic fatigue syndrome," *Health* 2(2): 175–193.

IDLER, ELLEN L.
  1995   "Religion, health, and nonphysical senses of self," *Social Forces* 74(2): 683–704.

IGLEHART, JOHN K.
    1993   "The American health care system: The End Stage Renal Disease Program," *New England Journal of Medicine* 328(5): 366–371.
    1998   "Physicians as agents of social control: The thoughts of Victor Fuchs," *Health Affairs* 17(1): 90–96.

ILLICH, IVAN
    1975   *Medical Nemesis: The Expropriation of Health.* London: Calder and Boyars.
    1992   *In the Mirror of the Past: Lectures and Addresses 1978–1990.* New York: Marion Boyars.

IM, EUN-OK, AFAF IBRAHIM MELEIS, AND KATHRYN A. LEE
    1999   "Symptom experience during menopausal transition: Low income Korean immigrant women," *Women and Health* 29(2): 53–67.

IMRIE, ROBERT
    1998   "Oppression, disability and access in the built environment," pp. 129–146 in T. Shakespeare, ed., *The Disability Reader.* London: Cassell.

IMSE, ANN
    2000   "Bankruptcy hits nursing homes, State's frailest citizens put trust in 58 facilities run by ailing companies," *Denver Rocky Mountain News,* October 22.

INDEPENDENT INQUIRY INTO INEQUALITIES IN HEALTH
    1998   *Independent Inquiry into Inequalities in Health Report* (The Acheson Report). London: The Stationers Office.

INHORN, MARCIA C., AND K. LISA WHITTLE
    2001   "Feminism meets the 'new' epidemiologies: Toward an appraisal of antifeminist biases in epidemiological research on women's health," *Social Science and Medicine* 53(5): 553–567.

INSTITUTE FOR WOMEN'S POLICY RESEARCH
    1994   *Women's Access to Health Insurance.* Washington, DC: Institute for Women's Policy Research.

IRWIN, SUSAN, AND BRIGITTE JORDAN
    1987   "Knowledge, practice, and power: Court-ordered cesarean section," *Medical Anthropology Quarterly* 1(3): 319–334.

ITO, YUTAKA, MARTIN H. TEICHER, CAROL A. GLOD, AND ERIKA ACKERMAN
    1998   "Preliminary evidence for aberrant cortical development in abused children: A quantitative EEG study," *The Journal of Neuropsychiatry and Clinical Neurosciences* 10(3): 298–307.

JACKSON, JEAN
    1994   "Chronic pain and the tension between the body as subject and object," pp. 201–228 in T. J. Csordas, ed., *Embodiment and Experience.* Cambridge, England: Cambridge University Press.

JACKSON, MICHAEL
    1983   "Knowledge of the body," *Man* 18: 327–345.

JACOBSON, ALAN M., AND JOAN B. LEIBOVICH
    1984   "Psychological issues in diabetes mellitus," *Psychosomatics* 25(1): 7–15.

JANES, CRAIG
    1986   "Migration and hypertension: An ethnography of disease risk in an urban Samoan community," pp. 175–211 in C. Janes, R. Stall, and S. Gifford, eds., *Anthropology and Epidemiology: Interdisciplinary Approaches to the Study of Health and Disease.* Dordrecht, Holland: D. Reidel.

JARVIS, WILLIAM R.
2001   "Infection control and changing health-care delivery systems," *Emerging Infectious Diseases* 7(2): 170–173.

JENSEN, GAIL A., MICHAEL A. MORRISEY, SHANNON GAFFNEY, AND DEREK K. LISTON
1997   "The new dominance of managed care: Insurance trends in the 1990s," *Health Affairs* 16(1): 125–136.

JERVIS, LORI L.
2001   "The pollution of incontinence and the dirty work of caregiving in a U.S. nursing home," *Medical Anthropology Quarterly* 15(1): 84–99.

JOHNSON, ALLEN
1978   "In search of the affluent society," *Human Nature* 1: 50–59.

JOHNSON, DANIEL M., J. SHERWOOD WILLIAMS, AND DAVID BROMLEY
1986   "Religion, health and healing: Findings from a southern city," *Sociological Analysis* 47(1): 66–73.

JOHNSON, ERNEST H., AND LARRY M. GANT
1996   "The association between anger-hostility and hypertension," pp. 95–116 in H. W. Neighbors and J. S. Jackson, eds., *Mental Health in Black America.* Thousand Oaks, CA: Sage.

JOHNSON, THOMAS M.
1987   "Premenstrual syndrome as a Western culture-specific disorder," *Culture, Medicine, and Psychiatry* 11: 337–356.

JOHNSON, THOMAS M., AND CAROLYN F. SARGENT
1990   *Medical Anthropology: A Handbook of Theory and Method.* New York: Greenwood Press.

JONAS, WAYNE B., AND JEFFREY S. LEVIN, EDS.
1999   *Essentials of Complementary and Alternative Medicine.* Philadelphia: Williams & Wilkins.

JONES, JAMES H.
1981   *Bad Blood: The Tuskegee Syphilis Experiment.* New York: Free Press.

JONES, KATHRYN
1993   "A hospital giant comes to town, bringing change," *New York Times,* November 21.

JONES, R. KENNETH
1985   "The development of medical sects," pp. 1–22 in R. K. Jones, ed., *Sickness and Sectarianism: Exploratory Studies in Medical and Religious Sectarianism.* London: Gower.

JONES, RUSSELL A.
1982   "Expectations and illness," pp. 145–167 in H. S. Friedman and M. R. DiMatteo, eds., *Interpersonal Issues in Health Care.* New York: Academic.

JORDAN, BRIGITTE
1997   "Authoritative knowledge and its construction," pp. 55–79 in R. E. Davis-Floyd and C. Sargent, eds., *Childbirth and Authoritative Knowledge in Cross-Cultural Perspective.* Berkeley: University of California Press.

KANE, ROSALIE A.
1993   "Delivering and financing long term care in Canada's ten provinces," pp. 89–101 in A. Bennett and O. Adams, eds., *Looking North for Health: What We Can Learn from Canada's Health Care System.* San Francisco: Jossey-Bass.

KAPLAN, JAY, STEPHEN MANUCK, THOMAS CLARKSON, FRANCES LUSSO, DAVID TAUB, AND ERIC MILLER
1983   "Social stress and atherosclerosis in normocholesterolemic monkeys," *Science* 220: 733–735.

KARASEK, ROBERT, AND TÖRES THEORELL
1990   *Healthy Work: Stress, Productivity and the Reconstruction of Working Life.* New York: Basic Books.

KARLSEN, SAFFRON, AND JAMES Y. NAZROO
2000   "Identity and structure: Rethinking ethnic inequalities in health," pp. 38–57 in H. Graham, ed., *Understanding Health Inequalities.* Philadelphia: Open University Press.

KASL, STANISLAV V., AND SIDNEY COBB
1966   "Health behavior, illness behavior, and sick role behavior," *Archives of Environmental Health* 12: 246–266.

KASSIRER, JEROME P.
1989   "Our stubborn quest for diagnostic certainty: A cause of excessive testing," *New England Journal of Medicine* 320: 1489–1491.
1995   "Our ailing public hospitals," *New England Journal of Medicine* 333(20): 1348–1349.

KASSIRER, JEROME P., AND G. A. GORRY
1978   "Clinical problem solving: A behavioral analysis," *Annals of Internal Medicine* 89: 245–255.

KASTENBAUM, ROBERT
1971   "Getting there ahead of time," *Psychology Today* 5: 52–54, 83–84.

KATES, ROBERT W.
1996   "Population, technology and the human environment: A thread through time," *Daedalus* 125(3), Summer: 43–71.

KATZ, ALFRED, HANNAH L. HEDRICK, D. H. ISENBERG, L. M. THOMPSON, T. GOODRICH, AND A. H. KUTSCHER, EDS.
1992   *Self-Help: Concepts and Applications.* Philadelphia: The Charles Press.

KAUFERT, PATRICIA
1988   "Menopause as process or event: The creation of definitions in biomedicine," pp. 331–349 in M. Lock and D. R. Gordon, eds., *Biomedicine Examined.* Dordrecht, Netherlands: Kluwer.

KAUFMAN, MARTIN
1971   *Homeopathy in America: The Rise and Fall of a Medical Heresy.* Baltimore: Johns Hopkins University Press.

KAUR, NARINDER
1990   "Impact of consumer culture on health," pp. 131–143 in B. Chaudhuri, ed., *Cultural and Environmental Dimensions on Health.* New Delhi, India: Inter India.

KAWACHI, ICHIRO, AND LISA BERKMAN
2000   "Social cohesion, social capital and health," pp. 174–190 in L. F. Berkman and I. Kawachi, eds., *Social Epidemiology.* New York: Oxford University Press.

KAWACHI, ICHIRO, BRUCE P. KENNEDY, VANITA GUPTA, AND DEBORAH PROTHROW-STITH
1999   "Women's status and the health of women and men: A view from the States," *Social Science and Medicine* 48: 21–32.

KAWACHI, ICHIRO, BRUCE P. KENNEDY, AND RICHARD G. WILKINSON, EDS.
1999   *The Society and Population Health Reader, Vol. I: Income Inequality and Health.* New York: The New Press.

KEARL, MICHAEL
  1993   "Dying American style: From moral to technological rite of passage," *American Journal of Ethics & Medicine* (Fall): 12–18.
KELAHER, MARGARET, NOELA BAIGRIE, LENORE MANDERSON, LAUREL MOORE, CINDY SHANNON, AND GAIL WILLIAMS
  1998   "Community perceptions of health, illness and care: Identifying issues for indigenous communities," *Women and Health* 28(1): 41–61.
KELLEY, DARYL
  1999   "Critical care: The number of patients turned away is rising," *Los Angeles Times,* January 24.
KELLY, MICHAEL P., AND DAVID FIELD
  1996   "Medical sociology, chronic illness and the body," *Sociology of Health and Illness* 18(2): 241–257.
KENNEDY, BRUCE P., ICHIRO KAWACHI, KIMBERLY LOCHNER, CAMARA P. JONES, AND DEBORAH PROTHROW-STITH
  1999   "(Dis)Respect and black mortality," pp. 465–473 in I. Kiwachi, B. P. Kennedy, and R. G. Wilkinson, eds., *The Society and Population Health Reader, Vol. I: Income Inequality and Health.* New York: The New Press.
KENNEDY, BRUCE P., ICHIRO KAWACHI, AND DEBORAH PROTHROW-STITH
  1996   "Income distribution and mortality: Cross-sectional ecological study of the Robin Hood Index in the United States," *British Medical Journal* 312: 1004–1007.
KERR, PETER
  1991   "Mental hospital chains accused of much cheating on insurance," *New York Times,* November 24.
  1992   "Centers for head injury accused of earning millions for neglect," *New York Times,* March 16.
KHIPPLE, SHEILENDR
  2001   "What's a bed plug? An L.O.L. in N.A.D." *New York Times,* May 13.
KIECOLT-GLASER, JANET K., AND RONALD GLASER
  1991   "Stress and immune function in humans," pp. 849–867 in R. Ader, D. Felten, and N. Cohen, eds., *Psychoneuroimmunology* (2nd ed.). New York: Academic Press.
KILBORN, PETER
  1996   "Factories that never close are scrapping the 5–day week," *New York Times,* June 4: A1.
KIM, JIM YONG, AARON SHAKOW, JAIME BAYONA, JOE RHATIGAN, AND EMMA L. RUBÍN DE CELIS
  2000   "Sickness amidst recovery: Public debt and private suffering in Peru," pp. 127–153 in J. Y. Kim, J. V. Millen, A. Irwin, and J. Gershman, eds., *Dying for Growth: Global Inequality and the Health of the Poor.* Monroe, ME: Common Courage Press.
KIM, RICHARD
  2001   "ACT UP goes global," *The Nation,* July 9: 17–19.
KING, PATRICIA A.
  1992   "The dangers of difference," *Hastings Center Report* 22(6): 35–38.
KING, RALPH T., JR.
  1996   "How a drug firm paid for university study, then undermined it," *Wall Street Journal,* April 25.

KIRCHER, TOBIAS, JUDITH NELSON, AND HAROLD BURDO
  1985   "The autopsy as a measure of accuracy of the death certificate," *New England Journal of Medicine* 313: 1263–1269.
KIRMAYER, LAURENCE J.
  1988   "Mind and body as metaphors: Hidden values in biomedicine," pp. 57–94 in M. Lock and D. R. Gordon, eds., *Biomedicine Examined.* Dordrecht, Netherlands: Kluwer.
KITMAN, JAMIE LINCOLN
  2000   "The secret history of lead," *The Nation* 270(211): 11–44.
KLEIN, DAVID, JACKOB NAJMAN, ARTHUR KOHRMAN, AND CLARKE MUNRO
  1982   "Patient characteristics that elicit negative responses from family physicians," *Journal of Family Practice* 14(5): 881–888.
KLEINMAN, ARTHUR
  1978   "The failure of Western medicine," *Human Nature* 1: 63–68.
  1980   *Patients and Healers in the Context of Culture: An Exploration of the Borderland Between Anthropology, Medicine, and Psychiatry.* Berkeley: University of California Press.
  1984   "Indigenous systems of healing: Questions for professional, popular, and folk care," pp. 138–164 in J. W. Salmon, ed., *Alternative Medicine: Popular and Policy Perspectives.* New York: Tavistock.
  1988   *The Illness Narratives: Suffering, Healing, and the Human Condition.* New York: Basic.
  1992   "Pain and resistance: The delegitimation and relegitimation of local worlds," pp. 169–197 in M. DelVecchio Good, P. E. Brodwin, B. J. Good, and A. Kleinman, eds., *Pain as Human Experience: An Anthropological Perspective.* Berkeley: University of California Press.
  1995   *Writing at the Margin: Discourse between Anthropology and Medicine.* Berkeley: University of California Press.
  1997   "The violences of everyday life," pp. 226–241 in V. Das et al., eds., *Violence and Subjectivity.* Berkeley: University of California Press.
KLEINMAN, ARTHUR, VEENA DAS, AND MARGARET LOCK, EDS.
  1997   *Social Suffering.* Berkeley: University of California Press.
KLEINMAN, ARTHUR, AND JOAN KLEINMAN
  1991   "Suffering and its professional transformation: Toward an ethnography of interpersonal experience," *Culture, Medicine and Psychiatry* 15(3): 275–301.
KLINKENBORG, VERLYN
  1997   "Awakening to sleep," *New York Times Magazine* (January 5).
KNICKMAN, JAMES R., AND KENNETH E. THORPE
  1995   "Financing for health care," pp. 267–293 in A. R. Kovner, ed., *Jonas's Health Care Delivery in the United States.* New York: Springer.
KNUTSSON, ANDER S., BJORN G. JONSSON, TORBJÖRN ÅKERSTEDT, AND KRISTINA ORTH-GOMER
  1986   "Increased risk of ischemic heart disease in shift workers," *The Lancet* 2: 86–92.
KOENIG, BARBARA
  1988   "The technological imperative in medical practice: The social creation of a 'routine' treatment," pp. 465–496 in M. Lock and D. R. Gordon, eds., *Biomedicine Examined.* Dordrecht, Netherlands: Kluwer.
KOGAN, MONROE D., GREG R. ALEXANDER, MARTHA A. TEITELBAUM, BRIAN W. JACK, MILTON KOTELCHUCK, AND GREGORY PAPPAS
  1995   "The effects of gaps in health insurance on continuity of a regular source of care among preschool-aged children in the United States," *Journal of the American Medical Association* 274(18): 1429–1435.

KOHN, LINDA T., JANET M. CORRIGAN, AND MOLLA S. DAVIDSON, EDS.
   2000   *To Err is Human: Building a Safer Health System*. Washington, DC: National Academy Press.

KOLATA, GINA
   1994   "Study says 1 in 5 Americans suffers from chronic pain," *New York Times*, October 21.

KONNER, MELVIN
   1987   *Becoming a Doctor: A Journey of Initiation in Medical School*. New York: Viking.

KOTARBA, JOSEPH A.
   1977   "The chronic pain experience," pp. 257–272 in J. Douglas, ed., *Existential Sociology*. Cambridge, England: Cambridge University Press.

KRAUT, ALAN M.
   1994   *Silent Travelers: Germs, Genes, and the "Immigrant Menace."* New York: Basic Books.

KRIEGER, NANCY
   1990   "Racial and gender discrimination: Risk factors for high blood pressure?" *Social Science and Medicine* 30: 1273–1281.
   1994   "Epidemiology and the web of causation: Has anyone seen the spider?" *Social Science and Medicine* 39(7): 887–903.
   2000   "Discrimination and health," pp. 36–75 in L. F. Berkman and I. Kawachi, eds., *Social Epidemiology*. New York: Oxford University Press.

KRIEGER, NANCY, AND ELIZABETH FEE
   1994   "Man-made medicine and women's health: The biopolitics of sex/gender and race/ethnicity," *International Journal of Health Services* 24(2): 265–283.

KROHNE, HEINZ WALTER
   1990   "Personality as a mediator between objective events and their subjective representation," *Psychological Inquiry* 1(1): 26–29.

KU, LEIGHTON, AND SHEETAL MATANI
   2001   "Left out: Immigrants' access to health care and insurance," *Health Affairs* 20(1): 247–256.

KUHN, THOMAS S.
   1970   *The Structure of Scientific Revolutions. International Encyclopedia of Unified Science, Vol. 2, No. 2*. Chicago: University of Chicago Press.

KUNISCH, JUDITH R.
   1989   "Electronic fetal monitors: Marketing forces and the resulting controversy," pp. 41–60 in K. S. Ratcliff, ed., *Healing Technology: Feminist Perspectives*. Ann Arbor: University of Michigan Press.

KUNZLE, DAVID
   1981   *Fashion and Fetishism: A Social History of the Corset, Tight-Lacing and Other Forms of Body Sculpture in the West*. London: Rowan and Littlefield.

LaCHEEN, CARY
   1986   "Population control and the pharmaceutical industry," pp. 89–136 in K. McDonnell, ed., *Adverse Effects: Women and the Pharmaceutical Industry*. Toronto, Canada: Women's Educational Press.

LACK, DOROTHEA Z.
   1982   "Women and pain: Another feminist issue," *Women and Therapy* 1(1): 55–63.

LADERMAN, CAROL, AND MARINA ROSEMAN, EDS.
   1995   *The Performance of Healing*. New York: Routledge.

LAGNADO, LUCETTE
   1997   "Hospitals profit by 'upcoding' illnesses," *Wall Street Journal*, April 17: B1, 10.

LAKE, EILEEN T.
    1998   "Advances in understanding and predicting nurse turnover," *Research in the Sociology of Health Care* 15: 147–171.

LAKOFF, ROBIN T., AND RAQUEL L. SCHERR
    1984   *Face Value: The Politics of Beauty.* Boston: Routledge and Kegan Paul.

LANDEFELD, C. SETH, MARY-MARGARET CHEN, ANN MYERS, RICHARD GELLER, STANLEY ROBBINS, AND LEE GOLDMAN
    1988   "Diagnostic yield of the autopsy in a university hospital and a community hospital," *New England Journal of Medicine* 318(19): 1249–1254.

LANDEFELD, C. SETH, AND LEE GOLDMAN
    1989   "The autopsy in clinical medicine," *Mayo Clinic Proceedings* 64(9): 1185–1189.

LAPLANTE, MITCHELL P.
    1996   "Health conditions and impairments causing disability," *Disability Statistics Abstract* 16 (September).

LARSON, MAGALI SARFATTI
    1979   "Professionalism: Rise and fall," *International Journal of Health Services* 9(4): 607–627.

LASSEY, MARIE L., WILLIAM R. LASSEY, AND MARTIN J. JINKS
    1997   *Health Care Systems around the World.* Upper Saddle River, NJ: Prentice-Hall.

LATOUR, BRUNO, AND STEVE WOOLGAR
    1979   *Laboratory Life: The Social Construction of Scientific Fact.* Beverly Hills, CA: Sage.

LA VEIST, THOMAS A.
    1993   "Segregation, poverty and empowerment: Health consequences for African Americans," *The Milbank Quarterly* 71(1): 41–64.

LAW, SYLVIA
    1974   *Blue Cross—What Went Wrong?* New Haven, CN: Yale University Press.

LAWRENCE, PHILIP
    1958   "Chronic illness and socioeconomic status," pp. 37–49 in E. G. Jaco, ed., *Patients, Physicians and Illness.* New York: Free Press.

LAZARUS, ELLEN S.
    1988   "Theoretical considerations for the study of the doctor-patient relationship: Implications of a perinatal study," *Medical Anthropology Quarterly* 2(1): 34–58.

LAZARUS, RICHARD, ED.
    1966   *Psychological Stress and the Coping Process.* New York: McGraw Hill.

LEAR, DANA
    1996   "Women and A.I.D.S. in Africa: A critical review," pp. 276–301 in J. Subedi and E. B. Gallagher, eds., *Society, Health and Disease.* Upper Saddle River, NJ: Prentice-Hall.

LEARY, WARREN E.
    1991   "With one disease defeated, another is attacked," *New York Times,* December 6.
    1995a   "Government gives up right to control prices of drugs it helps develop," *New York Times,* April 12.
    1995b   "Routine electronic monitoring of fetuses is challenged in study," *New York Times,* October 25.

LEDER, DREW
    1984   "Medicine and paradigms of embodiment," *Journal of Medicine and Philosophy* 9: 29–43.

LEICHTER, HOWARD M.
    1991   *Free to Be Foolish.* Princeton, NJ: Princeton University Press.

LEIDERMAN, DEBORAH, AND JEAN-ANNE GRISSO
    1985   "The GOMER phenomenon," *Journal of Health and Social Behavior* 26: 222–231.
LENNERLOF, LENNART
    1988   "Learned helplessness at work," *International Journal of Health Services* 18(2): 207–222.
LENNON, MARY CLARE
    1994   "Women, work and well-being," *Journal of Health and Social Behavior* 35: 235–247.
LEONHARDT, DAVID
    2001   "Health care as main engine: Is that so bad?" *New York Times,* November 11.
LERNER, MICHAEL
    1992   *Surplus Powerlessness.* Atlantic Highlands, NJ: Humanities Press, Intl.
LESLIE, CHARLES, ED.
    1976   *Asian Medical Systems: A Comparative Study.* Berkeley: University of California Press.
LETSCH, SUZANNE W.
    1993   "National health care spending in 1991," *Health Affairs* 12(1): 94–110.
LEVI, LENNART
    1978   "Quality of the working environment: Protection and promotion of occupational mental health," *Working Life in Sweden* 8.
    1981   *Preventing Work Stress.* Reading, MA: Addison-Wesley.
LEVIN, LOWELL S., AND ELLEN L. IDLER
    1981   *The Hidden Health Care System: Mediating Structures and Medicine.* Cambridge, MA: Ballinger.
LEVINE, JON D., N. C. GORDON, AND H. FIELDS
    1978   "Mechanism of placebo analgesia," *Lancet* 2(23): 654–657.
LEVINS, RICHARD, AND RICHARD LEWONTIN
    1985   *The Dialectical Biologist.* Cambridge, MA: Harvard University Press.
LEVIT, KATHERINE R., HELEN C. LAZENBY, AND LEKHA SIVARAJAN
    1996   "Health care spending in 1994: Slowest in decades," *Health Affairs* 15(2): 130–144.
LEWIN, TAMAR
    1987   "Company sues its workers' doctors," *New York Times,* June 9.
LEWIN, TAMAR, AND MARTIN GOTTLIEB
    1997   "In hospital sales, an overlooked side effect," *New York Times,* April 27.
LEWIS, CHARLES E.
    1976   "Health maintenance organizations: Guarantors of access to medical care?" pp. 220–240 in C. Lewis, R. Fein, and D. Mechanic, eds., *A Right to Health: The Problem of Access in Primary Care.* New York: Wiley-Interscience.
LEWIS, IOAN M.
    1971   *Ecstatic Religion: An Anthropological Study of Spirit Possession and Shamanism.* Harmondsworth, England: Penguin.
LEWTON, ELIZABETH L., AND VICTORIA BYDONE
    2000   "Identity and healing in three Navajo religious traditions," *Medical Anthropology Quarterly* 14(4): 476–497.
LIGHT, DONALD W.
    1992   "Excluding more, covering less: The health insurance industry in the U.S.," *Health/PAC Bulletin,* Spring: 7–13.

1993   "Countervailing powers," pp. 69–79 in F. W. Hafferty and J. B. McKinlay, eds., *The Changing Character of the Medical Profession*. New York: Oxford University Press.

2000   "The medical profession and organizational change: From professional dominance to countervailing power," pp. 201–216 in C. E. Bird, P. Conrad, and A. M. Fremont, eds., *Handbook of Medical Sociology*. Upper Saddle River, NJ: Prentice-Hall.

LILIENFELD, DAVID E.
1991   "The silence: The asbestos industry and early occupational cancer research— a case study," *American Journal of Public Health* 81(6): 791–800.

LINDHEIM, ROSLYN
1985   "New design parameters for healthy places," *Places* 2(4): 17–27.

LINK, BRUCE G., AND JO PHELAN
1995   "Social conditions in fundamental causes of disease," *Journal of Health and Social Behavior* (Extra Issue): 80–94.

2000   "Evaluating the fundamental cause explanation for social disparities in health," pp. 33–46 in C. E. Bird, P. Conrad, and A. M. Fremont, eds., *Handbook of Medical Sociology*. Upper Saddle River, NJ: Prentice-Hall.

LINK, BRUCE G., EZRA SUSSER, ANN STUEVE, JO PHELAN, ROBERT E. MOORE, AND ELMER STRUENING
1994   "Lifetime and five-year prevalence of homelessness in the United States," *American Journal of Public Health* 84: 1907–1912.

LITT, IRIS F.
1997   *Taking Our Pulse, the Health of America's Women*. Palo Alto, CA: Stanford University Press.

LITTLE, MARILYN
1982   "Conflict and negotiation in a new role: The family nurse practitioner," *Research in the Sociology of Health Care* 2: 31–59.

LITVA, ANDREA, AND JOHN EYLES
1994   "Health or healthy: Why people are not sick in a southern Ontarian town," *Social Science and Medicine* 39(8): 1083–1091.

LIVNEH, HANOCH
1991   "On the origins of negative attitudes toward people with disabilities," pp. 181–196 in R. P. Marinelli and A. E. Dell, eds., *The Psychological and Social Impact of Disability* (3rd ed.). New York: Springer.

LOCK, MARGARET
1990   "On being ethnic: The politics of identity breaking and making in Canada, or, Nevra on Sunday," *Culture, Medicine and Psychiatry* 14(2): 237–254.

1991   "Contested meanings of the menopause," *The Lancet* 337 (May 25): 1270–1272.

1993a   "The politics of mid-life and menopause: Ideologies for the second sex in North America and Japan," pp. 330–363 in S. Lindenbaum and M. Lock, eds., *Knowledge, Power, and Practice*. Berkeley: University of California Press.

1993b   *Encounters with Aging. Mythologies of Menopause in Japan and North America*. Berkeley: University of California Press.

1996   "Death in technological time: Locating the end of meaningful life," *Medical Anthropology Quarterly* 10(4): 575–600.

2000a   "Accounting for disease and distress: Morals of the normal and abnormal," pp. 259–276 in G. L. Albrecht et al., eds., *Handbook of Social Studies in Health and Medicine*. London: Sage.

2000b "On dying twice: Culture, technology, and the determination of death," pp. 233–262 in M. Lock, A. Young, and A. Cambrosio, eds., *Living and Working with the New Medical Technologies.* Cambridge, England: Cambridge University Press.

LOCK, MARGARET, AND PATRICIA KAUFERT, EDS.
1998 *Pragmatic Women and Body Politics.* Cambridge, England: Cambridge University Press.

LOCK, MARGARET, AND NANCY SCHEPER-HUGHES
1990 "A critical-interpretive approach in medical anthropology: Rituals and routines of discipline and dissent," pp. 47–72 in T. M. Johnson and C. F. Sargent, *Medical Anthropology: A Handbook of Theory and Method.* New York: Greenwood.

LOHR, KATHLEEN, R. H. BROOK, C. J. KAMBERG, G. GOLDBERG, A. LEIBOWITZ, J. KEESEY, D. REBOUSSIN, AND J. P. NEWHOUSE
1986 *Use of Medical Care in the Rand Health Insurance Experiment: Diagnosis and Service-Specific Analysis in a Randomized Control Trial.* Santa Monica, CA: Rand.

LONG, STEPHEN H., AND M. SUSAN MARQUIS
1998 "The effects of Florida's Medicaid eligibility expansion for pregnant women," *American Journal of Public Health* 88(3): 371–376.

LONGMORE, PAUL K.
1987 "Screening stereotypes: Images of disabled people in television and motion pictures," pp. 65–78 in A. Gartner and T. Joe, eds., *Images of the Disabled, Disabling Images.* New York: Praeger.

LONSDALE, SUSAN
1990 *Women and Disability: The Experiences of Physical Disability among Women.* New York: Macmillan.

LORBER, JUDITH
1997 *Gender and the Social Construction of Illness.* Thousand Oaks, CA: Sage.

LOUE, SANA, ED.
1998 *Handbook of Immigrant Health.* New York: Plenum.

LOW, SETHA M.
1985 *Culture, Politics, and Medicine in Costa Rica.* Bedford Hills, NY: Redgrave.
1994 "Embodied metaphors: Nerves as lived experience," pp. 139–162 in T. J. Csordas, ed., *Embodiment and Experience.* Cambridge, England: Cambridge University Press.

LUDMERER, KENNETH
1999 *Time to Heal: American Medical Education from the Turn of the Century to the Era of Managed Care.* Oxford, England: Oxford University Press.

LUFT, HAROLD S.
1999 "Why are physicians so upset about managed care?" *Journal of Health Politics, Policy and Law* 24(5): 957–966.

LUKOFF, DAVID, FRANCIS LU, AND ROBERT TURNER
1992 "Toward a more culturally sensitive DSM-IV: Psychoreligious and psychospiritual problems," *The Journal of Nervous and Mental Disease* 180: 673–682.

LUNDBERG, ULF
1976 "Urban commuting: Crowdedness and catecholamine excretion," *Journal of Human Stress* 2(3): 26–31.

LUNDBERG, ULF, ROLAND KADEFORS, BO MELIN, GUNNAR PALMERUD, PETER HASSMÉN, MARGARETA ENGSTRÖM, AND INGELA ELFSBERG DOHNS
    1994   "Psychophysiological stress and EMG activity of the trapezius muscle," *International Journal of Behavioral Medicine* 1(4): 354–370.

LUPTON, DEBORAH
    1994   *Medicine as Culture.* Thousand Oaks, CA: Sage.
    1995   *The Imperative of Health: Public Health and the Regulated Body.* Thousand Oaks, CA: Sage.
    1996a *Food, Body, and the Self.* Thousand Oaks, CA: Sage.
    1996b "Your life in their hands: Trust in the medical encounter," pp. 157–172 in V. James and J. Gabe, eds., *Health and the Sociology of Emotions.* Oxford, England: Blackwell.
    1998   "Medicine and health care in popular media," pp. 194–207 in A. Petersen and C. Waddell, eds., *Health Matters: A Sociology of Illness, Prevention and Care.* Buckingham, England: Open University Press.

LYNCH, JAMES J.
    1979   *The Broken Heart.* New York: Basic.
    1985   *The Language of the Heart.* New York: Basic.

LYNCH, JAMES J., AND PAUL J. F. ROSCH
    1990   "The heart of dialogue: Human communication and cardiovascular health," pp. 31–52 in H. Balner, ed., *A New Medical Model: A Challenge for Biomedicine?* Amsterdam: Swets and Zeitlinger.

LYNCH, JOHN, AND GEORGE KAPLAN
    2000   "Socioeconomic position," pp. 13–35 in L. F. Berkman and I. Kawachi, eds., *Social Epidemiology.* New York: Oxford University Press.

LYNCH, MARTY, AND MEREDITH MINKLER
    1997   "Impacts of the proposed restructuring of Medicare and Medicaid on the elderly," *International Journal of Health Services* 27(1): 57–75.

LYON, MARGOT L.
    1990   "Order and healing: The concept of order and its importance in the conceptualization of healing," *Medical Anthropology* 12(10): 249–268.

LYONS, BARBARA, ALINA SALGANICOFF, AND DIANE ROWLAND
    1996   "Poverty, access to health care, and Medicaid's critical role for women," pp. 273–295 in M. M. Falik and K. S. Collins, eds., *Women's Health: The Commonwealth Fund Survey.* Baltimore: Johns Hopkins University Press.

MACINTYRE, SALLY, AND ANNE ELLAWAY
    2000   "Ecological approaches: Rediscovering the role of the physical and social environment," pp. 332–348 in L. F. Berkman and I. Kawachi, eds., *Social Epidemiology.* New York: Oxford University Press.

MACLENNAN, CAROL A.
    1988   "From accident to crash: The auto industry and the politics of injury," *Medical Anthropology Quarterly* 2(3): 233–250.

MAIRS, NANCY
    1987   "Hers," *New York Times,* July 9.

MALTHUS, THOMAS ROBERT
    [1798] 1965   *Essay on the Principle of Population as It Affects the Future Improvements of Society,* reprinted as *First Essay on Population,* 1798. New York: Kelley.

MANSOUR, JARED
    1987   "Eating culture: Food as junk commodity," *Critique* 25: 14–16.

MARETZKI, THOMAS, AND EDUARD SEIDLER
    1985   "Biomedicine and naturopathic healing in West Germany: A historical and ethnomedical view of a stormy relationship," *Culture, Medicine, and Psychiatry* 9(4): 383–421.

MARKS, NADINE F.
    1996   "Socioeconomic status, gender and health at midlife," *Research in the Sociology of Health Care* 13(A): 135–152.

MARMOR, THEODORE R.
    1993   "Patterns of fact and fiction in the use of the Canadian experience," *American Review of Canadian Studies* 23(1): 47–64.
    1999   *The Politics of Medicare.* Hawthorne, NY: Aldine de Gruyter.

MARMOR, THEODORE R., AND JERRY L. MASHAW
    1997   "Canada's health insurance and ours: The real lessons, the big choices," pp. 482–492 in P. Conrad, ed., *The Sociology of Health and Illness.* New York: St. Martin's Press.

MARMOT, MICHAEL G.
    1996   "The social pattern of health and disease," pp. 42–67 in D. Blane, E. Brunner, and R. Wilkinson, eds., *Health and Social Organization.* London: Routledge.
    1999   "Acting on the evidence to reduce inequalities in health," *Health Affairs* 18(3): 42–44.
    2000   "Multilevel approaches to understanding social determinants," pp. 349–367 in L. F. Berkman and I. Kawachi, eds., *Social Epidemiology.* New York: Oxford University Press.
    2002   "The influence of income on health: Views of an epidemiologist," *Health Affairs* 21(2): 31–46.

MARMOT, MICHAEL G., M. KOGEVINAS, AND M. A. ELSTON
    1987   "Social/economic status and disease," *Annual Review of Public Health* 8: 111–135.

MARMOT, MICHAEL G., AND J. F. MUSTARD
    1994   "Coronary heart disease from a population perspective," pp. 189–214 in R. G. Evans, M. L. Barer, and T. R. Marmor, eds., *Why Are Some People Healthy and Others Not?: The Determinants of Health of Populations.* New York: Aldine de Gruyter.

MARQUIS, M. SUSAN
    1984   *Cost-Sharing and the Patient's Choice of Provider.* Santa Monica, CA: Rand.

MARTINEZ, BARBARA
    2001   "Gatekeepers in retreat," *Wall Street Journal,* February 21.

MASTROIANNI, ANNA C., RUTH FADEN, AND DANIEL FEDERMAN, EDS.
    1994   *Women and Health Research, Vol. 1: Ethical and Legal Issues of Including Women in Clinical Studies.* Washington, DC: National Academy Press/Institute of Medicine.

MAUSNER, JUDITH S., AND ANITA BAHN
    1985   *Epidemiology: An Introductory Text* (2nd ed.). Philadelphia: Saunders.

MAXWELL, STEPHANIE, MARILYN MOON, AND MISHA SEGAL
    2000   "Growth in Medicare and out-of-pocket spending: Impact on vulnerable beneficiaries," The Urban Institute, December 2000, retrieved from the World Wide Web at www.ui.urban.org on 23 March, 2002.

MAY, CLIFFORD
  1985   "Reporter's notebook: Images far from Ethiopia's famine," *New York Times,*
          April 7.
McCARTY, RICHARD, KARIN HORWATT, AND MARIA KONARSKA
  1988   "Chronic stress and sympathetic-adrenal medullary responsiveness," *Social
          Science and Medicine* 26(3): 333–341.
McCORMICK, JOSEPH, AND SUSAN FISHER-HOCH
  1996   *Level 4: Virus Hunters of the CDC.* Atlanta, GA: Turner Publishing.
McCREA, FRANCES
  1983   "The politics of menopause: The discovery of a deficiency disease," *Social
          Problems* 13(1): 111–123.
McDADE, THOMAS
  1996   "Prostates and profits: The social construction of benign prostatic hyperplasia
          in American men," *Medical Anthropology* 17: 1–22.
McELROY, ANN, AND PATRICIA K. TOWNSEND
  1985   *Medical Anthropology in Ecological Perspective.* Boulder, CO: Westview.
McGUIRE, MEREDITH B.
  1982   *Pentecostal Catholics: Power, Charisma, and Order in a Religious Movement.* Philadelphia:
          Temple University Press.
  1983   "Words of power: Personal empowerment and healing," *Culture, Medicine, and
          Psychiatry* 7: 221–240.
  1985   "Religion and Healing," pp. 268–284 in P. Hammond, ed., *The Sacred in a
          Secular Age.* Berkeley: University of California Press.
  1988   *Ritual Healing in Suburban America,* with the assistance of Debra Kantor. New
          Brunswick, NJ: Rutgers University Press.
  1996   "Religion and healing the mind/body/self," *Social Compass* 43(1): 101–116.
  2002   *Religion: The Social Context* (5th ed.). Belmont, CA: Wadsworth.
McGUIRE, MEREDITH B., AND DEBRA J. KANTOR
  1987   "Belief systems and illness experiences: The case of non-medical healing
          groups," *Research in the Sociology of Health Care* 6: 221–248.
McINTOSH, ALEX WM.
  1995   "World hunger as a social problem," pp. 35–63 in D. Maurer and J. Sobal, eds.,
          Eating Agendas: Food and Nutrition as Social Problems. New York: Aldine de Gruyter.
McKEOWN, THOMAS
  1979   *The Role of Medicine: Dream, Mirage, or Nemesis?* Princeton, NJ: Princeton Univer-
          sity Press.
McKINLAY, JOHN B.
  1996   "Some contributions from the social system to gender inequalities in heart
          disease," *Journal of Health and Social Behavior* 37(March): 1–26.
  [1974] 2001   "A case for refocusing upstream: The political economy of illness,"
          pp. 516–529 in P. Conrad, ed., *The Sociology of Health and Illness.* New York:
          Worth.
McKINLAY, JOHN B., AND SONJA M. McKINLAY
  1977   "The questionable effect of medical measures on the decline of mortality in
          the United States in the twentieth century," *Milbank Memorial Fund Quarterly* 55:
          405–428.

MCKINLAY, JOHN B., SONJA M. MCKINLAY, AND ROBERT BEAGLE ROLE
    1989   "Trends in death and disease and the contribution of medical measures," pp. 14–45 in H. E. Freeman and S. Levine, eds., *Handbook of Medical Sociology* (4th ed.). Englewood Cliffs, NJ: Prentice-Hall.

MCKINLAY, JOHN B., AND JOHN D. STOECKLE
    1988   "Corporatization and the social transformation of doctoring," *International Journal of Health Services* 18(2): 191–205.

MCKINLAY, SONJA M., D. J. BRAMBILLA, N. E. AVIS, AND JOHN B. MCKINLAY
    1991   "Women's experience of the menopause," *Current Obstetrics and Gynaecology* 1: 3–7.

MCMURRAY, CHRISTINE, AND ROY SMITH
    2001   *Disease of Globalization.* London: Earthscan Publication Ltd.

MCNEIL, DONALD G., JR.
    2001a   "AIDS and death hold no sting for fatalistic men at African bar," *New York Times,* November 29.
    2001b   "South African victims face rapists and H.I.V.," *New York Times,* November 30.

MCNEILLY, MAYA DOMINGUEZ, ELWOOD L. ROBINSON, NORMAN B. ANDERSON, CARL F. PIEPER, AKBAR SHAH, PAUL S. TOTH, PAMELA MARTIN, DREAMA JACKSON, TERRENCE D. SAULTER, CYNTHIA WHITE, MARGARATHA KUCHIBATLA, SHIRLEY M. COLLADO, AND WILLIAM GERIN
    1995   "Affects of racist provocation and social support on cardiovascular reactivity in African American women," *International Journal of Behavioral Medicine* 2(4): 321–338.

MECHANIC, DAVID
    1976   "Illness, illness behavior, and help-seeking," pp. 161–175 in D. Mechanic, ed., *The Growth of Bureaucratic Medicine.* New York: Wiley.
    1978   *Medical Sociology.* New York: Free Press.
    1999   "Issues in promoting health," *Social Science and Medicine* 48: 711–718.
    2000   "Managed care and the imperative for a new professional ethic," *Health Affairs* 19(5): 100–111.

MECHANIC, DAVID, DONNA D. MCALPINE, AND MARSHA ROSENTHAL
    2001   "Are patients' office visits with physicians getting shorter?" *New England Journal of Medicine* 344(3): 198–204.

MEDVEDEV, Z., AND R. MEDVEDEV
    1971   *A Question of Madness.* New York: Knopf.

MEE, CHERYL L., AND KATHERINE W. CAREY
    2001   "Nursing 2000 salary survey," *Nursing Communities,* retrieved from the World Wide Web at www.tnpj.com/nursingcommunities.htm on 22 December, 2001.

MEIER, BARRY
    1993   "Doctors' investments in home care grow, raising fears of ethical swamp," *New York Times,* March 19.
    1997   "Anglicans mull new step on baby formula," *New York Times,* March 3.

MELNICK, DANIEL, AND BEATRICE ROUSE, EDS.
    2001   *"Portrait of Health in the United States: Major Statistical Trends and Guide to Resources.* Lanham, MD: Bernan.

MELOSH, BARBARA
    1982   *The Physician's Hand: Work, Culture, and Conflict in American Nursing.* Philadelphia: Temple University Press.

MELZACK, RONALD, AND PETER WALL
    1983   *The Challenge of Pain.* New York: Basic.
MEMBERS OF THE WORKING PARTY
    1975   "Occupational accidents," pp. 65–90 in Members of the Working Party, eds.,
            *Research for a Better Work Environment: A Summary of Reports on Four Central Research
            Areas.* Stockholm: LiberFörlag.
MENGES, LOUWRENS J.
    1994   "Beyond the Anglophone world: Regular and alternative medicine," *Social
            Science and Medicine* 39(6): 871–873.
MERTON, ROBERT K., GEORGE C. READER, AND PATRICIA L. KENDALL, EDS.
    1957   *The Student Physician.* Cambridge, MA: Harvard University Press.
MESSING, KAREN
    1998   *One-Eyed Science: Occupational Health and Women Workers.* Philadelphia: Temple
            University Press.
MEYER, MADONNA HARRINGTON, AND ELIZA K. PAVALKO
    1996   "Family, work and access to health insurance among mature women," *Journal
            of Health and Social Behavior* 37: 311–325.
MILIO, NANCY
    1985   "Health policy and the emerging tobacco reality," *Social Science and Medicine*
            21(6): 603–613.
MILLEN, JOYCE V., AND TIMOTHY H. HOLTZ
    2000   "Dying for growth, part I: Transnational corporations and the health of the
            poor," pp. 177–223 in Kim et al., eds., *Dying for Growth: Global Inequality and the
            Health of the Poor.* Monroe, ME: Common Courage Press.
MILLMAN, MARCIA
    1976   *The Unkindest Cut: Life in the Backrooms of Medicine.* New York: Morrow.
    1980   *Such a Pretty Face: Being Fat in America.* New York: Norton.
MILLS, C. WRIGHT
    1956   *White Collar.* New York: Oxford University Press.
    1959   *The Sociological Imagination.* New York: Oxford University Press.
MINTZ, SIDNEY
    1979   "Time, Sugar, and Sweetness," *Marxist Perspectives* 8: 56–73.
MINZ, RENE
    1997   "Use of alternative health care by family practice patients," *Archives of Family
            Medicine* 5 (March/April): 181–184.
MISHLER, ELLIOTT
    1984   *The Discourse of Medicine: Dialectics of Medical Interviews.* Norwood, NJ: Ablex.
MITCHELL, JEAN M., AND ELTON SCOTT
    1992   "Physician self-referral: Empirical evidence and policy implications," *Advances
            in Health Economics and Health Services Research* 13: 27–42.
MITCHELL, JEAN M., AND JONATHAN SUNSHINE
    1992   "Consequences of physicians' ownership of health care facilities—Joint
            ventures in radiation therapy," *New England Journal of Medicine* 327(21):
            1497–1501.
MIYAJI, NAOKO T.
    1993   "The power of compassion: Truth-telling among American doctors in the care
            of dying patients," *Social Science and Medicine* 36(3): 249–264.

MIZRAHI, TERRY
    1986   *Getting Rid of Patients: Contradictions in the Socialization of Physicians.* New Brunswick, NJ: Rutgers University Press.

MOELLER, DADE W.
    1992   *Environmental Health.* Cambridge, MA: Harvard University Press.

MOELLER, SUSAN D.
    1999   *Compassion Fatigue: How the Media Sell Disease, Famine, Death and War.* New York: Routledge.

MOERMAN, DANIEL E.
    1997   "Physiology and symbols: The anthropological implications of the placebo effect," pp. 240–253 in L. Romanucci-Ross, D. Moerman, and L. Tancredi, eds., *The Anthropology of Medicine: From Culture to Method.* Westport, CT: Bergin and Garvey.
    2000   "Cultural variations in the placebo effect: Ulcers, anxiety and blood pressure," *Medical Anthropology Quarterly* 14(1): 51–72.

MOORE, J. STUART
    1993   *Chiropractic in America: The History of a Medical Alternative.* Baltimore: Johns Hopkins University Press.

MOORE-LAPPÉ, FRANCIS, JOSEPH COLLINS, AND PETER ROSSET, WITH LUIS ESPARZA
    1998   *World Hunger: 12 Myths.* New York: Grove Press.

MOOS, RUDOLF H., AND RALPH SWINDLE, JR.
    1990   "Person-environment transactions and the stressor-appraisal-coping process," *Psychological Inquiry* 1(1): 30–32.

MORANTZ-SANCHEZ, REGINA M.
    1985   *Sympathy and Science: Women Physicians in American Medicine.* New York: Oxford University Press.

MORGAN, MYFANWY, D. PATRICK, AND J. CHARLTON
    1984   "Social network and psychological support among disabled people," *Social Science and Medicine* 19: 489–497.

MORONE, JAMES A.
    1990   "American political culture and the search for lessons from abroad," *Journal of Health Politics, Policy and Law* 15(1): 129–143.
    1995   "Nativism, hollow corporations, and managed competition: Why the Clinton health care reform failed," *Journal of Health Politics, Policy and Law* 20(2): 391–398.

MORRIS, DAVID B.
    1998   *Illness and Culture in the Post-Modern Age.* Berkeley: University of California Press.

MULLEN, KENNETH
    1994   "Control and responsibility: Moral and religious issues in lay health accounts," *The Sociological Review* 42(3): 414–437.

MULLER, JESSICA H., AND BARBARA A. KOENIG
    1988   "On the boundary of life and death: The definition of dying by medical residents," pp. 351–374 in M. Lock and D. R. Gordon, eds., *Biomedicine Examined.* Dordrecht, Netherlands: Kluwer.

MUMFORD, LEWIS
    1963   *Technics and Civilization.* New York: Harcourt, Brace, and World.

MUNSON, MARTHA LITTLE
    1999   "Characteristics of elderly home health care users: Data from the 1996 National Home and Hospice Care Survey," *Advance Data,* 309. Hyattsville, MD: Centers for Disease and Prevention, National Center for Health Statistics, USDHHS.

MURPHY, ROBERT F.
   1987   *The Body Silent*. New York: Henry Holt.
MURRAY, CHRISTOPHER J. L., AND ALAN D. LOPEZ
   1996   "The global alternative epidemiological perspectives, discount rates, age-weights and disability weights," pp. 227–257 in Christopher J. L. Murray and Alan D. Lopez, eds., *The Global Burden of Disease*. Cambridge, MA: Harvard University Press.
MUSTARD, J. FRASER
   2000   "Healthy societies: An overview," pp. 3–14 in A. R. Tarlov and R. F. St. Peter, eds., *The Society and Population Reader, Vol II: A State and Community Perspective*. New York: The New Press.
MUWAKKIL, SALIM
   1996   "Moving mountains," *In These Times* 20(7), February 19.
NATIONAL ACADEMY OF SCIENCES, INSTITUTE OF MEDICINE
   2001   *Coverage Matters: Insurance and Health Care*. Washington, DC: National Academy of Sciences.
NATIONAL INSTITUTE ON ALCOHOL ABUSE AND ALCOHOLISM AND THE NATIONAL INSTITUTE OF MENTAL HEALTH
   1992   *Homeless Families with Children: Research Perspectives*. Rockville, MD: U.S. Department of Health and Human Services.
NATIONAL INSTITUTE ON DISABILITY AND REHABILITATION RESEARCH
   1987   "Low back pain," *Rehab Brief* IX(9).
NATIONAL SAFE WORKPLACE INSTITUTE
   1990   *Beyond Neglect: The Problem of Occupational Disease in the U.S.* Chicago: Author.
NAVARRO, VICENTE
   1988   "Professional dominance or proletarianization?: Neither," *Milbank Quarterly* 66(supplement 2): 57–75.
   2002a 'Neoliberalism,' 'globalization,' unemployment, inequalities, and the welfare state," pp. 33–107 in V. Navarro, ed., *The Political Economy of Social Inequalities: Consequences for Health and Quality of Life*. Amityville, NY: Baywood.
   2002b "The political economy of the welfare state in developed capitalist countries," pp. 121–169 in V. Navarro, ed., *The Political Economy of Social Inequalities: Consequences for Health and Quality of Life*. Amityville, NY. Baywood.
NEAL, HELEN
   1978   *The Politics of Pain*. New York: McGraw-Hill.
NELKIN, DOROTHY, AND MICHAEL S. BROWN
   1984   *Workers at Risk: Voices from the Workplace*. Chicago: University of Chicago Press.
NELSON, KARIN B., JAMES M. DAMBROSIA, TRICIA Y. TING, AND JUDITH K. GRETHEN
   1996   "Uncertain value of electronic fetal monitoring in predicting cerebral palsy," *New England Journal of Medicine* 334(10): 613–618.
NEWTON, THOMAS
   1995   *Managing Stress: Emotion and Power at Work*. London: Sage.
NEW YORK TIMES
   1989   "For mothers, elderly present second burden," May 13.
   1991   "Global checkup: Views in 10 nations," May 2.
   1992   "74% of Democrats and 53% of Republicans favor a national health insurance financed by tax money: The voters' views," November 4.
   1994a "Taxpayers may be paying twice for some drugs," July 12.
   1994b "Hmong protest girl's forced chemotherapy," October 19.

1996   "U.S. Healthcare to end limits on doctors' advice to patients," February 6.
1998   "Despite H.M.O.s: Doctors' incomes still healthy," April 22.
1999   "Social Security found to save third of elderly from poverty," April 9.
2002   "1 in 3 hospitals say they divert ambulances," April 9.

NIGHTINGALE, FLORENCE
1860   *Notes on Nursing: What It Is, and What It Is Not.* New York: Appleton.

NOBLE, KENNETH B.
1986   "Certain numbers can kill," *New York Times,* December 28.

NORDEN, MARTIN F.
1995   "Politics, movies and physical disabilities," *Kaleidoscope* Number 30 (Winter–Spring): 6–14.

NORRISH, BARBARA R., AND THOMAS G. RUNDALL
2001   "Hospital restructuring and the work of registered nurses," *The Milbank Quarterly* 79(1): 55–80.

NOVACK, DENNIS, ROBIN PLUMER, RAYMOND SMITH, HERBERT OCHITILL, GARY R. MORROW, AND JOHN M. BENNETT
1979   "Changes in physician attitude toward telling the cancer patient," *Journal of the American Medical Association* 241(9): 897–900.

NOVEK, JOEL, ANNALEE YASSI, AND JERRY SPIEGEL
1990   "Mechanization, the labor process, and injury risks in the Canadian meat packing industry," *International Journal of Health Services* 29(2): 281–296.

NUCKOLLS, KATHERINE B., JOHN CASSEL, AND BERTON V. KAPLAN
1972   "Psychosocial assets, life crisis, and the prognosis of pregnancy," *American Journal of Epidemiology* 95: 431–441.

NUMBERS, RONALD L.
1977   "Do it yourself the sectarian way," pp. 49–72 in G. Risse, R. L. Numbers, and J. W. Leavitt, eds., *Medicine Without Doctors: Home Health Care in American History.* New York: Science History.

OAKLEY, ANN
1984   *The Captured Womb: A History of the Medical Care of Pregnant Women.* Oxford, England: Basil Blackwell.

O'BRIEN, MARTIN
1995   "Health and lifestyle, a critical mess?: Notes on the dedifferentiation of health," pp. 191–205 in R. Bunton, S. Nettleton and R. Burrows, eds., *The Sociology of Health Promotion: Critical Analyses of Consumption, Lifestyle and Risk.* London: Routledge.

O'CONNELL, VANESSA
2002   "Drug requests are more specific," *Wall Street Journal,* April 15.

O'CONNELL, VANESSA, AND RACHEL ZIMMERMAN
2002   "Drug pitches resonate with edgy public," *Wall Street Journal,* January 14.

O'DONNEL, MARY
1978   "Lesbian health care: Issues and literature," *Science for the People,* May–June: 18–19.

OGLE, KATHLEEN M.
2001   "Sometimes the doctor is blind," *New York Times,* November 6.

OHRBACH, SUSIE
1981   *Fat Is a Feminist Issue.* New York: Berkeley.

OKEN, DONALD
    1961   "What to tell cancer patients—A study of medical attitudes," *Journal of the American Medical Association* 175: 1120–1128.

OLESEN, VIRGINIA
    2000   "Emotions and gender in US health care contexts," pp. 315–332 in S. J. Will, J. Gabe, and M. Calnan, eds., *Health, Medicine, and Society.* London: Routledge.

OLIVER, MICHAEL
    1996   *Understanding Disability.* London: Macmillan.

OMRAN, ABDEL R.
    1971   "The epidemiologic transition: A theory of the epidemiology of population change," *Milbank Memorial Fund Quarterly* 49: 509–538.

ONG, L. M. L., J. C. J. M. DE HAES, A. M. HOOS, AND F. B. LAMMES
    1995   "Doctor-patient communication: A review of the literature," *Social Science and Medicine* 40(7): 903–918.

ORGANISATION FOR ECONOMIC CO-OPERATION AND DEVELOPMENT (OECD)
    1999   *OECD Health Data 1998: A Comparative Analysis of 29 Countries,* Washington, DC: OECD CD-ROM.
    2001   *OECD Health Data 2001: A Comparative Analysis of 29 Countries,* retrieved from the World Wide Web at www.oecdwash.org/DATA/online.htm on 3, March 2002.

OSHERSON, SAMUEL, AND LORNA AMARASINGHAM
    1981   "The machine metaphor in medicine," pp. 218–249 in E. Mishler et al., *Social Contexts of Health, Illness, and Patient Care.* Cambridge, England: Cambridge University Press.

OSTERWEIS, MARIAN, ARTHUR KLEINMAN, AND DAVID MECHANIC, EDS.
    1987   *Pain and Disability: Clinical, Behavioral, and Public Policy Perspectives.* Washington, DC: Institute of Medicine, National Academy Press.

OTS, THOMAS
    1990   "The angry liver, the anxious heart, and the melancholy spleen: The phenomenology of perceptions in Chinese culture," *Culture, Medicine and Psychiatry* 14(1): 21–58.

OVERFIELD, THERESA
    1985   *Biologic Variation in Health and Illness.* Menlo Park, CA: Addison-Wesley.

PAGET, MARIANNE A.
    1983   "On the work of talk: Studies in misunderstandings," pp. 55–73 in S. Fisher and A. Todd, eds., *The Social Organization of Doctor-Patient Communication.* Norwood, NJ: Ablex.
    1988   *The Unity of Mistakes: A Phenomenological Interpretation of Medical Work.* Philadelphia: Temple University Press.

PALLEY, HOWARD A.
    1995   "The evolution of FDA policy on silicone breast implants: A case study of politics, bureaucracy, and business in the process of decision-making," *International Journal of Health Services* 25(4): 573–591.

PARSONS, TALCOTT
    1951   *The Social System.* Glencoe, IL: Free Press.
    1966   *Societies: Evolutionary and Comparative Perspectives.* Englewood Cliffs, NJ: Prentice-Hall.

1972   "Definitions of health and illness in light of American values and social structure," pp. 107–127 in E. G. Jaco, ed., *Patients, Physicians, and Illness*. New York:
Macmillan.

PATERSON, KEVIN, AND BILL HUGHES
2000   "Disabled bodies," pp. 29–44 in P. Hancock, B. Hughes, E. Jagger, K. Paterson,
R. Russell, E. Tulle-Winton, and M. Tyler, eds., *The Body Culture and Society*.
Philadelphia: Open University Press.

PAYER, LYNN
1988   *Medicine and Culture: Varieties of Treatment in the United States, England, West Germany,
and France*. New York: Henry Holt.

PEAR, ROBERT
1988   "Fate of newest treatments is often determined by Medicare," *New York Times*,
January 14.
1991   "AMA acts to curb profits from referrals," *New York Times*, December 12.
1999   "States called lax on tests for lead in poor children," *New York Times*, August 22.
2001   "Number of uninsured drops for 2nd year," *New York Times*, September 28.
2002a   "Many on Medicaid lack drugs, study says," *New York Times*, April 9.
2002b   "Medicare proposal promotes generic drugs," *The New York Times*, March 6.
2002c   "9 in 10 nursing homes lack adequate staff, study finds," *New York Times*,
February 18.
2002d   "Propelled by drug and hospital costs, health spending surged in 2000,"
New York Times, January 8.

PEAR, ROBERT, WITH ERIK ECKHOLM
1991   "When healers are entrepreneurs: A debate over costs and ethics," *New York
Times*, June 2.

PEAR, ROBERT, AND ROBIN TONER
2002   "Amid fiscal crisis, Medicaid is facing cuts from states," *New York Times*,
January 14.

PEARLIN, LEONARD I.
1983   "Role strains and personal stress," pp. 3–32 in H.B. Kaplan, ed., *Psychosocial
Stress: Trends in Theory and Research*. New York: Academic.

PEARLIN, LEONARD I., AND CARMEN SCHOOLER
1978   "The structure of coping," *Journal of Health and Social Behavior* 19: 2–21.

PEELE, STANTON
1989   *The Diseasing of America: Addiction Treatment Out of Control*. Lexington, MA:
Lexington Books.

PELLEGRINO, EDMUND D.
1976   "Prescribing and drug ingestion: Symbols and substances," *Drug Intelligence and
Clinical Pharmacy* 10: 624–630.

PELLETIER, KENNETH R.
1985   *Healthy People in Unhealthy Places: Stress and Fitness of Work*. New York: Dell.
1992   *Mind as Healer, Mind as Slayer* (2nd ed.). New York: Dell.

PELLETIER, KENNETH R., AND DENISE L. HERZING
1988   "Psychoneuroimmunology: Toward a mind-body model," *Advances: Institute for
the Advancement of Health* 5(1): 27–56.

PENDLETON, DAVID, AND STEPHEN BOCHNER
1980   "The communication of medical information in general practice consultations
as a function of patients' social class," *Social Science and Medicine* 14A(6):
669–673.

PERRY, SUSAN, AND JIM DAWSON
1985   *Nightmare: Women and the Dalkon Shield.* New York: Macmillan.

PESCOSOLIDO, BERNICE A., STEVEN A. TUCH, AND JACK K. MARTIN
2001   "The profession of medicine and the public: Examining Americans' changing confidence in physician authority from the beginning of the 'health care crisis' to the era of health care reform," *Journal of Health and Social Behavior* 42(1): 1–16.

PETERSEN, MELODY
2001   "2 drug makers to pay $875 million to settle fraud case," *New York Times,* October 4.
2002   "Methods used for marketing arthritis drug are under fire," *New York Times,* April 11.

PETERSON, CHRIS L.
1994   "Work factors and stress: A critical review," *International Journal of Health Services* 24(3): 495–519.

PETERSON, IVER
1986   "Surge in Indians' diabetes linked to their history," *New York Times,* February 18.

PFEFFER, RICHARD M.
1979   *Working for Capitalism.* New York: Columbia University Press.

PIERCE, JENNIFER L.
1999   "Emotional labor among paralegals," *Annals, AAPSS,* 561(January): 127–142.

PIERRET, JANINE
1993   "Constructing discourses about health and their social determinants," pp. 9–26 in A. Radley, ed., *Worlds of Illness.* New York: Routledge.

PILISUK, MARC, AND SUSAN H. PARKS
1986   *The Healing Web: Social Networks and Human Survival.* Hanover, NH: University Press of New England.

PINCUS, HAROLD A., ALLEN FRANCIS, WENDY WAKEFIELD DAVIS, MICHAEL B. FIRST, AND THOMAS A. WIDIGEN
1992   "DSM-IV and new diagnostic categories: Holding the line on proliferation," *American Journal of Psychiatry* 149(1): 112–117.

PINDER, RUTH
1995   "Bringing back the body without the blame?: The experience of ill and disabled people at work," *Sociology of Health and Illness* 17(5): 605–631.

PINNER, ROBERT W., STEVEN M. TEUTSCH, LONE SIMONSEN, LAURA A. KLUG, JUDITH M. GRABER, MATTHEW J. CLARKE, AND RUTH L. BERVELMAN
1996   "Trends in infectious diseases mortality in the United States," *Journal of the American Medical Association* 275(3): 189–193.

PODHORZER, MICHAEL
1995   "Unhealthy money: Health reform and the 1994 elections," *International Journal of Health Services* 25(3): 393–401.

POLEDNAK, ANTHONY P.
1989   *Racial and Ethnic Differences in Disease.* New York: Oxford University Press.

POLEFRONE, JOANNA M., AND STEPHEN B. MANUCK
1987   "Gender differences in cardiovascular and neuroendocrine responses to stressors," pp. 13–38 in R. Barnett, L. Biener, and G. K. Baruch, eds., *Gender and Stress.* New York: Free Press.

POLLACK, ANDREW
2000   "Biotechnology companies try to ward off generic drugs," *New York Times,* December 28.

POOLE, C. J. M., G. R. EVANS, A. SPURGEON, AND K. W. BRIDGES
1992   "Effects of a change in shift work on health," *Occupational Medicine* 42: 193–199.

POPAY, JENNIE, AND MEL BARTLEY
1989   "Conditions of labor and women's health," pp. 89–97 in C. J. Martin and D. V. McQueen, eds., *Readings for a New Public Health*. Edinburgh, Scotland: Edinburgh University Press.

POPE, GREGORY C., AND JOHN E. SCHNEIDER
1992   "Trends in physician income," *Health Affairs* 11(1): 181–193.

POPLIN, CAROLINE
1996   "Mismanaged care," *Wilson Quarterly* 20(3): 12–24.

POPPENDIECK, JANET
1995   "Hunger in America: Typification and response," pp. 11–34 in D. Maurer and J. Sobal, eds., *Eating Agendas: Food and Nutrition as Social Problems*. New York: Aldine de Gruyter.

POPULATION REFERENCE BUREAU
1982   *Population Bulletin* 37(2): 30–31.

PORTER, SAM
1992   "Women in a woman's job: The gendered experience of nurses," *Sociology of Health and Illness* 14(4): 510–527.

POSNER, TINA
1977   "Magical elements in orthodox medicine," pp. 141–158 in R. Dingwall, C. Heath, M. Reid, and M. Stacey, eds., *Health Care and Health Knowledge*. London: Croom Helm.

POST, STEPHEN G.
1992   "DSM-III-R and religion," *Social Science and Medicine* 35(1): 81–90.

PRESTON, JENNIFER
1996   "Hospitals look on charity care as unaffordable option of past," *New York Times*, April 14.

QUICK, ALLISON
1991   *Unequal Risks: Accidents and Social Policy*. London: Socialist Health Association.

RADLEY, ALAN
1994   *Making Sense of Illness*. Thousand Oaks, CA: Sage.

RAGGED EDGE
2001   "New figures from Census Bureau say half disabled people employed," *Ragged Edge* 3: 11.

RAGONÉ, HELÉNA, AND SHARLA K. WILLIS
2000   "Reproduction and assisted reproductive technologies," pp. 308–322 in G. L. Albrecht et al., eds., *Handbook of Social Studies in Health and Medicine*. London: Sage.

RAHKONEN, OSSI, EERO LAHELMA, ANTTI KARISTO, AND KRISTINA MANDERBACKA
1993   "Persisting health inequalities: Social class differentials in illness in the Scandinavian countries," *Journal of Public Health Policy* (Spring): 66–81.

RASELL, EDITH
1993   "A bad bargain: Why U.S. health care costs so much and covers so few," *Dollars and Sense* 186(May): 6–8, 21.

RASELL, EDITH, JARED BERNSTEIN, AND KAINAN TANG
1994   "The impact of health care financing on family budgets," *International Journal of Health Services* 24(4): 691–714.

RASKIN, VALERIE D.
  1997   *When Words Are Not Enough: The Women's Prescription for Depression and Anxiety.*
          New York: Broadway Books.

RATLIFF-CRAIN, JEFFREY, AND ANDREW BAUM
  1990   "Individual differences and health: Gender, coping and stress," pp. 226–253 in
          H. S. Friedman, ed., *Personality and Disease.* New York: Wiley.

RAY, WAYNE A., MARIE R. GRIFFIN, AND RONALD I. SHORR
  1990   "Adverse drug reactions and the elderly," *Health Affairs* 9(3): 114–122.

REDDY, PRABASHNI, AND M. MALONE
  1998   "Cost and outcome analysis of home parenteral and enteral nutrition," *Journal
          of Parenteral & Enteral Nutrition* 22(5): 302–310.

REID, JANICE, CHRISTINE EWAN, AND EVA LOWY
  1991   "Pilgrimage of pain: The illness experiences of women with repetition
          strain injury and the search for credibility," *Social Science and Medicine* 32(5):
          601–612.

REINHARDT, UWE E.
  1987   "Resource allocation in health care: The allocation of life styles to providers,"
          Milbank Quarterly 65(2): 153–176.
  1996   "Spending more through 'cost control': Our obsessive quest to gut the hospi-
          tal," *Health Affairs* 15(2): 145–153.
  1999   "Employer-based health insurance: A balance sheet," *Health Affairs* 18(6):
          124–132.

REINHOLD, ROBERT
  1987   "As hospitals close, rural America tries to cope with a void," *New York Times,*
          July 6.
  1988   "Crisis in emergency rooms: More symptoms than cures," *New York Times,*
          December 8.

RENNER, MICHAEL
  1988   "Rethinking the role of the automobile," *Worldwatch Paper,* No. 84. Washington,
          DC: Worldwatch Institute.

REVERBY, SUSAN
  1987   *Ordered to Care: The Dilemma of American Nursing, 1850–1945.* Cambridge,
          England: Cambridge University Press.

RHODES, ROBERT P.
  1992   *Health Care Politics, Policy, and Distributive Justice: The Ironic Triumph.* Albany: State
          University of New York Press.

RICHARDSON, JAMES T.
  1993   "Religiosity as deviance: Negative religious bias in and misuse of the DSM-
          III," *Deviant Behavior* 14(1): 1–21.
  1995   "Two steps forward, one back: Psychiatry, psychology, and the new religions,"
          International Journal for the Psychology of Religion 3(3): 181–185.

RICHARDSON, JOHN T. E.
  1995   "The premenstrual syndrome: A brief history," *Social Science and Medicine* 41(6):
          761–767.

RICHARDSON, STEPHEN A., NORMAN GOODMAN, ALBERT HASTDORF, AND STANFORD
DORNBUSH
  1963   "Variant reactions to physical disabilities," *American Sociological Review* 28:
          429–435.

RICHEY, FERRIS J., WILLIAM C. YOELS, JEFFREY MICHAEL CLAIR, AND RICHARD
M. ALLMAN
  1994   "Competing medical and social ideologies and communication accuracy in
          medical encounters," *Research in the Sociology of Health Care* 12: 189–211.
RIMER, SARA
  1997   "New, reviled college subject: Computer-linked injury," *New York Times,*
          February 9.
RISSE, GUENTER, RONALD L. NUMBERS, AND JUDITH W. LEAVITT, EDS.
  1977   *Medicine Without Doctors: Home Health Care in American History.* New York: Science
          History.
ROACH, STEPHEN S.
  2000   "Working better or just harder?" *New York Times,* February 14.
ROBBINS, THOMAS, AND DICK ANTHONY
  1982   "Deprogramming, brainwashing, and the medicalization of deviant religious
          groups," *Social Problems* 29(3): 283–297.
ROBERT, SETPHANIE A., AND JAMES S. HOUSE
  2000   "Socioeconomic inequalities in health: Integrating individual-, community-,
          and societal-level theory and research," pp. 115–135 in G. L. Albrecht et al.,
          eds., *Handbook of Social Studies in Health and Medicine.* London: Sage.
ROBERTS, HELEN, SUSAN J. SMITH, AND CAROL BRYCE
  1992   "Professionals' and parents' perceptions of A&E use in a children's hospital,"
          Sociological Review 40(1): 109–131.
  1995   *Children at Risk? Safety as a Social Value.* Buckingham, England: Open University
          Press.
ROBERTSON, ROLAND
  2001   "Globalization: Theory 2000+: Major problematics," pp. 458–471 in G. Ritzer
          and B. Smart, eds., *Handbook of Social Theory.* London: Sage.
ROBINSON, A. A.
  1988   "The motor vehicle, stress, and circulatory system," *Stress Medicine* 4: 73–76.
ROBINSON, JAMES C., AND MITA K. GIACOMINI
  1992   "A reallocation of rights in industries with reproductive health hazards," *The
          Milbank Quarterly* 70(4): 587–603.
RODIN, MARI
  1992   "The social construction of premenstrual syndrome," *Social Science and Medicine*
          35(1): 49–56.
RODWIN, MARC A.
  1993   *Medicine, Money and Morals: Physician Conflicts of Interest.* New York: Oxford
          University Press.
ROEDER, BEATRICE A.
  1988   *Chicano Folk Medicine from Los Angeles, California. Folklore and Mythology Studies,*
          Vol. 34. Berkeley: University of California Publications.
ROHRLICH, TED, AND NICHOLAS RICCARDI
  2001   "10% of ERs rejected patients, study finds," *Los Angeles Times,* July 13.
ROMANO, MICHAEL
  2001   "Unequal opportunities; Anesthesiologists, radiologists lead the pay parade,
          while generalists lag behind," *Modern Healthcare,* August 13.
ROOKS, JUDITH PENCE
  1997   *Midwifery & Childbirth.* Philadelphia: Temple University Press.

ROOT, ROBIN, AND CAROLE BROWNER
    2001   "Practices of the pregnant self: Compliance with and resistance to prenatal norms," *Culture, Medicine and Psychiatry* 25(2): 195–223.

ROSENBERG, CHARLES E.
    1987   *The Care of Strangers: The Rise of America's Hospital System.* New York: Basic.

ROSENBLATT, ROGER A., SHARON A. DOBIE, L. GARY HART, RONALD SCHNEEWEISS, DEBRA GOULD, TINA R. RAINE, THOMAS J. BENEDETTI, MICHAEL J. PIRANI, AND EDWARD B. PERRIN
    1997   "Interspecialty differences in the obstetric care of low-risk women," *The American Journal of Public Health* 87(3): 344–351.

ROSENBURG, TINA
    2001   "The Brazilian solution," *New York Times Magazine,* January 28.

ROSENHAN, DAVID L.
    1973   "On being sane in insane places," *Science* 179: 250–258.

ROSENTHAL, ELISABETH
    1993   "Drug companies' profits finance more promotion than research," *New York Times,* February 21.
    1997a   "Older doctors and nurses see jobs at stake," *New York Times,* January 26.
    1997b   "When a healer is asked, 'Help me die,'" *New York Times,* March 13.

ROSENTHAL, MARILYN M.
    1988   *Dealing with Medical Malpractice: The British and Swedish Experience.* Durham, NC: Duke University Press.
    1995   *The Incompetent Doctor: Behind Closed Doors.* Buckingham, England: Open University Press.
    1999   "Medical uncertainty, medical collegiality, and improving quality of care," *Research in Sociology of Health Care* 16: 3–30.

ROSS, H. LAURENCE, AND GRAHAM HUGHES
    1986   "Drunk driving: What not to do," *Nation* 243(20): 663–664.

ROSS, JERRY, AND GARY L. ALBRECHT
    1995   "Escalation in health care delivery," *Research in the Sociology of Health Care* 12: 241–260.

ROSSER, SUE V.
    1994   "Gender bias in clinical research: The difference it makes," pp. 253–264 in A. J. Dan, ed., *Reframing Women's Health.* Thousand Oaks, CA: Sage.

ROTH, JULIUS
    1972   "Some contingencies of the moral evaluation and control of clientele: The case of the hospital emergency service," *American Journal of Sociology* 77: 839–856.

ROWLAND, DIANE, B. SALGANICOFF, AND P. LONG
    1994   "Profile of the uninsured in America," *Health Affairs* 13(2): 283–287.

ROYAL COMMISSION ON ENVIRONMENTAL POLLUTION
    1994   *Transport and the Environment.* London: HMSO.

ROYER, ARIELA
    1995   "Living with chronic illness," *Research in the Sociology of Health Care* 12: 25–48.

RUBIN, BETH
    1996   *Shifts in the Social Contract: Understanding Change in American Society.* Thousand Oaks, CA: Pine Forge Press.

RUGGIE, MARY
    1992   "The paradox of liberal intervention: Health policy and the American welfare state," *American Journal of Sociology* 97(4): 919–944.

RUTLEDGE, ROBERT, THOMAS C. RICKETTS, AND ELIZABETH BELL
   1992   "Emergency medical services in rural areas," pp. 226–248 in W. M. Gesler and T. C. Ricketts, *Health in Rural North America: The Geography of Health Care Services and Delivery.* New Brunswick, NJ: Rutgers University Press.

RUZEK, SHERYL, VIRGINIA OLESEN, AND ADELE CLARKE, EDS.
   1997   *Women's Health: Complexities and Differences.* Columbus, OH: Ohio State University Press.

RYAN, WILLIAM
   1971   *Blaming the Victim.* New York: Vintage.

SACKS, KAREN
   1988   *Caring by the Hour: Women, Work and Organizing at Duke Medical Center.* Urbana: University of Illinois.

SACKS, OLIVER
   1984   *A Leg to Stand On.* New York: Summit.

SAGAN, LEONARD
   1987   *The Health of Nations.* New York: Basic.

SAKS, MIKE
   1995   *Professions and the Public Interest: Medical Power, Altruism and Alternative Medicine.* New York: Routledge.

SAKS, MIKE, ED.
   1992   *Alternative Medicine in Britain.* Oxford, England: Clarendon Press.

SALMON, J. WARREN
   1995   "A perspective on the corporate transformation of health care," *International Journal of Health Services* 25(1): 11–42.

SALTONSTALL, ROBIN
   1993   "Healthy bodies, social bodies: Men's and women's concepts and practices of health in everyday life," *Social Science and Medicine* 36(1): 7–14.

SAPOLSKY, ROBERT M.
   1982   "The endocrine stress-response and social status in the wild baboon," *Hormones and Behavior* 16: 279–292.
   1989   "Hypercortisolism among socially subordinate wild baboons originates at the CNS level," *Archives of General Psychiatry* 46: 1047–1051.
   1990   "Stress in the wild," *Scientific American* 252: 116–123.

SCHACHTER, STANLEY
   1968   "Obesity and eating," *Science* 16: 751–756.

SCHEDER, JO C.
   1988   "A sickly-sweet harvest: Farmworker diabetes and social equality," *Medical Anthropology Quarterly* 2(3): 251–277.

SCHENSUL, STEPHEN L., AND JEAN J. SCHENSUL
   1982   "Healing resource use in a Puerto Rican community," *Urban Anthropology* 11(1): 59–79.

SCHEPER-HUGHES, NANCY
   1992   *Death Without Weeping.* Berkeley: University of California Press.
   2000   "The global traffic in human organs," *Current Anthropology* 41(2): 191–224.

SCHEPER-HUGHES, NANCY, AND MARGARET M. LOCK
   1986   "Speaking 'truth' to illness: Metaphor, reification, and a pedagogy for patients," *Medical Anthropology Quarterly* 17: 137–140.
   1991   "The message in the bottle: Illness and the micropolitics of resistance," *Journal of Psychohistory* 18(4): 409–432.

SCHEPERS, RITA
  1985   "The legal and institutional development of the Belgian medical profession in the nineteenth century," *Sociology of Health and Illness* 7(3): 314–341.
SCHIFF, ROBERT L., DAIV ANSELL, JAMES SCHLOSSER, AHAMED IDRIS, ANN MORRISON, AND STEVEN WHITMAN
  1986   "Transfers to a public hospital," *New England Journal of Medicine* 314(9): 552–559.
SCHLESINGER, MARK, JUDY BENTKOVER, DAVID BLUMENTHAL, ROBERT MUSACCICO, AND JANET WILLER.
  1987   "The privatization of health care and physicians' perceptions of access to hospital services," *Milbank Quarterly* 65(1): 25–58.
SCHMALE, ARTHUR H.
  1972   "Giving up as a final common pathway to changes in health," pp. 20–40 in Z. Lipowski, ed., *Advances in Psychosomatic Medicine,* Vol. 8. Basel, Switzerland: S. Karger.
SCHMECK, HAROLD M.
  1985   "73% of Americans suffer headaches," *New York Times,* October 22.
SCHNALL, PETER L., AND ROCHELLE KERN
  1981   "Hypertension in American society: An introduction to historical materialist epidemiology," pp. 73–89 in P. Conrad and R. Kern, eds., *The Sociology of Health and Illness* (2nd ed.). New York: St. Martin's Press.
SCHNEIDER, JOSEPH W., AND PETER CONRAD
  1980   "In the closet with illness: Epilepsy, stigma potential, and information control," *Social Problems* 28(1): 32–45.
  1983   *Having Epilepsy: The Experience and Control of Illness.* Philadelphia: Temple University Press.
SCHOOFS, MARK
  1999   "Death and the second sex," *Village Voice,* December 7.
SCHOR, JULIET B.
  1992   *The Overworked American.* New York: Basic Books.
SCHREIBER, JANET M., AND JOHN HOMIAK
  1981   "Mexican Americans," pp. 264–336 in A. Harwood, ed., *Ethnicity and Medical Care.* Cambridge, MA: Harvard University Press.
SCHULZ, AMY, BARBARA ISRAEL, D. WILLIAMS, ADAM BECKER, AND S. JAMES
  2000   "Social inequalities, stressors and self reported health status among African American and white women in the Detroit metropolitan area," *Social Science and Medicine* 51(11): 1639–1653.
SCHWARTZ, MIRIAM
  1984   "A sociological reinterpretation of the controversy over 'unnecessary surgery'," *Research in the Sociology of Health Care* 3: 159–200.
SCOTCH, RICHARD K.
  1988   "Disability as the basis for a social movement: Advocacy and the politics of definition," *Journal of Social Issues* 44(1): 159–172.
SCULLY, DIANA
  1980   *Men Who Control Women's Health: The Miseducation of Obstetrician-Gynecologists.* Boston: Houghton Mifflin.
SECCOMBE, KAREN
  1996   "Health insurance coverage among the working poor," *Research in the Sociology of Health Care* 13A: 199–227.

SEGALL, ALEXANDER, AND LANCE W. ROBERTS
    1980   "A comparative analysis of physician estimates and levels of knowledge among patients," *Sociology of Health and Illness* 2(3): 317–334.

SELBY, W. GARDNER
    2002   "Kids' health insurance program facing deficit," *San Antonio Express News*, January 8.

SELIGMAN, MARTIN
    1992   *Helplessness: On Depression, Development, and Death.* San Francisco: Freeman.

SELYE, HANS
    1956   *The Stress of Life.* New York: McGraw-Hill.
    1975   *Stress Without Distress.* New York: New American Library.

SHABECOFF, PHILIP
    1987   "Vast changes in environment seen," *New York Times,* November 4.

SHAKESPEARE, TOM
    1996   "Power and prejudice: Issues of gender, sexuality and disability," pp. 191–214 in L. Barton, ed., *Disability and Society.* London: Longman.
    1999   "What is a disabled person?," pp. 25–34 in M. Jones and L. A. B. Marks, eds., *Disability, Drivers—Ability and Legal Change.* London: Kruwer Law International.

SHAPIRO, JOSEPH P.
    1993   *No Pity: People with Disabilities Forging a New Civil Rights Movement.* New York: Random House.

SHARMA, URSULA
    1992   *Complementary Medicine Today: Practitioners and Patients.* London: Tavistock/ Routledge.
    1995   "The homeopathic body: 'Reification' and the homeopathic 'gaze'," pp. 33–49 in H. Johannessen, S. G. Oleson, and J. O. Andersen, eds. *Studies in Alternative Therapy,* Vol. 2. Odense, Denmark: Odense University Press.

SHEILS, JOHN F., PAUL HOGAN, AND NICOLAY MANOLOV
    1999   "Paying more and losing ground: How employer cost-shifting is eroding health coverage of working families," *International Journal of Health Services* 29(3): 485–518.

SHELL, ELLEN RUPPEL
    2001   "New world syndrome," *The Atlantic Monthly* 287(6): 50–53.

SHI, LEIYU
    2001   "The convergence of vulnerable characteristics and health insurance in the U.S.," *Social Science and Medicine* 53(4): 519–529.

SHILTS, RANDY
    1987   *And the Band Played On: Politics, People, and the AIDS Epidemic.* New York: St. Martin's Press.

SHIVELY, CAROL A.
    2000   "Social status, stress and health in female monkeys," pp. 278–289 in A. R. Tarlov and R. F. St. Peter, eds., *The Society and Population Reader, Vol. II: A State and Community Perspective.* New York: The New Press.

SHIVELY, CAROL A., AND THOMAS B. CLARKSON
    1999   "Social status and coronary atheroschlerosis in female monkeys," pp. 393–404 in I. Kiwachi, B. P. Kennedy, and R. G. Wilkinson, eds., *The Society and Population Health Reader, Vol. I: Income Inequality and Health.* New York: The New Press.

SHIVELY, CAROL A., KATHY LABER-LAIRD, AND RAYMOND F. ANTON
1999   "Behavior and physiology of social stress and depression in female Cynomol-
gus monkeys," pp. 405–420 in A. R. Tarlov and R. F. St. Peter, eds., *The Society
and Population Reader, Vol. II: A State and Community Perspective.* New York: The
New Press.

SHORTER, EDWARD
1982   *A History of Women's Bodies.* New York: Basic.

SICHERMAN, BARBARA
1978   "The uses of a diagnosis: Doctors, patients, and neurasthenia," pp. 25–38 in
J. Leavitt and R. L. Numbers, eds., *Sickness and Health in America.* Madison:
University of Wisconsin Press.

SIEGRIST, JOHANNES, AND DANIEL A. KLEIN
1990   "Occupational stress and cardiovascular reactivity in blue-collar workers,"
Work and Stress 4(4): 295–304.

SIGERIST, HENRY B.
1960   *On the History of Medicine.* New York: M. D. Publications.

SILVERMAN, ED.
2001   "Lilly says Sarafem will help ease a severe premenstrual ailment: Critics call
the drug–Prozac by another name–a profit ploy," *Newark Star Ledger,* June 6.

SILVERMAN, MILTON, MIA LYDECKER, AND PHILIP R. LEE
1992   *Bad Medicine: The Prescription Drug Industry in the Third World.* Stanford, CA:
Stanford University Press.

SILVERSTEIN, BRET
1984   *Fed Up.* Boston: South End.

SIMMONS, ROBERTA G., AND SUSAN KLEIN MARINE
1984   "The regulation of high cost technology medicine: The case of dialysis and
transplantation in the U.K.," *Journal of Health and Social Behavior* 25: 320–334.

SINGER, MERRILL, AND HANS BAER
1995   *Critical Medical Anthropology.* Amityville, NY: Baywood.

SKOLNICK, ANDREW A.
1995   "Along U.S. southern border, pollution, poverty, ignorance, and greed
threaten nation's health," *Journal of the American Medical Association* 273(19):
1478–1482.

SMAJE, CHRIS
2000   "Race, ethnicity, and health," pp. 114–128 in C. E. Bird, P. Conrad, and A. M.
Fremont, eds., *Handbook of Medical Sociology.* Upper Saddle River, NJ: Prentice-
Hall.

SMEDLEY, BRIAN D., ADRIENNE Y. STITH, AND ALAN R. NELSON, EDS.
2002   *Unequal Treatment: Confronting Racial and Ethnic Disparities in Health Care.* Washington,
DC: National Academies of Science, Institute of Medicine.

SMITH, BARBARA ELLEN
1981   "Black lung: The social production of disease," *International Journal of Health
Services* 11(3): 343–359.

1987   *Digging Our Own Graves: Coal Miners and the Struggle over Black Lung Disease.*
Chicago: University of Chicago Press.

SMITH, DAVID BARTON
1999   *Health Care Divided: Race and Healing a Nation.* Ann Arbor, MI: University of
Michigan Press.

SMITH, DAVID G.
    1992   *Paying for Medicare: The Politics of Reform.* New York: Aldine de Gruyter.

SMITH, GEORGE D., KATHERINE CHARLSLEY, HELEN LAMBERT, SHEILA PAUL, STEVE FENTON, AND WAQAR AHMAD
    2000   "Ethnicity, health and the meaning of socio-economic position," pp. 25–37 in H. Graham, ed., *Understanding Health Inequalities.* Philadelphia: Open University Press.

SMITH, ROBERT C., AND GEORGE ZIMMY
    1988   "Physicians' emotional reactions to patients," *Psychosomatics* 29(4): 392–397.

SMOTHERS, RONALD
    1991   "Employers becoming targets of suits in the fight to halt drunken driving," *New York Times,* May 26.

SNOW, JOHN
    [1855] 1936   *On the Mode of Communication of Cholera,* reprinted as *Snow on Cholera.* New York: Hafner.

SNOW, LOUDELL F.
    1993   *Walkin' Over Medicine.* Boulder, CO: Westview Press.

SOBAL, JEFFERY
    1995   "The medicalization and demedicalization of obesity," pp. 67–90 in D. Maurer and J. Sobal, eds., *Eating Agendas: Food and Nutrition as Social Problems.* New York: Aldine de Gruyter.

SOBOL, RICHARD B.
    1991   *Bending the Law: The Story of the Dalkon Shield Bankruptcy.* Chicago: University of Chicago Press.

SOLDO, BETH J.
    1985   "In-home services for the dependent elderly," *Research on Aging* 7: 281–304.

SOLOMON, GEORGE F.
    1985   "The emerging field of psychoneuroimmunology," *Advances: Journal of the Institute for the Advancement of Health* 2(1): 6–19.

SORKIN, ALAN L.
    1986   *Health Care and the Changing Economic Environment.* Lexington, MA: D.C. Heath.

SPARROW, MALCOLM K.
    1996   *License to Steal: Why Fraud Plagues America's Health Care System.* Boulder, CO: Westview Press.

SPRUIT, INGEBORG P., AND DAAN KROMHOUT
    1987   "Medical sociology and epidemiology: Convergences, divergences, and legitimate boundaries," *Social Science and Medicine* 25(6): 579–587.

STAFFORD, RANDALL S.
    1991   "The impact of nonclinical factors on repeat caesarean sections," *Journal of the American Medical Association* 265(1): 59–63.

STALK, JEFFREY
    1992   "At issue in the Netherlands: Is sex for the disabled a right?" *International Herald Tribune,* August 4.

STARK, EVAN, AND ANNE H. FLITCRAFT
    1996   *Women at Risk: Domestic Violence and Women's Health.* Thousand Oaks, CA: Sage.

STARR, PAUL
    1982   *Social Transformation of American Medicine.* New York: Basic.

ST. CLAIR, JEFFREY
    1997   "Blowing smoke," *In These Times* 21(6): 24–26.

STEARNS, CAROL ZISOWITZ, AND PETER N. STEARNS
1986   *Anger: The Struggle for Emotional Control in America's History.* Chicago: University of Chicago Press.

STEBBINS, KENYON RAINIER
2001   "Going like gangbusters: Transnational tobacco companies 'making a killing' in South America," *Medical Anthropology Quarterly* 15(2): 147–170.

STEIN, HOWARD F.
1986   " 'Sick people' and 'trolls': A contribution to the understanding of the dynamics of physician explanatory models," *Culture, Medicine, and Psychiatry* 10: 221–229.

STEIN, LEONARD I.
1967   "The doctor-nurse game," *Archives of General Psychiatry* 16: 699–703.

STEIN, LEONARD I., D. T. WATTS, AND T. HOWELL
1990   "The doctor-nurse game revisited," *New England Journal of Medicine* 322: 546–549.

STEINBERG, CAROLINE ROSSI, AND RAYMOND J. BAXTER
1998   "Accountable communities: How norms and values affect health system change," *Health Affairs* 17(4): 149–158.

STEINMETZ, SUZANNE K.
1988   *Duty Bound: Elder Abuse and Family Care.* Newbury Park, CA: Sage.

STELLMAN, JEANNE
1977   *Women's Work, Women's Health.* New York: Pantheon.

STELLMAN, JEANNE, AND SUSAN M. DAUM
1971   *Work Is Dangerous to Your Health.* New York: Pantheon.

STELLMAN, JEANNE, AND MARY SUE HENIFIN
1983   *Office Work Can Be Dangerous to Your Health.* New York: Random House.

STERLING, THEODOR D., ELIA STERLING, AND HELEN D. WARD
1983   "Building illness in the white collar workplace," *International Journal of Health Services* 13(2): 277–287.

STEVENS, WILLIAM K.
1988   "Diarrhea kills surprising rate of U.S. young," *New York Times,* December 9.

STEWART, DAVID C., AND THOMAS J. SULLIVAN
1982   "Illness behavior and the sick role in chronic disease: The case of MS," *Social Science and Medicine* 16: 1397–1404.

STILLION, JUDITH M.
1995   "Premature death among males," pp. 46–67 in D. Sabo and D. F. Gordon, eds., *Men's Health and Illness.* Thousand Oaks, CA: Sage.

STILLWAGGON, EILEEN
1998   *Stunted Lives, Stagnant Economies: Poverty, Disease, and Underdevelopment.* New Brunswick, NJ: Rutgers University Press.
2001   "AIDS and poverty in Africa," *The Nation* 272 (20): 22–25

STIMSON, GERRY, AND BARBARA WEBB
1975   *Going to See the Doctor.* London: Routledge and Kegan Paul.

STOLBERG, SHERYL GAY
2001   "Reconsidering embryo research," *New York Times,* July 1.
2002   "AIDS fund falls short of goal and U.S. is given some blame," *New York Times,* February 13.

STONE, DEBORAH A.
1979   "Physicians as gatekeepers: Illness certification as a rationing device," *Public Policy* 27(2): 227–254.

STOUT, H. R.
   1885   *Our Family Physician.* Peoria, IL: Henderson and Smith.
STRAUB, LAVONNE A.
   1990   "Financing rural health and medical services," *Journal of Rural Care* 6(4): 467–484.
STRAUSS, ANSELM
   1975   *Chronic Illness and the Quality of Life.* St. Louis, MO: C. V. Mosby.
STREET, RICHARD L., JR.
   1991   "Information-giving in medical consultations: The influence of patients' communicative styles and personal characteristics," *Social Science and Medicine* 32(5): 541–548.
   1992   "Communicative styles and adaptations in physician-parent consultations," *Social Science and Medicine* 34(10): 1155–1163.
STRUCK, MIRIAM
   1981   "Disabled doesn't mean unable," *Science for the People,* September-October: 24–28.
STRUNK, BRADLEY C., PAUL B. GINSBURG, AND JOHN R. GABEL
   2001   "Tracking health care costs," *Health Affairs,* September 26, 2001, retrieved from the World Wide Web at www.healthaffairs.org on 12 December, 2001.
STRYKER, JEFF
   1996   "Life after Quinlan: Right to die," *New York Times,* March 31.
SUDNOW, DAVID
   1967   *Passing On: The Social Organization of Dying.* Englewood Cliffs, NJ: Prentice-Hall.
SULLIVAN, DEBORAH A.
   1993   "Cosmetic surgery: Market dynamics and medicalization," *Research in the Sociology of Health Care* 10: 97–115.
SULLIVAN, MARK
   1986   "In what sense is contemporary medicine dualistic?" *Culture, Medicine and Psychiatry* 10: 331–350.
SUNDQUIST, JAN
   1995   "Ethnicity, social class and health: A population-based study on the influence of social factors on self-reported illness in 223 Latin American refugees, 333 Finnish and 126 South European labour migrants and 841 Swedish controls," *Social Science and Medicine* 40(6): 777–787.
SUOMI, STEPHEN J.
   2000   "Early development in monkeys," pp. 131–142 in A. R. Tarlov and R. F. St. Peter, eds., *The Society and Population Reader, Vol. II: A State and Community Perspective.* New York: The New Press.
SUSMAN, JOAN
   1993   "Disability, stigma and deviance," *Social Science and Medicine* 38(1): 15–22.
SUSSER, MERVYN, AND EZRA SUSSER
   1996a   "Choosing a future for epidemiology: I. Eras and paradigms," *American Journal of Public Health* 86: 668–673.
   1996b   "Choosing a future for epidemiology: II. From black box to Chinese boxes and eco-epidemiology," *American Journal of Public Health* 86: 674–677.
SUTER, STEVE
   1986   *Health Psychophysiology: Mind-Body Interactions in Wellness and Illness.* Hillsdale, NJ: Lawrence Erlbaum.

SUTHERLAND, ALLAN T.
1981   *Disabled We Stand.* Bloomington: Indiana University Press.

SUTHERLAND, PRUDY
1987   "I want sex—just like you," *Village Voice* 32(14): 25.

SVENSSON, ROLAND
1996   "The interplay between doctors and nurses—Negotiated order perspective," *Sociology of Health and Illness* 18(3): 379–398.

SWANN, CATHERINE
1997   "Reading the bleeding body, discourses of premenstrual syndrome," pp. 176–198 in J. M. Ussher, ed., *Body Talk: The Material and Discursive Regulation of Sexuality, Madness and Reproduction.* New York: Routledge.

SWARNS, RACHEL L.
2002   "Grappling with South Africa's alarming increase in the rapes of children," *New York Times,* January 29.

2001   "A South African hospital fights AIDS and despair," *New York Times,* November 26.

SWEDLOW, ALEX, GREGORY JOHNSON, NEIL SMITHLINE, AND ARNOLD MILSTEIN
1992   "Increased cost and rates of use in the California workers' compensation system as a result of self-referral by physicians," *New England Journal of Medicine* 327(21): 1502–1506.

SYME, S. LEONARD
1996   "To prevent disease: The need for a new approach," pp. 21–31 in D. Blane et al., eds., *Health and Social Organization.* London: Routledge.

SYME, S. LEONARD, AND LISA F. BERKMAN
1976   "Social class, susceptibility, and sickness," *American Journal of Epidemiology* 104: 1–8.

SYME, S. LEONARD, AND JACK M. GURALNIK
1987   "Epidemiology and health policy: Coronary heart disease," pp. 85–116 in S. R. Levine and A. Lilienfeld, eds., *Epidemiology and Health Policy.* New York: Tavistock.

SZASZ, THOMAS S.
1970   *The Manufacture of Madness.* New York: Dell.

TAIPALE, ILKKA, HELENA MAKELA, KATI JUVA, AND VAPPU TAIPALE, EDS.
2001   *War and Health.* New York: Zed Books.

TARAGIN, MARK I., L. R. WILLETT, A. P. WILCZEK, R. TROUT, AND J. L. CARSON
1992   "The influence of standard of care and severity of injury on the resolution of medical malpractice claims," *Annals of Internal Medicine* 117(9): 780–784.

TAUSSIG, MICHAEL T.
1980   "Reification and the consciousness of the patient," *Social Science and Medicine* 14B: 3–13.

TAYLOR, FREDERICK
[1911] 1947   *Principles of Scientific Management.* New York: Norton.

TAYLOR, SHELLEY E., RENA L. REPETTI, AND TERESA SEEMAN
1999   "What is an unhealthy environment and how does it get under the skin?," pp. 351–378 in I. Kiwachi, B. P. Kennedy, and R. G. Wilkinson, eds., *The Society and Population Health Reader, Vol. I: Income Inequality and Health.* New York: The New Press.

TELLES, JOEL LEON, AND MARK HARRIS POLLACK
1981   "Feeling sick: The experience and legitimation of illness," *Social Science and Medicine* 15A: 243–251.

TEXAS HEALTH AND HUMAN SERVICES COMMISSION
1999   "Estimates of Texas population without health insurance by county," May 1999, retrieved from the World Wide Web at www.hhsc.state.tx.us on 29 March, 2002.
2001   "Texas Medicaid facts," retrieved from the World Wide Web at www.hhsc.state.tx.us on 29 March, 2002.

THEORELL, TÖRES
1991   "On cardiovascular health in women," pp. 187–204 in M. Frankenhaeuser, U. Lundberg, and M. Chesney, eds., *Women, Work and Health*. New York: Plenum Press.
2000   "Working conditions and health," pp. 95–117 in L. F. Berkman and I. Kawachi, eds., *Social Epidemiology*. New York: Oxford University Press.

THOITS, PEGGY A.
1983   "Dimensions of life events that influence psychological distress: An evaluation and synthesis of the literature," pp. 33–103 in H. B. Kaplan, ed., *Psychosocial Stress: Trends in Theory and Research*. New York: Academic.

THOMAS, CAROL
1995   "Domestic labour and health: Bringing it all back home," *Sociology of Health and Illness* 17(3): 328–352.

THOMAS, K. J., L. WESTLAKE, AND B. T. WILLIAMS
1991   "Use of non-orthodox and conventional health care in Great Britain," *British Medical Journal* 302: 207–210.

TIEFER, LEONORE
1992   "In pursuit of the perfect penis: The medicalization of male sexuality," pp. 450–463 in M. S. Kimmel and M. A. Messner, eds., *Men's Lives*. New York: Macmillan.
1994   "Women's sexuality: Not a matter of health," pp. 151–162 in A. J. Dan, ed., *Reframing Women's Health*. Thousand Oaks, CA: Sage.

TIERNEY, JOHN
1988   "Wired for stress," *New York Times Magazine,* May 15.

TILLMAN, ROBERT
1998   *Broken Promises: Fraud by Small Business Health Insurers*. Boston: Northeastern University Press.

TIMMERMANS, STEFAN
1999   *Sudden Death and the Myth of CPR*. Philadelphia: Temple University Press.

TIPTON, STEVEN M.
1982   *Getting Saved from the Sixties: The Transformation of Moral Meaning in American Culture by Alternative Religious Movements*. Berkeley: University of California Press.

TODD, ALEXANDRA
1983   "Discourse in the prescription of contraception," pp. 159–187 in S. Fisher and A. Todd, eds., *The Social Organization of Doctor-Patient Communication*. Norwood, NJ: Ablex.

TOLCHIN, MARTIN
1988a   "Curbs on tuition for doctors raising fears for care of poor," *New York Times,* July 25.
1988b   "Shift on Medicare to hurt hospitals in the inner cities," *New York Times,* October 19.

TONER, ROBIN
2001   "Sagging economy threatens health coverage," *New York Times,* November 12.

TOWNSEND, JOHN M., AND CYNTHIA L. CARBONE
1980 "Menopausal syndrome: Illness or social role—A transcultural analysis," *Culture, Medicine, and Psychiatry* 4: 229–248.

TOWNSEND, PETER
1990 "Individual or social responsibility for premature death: Current controversies in the British debate about health," *International Journal of Health Services* 29(3): 373–392.

TRAPPS, TYNISA E.
2001 "Nursing home abuse rising across nation," *Los Angeles Times*, July 31.

TROSTLE, JAMES A.
1988 "Medical compliance as an ideology," *Social Science and Medicine* 27(12): 1299–1308.

TROSTLE, JAMES A., W. ALLEN HAUSER, AND IDA SUSSER
1983 "The logic of noncompliance: Management of epilepsy from the patient's point of view," *Culture, Medicine, and Psychiatry* 7: 35–56.

TROTTER, ROBERT T., AND J. A. CHAVIRA
1981 *Curanderismo: Mexican-American Folk Healing*. Athens: University of Georgia Press.

TSING, ANNA L.
1990 "Monster stories: Women charged with perinatal endangerment," pp. 113–138 in F. Ginsburg and A. L. Tsing, eds., *Uncertain Terms: Negotiating Gender in American Culture*. Boston: Beacon.

TUDIVER, SARI
1986 "The strength of links: International Women's Health Network in the eighties," pp. 187–214 in K. McDonnell, ed., *Adverse Effects: Women and the Pharmaceutical Industry*. Toronto, Canada: Women's Educational Press.

TUFTS UNIVERSITY, CENTER ON HUNGER, POVERTY AND NUTRITION POLICY
2001 "Hunger in the U.S." February 2001, retrieved from the World Wide Web at http://hunger.tufts.edu/us.shtml on 22 December, 2001.

TURNER, BRYAN S.
1977 "Confession and social structure," *Annual Review of the Social Sciences of Religion* 1: 29–58.
1982 "The government of the body: Medical regimens and the rationalization of diet," *British Journal of Sociology* 33(2): 254–269.
1984 *The Body and Society: Exploration in Social Theory*. Oxford, England: Basil Blackwell.
1995 *Medical Power and Social Knowledge* (2nd ed.). Thousand Oaks, CA: Sage.

TWADDLE, ANDREW C.
1981 *Sickness Behavior and the Sick Role*. Cambridge, MA: Schenkman.

TYNES, SHERYL
1996 *Turning Points in Social Security: From Cruel Hoax to Social Entitlement*. Palo Alto, CA: Stanford University Press.

UBEL, PETER A.
1999 "How stable are people's preferences for giving priority to severely ill patients?" *Social Science and Medicine* 49(7): 895–903.

UNITED NATIONS DEVELOPMENT PROGRAMME (UNDP)
1995 *Human Development Report, 1995*. New York: Oxford University Press.
2001 *Human Development Report 2001*, retrieved from the World Wide Web at www.undp.org on 22 December, 2001.

UNITED NATIONS FOOD AND AGRICULTURE ORGANIZATION (FAO)
2000   *The State of Food and Agriculture, 2000*. Rome: Food and Agriculture Organization of the United Nations.
2001   "Mobilizing resources to fight hunger," Report of the Commission on World Food Security, June 2001, retrieved from the World Wide Web at www.fao.org on 13 January, 2002.

UNITED NATIONS HIGH COMMISSION FOR HUMAN RIGHTS
2000   "The right to food report," Report of the High Commission for Human Rights, January 2000, retrieved from the World Wide Web at www.unhchr.ch on 22 December, 2001.

UNITED NATIONS INTERNATIONAL CHILDREN'S EMERGENCY FUND (UNICEF)
1989   *Convention on the Rights of Children,* retrieved from the World Wide Web at www.unicef.org on 4 July, 2002.
2000   *The State of the World's Children, 2000,* retrieved from the World Wide Web at www.unicef.org on 17 September, 2001.

UNITED NATIONS PROGRAMME ON HIV/AIDS (UNAIDS)
2001a   "Aids epidemic update: December, 2001," retrieved from the World Wide Web at www.unaids.org/worldaidsday/2001 on 7 January, 2002.
2001b   "Children and young people and HIV/AIDS," retrieved from the World Wide Web at www.unaids.org on 30 March, 2002.

UNITED STATES ADVISORY COMMISSION ON CONSUMER PROTECTION AND QUALITY IN THE HEALTH CARE INDUSTRY
1997   *Consumer Bill of Rights and Responsibilities: Report to the President of the United States.* Washington, DC: United States Advisory Commission on Consumer Protection and Quality in the Health Care Industry.

UNITED STATES BUREAU OF THE CENSUS
1975   *Historical Statistics of the United States, Colonial Times to 1970.* Bicentennial edition, part 2. Washington, DC: Author.
1997   "Money income in the United States: 1996, *Current Population Reports,* P-60: 197. Washington, DC: U.S. Government Printing Office.
2000a   "The foreign-born population of the United States," *Current Population Reports.* Washington, DC: Author.
2000b   "Historical income tables—households," retrieved from the World Wide Web at www.census.gov on 10 September, 2001.
2000c   "Low income uninsured children by state: 1996, 1997, and 1998," *Current Population Survey, March 1997–1999,* retrieved from the World Wide Web at www.census.gov/hhes/hlthins/liuc98.html on 22 October, 2001.
2000d   *Statistical Abstract of the United States: 2000.* Washington, DC: Author.
2001a   "Census 2000," Summary File, American FactFinder, retrieved from the World Wide Web at http://factfinder.census.gov on 29 January, 2002.
2001b   "Nation's median age highest ever, but 65-and-over population's growth lags, Census 2000 shows," 15 May, 2001, retrieved from the World Wide Web at www.census.gov on 29 January, 2002.

UNITED STATES BUREAU OF LABOR STATISTICS
2001   "Annual demographic survey," table HI10, 12 September, 2001, retrieved from the World Wide Web at http://ferret.bls.census.gov on 3 December, 2001.

UNITED STATES CENTER FOR DISEASE CONTROL (CDC)
2000   "HIV/AIDS surveillance report," 2000 Year-end edition, Vol. 12(2), retrieved from the World Wide Web at www.cdc.gov on 20 March, 2002.

2001a "Cigarette smoking–related mortality," June, 2001, retrieved from the World Wide Web at www.cdc.gov/tobacco/ on 30 March, 2002.

2001b "Women and smoking: A report of the Surgeon General–2001," retrieved from the World Wide Web at www.cdc.gov on 17 March, 2002.

2002a "Need for sustained HIV prevention among men who have sex with men," 22 March, 2002, retrieved from the World Wide Web at www.cdc.gov on 30 March, 2002.

2002b "New CDC report shows decline in infant mortality rate in 1999, analyzes patterns of infant mortality," retrieved from the World Wide Web at www.cdc.gov on 17 March, 2002.

UNITED STATES CONFERENCE OF MAYORS

2001 "Hunger and homelessness, 2001," Report of the United States Conference of Mayors, December 2001, retrieved from the World Wide Web at www.usmayors.org on 22 December, 2001.

UNITED STATES CONGRESS

1997 "Medicare and health care chart book," House Ways and Means Committee, retrieved from the World Wide Web at www.access.gpo.gov on 2 March, 2002.

UNITED STATES DEPARTMENT OF HEALTH AND HUMAN SERVICES (USDHHS)

1989 *International Classification of Diseases.* Public Health Service, Health Care Financing Administration. Washington, DC: Government Printing Office.

1996 *Monthly Vital Statistics Report* 44(11S): 15–16, 68.

2000 *Health United States, 2000.* Hyattsville, MD: National Center for Health Statistics.

2001a *Health United States, 2001.* Hyattsville, MD: National Center for Health Statistics.

2001b "The Surgeon General's call to action to prevent and decrease overweight and obesity," December 2001, retrieved from the World Wide Web at www.hhs.gov on 22 December, 2001.

UNITED STATES DEPARTMENT OF LABOR

1981 "Workers on late shifts," Bureau of Labor Statistics, September Summary: 81–103.

UNITED STATES FEDERAL INTERAGENCY FORUM ON AGING-RELATED STATISTICS (FIFA)

2000 *Health Care: Older Americans 2000,* August 2000, retrieved from the World Wide Web at www.agingstats.gov on 2 March, 2002.

UNITED STATES FORUM ON CHILD AND FAMILY STATISTICS

2000 "Behavior and social environment indicators: Regular cigarette smoking," retrieved from the World Wide Web at www.childstats.gov on 30 March, 2002.

UNITED STATES GENERAL ACCOUNTING OFFICE (GAO)

1997 *Employment Based Health Insurance: Costs Increase and Family Coverage Decreases.* GAO/HEHS 97-35. Washington, DC: Author.

2001 GAO-01-750T, testimony before the U.S. Senate on direct care health workers, May 17.

UNITED STATES HEALTH CARE FINANCE ADMINISTRATION (HCFA)

2000 "Highlights–National health expenditures, 2000" retrieved from the World Wide Web at www.hcfa.gov on 23 March, 2002.

2001 "State Children's Health Insurance Program: Aggregate enrollment statistics for the 50 states . . . 2000," retrieved from the World Wide Web at www.hcfa.gov on 23 March, 2002.

2002 "National health expenditures, 2000," retrieved from the World Wide Web at www.hcfa.gov/stats/ on 23 March, 2002.

UNITED STATES NATIONAL INSTITUTE FOR OCCUPATIONAL SAFETY AND HEALTH (NIOSH)
  1999   "Traumatic occupational injuries," updated 1999, retrieved from the World
         Wide Web at www.cdc.gov/niosh/injury/trauma.html on 29 March, 2002.

VALACH, LADISLAV
  1995   "Coping and human agency," pp. 249–265 in I. Markova and R. M. Farr, eds.,
         Representations of Health, Illness and Handicap. London: Harwood.

VANDENBURGH, HENRY
  1999   *Feeding Frenzy: Organizational Deviance in the Texas Psychiatric Hospital Industry.*
         Lanham, MD: University Press of America.

VEDANTAM, SHANKAR
  2001   "Renamed Prozac fuels women's health debate," *Washington Post,* April 29.

VERBRUGGE, LOIS M.
  1986   "From sneezes to adieux: Stages of health for American men and women,"
         Social Science and Medicine 22: 1195–1212.
  1990   "Longer life but worsening health?: Trends in health and mortality of middle-
         aged and older persons," pp. 14–34 in P. R. Lee and C. L. Estes, eds., *The
         Nation's Health.* Boston: Jones and Bartlett.

VERBRUGGE, LOIS M., AND FRANK J. ASCIONE
  1987   "Exploring the iceberg: Common symptoms and how people care for them,"
         Medical Care 25(6): 539–569.

VINES, GAIL
  1993   *Raging Hormones.* Berkeley: University of California Press.

VUCKOVIC, NANCY
  2000   "Self-care among the uninsured: 'You do what you can do'," *Health Affairs*
         19(4): 197–200.

WADSWORTH, MICHAEL
  1996   "Family and education as determinants of health," pp. 152–170 in D. Blane
         et al., eds., *Health and Social Organization.* London: Routledge.

WAGNER, MELINDA BOLLAR
  1983   *Metaphysics in Midwestern America.* Columbus: Ohio State University Press.

WAITZKIN, HOWARD B.
  1971   "Latent functions of the sick role in various institutional settings," *Social Science
         and Medicine* 5: 45–75.
  1979   "A Marxian interpretation of the growth and development of coronary care
         technology," *American Journal of Public Health* 69(12): 1260–1268.
  1984   "The micropolitics of medicine: A contextual analysis," *International Journal of
         Health Services* 14: 339–378.
  1985   "Information giving in medical care," *Journal of Health and Social Behavior* 26:
         81–101.
  1989   "A critical theory of medical discourse: Ideology, social control, and the
         processing of social context in medical encounters," *Journal of Health and Social
         Behavior* 30(2): 220–239.
  1991   *The Politics of Medical Encounters: How Patients and Doctors Deal with Social Problems.*
         New Haven, CT: Yale University Press.
  2000   "Changing patient-physician relationships in the changing health-policy envi-
         ronment," pp. 271–283 in C. E. Bird, P. Conrad, and A. M. Fremont, eds.,
         Handbook of Medical Sociology. Upper Saddle River, NJ: Prentice-Hall.
  2001   *At the Frontlines of Medicine.* Lanham, MD: Rowman and Littlefield.

WAITZKIN, HOWARD B., AND JOHN D. STOECKLE
  1972   "The communication of information about illness," *Advances in Psychosomatic Medicine* 8: 180–215.
WALDRAM, JAMES B.
  2000   "The efficacy of traditional medicine: Current theoretical and methodological issues," *Medical Anthropology Quarterly* 14(4): 603–625.
WALDRON, INGRID
  1994   "What do we know about causes of sex differences in mortality?" pp. 42–55 in P. Conrad and R. Kern, eds., *The Sociology of Health and Illness* (4th ed.). New York: St. Martin's Press.
WALLSTON, BARBARA S., S. W. ALAGNA, B. M. DEVELLIS, AND R. B. DEVELLIS
  1983   "Social support and physical health," *Health Psychology* 2: 367–391.
WALSH, DIANA CHAPMAN
  1987   *Corporate Physicians: Between Medicine and Management.* New Haven, CT: Yale University Press.
WALTERS, VIVIENNE
  1982   "Company doctors' perceptions of and responses to conflicting pressures from labor and management," *Social Problems* 30(1): 1–12.
WARD, MARTHA C.
  1986   *Poor Women, Powerful Men: America's Great Experiment in Family Planning.* Boulder, CO: Westview.
WARDWELL, WALTER I.
  1993   *Chiropractic History and Evolution of a New Profession.* St. Louis, MO: Mosby-Year Books.
  1994   "Alternative Medicine in the United States," *Social Science and Medicine* 38(8): 1061–1068.
WARE, JOHN E., JR., MARTHA S. BAYLISS, WILLIAM H. ROGERS, MARK KOSINSKI, AND ALVIN R. TARLOV
  1996   "Differences in 4-year health outcomes for elderly and poor, chronically ill patients treated in HMO and fee-for-service systems," *Journal of the American Medical Association* 276(13): 1039–1047.
WARE, NORMA C.
  1992   "Suffering and the social construction of illness: The delegitimation of illness experience in chronic fatigue syndrome," *Medical Anthropology Quarterly* 6(4): 347–361.
WATSON, WILBUR H., ED.
  1984   *Black Folk Medicine: The Therapeutic Significance of Faith and Trust.* New Brunswick, NJ: Transaction.
WAXLER, NANCY E.
  1980   "The social labeling perspective on illness and medical practice," pp. 283–306 in L. Eisenberg and A. Kleinman, eds., *The Relevance of Social Science for Medicine.* Dordrecht, Netherlands: D. Reidel.
  1981   "Learning to be a leper: A case study in the social construction of illness," pp. 169–194 in E. Mishler, L. AmaraSingham, S. Hauser, R. Liem, S. Osherson, and N. Waxler, *Social Contexts of Health, Illness, and Patient Care.* Cambridge, England: Cambridge University Press.
WAXLER-MORRISON, NANCY, T. GREGORY HISLAP, BRONWEN MEARS, AND LISA KAN
  1991   "Effects of social relationships on survival for women with breast cancer: A prospective study," *Social Science and Medicine* 33(2): 177–183.

WAY, KAREN
  1995   "Never too rich . . . or too thin: The role of stigma in the social construction of anorexia nervosa," pp. 91–113 in D. Maurer and J. Sobal, eds., *Eating Agendas: Food and Nutrition as Social Problems.* New York: Aldine de Gruyter.

WAZANA, ASHLEY
  2000   "Physicians and the pharmaceutical industry: Is a gift ever just a gift?" *Journal of the American Medical Association* 283(3): 373–380.

WEBER, MAX
  [1904] 1958   *The Protestant Ethic and the Spirit of Capitalism.* New York: Charles Scribner's Sons.
  [1922] 1963   *The Sociology of Religion,* E. Fischoff, trans. Boston: Beacon.

WEIL, ANDREW
  1988   *Health and Healing* (rev. ed.). Boston: Houghton Mifflin.

WEIL, ANDREW, AND WINIFRED ROSEN
  1993   *From Chocolate to Morphine* (rev. ed.). Boston: Houghton Mifflin.

WEINER, HERBERT
  1992   *Perturbing the Organism: The Biology of Stressful Experience.* Chicago: University of Chicago Press.

WEIR, DAVID, AND MARK SHAPIRO
  1981   *Circle of Poison.* San Francisco: Institute for Food Development Policy.

WEISS, KAY
  1983   "Vaginal cancer: An iatrogenic disease?" pp. 59–75 in E. Fee, ed., *Women and Health: The Politics of Sex in Medicine.* Farmingdale, NY: Baywood.

WEISS, LAWRENCE D.
  1997   *Private Medicine and Public Health: Profit, Politics, and Prejudice in the American Health Care Enterprise.* Boulder, CO: Westview.

WEISSMAN, ROBERT
  2001   "The AIDS Fund fight," *The Nation,* July 9: 14.

WELCH, W. PETE, DIANA VERRILLI, STEVEN J. KATZ, AND ERIC LATIMER
  1996   "A detailed comparison of physician services for the elderly in the United States and Canada," *Journal of the American Medical Association* 275(18): 1410–1416.

WELLMAN, BEVERLY
  1995   "Lay referral networks: Using conventional medicine and alternative therapies for low back pain," *Research in the Sociology of Health Care* 12: 213–238.

WERTZ, RICHARD W., AND DOROTHY C. WERTZ
  1979   *Lying-In: A History of Childbirth in America.* New York: Schocken.

WEST, CANDACE
  1983   " 'Ask me no questions . . . ': An analysis of queries and replies in physician-patient dialogues," pp. 75–106 in S. Fisher and A. Todd, eds., *The Social Organization of Doctor-Patient Communication.* Norwood, NJ: Ablex.
  1984   *Routine Complications: Troubles with Talk Between Doctors and Patients.* Bloomington: Indiana University Press.
  1993   "Reconceptualizing gender in physician-patient relationships," *Social Science and Medicine* 36(1): 57–66.

WEST, PATRICK B.
  1979   "Making sense of epilepsy," pp. 162–169 in D. J. Osborne, M. M. Greenberg, and J. R. Eiser, eds., *Research in Psychology and Medicine: Social Aspects, Attitudes, Communication, Care, and Training,* Vol. 2. New York: Academic.

WESTLEY, FRANCES
    1983   *The Complex Forms of the Religious Life: A Durkheimian View of New Religious Movements.* Chico, CA: Scholars Press.

WETHINGTON, ELAINE, AND RONALD C. KESSLER
    1986   "Perceived support, received support, and adjustment to stressful life events," *Journal of Health and Social Behavior* 27: 78–89.

WHARTON, AMY S.
    1999   "The psychosocial consequences of emotional labor," *The Annals of American Academy of Political and Social Sciences* 561 (January): 158–176.

WHITE, RONALD D.
    2002   "Baby boomers fuel surge in drug spending," *Los Angeles Times,* March 30.

WHITE, WILLIAM D., J. WARREN SALMON, AND JOE FEINGLASS
    1994   "The changing doctor-patient relationship and performance monitoring: An agency perspective," pp. 195–224 in J. W. Salmon, ed., *The Corporate Transformation of Health Care #2.* Amityville, NY: Baywood.

WHITEIS, DAVID, AND J. WARREN SALMON
    1987   "The proprietarization of health care and underdevelopment of the public sector," *International Journal of Health Services* 17(1): 47–64.

WHYTE, SUSAN, AND BENEDICTE INGSTAD
    1995   "Disability and culture: an overview," pp. 3–31 in B. Ingstad and S. R. Whyte, eds., *Disability and Culture.* Berkeley: University of California Press.

WIKLER, DANIEL, AND NORMA J. WIKLER
    1991   "Turkey-baster babies: The demedicalization of artificial insemination," *The Milbank Quarterly* 69(1): 5–40.

WILKINSON, RICHARD G.
    1986   "Socio-economic differences in mortality: Interpreting the data on their size and trends," pp. 1–21 in R. Wilkinson, ed., *Class and Health: Research and Longitudinal Data.* New York: Tavistock.
    1996   *Unhealthy Societies.* London: Routledge.
    1999a   "The epidemiological transition: From material scarcity to social disadvantage?," pp. 36–46 in I. Kiwachi, B. P. Kennedy, and R. G. Wilkinson, eds., *The Society and Population Health Reader, Vol. I: Income Inequality and Health.* New York: The New Press.
    1999b   "The Culture of Inequality," pp. 492–498 in I. Kiwachi, B. P. Kennedy, and R. G. Wilkinson, eds., *The Society and Population Health Reader, Vol. I: Income Inequality and Health.* New York: The New Press.
    2000   *Mind the Gap: Hierarchies, Health, and Human Evolution.* London: Widenfeld and Nicolson.

WILLEN, RICHARD S.
    1983   "Religion and law: The secularization of testimonial procedures," *Sociological Analysis* 44(1): 53–64.

WILLIAMS, DAVID R.
    2000   "Race, stress and mental health," pp. 209–243 in C. J. R. Hogue, M. A. Hargraves, and K. S. Collins, eds., *Minority Health in America.* Baltimore: The Johns Hopkins University Press.

WILLIAMS, GARETH, AND HELEN BUSBY
    2000   "The politics of disabled bodies," pp. 169–185 in S. J. Williams, J. Gabe, and M. Calnan, eds., *Health, Medicine and Society.* London: Routledge.

WILLIAMS, GARETH, JENNIE POPAY, AND PAUL BISSELL
  1995   "Public health risks in the material world: Barriers to social movements in health," pp. 113–132 in J. Gabe, ed., *Medicine, Health and Risk*. Oxford, England: Blackwell.

WILLIAMS, RORY
  1990   *A Protestant Legacy: Attitudes to Death and Illness among Older Aberdonians*. Oxford, England: Clarendon Press.

WILLIAMS, SIMON J.
  2000   "Emotions, social structure and health," pp. 296–314 in S. J. Williams, J. Gabe, and M. Calnan, eds., *Health, Medicine and Society*. London: Routledge.
  2001   *Emotion and Social Theory: Corporeal Reflections on the (IR) Rational*. London: Sage Publications.

WILLIAMS, SIMON J., AND GILLIAN BENDELOW
  1996   "Emotions, health and illness: The missing link in medical sociology?" pp. 25–53 in V. James and J. Gabe, eds., *Health and the Sociology of Emotions*. Oxford, England: Blackwell.

WILSON, SHARON
  1991   "The unrelenting nightmare: Husbands' experiences during their wives' chemotherapy," pp. 237–313 in J. M. Morse and J. L. Johnson, eds., *The Illness Experience: Dimensions of Suffering*. Newbury Park, CA: Sage.

WOLFE, KATHI
  1995   "Bashing the disabled," *The Progressive* (November): 24–27.

WOLFE, SIDNEY M.
  1996   "Why do American drug companies spend more than $12 billion a year pushing drugs?" *Journal of General Internal Medicine* 11: 637–639.

WOLFF, EDWARD N.
  2000   "Recent trends in wealth ownership, 1983–1998," Working Paper No. 300, Jerome Levy Economics Institute, April 2000, retrieved from the World Wide Web at www.levy.org/docs/wrkpap/papers/300.html on 28 August, 2001.

WOLPE, PAUL ROOT
  1985   "The maintenance of professional authority: Acupuncture and the American physician," *Social Problems* 32(June): 409–424.
  1990   "The holistic heresy: Strategies of ideological challenge in the medical profession," *Social Science and Medicine* 31(8): 913–923.

WOODS, NANCY FUGATE
  1995   "Women and their health," pp. 1–22 in C. I. Fogel and F. G. Woods, eds., *Women's Health Care: A Comprehensive Handbook*. Thousand Oaks, CA: Sage.

WOOLHANDLER, STEFFIE, AND DAVID U. HIMMELSTEIN
  1997   "Costs of care and administration at for-profit and other hospitals in the United States," *New England Journal of Medicine* 336(11): 769–774.

WOOLHANDLER, STEFFIE, DAVID U. HIMMELSTEIN, AND JAMES P. LEWONTIN
  1993   "Administrative costs in U.S. hospitals," *New England Journal of Medicine* 329(6): 400–403.

WORLD BANK GROUP, THE
  2001a   *Global Economic Prospects and the Developing Countries, 2001,* retrieved from the World Wide Web at www.worldbank.org/poverty/data/trends/ on 22 December, 2001.
  2001b   "Social Indicators—The Environment," retrieved from the World Wide Web at www.worldbank.org/poverty/data/trends/water.htm on 28 September, 2001.

2001c   "Social indicators—Health: Health status and health care services for the poor," retrieved from the World Wide Web at www.worldbank.org/poverty/data/trends/healts.htm on 28 September, 2001.

WORLD HEALTH ORGANIZATION
2000   "Healthy life expectancy rankings," *World Health Report 2000.* Copenhagen, Denmark: World Health Organization.
2001   *Report of the Commission on Macroeconomics and Health,* December 2001. Retrieved from the World Wide Web at www.who.int/whosis/cmh/cmh_report/e/htm on 22 December, 2001.

WRIGHT, BARBARA DRYGULSKI
1987   "Women, work, and the university-affiliated technology park," pp. 352–370 in B. D. Wright, ed., *Women, Work, and Technology: Transformations.* Ann Arbor: University of Michigan Press.

WU, W. C., AND R. A. PEARLMAN
1988   "Consent in medical decision-making: The role of communication," *Journal of General Internal Medicine* 3: 9–14.

YATES, ALAYNE
1991   *Compulsive Exercise and the Eating Disorders.* New York: Brunner/Mazel.

YELIN, EDWARD
1986   "The myth of malingering: Why individuals withdraw from work in the presence of illness," *Milbank Quarterly* 64(4): 622–649.

YOELS, WILLIAM C., AND JEFFREY MICHAEL CLAIR
1995   "Laughter in the clinic: Humor as social organization," *Symbolic Interaction* 18: 39–58.

YOUNG, ALLAN
1976   "Some implications of medical beliefs and practices for social anthropology," *American Anthropologist* 78(1): 5–24.
1978   "Mode of production of medical knowledge," *Medical Anthropology* 2: 97–124.
1980   "The discourse of stress and the reproduction of conventional knowledge," *Social Science and Medicine* 14B: 133–146.

YOUNG, ERNIE, AND DAVID K. STEVENSON
1990   "Limiting treatment for extremely premature, low-birth-weight infants (500–750 g.)," *American Journal of Diseases of Children* 144(5): 549–552.

YOUNG, GARY J., K. R. DESAI, AND F. J. HELLINGER
2000   "Community control and pricing patterns of nonprofit hospitals: An antitrust analysis," *Journal of Health Politics, Policy and Law* 25(6): 1051–1081.

ZARLING, EDWIN J., HAROLD SEXTON, AND PERVIS MILNOR, JR.
1983   "Failure to diagnose acute myocardial infarction: The clinicopathologic experience at a large community hospital," *Journal of the American Medical Association* 250(9): 1177–1181.

ZBOROWSKI, MARK
1952   "Cultural components in response to pain," *Journal of Social Issues* 8: 16–30.

ZERNIKE, KATE, AND MELODY PETERSEN
2001   "Schools' backing of behavior drugs comes under fire," *New York Times,* August 19.

ZIELINSKI GUTIÉRREZ, EMILY C., AND CARL KENDALL
2000   "The globalization of health and disease: The health transition and global change," pp. 84–99 in G. L. Albrecht et al., eds., *Handbook of Social Studies in Health and Medicine.* London: Sage.

ZOLA, IRVING K.

  1982   *Missing Pieces: A Chronicle of Living with a Disability.* Philadelphia: Temple University Press.

  1983   *Socio-Medical Inquiries: Recollections, Reflections, and Reconsiderations.* Philadelphia: Temple University Press.

  1993   "Self, identity and the naming question: Reflections on the language of disability," *Social Science and Medicine* 36(2): 167–173.

ZUGER, ABIGAIL.

  1999   "Arming unsung heroes of health care," *New York Times,* October 26.

AUTHOR INDEX

Subject Index